MAURY COUNTY, TENNESSEE
WILL BOOKS A, B, C-1, D AND E

1807-1832

by
Jill Knight Garrett
and
Marise Parrish Lightfoot

Please direct all correspondence and orders to:

www.southernhistoricalpress.com
or
SOUTHERN HISTORICAL PRESS, Inc.
PO BOX 1267
375 West Broad Street
Greenville, SC   29601
southernhistoricalpress@gmail.com

ISBN #0-89308-362-3

Printed in the United States of America

MAURY COUNTY

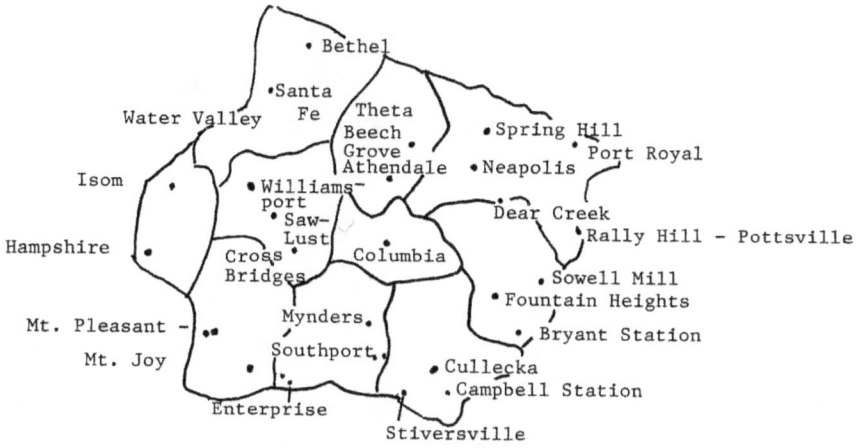

- Bethel
- Santa Fe
- Water Valley
- Theta
- Beech
- Grove
- Athendale
- Spring Hill
- Port Royal
- Isom
- Neapolis
- Williams-port
- Saw-Lust
- Dear Creek
- Rally Hill – Pottsville
- Hampshire
- Cross Bridges
- Columbia
- Sowell Mill
- Fountain Heights
- Mt. Pleasant –
- Mynders
- Bryant Station
- Mt. Joy
- Southport
- Cullecka
- Campbell Station
- Enterprise
- Stiversville

WILLS AND SETTLEMENTS, BOOK A, VOLUME 1, 1807-1810
MAURY COUNTY, TENNESSEE

page 1   Will of William WHITSON, deceased. Wife, Ann. My
          children, except my three oldest, John, Thomas, and
          Joseph. "...as I have sold my lands in this county
          except one tract on Ivey (?) and one on Rosses (?)
          Creek. Witness: William SMITH and William YOUNG.
          Dated 6 November, 1806.

page 3   Inventory by Alexander and Joseph MCDONALD, adminis-
          trators for John MCDONALD, deceased. Among items:
          note on Michael KINSEY of (KINZER?) Montgomery County,
          Virginia; note on Richard MCDONALD of Washington
          County, Kentucky; note on Parson CROFFORD now in Court
          of Chancery in the Federal City. 22 December, 1807.

page 4   Inventory and sale of John MCDONALD, deceased. 26
          January, 1808. Those buying at sale:
          Elizabeth MCDONALD   Amos CALDWELL
          John MCDONALD   William CALDWELL
          Alexander MCDONALD   Abraham BOGARDS
          Robert MCDONALD   James BOGARD
          William ALEXANDER   Matthew YOCUM
          Mrs. WALTON   Joseph PHARARER
          John MCCURLEY   Richard COCK
          Lazarus DOTTSON   James WREN
          Col. RUSSELL   Jesse YOCUM
          James MCDONALD   Hugh ROSS
          John MILLER,Esqr.   John WELLS
          Anthony I. TURNER   John GIVEN
          William TRESS (?)   Aguiler NOW (?)
          Abner FRANKLIN   Joseph LAND
          John MCKNIGHT   John WILLIAMS
          Thomas MORGAN   John HUGHEY

page 9   Sale of Ezekial LINDSEY, deceased. Sale held
          22 December 1807. Those buying:
          Hannah LINDSEY   John ANDERSON
          Edward LINDSEY   Thomas H. HARDEN
          Isaac LINDSEY   Joseph LEMASTER
          John LINDSEY Senr.   William COLLINS
          Joseph YOKEM   George DAVIDSON

page 10   Sale by Richard CHURCHWELL, administrator of Ephriam
          CHURCHWELL, deceased no date. Those buying:
          Richard CHURCHWELL   Robert HILL
          William CHURCHWELL   Harrison BLAGRAVE
          Thomas MCLAUGHLIN   Samuel WILLIAMS
          Mrs. HANKS   Joseph TAYLOR
          Margaret REANY   Aaron HUNTER
          Mrs. COCKRAN   Samuel COCKRAN
          William TOLLEY   William ESHAM
          Daniel KEETCH   Thomas BROOKS
          Ayres DOSS (?)   Spencer GRIFFIN

page 15   Sale by Elenor and William HAYS, administrators of
          Jesse HAYS, deceased no date. Those buying:
          Eleanor HAYS   Thomas AYDELOTT

Jonathan HAYS   James BIRMINGHAM
George HAYS   John LOVE
Margaret HAYS   Spencer HILL
William HAYS   William LEE
Mary LOVE   Robert LOVE
Ephriam MC LEAN

page 18   Sale by Traves HARMICK (or HAMRICK), Administrator of
Jeremiah HARMICK, deceased, held on 16 April 1808.
Those buying:
Yelvonton HARMICK   James CRAIG
Traves HARMICK   Joseph BROWN
Anna HARMICK   Joseph KINCADE
Anthony COPELAND

page 19   Amount of Sales, Number of Lotts and purchasers names
in town of Columbia:

Lot No.	Purchaser	Lot No.	Purchaser
1	C. STUMP	45	Isaac ROBERTS
2	Thomas DEIDRICK	46	Joseph RHODES
3	Perry COHEA	47	Isaac CROW
4	Kinshen MASSINGALE	48	NEILSON and CAMRON
5	John WILLIAMS	49	Samuel MC CLUSKEY
6	John M. GOODLOE	50	John WHITE
7	C. STUMP	51	William W. THOMPSON
8	John M. GOODLOE	52	James DOBBINS
9	Abner PILLOW	53	O. P. NICHOLSON
10	John DAVISON	54	Lucey WHITE
11	Peter BASS	55	Lucey WHITE
12	C. STUMP	56	John WHITE
13	C. STUMP	57	Thomas H. HOLLAND
14	John CARUTHERS	58	Alexander MC GILBERT
15	CRAIG and WASHINGTON	59	William LINTZ
16	Robert WEAKLEY	60	James M. LEWIS
17	Norton GUMM	61	John WILLIAMS
18	William MC GEE	62	Richard GARRET
19	John LYON	63	Z. DRAKE
20	Allen YATES	64	John WILLIAMS
21	SHANNON and SAWYERS	65	Lawrence THOMPSON
22	John KEANON	66	David HUGHES
23	William BRADSHAW	67	John BELL
24	HODGE and MOBIN	68	John LINDSEY
25	William M. BERRYHILL	69	William FRIERSON
26	William BRADSHAW	70	William DANIEL
27	Nichilas T. PERKINS	71	NICHOLSON and GOODLOE
28	James WELCH	72	William W. THOMPSON
29	John PALMER	73	Samuel TAYLOR
30	Peter CHEATAM	74	John WILLIAMS
31	William LINTS	75	Samuel TAYLOR
32	John RAINS	76	Richard HANKS
33	OLDHAM and O'NEAL	77	John RUSSEL
34	John SPENCER	78	Benjamin WOOTON
35	Newton COMRON	79	Joseph B. PORTER
36	Henry ANDERSON	80	Robert MC LANE
37	James BRUCE	81	Joseph BROWN
38	James GULLET	82	David ORTERE (?)
39	L. B. ESTES	83	Richard ORTON
40	L. B. ESTES	84	Dennis WRIGHT
41	George COCKBURN	85	Jabus NOWLIN
42	James GULLET	86	James WELSH
43	John M. GOODLOE	87	Richard HANKS
44	John M. GOODLOE	88	Thomas HARNEY

Lot No.	Purchaser	Lot No.	Purchaser
89	James WELSH	100	John SPENCER
90	John SPENCER	101	Micajah DAVIS
91	William BADGER	102	Samuel CAMRON
92	David SHANNON	103	Nicholas COBLER
93	Isaac ADAIR	104	Hezekiah ALMON
94	Jabus NOWLIN	105	Richard HENDERSON
95	Thomas H. HARDEN	106	John WIBLE
96	John SPENCER	107	Hezekiah SHACE
97	John M. GOODLOE	108	Edmund HARRISON
98	Faulker COX	109	George COCKBURN
99	Joseph LEMASTER		

page 23   Will of Richard SCOTT. Wife, Rebecca, one half land.
Daughter Polley, other half land. Robert CARSON, a
mare and "all my carpenter's tools.....hogs and
farming utensils for use of family until said Robert
comes of age and then he is to have them as his
property.." Cable MURRY to have privilege of living
on part of land I now live on for ten years. Josiah
TEMPLE and wife Rebecca SCOTT Executors. 17 November
1808. Witness: Capel MURRAY, Shadrack HOWARD, Thos.
MC GRATT

page 25   Agreement on 2 September 1808 between John M. GOODLOE
and Osborn P. NICHOLSON of Davidson and Williamson
Counties and Commissioners of town of Columbia to
build a brick court house. Description. Commissioners:
Joseph BROWN, John LINDSEY, William FRIERSON, and
Isaac ROBERTS. For amount of $6,990.

page 29   Will of James TURNER. James T. SANDFORD to receive
negro Lucy and 6 children. Son, James TURNER. Betsey
MORGAN to receive one side saddle and $200. Balance
"among my 4 children." James T. SANDFORD, Executor.
5 April 1809. Witness: Donald CAMPBELL and John C.
SMOOT.

page 31   Division of estate of James TURNER, deceased. Oldest
son-in-law, James T. SANDFORD; son, William TURNER;
and Anthony I. TURNER. 14 August 1809.

page 32   Will of Benjamin HOWARD. Two negroes Sharp and Tenny
to be emancipated. Daughter Polley. "when youngest
child comes of age to be divided among them"...Wife
Emith(?). James HOWARD, brother and Andrew GAMBLE,
friend, Executors. 12 November 1810. Witness: James
WALSON, Eli and Robt MC CAIN

page 33   Will of Andrew GOFORTH. Jane HOOD to have household
furniture, etc. Three sons, Andrew, William, and
Hiram. 20 November 1810. Witness: Wm. Halcomb, Wm. A.
CALDWELL, Amos CALAWELL (?)

page 37   Sale of property of Isaam CHRISTIAN, deceased, sold
29 October 1811. (see Book B, page 11.) Those buying:

Ann CHRISTIAN	Jodiah PECK
Polly CHRISTIAN	William JOHNSON
Nathaniel CHRISTIAN	Jane RAYE
Nancy CHRISTIAN	William MC BRIDE
A. W. RAYE	Robert PATAN
Silas ALEXANDER	Henry PAYTON

Jane CHRISTIAN   James DUNCAN
Betsy CHRISTIAN   John WILLIAMS
Patsy CHRISTIAN   Pleasant SCRIBNER
Elizabeth CHRISTIAN   Thomas POWELL
Moses PAYTON

page 40   Will of John LOVE, 12th day of _____, 1811. Wife,
           Jane. Son, Wilson, when comes to be 12 years old.
           Edom, Eli, and Nathan, my sons and Easter, my
           daughter. Son Robert. Daughter-in-law, Mary Lee (?),
           Son John; son Joel; daughter Betsy. Joel and Edom
           LOVE, Executors. Witness: Robert LOVE, Alexander
           CATHEY.

page 42   Will of Robert FRIERSON. Son, Thomas JAMES; son
           Samuel ELIJAH; wife, Elizabeth; three daughters, Mary
           MAYS, Elizabeth Martha FRIERSON, and Susannah BROWN;
           son Robert. Friends Dr. Samuel MAYS and William
           FRIERSON, Executors. 31 April 1808.

page 44   Oral will of William HARRISON (living on the double
           branch of Rutherford Creek) to John OVERTON. Named
           wife, Sarah and children. 16 September 1811.

page 45   John PIERCE will. Brother, Spencer; Samuel PIERCE.
           Two little nephews Joseph and Jesse; brother, Robert;
           nephew, William; two nieces, Lucenda PIERCE and Betsy
           PIERCE. 10 January 1812. Witness: Robt. MACK,
           Nathan MURPHEY.

page 46   Will of Drury BRIDGES. Wife, Molley and all my
           children. Wife and brother Daniel G. BRIDGES
           Executors. 29 January 1812. Witness: Daniel S.(?)
           BRIDGES, James PAISLEY.

page 47   Robert MC KEAN will. Wife, Elizabeth and children.
           20 January 1812. Witness: James BROOKS, Thos. MAHON,
           Tandy YOUNG.

page 48   Sale of Robert MC KEAN. No date. Those buying:
           Jacob ROGERS, Richard MC MAHON,Thomas MC MAHAN,
           Phillip LINDSEY (TINSLEY?), John BECKENSTAFF, Chales
           PATE, Anthony I. TURNER, Robert GOAD, Thomas MAKIN,
           Stephen BROOKS, John HOLDER, James MORRISON, John B.
           MC MAHAN, Hezekiah BROOKS, William TURNER, Dudley
           BROOKS, Abel WILSON, Mack MILLER, Mark HARDIN,
           William FALIM, William PURDY, David MONTGOMERY.

page 48   Inventory of William GREEN, by Laurence HALCOMB,
           administrator. No date.

page 50   Inventory of John DOBSON, by Phebe DOBSON and George
           B. DOBSON, 16 June 1812.

page 50   Inventory of Henry LUSK. Notes of Alexander SUNDIAL,
           10 April 1794; Amos BALOH, 19 January 1797. James
           LUSK 3 May 1811.

page 52   Inventory of Patience SELLARS, 15 June 1812.

page 53   Sale of Thomas FORE, by Samuel H. WILLIAMS, and
           Polina FORE. Buying: Matthew BRANCH, andrew
           LAFFERTY, Charles COATES, John POWELL, Robert NEELEY,

Thomas HUDSPETH, Harrison COOPER, Nancy BRANCH, Robert HILL, Simpson HARRIS, Henry BRANCH, Reddick ROBISON, Polina F. FORE, John MATTOS, Joseph WALES, Wiley GRIFFIN. 1 January 1810.

page 53   Inventory of Drury BRIDGES, June term, 1812, Daniel G. BRIDGES and Poley BRIDGES.

page 56   Inventory of James OGLESBY; no date, by Hugh W. STEPHENSON.

page 60   Inventory and Sale of George BURNS. No date. Those buying: George BURNS, Thomas STANFIELD, John HARRIS, Charles GRAY, Laurence BURNS, Isaac STANFIELD, Robert OLIPHANT, Isaac MC COLLUM, Francis PARKER, David FARRIS, _____kiah WALDROP, Jacob STANFIELD, William MC INTOSH, John ALLEN.

page 61   John STANFIELD will. Wife, Sarah; son, Isaac; Sarah MC CARTY, daughter of mine; sons, Jackson, Jonathan, and John; daughter, Elizabeth HARRIS; daughter Rebecca STANFIELD. No date.

page 62   Inventory of Luke GRIMES, deceased, taken 15 September 1812.

page 62   Inventory of James STANFIELD

page 63   Inventory of George KNOX, deceased, taken 24____ 1812.

page 63   Inventory of James KNOX, deceased, taken 23 September 1812.

page 64   Estate of Honay HOGSON(?), deceased, "who departed this life on 3 August 1812 at house of L.B. ESTES."

page 65   Inventory of Thomas H. HOLLAND, by James HOLLAND, administrator.

page 65   Will of John JAMISON. To my (first)?? children, George JAMISON, Rebecca F____ay?; Elizabeth JAMISON and also John JAMISON. Son, Robert; son Samuel?; son Hosia?; daughter, Margaret DOUGLASS; son, James; son Allen, when he is 21; beloved wife, Rhoda. 13 October 1811.

page 65   Add to Will of John JAMISON; John DOUGLAS, executor. Witnesses: Wm. HOLT, Joseph IRWIN (?).

page 67   Inventory of goods of George DAVIDSON, deceased, 1 September 1812.

page 68   Sale of goods of James KNOX, deceased, 23 November 1812. Buying: Joseph CHOATE; Daniel COATES; Ambrose POWELL; Alexander KELLEY; Thomas EDWARDS, Esquire; Thomas LOWD; John PHILLIPS; Jonathan BULLOCK; Doctor Garrett (?) GREENFIELD; James LOVE; William DUDLEY; Robert OLIPHANT; Walker KNOK; Squire CHOSTE; ADONIJAH.
Division of negroes of James KNOX, deceased, among

5

heirs: Widdow Peggy POWELL; Sally, youngest daughter; Joseph CHOATE who married Jenny KNOX, daughter of James KNOX. 24 October 1812. Signed William FRIERSON and Henry KIRK.

page 70   Sale of Luke GRIMES, deceased, December session, 1812. Those buying: Nancy GRIMES; Loyed GRIMES; Cathy GRIMES; John GRIMES; William GRIMES; James BEATY; Henry KOONCE; William STOCKARD; David CRAIG; John CLOUD; William HUNTER; John TOMLINSON; Redding WOMBLE; Henry PICKARD; John FROST; Lewn (?) FORKINER; Isaac LITTLETON; Lewis FORKNER . Signed, Nancy GRIMES, Administrator.

page 71   Sales of property of George DAVIDSON, deceased, December, 1813, by E. E. DAVIDSON. (Note: see will book C-1, page 91 for will). Those buying: Widdow; Henry THOMPSON; James PURSELL; James HANNAH; Green WILLIAMSON; George DAVIDSON; John E. DAVISON; G. F. DAVIDSON; James L. DAVIDSON; Louisa S. DAVIDSON; Joshua SMITH; SAMUEL B. MC KNIGHT; Samuel J. ROGERS; Thomas NATION; William A. MAXWELL; Signed: Gilbreath F. DAVIDSON and James L. DAVIDSON, Administrators.

page 72   Inventory of Daniel NEEL, by Samuel OLIPHANT, administrator, December, 1812.

page 72   Inventory of sales of George KNOX, deceased. Sale held 7 November 1812. A. CATHEY, administrator. Those buying: Joshua NEWMAN; A. CATHEY; James FOLLIS; William WILLIAMS; James KNOX; Walker KNOX.

page 73   Inventory of Estate of Ayres DOSS, deceased, March term, 1813.

page 73   Sale of property of Thomas HOLLAND, deceased, March session, 1813. James HOLLAND, Administrator. Many books listed, medical books and others. Those buying: John REED; James HOLLAND; John CAMPBELL; Robert MACK; Robert P. CURRIN; Horatio DE PRIEST; Doctor SANSOM.

page 74   Inventory of estate of James AIKIN, deceased, March term, 1813.

page 75   Will of James AIKIN. Wife, Lucretia. Our children, Stephen, Jinsey, Lucy, and John. 20 January 1813. Witness: Ezekial AKIN, Wm. WOODS.

page 77   Osburne P. NICHOLSON will. Wife, Sackey; daughter Maria; son, Calvin; son, Alfred. Wife, Samuel CRAIG, and Doctor L. B. ESTES Executors, 14 November 1812.

page 79   Will of William ISHAM. Son, William; son, Henry; son, Dudley; son, Charles; son, George; son, Arthur; son, Jonathan. Executors: son, William ISHAM and Joseph PAYTON. 12 February 1813.

page 81   Will of William DEVER. Jane DEVER Executrix. Son, William; daughter, Elizabeth REED; daughter, Margaret O'NEAL; daughter, Mary DEVER; daughter, Jane DEVER. Witness: Elisha HURT, Elizabeth HURT, Osphia RUTLEDGE, 1 August 1812.

page 82   Inventory of William ISHAM, now deceased. Taken
          16 March 1813.

page 83   Will of Samuel CARTER. (Note: This may be CHARTER-
          in the body of the will "h's had been inserted between
          the C and a in some of the names and between the a and
          r in others. This is very confusing.) Wife
          Elizabeth; daughter, Winney; son Theophillis CAHRTER;
          son, Shadrack CARHTER: son, Samuel CARTER; daughter,
          Lucy L. CHARTER. 16 April 1813.

page 83   Will of William SIMS. Wife, Judith; unmarried
          children. 150 acres conveyed to myself, John SIMS,
          and John P. ELLIOTT by Alexander G. ROGERS, 20 July
          1812, part of 2000 acres tract granted to Alexander
          MARTIN, Esquire, by N. C. (reserving one acre
          forever for graveyard). William SIMS, Junr. now lives
          on the said land. 3 February 1813. Witness:
          Harrison BLACKGRAVE, Thomas T. GREENFIELD, John SIMS.

page 84   Will of William SIMS. Land in Hanover County,
          Virginia. My children. Daughter, Jenny WINN; Wife,
          Judith; son, John; daughter, Elizabeth HARLIN;
          daughter, Polly SIMS; son, William SIMS, Junr;
          daughter, Milly GRIMHAW (?); daughter, Nancy SIMS;
          daughter, Patsey SIMS; daughter, Turkey MC COLLISTER;
          son, Thomas; daughter, Sarah GILASBY; daughter,
          Francis SIMS; (daughter Polly, Nancy, Patsey, and
          Frances). 14 March 1813.

page 91   Will of Jonathan ISHAM. (see BOOK B., page 232).
          Wife Elizabeth; daughter, Ursula; son, John; daughter,
          Elizabeth; daughter, Sally; daughter Jinny; daughter,
          Polly; son, George; daughter, Janney. 15 September
          1813. Witness: John PAYTON and Andrew KENNEDY.

page 93   Will of Francis WRIGHT. 30 May 1809. Son Robert;
          son-in-law Robert MC CASTER (MC CARTER?); son, John;
          son, Francis, Junr.

page 94   Inventory of property of David PICKINS, deceased.
          23 July 1813.

page 95   Inventory of property of John MURHEAD, deceased.
          2 August 1813. Notes on Joseph MC CAVEN; in hands of
          John LOVE on Abner BLAIR; on Perminas BRINS (?);
          Resin L. BISHOP; Samuel MONTGOMERY; Coles MEDE; John
          JULER(?); Joseph O'NEAL; Jacob MC KEE; Frederick C.
          SIMPSON; Col.Joseph LEMASTER; David HUDSTOCK; John B.
          WILLS; Samuel OLIPHANT; Absalom RICHARDSON; Thomas
          MALONE; Samuel KENNEDY. Signed Martha (her mark)
          MUIRHEAD, Robert OLIPHANT, and James LOVE.

page 97   Inventory of Samuel CARTER, deceased, 4 August 1813.

page 98   Inventory of Henry Payton, deceased. No date.

page 98   Inventory of John STANFIELD, deceased, 16 September
          1813.

page 100 Heirs of Joseph MC GEE,deceased- bond of division to
          C. MC GEE. Polly MC GEE, widow of the late Reverend
          Joseph MC GEE, Abner PREWITT and Nancy his wife and

7

Polly MC GEE daughter of said Joseph, all heirs and legatees. 13 November 1812. Bound unto Chiles MC GEE of the state of Tennessee for $2000. "The conditions of the above obligation are such that whereas the above bound Polly MC GEE, Abner PREWIT and Nancy, his wife, and Polly MC GEE, Junr., heirs and legatees of aforesaid Joseph MC FEE, deceased, being desirous of leaving the Mississippi Territory and removing to Tennessee and for purpose of enabling them to do so, the before mentioned Chiles MC GEE was prevailed upon to undertake the settlement of the estate." Chiles MC GEE, executor desontart??.

page 102   Inventory of property of William TURNER, deceased, 21 December 1913.

page 103   Sales of property of John MUIRHEAD, deceased, on 15 October 1813. Buying: Hezekiah WALDRUP; George MARTIN; John LEEPER; John THOMAS; James WHITTON; Joseph HAMPTON; James LOVE; Samuel OLIPHANT; William REGION; John JOHNSON; Robert PUREY (PEERY?); Richard ROBERTS; John H. GATLIN; Samuel SNOODY; James DOBBINS; Rezin L. BISHOP; Martha MUIRHEAD: Caleb ZACKERY; Terry BRIDGES; Thomas C. FARRIS; Kemp HOLLAND; Thomas MC GEE; Joseph LYNN; Hugh WHITESIDE; Jeremiah BOLEN; Miles MORRISON; Robert COWAN; Barton DAVIS; Isaac STANFIELD; John G. BERRY; Sarah MC CAFFERTY; Joseph HOPKINS; John JACKSON; Jonathan J. STANFIELD; William D. LEEPER; Stephen MILLER; John PREWITT; Thomas DUFF.

page106   James MILICAN, deceased. Sale, 5 October 1813. Buying: Elizabeth MILICAN; N.B. PHILLIPS; Joseph B. HOWELL; Isaac, Thomas, and James MILICAN; Henry KIDDY; Jacob REED; George A. BROCK (?); Jane REYNOLDS; David BUTTER; Michael PREWITT; Isaac BUTTER; Samuel BEARD; James THOMAS; Hugh GILBREATH.

page 108   Sale of Henry PAYTON, deceased. No date. Buying: Robert PAYTON; Jesse MC LEAN; Conrad KYMES; Peter MILLER; Moses HUDSPETH; John GOFF; William KYMES; Richard JOHNSON; Elias J. ARMSTRONG· John WILLIAMS: Tilman SPENCER; William L. KING; George WEBSTER; Peggy PAYTON; James DUNCAN; Thomas WORTHAM; Thomas NATION; Gideon JOHNSON; Henry PAYTON; Nancy MC LEAN; James PEYTON; Edward NATION; John PEERY; Adam KLYCE; Burwell CANNON.

page 111   Will of John BROWN the Elder of Wilkes County, North Carolina. Wife, Jane; Sons, Hugh, Hamilton, Thomas, and Allen; daughters, Ann and Margaret. Daughter, Elizabeth STEWART. Land on which I now live in North Carolina. 2000 Acres on Knob Creek, Tennessee. Son, John; son, James; William. 3 Feburary 1812.

page 114   Inventory of Moses G. FRIERSON. 17 December 1813.

page 115   Estate of Col. John STANFIELD, deceased. Sold on 27 October 1813, by Jonathan STANFILE. Buying: Sarah STANFILL; Eli WARD; Stephan Phillips; Issac STANFILL; Jackson STANFILE; John STANFILE; George TURNBOW: John JACKSON; Joseph HART; Josiah WHITE;

Ebenezer MILLER; Stephen MILLER; William STANFIELD; John DAVIS; John PHILLIPS; Toliver BRADY; Charles GRAY; Sally MC AFERTY; John WILEY; James BRADY; Rebecca STANFILL; Samuel OLIPHANT.

page 116   Inventory of estate of Ezekial ALEXANDER, deceased. No date.

page 117   John JOHNSON will. Wife, for support of her and Elijah. Nancy MONTGOMERY. Three daughters. Son, Thomas; son, Joseph; son, William ; son Elijah; Daughters Nancy, Elizabeth, and Polly. 9 September 1813. Executors: Joseph HERNDON; John MONTGOMERY; Joseph JOHNSON. Witness: John HODGE, Patrick MC QUIRE, and John MC MANUS.

page 119   Will of Jane SANDERS. Sons William AND Peter; two sisters' children, Jane MALONE and Lucy A. HUNT (HURT?) . Executors: Peter LYON and Hallery MALONE. 29 November 1813.

page 120   Will of Alexander BRECKINRIDGE, Senr., of county of Bourbourn, state of Kentucky. Wife Polly; son Edda Linn BRECKINRIDGE; sons George, Robert James, Alexander, and John. Daughters Ann, Rachale, and Elizabeth; sons Preston, Washington, and Roddy H. BRECKINRIDGE, land on Lytle's Creek, Maury County, Tennessee - divided between the three brothers - George BRECKINRIDGE their guardian until they come of age. Daughter Jinny. 2 June 1813.

page 124   Sale of property of William TURNER, deceased. Held 13 and 14 January 1814. Buying: Mrs. Nancy TURNER: Colonel James T. SONFORD; John MILLER, esqr.; William Abner CLEVELAND; Captain Benjamin SMITH: Mc Daniel HUTCHESON; William YANCY; John M. NAPPIER; Thomas H. JENKINS; Jacob DAIMWOOD; James GULLET; William KILCREASE; Colonel Albert RUSSEL; William WEBB; Edward B. LITTLEFIELD; Robert BENTON; Dudley BROOKS; James HIGS; Waston HARDIN; James MONTGOMERY;
ff   Abel WILSON; Garrett VOORHIES; John D. DAVIDSON; Henry COOKE; John COCKRILE; Doctor A. WHITESIDE; James PEARCILE; James HUEY; Major WILLIS; Joseph SAULTERS; Benjamin LEWIS; Caden Johnson; John Bolton; William WADE; John WILLIAMS; John BUTTER; Richard COCKE.

page 127   Inventory of property of Joseph MOORE, deceased, 16 May 1814.
            Inventory of property of John LOVE, deceased, 5 March 1814.

page 128   Inventory of property of Luke H. DEAN, deceased, May term, 1814.
            Inventory of property of Samuel WILLIS, deceased, 20 February 1814.

page 129   Inventory of sale of Esham CHRISTIAN, deceased, February session, 1814. One negro sold of Ann Christian.

page 130   Sale of Thomas Edwards, deceased, 19 March 1814.

Buying: Mary EDWARDS; A. JOHNSON; G. SHARP; William MAXEY; Zebinon SPENCER; Magness DAVIS; William DAVIS; William HUNTER; Davis GURLEY; Benjamin ADAIR; Samuel GRIFFITH; Hugh GILBREATH; Stephen EDWARDS; William BRYAN; George MURPHEY; Noble OSBOURNE; Henry SHARP; Sherwood WHITE.

page 131   Will of James WATTS. Written 22 February, A.D. 1793.
James WATTS of county of Iredell, North Carolina.
Beloved wife Mary "plantation I now live on".
Eldest daughter Margaret. Daughters Mary, Rebeccah,
and Rosanna. Sons William, Andrew, and John.
Granddaughter Ann PITCHEY. Filed Iredell County,
North Carolina, 14 June 1813.

page 134   Power of attorney from heirs of James WATTS,
deceased, to Daniel KILLIAN. heirs John MC CLELLAND
and Rosanna his wife, alias Jane WATTS; Ann PITCHEY,
daughter of Ann PITCHEY, alias WATTS, all of Iredell
County, North Carolina appoint our friend and

brother-in-law Daniel KILLIAN who intermarried
with Mary WATTS, also of Iredell County. Signed:
J. MC CLELLAND, Rosy MC CLELLAND, James WOODS, Jean
WOODS, Margaret (her mark) WATTS, Polly KILLION,
Anne PITCHEY. 9 June 1813.

page 136   Inventory of chattel property owned by James LATTA,
deceased, late of Maury County, Tennessee 15 May
1815, signed by John LATTA.

page 137   16 June 1815. Sale of James LATTA, deceased.
Buying: Thomas TAYLOR; Thomas J. HARDAMAN; Martha
LATA; William WEBB; Josiah HOGAN; Thomas GOAD; John
LATTA; John POLK; Pleasant CREWS; William HENTY;
Joseph WINGFIELD; John KINDOWS; Thomas LATA; James
ONEAL; David WHERTON; Julius BURTON; John CANADA;
William SEALLARS; Charles NEELY; Andrew MILLS;
William GRANT; John P. POWELL; John DUCKWORTH;
Allen RAINY; Luke PATTERSON; Shadrick CHANDLER;
Green B. ROGERS.

page 141   Inventory of sale of Walker KNOX, deceased. Among
items: year's rent on plantation maintained one
discharge for tour of duty in Captain John GORDON'S
Company of "spiez" for term of seven months; one
discharge for a tour of four months and fifteen days
in the Tennessee Militia under command of Major
General Wm. CARRELL; notes on Cornelius DABNEY;
Ambrose POWELL; Daniel FERGESEN - 21 day of August,
1815. Also money in hands of Joseph CHEATNIM (?)
and Joseph CHOATE. James KNOX, administrator.

page 142   Sale of Aron HUNTER, deceased, 1 July 1815. Buying:
Mary HUNTER; Ephraim MC LEAN; John FITZGERALD;
Robert HILL; Daniel KEETCH; John B. NEELY (?);
Robert WILLIAMS; Isaac BROOKS; Amos DICKSON;
Absalom YARBOROUGH; Thomas BROOKS of Williamson
county; Thomas BAKER; By Robert HILL, Administrator
and Mary HUNTER Administrix.

page 144   Estate of Charles COURT, deceased. Thomas HEDGEPATH

10

Administrator. "Money in the clerk's office coming
to Charles COURT and his wife for their attendance
as witnesses in a suit between Thomas HEDGEPATH and
Ambrose POWEL." 5 June 1815. William RUSSELL and
Sam P. MC LEAN.

page 145   Inventory of estate of Isaiah MC BRIDE. Signed:
           21 August 1815, Francis MC BRIDE and Samuel MC BRIDE.

page 145   Inventory of estate of William LONG, deceased,
           (Bible, sermon book, hymn book). Johnson CRAIG and
           John HUNTER, Administrator. No date.

page 146   Inventory of estate of Jesse BROWN, deceased,
           18 August 1815, John ATKISON, Administrator.

page 146   Laying off year's provision for Hannah SCOTT, widow
           of Samuel SCOTT, deceased, 2 june 1815. Thomas
           JONES, Silas ALEXANDER, John MATHIS.

page 147   Estate of Lucy HUNT -sale- no date. Buying: Samuel
           POLK; Horatio DE PRIEST; Daniel BROWN; John CAMPBELL;
           William R. BRADLEY; Albert RUSSELL; Nathaniel SCOTT;
           William LION; Peter LION; John CHISM; William
           SELLARS; Elizabeth HUNT; Jethro BROWN; John BOLTON;
           Burrel AKIN; Lewis PETMO_ON (?); Nathaniel CHEARS.

page 147   Sale of June 6, 1815, property of William KELLY,
           deceased. Buying: John CECIL; James SHALBY; Thomas
           RANDLE; John HEWEY; Charles SHEARMON; Isaac
           SEAGRAVES; Charles PARTEE; Vinson SEGRAVES; Polly
           KELLY; Ambrose YARBOROUGH; James MITCHEL; Andey
           MITCHEL; James REEVES; (Polly KELLY bought all
           Household goods), William MC LEAN John LOCKART
           George MITCHEL; Thomas LOCART.

page 150   William JORDEN, deceased, at New Orleans on the
           25 of Febuary 1815. Thomas JERDEN, Administrator.

page 150   Account of hire of negroes of estate of Thomas
           EDWARDS for the year 1815 by Mary EDWARDS and Davis
           GURLEY (administrator and admintrix)

page 151   Property of Jesse Yarberough, deceased, 6 June 1815.
           Buying: Absalom YARBOROUGH Administrator Thomas
           LOCKART, and Benjamin LITTEN.

page 151   Inventory of Samuel NEELY, deceased, 17 August 1815.

page 151   Inventory of Grant HAWKINGS, deceased. William
           HAWKINS, Administrator, 21 August 1815.

page 152   Inventory of Fereby RICE- Pherreby RICE, Admintrix.

page 152   Inventory of William JONES, deceased.

page 153   Inventory of John CHURCHWELL, deceased, 24 August
           1815. Elizabeth CHURCHWELL, Admintrix, Sam'l B.
           MC KNIGHT. "His discharge not known."

page 153   Inventory of Thomas SMITH, deceased.

11

page 153   Estate of David JONES, deceased, (Notes in North
            Carolina) Isabells JONES bound as Administrator.

page 154   Inventory of Abner KING, deceased, "his claim on the
            United States for his services in Captain MC MAHEN'S
            Company of mounted men from 28th of September until
            as will appeared by the muster rolls."

page 154   Inventory of John HOOD, deceased, 10 June 1815.
            Agnes HOOD, Executrix.

page 155   Inventory of William CARR, deceased. 18 August 1815
            "his services for a touer of duty against the Creek
            Indians in Captain John GORSON'S Company of 'spees'
            commanded by Major General JACKSON from 30 September
            1814 until first day of April 1814???- enclosed his
            services for a touer of duty in Captain MC MAHEN'S
            Company at New Orleans under the command of Major
            General Andrew JACKSON which touer he dyed".
            Alexander CATHEY, Administrator.

page 156   Inventory of Daniel YATES, deceased, 23 August 1815.
            Roswile SEATON, Administrator.

page 156   Inventory of William KELLY, deceased. "Certificate
            for lost property in the army". Wages for a tour
            of duty to New Orleans. Polly KELLY, Administrix.

page 157   August term, 1815. Petition of Roswell SEATON and
            Martha SEATON his wife, former Marthe YATES of Maury,
            she that same Martha some years past intermarried
            with the same Daniel YATES who on 1 Feburuary 1815
            was secured of a tract of land. . . . and the said
            Daniel YATES has since the first day of February
            departed this life. . . . the said Martha YATES has
            since his death intermarried with your petitioner
            Roswell SEATON.

page 159   Sale of property of James HUNT, deceased, sold by
            Elizabeth HUNT, an Administrix, 9 June 1815. Buying:
            James Higgs; William BEARD; John P. NORVEL (?);
            Cluff LAVENDER; Lewis PETMON; Peter LYONS; Joseph
            MILLER; Swann HOLDEN; Samuel ANGLIN; Henry MALONE;
            Abner CLEVELAND; Ezekial AKINS; William R. BRADY;
            James EVINS; William CRAWFORD; William WEBB; William
            LYON; John NULTS (?); John BOLTON; Abner FRANKLIN;
            Joseph WINKFIELD; William WINDFORD; William DEAN.

page 161   Estate of Luke GRYMES, deceased. Paid to John
            GRIMES, heir; Loyd GRIMES, heir; Catherine GRIMES,
            heir; William GRIMES, heir;by self, heir; demands
            against estate by William GRIMES, Sr, 19 August
            1815. Nancy PICARD, Administrix.

page 162   Estate of Thomas Segraves, deceased. Sarah
            SEGRAVES, Administrix.

page 162   Estate of Henry MC CULLA, deceased, 24 August 1815.
            James ADMINISTRONG (?), Elexander DOBINS, and
            George DICKY, appointed appraisors. Signed by
            James ARMSTRONG.

page 164	May term, 1815. Settlement with William ISOM and Joseph PAYTON executors of estate of William ISOM, deceased. Settled with all heirs accept Henry ISOM who is not yet of age, 9 August 1815. A. CATHEY and Joel (?) THIMPSON, Administrators.
page 165	Estate of Samuel NELSON, deceased, 19 August 1815, Abner HENDRIX, Administrator.
page 165	Estate of Edward BEANLAND, deceased, William DOOLY and Polly BEANLAND, Administrators.
page 166	Inventory of Thrasher MC COLLUM, late of Maury County, 22 June 1815. (see Book B. page 241). Mary MC COLLOM, Administrix.
page 171	Sale of estate of Thomas POWEL, deceased, on March 25, 1815. Elisha POWEL, Zepparah POWEL. "Observe Flora POWEL, Senior, is the widdow who in the amount of sailes is called widdow--Flora POWEL named in thr amount of sales is the daughter of the deceased." Elisha POWEL, Administrator.
page 174	Account of estate of Robert NEELY. William NEELY, Administrator, 28 October 1807. "To amount _____ the testator (?) in South Carolina, Chester District, 17 June 1811--amount of vandue bill as made by administrator." 1812--To William LATA note for a horse (?) in schooling; note on John GILMORE due 17 January 1805 note on John LATTA ; Henry BRANCH; William RODGERS. To account on Joshua DALE, Thomas HEDGEPATH, AYDELOT, James LURK, Patenr FARE, Widow WHITSON, Hugh DOUGLASS, paid Richd BASKERVILLE, George HANKS, A. WHERTON, Samuel H. WILLIAMS, ____ EARTHMAN, John CHAMBERS, James WALKER. Peter R. BOOKER, Harrison Coffe ____, Stephen EDWARDS, Hughe NEELEY, WILLIAM BRADSHAW, Benjamin THOMAS, Harrison COOPER, Doctor MC CLEAN (paid for attendance), Thomas HEDGEPATH (for attending), Robert BUFORD, Ambrose POWEL, Marker Mellon REDENGRIDE (?), William RAY, Doctor John DEWEARS, James MC ALISTER, Thomas JELETOTTE(?).
page 176	Estaet of Samuel SCOTT, deceased, 2 June 1812 (or 1813?). Buying: Hannah SCOTT; Baily BROOKS; Samuel M. JOHNSON; West HARRIS; Silas ALEXANDER; Isaac NEEDHAM; Robert DAVISON; John MATTHEWS; William JOHNSON; George JOHNSON; George FERRIL; Isaac J. THOMAS; Samuel B. MC KNITE; Orin STANDPACE; Jacob WILLIAMS; Barwell CANNON; Hugh W. STEPHENS; Stephen EDWARDS; Thomas BROOKS; George BROOKS; Hezakiah JONES; John TIDWELL; James REECE; John GARRIGAN; John H. JOHNSON; Ann (?) STANDFORD; Samuel BEARD; David JONES; Andrew J. PORGEY; Zilman SPENCER; Henry BECKINS; Lewis NEEDHAM; Isaac WILLIAMS; Hannah SCOTT; Lewis NEEDHAM; Administrators, of estate.
page 179	21 October 1815. Division of negroes of James C. ALDERSON, deceased. Sarah ALDERSON, first; Nancy, second legatee; Betsy, third legatee; Polly, fourth legatee; and Jinny, fifth legatee.

page 180   Sale of Abner KING, deceased, 15 Septembet 1815.
            Ellen PICKARD, Administrix, (Alexander PICKARD
            bought item).

page 181   Property of Walter (or Walker) KNOX, deceased.
            James KNOX, Administrator.

page 181   17 November 1815. More property of Robert NEELY,
            deceased. William NEELY, Administrator.

page 181   Memorandum of items sold, Arthur AYDELOTTE, deceased.
            Jodiah AYDELOTT, Administrator.

page 182   Inventory of estate of Grant HAWKINS, deceased.
            "Discharge for six minths under command of General
            JACKSON, Captain JACKSON'S company." William
            HAWKINS, Administrator, 17 September 1816.

page 182   List of goods of Andrew GOAN, deceased. Nathaniel
            SIMS, Administrator.

page 182   Estate of Robert JOHNSON, deceased, 24 June 1815.
            Isham JOHNSON, Administrator.

page 183   Estate of William TONEY, deceased, 22 August 1815.
            Cynthy TONEY, Administrator.

page 183   Inventory of property of David JONES, deceased, to
            be returned to November term 1815 by Isabel Jones,
            Administrator.

page 184   Widow provision for Mary HUNTER and nine of a
            family, late the wife of Aron HUNTER, deceased,
            27 May 1815.

page 185   Sale of William JONES, deceased, 23 September 1815.
            Buying: David MONTGOMERY; Samuel MC LEAN; John
            MOULTON; Stephen COLLINS; Willie GITFON(?); Milley
            JONES; John SELLARS; James PORTER; Henry GOODNITE;
            Thomas RANDLE; James B. MC LEAN; Jethro BROWN;
            Samuel CRAWFORD; Joseph TAYLOR; Reuben GOOD; William
            HENRY; David HOGAN; Robert GOOD; Jeremiah GURLEY,
            Administrator.

page 186   Estate of O. P. NICHOLSON, deceased. Belonging to
            heirs of Sarah NICHOLSON, now Sarah VOORHIES--1/4
            part of property-- said part to settle on Garrett
            L. VOORHIES as his wife Sarah's part, sold
            28 October 1815 by me, James T. SANDFORD. Buying:
            Walter S. JENKENS; Daniel BROWN, Senior; Molliky
            NICHOLS; James HUGHEY; James SWANSON; Patrick
            CHAIRS; Frederick MILLER; John MILLER; John NELSON;
            Thomas H. JENKINS; Jethro BROWN; Thomas BODDIE;
            George NICHOLSON; Green B. ROGERS; Anderson MILLAR;
            Calvin H. NICHOLSON; Alfred A. NICHOLSON (purchased
            by his guardian James T. SANDFORD).

page 189   Estate of Samuel SRIGLEY, deceased, sold 7 May 1815.
            Buying: George HOFTER; John JONES; Ebenezar RICE;
            William Covey, David HANKINS; Joseph EAST; John
            GRIMES; Christopher HUTIONS(?); David KINCAID;
            Lewis (?) KENDRICK; George WEBSTER; J. B. BECKINS;

James PACERLY; Elijah IRINA; Richard FOSTER; William
GRIMES; John GOODNOE; Jesse TYNUM(TYNER); Shedrick
DUGGER; Akin MOORE; James E. Edmundson; _____ SRIGLEY;
Jesse EVENS, Esquire; John GRIFFIN; Thomas MITCHELL;
Thomas PORTER.

page 191   Property of Daniel YATES, deceased, 2 September_____
Raswell SEATON and Adam ANDREWS, Administratiors.

page 192   Property sale of William LONG, deceased. Buying:
Mrs. LONG; William STOCKARD; John COOPER; William
PICKARD (purchased Bible); Henry PICKARD; John
GORDON; James BEATY; James GORDON; John HUNTER,
Administrator.

page 193   Ordered that James MITCHELL, James BEATY and Johnson
CRAIG apportion to Rebecca KING, late widow of Abner
KING, deceased, years portion.

page 194   Above order carried out 16 September 1815.

page 194   Estate of Thomas J. JOHNSON, deceased, 14 October
1815. George JOHNSON, Thomas BROOKS, William
MC NUTT. George JOHNSON, Administrator.

page 194   Order that William STOCKARD, Esquire, James BEATY,
John COOPER, apportion to Margaret LONG year's
provision and make return August 1815.

page 195   Inventory of Thomas DAWSON, deceased, taken
18 November 1815 by John M. GOODLOE, Administrator.
"Discharge for six months tour of military duty
signed by Colonel P. PIPKINS, dated 27 January 1815.

page 195   May term 1815. Lemuel PREWETT, George BRECKENRIDGE,
and John GILLESPIE laying out year's provision for
Rachel SRIGLEY, late wife of Samuel SRYGLEY,
deceased.

page 196   Additional inventory of Edward BEANLAND, deceased.
William DOOLEY, Administrator, 19 June 1815.

page 196   William STAGGS, Nancy WADSWORTH, Martin STAGGS,
Absalom FRY, John WARNERSON, Joseph STAGS, Pherrby
RICE, William AI.TREASE, John BANER, George BURPO,
"a true copy of sale of property of Pherriby RICE,
widow of Roland RICE, deceased."

page 197   Sale of property of Thomas (O.) SMITH, deceased
3 October 1815. Widow, John MITCHELL, Frances
SEACREASE, Robert ELLIOTT, Charles SHEARMAN,
Nicholas BRANCH, John MC INTERE, L___GRIFFIN,
Buyers. Sarah SMITH, Adninistratior.

page 198   Memorandum of property of late John P. CRAIG,
deceased. Isaac ACUFF, Administrator.

page 199   Inventory, not headed, follows above entry. Buying:
Charles M. PARTEE; Widdow H. BROOKS; John BOOLER;
Hezakiah BROKS; Geremiah GERLEY; Charles SHEARMAN;
Ephraem MC LEAN; _____ HOGAN; Isaac SELLARS; Benton
BAGETT (or BAUGUS of BADGETT); James MC CLEAN;
David HINES; Samuel MC LEAN; Marks PIPKIN; Hiram

15

PARTEE; Isah HOGAN; James RUTLEDGE; John DUCKWORTH:
Edward COSTET (?); Abner PARTEE; Micager PAIN;
Robert SELLERS.

page 202 Estate of William TONEY, deceased, sold 15 and 16
September 1815. Signer, Cythia TONEY.

page 205 Memorandum of sale of Thomas LADD, deceased. Buying:
Jehosophat LADD; Polly HANKS; Thomas AYDELOTT;
James ERWIN; Thomas BROOKS; William DUNCAN; Daniel
AYDELOTT.

page 206 Widow's provisions for Pherriba RICE, late widow of
Roland RICE, deceased, November session 1815.
Jesse EVANS, Lemuel PREWITT, Pleasant MC GREARY.

page 206 Sale of corn held 24 March 1815. Buying: Jonathan
MC MANNAS; Nicholas THOMPSON; John KILLINGWORTH;
John COUSAT; Deborech TAYNER; John RENFRO. "sold by
us--Mary RECORD, John W. RECORD, Sion RECORD and
Elisha HUNTER, executors."

page 207 Inventory of estate of James MC CAULEY, deceased,
taken 23 November 1815. Major DAVIS, Administrator.

page 208 Widow's provision for Jane MC BRIDE, widdow of
Isaiah MC BRIDE, deceased, made by S. B. MC KNIGHT,
James HANNAH, and J. J. ZOLLICOFFER.

page 208 Widdow's provision for Catharine MC CAWLEY, widow of
James MC CAWLEY, made by Eilliam RODGERS, Amus
JOHNSON, and Chiles MC GEE, 14 December 1816.

page 209 Sale of _____ by Abraham WHITESIDE, Administrator.
Buying: Jonathan WEBSTER; Thomas C. FARRIS; George
KELSY; John SKIPPER; John HAWKINS; Uzzial HAWKINS;
Hugh DOUGLASS; Reason L. BISHOP; William F. SCOT;
Benone DICKEY; Joshua NEWMAN.

page210 Estate of Mary WARD, deceased, listed 19 February
1816. Benjamin SMITH, D. BROWN, James T. SANFORD,
Executors.

page 211 Sales of James MC CARTY, deceased, sold 14 December
1815. Buyers: Nancy MC CARTY; Nathaniel MC CARTY;
Katherine MC CARTY; Polly MC CARTY; William DAVIS;
Magnus DAVIS; Henry SHARP; Samuel GRIFFITH; Joseph
STOCKARD; James THOMAS; William MC GEE; Elisha
THOMAS; Moses TOMLIN; Nathaniel FISHER; Major
DAVIS, Administrator.

    (NOTE: MC COULEY; MC CAWLEY; MC CARTY; on
      pages 207, 208, 211 must be same.)

page 212 Estate of Mrs. Roann JOSY, 1 Jamuary 1916,
J. WEBSTER, "Guardeen".

page 213 Inventory of property of Jesse RADFORD, deceased,
taken 1 February 1816.

page 214 Inventory of estate of John DICKEY, deceased,
25 November 1814 signed by Nancy DICKEY.

page 214   Sale of estate of John DICKEY, deceased, 24 December 1814. James T. SANDEFORD, Administrator.

page 215   Inventory of property of Isaac PATTERN, deceased, taken by Samuel PATERN, Administrator, November term 1814.

page 215   Account of chattel estate of Jesse BROWN, deceased, many books, John ATKISON, Senior, Administrator.

page 216   Inventory of goods of Luke H. DEANS, deceased, 19 August 1814. P. CUTTHAM. Administrator.

page 217   Widow's portion, Agnes HODGE, late widow of John HODGE, deceased, 23 March 1815. A. (?) CATHEY, William ERWIN, Joseph HOPKINS.

page 217   Sale of Alpia RICHARDSON, deceased. Richd. JENNINGS, Administrator.

page 218   Inventory of sale of John M. MURPHEY, deceased. "Wages for a tour of duty to Orleans". Nathaniel MURPHEY signed.

page 218   List of property of John HODGE, deceased, sold 23 March 1815. Buyres:

Edward NUNNALEE	Agnes HOAG
John BERRY	John JOHNSON
James THOMPSON	Samuel OLIPHANT
Thomas GREENFIELD	Joshua NEWMAN
Caleb FARRIS	Eleaner CATHIN
James KERR (?)	John ADAIR
George HODGE	Iaven SHELBY
Thomas C. FARRIS	John WATTS
William STANFIELD	John CAERY
Agnes HODGE	Thomas SHELBY
Reason BISHOP	James LANCK
Thomas Hopkins	John KINGTON
Robert WILEY	

page 220   Debts of Late L. B. ESTUS, deceased: John ALDERSON; James ALLEN; Major John BROWN; William ARMSTRONG; Zachariah BUTLER; William BRADSHAW; Dudley BROOKS; James BURNES; Simeon BATTEMAN; William BURKET; William M. BERRYHILL; Elijah BLOCKER; Peter R. BOOKER; William BEARD; George CAMPBELL; David CAMPBELL; William CATTES; John COOPER; Thomas CRENSHAW; Moses CHAFIN; Thomas ONELL; Jesse EVANS; William A. DAVIS; Jesse FOSTER; James FEITTON; Samuel CHAPALEAN; Bartlet ESTUS; Chesley ESTUS; John B. ESTUS; Josiah ALDERSON; Joshew MC DOWELL; J. L. BROWN; Lard B. BOYD; John M. GOODLOW; Lewis COCKRIL; Reuben A. CARTER; James DEWANEY and Andrew_____; Duncan MC INTERE; W. G. GILL; Robert YARBOROUGH; Solomin WATKINS; James FITTZGERELL; LAUGHLIN and EDWARDS; John ARMSTRONG; Thomas CAMPS; William H. RAMSEY; William G. GILLIAM; John GARNER; Thomas GREEN; James GULLIT; Spencer GRIFFIN; John COLEMAN; Doctor G. GREENFIELD; Robert GOOD; William ROSS; Benjamin H. LEWIS; Stephen NOBLE; Charles P. NEILSON; George

NICHOLSON; James L. NEELEY; John MYRICK; A. B.
MAYFIELD; Mrs. MANGEE; Joseph C. MC DOWELL;
Mollicky NICHOLSON; Walter MYRICK; John MILLAR;
John MC WILLIAMS; Thomas MUCHER; Thomas MC LEMORE;
Ed B. LITTLEFIELD; Humphrey LIECH; Robert HENDERSON;
Cauron HOLLAND; James GORDON; David AMES; John
HENDY; Willis RICHARDSON; Hugh ROSS; Jonah
RICHARDS; Nicholas PERKINS; Daniel PAYNE; Edw.
PUCKETT; William PHILLIPS; Andrew NEELY; William
STOCKARD; Jordan REECE; Joseph BODDES; Isaac
TURMAN; Alexander SMITH; John TULLEY; A. J. TURNER;
William VOORHIES; A. J. WALTON; Jonathan WEBSTER;
William RUTLEDGE; James C. MARTEN; William WHITE;
Dennis BRIGHT; Colonel Samuel H. WILLIAMS; General
Richard WINN; John C. WORMBRY; James WHITE; Thomas
WHITE; Doctor A. WHITESIDE; David OGLEVIE; Joshua
SMITH; John ROSS; Mack EDWARDS; Adam BAWYER; _____
MC KENON; _____ MC KEE; Jerry CHERRY; John
DOWNELLY; William WILLIAMS; Samuel MC MAHEN; James
MC MAHEN; Thomas SOUTHERLAND; David WHARTON;
Samuel CRAIG; Peter J. VOORHIES; William DUNN;
Alfred WHITE; John WHITE; John HAYNNIE; Allen JONES;
Lawrence BASS; John LAYMASTER; Robert WILLIS; James
SANDERS; William SCRIBNER; John P. CRAIGE; William
H. RAMSEY; James LAYMASTER; Daniel BROWN; John
MEECE (unknown); William BUTLER; John DANIEL;
William COOPER; William MITCHEL; Augustin BROWN;
George COCKBURN; John ALDERSON; William PILLOW;
Chares STATLER; John HOWELL; David MARTIN; William
GENNGER; John GARNER; John H. ESTES; Doctor H.
DEPRIEST; Been DAVIS; Lewis COCKRILL; Perry COHEA;
Captain Robert CAMPBELL; Saeky NICHOLSON; James
WALKER; Joseph B. PORTER; John BITTEMAN; Robert
REED; Dudley BROOKS; Meredith and Fielding HELMS;
"A list of the debts due to the estate of L. B.
ESTES, deceased."

page 233   Inventory of property of Samuel NELSON, 19 May 1815,
            Abner HENDRIX, signer.

page 233   20 February 1815. "It is my desire that Richard
            MC MAHEN and Calloway HARDIN should administer on
            the estate of my husband, deceased.....Polly
            MC MAHON."

page 233   Property of estate of James MC MAHEN, deceased,
            taken 20 February 1815, signer Robert MC MAHEN AND
            Calloway HARDIN.

page 234   "I appoint Jacob RODGERS to act and do for me as
            administrator in Jacob PATTERSON'S deceased
            property, this 16 day of May 1815, Nancey
            PATERSON."

page 234   Inventory of Joab PATERSON, deceased, 15 May 1815.

page 235   Widow's provision for Elizabeth PICKINS, wife of
            Aron PICKINS, deceased, 14 March 1815, Josiah RICE,
            James SMITH, and Samuel SMITH, Administrators.

page 236   Inventory of Jesse YARBOROUGH, deceased, 19 April
            1815. Signer: Absalem YARBOROUGH, "his services
            to New Orleans in the late expedition."

page 236   Inventory of sale of James MC MAHON, deceased, May
            term 1815. R. MC MAHON and Calloway HARDIN,
            Administrators.

page 240   Inventory of estate of John DODSON, deceased, taken
            by Pheby DODSON and George DODSON, Adninistrators,
            16 June 1812. (or DOBSON)

page 241   Will of John NICKLES, 25 February 1816. My
            daughters now living with me, Peggy and Kizzy.
            (Interest on three notes on Andrew NEELY in Samuel
            B. MC KITE'S hands).. Gives to Robert CHAFEN and
            his wife Amelia... Gives to son Robert NICKLES
            same amount as above ... to Jonah (?) WOODS-- all
            my wearing apparel. Robert HAFFIN, executor.
            Witnesses: Samuel B. MC KNIGHT; Robert CHAFEN,
            Senior.

page 243   Inventory of balance of property of John NICKLES.
            21 May 1816.

page 243   Will of James JOHNSON. My wife and children. Son
            Joseph. Rest of my children. My daughters. Wife
            Elizabeth JOHNSON and Matthew JOHNSON, executors.
            25 May 1816.

page 245   Edward NATIONS, Thomas NATIONS, and Eli NATIONS,
            the lawful heirs of Thomas NATIONS, who had no pen
            and ink to make will ... desired that ... Nancy
            NATIONS, his wife. 28 May 1816.

page 246   Will of Washington WALKER...wife Elizabeth...
            brothers and sisters, accept Su--ey GANOWAY and
            her heirs... father's estate, five pounds in
            Virginia money. Wife and friend Joseph BROWN

executors. 29 September 1813.

page 248   17 April 1814. Will of Lewis FORKNER. "As I am
            about to go in campaign to the Creek Nations."
            Sally, my wife--if she remarries to have a child's
            part. Witnesses: Francis MC BRIDE and Francis
            DONALDSON.

page 249   Will of James FARRIS, daughter Polly, my wife Mary,
            sons Lindsey and Robert. Rest devided among my
            children. James HILE (?) and Moses ROBISON,
            executors. 26 August 1815.

page 250   Will of John Forsythe, December 7, 1814...have
            given to all my girl children already married and
            left me: namely to Thomas HILL'S wife; to Benjamin
            HIGHFIELD'S wife; to Francis HOGG;S wife ; Randle
            TOEN;S wife; sons Thomas, John, James, William;
            daughters: Lucy; Milley; and wife Martha FORSYTH.
            Witness: James FROSYTH, Milderd FORSYTH.

page 251   Inventory of property of Aron HUNTER. Note of
            Spencer GRIFFON due in February or March 1813.
            "His wages as Lieutenant under Major General
            Andrew JACKSON to New Orleans." 16 February 1816.
            Mary HUNTER and Robert HILL, Administrators.

page 252   John LINDSEY and Randolf WEBSTER make oath that on
            4 September 1815 William MICHAEL of Maury "of which
            sickness on Thursday followiog to wit, September 7,
            he died, he dictated his will..... wife and
            children til youngest child comes of age."
            12 September 1815.

page 255   Mrs. Jenny ALDERSON, Mrs. Sarah ALDERSON, Mrs.
            Agnes ALDERSON, Miss Elizabeth ALDERSON, AND Mrs.
            (?) Mary ALDERSON. Court to appoint John CAMPBELL,
            Thomas MC NEAL, and John ALDERSON committee to
            divide estate of James ALDERSON, deceased, John
            PEEK, executor.

            END OF BOOK A-1, MAURY COUNTY, TENNESSEE WILLS
            AND SETTLEMENTS (covering 1807 to 1816)

MAURY COUNTY, TENNESSEE WILLS AND SETTLEMENTS BOOK B

page 1   Will of James TURNER. (See Book A, page 29)

page 1   Will of John LINDSAY: Dearly beloved wife; son
            Abram; son John; son Isaac; daughter Ruthy BARNETT;
            daughter Mary CUNNINGHAM; son Josiah; son Jacob;
            ____ EZEKIAL; Mabourne (?) BARNET. Sons Jacob
            and Ezekial, executors. 22 January 1810.
            Witnesses, Thomas BARTLET and Rutha ADAIR.

page 3   Will of William BRADSHAW: Sally, my dearly
            beloved wife; land in Bourbon County, Kentucky,
            under management of Robert TRIMBLE my attorney;
            three beloved children; William BRADSHAW, James

BRADSHAW, and Jane BRADSHAW. Nephew William BRADSHAW,Jr., and wife, executors. 4 March 1814. Witnesses: Lewis COCKELL; Hugh B. PORTER; And John HAMBUE. (?)

page 5   Will of James TROUSDALE: Beloved wife Sarah TROUSDALE; daughter Allender (Elendor?) PORTER; daughter Sarah TROUSDALE; daughter Elizabeth TROUSDALE; daughter Mary TROUSDALE; daughter Jane TROUSDALE; son David F. TROUSDALE; son James TROUSDALE; son William TROUSDALE. Wife Sarah and son William, executors. 6 June 1816. Witnesses: Edward TANNER and John WILEY.

page 6   Will of John MACK, deceased; loving wife Sarah MACK; son Constantine; James MACK; John MACK, Junr; Polly MURPHY; Robert MACK; William MACK; James H. MACK and Sally NANCE, my other children. Robert and William MACK, executors. 31 May 1813. Witnesses: Andrew BOYD and James BOYD.

page 7   Will of Parmenus HOWARD. Emancipated negroes Tharp and Launy; daughter Polly..."until my youngest child becomes of age and then for it to be equally divided among them." Wife Emmitter. Friends Andrew GAMBLE and James HOWARD, executors. 10 November 1810. Witnesses: John MASSON (?); Eli MC CAIN; and Robert MC CAIN. (See Book A, page 3D) ?? page A-32?? (Benjamin HOWARD)

page 8   Will of James CAMPBELL, beloved wife Sarah ...three youngest sons a complete English education (to wit) William Harvey CAMPBELL, Alvin Cook CAMPBELL, and George Washington CAMPBELL." Wife Sarah, executor. 16 February 1816.

page 9   Will of John CAMPBELL, 21 April 1816. "Being on the eve of a long jorney and the sickness of the seasons has induced me to make ny last will and testament... Wife Matilda... as my children becomes of age... as my wife is now pregnant." Wife Matilda and son Robert CAMPBELL, when he becomes of age. executors. Witnesses: John MC MEEN and Samuel GRAHM

page 10   Will of William GIPSON: of County of Lagan, State of Kentucky; beloved wife Margaret GIPSON; land in Overton County, Tennessee... "to her and her heirs forever." No date. Witnesses: William GRIGGS and Jacob YOIST.

page 12   Will of Wilson HENDERSON: son William HENDERSON; son Wilson HENDERSON; elder daughter Susannah MAYFIELD. (Three beforementioned each received " "one cent together with the estate already given".) Daughter Elizabeth; son James HENDERSON; son John HENDERSON; daughter Mary; son Jesse URIA (?) HENDERSON; beloved wife Molley. Wife Molley, son Wilson HENDERSON, and Joseph BROWN, executors, 17 May 1809. Witnesses: Joseph BROWN; James PATTON; Nimrod PORTER; Robert WEALTEY. Signed William X HENDERSON.

page 13	Will of Elijah ROBERTS: 3 January 1816. Brothers and sisters. Brother Moses Firk, to father and mother. "My wearing apparel now in Nashville to my brother Mark ROBERTS." Sister Nancy Roberts; Ephriam H. FOSTER; to my friend ___turby___(?) ROBERTSON; father, Isaac ROBERTS, executor. Witnesses: Was. L. HANNUM, Elijah ROBERTSON, and Martha COCKRILL.
page 14	Will of Daniel YATES. Beloved wife Martha... if wife remarries, to be put in trust for children until become of age...children Mirah YATES, James YATES, William YATES, John YATES, Sarah YATES, and Akilla (?) YATES. "when my son James YATES arise to age of 14..." Wife Martha, John MC FALLS and James HILL, executors. 21 November 1814. "But in case my wife does not keep Martha YATES and James YATES together children (?)...notes to be put to their support." (See also page 237 of Will Book B)
page 15	Will of General Isaac ROBERTS. "We heard General Isaac ROBERTS say on the day before his death that it was his will...Wife Polly ROBERTS... we set out hand, 28 February 1816, Daniel X Evans and Elizabeth X EVANS."
page 15	Will of Money GANOWAY. 24 March 1815. Wife Denesslla (?), seven youngest children: Gregory; James; William; Jane; Mary; Patsy; and Edmund; two oldest children not named already given their parts; son James and wife named executors. Signed: Money X GANAWAY. Witnesses: Ebenezer RICE; Jeremiah BLACKARD; and Susannah X LANCASTER.
page 16	Will of Thomas RICHARDSON. Two oldest sons, Amos and Willis; two other sons, Allen and Thomas; dearly beloved wife Jane, after her death or marriage. "Jinny, Hulda, Frances, and Levoy have.. equal to that Cresy CANNON and Anna PULIN had when they married." My six daughters. Wife Jane, son Willis, and brother John RICHARDSON executors. 18 May 1815. Witnesses: Lemuel PREWETT, Samuel GAMBLE, and Wiley RICHARDSON.
page 18	Will of John JINKENS: Daughter Nancy JONES; daughter Peggy JONES; Farther Thomas JINKENS; wife Ann JINKENS...schooling for my five youngest children "with...advice of Richard F. STEPHENS." Witnesses: John X JINKINS; Thomas NEELY; and Mary JINKENS.
page 19	Will of John RECORD. 20 July 1814: My dear beloved Mary RECORD; daughter Elizabeth HUNTER; "all my children"; "also to one that may be born after my death"; sons John Junior and Sion RECORD, wife Mary, and son-in-law Elisha HUNTER, executors. Witnesses: William PATTON, James BOYET, and James Y. GREEN.
page 23	Will of William DEAN: Allice, my wife; Eliza, bod and bodding when she marries; Hannah; Matilda, as much as the other girls; four sons; John, William,

Alexander, and Benjamin; land on Rutherford Creek;
my sons and daughters when all become of age. Mark
L. ANDRES and John BLANTON, executors.
16 September 1816. Witnesses: John DEAN and
Elizabeth DEAN. (Add: Elizabeth, property she now
has.)

page 25   Will of Thomas SHELBY, Clarksville, 24 November
1814, in form of letter to his mother, as follows:

Dear Mother. I have a few words to say to you
respecting the situation I am now in and will be
in when I get home. I am at this time well
clothed, but I shall take the greater part of them
with me. Mother, you know the wool I left in your
possession. I want you to have me two complete
suits made, one a dark mixed, the other just like
the black patron farther has got and the weatcoat
like the white streaked patron if now you know
C. FARRISS cannot weave like the patron get T. C.
FARRIS to weave it____and I will pay him, so send
to my and it will be done complete. I request you
to pay yourself out of my wool for your work and
for the the cotton you make use of. Some of my
money that is in the hands of T. C. FARRIS to get
indego and cossess to the work of all the blue the
cloth. I got of Miss CAMPBELL was black wool and
when it gets wet it stains my clothes as black as
it is nearly. Give my complements to sister Polly
and tell her I make a present of that cow and
calf to John WILEY that is due me on Cathy's Creek
as my part to help buy her a house, but in the
main time you give her my corn and tell her I
shall want a complete slive cotton or flax shirt.

A few words to farther.
Dear Farther. I am started to meet a vetern for
where the cannons will soar and the bullits come
perhaps it may be to my toll to fall in the
defense of our liberty and I say my wish
respecting my land is that after Thomas P. SHELBY
gets his fifty acres off my west fork land that
I am due him, then divide the rest of the tracts
between him and Isaac SHELBY and my Duck River
land I shall give to my nephew Wright.

A few words from Clarey (?). She wishes to be
visited by her friends while we are absent and
for the lords sake tell George W. SHELBY come
and stay until we return he can with the help of
friends here get our little crop of 7 or 8 acres
planted perhaps our friends has drew an idea that
we draughted and are going off with reluctance,
but you must give over that idea. We volunteered
ourselves as first and second sargents. We done
this because we considered this tour more
favourable than the next and we have not repented
what we have done but a cannon ball can take us
as easy as some that is in camps and crying to
go and see their poor wives. We have had one man
made an example for desertion, he had to ride
trukton (?) twenty minutes.

23

Give my complements to Captain J. G. SMITH and
Captain GREENFIELD and all the neighbors
particularly Captain J. MICHAEL.

                              Farewell

                                    John H. SHELBY

Witnesses: Evin SHELBY, William SHELBY, Eli
SHELBY

page 26

Will of Mary WARD: brother James SMITH; brother
Charles SMITH; brother Benjamin SMITH; my niece,
Mary S. NAPIER; Samuel S. NAPIER, my nephew;
under government and direction of my brother
Benjamin SMITH, "my sister Sarah M. NAPIER now
being separated from her husband John M. NAPIER
and seeking to obtain a devourse from him and
therefore should she obtain a devorse from him and
never hereafter live with him then and in that
case and on that condition, I give and bequeath to
her....but if the said Sarah N. NAPIER should not
obtain a devorse from the said John M. NAPIER,
then and in that case it is my will that the above
named property in this case shall be placed in the
hands of my brothers James SMITH and Benjamin
SMITH for the use and benefit of the said Sarah M.
NAPIER during her life and after her death the
said property to be equally divided, etc...;" to
my friend Silvester CHUNN; my brothers James and
Benjamin SMITH; my trusty friend James T.
SANDFORD, and Duncan BROWN, executors.
16 January 1816. Witnesses: Duncan BROWN;
William CHUNN; and Elizabeth STRATTON.

page 27

Will of John ISOM: Brother James. 30 March 1813.
Witnesses: Andrew KENEDY and Priscilla KENEDY.

page 27

Will of John HOOD: Wife Nancy, my children.
10 September 1814. Witnesses: Jethro BROWN and
William AKLIN.

page 28

Will of John Joseph LONG: "undivided part of my
father's estate of which I have two shares(to
wit) one in my own name and the one as legatee of
McKinnie LONG--on waters of Cumberland River,
counties of Umphries and Stuart;" beloved wife
Francis Scott LONG; my children. My wife and my
four friends Nathaniel WILLIS, Doctor Edward
FISHER, Samuel MAYS, and William FRYERSON, Esquire,
executors. Witnesses: John FRIERSON; David
GLASS; James NEELY; and Isaac WHITE. 20 August
1816.

page 29

Will of Drury BRIDGES: Wife Molley; all my
children. Wife and brother Daniel BRIDGES,
executors. 29 Janurary 1812. Witnesses: Daniel
BRIDGES and James PAISLEY.

NOTE:

Although Shelby will is headed "Will of Thomas
Shelby", it is actually will of John H. SHELBY.
Thomas SHELBY was his father.

page 29	Will of John M. GOODLOW: first to my woman of colour, Rachel, $100, bed, furniture, and be emancipated at my death; wife Mary Hurt (?) GOODLOW; daughter Martha Eliza GOODLOW; my sister Elizabeth JONES. Wife, friends Peter R. BOOKER and Daniel GRAHM, executors. 1 December 1816. Witnesses: C. LANGLEY; John P. ELLETT; Sophronia LANGLEY; and Druscilla FLEMAN (?).
page 32	Will of Joshua FRYERSON: wife Elizabeth; son Samuel DEADRIDGE; son John JAMES; son Joshua BUNYAN; wife and friend David FRYERSON, executors. 5 November 1816. Witnesses: Benona DICKEY and Thomas F. FLEMMEN. Codical, 28 Janurary 1817, son Joshua BUNYAN be made executor when he becomes twenty-one. Witnesses: John FRYERSON; Thomas Joseph FRYERSON; and William FRYERSON.
page 33	Will of Thomas PARKER: Son Thomas; daughter Molley; grandson Artimus. 8 Janurary 1817. Witnesses: John MACK and Nathaniel X MURPHEY.
page 33	Inventory of William GANT, deceased, 16 November 1816. Notes on Thomas MC NEAL, Peter CHALTHAM, Josiah BROWN, Maclaja BROOKS, Stephen NOBLES, James CALLIAS, Charles KAVENAUGH, A. WADDLE administrators: Jesse GANT; P. R. BOOKER; D. N. SANSOM; Patrick MAGUIRE.
page 35	Sale of estate of John ADKINS, deceased. William ADKINS, John ADKINS, William WHITSON, James PORTER. November session 1816. William ADKINS, administrator.
page 35	Inventory of Charles ISHAM, deceased. 19 November 1816. Notes on Thomas CATES, note on "the young Facter", one uniform coat.
page 36	Inventory of James BURNS, deceased. John MC FAWLS, administrator. Inventory of William DEAN, deceased. November 1816. M. L. ANDREWS, administrator. Inventory of William GRIMES taken by David CRAIG, 26 November 1816.
page 37	Inventory of John CAMPBELL, deceased. 9 september 1816. Taken by James BLACK, Thomas MC NEAL and William (?) JOHNSTON.
page 38	Property of Joseph ROBB, deceased, by John ROBB, administrator, 28 September 1816. Buying: Thomas WHITESIDE; James LOVE, Esquire; Joseph AYRES; William JONES; Ann ROBB; Hugh JONES; John MC FALL; Nathaniel BIFFLE; Isaac STANFIELD; Daniel MC COLLUM; Nicholas SHOAT: Alexander ERWIN; Alexander WILLEY; Abram WHITESIDE; Harvey (?) G. THOMAS; George TURNBOUGH; David LEACH; Thomas BELL; Samuel JOHNSTON; Thomas JONES; Frederick MAYBERRY; Lewis GARNER; George MARTIN; George ISHAM; James DOBINS; Charles BROWN.
page 42	Inventory of John JINKINS, deceased. Anny JINKINS, executrix. Sale of L. B. ESTUS, deceased--1816--David MARTIN, administrator.

page 43	Inventory of sales of Agnus HODGE, deceased, 12 September 1816. Buying: James THOMPSON; Moses WILEY; Robert KELSEY; William FARNER; Cabel HARRIS; John KENDRICK; Thomas BOWMAN; Ebenezer THOMPSON; John EDWARDS; Loyd GRIMES; James LOVE; Silas HAWKINS; John JOHNSTON; Robert LYLE; Isaac STANFIELD; Thomas DUFF; Joseph HOPKINS; Hamilton GATLIN; John WATTS; William POOL; Griffith CATHEY; Zachariah TRANTHAM; Caleb FARRIS: George HODGE; Daniel HOLCOMB; James CARR; James GAUNT; Craige FARRIS; Polley BROWN; John PHILLIPS; Thomas GREENFIELD; John WISE. 8 November 1816, James LOVE, administrator.
page 44	Inventory of David JONES, deceased. November term 1815. Isabel JONES, administrator.
page 46	Inventory of Thomas LADD, deceased. "One discharge in the volunteer horse company commanded by General COFFEE." 17 May 1815. Jane X. LADD, administrator.
page 46	Inventory of Robert JOHNSTON, deceased. Notes on Samuel WATKINS, Stephen HARRIS, and Joseph WILLIAMS. 15 May 1815. Isham JOHNSTON, administrator.
page 47	Inventory of William KELLEY, deceased. Polly KELLY, administrator.
page 48	Amount of sale of William JONES, deceased. Sold 23 September 1815.. Buying: David MONTGOMERY; Samuel MC LEAN; Stephen COLLINS; John MOULTON; Willie GRIFFIN; Milley JONES; James PORTER; Henry GOODNIGHT; Thomas RANDAL; James D. MC LEAN; Jethro BROWN; Samuel CRAWFORD; Joseph T. TAYLOR; Robert GOOD; William HENLEY; David HOGAN. Jeremiah GURLEY, administrator.
page 49	Sale of James MC CAWLEY, deceased. 14 December 1815. Catherine MC CAWLEY, Nancy MC CAWLEY, Polley MC CAWLEY, Nathaniel MC CAWLEY, William DAVIS, Magnuss DAVIS, Henry SHARP, Samuel GRIFFITH.
page 50	November session 1816. John MILLER, Samuel POLK, Esquires, and Thomas MC NEIL to lay off provision for Lesse GANT, late widow of William GANT, deceased.
page 51	Estate of John H. SHELBY, deceased, by Thomas SHELBY, administrator.
page 51	Inventory of sale of William GRIMES, deceased, 17 December 1816. Buying: David CRAIG; James GRIMES; John GRIMES (of Luke); John GRIMES (of William); William GRIMES, Senr.; Lloyd GRIMES; William GRIMES (of William); John GIBSON; John P. ELLIOTT; Brice HADNOT(?); James CAMPBELL; Tilman IRISH (?); John BEATY; William GRIMES (of John); William WILLIAMS; Daniel CUTBIRTH; John GRIMES (of Luke); Nancy PICKARD; Isaac PICKARD; Samuel

ARENTON; Green HOLDEN; John GRIMES, Senr; John
GRIMES (of Luke); Jane STOCKARD; Arthur BEATY;
Francis DONALDSON; John GRIMES (of William); Joseph
HUDDLESTON; James STOCKARD; Robert M. COOPER;
Alexander PICKARD. David CRAIG, administrator.

page 53 Estate of Elisha RHODES, deceased, (part of estate),
by Sampson PROWEL, administrator, 17 February 1817.
Widdow RHODES, Jessee OAKLEY, John THOMPSON.

page 54 Sale of Samuel WILLIS, deceased, 16 June 1816.
Buying: William NEAL; John M. NAPIER; Obediah
TRANTHAM; Robert MC CASTER; John WILLIS; James
BRADY; Abraham PICKENS; Josiah (Bird) REA (?);
James HALE; Hugh REID; William NIX; Robert
HENDERSON; Daniel W. HARRISON; William FOX; Zador
AYDELOTTE; Henry REED; John WARREN; Thomas MC CALL;
Samuel REED; Curtis WOODS; Simon JOHNSTON; William
GILLEM; Asar REED; John TANKASLEY; Samuel MORGAN;
Rhoderick RIGHT; William RICHMOND; Hugh MC WITER;
George JULIAN; Obediah LANGSTON; James BRALEY;
Nelson JACKSON; Srigley REEVES; Henry CRESSWELL;
Robert HENDERSON; Lewis JONES; Joseph MOREHEAD;
Samuel GULLET; Julius FLEMMIN: Presley RIEVES.
William NEEL and Piety WILLIS, administrators.

page 56 Estate of William MINNEFEE (?). Administrator,
John MINNEFEE. Note on Morgan BODIMAS; James J.
WASHINGTON, one name illegible; 1 August 1809;
note on Duglas BLUE 25 November 1809; note on
Isaac RENTFORD due 15 April 1819; Jared MINNIFEE
due 1 May 1818. Buying: Widdow MINNAFEE: David
BUCKNER (?), (or BRECKEM); Linday MINNEFEE; John
LASLY; Polly MENFE; Jonathan RIDGWAY; David
CRICNER; Thomas MC LAUGHLEN; William MINNAFEE;
Robert STEWART; John YOUNG; James FINDLEY; John
LAMB; Isaac CRAWSON; John CLICK; Thomas WHITSON;
Benjamin LONG; Littleton DUTY; Cindy MINAFEE; John
ALSOP; Joseph LOWD (?).

page 60 17 March 1812. Memo of property of Robert MC CAIN,
deceased, by Elizabeth MC CAIN and William NUTT,
executors.

page 61 11 February 1815, William Daniel, administrator.

page 61 Sale of Thomas FORE, deceased, returned by Samuel
H. WILLIAMS, acting administrator, 21 September
1809.

page 61 E. ALEXANDER sale. Polly ALEXANDER bought most
household goods, the other buyers included: John
G. BARRY; Caleb FARRIS; Edward NUNNALE; Nicholas
PERRISH; John FARRIS; William ERWIN; Griffith
CATHEY; Robert JOHNSTON; John CATHEY; George M.
ADDAMS; James ROBERTSON; Robert LYELL; George
MARTIN; Robert DUNNAM; Alexander P. DUNHAM;
Kinchen RHODES; Alex B. LITTON; and Thomas G.
HARVEY.

page 63 Sale of Ayres DOSS(?). Daniel CONDER,
administrator.

page 64   Estate of Patience KIRK, deceased, 13 April 1813.
Note on Roderick RIGHT, due 28 May 1812; note on
John MYRACK due 1 August 1812; note in hands of
Joseph RIGHT in North Carolina due____1808; Note on
John WHITAKER, James NIGHT. Buying: Natus KIRK;
William DANIEL; Nancy NIGHT; John J. ZOLLICOFFER;
Washington WALKER; John FACHETT; John PACE; Plesant
MC QUICY (?); William MICHAEL; Monny GANNAWAY; John
EMMERSON; Hosea JAMMESON; Mychael LANDS; Joseph EAST;
William COVEY.

page 66   Thomas H. O'NEAL administrator of Marmaduke O'NEAL,
deceased. Add to account of -----1809, 19 of___1809.

Inventory of John LINDSAY, deceased. Notes:
Gregory WATKINS, William HUDSON (?); B. HURT; taken
15 June 1810. J. H. LINDSAY and Ezekial LINDSAY,
executors.

page 67   Inventory of sale of William ISOM, deceased,
22 April 1813. Buying: James ISOM; Moses
PENNINGTON; James LOCK; Stephen MILLAR; George ISOM;
William LOVELL; William GARNER; Andrew HAMILTON;
Charles BROWN; John WHITESIDE; Doctor James G.
SMITH (?); Frederick MAYBERRY; Ezekial SMITH;
Charles ISOM; Andrew MC MAKIN; John BURY; William
MAYFIELD; James FILES; James RAIL; Hugh BRADFORD;
David MAYBERRY; James DOBING; William COTTLE; Jacob
BIFFLE; William NICKERSON; Warner FALKNER; Abram
MAYBERRY; Lewis GARNER; Alexander ERWIN; William
COCKS; Jacob YOUNG; Samuel MAYFIELD: John SELLARS;
Jonathan J. STANFIELD; Samuel AKIN; Charles CHOAT;
John CAMBELL; Miles BURNS; Samuel YOUNG; Joseph
TOD; Captain James LOCK; Andrew KENNEDY; Starling
BELLS; Jackson STANFIELD; Joseph TATE; Thomas CATES;
Samuel LUSK; James LANKFORD; John DAVIS; Nathaniel
DOBBS; Arthur ISHAM; William ISHAM; and Joseph
PAYTON; George ISHAM.

page 71   Repeat of the estate of MENNAFEE on page 56.

page 75   Inventory of Patience SELLARS, deceased, taken
15 June 1812 by Milley GRIFFIN.

page 75   Estate of Ezekial ALEXANDER, deceased.

page 76   Inventory of James OGLESBY, deceased, 14 December
1811, by Hugh W. STEPHENSON and Daniel OGLESBY.

page 77   Inventory of Thomas FORE, deceased, turned in
22 June 1819. Samuel H. WILLIAMS and Pollina F.
FORE, administrators.

page 77   Inventory of James C. FENNEAL (?), deceased, by
Joseph B. PORTER, March term 1810.

page 77   December term 1813. Abner FRANKLIN, John MILLER,
Abner CLEVELAND, appointed to lay off widow's
portion to Nancy (Mary?) TURNER, widow of William
TURNER, deceased.

page 78   Provision for Nancy TURNER, widow of William
TURNER. 8 Janurary 1814.

page 80   Inventory of John CRAIG, deceased, 12 December 1815,
           by Isaac ACUFF and Betsy CRAIG, administrators.

page 83   Widow's provision for Catherine MOORE, relict of
           Joseph MOORE, deceased, 24 May 1815. William COVEY,
           William DANIEL, Benjamin WEEK (?).

page 84   Widow's provision for Sarah ESTUS, late widdow of
           Doct ESTUS, deceased, November term 1814, by Samuel
           CRAIG, Esquire, Doct Horatio DE PRIEST and Patrick
           MC GUIRE. Next term, apportionment, Sarah ESTUS,
           widow and relict of L. B. ESTUS, deceased.

page 85   Inventory of estate of Samuel T. BROOKS, deceased.
           Notes on Joseph DARNELL, Peter GOOD, estate of
           William TURNER, deceased, John GOODNIGHT, John S.
           WADE, William GANT, Hugh LEEPER, William GREEN,
           Nashville. "appointment as lieutenant in Captain
           James W. MAKIN'S company commanded by Brigadier
           General John COFFEE to Mobile,New Orleans, and the
           time of service nor the amount due not yet
           ascertained, one steer and a certificate if property
           to the amount of $29 lost in the Creek Nation by
           Samuel BROOKS while under the command of Major
           General A. JACKSON, but very uncertain whether or
           not it will be recovered." Signed: Samuel BROOKS,
           no date.

page 85   Inventory of property of William WILLIAMS, deceased.
           Buying at sale: Michael LANCASTER; Daniel BRIDGES;
           James GANNAWAY; Thomas WILLIAMS; Henry HAWKINS;
           James BOWDEN; Alexander MOLLERE. Statement at May
           term 1815 by Martha WILLIAMS, administratrix.

page 86   Widdow;s provision for Mary HAWKINS, widdow of late
           Reverend William HAWKINS, 3 December 1814, made by
           James ROBERTSON, Joshua NEWMAN, James HOLLIS.

page 86   Inventory of property of Thomas POWEL, deceased,
           16 February 1815, by Elisha POWELL.

page 87   Widow's provision for Flora POWEL, late widdow of
           Thomas POWEL, deceased, 24 May 1815, by Amos
           JOHNSTON, John GILCHRIST, William RODGERS.

page 88   Inventory of John HODGE, deceased. Agnis HODGE,
           administrator, and James LOVE, administrator.

page 88   Inventory of Moses G. FRIERSON.

page 90   Widow's provision for Peggy MC LEAN and her family,
           late wife of William MC LEAN, made by Anthony I.
           TURNER, William GANT, Robert SELLARS, 29 November
           1814.

page 90   Inventory of William HAWKINS, deceased, 15 November
           1814.

page 91   Widow's provision for widow and family of Samuel
           WILLIS, 16 June 1814, by Isiah REID, Abraham
           PICKINS, and Thomas MC CALL. Will NEAL,
           administrator.

page 91   29 November 1814. Martha PARTEE, widow of Locker
           PARTEE, deceased, resignes her right of
           administration to Robert SELLARS. Witnesses:
           Charles PARTEE, A. PARTEE.

page 92   Inventory of Lockar PARTEE, 14 October 1814, by
           Robert SELLARS.

page 92   List of property purchased by Mary BROOM, widow and
           administrator of Jonathan BROOM, deceased. Other
           buying: John HODGE; Evan SHELBY; Captain
           GREENFIELD; Stephen MILLAR; Levi SHELBY; Thomas
           SHELBY; Regin L. BISHOP; Griffith CATHEY.

page 93   Sale of property of John LOVE'S estate, late
           deceased, 20 July 1814. Buying: Edam LOVE; Thomas
           HARVEY; John MICHAEL; Harrison BLAGRAVE; Wilson
           LOVE; Adam LOVE; Robert LOVE; William CHURCHWELL;
           James WHITE; Joel LOVE; Aron HUNTER; Robert HOLMES;
           Jane KINDRICK James OWEN; Andrew BAKER; James
           AYARES; John MITCHELL; Moses HAMES (?); Isaac
           MC COLLUM; William BURRIS; Charles BURNS; James
           ELLIOT, (page 95), (see note) Sion RECORD; David
           LAWRANCE; Hopson ARNOLD; John W. RECORD; Elisha
           HUNTER; Signor CAWLLEY; Jonathan MC MORRIS; John
           BRADFORD; James MC CANDLESS; John MASSEY; Joseph
           HALL; David LYLE; Anderson POWELL; Drum (?) COLLINS;
           Jesse MCLAIN; Benjamin JORDAN; John AUSBURN; Robert
           MADDEN; John MAYSE; Mary RECORD; Sherwood RECORD;
           Joshua CUDDLE; William MILLAR; Sterling C.
           ROBERTSON; Cumford RECORD; Thomas ACRE; Edmund MAY;
           Francis KENEDAY; Joshua NICHOLS; Thomas MARTIN;
           James A. YOUNG; Thomas SMITH; Elijah MEADOWS; David
           ARNOLD; William ARNOLD; William COWDER (?); Lewis
           JONES; John RADFORD; Jeremiah CHEEK (?); William
           POLK; Edw FAGGARE (?); Joseph WEAVER (?); James Y.
           GREEN; Laurance MC MANIS; Benjamin HALE; Joshua
           WILLIAMS; Nathan GLASGO; Edmund HAGGARD; David
           ANDREWS; Jesse BOYETT; John COCKRILL; Deborah
           TERARAR (?); William RECORD; James C. RECORD.
           "used for the sale 10 gallons of whisley; used for
           the family, 15 gallons of brandy." Mary RECORD,
           executrix, John W. RECORD, Sion RECORD, AND Elisah
           HUNTER, executors.

           (Note: the above entry is believed to be two
           separate entries. The first being the estate
           settlement of John LOVE, with Robert LOVE,
           administrator. The second being the estate
           settlement of ____ RECORD, beginning on page 95.
           There was no heading on page 95, but at the end of
           the record there is notation saying that John
           RECORD made the account of the sale.

page 99   Inventory of estate of Charles COATS, deceased, late
           of the county of Hardin, state of Kentucky. "that
           I can find in this state." (Tennessee.) Account
           against Joshua DEAL. Mari MILLIN reading (?).
           B. ROBERTSON, 16 August 1814. Thomas HAGEPETH,
           administrator.

page 100   Sale of John JINKINS, deceased. Buying: Ann
            JENKINS; Robert PATTEN; Jacob LANGSTON; Anney
            JENKINS, executrix.

page 101   Sale of Doctor L. B. ESTUS, deceased, December 1815.
            (Sale is from page 101 to 108, with no names
            listed.)

Page 105   Will of Joseph SANDFORD. Proved Janurary session
            1818. Brother James T. SANDFORD, brother-in-law
            William YANCEY, Susannah SHACKELFORD. "rest of
            relations hereby debarred from any part of my
            estate." 2 April 1817. Witnesses: James X
            SANDERS; Benjm LITTEN.

page 108   Sale of Joseph MOORE, deceased. Buying: Catherine
            MOORE; William COVEY, Junr.; John JONES; Richard
            LYON; Samuel JIMESON; John THOMPSON; Jesse TYNER;
            John SAGE; Jesse EVANS; Ebenezar RICE; Thomas
            MICHAEL; William RUDD; Plesant MC QUARY; Money
            GANNOWAY. Signed: William HOLT; Catharine MOORE.

page 109   "John FILES, discharge, borne on Captain CRAWFORD'S
            pay--$73.30." James FILES, administrator.

page 110   Inventory of estate of Samuel SCOTT, deceased,
            Taken 11 May 1815. Note on Rachel BROWN, James S.
            BAILES, and on William SULLIVANT. Signed: Lewis
            NEEDHAM and Hannah SCOTT.

page 110   Widow's provision for Polly ALEXANDER, widdow and
            relict of Ezekial ALEXANDER, deceased. December
            session 1813. Provision made by Isaac FARIS,
            Alexander CATHEY, Senr., and Alexander CATHEY,
            ESQUIRE.

page 111   List of property of James JOHNSTON, deceased.

page 111   Inventory of property of estate of Joseph MOORE,
            deceased. 16 May 1814. (See Book A, page 127,)
            Notes on John SION, Robert MACK, Rhoderick NITE,
            Richard LYON. Catharine MOORE, administratrix,
            William HOLT, administrator.

page 112   Inventory of estate of William LONG, deceased.
            Recorded in Book A, page 145. Add "one note for
            $6, his services in a tour to New Orleans."

page 114   Widow's provision for Lesse GANT, late widdow of
            William GANT, deceased. November session 1816.
            John MELTOR, Samuel POLK, Esquire, and Thomas
            MC NEIL.

page 114   John BROWN, John SPENCER, James T. SANDFORD, and
            Abner FRANKLIN appointed to make division of estate
            of William TONEY, deceased. 24 May 1816. "Met at
            house of Sinthy TONEY." Allotted to Synthia
            TONEY, widow of William TONEY, deceased. Martin
            Tony, Hardin TONY, Washington TONEY, Jefferson
            TONEY, Mark TONEY, Pinkney TONEY, Henry TONEY,
            Susan TONEY, Elizabeth TONEY, now Elizabeth
            WHITSON.

page 116   Sale of property of Isham CHRISTIAN, deceased, sold
           29 October 1814 (?). Buying: Ann CHRISTIAN; Patsy
           CHRISTIAN; Nathaniel CHRISTIAN; A. W. REESE (?);
           James REESE (?); Silas ALEXANDER; William MC BRIDE;
           Nathan D. CHRISTIAN; Betsy CHRISTIAN; Patsy
           CHRISTIAN; Jodiah PICK; Robert PAYTON; Pleasant
           SCRIBNER; James DAWKIN; James DUNCAN; W. MENIDE (?);
           James BARDAL (?); William J. JOHNSTON; Thomas
           CARNELL; Henry PAYTON; Polly CHRISTIAN; Moses
           PAYTON; Jane CHRISTIAN; John WILLIAMS; Elizabeth
           CHRISTIAN; Nancy CHRISTIAN; Charles CHRISTIAN.
           Nathaniel CHRISTIAN, administrator.

page 118   Sale of Samuel SCOTT, deceased. (See Book A,
           page 176.)

page 122   Inventory of property of Balias GRAVES, deceased.
           "consisting of his bounty of land as an enlisted
           soldier during the war in the service of the United
           States." Jacob GRAVES, administrator,
           18 February 1817.

page 122   Sale of Abner KING. (Recorded in Book A.
           page 180.)

page 122   Inventory of estate of Hetty SHEARMAN, deceased,
           18 February 1817. "Cash in the hands of Abner
           PARTEE." Charles SHEARMAN, administrator.

page 123   Inventory of Jesse RADFORD estate, taken 10 April
           1816. Buying: Hannah RADFORD; James SCOTT;
           William LIGGETT; Thomas ARNOLD; Stephen COOK. A
           discharge for three months and four days--$69.40,
           amount of property lost in battle--$31.00.

page 124   Inventory of Mary GREEN, deceased. 7 February 1817.
           Signed: Joshua CAUDLE.

page 124   "Columbia, 21st 1816. After deducting the amount
           that Robert LAMPKLINGS, deceased, was owing to me
           there is still due his estate the further sum of
           $70." Signed: John HODGE. Ezekial ANDMOND (?)
           administrator.

page 125   Sale of James BURNS, deceased. Buying: Jane
           BURNES; James HILL; May term 1816. John MC FALLS
           and Jane BURNS, administrator and administratrix of
           James BURNS, deceased.

page 126   Inventory of Gideon KIRKSEY, deceased. Mary
           KIRKSAY, administratrix.

page 126   Inventory of Thomas LARIMORE, deceased, taken
           19 February 1816. Tankersley N.P. HARDIMAN,
           administrator.

page 127   Inventory of John SUTHERLAND, deceased, taken
           19 May 1817. "one discharge for three months,
           11 days--$26.68. "James BOWDEN, administrator.

page 127   Inventory of estate of Osburne P.NICHOLSON,
           deceased. Notes on William WALLICE. Joel DOWELL,

32

accounts in copartnership with John M. GOODLOE, on Green WILLIAMSON. David RUSSELL, Patrick MC GUIRE, Perry COHEA, Lawrence BASS, Jeremiah CHERRY. Signed: Garrett VOORHIES, executor of O. P. NICHOLSON in right of his wife Sackey VOORHIES. 20 May 1816.

page 129   Property of Benjamin SHIPLEY, 19 February 1815. "The service money of Benjamin SHIPLEY for three months tour against the Creek Indians as an insighn." Accounts of Henry HALL, Obedia LANKSTON, Indian FLEMMAN, William MILLAR.

page 129   Inventory of property of David PICKENS, deceased, Signed: Susanna PICKINS; William BUYERS; John G. PICKINS, administrators.

page 130   Inventory of property of Abram PICKINS, deceased, taken 22 Febuary 1815. William NEEL, administrator.

page 131   Inventory of James KENDRICK, deceased. Notes on Abner PREWETT, Samuel GATTES, and ____JAMESON. ____KINDRICK, administrator.

page 132   Inventory of David COPELAND, deceased. Notes on Anthony COPELAND, Silas DOBBINS, James COPELAND, David COPELAND, Junr., Henry COPELAND, A. W. COPELAND, James H. BOWMAN. Signed: James COPELAND and David COPELAND, administrators.

page 133   Division of estate of William MC LEAN, deceased. Allot to his widdow and her children; to Margarett MC LEAN, widow and relict of said William MC LEAN, deceased, $401.94, being her sixth part of the estate. 20 November 1816. Signed: Joseph SANDFORD; William YANCY; James PORTER; Samuel E. FRYERSON; Elijah HANKS; William WILLIAMS; Daniel PAYNE; Moses HANKS; James WILLIAMS; Robert WILLIAMS; David WEATHERSPOON; Isiac SUTHERLAND.

page 133   Inventory of property of William MC LEAN, deceased, Notes on John MC GIMSEY, Peter BIGGS; John DUCKWORTH; and John DAUTTORY.

page 135   More on widdow's share for Margaret MC LEAN and her five children. Samuel MC LEAN, administrator.

page 136   Estate of Samuel Pryerson. James T. SANFORD, William MC BRIDE, John MERCER, William SMITH, John T. MOORE, T. HENDERSON, J. T. RICLEY (for schooling), J. T. WHITE, J. T. STEPHENSON, James SEALLARS.

page 137   Sale of estate of Daniel NEIL, deceased, sold 16 January 1813. Buying: Thomas LANE; Barten DAVIS; John H. GATTLING; Ezekial WALDRUP; John HAINESS; John WILIE; Phillip COMPTON; John PREWITT; Daniel HALKIM; James OLLIPHANT; Samuel OLLIPHANT; Jacob STANFILL; James THOMPSON; Ebenezar MILLER; Charles BROWN; John GORDON; Daniel MC COLLUM; William LEEPER; Jones MORGAN.

page 138   Sale of William MC LEAN, deceased, made 16 December 1814.

page 142   Inventory of O. P. NICHOLSON, recorded Book A
            page 186.

page 145   Inventory of estate of late Samuel FRYERSON of
            Maury County. 18 November 1815. Signed: Thomas
            Stephenson, John W. STEPHENSON, Thomas F. FLEMMING.

page 147   Estate of Jeremiah GURLEY, deceased, by Davis GURLEY,
            administrator. To account of James WALKER, John
            COOPER, Andrew KENEDY, MC NICK and MOORE, Barns
            THOMAS, estate; Thomas EDWARDS estate, Henry
            SHARPE, James AKIN, William KENDRICK.

page 148   Settlement of estate of Jeremiah GURLEY, deceased.
            Signed: D. CRAIG and John GILCHRIST. 16 May _____.

page 149   Estate of Thomas EDWARDS, deceased, in account with
            Mary EDWARDS, administratrix, and David GURLEY,
            administrator. Widow's dower; Account of G. B.
            WILLIAMS, H. BOYCE, William DAVIS, John DAVIS,
            Jeremiah GURLEY, deceased; Barns THOMAS estate,
            Amos JOHNSTON, Lewis JOHNSTON, James MC CAULEY,
            Mikajiah EDWARDS, MC NEIL and MOON, Henry SHARP,
            Elisha THOMAS, Jeremiah GURLEY, Polly GURLEY legacy,
            Samuel WILLIAMS; clerk's fee in North Carolina;
            D. GURLEY legacy and rent of plantation; Stephen
            HARMON, P. MARCUS; traveling to North Carolina and
            back; by notes on North Carolina.

page 150   Settlement of estate of Thomas EDWARDS, deceased.
            Signed: D. CRAIG and John GILCHRIST, 16 May 1816.

page 150   Inventory of William DEAN, deceased. "Inventory of
            property not specifically named by the testator in
            his last will and testament," 17 February 1817.
            Mark L. ANDREWS, executor.

page 152   Inventory of Betsy SAWYERS, deceased. 20 April 1818.

page 152   Remainder of John CAMPBELL'S property, deceased,
            sold on 15 February 1818. Property purchased by
            the widdow.

page 152   Inventory of estate of Dabney WADE, deceased.
            William J. WADE, administrator, 18 January 1817.

page 153   Widow's provision for Catharine MUSE, late widow
            of John MUSE, deceased, by A. I. TURNER, James
            RUTLEDGE, William COOPER, 12 December 1817.

page 154   Inventory of William ADKINS, deceased. Notes on
            Calib LONGLEY, White DOUGERTY, John C. HAMILTON,
            Abel WILSON, Timothy BRINKLEY, Ray SELLARS, Robert
            MC CULLOCK, Bynum SELLARS, Thomas LOCKARD, Joseph C.
            MC DOWD, John MIDDLETON, Jonathan STANFELL, John
            LATTA, James GIBSON, Benjamin YARDLY, O'NEAL and
            WITHERSPOON, John THOMPSON, Absalum YARBOROUGH,
            Joseph WAKEFIELD, James MICHELL; widow's provision
            for Jane ADKINS, widow of William ADKINS, deceased,
            her own fifth part. 16 December 1817. Signed:
            A. I. TURNER; William YANCY; James D. MC LEAN;
            Hezekiah BROOKS; Robert SELLARS; Edmund FITZGERALD

34

(FITZJARROLD); Samuel MC LEAN: Westly WEATHERSPOON;
Matthew HARBINSON; William COOPER; David
WEATHERSPOON; Georg BRECKENRIDGE.

page 160   Jane ADKINS, widow of William ADKINS, deceased.
Legal DOWER. November 1817.

page 160   Sale of Propert of William WINNS, deceased,
22 December 1817. Buying: Mary WINNS; Charles
WINNS; Nancy WINNS; John TOOMS; Shadrick DUGGAR;
Joseph ROYAL; William ALLEN; William RENFRO; Samuel
ROGERS; James KNIGHT; John ELLIOTT; John ASBURN;
Johnston WINSTEAD; Joshua ORR; Matthew NELSON;
Ichabod TUTTLE; Samuel COLE; David DUGGER; Armstead
REDDING; Richard ROYAL; William RUST; William CRAIG.
Also sold on January 10, 1818.

page 164   More on widow's provision for Jane ADKINS, widdow
of William ADKINS, deceased. 13 December 1817.

page 164   Elizabeth JOHNSTON relinguishes her right of
administratrix of estate of James JOHNSTON,
deceased, and names William RUSSELL, Esquire,
21 August 1816.

page 165   Inventory of Nathan SUNDERLAND, deceased. "his
services for a tour of 12 months as a regular
soldier in the service of the United States, two
bonds in the amount of $40, due in December 1817."
19 August 1816, A. CATHEY, administrator.

page 165   Estate of Robert LUMPKINS, deceased, sold by
Hezekiah ALLMAN, 13 June 1816. Buying: Hezekiah
ALDMOND; Joseph MOOREHEAD; James MONTGOMERY; Robert
STEEL (?); Abner CLEVELAND; Robert HENDERSON;
Joseph LONG; Benjamin SMITH.

page 167   Inventory of John ADKINS, deceased. Notes on:
William HESTER; William COE; E. TURNER; Eli NEWMAN;
James HARRELL; John WHITESIDE; Samuel POLK; Samuel
LEEPER; J. HOLDER; William GARDNER; ____ MC BEE;
James Usher; M. LEWALLYON; E. GIVINS; R. ROBERTSON;
Henry NEELY; Thomas CLARK; Peter PARKER; Samuel
WHITESIDE; Wright WILLIS.

page 168   Inventory of David OGLEVIE, deceased. Returned
24 August 1816. Elizabeth OGLEVIE, administratrix,
and Will BRADSHAW, administrator.

page 168   Widow's provision for Sarah RHODES, widow of
Elisha RHODES, deceased, 11 June 1816, by Samuel
LONG, Thomas PROWELL, and William CRAWFORD.

page 169   Sale of Nimrod DILLIANS, deceased. Joseph DILLIAN
bought all.

page 170   Inventory of Joseph ROBB, deceased.
Inventory of Lewis FORKNER, deceased. "One
discharge to a six months tour of duty in the
militia." One negro woman and child in possession
of Doctor JENNINGS. 20 August 1816. Jonathan
BAILEY, administrator.

page 170   Inventory of Thomas DAVIDSON, deceased. Signed:
            George DAVIDSON.

page 171   Inventory of Thomas RICHARDSON, deceased.
            16 October 1816. John RICHARDSON, executor.

page 171   Inventory of Elisha RHODES, deceased, 16 May 1816.

page 173   Sale of Elisha RHODES, deceased, 3 June 1816.
            Buying: Widdow RHODES; James SKELLY; William
            RAGSDALE; Robert OAKLEY; Daley WARRINGTON; James
            HOPKINS; James ROOTS; George SMITH; John STABOUGH;
            Peter BROWN; Samuel BRADSHAW; Stephen PIGG; Joel
            PRUIT; Henry MAYBERRY; Sally MAYS; Edward CAMPBELL;
            Thomas LINTEY; Simeon ROACH; Thomas CRAIG; William
            DEMOSS; Abram MAYBERRY; Lewis DEMOSS; Nicholas
            BRANCH; James WARRINGTON; George PIELER; Rebecca
            RHODES; William GRAY; Patsy SMITH ; Michael
            MAYBERRY; Elijah WALKER; William QUILLEN; William
            SPARKMAN; John THOMAS, William SEGAR.

page 177   Further inventory of Robert LUMPKINS, deceased.
            "State of Tennessee, County of Davidson--to any
            lawful officer to execute and return, you are
            hereby commanded that of the goods, and chattels,
            lands and tennements of Robert LUMPKINS you cause
            to be made the some of $83.06 and costs of suit to
            satisfy a judgment obtained by BROWN and LITTLEJOHN
            on 18 November 1815 against said Robert LUMPKINS
            before J. R. MARTEN of Williamson County, etc." by
            E. J. HALL, 10 May 1816.

page 179   Inventory of property of Agnes HODGE, deceased,
            5 August 1816. Made by James LOVE.

page 180   Inventory of James FARRIS, deceased, 19 August 1816.
            By Moses ROBERTSON and James FILES.

page 181   No heading. Inventory of sale of estate of Gideon
            KIRKSEY, deceased. 30 June 1816. Signed: Mary
            KIRKSEY; administratrix. "Names of Persons";
            Robert JOHNSTON; Samuel MAYFIELD; James ISOM; John
            MC LISH; John KIRKSEY; John LANKFORD; James S.
            ROBERTSON; Joshua SHARP; Lemuel BLACKBURN.

page 182   Inventory of personal property of John CAMPBELL,
            deceased, made 20 August 1816, by Matilda CAMPBELL,
            executrix, and Robert CAMPBELL, executor.

page 184   Inventory of Ezekial LINDSEY, 22 December 1809, by
            Hannah X LINDSEY. Compared Book A, page 8.

page 184   "Property now in my possession of estate of my
            father Laurence BURNS." 1 April 1811. Signed:
            George X. BURNES.

page 185   March 1808. Elenor HAYS and William HAYS,
            administrators for Jesse HAYS, deceased--allowance
            for administrators. Signed: J. BURMINGHAM and
            Robert HILL.

page 186   Inventory of sale of Thomas FORE, deceased.
            1 August 1809. Buying: Pollinia F. FORE; Samuel
            H. WILLIAMS; Matthew BRANCH; Andrew LAUGHERTY;
            Charles COATS; John POWEL; Robert NEELEY; Thomas
            HEDGEPATH; Harrison COOPER; Henry BRANCH; Simpson
            HARRIS; Reddick ROBERTSON; Andrew LAFERTY; John
            MOTTON; Joseph WALLS; Wyley GRIFFIN.

page 188   Inventory of Henry LUCK, deceased. One note on
            Amos BATCH dated 19 June 1797. By David LUCK,
            administrator, 15 June 1812.

page 190   Joseph CHOAT and James LOVE, administrators of
            estate of James KNOX, and Samuel WEATHERSPOON, Henry
            KIRK, and William FRYERSON, appraisers of said
            estate. 23 September 1812.

page 191   "Articles purchased by me Francis WRIGHT, Junr., at
            the sale of Francis WRIGHT, Senior, deceased."
            17 February 1814.

page 191   Inventory of estate of William GREEN (or GREER),
            deceased, by Laurence HALCOMB.

page 192   Inventory of James TURNER, deceased. Compared in
            Book A, page 30.

page 193   Report of inventory of Hugh ROSS, deceased, by
            Hezekiah BROOKS, administrator.

page 193   Inventory of property of Patience SELLARS, deceased.
            "Sold by me, Wyley GRIFFIN on 28 July 1812.

page 195   Supplemental inventory of Elo-zor ALEXANDER. "a
            rect of Abdon ALEXD dated 6 May 1808 for two notes
            payable by Robert and Andrew CROCKETTS." By
            Margaret ALEXANDER, administratrix.

page 196   Inventory of estate of Elliazor ALEXANDER, 14 June
            1811. "Notes left in North Carolina, amount not
            known." Signed: Margaret ALEXANDER. Sale follows
            with articles and amounts.

page 198   Estate of Andrew GOFORTH, deceased. 28 September
            1811. Andrew H. GOFORTH, executor of estate of
            Andrew GOFORTH, deceased.

page 199   Inventory of Ephriam CHURCHWELL, deceased. See Book
            A, page 10.

page 202   3 June 1814. Widow's provision for Mary EDWARDS,
            widow of Thomas EDWARDS, deceased, by A. J. JOHNSTON,
            John GILCHRIST, Chiles MAGE, Duncan GILCHRIST.

page 203   Jury appointed to inquire into insanity of Andrew
            Miller. His reason impaired and incapable of
            managing his person or property--under care of
            guardian--20 July 1814. Signed: A JOHNSTON; Lewis
            JOHNSTON; Thomas EDWARDS; Solomon THOMAS; Barns
            THOMAS; Elisha THOMAS; Phillemon X WHITE; Moses X
            SPRINKLE; Phillip X MARCUS; James NEWLID; Martin
            ADAMS; Alexander CRAWFORD.

page 204	Sale of Jeremiah GURLEY, deceased, 25 June 1814. Buying: Davis GURLEY; Hugh GILBREATH; James HIGGS; Stephen EDWARDS; Polly GURLEY; Major DAVIS; William DAVIS.
page 204	Sale of Thomas EDWARDS, deceased. Buying: William DAVIS; Ebenezar SMITH; William EDWARDS; Mary EDWARDS; Stephen EDWARDS; and Henry DAVIS.
page 205	Inventory of Thomas EDWARDS, deceased.
page 206	Sale of Marmaduke ONEAL, deceased, 11 February 1809. Thomas H. ONEAL, administrator.
page 206	Joseph BROWN and William DONLEY appointed to settle with Alexander MC DONALD and Joseph MC DONALD, administrators of John MC DONALD, deceased, March 1811.
page 206	Inventory of Ephriam CHURCHWELL, deceased, by Richard CHURCHWELL. See Book A, page 11.
page 208	Inventory of Jeremiah GURLEY, deceased. 31 February 1814. (?)
page 208	Inventory of Asa RICHERSON, deceased, returned by Richard JENNINGS, administrator.
page 208	Silas ALEXANDER, Nimrod PORTER, and John DAVIS have proportioned to Polly BEANLAND, late widdow of Ed (Ewd?) BEANLAND, deceased, year's provision, 17 May 1815.
page 209	Inventory of Edw BEANLAND, deceased, May term 1815. "Wages for six months tour of duty." Polly BEANLAND, administratrix, and William DOOLEY, administrator.
page 210	Inventory of Edw BEANLAND, deceased, see Book A, page 196.
page 210	Inventory of estate of E. ROBERTS, deceased. (See page 179???) Polly ROBERTS, executrix.
page 211	Isaac ROBERTS Inventory. Polly ROBERTS.
page 212	Robert NEELEY'S sale. Buying: Thomas WEIR; John NEELY, Harrison COOPER; Max Miller REDDIN; Elijah P. CHAMBERS; Widow NEELY, Hugh NEELY.
page 213	Inventory of estate of Washington WALKER, deceased, by Elizabeth WALKER, 29 November 1814. Part of property "came by sd Washington WALKER," and part" came by Elizabeth WALKER." Signed by Elizabeth WALKER, executrix of the last wife of Washington WALKER, deceased.
page 214	Sale of Washington WALKER.
page 216	Inventory of estate of David HINES, deceased, by Stephen COLLINS, administrator, and Anna HINES administratrix, 14 November 1817.

page 217   Inventiry of Littleberry HAMBLET. 20 December 1817.
            By William YANCY, administrator.

page 217   Inventory of estate of Milan ANTHENEY. (?)

page 218   blank

page 219   blank

page 220   Inventory of William WINNS, deceased, 7 November
            1817, by Mary X WINNS, administratrix, and Charles
            WINNS, administrator. 17 November 1817.

page 221   Inventory of estate of Joseph SANDFORD, deceased,
            taken 21 Janurary 1818 by James T. DANDFORD,
            executor.

page 222   Estate sale of John JOHNSON, March 10, and 11, 1814.

page 222   Inventory of David HINES, deceased, see page 216,
            Book B.

page 223   Sale of David COPELAND, "taken by Exrs lawyers and
            filed with papers of suit."

page 224   Widow's provision for Mary WIMS, (?), widdow of
            William WIMS. 22 December 1817, by William NOTT,
            John LINDSEY, and James GHOLSON. Francis GHOLSON
            was appointed to lay this out but James GHOLSON
            evidently took his place.

page 225   Inventory of Washington WALKER taken by Elizabeth
            WALKER 29 November 1814. Some property "came by
            Elizabeth WALKER." Elizabeth, executrix of last
            will of Washington WALKER, deceased.

page 226   Sale of William CARR, deceased, 17 January 1818.
            "one tour of duty in Captain GORDON'S company--
            $137.25; one tour of duty in W. MAKIN'S company--
            $75.87." Notes on Thomas KELSEY, Hugh SINCLAIR,
            and Thomas CORBEAR (?), Aron Carter LAND and
            Lewis MATTHEWS; James KELSY; Solomon HUFFLESTUTLER;
            William LONG; Alexander CATHEY; Nathaniel WILLIS;
            Captain Sam (?) CRAWFORD. Alexander CATHEY,
            administrator,

page 227   John ASKEW'S account of sales. 17 November 1817 by
            Zephaniah NUNN, administrator.

page 229   Sale of Enos HOLLAND, deceased, 21 May 1817, by
            John JOHNS, administrator. Buying: John COOK;
            Alexander P. DENHAM; William KIRK; Thomas WILLIAMS;
            Robert KELLY; Elijah P. CHAIMBERS; John HART;
            John JOHNSTON.

page 229   Inventory of Charles POWELL, deceased, taken
            19 October 1818. Notes on William MC MUNN,
            William D. POWEL, John WILSON, John T. MOORE,
            Martin WILSON.

page 230   Inventory of Charles POWEL, deceased, 24 November
            1818. Buying: Jesse GLOVER; Mrs. D. POWELL;

Solomon ROSWELL; William CUNNINGHAM; William
MC WILLIAMS; James T. SANDFORD; Samuel STRAMLES;
Josiah ALEDERSON; Darrel N. SANSOM; William EMERSON:
James DAVIS; Sion ROGERS; Blackston HARDEMAN; James
ROBINSON; P. CHEATHAM; David ANDREWS; Alexander
GILLESPIE; Morgan FITZPATRICK; William CRAIG;
John HALEBET; Thomas STONE; P. NELSON; William D.
NELSON; Elisha HUNTER; Sally POWEL.

page 231   October 28, 1818. "I Blackstone HARDEMAN, guardian
of Anna H. LARRAMORE, John H. LARRAMORE, James
LARRAMORE; Patsy LARRAMORE, Polly LARRAMORE, AND
Leah LARRAMORE have this day recerived from Thomas
HARDEMAN, Junr., one of the executors of Thomas
LARRAMORE, deceased, the sum of $156.40 and
7 mills, being the amount due said heirs from said
administrator."

page 232   Will of Jonathan ISHAM: beloved wife Elizabeth;
daughter Ursula, Elizabeth, Sally, Polly, Jenny,
Fanny; son, George. "will that my beloved wife
give to each of the above named daughters at
eighteen years of age..my son John sell all the
land that I hold in the state of Virginia,
Montgomery County." Wife and son John, executors.
15 September 1813. Witnesses: Joseph PAYTON and
Andrew KENNEDY.

page 233   Will of James M. WRIGHT: 29 August 1817. Wife
Margaret M. WRIGHT sufficient property to maintain
Patsey MACK WRIGHT her life time. Balance divided
between John M. WRIGHT and Matthew M. WRIGHT and
Polly M. WRIGHT. Witnesses: William GILLIAM;
John MC FALLS; and James HILLS. (Possible thet
the surname should be MC WRIGHT.)

page 235   Nuncupative will of John J. WEBB of Hickman County.
Witnesses: David KELLOUGH; Gabriel FOWLES; Horatio
CLAGETT; George P. TYLER; Wife: Elizabeth G. WEBB.
11 January 1822.

page 235   Will of Moses CHAFFIN: Wife Jean and my children.
"When youngest child comes of age..." No date,
proven 182_. Witnesses: E. E. DAVIDSON; V. RIDLEY;
and James F. HOUSE.

page 236   Jacob MC KEE, will: Proven 182_. Wife Elizabeth
and my seven(???) children: Anne; Polly; Jane;
Matilda; Sally; Minerva; Betsy; Malinda; and
Nancy Lucinda. Brother Thomas MC KEE and
A. R. ALEXANDER, executors. 28 September 1818.
Witnesses: George E. EGNEW and William A. MAXWELL.

page 237   Will of Daniel Yates: Wife Martha...Mariah YATES,
James YEATS, John YEATS, William YEATS, Sarah
YEATS, and Arilla YEATS... when my son James YEATS
arrives of age of 14 (?)...wife Martha, John
MC FALLS, and James HILL, executors, 2 November
1814. Witnesses: Alx HILL and Edward WHITE.
Codicil: "in case wife does not keep Mariah and
James YEATES together with other children, notes
to be put to their support."

page 238   Will of William ADKINS. 2 September 1807. Wife,
             Jane....all my children....wife and George PATTON,
             executors. Witnesses: Samuel MC LEAN; James PORTER;
             and John X DUCKWORTH.

page 239   Inventory of estate of Donald MC DONALD, 21 November
             1814. "600 Acres of land in Georgia." Catharine
             MC DONALD, administrator.

page 239   Inventory of estate of John ASKEW, deceased,
             18 August 1817, by Zephaniah NUNN, administrator.

page 240   Sale of Charles ISHAM, deceased, 7 December 1816.
             Buying: George ISHAM; John MC CLISH; John M. GILL;
             Abram MAYBERRY; Thomas KELLOUGH; Heckey BROWN; Joel
             DABLES; William WHITESIDES; John ISHAM; Arthur T.
             ISHAM; George SHAW.

page 241   Sale of Thresher MC COLLOM, deceased, 22 June 1815.
             Buying: Mary MC COLLUM (bought most); Joseph
             WEALTHERINTON; John RANDOLPH; James S. RILEY; John
             MC INTIRE; Alexander THOMPSON; Nathaniel NOBLE;
             James SKELLY; Abraham WEATHERTON; Enoch P. GALLOWAY;
             Stephen PIGG; Andrew LIONS; Barnabas DOLLISON.
             Mary MC COLLUM, administrator.

page 242   Inventory of Obediah LANGSTON, deceased,
             20 February 1815.

page 242   Sale of property of Donald MC DONALD, held
             22 January 1814. Catherine MC DONALD,
             Asministratrix.

page 243   Inventory of Theophelus FRAME, deceased, February
             term 1815 by Daniel L. Bridges, administrator.

page 244   Inventory of Francis WRIGHT, deceased, 15 December
             1813. "......give to my son John." Signed:
             Francis WRIGHT.

page 244   Additional inventory of William ADKINS, deceased.
             22 April 1820. Notes on: John BLACKBURN; James
             BLACKBURN; Joseph BLACKBURN; Hugh BROWN; Robert
             CHURCH, Snr.; David DOBBINS; Reuben OWENS; Jacob
             SEAGROVES; Charles SHEAMATE; Stephen PIGG;
             Masterson FITZJARRELL; Elijah PATTON.

page 245   Inventory of John RECORD, deceased, 16 August 1814.
             By Elisha HUNTER, Sion S. RECORD, John M. RECORD,
             Mary RECORD, administrators.

page 246   Additional inventory of James MC MAHON, deceased,
             November term 1817. Notes and accounts: Henry
             REED; Soloman HUFFSTATLER; Samuel CRAWFORD; "wages
             while in service of United States--$280, amount
             collected for lost property while in service of
             United States--$148.50." R. MC MAHON and Callaway
             HARDIN, administrators.

page 256   Sale of Jesse BROWN, deceased, 15 December 1814.
             Buying: William H. HILL; Samuel ATKINSON; William
             TIMMONS; Richard ROADS; Daniel BROWN; William

FARRER; Hugh BROWN; Nathaniel CHAIRS; Nathan USSERY;
Walter JENKINS; Burwell AKIN; Goldman KIMBROW;
Daniel B. MILLER; Reuben SMITH; Samuel POLK;
Ebenezer MILLER; Elizabeth JONES; Frederick MILLER;
Oliver WILLIAMS.

page 249   Inventory of Robert FOSTER, deceased, appraised by
           Samuel FREERSON, Thomas STEPHENSON, and Doctor
           Samuel MAYES. 9 March 1815.

page 250   Account of sale of Daniel DAVIS, deceased.
           30 November 1820. Buying: William RICHARDS;
           Charles V. BROWN; Matthew G. PICKINS; Robert M.
           RICHARDSON; William ALLEN; Constantine DAVIS; Willis
           RICHARDSON; David DUGGER; Allen RICHARDSON; Howard
           CANON; Lydia DAVIS (house-hold furniture); William
           BOAZ.

page 252   Inventory of Joseph DENTON, deceased, by Elleanor
           DENTON, executrix. ____term 182_.

page 252   Inventory of estate of Tyre DOLLINS, deceased.
           "horse in equal partnership with J. MC CAFERTY and
           Tyro DOLLINS." ____term 182_.

page 152   Inventory of estate of Daniel DAVIS,___term 18__.

page 153   Widow's provision for Elizabeth DICKSON, 14 November
           1819, widow of John DICKSON, deceased. By Johnston
           CRAIG, John PICKARD, and William GLASS.

page 254   Sale of Tyre DOLLINS, ____term 182_. Buying: John
           D. DAVIDSON; Walter MC CONNELL; Andrew NEELY;
           Pleasant SCRIBNER; James MC CAFERTY; Widdow DOLLINS;
           Joseph HACKNEY; Nicholas MC MILLAN; Howard CANNON;
           William MC CONNELL; David EDDLEMON; William ESOM;
           James THOMAS; George W. JOHNSTON; Mrs. BILL; George
           WHITE; James STONE; Drury PAGET; David W. MC REA;
           Phillip HOLLINGER; George HAAZE; William CURRY;
           Edward COLE; Joel COFFEE; William COMBS; James
           Smith; John EDLEMON; Wright TRIGG (or GRIGG); Abner
           JOHNSTON; James NEELEY; Robert WORTHAM; Ambrose
           HARVELL; Aron WILCOXEN; Polly PERRY (or BERRY, OR
           TERRY); Travis HAMRICK; Merideth WEBB; William
           PATTERSON; John CANNON; William SANDS; Thomas
           CARDEN; Moses MAY; Evender KENEDY; Benjamin WHITE:
           John WASSON; James LYNCH; Jeremiah THOMASON; Bailey
           BROOKS; Thomas OSBURNE; Elisha MERRYMAN; Peter R.
           VOORHIES; William VORRHIES; John CLANTON; Agnes
           BLACK; Joseph PERKINS; Reese PORTER and Caleb
           THOMAS; Ephriam ABERNATHA; William ROPER; William
           FENE; Simeon PEERY; William RODGERS; Thomas DUE;
           Edmond GWIN; Allen JONES; Hugh TERRANCE.

page 257   Inventory of estate of Joseph DYAL, ____term 182_.

page 257   Widow's provision for Lydia DAVIS, widdow of Daniel
           DAVIS, deceased; for year 1821, by John RICHARDSON,
           William RICHARDSON, John CANNON, 19 November 1820.

page 266   Sale of Jacob MC KEE, deceased, held 25 November
            1819. Buying: George WEBSTER; Robert WALLIS;
            William A. MAXWELL; Solomon P. MAXWELL; Andrew
            NEELEY; Samuel GODWIN; Curtis WOODY; A. B. MAYFIELD;
            John GILBREATH; Levin COVEY.

page 267   John ASKEW, additional sale. 1 November 1819. By
            Zephaniah NUNN, administrator.

page 267   Widow's provision for Elizabeth ALDERSON, widow
            of John ALDERSON, deceased, 24 August 1819. By
            Edward WILLIAMS; James G. SMITH; and John
            MC FALLS, Jr.

page 267   Inventory of William JACOBS, deceased, 26 July
            1821. "the property that William JACOBS gave to
            his daughter Sally JACOBS"...Allen (?) RAINEY,
            administrator.

page 268   Sale of Aron ALDRIDGE, deceased. 20 July 1821.
            Buying: William ALDREDGE; Nancy ALDRIDGE;
            Samuel ALDRIDGE; (these three bought all but two
            items) Eli SMITH (bought rest). By William
            ALDRIDGE and and Samuel ALDRIDGE.

page 270   Sale of John ALDERSON, deceased, 17 and 18 February
            1819. Buying: Elizabeth S. ALDERSON; John D.
            ALDERSON; John EDWARDS; Lucy ALDERSON; Jeremiah
            ALDERSON; Fortunatus ALDERSON; Daniel KEETCH; James
            GRAY; John W. LEMASTER; Samuel A. BAKER; Joseph
            H. MC EWING; James BECK; Benjamin POLK; Thomas
            COLEMAN; William B. ALDERSON; Sherwood HELMS;
            Josiah ALDERSON; John STEWARD; Robert CAMPBELL;
            John MC FALLS; Arthur W. DUE; George TATE; Richard
            LEWIS; E. G. (or L.) ALDERSON; Horatio CLAGETT;
            Thomas WALKER; George P. LYLE; William ALDERSON;
            George Hicks, By L. COLEMAN, clerk.

page 274   Year's allowance for Polly ALEXANDER, 11 January
            1814, widow and relict of Ezekial ALEXANDER and
            her children by A. CATHEY, Alexander CATHEY, Sr.,
            Isaac FARRIS.

page 274   Additional inventory of John ASKEW, deceased,
            1 November 1818. Zephaniah NUNN, administrator.

page 274   Year's provision for Nancy ALDRIDGE, widow of
            Aron ALDRIDGE. 16 June 1821, by Samuel MC DAVID,
            Samuel SMITH, and Nathan SMITH.

page 274   Inventory of Moses ALEXANDER, deceased, 15 June
            1822. "one note in Notrh Carolina;" by Obediah
            ALEXANDER.

page 275   Sale of William BYNUM, deceased. No date, 182_.
            Buying: Moses HILL; James SELLARS; Luke SELLARS;
            Asa PUCKET; John SAUNDERS; Jonathan WILLIAMS;
            Joseph LAYMASTER; Mark BYNUM; Robert SELLARS;
            Daniel MAY; Badford BYNUM; James SPADLING
            (SPRADLING?); Shelby POLK; by Robert SELLARS,
            James SELLARS, and Luke SELLERS, executors.

page 275　　　Personal estate of Robert FOSTER, deceased,
　　　　　　　produced February term 1815. Buyers: Mrs. EVANS;
　　　　　　　Elias J. ARMSTRONG; David LUCK; Thomas FLEMMING;
　　　　　　　Thomas J. FRIERSON; Samuel FRIERSON; Thomas C.
　　　　　　　FARRIS; James JOSEY; John W. STEPHENSON; Samuel
　　　　　　　WEATHERSPOON; John GURLEY; John F. WHITE; James M.
　　　　　　　FRIERSON; Thomas WILLIS; James ROBESON; William
　　　　　　　BLAKELEY; James ROSS; Mary FOSTER; Jane DAVIS;
　　　　　　　Michael WALDRUP; Nathaniel YOUNG; Nathaniel
　　　　　　　STEPHENSON; Thomas WILLIS; Thomas STEPHENSON; Isaac
　　　　　　　ROSS; Thomas F. FRIERSON; Elias FRIERSON; John
　　　　　　　Loate (?) MAYES; George DICKEY, by Samuel
　　　　　　　WEATHERSPOON and John W. STEPHENSON, administrators.

page 278　　　Year's provision for Susanna BOGARD, husband's name
　　　　　　　not given, 23 November 1820, by Benjamin WILKES,
　　　　　　　John GILLESPIE, Robert MC DONALD .

page 279　　　Inventory of Jethro BROWN, deceased, by James T.
　　　　　　　SANDFORD, administrator, 19 October 1818.

page 279　　　Inventory of Jethro BROWN, 19 October 1818.

page 279　　　Inventory of E. ROBERTS, 10 May 1816, Polly ROBERTS,
　　　　　　　administratrix. Notes on Jacob AVORAL, E. D.
　　　　　　　GRIGORY, Andrew GREEN, N. PARKINS, Ged HENSLEY (?),
　　　　　　　James WHITSON, J. B. PORTER, Tom NORTON, William
　　　　　　　BOYD, William MARTEN.

page 280　　　Inventory of Joseph SANDFORD, 21 January 1818,
　　　　　　　James T. SANDFORD, executor.

page 280　　　Inventory of John KINDRICK, 8 December 1821, notes
　　　　　　　on James G. SMITH.

                    THE END OF WILL BOOK B

     MAURY COUNTY, TENNESSEE WILLS AND SETTLEMENTS BOOK C-1

page 1　　　　Division of estate of John CAMPBELL, deceased,
　　　　　　　11 shares, 19 December 1822. Joseph H. MILLER;
　　　　　　　Robert CAMPBELL; _____ ALEXANDER; Ezekial M.
　　　　　　　CAMPBELL; John P. CAMPBELL; William C. CAMPBELL;
　　　　　　　Matildy L. CAMPBELL; Junious T. CAMPBELL; Caroline
　　　　　　　CAMPBELL; Samuel P. CAMPBELL; and Matildy G.
　　　　　　　CAMPBELL, widow of late John CAMPBELL and now
　　　　　　　Matildy G. JINKINS, wife to Phillip JINKINS.
　　　　　　　James T. SANDFORD and James BLACK, commissioners.
　　　　　　　(Note: should be Caroline H. CAMPBELL.)

page 1　　　　Petition for division of estate of George DAVIDSON,
　　　　　　　deceased. 7 shares. Heirs: Rosanna DAVIDSON,
　　　　　　　widow; Samuel J. ROGERS and his wife Sarah C. ,
　　　　　　　formerly Sarah DAVIDSON, for their part and right
　　　　　　　of purchase of George DAVIDSON and John E.
　　　　　　　DAVIDSON; John HENDERSON and wife Emeline,
　　　　　　　formerly Emeline DAVIDSON; Joseph KNOX and wife
　　　　　　　Louisa, formerly Louisa DAVIDSON; James C. KING
　　　　　　　and wife Isabella, formerly Isabella DAVIDSON,
　　　　　　　and Jane DAVISON (Minor) by her guardian James C.

KING; and equally the heirs of James L. DAVIDSON, deceased; also Polly DAVIDSON, widow and relict of Gilbreth F. DAVIDSON, deceased, for herself and her orphan children, "all of us being heirs and distributees of George DAVIDSON."

Signed: 15 January 1823
Rosanna DAVIDSON
Samuel J. ROGERS)--for themselves and right of
Sarah C. ROGERS)   purchase for George DAVIDSON,
                    Jr., and John E. DAVIDSON.
Joseph KNOX
Louisa KNOX
James C. KING
Isabella KING
John HENDERSON
Emeline HENDERSON
James C. KING, guardian for Jane DAVIDSON
Polly DAVIDSON, widow of Gilbreth DAVIDSON

page 3   Estate settlement with Thomas G. BLACK, executor of estate of Edward CALLIHAN, 17 January 1823.

page 3   Settlement of estate of William MADDIN, deceased, 27 January 1823.

page 3   Commissioners return on division of estate of William BYNUM, deceased, April term 1823. "property was not surrendered for division by the executors." Isaac BILLS, Swan HARDEN, Thomas HUDSPETH, John MILLER, commissioners.

page 3   Dower for Elizabeth WILKS, widow of John B. WILKES, deceased, made 19 July 1823. Commissioners: John HALIBERT; William A. JOHNSON; J. D. LINDSAY; William _____; Alexander JOHNSON; John KERR; W. B. ANDERSON; John ANDERSON; James BRANCH; Andrew M. KERR; John M. JONES; Isaac BILLS.

page 4   Estate settlement of Parmenes HOWARD, deceased. James HOWARD, executor. Accounts against estate: Doctor WHITESIDES; Doctor W. W. THOMPSON; John GOFF; John SAMPLE; John ALEXANDER; James MC CLEUR; John BOYD; Theron E. BALCH; Andrew HAUTH; Nathaniel W. (?) MOODY; Robert DAVIDSON; William ASBURN; Hugh W. STEPHENSON; John MC CRERY; Jesse NEEDHAM; Jacob WILLIAMS; Isaiah WAFOR; Robert MC CAIN. 23 May 1823. Witnesses: John MACK; John MATTHEWS: Alexander JOHNSON.

page 6   Heirs of Green WILLIAMSON, deceased. Division and distribution of negro property. Commissioners: Wilkison BARNS; Samuel H. WILLIAMS; William BRADSHAW; William PILLOW; and John HODGE.

          Division among heirs:
          Lot Number 1 --Mariah G. WILLIAMSON
          Lot Number 2 --Russel M. WILLIAMSON
          Lot Number 3 --Martha A. WILLIAMSON
          Lot Number 4 --Ann H. K. WILLIAMSON
          Lot Number 5 --Elizabeth P. WILLIAMSON

                    Lot Number 6 --William H. WILLIAMSON
                    Lot Number 7 --Patsey H. WILLIAMSON
                    Lot Number 8 --_____ H. WILLIAMSON

page 7   Estate Settlement of Ambrose Blackburn, deceased,
                by John BLACKBURN, administrator, 28 July 1823.

page 7   Nicholas J. LONG--partition of lands. Lotts 5 and
                6 to Richard H. LONG, said lotts being a part of
                the tract of land which was granted by the state of
                North Carolina to Colonel Nicholas LONG.

                Plat shows Nicholas J. LONG received 175-½ acres
                bounded by Richard H. LONG and Louisa LONG'S
                351 acres. Dated 14 July 1823. Signed: H. GROVE;
                James DOBBINS; and John MATTHEWS.

page 8   Settlement with John W. Jones, guardian of Elenor
                C. GLOVER. April term 1823. Receipts on:
                P. GLOVER; L. KILLUM; J. ALDERSON; and J. GLOVER.

page 10   Estate of James THOMPSON, deceased. December term
                1823. James DOBBINS and S. OLIPHANT,
                administrators. Notes on John and Fieldin GORDON,
                Charles HICKS, George E. MC FALL, and H. R.
                CHAMBERS, John WILKINS, William B. MARTIN, George
                HICKS, and John D. ALDERSON.

page 11   John NELSON, deceased, petition for distribution
                of estate. Mary NELSON is the widow of John NELSON,
                Senr., deceased, and other petitioners are children
                and legal heirs of John NELSON, Senr., deceased,
                who died intestate. Petitioners: Mary NELSON;
                Elizabeth ULAND. widow of Thomas Uland, deceased,
                formerly Elizabeth NELSON; Abram TRIBLE and Polly
                his wife, formerly Polly NELSON; Sally POWEL,
                widow of Charles POWEL, deceased, formerly Sally
                NELSON; William POWEL and Nancy, his wife, formerly
                Nancy NELSON; Mathew NELSON; William D. NELSON;
                James NELSON; John NELSON, Junr.; Pleasant NELSON.

                Swan HARDIN, Edward W. DALE, Esquire, and Major
                John BROWN appointed committee to report to
                January term 1823. Follows division. Dated
                27 January 1823.

page 13   Settlement with Simpson PERRY and Hugh FORGEY,
                administrators of estate of Andrew FORGEY, deceased.
                22 January 1823.

page 14   Thomas W. VINCENT, a minor, in account with his
                guardian, John JENKINS, January, February, April,
                October, December 1821, January,-December, 1822.
                Among items: "schooling said Vincent."

page 14   James T. SANDFORD and James BLACK, Justices of the
                Peace of county, make settlement with John JENKINS,
                guardian of Thomas W. VINCENT, a minor.
                27 January 1823.

page 15   Recorded 21 December 1823. Thomas JONES, Doctor,
                to Marthey WILLIAMSON--1/8 part of hire of negroes

                                    47

and rent for 1821 and 1822; Thomas JONES, Doctor,
to Ann H. K. WILLIAMSON--1/8 part of hire of
negroes and rent, for 1821 and 1822; Thomas JONES,
Doctor, to Mariah G. (?) WILLIAMSON, same as above
entry; Thomas JONES, Doctor, Guardian to Russell
Mc Cord WILLIAMSON, same entry as above. Court
directed to make settlement with Thomas JONES,
guardian of Martha WILLIAMSON, Ann H. K. WILLIAMSON,
Maria G. WILLIAMSON, and Russell Mc Cord
WILLIAMSON, 28 January 1823. Edward W. DALE,
Justice of the Peace, and James WALKER, Justice of
the Peace.

page 16   Doctor Dorrel N. SANSOM, James K, POLK, and
     21   E. E. DAVIDSON, administrators of estate of
           Abraham WHITESIDE, deceased.

October -1821--John GORDON, administrator of his
                     father's estate.
November 1821--William MC NEIL
January 1822--William B. ALDERSON, J. J. _____,
                     L. KENCHIN, Matthew SARRAGE, Joel
                     R. SMITH, P. COHEA, Alexander
                     ALEXANDER, William B. ALEXANDER
                     (amount of his father's account),
                     J. C. MC KEAN, amount of PLUMMER'S
                     Purchased at sale.
February 1822--J. M. GILLIAM, Henry TURNEY, John T.
                     PORTER, J. W. EGNEW, Joshua
                     WILLIAMS, Elisha UZZELL, Madison
                     CARUTHERS, Matthew REAH.
March   1822--Benjamin B. SMITH, A. B. MAYFIELD,
                     John HODGE, Silas M. CALDWELL,
                     BROWN and MC GIMSEY, William K.
                     HILL, Joseph COE, William H.
                     WILLIAMSON (or William G. DICKINSON)
                     amount of Mrs. WILLIAMSON'S account
                     and amount of David MARTIN's
                     account, P. MAGUIR, R. H. VAIL,
                     Nimrod PORTER, J. B. PORTER.
April   1822--Mr. RAMSEY, William VOORHIES, James
                     R. SHELTON, William S. HENDERSON.
May   1822--Augustine WILLIS.
June   1822--John O. (?) DAVIDSON, amount of
                     Jesse DOLLINGS' account.
July   1822--Edward B. LITTLEFIELD, Pleasant
                     NELSON, John FORNEY.
October 1822--Henry E. TURNER, Solomon P. MAXWELL.
January 1823--Edward W. DALE

1821: August, William J. JOHNSON; September,
William DONLEY; July, Duncan MC INTYRE; September,
William COVEY, George MARTIN; November Jasper R.
SUTTON; Adam CLIN; January 1822, Patrick MAGUIRE,
John J. BRIGGS, Richard B. PASSMORE, administrator
of John MC LEAN, deceased; March, Robert
CARUTHERS, Andrew BOYD, Samuel MC DOWELL, Esquire;
April, Charles LEULLIN; May, Oscar WILLIS;
December, Jesse T. ROSS; January 1823, D. N.
SANSOM; September 1821, Redden TAYLOR, Allen
TAYLOR; October 1822, estate of West HARRIS,
deceased; estate of Jesse DOLLINS, deceased;

Samuel DAVIS; Samuel SAVAGE; James HOLLAND; Henry
E. TURNER; John H. ESTES; Isaac J. THOMAS; 1823,
Thomas O. CLARK; William B. MARCH; E. DAVIDSON.

1822: Samuel RANKIN; Patrick MAGUIRE for coffee
and sugar furnished Mrs. WHITESIDES for her year's
allowance; Simon P. JORDAN for Richard's tuition;
John SKELTON; D. CRAIGHEAD'S allowance for
erecting a tomb over A. WHITESIDES, deceased--
$38.00; money advanced to Mrs. R. WHITESIDES;
John W. P. MC GIMSEY; advanced to Mrs. Ruth M.
WHITESIDES; George CAMPBELL, J. BROWN and son;
E. ERVIN for ADKINSON; _____CHITTENDEN; Thomas
DIXON; James HAYS.

1823: Jonah ALDERSON, John MACON.

page 21   October term 1822. Settle estate of Doctor
Abraham WHITESIDE, deceased. 14 January 1823.
I. BILLS, J. S. ALDERSON, E. W. DALE, Justices
of peace.

page 21   Robert, Luke, and James SELLARS, executors of
William BYNUM, deceased. 28 April 1823. Andrew
BAKER account; Robert SELLERS account; John
MILLER; Swan HARDEN; Edward W. DALE, Justices of
the Peace.

page 22   Recorded 22 December 1823. John M. JONES,
guardian of heirs of James OGLESBY, deceased.
1820 Balance. 27 January 1823. Isaac BILLS and
Edward W. DALE, Justices of the Peace.

page 23   Hiram GOFORTH, administrator of Andrew H. GOFORTH,
deceased. Money received.

1821--Joseph HERNDON, Hugh CANNON, John BOYAR,
William WALTON, William KILCREASE, Lewis RENFORW,
Moses F. ROBINS, James HERNDON, _____HOLLAND,
Ephriam FARTHER, John RENFROW, Shelton RENFROW,
William DISON, Isaac RENFROW, Abram JOB.

1822--Thomas CALDWELL, William HALCOMB, Samuel
HAYS, John W. BEASLEY, Richard J. COCKS, David
CALDWELL, John MUTS, William J. BAUCUM, James
MALCOMB, David RANKIN, David FORTNER, Willey
SCOTT, Alphred MEDLEY, Samuel JOHN, Robert RANKIN,
Bennet M. MOORE, William JOHNSTON, William DENNEY,
James RANKIN, Samuel HAYS, John CHISM.

1823--Brittain J. BAUCUM, Moses RANKIN, Lawrence
HALCUM, Powel HALE.

1821--paid out for widow; paid COHEA for Widow
YEATMAN; Thomas; Joseph SEWELL; Richard GORDON.

1822--Ezekiel AIKEN; James C. ORILEY; Reuben R.
CARTER. John C. WORMELEY and John GORDON,
Justice of the Peace.

page 25   27 January 1823. Settlement with John JENKINS, guardian of William B. VINCENT, a minor. "boarding at Esquire HERNDON'S."

page 26   15 January 1823. Settlement with executors of last will and testament of Samuel SHAW, deceased. David CRAIG account, Michael BAILEY; Doctor G. B. WILLIAMS; John PINKARD, Senr. Signed: William STOCKARD; Samuel GRIFFETH, Justices of the Peace.

page 26   26 November 1822. Commissioners (James P. PETERS, Isaac RAINEY, and Nathaniel CHEARES) appointed to allot Nancy HOBSON, widow of Jeremiah HOBSON, deceased, one year's provision.

page 27   19 July 1823. Settlement with Charles PARTEE, guardian of minor heirs of Squire SHURMAN, deceased--to Nancy SHURMAN _____; Board and clothes for five children for 1822; Richard B. PASSMORE'S fee; Swan HARDEN'S fee; for rent of land in North Carolina. Signed: Richard B. PASSMORE; Swam HARDEN, Justices of the Peace.

page 28   Estate of William FRIERSON, deceased.
35

        1820--_____ BUFORD; M. D. COOPER: G. DICKEY, BLAKELY; Mr. STEPHENSON; Mr. T. JONES.
        1821--Jennings; James N. BROWN; P. FULTON; SAVAGE; Frederick MILLER; Thomas JONES; B. DICKEY; Elias J. ARMSTRONG; Henery TURNEY; Samuel WHITESIDES; James ARMSTRONG; UZZELL; Simpson WALKER; William PILLOW; John RENFROW; W. J. FRIERSON; P. MC GUIRE; estate of Moses G. FRIERSON; John FRIERSON; David FRIERSON; J. LAMASTER; Nathaniel YOUNG; Samuel BLAKELY; Alexander WILLIAMS; E. B. LITTLEFIELD; Valentine PAULEY; Thomas F. FLEMING; John BLACKBURN; John BRIGGS; Thomas JONES; W. R. DICKEY; James DOBBINS; Samuel H. ARMSTRONG; J. M. FRIERSON; James R. PLUMMER; Jesse GOODMAN; Hugh SHAW; R. B. NEWSON; William P. ARMSTRONG; John W. GREEN; Peter JOICE; David MARTIN; Alexander HENDERSON; Francis PERRY; George EGNEW; PEYTON; MICHEL and WEBSTER; Lorenzo HICKCOCK: John LONGLEY; Alexander MC KAY; Thomas SUTHERLAND; R. G. KELSEY.
        1822--L. C. OLIPHANT, Mary J. FRIERSON, William J. ROBERTS, Edward ENGLISH, William WAGGONER, John WINN, J. B. FOAG, Doctor MAYES, D. CRAIGHEAD, David RUSSELL.
        1823--DUPREST, N. J. LONG, J. PURCELL, Alexander MACKEY.

        Paid Out:
        1820--August 29, paid Walker for coffin, $10.00; John LAWRENCE; DUNCAN'S board; Mr. BARKE.
        1821--A. DOBBINS for Doctor AVEY; schooling for Edmund; Captain SAVAGE; Gideon BALCKBURN, D. D.; HODGE; COOPER; Sansom SHAW; GROVES and SMITH; ERVIN; Francis B. FOGG; James S. WALKER; E. H. CHAFFIN; Thomas OLA; John B.

HAMILTON; Adam CLIES; E. A. BARKER; L. BROOKS
L. BROOKS; Doctor AVERY; John W. GREEN;
William BLANK; MC NEAL and MORE; William
LITTRFIELD; Thomas SUTHERLAND; James H. OTEY
for tuition.
1822--Mrs. SHAW; wine for EDMUND; "D. CRAIGHEAD
for advice--$20.00;" John HODGE; S. P.
JORDAN; J. ALDERSON.
1823--R. L. COBBS "for advice--$15.00;" Thomas
YATEMAN.
1822--Doctor TURNER; D. N. SANSOM; LANGTREY; John
TERREL.
1823--William R. MILLER; E. CLACK; L. C. SHAW,
executrix of C. MILLER; William and L.
GAGGERS. Signed: David CRAIG; William
STOCKARD; and Hugh DOUGLAS, Justices of
the Peace.

page 36   Account of sale of Nathaniel WILLIS, Peter R. BOOKER,
and John MATTHEWS, executors of estate of West
HARRIS, deceased: James R. PLUMMER, Mrs. Milley
HARRIS, Patrick MAGUIRE, George JOHNSTON, John M.
DANIEL, Baley NEEDEM, WALKER and HODGE, John
WILLIAMS, William EDWARDS, Andrew MC CARTY, John
MATHEWS, Jacob WILLIAMS, Abraham WHITESIDES'
executors, WILLIAM and LEE, John HODGE, Thomas
BROWN, M. HELM, William H. STEPHENSON, Sarah
BRADSHAW, William PACKEY, Silas ALEXANDER, Moses
D. HARPER, John ALEXANDER, Edward COLE, Minta P.
ABERNATHY, John WILLIAMS, EWING, Joseph B. POARTER.
19 September 1823. Isaac BILLS and Edward W. DALE,
Justice of the Peace.

page 37   Nathaniel WILLIS, one of executors of West HARRIS,
deceased, in October with minor heirs:

1820--Solomon P. MAXWELL for his store account
against Olive HARRIS for year 1820; same for
West HARRIS; Bond of West HARRIS paid Daniel
WILLIAMS; same year for board of Olive
HARRIS having paid Wyatt HARRIS; advanced to
Henry HARRIS to bear traveling expenses to
Georgia in 1821.
1822--To William MACON for schooling of Olive
HARRIS when taught by Mr. Edward COTTON in
1822; to William H. LEE for schooling West
HARRIS in 1822; cash paid Benjamin R. HARRIS,
one of the nine heirs of said deceased--
$50.57, it being his proportion of the hire
of negroes belonging to the minor heirs
after deducting therefrom the maintenance,
clothing, and schooling of the three
youngest children and $25.00 which he
recieved more than an equal share of the
negroes, his Lot being worth that amount
more than the remaining lots. 19 September
1823, signed: Isaac BILLS, Edward W. DALE;
Justices of the Peace.

page 39   Division among heirs of Elijah ROBERTSON to an
undivided tract of 5,000 acres. Divided (viz)
Eldridge B. ROBERTSON, Sterling C. ROBERTSON,

51

John CHILDRESS' heirs and Washington L. HANNUM.
21 October 1823.   James N. GILL and Thomas GILL.

page 39   Commissioners settlement with administrator of John
            J. WEBB, deceased, met 7 October 1823 at house of
            Doctor James G. SMITH at Williamsport. Signed:
            T. COLEMAN and William EDMONDSON, Justices of the
            Peace.

page 40   Settlement with executors of William K. MATTHEWS,
            deceased.   Receipt from David and Hannah BRACKEN-
            RIDGE, former widow of said MATTHEWS, deceased,
            MC GIMSEY; Moses HARPER; John GILLESPIE; the minor
            heir Margaret Ann MATTHEWS. 5 August 1823. Isaac
            BILLS and John MACK, Justices of the Peace.

page 41   Settlement with Lawrence MC MINAS, administrator of
            estate of William MC LEOD, deceased. 12 September
            1823. Signed: Thomas G. BLACK, John W. RECORD,
            Justice of the Peace

page 41   Settlement with Moses ROBINSON, administrator of
            estate of Robert FARIS, deceased. 29 September 1823.
            Signed: A. CATHEY, John O. COOKE, Justices of the
            Peace.

page 42   Nashville, 23 May 1821. Sary THOMPSON, daughter of
            James THOMPSON, deceased, Doctor to William G.
            GOODWIN, her guardian. Received from James DOBBIN,
            administrator of James THOMPSON, deceased.
            20 October 1823. Joseph B. PORTER, clerk.

page 43   Credit Calvin H. NICHOLSON, minor, in account with
            James L. WALKER, guardian--1821, 1822, 1823. James
            WALKER, Garret L. VOORHIES, William HARMON, John
            BILLS, Simon E. JORDON, WALKER and HAYS, Buford
            TURNER, T. D. CLARK, WALKER and HARRIS.

            Calvin G. NICHOLSON, minor heir of O. P. NICHOLSON,
            deceased. 15 April 1823. Signed: James T.
            SANDFORD, Esward W. DALE, Justices of the Peace.

page 44   Settlement and distribution of estate of Aaron
            ALDREDGE, deceased. 8 April 1823. Caleb HEADLEE,
            Joseph B. WALLACE, Thomas G. BLACK, commissioners.
            List of legatees: widow; William ALDREDGE; John
            FLEMING; Eli AMECK; Samuel, John, Sarah, James,
            Betsey, and Nancy ALDREDGE.

page 44   Year's provision for Margaret FREELAND and family,
            widow of Joseph FREELAND, deceased. 8 February
            1823. William HOLT, Daniel DAVIS, Thomas BATY.

page 45   Year's provision for Selah FITTSPATRICK, the wife
            of Andrew FITTSPATRICK, deceased. 11 September
            1822. Andrew SMITH, Morgan FITTSPATRICK.

page 45   William H. CAMPBELL, Alvin C. CAMPBELL, George W.
            CAMPBELL, minor heirs of Sarah CAMPBELL, deceased,
            in account with John BROWN, their guardian.
            P. NELSON, GANNT and MEAS, Alexander WHITE.
            21 April 1823. William EDMONDSON, commissioner.

page 46   Supplematory inventory of estate of James M. LEWIS,
           made 22 October 1822, recorded 24 December 1823.
           Notes:

Shadrick WALKER
John HATCHETS
Waller KENNARD
Samuel LONG
John JACKSON
Andrew WALLACE
E. GANT
John GRAY
Richard C. HARRIS
John BOKER
Jacob WILKASE
James MARLOW
John G. POWELL
Charles HAVENDRE
James GOODWIN
James MC CUTCHINS
L. HARNEY
William O. EDD
Allen YATES
Thomas REYNOLDS
David MARTIN
William BRADSHAW and
        William PILLOW
Joseph HERNDON
Wade L. HENDERSON
Silas ENYART
Avery L. LONG
Bird M. TURER
John D. ROBISON
Joshua BADDES
James BIFLEY
John CAMPBELL
O. M. BIRD
Mr. ADAMS
Mr. ROSS
James L. ROBINSON
W. C. COWEN
Thomas ALLEN
R. DAMSON
John DUCKWORTH
Banoni DICKEY
Mark EDWARDS
John ELEATT
R. BOYD
Stephen CHILDRESS
Reuben ELEATT
Hezekiah DAVIS
James BLACKBURN
        CANIDY
Josiah DAVIS
Major BATY
George BRISCOO
William BURROW
George CAMPBELL
Daniel CRAIGHEAD
Luke BENUM
Reubin A. CARTER
John CARTER

Captain KEESEY
Cader Knight
James LINCH
Joel LOVE
John MACON
James MC CAIN
Benjamin H. and
    Will T. LEWIS
William MC MAHON
Stephen NOBLE
W. C. MAYFIELD
John PORTER
Hugh B. PORTER
William A. MAXWELL
Captain PERRY
John LINDSEY
William MITCHELL
George MC FALL
Thomas MC NUTT
Nathaniel MURPHEY
Thomas MC DINEL
John MILLER
William MC CARTER
Charles PORTER and Sons
Louis JOHNSON
James HARDIN
Richard C. HARRIS
Gideon HENSLEY
John KNOX, Jnr.
William FRIERSON
Powel HALL
Benjamin HAYES
Samuel HUNTER
Henry GIPSON
William HOLCOMBE
Caleb HENLEY
Hiram GOFORTH
Mr. GILCHREST
Thomas FROSYTHE
Allen JONES
John SIMMONS
Charles REESE
Robert REED
John REECE
Reubin SHOTE
Benjamin G. STUART
Ley TERREL
Samuel SAVAGE
William STOCKART
Reubin REEVES
Matthew SWAN
Thomas STRIPTER
William STEPHENS
Stephen SNELL
Elijah REEVES
ROSS and RUSSEL
Peter RAGSDALE
Shadrack STARLING

D. L. T. CAMPBILL
Joel BARROW
Joseph COE
Joshua DAVIS
William BLAKELY
Isaac ACUFF
John BROWN
William COOPER
John DANILY
J. C. DEERIN
Robert MACK
Vincent PILLOW
Lemuel PHILIPS
Joseph B. PORTER
Joshua ORR
William MC WILLIAMS
William KIRK
Alexander LARD
James LOCK
Duncan MC INTYRE
John MC CLOY
Robert A. NELSON
William MC MAN
Lemuel PREWITT
David MITCHELL
James NEWELL
R. B. PORTER
Mordica PILLOW
Peter LEGGEN
A. B. MAYFIELD
Plesant MC QUERY
Henry MILLER
Andrew MC MAKINS
Clement MULLEN
Thomas MABA
A. MC KINDSY
Robert MC CARTER
Andrew MC CARTER
James Y. GREEN
Samuel JONES
Archibald HIGHT
Gideon JOHNSON
William FINDLEY
William FORGEY
Lewis JOHNSON
Simpson HARRIS
William HUNTER
Sion HARDIN
John HATCHET
Thomas HUDSPETH
Frances GHOLSON
Joshua GURT
John GRAVES
Morgan FITTSPATRICK
Doctor HAYWOOD
James RUTLEDGE
Joseph RHODES
John RANKINS
William RUTLEDGE
John SHADDON
James T. SANFORD
Thomas STONE

Anthony J. TURNER
Mr. SEATON
John L. SMITH
Joseph YOUNG
John MITCHELL
Mr. WILKES, Jr.
Thomas WILLOFORD
Michel WALDROP
John WILLSON
John WRIGHT
Samuel WINN
James WRENN
John WEBB
Datin YOUNG
William L. WILLSFORD
Abram YARBOROUGH
Alen MC COLOUGH
Joel REEVES
Abner PILLOW
John M. NAPIER
Joshua GUEST
B. HALCOMB and John
James READ
Dougherty LONGLEY
Joseph CALMAR
R. B. PORTER
Thomas MITCHEL
David W. MC KEA
Alexander MC COLOUGH
James REEDE (or RUDE?)
Charles JONES
Thomas DUE
Joel LEWIS
George MARTIN
W. L. JAMES
William RAMSEY
Benjamin REYNOLD
Henry MILLER
J. C. O'RILEY
John L. FIELDER
William W. THOMPSON
William ROBERTSON
E. SMITH
Daniel DAVIS
Martin GUM
Jacob BURGER
A. BLACKBURN
Buford TURNER
Charles A. TILLER
Major BRIGGS
John FLRMING
A. R. ALEXANDER
Mr. BEASLEY
William A. DAVIS
George M. DICKEY
Thomas DAVIS
W. EDWARDS
William EASTHOR
William BRADSHAW
John BRANCH
John BALCKBURN
G. BURNS

John W. BERN
Nathaniel SMITH
Joseph SHADDEN
James STACY
Samuel CRAWFORD
Jesse SANDERS
Buford TURNER
William RUSSELL
Tyre ROBERTSON
David FERREL
Bird M. TURNER
Jeremiah GURLEY
John SHELTON
William YANCEY
James VENTRESS
James WHITSON
Isaac WHITSON
Samuel H. WILLIAMS
Abram WHITESIDE
John WHITE
Green WILLIAMSON
James WILKINS
William W. WOOD
John L. WOOD
Jonathan WEBSTER
Minor L. WILKES
Thomas SCOTT
Edward H. FASE
Calvin L. HANEY
Gideon HENSLY
Henry GIPSON
Robert CAIN
Jonathe JONES
Elijah SIMPSON
Merideth L. F. HELM
Thomas OSBORN
Thomas EDIMONSON
John COWEN
Stephen DYE
Josel HOWES
Charles TUELL
Allen JACKSON
John KIRKMAN
John HARROD
Willis GOODWIN
N. PORTER
Richard HOUSTER
F. PRENIE
Gabriel LOVING
Ezekial LINDSEY
Reuben A. CARTER
William GILLEAN
Samuel SMART
John MILLER
James WEATHERS
J. HUNT
James LEWIS
Benjamin JOHNSON
L. B. ESTLE
William P. ANDERSON
Augustine BROWN
James RUMMAGE

_____ DOWER
William CURREY
Robert ALDERSON
_____ ALEXANDER
Peter BRIGGS
Daniel CAMPBELL
A. M. COPLAND
Abrom CASSELMAN
Ambroes CAUNN (?)
Levi FLECHER
S. L. CARTER
John T. ALDERSON
Pleasant CREW
Samuel BROOKS
Martin BEARD
Moses CHAFFIN
James DUNCAN
Samuel CRAIG
Willian DOOLEY
Daniel DEER
John MC FALL
Mack PIPKIN
Green PRIOR
Abner PILLOW
Charles NEELY
James ONEAL
David KELCHNUT
Pairor T. KIRK
James LOVE
James LEWIS
Richard MC MAHAN
Allen PILLOW
John LOFTAND
Samuel NORTHERN
Abraham LOONEY
Drewry MIDDLETON
Nimrod PORTOR
Samuel POLK
Alexander MC KEE
Pleasant NELSON
Edward MC FADE
John MC WILLIAMS
John MILLER
James MAYES
Patrick MCGUIRE
Joshiah MC BRIDE
Joseph MC NUTT
David W. MC REE
William GILLIAM
John C. HAMILTON
Solomon HERRIN
Abraham JOBE
_____ FORGEY
Abner JOHNSON
George W. HUMPHREY
John HODGE
Travis HAMBRICK
Joseph HART
Martin HARDIN
John GRIFFIN
John GORDON
Joseph GILMORE

Esquire BLACK
Samuel CUNNINGHAM
Charles R. DUIN
Thomas DUE
Daniel EVINS
Barlett ESTES
Sandy ESTES
Joseph CRENSHAW
Jacob DAMEWOOD
James ALLEN
WILLICO
Joseph BLACKBURN
John H. BILLS
Veridman ANDERSON
John BOLD
George BECKERSTAFF
Jesse BRIDGES
Daniel CAMPBELL
William CRAIG
Samuel CAMPBELL
Littleberry CHEER
Peter R. BOOKER
John CLOUD
Robert CHAMP
Perteyman DYE
William DAVIS
Edward H. CHAFFIN
Stockley DONNELS
Cornelius DABNEY
James DICKSON
Peter PRIOR
Jahn PILLOW
Gideon PILLOW
John T. PORTER
Joseph LAMASTER
John HODGE,
   administrator

John FAINEY
George JOHNSON
N. ROGERS
Mack **ROBERTS**
Samuel RUTLEDGE
Henry REECE
Aaron SMITH
Samuel SMITH
William SIMMONS
Thomas TRUELOVE
Charles L. HEARMAN
Abner STAGS
Robert SELLARS
Samuel SMOOT
Thomas TAYLOR
Joseph SANDERS
Jesse ROSSE
David RUSSEL
Moses D. PAYTON
Jobe H. THOMAS
Sterling TUCKER
Martin SHADDEN
James WHITE
Venable WILLIAMS
Mathas WARFIELD
John C. WORMLEY
William WEBB
George WEBBER
John WILKES
William H. WILLSON
Jesse WALTER
John L. WALLER
Nathaniel YOUNG
Garret VOORHIES
Dabney WADE
William VOORHIES

page 57   Dower of land for late widow of James THOMPSON; the
           total the deceased died possessed of: 572 acres.
           Widow, 164 acres; the one-third part of tract.
           27 February 1823. James H. BROWN, Thomas WHITESIDE,
           Robert WHITESIDE, Richard ANDERSON, Thomas KENDRICK,
           Samuel LUSK, Robert LUSK, John REBB, William SCOTT,
           Francis SPENSER, A. WHITESIDE, commissioners.
           Nimrod PORTER, sheriff.

page 58   Settlement with Greenberry WILLIAMS, surviving
           executor of estate of James H. WILLIAMS, deceased.
           Parmenus WILLIAMS, deceased, was executor of estate.
           Bondsmen: T. H. SILLIMAN; Phillips P. WINN.
           15 March 1823. William STOCKARD and Robert WORTHAM,
           Justices of the Peace.

page 59   Report of Doctor Garrett L. VOORHIES, executor of
           O. P. NICHOLSON, deceased. Suit O. P. NICHOLSON
           executed versus GOODLOE'S executors; WALLACE;
           James S. WALKER; James K. POLK'S fee.   25 April
           1823. James T. SANFORD and Edward W. DALE,
           Justices of the Peace.

page 60 Credit Alfred O. NICHOLSON, a minor heir, in account with James T. WALKER; J. BILLS; William IRWIN; Simon P. JORDAN; WALKER and HARRIS; B. TURNER; SANSOM and HAYS; Thomas D. CLARK; WALKER and HARRIS. Alfred O. NICHOLSON, a minor heir of Osborn P. NICHOLSON. 15 March 1823. James T. SANDFORD and Edward W. DALE, Justices of the Peace.

page 60 Settlement with Joseph JOINS and Esther HAWKINS, former administrators of estate of Allen HAWKINS, deceased. Note on Joel ALEXANDER. John SKIPPER and Joseph SKIPPER, present administrators. 21 April 1823. A. CATHEY and Richard ANDRES, Justices of the Peace.

page 61 Settlement with George M. MARTIN, guardian of William T. ROBERTS, minor heir of Isaac ROBERTS, deceased. Cash lent Mrs. Polly ROBERTS, 22 March 1823. Isaac BILLS and J. S. ALDERSON, Justices of the Peace.

page 62 Debit John MILLER in account with his ward William GANT, 1821, 1822, 1823. J. P. VOORHIES, Thomas SMITH, William VOORHIES. 28 April 1823. James T. SANDFORD and James BLACK, Justices of the Peace.

page 62 Debit John MILLER in account with his ward Jane GANT, 1821, 1822, 1823. P. J. VOORHIES, Thomas SMITH, William VOORHIES. 28 April 1823. James T. SANDFORD and James BLACK, Justices of the Peace.

page 63 Heirs of Jacob MC KEE, deceased, in account with Isaac BILLS, Guardian. John BOYD, Alexander MC INTIRE, James W. WALKER, John R. KENNEDY, William FINLEY, Richard WILKES, L. MARTIN, James MIGHT, and D. COPELAND. 23 April 1823. Edward W. DALE, John S. ALDERSON, Justices of the Peace.

page 64 Heirs of Alexander BRECKENRIDGE in account with Isaac BILLS, Guardian. 1821, 1822, 1823. W. L. WILLEFORD; N. PORTER; George BRECKENRIDGE, former guardian; Joseph B. PORTER; W. A. JOHNSON; Abraham LOONEY. 23 April 1823. Edward W. DALE, J. S. ALDERSON, Justices of the Peace.

page 65 Robert SELLERS, James SELLERS, and Luke SELLERS, executors of William BYNUM, deceased. 28 April 1823. Settlement. John MILLER, Swan HARDIN, E. W. DALE, Justices of the Peace.

page 66 Wilson WHITE, administrator of estate of James WHITE, deceased. January 1821, January 1822, January 1823. Paid to Eliza WHITE, John WHITE, Catharine WHITE, John RHINE, Bartlott ESTES, L. HITCHCOCK, Thomas WHITE (alias Reubin SMITH), Henry GIPSON, John ARNOLD, Martin SUTHERLAND, Josiah ALDERSON, H. MC DOWEL and P. NELSON, John L. SMITH. 19 April 1823. J. S. ALDERSON and Edward W. DALE, Justices of the Peace.

page 67	Amount of Goods and Chattles sold of the estate of Peter YOUNG, deceased, by Sarah YOUNG, executrix. 28 April 1823. Sarah YOUNG.
page 68	Settlement with William HOLT, Esquire, guardian of Thomas H. HEADIN and Ann Maria HEADIN. James LINDLEY's receipt for boarding, 1 January 1820; schooling 1820, Thomas J. KENNEDY; Robert MC NUTT for boarding 1819 and 1820; M. BLALOCK; Willis RICHARDSON; William MC WILLIAMS; John HOLT; Jesse MORTON; Willis BOBO; John WEBB; Rebecca DARK; Samuel BRASIN; William HARK'S. John HATCHETT and Alexander JOHNSON.
page 70	Settlement with John BROWN, administrator of estate of Sarah CAMPBELL, deceased. Margery CAMPBELL'S note, 2 October 1819; G. M. RIVES; GANNT and MEASE; Lowery HENDERSON; 21 April 1823. William Ed MONSON.
page 71	Settlement with Edmund and Greenberry WILLIAMS, executors of estate of Permenas WILLIAMS, deceased.

Collected from William HUNT of North Carolina; HOWEL and SAMPLE; Samuel GRIFFITH; William SIMS; Paid to A. A. SMITH; bill in equity Raleigh, North Carolina; MORDECAI and DEVERAUX; Thomas YEATMAN; Duke WILLIAMS rendered estate in North Carolina; Elijah HARLAND; John FRIERSON; John ROYAL; Mary STITH; Peter JOYCE; Anderson WILLIAMS; Samuel SAVAGE; William DEVER; Duke WILLIAMS expenses to North Carolina on business of estate; E. W. DALE; John TILLACON; John SHULE. 13 March 1823. William STOCKARD and Robert NORTHARN, Justices of the Peace. |
page 72	John CRAWFORD, in account with estate of Thomas CRAWFORD; legacy due Eliza DUNLAP; legacy due Thomas H. DUNLAP. 23 April 1823. James T. SANDFORD and John MILLER, Justices of the Peace. Negroes were willed to Elizabeth BLAIR, wife of George D. BLAIR.
page 73	Settlement with Elizabeth DICKSON, guardian of minor heirs of John DICKSON, deceased. Notes on James T. CRAFFORD and John COOPER; James MC GOWEN; William H. PATTEN; Robert C. and James DICKSON; Alexander PICKARD. 15 April 1823. David CRAIG, William STOCKARD, Justices of the Peace.
page 74	Settlement with Samuel MC LEAN, guardian of minor heirs of William MC LEAN, deceased. Margaret DENNY'S account for clothing, schooling, and boarding said minors. 16 April 1823. Richard B. PASSMORE and Robert SELLARS, Justices of the Peace.
page 74	Record 27 December 1823, Inventory of property of Peter GLASSCOCK, deceased, by James GLASSCOCK, administrator.
page 75-82	29 August 1820. Account of sales of estate of William FRIERSON, deceased. Purchasers:

Hugh SHAW	Samuel E. FRIERSON
James M. FRIERSON	Benoni DICKEY
Tilman A. CRISP	Alexander HENDERSON
James W. STEPHENSON	Doctor TURNER
John FRIERSON	Colonel Wm. PILLOW
William BLAKELY	Joseph LEMASTER
Nimrod PORTER	William JENNINGS
Jacob BIFFLE	William BLANKS
David FRIERSON	Paul FULTON
Jesse EGNEW	Samuel WHITESIDES
William ARMSTRONG	James COLLINGS
Matthew D. COOPER	John FERRELL
Robert G. KOLSIP	J. R. PLUMMER
John LONGLEY	James ARMSTRONG
John J. BRIGGS	Elias J. ARMSTRONG
Alexander DOBBINS	Samuel BLAKELY
Thomas SUTHERLAND	George DICKEY
Lembert C. OLIPHANT	William J. FRIERSON
Alisha GOODMAN	William G. ARMSTRONG
Nicholas J. LONG	Thomas F. FLEMING
John SMISER	John MECCAN
David LEECH	Samuel WHITESIDES
Augustus BROWN	Edward B. LITTLEFIELD
Daniel YOUNG	Henry E. TURNER
James BARLOW	E. PETON
James ROBINSON	Simpson WALKER
Simpson SHAW	Josiah ALDERSON
James N. BROWN	James DOBBINS
Alexander WILLIAMS	Elisha UZZEL
Thomas J. FRIERSON	Edward ENGLISH
Elizabeth FRIERSON	Patrick MC GUIRE
Thomas J. ARMSTRONG	William HAWKINS
Samuel E. FRIERSON	William R. DICKEY
John RENFROW	John SMOTHERS
John D. FLEMING	William WAGGONER
Willis RIDLEY	Nathaniel YOUNG
Samuel J. ROGERS	William BROWN
George EGNEW	James PURSELL
Nat WILLIS	

16 May 1823--Samuel MC DANIEL, Allen LEEPER, Robert CONDEN, Thomas G. BLACK

page 82   Received of John L. WOOD and John STEEL, executors of estate of James REED, the negroes assigned to us agreeable to the division, assigned according to the last will and testament of said deceased. Received by us 16 May 1823: Hugh REED; Josiah (by his mark) REED; John REED; William REED.

page 83   Received of John L. WOOD and John STEEL, executors of estate of James REED, deceased, the negroes assigned to us agreeable to the division, assigned according to last will of testament of said deceased. Received 16 May 1823: Samuel STEEL; James STEEL; James R. FULLERTON; Robert L. FULLERTON; Robert COWDEN; William H. FULLERTON.

page 83   Inventory of property of James STEEL not disposed of in his will. Notes: John WEBB; William STEEL; Philip ANTHONY; Nathaniel H. STEEL; James SCOTT. 31 July 1823. Nathaniel H. STEELE and Aaron STEELE.

page 84	Inventory of property of Thomas WALKER, deceased. Recorded 28 December 1823 by John SELLERS, James N. BROWN.
page 84	Inventory of estate of John NICHOLSON, deceased. Recorded 28 December 1823. Notes on: Thomas C. H. GANT; Lorenzo HITCHCOCK; John THENTON; Wright NICHOLSON; David CAMPBELL; James SANSON; executors, 22 January 1822.
page 85	Amount of sales of property of John GOSSETT, deceased. Buyers: Elijah GOSSETT; William SHINAULT; Walter SHINAULT; Willey JONES; William GROOMS; John BUTLER; U. D. GOSSETT; Polly GOSSETT; Robison ROSS; Edmund MORRIS; Samuel DUNLAP; Richard VAUGHTERS.
page 86	Inventory of property of John FORSYTH, deceased. Recorded 28 December 1823.
page 87	Inventory of property of Mark BYNUM. Recorded 28 December 1823. Anderson WILLIAMS, administrator.
page 87	Sale of Peter YOUNG, deceased. 14 June 1823. By Sarah YOUNG, executrix.
page 87	Eleaner C. GLOVER's estate by John W. JONES, 10 February 1821.
page 87	Inventory of property of Patrick BUCHANAN, deceased. Recorded 28 December 1823. "All remain in possession of Margaret BUCHANAN... she being the sole devisee." Margaret BUCHANAN, executrix, and John BROWN, executor. 2 July 1823.
page 88	Amount of sale of estate of James REED, deceased, 22 May 1823. Buying:

Andrew STEELE	James PATTERSON
Basel WILLIAMS	Johnathan SMITH
David HEADLEE	John S. WOOD
Eli CHEEK	Nancy ALDREDGE
Hugh REED	Robert FULLERTON
Joseph HEADLEE	Richard HIGHT
James FULLERTON	William HILL
John STEELE	Aaron WILSON
John MULREY	Caleb HEADLIE
John BECK (?)	Daniel REED
John CHEEK	George ROW
Peggy FULLERTON	John FOX
Turson PERSONS	John F. CAR
William FOX	John WRIGHT
Alexander MARTIN	Josiah B. ____
Claude CARTER	Joseph MOREHEAD
Daniel HEADLEE	John STOKES
Ezekial BILLINGTON	Nathaniel SMITH
Josiah REED	Samuel STEELE
James A. MC CALL	William FULERTON
John REED	William WILLSON

page 89	Probable value of estate of James HOLLAND, deceased, recorded 28 December 1823.

page 89	"At home, July the 21st, 1823. To the honourable Court of Maury County. I understand that some of the minor heirs of Squire Sherman, deceased, by the influence of their mother, will make a motion to you this court, for to make a new guardian. It is out of my power to attend court, therefore I considered it my duty to write you a few lines. I as their guardian at this time am perfectly willing you should appoint any person you think proper, and release me as their guardian. I am your most obedient and very humble servant, Charles PARTEE."
page 90	16 November 1822. Commissions laying off provision. (Does not show for whom.) Wilson HENDERSON, Thompson PORTER, Solomon BRADSHAW.
page 90	19 April 1823. Settlement with Benjamin WILKES, Minor WILKES, and Jesse WILKES, executors of Daniel WILKES, deceased. Paid out: Ebenezer RICE; Marine THOMAS; BROWN and MC GIMSEY; W. L. WILEFORD; John ALEXANDER; C. MACK; Elizabeth WILKES, widow; to Benjamin, Jesse, and Minor WILKES; TO Henrietta and three executors by will. Signed: John HATCHETT; Alexander JOHNSON; and John MATTHEWS.
page 91	Inventory of estate of George SLAUGHTER, 29 December 1823.
page 91-96	Recorded 29 December 1823. Division of lands of George DAVIDSON, deceased, by William HOLT, John MATTHEWS, Alexander JOHNSON, Wilson HENDERSON, and Samuel KING.

Land on Fountain Creek
1. for Rosanna DAVIDSON, widow
2. Samuel J. ROGERS and wife Sarah, by right of his wife Sarah
3. Jane DAVIDSON, minor daughter
4. Gilbreth F. DAVIDSON, deceased, heirs
5. Joseph KNOX and wife Louisa, John HENDERSON and wife Emeline, and James C. KING and wife Isabella.
Mentions share of James L. DAVIDSON, deceased.

page 96	Inventory of estate of Green B. WILLIAMS, deceased. Recorded 29 December 1823. Accounts on:

Hyrney SPENCER	Edmond WILLIAMS
Lot HACKNEY	Philip WIRE
Hugh SHAW	Doctor HAMILTON
John M. DANIEL	Doctor SANSOM
John SIMS	Thomas J. FRIERSON
John BEATY	Philip PENN
Susanna B. WILLIAMS (all household, Holy Bible.)	
Thomas WORTHAM	John P. ELLIOTT
Hardin WILLIAMS	James BEATY
Alexander WILLIAMS	James W. BRISCOE
James M. FRIERSON	Jordan TUCKNESS
Moses HOGUE	Samuel H. SMITH
Elias PEYTON	Doctor HALL
Daniel JOB	John ALEXANDER

Thomas SIMS
John BRISCOE
Samuel JONES
Oliver CROSS

Samuel SHELL
James STOCKARD
P. P. WINN

Articles sold indicate that he was probably a
doctor: surgical tools, all kinds of medical
books, and drugs.

page 99   Delila GARRISON requests that Isaiah GARRISON be
appointed administrator of the estate of John
GARRISON, deceased. 21 April 1823.

page 99   Inventory of sale. (Does not state whose, possibly
George DAVIDSON.) Recorded 29 December 1823.
Buying:

Alexander NICHOLS
George DAVIDSON
James SHIELDS
Shadrach DUGGAR
Jeremiah CHERRY
Wilson HENDERSON
Samuel MONTGOMERY
Samuel J. ROGERS

Joseph KNOX
William B. SHIELDS
William ALLEN
Rosannah DAVIDSON
Charles J. BAILEY
William B. SHIELDS
John HAMBRICK
John MC DONALD

page 100   Inventory of sale of estate of Benjamin HERNDON
made on 16 November 1818. Sold to:

Sarah HERNDON, widow
John WRIGHT
Samuel SMITH
James HAYS
Samuel M. KING
Hardy W. CRAWFORD
William WILLIAMS
William WADE
William A. DAVIS
John KNOX
John GORDON
Abraham JOB
James C. O'REILLY
Andrew VANNOY
James JOES

Mr. PATTERSON
Peter I. VOORHIES
Hiram GOFORTH
Jesse WALTON
William P. CRAWFORD
James RANKIN
Thomas GILLAM
Joshua W. KILPATRICK
Alfred H. WORTHAM
Francis PORTER
Amos CALDWELL
John BICKENSTAFF
Allen MORRIS
Joseph HERNDON,
   administrator

page 101   List of property of William R. MATTHEWS, deceased,
dated 1 March 1822. Recorded 30 December 1823.
Buying:

Moses D. PAYTON
James T. SANDFORD
James O. ALEXANDER
James SCOTT
John MATTHEWS
William PILLOW
Moses D. PEYTON
Matthew SWANN
John GOODMAN
Allen TAYLOR
George W. JOHNSON
James STOCKARD
John GARRAGUS

Elijah PEYTON
Thomas WORTHAM
Elisha MERRYMAN
Phillip PENN
John EDMON
Robert F. MATTHEWS
A. S. CRAFFORD
James T. CRAFFERD
Charles MERRYMAN
Jeremiah GOODWIN
A. B. ALEXANDER
Ozni ALEXANDER
Drewey BROCK

62

John GILLESPIE   Fleming GOODMAN
Isaac J. THOMAS   Joseph MATTHEWS
Richard BROOKS   Samuel NORMAN
James D. MATTHEWS

page 103   Sales of Mark BYNUM, deceased, 16 August 1823.
             Buying:

Anderson WILLIAMS   Keblet HUGHES
Richard SCOTT   Murdock MC CLANE
Jonathan PICKETT   John BOOKER
Luke BYNUM   Charles PARTEE
John MILLS   Isaac SELLARS
Richard SCOTT   Daniel PAYNE
Robert PAYNE   Bradford BYNUM
A. Y. PARTEE   William BYNUM
Isaac BADGETT   Anderson WILLIAMS, admr.

page 104   Sale of _____HANCOCK, recorded 30 December 1823.
             Buying:

Elizabeth HANCOCK (household goods)
Powel HALE   J. W. HANCOCK
William A. STEPHENSON   Lewis PERRY
John HANCOCK   Stephen M. HANCOCK
John B. TOLIVER   Francis GORDON
Thomas SCOTT   John TOLIVER
Richard C. HANCOCK   Samuel FOGLEMAN
Lewis PEERY   William STRATON
Mark DODD   Lucinda HANCOCK
Samuel M. KING
William and Thomas WILLS

page 105   Inventory of sale of Hopson ARNOLD, deceased.
             Recorded 30 December 1823. Buyers:

James YARBER   William ARNOLD, Jr.
John NITT   Joshua CAUDLE
Avery ARNOLD   William GREEN
Freeman KILLINGSWORTH   Wyatt HILL
Robert NITT   Hezekiah DAVIS
Matthew WIGGS   Isaac HILL
Shearwood P. RECORD   James A. ELLIOTT
Thomas ARNOLD   John ROYAL, Sr.
William HIGDON   Ebenezar ELLIOTT
Milly NITT   Jesse BURKUM
John ARNOLD, Sr.   William ARNOLD, Sr.
John WILKINS   David FESSET (?)
James L. ARNOLD   William NITT
Yearby NITT   Richard ROGERS
Sion RECORD

             Returned 12 August 1823, James C. RECORD, Thomas
             NITT, and Robert NITT, administrators. Notes on
             Jonathan and Williamson SMITH, Stepehn COOK,
             Eskard ROLLER.

page 107   Inventory of Goods of James JONES, deceased.
             28 October 1823. E. D. JONES and David GLASS,
             administrators.

page 107   Notes belonging to estate of Andrew FITZPATRICK,
            deceased, on Samuel FITZPATRICK, William SMITH,
            Robert KERR, by Celia FITZPATRICK, executrix.
            Recorded 30 December 1823.

page 108   Amount of sale of Signee CAWLEY, sale on 23 and 24
            of May 1823.

Miner WINN	James LEGETT
John BECK	John CHEAK
Patsey CAWLEY	James L. ARNOLD
Wiett HILL	Alexander BALDRIDGE
Hezekiah DAVIS	John SMITH
James J, MAXWELL	Joel GILLIAM
Shurwood RECORD	Richard HIGHT
Samuel WOOD	John CANADA
William EWING	John RAY
Joseph EWEL	Fred WIN
John ARNOLD	William GIFFORD
George ROAN	Nathaniel WOOLARD
Daniel REED	Samuel MORGAN
Eli CHEECK	Reubin A. CARDER
Thomas MOSS	Conner DOWD
John NICKS	N. MOORE
Rolley MORGAN	John BECK
James YARBROUGH	Boswell WILLIAMS
William CAWDEL	William FOX
Joffery BECK	Thomas ROSS
William MC WHERTER	Daniel REED
George J. PURDON	William LEGETT
James ELLIOTT	John BLACK

            Patsey CAWLEY and Samuel MORGAN, administrators for
            Signor CAWLEY, deceased.

page 110   Supplemental inventory for Jeremiah CHERRY, deceased.
            1 January 1822. To: James T. SANDFORD; Janes
            RANKIN; Jeremiah CHERRY; Polly CHERRY. From: Davis
            KILLCREASE; James C. O'REILLY; William WILLIAMS,
            Joseph HERNDON; Jacob ROGERS; John MILLS;
            Mrs. HERNDON.

            2 January 1823 to Jeremiah CHERRY, Mrs. Polly CHERRY,
            Francis SLAUGHTER, Thomas NORTON. James T.
            SANDFORD, administrator, 25 January 1823.

page 110   Sale of Thomas SHELBY, deceased, _____1822.
            Recorded 30 December 1823. Buyers:

George SHELBY	Widow SHELBY
John PRUVETT (?)	Samuel MONTGOMERY
William STANFILL	William SHELBY
William REGION	Wade SHELBY
William PRUNETT	Isaac FARRIS
L. C. OLIPHANT	A. T. ISOM
James BEARD	William BRIGGS
John BRADY	Vardaman SHELBY
Evin SHELBY	Calib FARRIS
Wade H. SHELBY	William MC INTOSH
Levi SHELBY	Richard JONES

```
Ebenezar ROSS                      E. CANTRELL
E. SHELBY                          George SHELBY
Alexander CATHEY                   James BECK
```

28 April 1823. William SHELBY, Evan SHELBY,
administrators.

page 112   Sale of estate of Sion P. RECORD, deceased.
             Recorded 31 December 1823. Buyers:

```
Joshua CAWELL                      Horatio PHILLIPS
Mary RECORD                        Joshua CAWDLE
William DUNCAN                     Lindsey ARNOLD
William CAWDLE                     George W. RECORD
Thomas D. KENNEDY                  James C. RECORD
Sherwood P. RECORD                 John ARNOLD
John W. RECORD                     Joseph DUNCAN
```

Notes on:

```
Robert CAPPS                       Henry KILLINGSWORTH
John A. POWELL                     Thomas FISHER
Shadrack TILMAN                    John HALL
John WILLIAMS                      Joseph T. ELLIOTT
James Y. GREEN
```

By James C. RECORD, administrator.

page 113   Sale of estate of Allen H. YOUNG, deceased. April
             term 1823. Sale held 22 February 1823.
             "some papers belonging to the deceased having
             fallen into my hands, purporting to be accounts for
             tuition of musick and for musick books on persons
             said to reside in the state of Alabama....Alexander
             JOHNSON, administrator."

page 114   Inventory of goods and effects of the estate of the
             late Signer CAWLEY, deceased, taken 28 April 1823.
             Property in the state of Louisiana inventoried by
             S. MORGAN in said state. Amount in State of
             Mississippi. Amount in State of Tennessee; amount
             in Maury County, Tennessee, unsold. Samuel MORGAN
             and Patsey CAWLEY, administrators.

page 115   E. W. DALE and Swan HARDIN - widow's allowances
             for Mary NELSON, widow of late John NELSON,
             deceased. 20 January 1823.

page 115   Personal property of Abner H. H. BUSH, deceased.
             January 1823. Note on John PAYTON, David LOVE.
             J. HAMILTON, administrator.

page 115   Amount of sales of Joseph SANDERS, deceased.
             Recorded 31 December 1823. Buyers:

```
Widow SANDERS                      Fleming GOODMAN
John RENFROE                       John GOODMAN
Jesse GOODMAN                      R. WORTHAM
James BARLOW                       James STOCKARD
P. PENN                            Toliver GOODMAN
W. JETT                            William DUE
A. ATKINSON                        Alisha GOODMAN
```

Moses D. PAYTON   William GARRET
Alexander GOODMAN   Thomas ADKINSON
Samuel NORMAN   K. GOODMAN

page 117   Sale of West HARRIS, 18 December 1819. Buyers:

Isaac WILLIAMS   Baily NEEDHAM
Thomas OSBURN   William LACKY
Nathan COFFEE   Andrew MC CARTY
John RENFRO   James GUNN
James O. (P.?) ALEXANDER Henry PEDIN
A. O. HARRIS   John RENFRO
Butler NOLES   William LACKIE
John M. DANIEL   Wyatt HARRIS
Robert WORTHAM   Josiah ALDERSON
Andrew FORGEY   A. B. MAYFIELD
Mrs. SCOTT   John WILLIAMS
William KINAMORE   James BALL
P. R. BOOKER   John CROSSTHWAIT
John ALEXANDER   John MATTHEWS
William GARROTT   John TIDWELL
M. HELM   Nathan CIFFA
Isaac J. THOMAS   James BELL
Perry COHEA   Samuel DAVID
N. WILLIS   Thomas BROOKS
Goerge JOHNSON   W. J. WADE
John MASON   Joseph PERKINS

by Nathaniel WILLIS, John MATTHEWS, and
P. R. BOOKER.

page 120   "as directed at July term 1823, we the
underassigners have met and laid off to the widow
as follows..." No name of widow given. Signed:
James P. RECORD, Esquire, Joshua CAWDEL, Jesse
CAWDLE.

page 120   Inventory of property of John B. KENADY, deceased.
Recorded 1 January 1823, by James L. BALDRIDGE,
Richard F. _____, Thomas MC KEE, Richard H._____.

page 121   Inventory of James STEELE, deceased, recorded
1 January 1823. Inventory made 20 October 1823, by
Nathaniel H. STEELE and Aaron STEELE.

page 122   Sale of William HENDERSON, deceased, sold
14 November 1822. Buyers:

James BOYD   Green MURPHY
Thomas RAMSEY   Simpson PERRY
George PATTON   Edward W. DALE
Elias PEYTON   John MERICK
John WEBB   James BALDRIDGE
John JONES   John BALDRIDGE
George W. JOHNSON   Nathaniel
John S, CURRY   Elijah PEYTON
John WEBB   John FORGY
B. CARTER   John GALBREATH
Edward R. HUSON   Sarkin PILKINTON
Ezekial HENDERSON   George PATTON
William S. HENDERSON   Thomas W. STONE

66

James R. PLUMMER   William W. LEE
James BOWMAN   John HENDERSON
Samuel D. MACK (?)

page 124   Francis WADE (non compos mentis)
            17 January 1823. Joseph WINGFIELD, Guardian.
            Accounts from 1 January 1817. "1 June 1818...to
            Robert MACK'S fee for getting the state of your
            mind inquired into, by wit, and guardian appointed.";
            Doctor MC NEAL, Doctor J. C. O'RIELEY; Messrs
            SANSOM and HAYS; E. WADE; "1 August 1822, by cash
            from Jacob Scott on account of your interest in
            Louisa WADE'S estate"; Due to Frances WADE. Joseph
            WINGFIELD as guardian of Frances WADE. Witnesses:
            John C. WORMELEY and John GORDON.

page 125   Moses STEVENS, administrator for Mylland PETERS,
            deceased. 21 October 1823. Witness:
            J. S. ALDERSON.

page 126   Account of sale of estate of Ambrose BLACKBURN,
            deceased, superintended by John BLACKBURN,
            administrator, 7, 29, 30, December 1820.
            Purchasers:

            Frances BLACKBURN   James BLACKBURN
            Josiah BLACKBURN   John ALTON (?)
            William HENSLEY   John SHARP
            William MAYFIELD   James ISAM
            Lemuel BLACKBURN   James TARRANT
            John BLACKBURN   Hugh BROWN

page 127   Inventory of estate of late Signor CAWLEY, deceased,
            taken 28 April 1823. Property in state of
            Louisiana; appointed administrator in state of
            Louisiana before appointment in Tennessee; amount
            in state of Mississippi; property in Tennessee;
            slaves martgaged to John SMISER; William MC NEAL;
            by Samuel MORGAN and Patsey CAWLEY, administrators.

page 128   Inventory of estate of Joseph SAUNDERS, deceased,
            by Jesse GOODMAN and Alexander GOODMAN,
            administrators. Recorded 5 January 1824.
            "Accounts due deceased at time of his death on men
            believed to be insolvent or moved away and worth
            nothing:"

            George DEWOODY   Isaac ANDERSON
            William BROWN   R. GILLESPY
            Mr. PURNETT   Henery FRANCIS
            W. W. NELSON   John W. WARREN
            J. CAMPBELL   Mr. PAYNE
            Richard FINES   Doctor SHANNON
            Samuel NORMAN   J. WILLIAMS
            Benedict BROWN   George GRAY
            Charles E. IRVINE   Mr. DICKENSON
            William WELCH

page 130   Schedule of money, notes, and debts of Willard
            PETERS, deceased. (or Wyllard PETERS). By Moses
            STEVENS, 21 October 1823.

page 130   Inventory and sale of estate of Jeremiah HOPSON, deceased, taken by James T. SANDFORD, administrator, 1 January 1823. Buying:

John B. HAYS	William OWEN
Abraham HAMMON	Young E. BONE
William WEBB	Thomas SMITH
William YANCEY	Nancy HOPSON
Willis DODSON	James PETERS
William BYNUM	Walter S. JINKENS
Thomas WALLS	Daniel C. BROWN

page 132   Will of Thomas WALKER; son Thomas; son John; son Joseph; son Andrew; I have given to my daughter Jane, a negro girl......by a deed of Gift, recorded in Chester, South Carolina; son Nixen; youngest son Joseph. Executors: John SELLERS and James N. BROWN; dated 13 May 1823. Signed: Thomas X. WALKER. Witnesses: William HART and James SESSONS. Recorded 5 January 1824.

page 133   Will of Patrick BUCHANAN: sons: Patrick, Daniel, James; daughter, Margaret; grandchildren: James, Martha, and Mary Ann ("that is my son John's children"); having heretofore given to son John. Beloved wife Margaret, all my land, willed to me by my son John; as my son Duncan is not compos mentis, it is my will that my beloved wife Margaret shall support and maintain him...wife Margaret, executrix, and friend John BROWN, executor. Dated 24 January 1819. Signed: Patrick X BUCHANAN. Witnesses: Hugh BROWN; John BROWN. Recorded 5 January 1824.

page 134   Will of James REESE: brothers Hugh REED, William REEDE, Isaiah REEDE, John REEDE; my deceased wife's, Mary REEDE children, Janey STEELE, Martha STEELE, and Hannah FULARTON, deceased heirs; divide negroes between my brothers and my deceased wife's children, to be divided by Samuel MC DANIEL; Allen LEIPER; Robert CANDON, and Thomas BLACK; "to Jinney STEELE and Mary CONDON; also my deceased wife's saddle, Anny FULARTON, wife if James FULARTON." John STEELE and John S. WOOD, executors. 6 June 1822. Signed James X REEDE. Witnesses: John L. WOOD and Samuel MC DANIEL. Codical dated 5 March 1823. Recorded 5 January 1824.

page 135   Jesse BRIDGES and David TUTTLE swore they were called upon by John FORSYTHE, now deceased; nuncupative will of John FORSYTHE named Thomas GILLUM executor...mentions his wife and family. 1 March 1823. John GORDON, Justice of the Peace, recorded 5 January 1824.

page 136   Will of James STEEL: beloved wife Hannah. Son James STEEL, all my lands lying on Silver Creek in Maury County; daughter Rachel; Daughter Jane SCOTT; daughter Esther SCOTT; granddaughter Betsey S. MC NUTT, the daughter of my daughter Elizabeth, deceased. All my children, to wit, Nathaniel H.

STEEL; William STEEL; James STEEL; Jane SCOTT; Esther SCOTT; Rachel STEEL. Nathaniel H. STEEL and Aaron STEELE, executors. 3 June 1823, James STEELE. Witnesses: William HOLT; Richard FAUCETT; Aaron TURNER. Recorded 5 January 1824.

page 137   Will of Peter YOUNG. Beloved wife Sally, sole executrix. "divide the remainder of my estate into ten equal parts amongst my beloved wife and children. That is to say, to my daughter Margery P. YOUNG, one part, to my son Peter R. YOUNG, one part, to my daughter Sally YOUNG, one part, to my daughter Cynthia YOUNG, one part, to my daughter Evelina YOUNG, one part, to my daughter Minerva YOUNG, one part, to my daughter Permelia YOUNG, one part, to my daughter Helena YOUNG, one part, to my beloved wife Sally YOUNG, one part." 16 November 1822. Signed: Peter YOUNG. Witnesses: Joseph H. CALVERT; Katharine CALVERT. Exhibited in open court, January sessions 1823. Recorded 6 January 1824.

page 138   Will of Mary REED: brother John REED; at death of brother John, to be sold and divided into five equal parts, viz., equally between my nieces, Elizabeth BELL, Peggy REED, and Polly PATTERSON, and my nephew Daniel REED, and the children of my nephew Hugh REED, deceased, that is, William Bell REED and Polly Elenor REED, in the state of North Carolina; my little cousin James Reed BELL, son of my niece Elizabeth BELL. Executors: Nephews Daniel REED; Samuel REED; and James PATTERSON. 17 April 1821. Signed: Mary X REED. Witnesses: James N. SMITH, Richard HIGHT. Recorded 6 January 1824.

page 139   Will of George NICHOLSON: Loving wife Jane; daughter Elizabeth ZALIAFER; daughter Polly SWANSON; son John NICHOLSON; granddaughter Maria WALKER; grandson Alfred. Executors: John NICHOLSON; John Jacob ZALIAFER (ZOLLICOFFER); and James SWANSON. 3 August 1820. Signed: George NICHOLSON. Witnesses: Nancy X ELY, J. POPE. Produced at January term 1823, recorded 8 January 1824.

page 140   Will of John CATHEY: Mary, my beloved wife; granddaughter Susanna CATHEY; son Alexander; daughter Polly; to her son and my grandson John Pinkney ERWIN; to my daughter Susannah's son John CATHEY; daughter Peggy's daughter Nancy LOCK; daughter Hannah; grandchildren: Jane KENNEDY, now ERWIN; Patsey KENNEDY, now MILLER; _____ KENNEDY, now STAMFIELD; Eliza KENNEDY, now ISAM; and George KENNEDY; grandchildren: Alexander CATHEY and David CATHEY; appoint my son Alexander CATHEY and Griffith CATHEY executors. 18 June 1821. Signed John CATHEY. Witnesses: Moses ROBISON, Benjamin ROBISON. Recorded 8 January 1824.

page 142   Will of Peter WOOSLEY, late of the United States Army: well beloved friend Sarah VENABLE the 160

69

acres of land due me from the United States and
her daughter Jane VONABLE. Friend William VENABLE,
executor. 18 November 1818. Signed: Peter X
WOOSLEY. Witnesses: Polly MYERS and Elizabeth
VENABLE. Recorded 8 January 1824.

page 143   Will of John NICHOLSON: mother Jane NICHOLSON,
sisters Elizabeth ZALACOFER and Mary SWANSON.
Maria WALKER, Calvin NICHOLSON, and Alfred NICHOLSON.
James SWANSON, executor. 20 June 1822. Signed:
John NICHOLSON. Witnesses: S. TURNER, Ephraim
JONES. Recorded 8 January 1824.

page 144   Will of James LONGLEY, Sr.: beloved wife, Elizabeth
LONGLEY; daughter Mary_____; Eliza PLUMMER; Jane
C. W. LONGLEY; Catharine LONGLEY; Rachael LONGLEY.
James R. PLUMMER and Edward W. DALE, executors.
29 September 1820. Signed: J. LONGLEY. Witnesses:
P. COHEA and Isaac J. DOBBINS. Recorded 8 January
1824.

page 144   Will of Lance FOX: wife Margaret FOX; daughter
Jinny. My five children. No date. Signed: Lance
FOX. Witnesses: Joshua X CAUDLE, Willis BRIDGES.
Recorded 8 January 1824.

page 145   Will of James HOLLAND: wife, daughter Cynthia
RHODES; daughter Sally MIRA; son James; three
daughters, Sally Mira, Solina Sophia, and Polly
Louisa; wife executrix; my son James and my two
sons-in-law Tyree RHODES and Hardin PERKINS,
executors. 25 February 1816. Signed: James
HOLLAND. Witnesses: Joseph HERNDON, James C.
O'RIELY. Recorded 8 January 1824.

page 146   Will of Edward CALLIHAN. 22 July 1819. "having
done all I could do for my first wife and children."
My present wife Elizabeth CALLIHAN (also calls her
Betsey). "my daughter Polly to be schooled...as
soon as she is capable of receiving instruction."
Thomas G. BLACK executor and Betsy CALLAHAN, my
present wife, executrix. Signed: Edward X
CALLAHAN. Witnesses: John MCRIGHT; Matthew
MCREIGHT; Jeremiah HARDISON. Recorded 9 January
1824.

page 147   Will of William BYNUM: beloved wife Rebecca; my
boys, to wit; James BYNUM, my son, and Norwood
BYNUM, my son, and Chesley BYNUM, my son, and
Paterson BYNUM, my son. and Lard BYNUM, my son,
and the child my wife is pregnant with. All my
children, male and female. Friends Luke SELLARS,
Robert SELLARS, and James SELLARS, executors.
20 January 1820. Signed: William X BYNUM.
Witnesses: Josiah RICHERSON, John T. RICHERSON.
Proven 24 February 1820.

page 148   Will of Permenas WILLIAMS: beloved wofe Dolly--
land, 250 acres bought of Pleasant HENDERSON; 150
acres bought of Thomas LEARCY; 150 acres bought
of Alexander MARTIN. My children, that is, Thomas,
Nancy, Betsey, Polly, Edmund, Greenberry, and

Alexander. Claim to John T. TODD for services in
Giles County....interest in concern of Galloway and
Company land bought of William HUNT to be equally
divided between Thomas WILLIAMS, Nancy WORTHAM,
Betsy JOHNSON'S six children as one individual,
Polly COLEMAN, Edmund WILLIAMS, and Alexander M.
WILLIAMS. Granddaughter Emily E. WILLIAMS. Wife
Dolly WILLIAMS executrix; sons Edmund and Greenberry,
executors. 8 June 1820. Signed: Permenas WILLIAMS.
Witnesses: Sally X GRISHAM, D. BROWN, William
NEWSUM. Proven 9 March 1821.

page 151   Will of Peter LYONS: wife and children; daughter
Caty MALONE; son John LYONS; son James Lyons;
beloved wife Elizabeth LYONS; son William LYONS;
daughter Jenny SANDERS, deceased; son Peter LYONS;
daughter Elizabeth HUNT (relict); William and Peter
SANDERS; friend Henry MALONE, executor. 27 February
1819. Signed: Peter LYONS, Senior. Witnesses:
Reubin SMITH, Frances X KILCREASE, Elizabeth X HUNT,
John KENNEDY. Recorded 9 January 1824.

page 153   Will of ALexander FARIS: beloved wife Elizabeth
FARIS; oldest children, Thomas C. FARIS, Moses A.
FARIS, and Mary Ann FARIS, now WALKER; daughter
Sarah FARIS, now KIRK, "provided John KIRK hath
drew a suit he commenced against me, nor shall
institute any others...", sons John FARIS and Adam
FARIS; son Alexander FARIS; son Caleb FARIS; Leah
FARIS, now ALEXANDER; Mary A. FARIS, and Rody E.
FARIS. "to have equal divide in the negroes
hereafter named together with....which I leave and
bequeath all my negroes at my wife's death, not
other wise apportioned by this will." Wife and
faithful son Alexander FARIS and my neighbor Hugh
DOUGLAS, executors and executrix. 9 May 1820.
Signed: Alexander FARIS. Witnesses: John _____,
Daniel MC KENNON, Edward MC FADDEN, Junior.
Recorded 9 January 1824.

page 154   Will of Andrew MITCHELL: wife Polly MITCHELL; son
James MITCHELL, 120 acres where Archibald HOLMS
now lives; son George, 120 acres where James
MITCHELL, son of John, settled; son John MITCHELL,
120 acres where he now lives; daughter Jennet
HOLMES, 60 acres, the place whereon her husband
Robert HOLMES now lives; daughter Polly FLY, 60
acres, the place whereon James REAVES now lives;
son David MITCHELL, remaining part, including
place whereon I now live, except a tract of land on
Beech Creek, joining the lands of Ephraim MC KEACEN,
and a tract of 130 acres on Elk River; daughters
Elizabeth and Peggy; 3 October 1817. Signed:
Andrew MITCHELL. Witnesses: Archibald HOLMES,
Moses HOLMES. Recorded 9 January 1824.

page 155   Nuncupative will of Robert FARIS: made on 31 July
1821 to Will CATHEY and Moses ROBISON. Wife,
"expected his wife to be delivered of an heir."
"Land left me by my father's will; at my mother's
death I wish my child to have it if my wife is ever
delivered of one..." Dated 4 Auguat 1821.

page 156   Sale of Property of estate of James LONGLEY,
            deceased by J. R. PLUMMER, executor. Buying:

Perry COHEA   Henry MILLER
J. CHERRY, Junr.   John ROYAL
William ANDERSON   James ANDERSON
A. LAIRD   C. LONGLEY
Samuel SMITH   Daniel BROWN
John W. JONES   E. LONGLEY
J. CHERRY   Joseph COE
Thomas WHITE   E. DOOLEY
Elijah BROWN   P. J. VOORHIES
J. LONGLEY   Alexander HENDERSON
P. CHEATHAM   Jesse LEFTWICH
Thomas SPACE   E. B. DOOLEY
Thomas JONES   L. KETCHUM
John S. LONGLEY   R. LONGLEY
H. B. PORTER
Recorded 9 January 1824.

page 159   Will of Daniel WILKES: body to be buried by my
            wife and children; daughter Polly WILKES; son John
            WILKES; daughter Sarah WINCALE (?); son Daniel
            WILKES, land on Lunenburg County (that came by his
            mother) called Williamson's tract; daughter
            Elizabeth R. _____; son Benjamin WILKES; son Minor
            WILKES; son Jesse WILKES; daughter Heneriter WILKES;
            wife Betsy WILKES; at her death to be divided
            between three sons, Benjamin, Minor, and Jesse;
            balance divided between Polly WILKS, John WILKS,
            Sally COLE, Elizabeth R. GUNN, and Henritta
            WILKES. Three sons, Benjamin, Minor, and Jesse,
            executors. 31 May 1821. Signed: Daniel WILKES.
            Witnesses: James HOWARD, John DICKIE, Jesse H.
            THOMAS. Recorded 9 January 1824.

page 162   Will of John ROYAL, Senior: wife Catharine ROYAL,
            and beloved son William ROYAL, executors; beloved
            daughter Elizabeth HILL, wife of Richard HILL; son
            John ROYAL, Junior; daughter Susannah ROYAL, wife
            of Joseph ROYAL; Sally Smith ALLEN; daughter
            Catharine ROYAL; daughter Sally ROYAL;
            granddaughter Mary DICKENSON; grandsons Archillus
            A. DICKENSON and Washington Ribon DICKINSON, heirs
            of my daughter Nancy DICKINSON, deceased. Beloved
            grandchildren, heirs of my beloved son Richard
            ROYAL (names not recollected); son Joseph ROYAL;
            grandchildren.....heirs of my daughter Susannah
            ROYAL, wife of Joseph ROYAL....."that Joseph ROYAL
            shall not have any controle over the portion of my
            estate given to the grandchildren by me...."
            Signed: John ROYAL, Sr. Witnesses: John SESSIONS,
            J. (or I.) S. BILL. Recorded 10 January 1824.

page 164   Petition for division of negroes of John NELSON,
            Senior, deceased, by Mary NELSON, widow of John
            NELSON, Sr., deceased; Elizabeth ULAND, widow of
            Thomas NELSON, Sr., deceased, formerly Elizabeth
            NELSON; Abram TRIBLE and Polly, his wife, formerly
            Polly NELSON; Sally POWEL, widow of Charles POWEL,
            deceased, formerly Sally NELSON; William POWEL and
            Nancy, his wife, formerly Nancy NELSON; Matthew

NELSON, William D. NELSON, James NELSON, John
NELSON, Junior, and Pleasant NELSON, all children
and legal heirs of said John NELSON, Sr., deceased.
"all over the age of twenty-one years of age, and
all the only heirs of said John NELSON, deceased."
January term 1823. All signed. Commissioners
appointed to divide: Swan HARDEN, Edward W. DALE,
Esquire, and Major John BROWN. Recorded 10 January
1824.

page 165   Sale of property of heirs of Jacob MC KEE on
             9 February 1822. Received of Thomas MC KEE, former
             guardian of heirs of Jacob MC KEE, deceased, by
             Isaac BILLS, guardian for the heirs of Jacob MC KEE,
             deceased.

page 167   Settlement with executors of Jacob MC KEE, deceased.
             20 October 1821. Isaac BILLS and John HATCHETT,
             Esquire.

page 169   Settlement with Thomas MC KEE, guardian for the
             heirs fo Jacob MC KEE, deceased. 22 January 1822.
             John W. RECORD and J. S. ALDERSON.

page 169   Division of land of Jacob MC KEE between his heirs
             into 8 lots. 31 January 1822.

             Lot Number 1--Jacob Hamilton MC KEE
             Lot Number 2--Jane MC KEE
             Lot Number 3--Nancy Lucinda MC KEE
             Lot Number 4--John BOYD and his wife Anny
             Lot Number 5--Betsey Malinda MC KEE
             Lot Number 6--Malinda MC KEE
             Lot Number 7--Sally Manirva MC KEE
             Lot Number 8--Alexander MC INTYRE and his wife Polly
             Commissioners: Solomon P. MAXWELL, John H. BILLS,
             John GILLESPIE.

page 172   Account of sales of estate of Jacob MC KEE,
             deceased, made 19 November 1818. Buying:

             Isaac BILLS   Robert WALLACE
             James EDMONDSON   Bird M. TURNER
             Ebenezer SMITH   John S. ALDERSON
             Henry THOMPSON   William DANIEL
             Hugh MC DUGLE   George GULLET
             A. B. MAYFIELD   Meredith HELMS
             George CAMPBELL   Joseph GILMOER
             Josiah ALDERSON   Thomas MC KEE
             Joshua GUIST   James PURSWELL
             Allen TAYLOR   Ephraim E. DAVIDSON
             Widow   William W. WOODS
             Alexander MC KEE   Williamson ROGERS
             Richard HENDERSON   James M. LEWIS
             Joseph KINCAID   James WRIGHT
             Samuel MC KEE   David SOPELAND
             James LONGLEY

             By Thomas MC KEE, Adam B. ALEXANDER, executors.

page 176   Will of Robert MATTHEWS, 14 February 1822. Wife
             Hannah; daughter Margaret Ann; my trusty friend,

_____; my uncle, my executor; signed: Robert
MATTHEWS. Witnesses: John MATTHEWS; George M.
_____; Daniel Y. _____; Michael C. YOUNG. Recorded
15 January 1824.

page 176   Will of Philip MEEC, 12 May 1820. Two sons, Adam
MEEC and Alexander MEEC; wife Mary MEEC; daughter
Sely H. POWEL; executors Thomas WILSON and Adam
MEEC. Signed: Philip _____; witnesses: John
MC CANNEL; John _____. Recorded 15 January 1824.

page 177   Will of William PERRY: son Francis S. PERRY;
Simpson PERRY; daughter Elizabeth; rest of my
children; wife Elizabeth and sons Francis and
Simpson, executors. 23 February 1822. Signed:
William X PERRY. Witnesses: John MACK and S. R.
HOUSTON. Recorded 15 January 1824.

page 178   Will of Sarah FRIERSON. Grandchildren Ludlow
DICKEY and John Frierson DICKEY, sons of my daughter
Margaret, when they reach twenty-one; grandchild
Sarah Elmire FRIERSON, daughter of my daughter
Isabella, when she is twenty-one; son John Wilson
FRIERSON, to provide him schooling; nieces Mary
BRADLY, Sarah STEPHENSON, Selina STEPHENSON, _____
STEPHENSON, and Sarah M. FRIERSON; Children, viz,
James MADISON, William VINCENT, Samuel DAVIS, and
John WILSON. Friend Thomas F. FLEMING and beloved
sons James MADISON and William VINCENT, executors.
2 January 1820. Signed: Sarah FRIERSON.
Witnesses: William FRIERSON, Thomas STEPHENSON,
and Benoni DICKEY. Recorded 17 January 1824.

page 180   Will of Richard WINN. Sons Samuel WINN; wife
Priscilla WINN; son Benjamin; son Thomas WINN, my
_____, her children.....where her husband Thomas
SIMS now lives; my daughter Priscilla BLOCKER; son
John; when my sons Richard and William marry.
Pricilla WINN, my wife, executrix, Doctor Benjamin
WINN and Samuel WINN, executors. 28 February 1818.
Signed: Richard WINN. Witnesses: William NICHOLS,
J. H. MC KENZIE, W. MC MUNN. Codicile: David R.
EVANS marries my daughter Margaret; Doctor William
BRATTON married my daughter Cristine. Recorded
20 January 1824.

page 181   Will of West HARRIS: wife Milly HARRIS; son West,
when he reaches twenty-one; son Wyatt HARRIS; seven
younger children--three youngest children, Henry,
West, and Olive to be educated; two oldest children,
Eli HARRIS and Sally STUBBLEFIELD; friends Peter
R. BOOKER, John MATTHEWS, and Nathaniel WILLS.
31 August 1819. Signed: West HARRIS. Witnesses:
Edward HUDSON, Silas ALEXANDER, Daniel WILLIAMS.

page 184   Will of Bennett WILLIAMS, 19 January 1820. Mother
Margaret WILLIAMS; sister Fanny ELINGTON; brother
William WILLIAMS; brother Zachariah WILLIAMS;
sister Betsy; sister Nancy WILLIAMS; friend Thomas
WORTHAM; land left me by will of brother Leonard
WILLIAMS, lying on Dick's Branch, the waters of
Nut Bush Creek, Warren County, North Carolina.

74

Executors: Thomas WORTHAM and William H. WORTHAM.
Signed: Bennett WILLIAMS. Witnesses:
W. M. GARRETT, John X SMITH, Robert WORTHAM.
Recorded 23 January 1824.

page 186   Will of James C. ALDERSON: "Court held for the
county of Roane, Tennessee, courthouse in Kingston
on third Monday in April 1811...last will...of
James C. ALDERSON was produced for probate." Will:
James C. ALDERSON of county of Sumner, state of
Tennessee; beloved wife; youngest daughter Jinney
STEPHENSON; John POLK and wife Jane, executors.
27 October 1810. Signed: J. C. ALDERSON.
Witnesses: Jared HOTCHKISS, H. W. HOTCHKISS.
Henry BRAZEALE, clerk of court of Roane where will
probated.

page 189   Will of Isaac B. HARDIN of town of Columbia, Maury
County; wife Sally P. HARDIN; three children,
William F. HARDIN, Benjamin Franklin HARDIN, and
Isaac B. HARDIN on their coming of age; friends
John HODGE and Robert MACK, executors; 13 May 1819.
Signed: Isaac B. HARDIN. Witnesses: Samuel
MC DOWELL and Samuel POLK. Recorded--no date.

page 190   Will of William FRIERSON: son Edmund; daughter
Caroline; rest of my children; two oldest daughters.
Executors: William James FRIERSON, David FRIERSON,
and John FRIERSON. 12 April 1820. Signed:
William FRIERSON. Witnesses: Nathan AVERY; Benoni
DICKEY, and William BLACK. Recorded 24 January
1824.

page 191   Will of Malcolm GILCHRIST, Senior: wife Catharine
GILCHRIST; "my children that are married"; son
Archibald GILCHRIST; son John GILCHRIST, land I
gave him in North Carolina; son Duncan GILCHRIST,
land I gave him in Moore County, North Carolina;
daughter Sarah MC MILLAN; daughter Ann LEACH; son
Malcolm GILCHRIST; daughter Catharine DOBBIN;
Malcolm GILCHRIST, my nephew, son of John GILCHRIST,
and nephew Malcolm GILCHRIST, son of Duncan
GILCHRIST; son Daniel GILCHRIST; son William
GILCHRIST. Executors: faithful sons Malcolm and
William GILCHRIST; _____1819. Signed: Malcolm
GILCHRIST, Senior. Witnesses: Moses SMITH, Chiles
MC GEE, and Samuel GRIFFITH. Recorded 24 January
1824. Probated 23 April 1821.

page 196   Will of William HENDERSON: beloved wife Nancy
HENDERSON; son Ezekiel; son William S.; son Richard;
grandson Thomas C. MILLER; daughter Susanna RAMSEY;
daughter Mary HOUSTON; daughter Narcissa BALDRIDGE;
daughter Asenath MATTHEWS; daughter Betsey P. BOYD;
Arabella W. MC KNIGHT; my land on west side of
Tennessee River to be equally divided between my
wife and children now living and Arabella W.
MC KNIGHT. My friend John TATE; executors, wife
Nancy and three sons William S, Ezekiel, and
Richard. 15 September 1822. Signed: William X
HENDERSON. Witnesses: Samuel SCOTT, Margaret
BALDRIGE, Manuel BALDRIGE. Recorded 24 January 1824.

page 199   Will of Samuel LUSK, Senior: Beloved wife Margaret; daughter Elander; son Samuel; daughter Margaret; son Robert; grandson John MC GILL; executors, sons James and Samuel and Robert. 10 September 1810. Signed: Samuel LUSK. Witnesses: Joseph PEYTON, Andrew KENNESY, Henry YOUNG. Codicil: Daughter Elenor WHITESIDE of south Carolina, York District; dated 15 January 1816. Witnesses: Thomas X WALKER, Andrew WALKER, Robeson WHITESIDE. Recorded 24 January 1824.

page 202   Will of James HAYNES: 20 July 1820. Wife Sally, my small shildren; executors: wife Sally and brother Robert HAYNES. Signed: James HAYNES. Witnesses: John LOWRANCE, Elenor LOWRANCE. "This testament, I wish to stand, August 4, 1818, James HAYNES." Witnesses: Joseph ARMSTRONG, Amanaud (?) MC CONNEL. Recorded 24 January 1824.

page 202   Will of John HAIL. Verbally made 25 August 1818. "present wife Nancy." Son Stephen M. HAIL. Daughter Margaret STONE and her husband Macajah STONE. Witnesses: Samuel SMITH, Martha SMITH, Elenor REESE. Recorded 25 January 1824.

page 203   Will of Edmond FALLEN. Son William FALLEN; daughter Esther FALLEN; grandson Edmond FALLEN, son of Peter FALLEN. Grandchildren Billy and Peggy GRIGGS; son William, executor. 9 March 1818. Signed: Edmond FALLEN. Witnesses: George BRADBURY, Jacob BRADBURY. Recorded 25 January 1824.

page 204   Will of John BUCHANAN "about to travel far from home and uncertain whether I shall ever return"...... father Patrick BUCHANAN. Wife Catharine BUCHANAN and my three shildren, viz, James, Martha, and Mary Ann. Executors: my friends Hugh BROWN, Duncan BROWN, and John BROWN. 2 July 1818. Signed: John BUCHANAN. Witnesses: Duncan BROWN, William BUYERS, Hugh BROWN. Recorded 25 January 1824.

page 205   Will of David HINES: beloved wife and children until they all arrive at twenty-one years of age, the boys and the girl when she reached eighteen years or marries--three children. Executors: Stephen COLLINS, Jeremiah GURLEY, and Ann HINES, my wife. 6 July 1817. Signed: David X HINES. Witnesses: William YANCEY, Aaron CUNNINGHAM; Sally X COLLINS.

page 206   Will of "Anney MC INTRYE of Chatham...." 9 October 1812. Son John MC INTYRE; all my children, viz, Archibald MC INTYRE, John MC INTYRE, Nancy WRIGHT, Catharine WRIGHT, and Christian MC INTYRE. Executors: John _____ and Philip ASHTON. Signed: Anney X MC INTYRE. Witnesses: Philip ASHTON and Alfred YARBROUGH. 25 January 1824.

page 207   Will of Samuel BROOKS: wife Keziah BROOKS; my two sons Hesekiah BROOKS and Meedjiah BROOKS execu executors. 18 July 1821. Signed: Samuel X BROOKS. WITNESSES: Reubin SMITH, William J. JOHNSON. Recorded 26 January 1824.

page 207   Will of Margaret WILLIAMS of Hawkins County, Tennessee.
            Servant Easter; my children. Executors: son William
            WILLIAMS and friend Samuel SMITH, Senior, both of
            Maury County, Tennessee. 15 September 1821.
            Witnesses: Samuel SMITH, James SMITH. Signed:
            Margaret WILLIAMS. Recorded 26 January 1824.

page 208   Will of William HILL: wife Mary; son Andrew; son
            Robert HILL: daughter, now Easter WYLIE: balance of
            my children; viz, Elizabeth FINCH, Mary DUCKWORTH,
            John HILL, Thomas HILL, Margaret GRAY, Robert HILL,
            Easter WYLIE, and Andrew HILL. 27 April 1821.
            Signed: William X HILL. Witnesses: D. RUSSELL,
            Joshua DALE, Obediah ALEXANDER. Recorded 26 January
            1824.

page 209   Will of David COPELAND, Senior. 24 July 1817. Loving
            children, Sarah CARSWELL, and my son James COPELAND,
            and my son David COPELAND, and my daughter Polly CRAIG,
            and my son Anthony M. COPELAND, and my daughter,
            Betsey MC CARNISH (?), and Matthew L. WHITE. Daugh-
            ters Sally and Polly. Signed: David COPELAND.
            Witnesses: Daniel DOUGLASS, John DOUGLASS.
            Recorded 26 January 1824.

page 210   Will of David ROBINSON: wife Elizabeth ROBINSON; son
            Charles; "Asa HARDISON, 40 acres of land or $50 when
            it is collected from North Carolina"; son Mark; son-
            in-law Silas WOLLARD; son Charles; daughter Nancy;
            daughter Martha. Wife Betsey and Mark ROBINSON,
            executors. 6 February 1817. Signed: David ROBINSON.
            Witnesses: John_____and John_____. Recorded
            26 January 1824.

page 211   Will of James KERR: wife; five oldest sons; son James
            KERR; son David KERR; daughter Mary ODIL; daughter
            Nancy MC GERVIN (or MC GOWIN); five oldest sons, viz,
            William, John, Andrew, James, and Samuel; executors,
            my three sons William, John, and Andrew. 10 November
            1817. Signed: James KERR. Witnesses: John BUCHANAN,
            Noah WADE. Recorded 26 January 1824.

page 213   Will of William JACOBS, 18 February 1821. Daughter
            Sally JACOBS; wife Rachel JACOBS; Jesse JACOBS and
            Joseph JACOBS, my two sons. Executor, John GARRISON.
            Signed: William X JACOBS. Witnesses: Allen RAINEY,
            James T. FURGUSON. Recorded 27 January 1824.

page 214   Will of William HARDIN of the State of Georgia, and
            county of Franklin: wife Sarah; two sons Martin and
            Richard; all my children (to wit) Henry, Mark, Swan,
            Martin, Richard, Cynthia, Sarah, and Sucky. Executors:
            sons Mark, Martin, and Swan. 17 October 1803.
            Signed: William HARDIN. Witnesses: Mary WHITNEY,
            Gadwell AYERS, Obadiah TRIMMUR. Frederick BEALL,
            clerk of court, Franklin County, Georgia, states
            true copy of William HARDIN's will in his office,
            15 November 1810.

page 217   Will of Eley DRAKE: son Hubert DRAKE; daughter
            Diana; daughter Annah; daughter Demarius (?); wife
            Nanny. 29 October 1821. Executor, friend Thomas

GRANT. Signed Eley X DRAKE. Witnesses: R. HILL, Betsey X JOHNSTON. Recorded 27 January 1824.

page 217   Will of Jesse CLARKE, codicil to former will: property in hands of Barnes CLARKE and Champion BLYTHE; give to Clarissa CANNON mare now at Doct. James C. O'REILLY's; Hugh CANNON; Barnes CLARKE. 22 May 1817. Signed: Jesse CLARKE. Witnesses: Benjamin H. LEWIS, J. C. O'REILLY, James RANKIN. Recorded 27 January 1824.

page 218   Will of Mary CLARK: money due me in North Caroline in March 1819 and in hands of _____SHAW, son of Daniel SHAW in North Carolina; nephew Malcolm Clark BASKET, alias Malcolm Clark MIDDLETON; brother Archibald CLARK's children and sister Ann _____ children; Aunt Catherine GILCHRIST; cousin Sarah MC MILLAN and her daughter Catherine; cousin Ann LEACH; cousin Effy GILCHRIST; cousin Catherine DOBBIN and her daughter Jennet Malvina DOBBIN; niece Nancy CLARK, daughter of brother Archibald CLARK; rest to be divided by Aunt Catharine GILCHRIST between cousin Sarah MC MILLIN, cousin Ann LEACH, cousin Catharine DOBBIN, herself, and to cousin John GILCHRIST's daughters. Executors: friends David DOBBIN and William GILCHRIST. 1 November 1818. Signed: Mary CLARK. Witnesses: John GILCHRIST, Daniel BUIE. Recorded 27 January 1824.

page 220   Will of Branch JACKSON: mother Henaritta JACKSON; sister Polly Ann. 30 March 1818. Mother executrix. Signed: Branch X. JACKSON. Witnesses: William H. CALDWELL, Thomas WHITE, Junior, William ALLEN. Recorded 27 January 1824.

page 221   Will of Robert WILEY. Wife Sarah; my children, viz, John WILEY, Thomas WILEY, William WILEY, Moses WILEY, Andrew WILEY, Polly, and Margaret. Son Alexander WILEY; daughter Sarah THOMPSON; wife and son Alexander, executors. 31 August 1820. Signed: Robert X WILEY. Witnesses: Jasper R. _____, Francis S. PERRY, John BARNES. Recorded 27 January 1824.

page 222   Will of George DIXON. Bonds in State of Virginia, to my daughters Rachel and Anna; five grandchildren, sons and daughter of my daughter Mary; sons Thomas and Adam. Sons Thomas and Adam, executors. Signed: George DIXON. Witnesses: Henry TURNEY, John SMISER, Jones IRVIN. 4 September 1819. Recorded 28 January 1824.

page 223   Verbal will of Baynes BRIDGES, deceased, given to Jesse BRIDGES and Joel REAVES on Friday morning, 25 September 1818, a few hours before his death. Wife and children. 29 September 1818. Signed: Joel X REAVES, Jesse BRIDGES.

page 224   Verbal will of Samuel SHAW, legatees; executors, David CRAIG, Esquire, William SHAW, and Hugh SHAW. 10 July 1818. Witnesses: Hugh SHAW, Levi SHAW.

page 224   19 July 1818. Jane X SHAW, states her late husband Samuel SHAW made the nuncupative will as above.

page 225   Will of Jane SHAW: daughter Nancy SHAW; my children; David CRAIG, executor; 19 November 1819. Signed: Jane X SHAW. Witnesses: David CRAIG and William GORDON. Recorded 28 January 1824.

page 225   Will of James H. WILLIAMS: appoint father, brother Edmund, brother Green B. WILLIAMS, and brother Alexander M. WILLIAMS, executors. Signed: James H. WILLIAMS, 12 May 1818. Witnesses: Bennett WILLIAMS, George GRISHAM, William FAULLIN. Recorded 28 January 1824. Codicil witnessed by Sally X GRISHAM and Bennett WILLIAMS.

page 227   Will of Joseph DENTON: wife Elenor; daughter Phebe SMITH; daughter Martha JOHNSON; daughter Elenor CAMPBELL; son Abram DENTON; son Benjamin DENTON; daughter Hannah HILLEY (or WILLEY); daughter Polly CAMPBELL; daughter Elizabeth HOPKINS; daughter Rhoda MC CUTCHEN; grandson Charles DENTON. Nine mentioned legatees. Wife Elenor DENTON, executrix. 30 July 1818. Signed: Joseph DENTON. Witnesses: William WILLEY, Ambrose B. RICHARDS, Nathan GARNER. Recorded 29 January 1824.

page 228   Will of Ephraim MC LEAN, Junior. Wife Polly; daughter Patsey, son John, and son Ephraim having been provided for, son Alvey; daughter Betsey; daughter Cynthia; two sons Cavel B. MC LEAN and James B. MC LEAN; wife Polly, and son Cavel B. MC LEAN, executors. 26 March 1818. Signed: Ephraim MC LEAN. Witnesses: Charles SHEARMAN, Robert_____, John MITCHELL. Recorded 29 January 1824.

page 229   Will of Thomas CRAWFORD; daughter Eliza DUNLAP: grandson Thomas H. DUNLAP; son John CRAWFORD; daughter Elizabeth BLAIR; friend James W. STEPHENSON, D. D., and son John CRAWFORD, executors. 31 May 1821. Signed: Thomas CRAWFORD. Witnesses: Duncan BROWN, Moses D. STEPHENSON, Daniel KERR. Recorded 25 January 1824.

page 230   Will of Tyree DOLLINS: "will...that the occupant law as past in Murfreesboro in the State of Tennessee in 1819 shall take effect, that provided James MC LAFFERTY does procure a land warrant and make an entry on the same, so as to include my present place of residence ..." wife Alvira, "provided the...legacy shall not come into the possession of my beloved wife Alvira's hands until she becomes of lawful age or is married"; nephew Tyre DOLLINS, son of John DOLLINS; brother Jeremiah DOLLINS my part of my father John DOLLINS estate in Albemarle County, Virginia. Executors: James MC LAFFERTY and Ephraim E. DAVIDSON. 28 July 1820. Signed: Tyre DOLLINS. Witnesses: J. WATSON, William MC CONNELL. Recorded 29 January 1824.

page 232   Will of Robert SCOTT. Friend John M. DANIEL "interest in store of merchandise which said John M. DANIEL and myself are in copartnership." 13 May 1817. Signed: Robert SCOTT. Witnesses: John_____, Jonathan BAILEY, Jurat. Recorded 29 January 1824.

page 232   Will of Thomas SHELBY: wife Hannah, my son Evan, Polly, Beck, Nolly POLK, Eli, Levi, William, and

George. Son George. Executors: sons Evan and William. 20 September 1822. Signed: Thomas SHELBY. Witnesses: Isaac MC CALLUM, Vardernam X. SHELBY. Record 29 January 1824.

page 233   Will of Alexander B. SMITH: wife Jane, 4 November 1819. Signed: Alexander B. SMITH. Witnesses: William STRATTON, Bird S. HURT. Recorded 29 January 1824.

page 234   Will of James AKIN: son Ezekiel and his (Ezekiel's) children Eliza, Polly, James; daughter Martha AKIN, wife of Burwell AKIN; grandchildren Ginsey AKIN and Lucy AKIN, daughters of my son James AKIN, deceased; grandson Green AKIN, son of Burwell AKIN; son Pleasant AKIN; executor: son Ezekiel AKIN and friend Samuel POLK. 14 October 1821. Signed: James X AKIN. Witnesses: Robert ROGERS, Isaac FORD, Wiley SCOTT, John KILCREASE, Silas M. CALDWELL. Recorded 29 January 1824.

page 235   Inventory of property of James STEELE, deceased, by Nathaniel H. Steele and AARON Steele, executors. Recorded 29 January 1824.

page 235   Dr. Thomas JONES, guardian of Ali ROGERS. Guardian's settlement report. 29 January 1824; by E. W. DALE and James WALKER.

page 236   Commissioners report for division of 5,000 acre tract granted to Robert BURTON and William SMITH from State of Tennessee, grant no. 14648. Allotted to:

    Samuel G. SMITH, 260-142/160, Lot No. 1
    James W. SMITH, 898 Acres, Lot No. 2
    Heirs of William SMITH, 416 Acres, Lot No. 3
    Samuel G. SMITH, 220 Acres, Lot No. 4
    Richard SMITH, 525 Acres, Lot No. 5
    William SMITH's heirs, 978 Acres and 80/160,
        Lot No. 6
    James W. SMITH, 978 Acres, Lot No. 7
    Heirs of William SMITH, 146 Acres and 64/160,
        Lot No. 8
    James W. SMITH, 219-120/160 Acres, Lot No. 9

    Dated 6 December 1823. Signed: John MATTHEWS, James STOCKARD, and Samuel GRIFFITH.

page 240   Estate settlement with Samuel HUCKABY as administrator of John HUCKABY, deceased. Court order, July 1823, and renewed at October term 1823. 15 January 1824. Signed: E. WILKS and I. S. BILLS.

page 240   Settlement with executors of John J. LONG for years 1820, 1821, 1822, 1832. Persons named:

Stephen SMITH; land in Stewart County; Col. WILLIS; Nicholas LONG; Thomas WORTHAM; legacy in North Carolina; Thomas B. CRAIGHEAD; Mrs. Frances LONG; Alfred BALCH; A. C. HAYES; George M. MARTIN; John BROWN, Samuel MAYS, Mrs. PARKER, E. J. ARMSTRONG, Duke WILLIAMS, Darrel N. SANSOM, Lemuel LONG, Thomas J. KENNEDY, "for Edward LONG"; "Board and expenses

for Mary LONG"; "Board and schooling of John LONG";
"Board and schooling for Nicholas LONG"; "Board and
schooling of George LONG"; "Board and expenses for
E. LONG"; board and expenses for Mary LONG; board
and expenses for Frances LONG; William H. MACON.
27 January 1824. Signed: R. B. NEWSUM, John MATTHEWS.

page 242   January term, 1824, petitioner Mada FRIERSON...she is
            the widow of George FRIERSON...who died about the
            year 1818, leaving his widow and six children...
            wishes her widow's dower.

page 243   Inventory of James HOLLAND's property by James
            HOLLAND, Harden PERKINS, recorded 31 January 1824.

page 243   Widow's provision laid off 21 December 1823 for
            Patsey SLAUGHTER, by Samuel _____ and George X
            DAVISON.

page 244   Amount of sale of property of Joseph FREELAND, dec-
            eased, sold 8 February 1823, by R. D. FREELAND,
            Margit FREELAND, administrator and administratrix.

page 244   Will of William DOOLEY: "whenever my daughter
            Levisa choses to leave my family or the day of her
            marriage...; whenever my daughter Cynthia chooses to
            leave my family or on the day of her marriage...;
            wife Jane and her two daughters Levisa and Cynthia,
            executrixes and all my other children in turn as
            they become of age"; 30 January 1823. Signed: Wm.
            DOOLEY. Witnesses: John SMISER, James COPELAND,
            John _____, Adam DIXON.

page 247   22 January 1822. Settlement with Edward BLACKBURN,
            administrator of John HOCKINS; accounts: Doctor
            MC GIMSEY, James KNOX, Polly HOCKINS: by Isaac BILLS
            and John MATTHEWS.

page 247   Guardian's settlement with Samuel DAVIS, guardian of
            Jane DAVIS. October term 1823; 24 January 1824, by
            John MATTHEWS and James STOCKARD.

page 248   Settlement with Robert SELLARS, guardian of minor
            heirs of William BYNUM, deceased, vix, Laird S. BYNUM,
            Buth (?) W. BYNUM, Isafeney BYNUM, and Sarah S. BYNUM.
            24 January 1824, by Richard B. PASSMORE and J. S.
            ALDERSON.

page 249   Guardian's report: Dr. Thomas JONES, guardian of
            R. M. WILLIAMSON, Martha WILLIAMSON, Ann H. K.
            WILLIAMSON, Maria G. WILLIAMSON. 22 January 1824,
            by Isaac BILLS and Ewd. W. DALE.

page 250   Settlement with Jeremiah CHERRY, guardian of Sally
            COOPER; cash received for Thomas GILL and John JONES;
            cash received from John _____, administrator of
            Joel COOPER, deceased; cash received from Mr. BROWN,
            administrator of COOPER a minor; settlement made
            6 July 1822. Recorded 2 February 1824; by Alex.
            JOHNSON and Thomas GILL.

page 251   Inventory of sale of George SLATER, deceased. Buying:
            Andrew BURNS, Andrew SLATER, Edward HARRIS, Lewis

RING, Patsey SLATER: by Patsey X. SLAUGHTER. Recorded 2 February 1824.

page 251   Sale of John B. KENNADY, deceased. Buying:

John ANDREWS	Alexander FAUCETT
Edward HAGGER	James DAVIS
Frances H. KENNEDY	William HOLT
Isaac H. HILL	Isaac W. WILLIAMS
Benjamin BALDRIDGE	Elizabeth KENNEDY
Collin FORBES	Demsey HUBBARD
Thomas D. KENNEDY	Edmund HAGGARD
John BALDRIDGE	John GILLESPIE
David ANDREWS	Robert MADEN

by James L. KENNEDY, administrator. Recorded
2 February 1824.

page 252   Inventory of sale of estate of Hopson ARNOLD, deceased,
held 1 January 1824. Buying: Richard RAGGEN, William
G. PERKINS, Robert NIX; administrators: James C.
RECORD and Robert NIX.

page 252   Settlement with Samuel MC LEAN, guardian of minor
heirs of William MC LEAN, deceased: schooling for
Andrew MC LEAN; schooling for NANCY MC LEAN; schooling
for Harvey William MC LEAN. 24 January 1824, by
Richard B. PASSMORE and Robert SELLARS.

page 253   Laying off one year's provision (no name) by William
STOCKARD, James BAITY and Jno. COOPER. Recorded
2 February 1824.

page 254   "Received May 20, 1816, into my hands as guardian for
the heirs of Robert _____, deceased.... Signed:
William WALLACE, guardian for the heirs of _____,
deceased." Recorded 4 February 1824.

page 253   Sale bill of John LOVE's estate, late deceased
July 20, 1814; buying:

Edom LOVE	Robert HOLMES
Wilson LOVE	James OWEN
James WHITE	Moses HOLMES
Aaron HUNTER	James William BURNS
Jane KENDRICK	Harrison BLAGRAVE
James AYRES	William CHURCHWELL
James KENDRICK	John LOVE
James ELLIT	Thomas G. HARVEY
John MITCHELL	Andrew BARKER
Robert LOVE	Isaac MC COLLUM
Joel LOVE	Charles BURNS

by Robert LOVE, administrator. Recorded 4 February
1824.

page 254   Sale of property of Jehosephat LADD, deceased. Buying:

David DOBBINS	Booker CHARTER
William CHAMBERLAIN	Samuel BAKER
Isaiah DAVIS	George SHELBY
William HAWKINS	Isaac FARIS
Joel ALEXANDER	F. J. ALDERSON

William SAVAGE
Thomas BRADY
William PREWETT
Edward MC FADDEN
Bowling GORDON
John WALKER
Baird (?) SHELBY
Abram SHELBY
William KIRK
Randolf WALKER
Thomas B. MALONE
Henry E. TURNER
John C. HAMILTON
Evan SHELBY
Levi SHELBY
Charles PISTOL

Caleb FARRIS
Elezar ROSS (?)
William RIGGAN
Jeremiah ALDERSON
John GORDON
Richard ANDERSON
Robert G. KELSEY
Robin GORDON
Ezra BRESEL
John PREWETT
John KENDRICK
O. B. MITCHELL
Daniel HALCOMB
Thomas THRANTHAM
Richard JONES

Property sold on 16 and 17 November 1821, by Hugh
DOUGLAS and Wm. HAWKINS, administrators. Notes on
Constantine LADD, John D. ALDERSON, Mary HUNTER.
13 April 1822. Recorded 5 February 1824.

page 258   Inventory of James M. LEWIS: "Negroes disposed of by
James M. LEWIS in the year 1814 and the title vested
in Benjamin H. LEWIS and William T. LEWIS..." John
HODGE, administrator, 25 April 1822.

page 259   Year's provision for widow and orphans of Thomas
LAREMORE, deceased. 11 March 1816, by William HOLT
and Joshua GLOVER.

page 259   Account of sales of estate of Thomas LARAMORE,
deceased, sold at his late dwelling on Globe Creek,
11 March 1816. Purchasers:

M. C. DAVIS
Peter YOUNG
Adam ANDREWS
James STEEL
John LORENCE
David ANDREWS
Milton ANTHONY
Joel YORK
James DAVIS
Morgan FITZPATRICK
Thomas GRANT
Jesse HOSEY
William PACE
Joel BURROW
Besey LARAMORE
John WEBB

Alexander TURNER
H. STEEL
Merideth WELL
James DUNCAN
John WEBB
William HOLT
Samuel BIRD
Rees PICKINS
Archelus DAVIS
Stephen HOSEY
J. SUMMERS
Robert MC NUTT
Thomas SHANNON
James ORR
Robert LOGAN

Signed: N. P. HARDEMAN, administrator of Thomas
LARAMORE; settlement with Thomas H. PERKINS, executor
of Nicholas P. HARDEMAN, deceased, as administrator
of estate of Thomas LARAMORE, deceased. 20 July 1818.
Signed: John MACK.

page 261   Sale of John LOVE, deceased, sold 9 August 1819.
Adam LOVE, Eli LOVE, and Nathaniel LOVE. Signed:
Thomas KENDRICK, guardian.

page 262   Inventory of property of Samuel LUSK, deceased.
            15 April 1820. By James LUSK, Samuel LUSK, and
            Robert LUSK, executors.

page 263   Widow's provision for Elizabeth LONGLEY, widow of
            late James LONGLEY, deceased, and the two youngest
            children. 25 July 1821, by E. W. DALE, Saml.MC DOWELL.

page 263   Inventory of estate of Jesse LIVESEY, deceased.
            9 February 1817. By Robert LIVESAY.

page 264   Widow's provision for Mrs. Mary B. LEWIS, widow of
            the lately deceased James M. LEWIS. 31 May 1822, by
            George M. MARTIN, William MC NEILE, and Samuel
            MC DOWELL.

page 264   Inventory of estate of Dr. John J. LONG, deceased,
            1817, by Frances S. LONG and Samuel MAYES, executors.

page 265   Sale of _____, sold 15 May 1815 by Catharine
            LANGSTON. Buying:

George ROAN   Elias CHEEK
Isaac LANGSTON   David ARNOLD
Henry HALL   Nalns KIRK
Curtis WOOD   Rodarick WRIGHT
Catharine LANGSTON   John PATTON
John WARREN

page 266   George P. Tyler in account with the estate of John J.
            WEBB, deceased. Goods sold 22 February 1822. Notes
            on:

John E. WILLIAMS   Samuel WINN
David R. MITCHELL   Edward WILLIAMS
Cyrus GILES   John WINN
Howard BENNET   Thomas SIMMS
Horatio CLAGETT   William PREWETT
George HICKS   Samuel ROBBINS
Thomas J. MORTON   James WILLIE
Benjamin AYRES   William BLACKBURN
James BEEK   William REGION
John KENDRICK   George H. LARETT
J. MC KENSEY   Capt. YANCEY
William TYLER, Sr.   Jesse GRIFFIN
Job HUNT   Moses R. WILEY
Peter GRAHAM   John PEWRY
James H. GILES   Stewat STALLINGS
George P. TYLER   Samuel A. BAKER
E. W.   Samuel SATERFIELD
James DOBBINS   Peter GRAHAM
Charles SOWEL   John WOOLDRIDGE
John GRIMES   Ebenezar ROSS
Andrew MITCHELL   Isaiah DAVIS
William H. AKIN   Thomas WALLACE
Isaac FARRIS   John WOODRIDGE
John WILSON   _____ BARNHILL
John GRIFFITH   G. S. TYLER
Booker R. CHARTER   Hugh MC CABE
John COOPER   John GORDON
GREENFIELD & SMITH   Abram MAYS
John ERVIN   David KILLAUGH
James ERVIN   Capt. Thomas CHOATE

Jesse S. ROSS	J. R. MC ALISTER, constable
George GARNETT	Thomas WALKER
James JOSEY	Thomas CHOATE
Ambrose R. RICHARDS	Jonathan WEBSTER
Wm. WHITESIDE	Edom LOVE
Joseph AYRES, Sr.	Joseph ALLEN
Mrs. Dolly GORDON	Robert HARRING
Edward ENGLISH	Polly JONES
Jesse OAKLY	Thomas SILLIMAN
Spencer TINSLEY	Neale HOPKINS
Redmond CHOATE	Benjamin H. MARTIN
Thomas KENDRICK	Joseph M. BAIRD
Alexander OAKLEY	Jonathan TOLLY
David H. TRUE	Thomas WEBB
Luke WHITE	William STRAYHORN
Hugh WHITESIDE	James CHOATE
James TRAVIS	John DAVY
Alston JONES	John SELLERS
George GREER	Isaac B. LINDSEY
Joseph CHOATE	James G. KILLOUGH
William CROFFORD	Eli SHELBY
John C. HAMILTON	Robert HAMILTON
James ERVIN	William HICKS
Thomas T. GREENFIELD	Thomas CLAIBOURN
Daniel PERITT	G. T. GREENFIELD
Col. Thomas COLEMAN	David KILLOUGH, Esqr.
Thomas J. MARTIN	William DANIEL, constable

"since the death of Mrs. WEBB."
8 January 1824, T. COLEMAN, J. P., and Wm. _____.

page 272   Sale of John P. POOL held 18 May 1822. Purchasers:

Thomas J. FRIERSON	Robert G. KELSEY
Willis BEDDY	David DOBBIN
James WALKER	James BLAKE
John MACON	Nathn. GRAVES
Catharine POOL	William KIRK
James DOBBINS	William ROBERTS
John PATTERSON	Perry O. MALOEN
Edward F. ENGLISH	

by Nathl. GRAVES, administrator.

page 275   Inventory of estate of John P. POOL, deceased
            18 April 1822. Nathl. GRAVES, administrator.

page 276   Apportionment for _____ 30 October 1818, by
            William HOLT, Alexander GILESPIE, Benjamin THOMPSON.

page 276   Petition to court October term 1819 by John PATILLO
            ...."William ADKINS, deceased some time in the year
            1817, leaving his wife Jane ADKINS and George PATTON,
            his executor and executrix and four children, one of
            whom named Margarett, is since intermarried with
            petitioner..." wanted estate divided. Recorded
            12 February 1824.

page 277   Return of hire of negroes by estate of William H.
            WILLIAMS for 1823 and 1824 by Stephen SMITH and John
            W. SMITH, administrators.

page 278   Amount of sale of James PERCELL, deceased. 27 March
            1822 by Richard FAUCETT and Alexander BALDRIDGE.

page 278   One year's provision for Sally PERCELL, 11 February
            1822, by E. W. DALE, James WALKER, Mathias WOFIELD.

page 278   Inventory of property of William PERRY, deceased.
            5 July 1822. By Elizabeth, Francis S., and Simpson
            PERRY.

page 279   Inventory of property of Abraham PICKENS, deceased,
            taken 22 February 1815 by Will NALL (?), administrator.

page 279   Sale of property of Abraham PICKENS, deceased, held
            14 March 1815. Purchasers:

Elizabeth PICKENS   Hugh MC LEDEN (or MC LERLEN?)
Joel BURROW   Widow PICKINGS
William NEIL   James SMITH
Flemin R. SIMMONS   Thomas MC CALL
Robert PARKS   Elijah WARD
William BRANFORD   James HALE
Benjamin HENDERSON   James N. SMITH
Robert REID   Hannah PICKENS
John MASSEY   Isiah REID
William BOROUGH   Samuel SMITH
Beton BOCAM   David LILES
Joseph MOREHEAD   Christian SHIRES
Richard COCKE   Presley RIEVE
Richard JONES   William HALCOMB
Richard C. HARRIS   William GOFORTH
Will NEEL, administrator   Samuel GULLET
Fanny PICKINS   William G. PICKINS
William PICKENS   William GILLAM
Daniel REID   Jean PICKENS
Robert HENDERSON   George GULLET
Richard LOCKE   John GILCHRIST
Benjamin HERNDON   John PICKENS
Jno. GORDON

page 283   Will of Cornelius WILSON: wife Anney WILSON; daugh-
            ter Nancy WILSON (should she marry before the death
            of her mother);...equal share to that of the rest of
            my children heretofore married; son Henry Stephens
            WILSON...when he shall arrive at the age of 20 years;
            daughter Elizabeth TRANERM (?); son John WILSON;
            daughter Mary HARDISON; son Alexander WILSON; wife
            Anney WILSON, son John WILSON, son-in-law Thomas
            HARDISON, executrix and executors. 24 April 1821.
            Signed: Cornelius WILSON. Witnesses: Edward
            BAGSDALE, Henry S. WILSON, Jeremiah TRANUM.
            Recorded 24 February 1824.

page 284   October term 1823. James P. PETERS, Reuben SMITH,
            John KENNEDY, John MILLER, and Simon TURNER appointed
            to divide personal property of Jeremiah HOBSON,
            deceased, between Nancy HOBSON, widow of said
            deceased...and make return third Monday in October
            1823.

            Division follows: negroe slaves of Jeremiah HOBSON,
            deceased, between Nancy HOBSON, widow and relict of

said Jeremiah, and Jeremiah HOBSON, minor heir of said Jeremiah, deceased. 30 December 1823. Signed: by above named commissioners.

page 284   Edward PUCKET and James L. BALDRIDGE met on 5 September 1823 to say what Richard FAUCETT should be allowed for the maintenance of the minor heirs of James PERCELL, deceased.

page 285   Inventory of property of William H. WILSON, deceased. "Papers on Samuel DAVIS"; note on John CLARKE due 25 December 1822; "his school articles for the year 1821 not settled." Dated 15 February 1822.

page 285   Inventory of money collected by administrators of James PERSELL, deceased. Rents for year 1822. Dated 19 February 1824. Signed: Alex BALDRIDGE and Richard FAUCETT.

page 286   January 1824 "At the request of the representatives of Jacob HUNTER, deceased, to wit: Mrs. HUNTER; Eliza H. HUNTER by her guardian Micklejohn KITREL; James KIMBLE; William HUNTER, John DAWSON, and Micklejohn KITREL...undersigned have made following division of negro property between the representatives of the said Jacob HUNTER:

To Mrs. HUNTER, the widow............10 slaves
To M. KITREL.......................7 or more
To Elisa H. HUNTER.................10 slaves
To James KIMBLE....................10 slaves
To William HUNTER...................7 slaves
To John DAWSON......................8 slaves
....and for the purpose of making the lots equal between said representatives the following sums of money to be paid to wit....

Signed: P. R. BOOKER, William PILLOW, Thomas JONES.

page 287   Acknowledgement of receipt of full portion of negro property of the administrators of Jacob HUNTER, deceased, signed by representatives of Jacob HUNTER. 2 January 1824. Signed by: Micklejohn KITRELL, Micklejohn KITRELL, guardian for Eliza H. HUNTER; William HUNTER; James KIMBLE; John DAWSON; Patience X HUNTER. Witnesses: James L. WALKER, P. PENN.

page 288   Petition by Jeremiah CHERRY and Mary B., his wife, formerly Mary B. COOPER, and Sarah COOPER, an infant under the age of 21 years, by her guardian Jeremiah CHERRY....to divide negroes between the petitioners ....January 19, 1824.

Court appoints Thomas GILL and Alexander JOHNSON, Esquire, to make said division. Division made 24 January 1824 by Thomas GILL and Alexander JOHNSON.

page 289   Settlement by Thomas GILL and Alex JOHNSON with Charles WEEMS, administrator of William WEEMES, deceased. "amount charged by the commissioners 16 September 1819..." "....land sold to Thomas ADAMS by the deceased before his death...." ".... charge for making division of land among the heirs and reporting same with this settlement." (Abstractor's note: division does not follow.??) Recorded 27 February 1824.

page 290 Report made by Jesse M. GORDON, guardian for James and William SHAW, minor heirs of Samuel SHAW, deceased. "Received on 8th day of May, 1823 of Hugh SHAW, William SHAW, and David CRAIG, executors of Samuel SHAW, deceased, and David CRAIG, executor of Jane SHAW, deceased." "Tax and charge for land in Shelby County, Western District." Tax on lands in Maury County. Record 27 February 1824.

page 290 Report made by David CRAIG, Junior, guardian for Nancy SHAW, heir of Samuel SHAW, deceased. About same as above report. Recorded 28 February 1824.

page 291 Report made by David CRAIG, acting executor of Samuel SHAW, Junior, deceased of the estate of John SHAW, minor heir of said SHAW, deceased. "for use and repair done to a Deaburn wagon to convey said John SHAW to Danville, Kentucky, and home." 15 January 1824.

page 291 "July 20, 1818, to the Honourable Court of Maury will receive this as my resignation I am yours with respect ---John POLK."

page 292 Sale - no indication as to whose or when. Recorded 28 February 1824. Purchasers:

Charles M. PARTEE	David HINES
John BOOKER	Hiram PARTEE
Jeremiah GERLEY	John DUCKWORTH
Isah HOGAN	Robert SELLERS
James MC LEAL (?)	Widow H. BROOKS
Mark PIPKIN	Hezekiah BROOKS
Hardaman SELLARS	Ephr. MC LEAN
Edward COSTELA	Benton BADGETT
John SMITH	Samuel MC LEAN
widow	James RULEDGE
A. PARTEE	Micajah PAIN
Charles SHEARMAN	Miager (?) PARRIS
Isaac SELLARS	

page 294 Recorded 10 December 1811 and transferred to this Book 28 February 1824.

William LAW (?)   Thomas GILLIAM   Edward MOORE Wm. GILLIAM and David LONG divide tract of land in Maury on north side of Duck River granted to Minican HUNT and Benja HERNDON, Jr., by the state. Lot No.1 allotted to representative of said HUNT. Lots Nos. 2 and 3 to Benjamin HERNDON, Junior.

page 295 Sale of property of Joel PATTERSON, deceased, sold on 25 August 1816 by Jacob ROGERS, administrator. Purchasers: Jesse MORRIS, John MILL, Briant BAGUS (or BOGUES), widow, William SLENS (?), Bennet FEELS, Huey, Asa MORRIS, Ezekial AKINS.

page 296 Settlement between Charles PARTEE former guardian

88

and Simpson SHAW; present guardian, of the estate of the minor heirs of Squire SHEARMAN, deceased. "Note on Thomas MC GIMPSEY" "hire of negroes for years 1822 and 1823" 29 December 1823 by Hugh DOUGLAS, James BLACK, and Swan HARDIN.

page 296   January 1824. Widow and relict of Thomas G. BLACK, deceased, to come in before the next Monday of the present term of court and shew cause if any she hath or why the noncupative will of said Thomas G. BLACK, deceased, be not recorded. Third Monday in January 1824.

page 296   On the back of the foregoing process was written "Ipd 19th Feby, 1824. I do by these presents authorise William BLACK to execute and return this Spa agreeable to law. Nimrod PORTER, Shf." January 19, 1824.

page 297   Inventory of estate of Ambrose BLACKBURN, deceased, December 28, 1820, by John BLACKBURN, administrator of Ambrose BLACKBURN, deceased.

page 297   Widow's provision for widow of Ambrose BLACKBURN, deceased, 2 December 1820, by William CATHEY, Samuel WHITESIDE.

page 298   Memorandum of sale of property of John BARNES, deceased, recorded 1 March 1824. Purchasers:

Nathaniel YOUNG	Asa WILLIAMS
Joseph R. SUTTON	Alexander WILEY
William WILLIS	Royal FURGISON
Luke WHITE	John WALKER
Joseph LAYMASTER	John NEELY
Henry E. TURNER	Jesse BROWN
William BROWN	Andrew ALEXANDER
Jasper R. SUTTON	Obediah ALEXANDER
George JENNINGS	John ALEXANDER
H. H. HOPKINS	George HARRISON
John SEWELL	Eli ALEXANDER
Robert WILEY	Richard MILLER
Allen DODD	Peter JOYCE
Jane W. BARNES (bought	John L. SMITH
most of household	John BULLOCK
furniture and slaves)	David RUSSELL
Reuben HILL, Senr.	John WILLIS
Andrew HILL	Allen WILEY
E. B. LITTLEFIELD	Jane BARNES

Notes on:
Thomas M. FOWLER	Thomas H. JENKINS
Peter GRIMES	Andrew MC MACKIN
George ROSS	Thomas G. KELSEY

page 302   Widow's provision for Mrs. Jane BARNES and family, recorded 2 March 1824 by John ALEXANDER, Nicholas YOUNG and Obediah ALEXANDER.

page 302   Additional inventory of estate of Jesse BROWN, deceased, by John ATKINSON, administrator, 20 February 1815.

page 302   Lucy BITTLEMAN relinquishes her right of administra-
           tion in estate of her husband John BITTLEMAN, deceased,
           in favor of William VOORHIES, John FARNY, and Henry
           TURNEY, 30 July 1819. Witness: James WALKER.

page 303   Inventory of Jonathan BROOM's estate, deceased 12
           August 1814.

page 303   Widow's provision for Sarah BROWN, late widow of
           Jethro BROWN, deceased, 18 November 1818. (Order
           made at October term 1818.) By Reuben SMITH, John
           KENNEDY, Edward SAUNDERS.

page 304   Inventory of sale of Benton BADGETT, deceased, 1 July
           1822. Recorded 3 March 1824. Accounts due:

           John WOLVETON   Charles PARTEE
           A. Y. PARTEE   Peter JOICE
           Hiram PARTEE   John BOOKER
           William YANCEY   Joseph G. KELSOE
           James WOLVERTON   Thomas HANKES

           by Levenah BADGETT, administrator.

page 305   Supplement to inventory of estate of John BUCHANAN,
           deceased, by H. BROWN, D. BROWN, John BROWN, executors.
           Recorded 3 March 1824.

page 306   Inventory of estate of Jacob BOGARD, by Wm. and James
           BOGARD, administrators.

page 307   Amount of sale of Richard BUTLER, deceased, property
           sold on 3 July 1820 by William BRYAN.

page 308   Inventory of property of John BUCKHANON, deceased,
           recorded 3 March 1824.

page 308   Inventory of goods of estate of Barnes BRIDGE,
           deceased, valued by Joel REEVES and Nat. MURPHEY,
           14 November 1818.

page 309   Inventory of property of estate of John BITTLEMAN,
           deceased. Recorded 3 March 1824.

Notes	When given	When due
Henry C. DAWSON	17 July 1819	1 January 1820 Greensborough, Georgia
Henry KINGSBURG & H. C. DAWSON	6 August 1819	Do
H. M. MACKEY & Jonathan MACKEY	6 January 1819	Do near Natchez
N. HOOPER	5 February 1819	Do Greenville,Miss.
John COLEMAN	10 December 1818	March 1819 Woodville, Miss.
Jasper R. SUTTON	30 April 1819	June 1819 Maury, Tenn.
Edned (?) BURTON & E. ANDERSON	13 January 1819	June 1819
Letter from Hiram SMITH		

Jesse LAMBERT   1 January 1817, on day after date
William CROCKET   6 August 1814
       ROLSTON   28 June 1813
Joseph BAILEY and
    John MC GINNIS   25 February 1810
G. W. HUMPHRIES   24 May 1817
Vance GREER (?), deed for 2,250 acres in Kentucky
Bond for Robert ERWIN for 180 acres
One-fourth of lot No. 30 corner of Market and Embargo
    Streets
By William VOORHIES, John FEARNY, Henry TURNEY,
administrators.

page 310   Andrew BOYD and _____ HACKET petition for division
            of jointly held land on waters of _____ Creek
            adjoining John MIRICK and East of William HENDERSON.
            Commissioners: William HENDERSON, Sr., John TATE,
            William COVEY, Sr., Capt. DANIEL, and John MIRICK.
            April term 1820.

page 310   October term 1820. Samuel DAVIS, Alexander M.
            WILLIAMS, and Wilkinson BARNS appointed to lay off
            widow's provision for Peggy ROGERS, late widow of
            James W. ROGERS, deceased.

page 311   List of accounts due. No name. No date. Recorded
            4 March 1824. Persons named:

Hugh LEEPER   William HENSON
James ALLEN   Spence HUNT
Joseph AYRES   A. HAMILTON
Samuel W. LEAPER   Robin MEULLAS (?)
William HARPER   Jesse TEMPLES
William THOMAS   Allen PILLOW
John FUZELL   John GILBERT
William STONE   Tilman GOSSETT
Gideon F. DIXON   Green HOLLEN
James B. NAPPER   Patten SPEAN
John FRACE   Richard N. C. LAMBIRD
James ROBERTSON   Jewless BLAYCOCK
John M. BAYRES
Fanney MC CORNAL   Scott COALMAN
David CATWELL   Wiley B. PAIN
Stephen SMITH   Samuel MC GOWEN
Claborn SPICER   Henry KING
William HUSTER   Isaac HUNTER
William STONE   Sara MAY
Alexander WILKINS   Thomas TULB (?)
Edward FOSTER   Charles HULSEY
Lewis THOMPSON   Polly WAST
John SPENCER   Moses GAMBRILL
David MILLER   William SLATER
Henry M. JAMES   William CAPHREY
James RILEY   Patsey GOODWIN
George EVANS   John RICHARDSON
James BAKER   Mary KENDRICK
Matthew TULES   James JONES
Stoakley UMPHRIES   William WIRIGATE
William KIRK   Nathan NEWLEY
Joseph AYRES   Alexander CHISERBALE
Jane BETHERY   Carter MORRIS
William DOWEL   George H. WALKER
James M. THOMAS   Jesse OAKLEY, Maury County

Benjamin B. SMITH
Cesar TAYLOR
Jacob WALKER
Joseph F. CLOUD
Isaac MC LAYER
Daniel HUNT
Pleasant BAUGUS
Ben T. WYATT
James D. BROWN
John MC FALLS
Dudley ISOM
John GAMBRILL
John M. RAY
Pewell BAWSE
Benjamin WATTES (?)
Mosy BOSS
John EDWARDS
Phebe COOKSEY
John SHEHAN
Rickman BAKER
James NESBITT
James FREEMAN
Samuel RICHARDSON
George VINERFORD
Nancy EANCE
John EPERSON
Jonith WILLEY
James SCOTT
Eduson (?) CAMBREEL
Harberd PARRISH
Richard BATSON
Calob PARRISH
Lewis SHEHOEN
Michael GAFFORD
John ROBERTSON
Nicholas BAKER
Joseph KELLEY
Absalom ROBERTSON
E. PARRISH
John DAMELEY
W. & J. L. RAY
W. B. HADDEN
Sam LOWRANCE
Thomas PENAL
William EDWARDS
William NEAL
Jeremiah BRASSE
Mark HOLLEN
John JINKINS
Joseph ROBERTS
WHITESIDE & WILLIS
Berramin STOKES
George HICKS

William TOLLEY
Lenard HUFF
James HARNEY
John NIXON

Joshua DALE
John H. GATLIN
Jeremiah FERGERSON
E. SHELBY
James BIGHAM
Isom POWELL
Robertson HAMILTON
John CERSY
John POWELL
Tilmon GARRETT
C. STEAL
HICKS & NIX
David MAYS
Terry SATTERFIELD
E. P. CHAMBERS
Council HEDGEPATH
Charles WILLIAMS
John BROWN
William STANFIELD
Abner CANON
Thomas STERLING
George MC FALLS, Sr.
John SHEHORN
Jonathan BULLOCK
Alexander CATHEY
Moses MC AFFEE
Joshua FLY
William MC INTOSH
John CAMBLY
James ERWIN
F. S. ELLIS

James D. GRAY
John THORNBURY
Nancy BAREFOOT
Richard HARREL
William TURNAGE
T. T. GREENFIELD
Jane GOALSBY
Nathan LOFTEN
Thomas CHOAT
James O'NEAL
Jonathan HILLAMS
Moses A. WILEY
William FURGESON
Matthew NEEL
James CURRY

page 313   Noncupative will of Thomas G. BLACK by dispositions
of William BLACK and Mary HURT...his beloved wife for
her and family and at her death to be equally divided
among the heirs of her body. Signed 9 January 1824
before James L. BALDRIDGE, J.P.

page 314   Agreement made 21 November 1814 between Samuel
ATKINSON and Nancy, his wife, William H. HILL and
Sally, his wife of county of Williamson and Daniel

BROWN of county of Maury and Milly H. BROWN of county
of Williamson by her father Oliver WILLIAMS, touching
the estate of Jesse BROWN her husband lately deceased.

"Jesse BROWN, son of said Daniel BROWN of county of
Maury lately intermarried with the said Milly H.
WILLIAMS has died intestate leaving to his heirs and
next of kin his said wife and Sally HILL, wife of
said William H. HILL, and Nancy ATKINSON, wife of
said Samuel ATKINSON and Daniel BROWN, Junior, infant
son of Daniel BROWN, Senior...Oliver WILLIAMS wishes
his daughter Milly H. BROWN to retain possession of
property he (said Oliver WILLIAMS) gave her at time
of her marriage for which she relinquishes all claim
as administrator of estate of Jesse BROWN in favor of
John ATKINSON." Signed: Nancy ATKINSON; Sally HILL;
Samuel ATKINSON; William H. HILL; Daniel BROWN,Senior.
Witnesses: W. W. CUNNINGHAM, Armstead ATKINSON, John
ATKINSON, John ATKINSON, Senior. November 1814.
Milly H. BROWN signs relinquishment of administration.
20 November 1814. Witnesses: O. WILLIAMS, Wm. THOMAS.

page 316   Inventory of property of William BYNOM, deceased, by
Robert SELLARS; James SELLERS, and Luke SELLERS.
Recorded 5 March 1824.

page 317   December 7, 1820. Sale commenced agreeable to
advertisement of Jacob BOGARD, deceased, of personal
property of _____Susan BOGARD, bed and household
furniture. Buying:

Thomas TIDWELL   Thomas GOODRUM
Susanna BOGARD   William BOGARD
Archibald W. WINN   John KERR
David KINGKAID   Abraham BOGARD
William A. JOHNSON   John J. BOGARD
Robert MC DANIEL   John GARRISON
James BOGARD   George DYER
Armstead REDDING   John WILKES
Gardner GILL

page 319   List of property sold at second sale of William
BYNOM, Senior, deceased. Buying:

James TURNEY   Isaac SELLERS
Thomas GRANT   Luke SELLERS
Caleb GOOD   Richard CHAPEL
John BOOKER   James SELLERS
Chestly BYNOM   Micager PAIN
Reuben GOOD   Joseph G. KELSOE
James BYNOM   Joseph PUCKET
Robert SELLERS   Radford BUTT

By Robert SELLERS, James SELLERS, Luke SELLERS,
executors. Recorded 6 March 1824.

page 321   Inventory of estate of Jethro BROWN, deceased, by
James T. SANDFORD, administrator. 13 September 1820.
Notes On:

John BYNUM   Isaac BROOKS
William BYNUM   Abe WILSON
William CRAIG   John W. WADDE (?)

93

William JACOBS
Samuel MARTIN
Robert GOOD
Martin TONEY
John SEWELL
William HICKMAN
William WILLS
Mark BYNUM
Micajah BROOKS
James HUEY
William STEPHENS
William YANCEY
Beverly PHILLIPS
William SELLERS
Martin HARDIN
Thomas HELEY
_____ JORDAN
David W. MC KEE
William ROBERTSON
Abram OLDHAM
James WILLIS
Martin BEARD
Thomas ELLIS
George CASEY
Radford BUTT
John SHADD
John MILLS
Littleberry HAMBLET
William HARDIN
Samuel D. MC MAHAN
Thomas MAHON
Mark PIPKIN
John S. WADDLE
Julius BERTON
Thomas TRUELOVE
Green B. ROGERS
Tyre ROBERTSON
Lucretia AIKIN
Samuel CRAWFORD
James MILLS
Pleasant CREWS
_____ SPARKS
Thomas RANDAL
David HOGAN
James MILLS
David MAIZE & CRAWFORD
Tapley BINOM
Eli HOPE
Peter BIGGS
William JENKINS
William R. BRADLEY
Willie JOHNSON

Callaway HARDIN
Luke BYNUM
Veles (?) SYON
Shadrick CHANDLER
William KERR
Nancy WADE
James PORTER
Stephen BROOKS
Robert ALDERSON
Andrew WHITE
Redrick ROBERTSON
Samuel BROOKS
Jacob ROGERS
Robert PAYNE
John MILLER
Solomon HERAN
Luke MORE
William MC MAHAN
John MEES
David HAYS
Robert LOCKRIDGE
Widow HOOD
TUNN
John KENNEDY
William COOPER
Jesse OVERTON
S. SHEPHERD
Robert CAMPBELL
John HOGAN
Ezekial AIKEN
William GRIFFIN
Daniel BROWN
Robert WHITE
James T. SANDFORD
Thomas MC NEAL
Samuel POLK
William JOHNSON
Thomas SMITH
George NICHOLSON
William ROGERS
Isiah HOGAN
Anderson HOGAN
Micajah PAYNE
Aaron CUNNINGHAM
James LOCKRIDGE
Thomas GRANT
Rubin GOAD
David CAMPBELL
Green HILL
Tapley ISBY
Drewey SMITH

page 323   Sale of estate of Jethro BROWN, deceased, by James
            T. SANDFORD, administrator, on 20 and 21 November
            1818. Buyers:

Sarah BROWN
John MILLER
Josiah ALDERSON
Bryant BAUGUSS
Richard HOUSTON
John GORDON

William MC MUNN
Jacob DAMERWOOD
Luke MOORE
Esom POLK
Samuel SMITH, Jr.
Caleb HENLEY

94

William JACOBS
James H. MILLER
Julius WOODARD
Meridith HELM
William ROBERTSON
Benoni DICKEY
James WALKER
Daniel GOODRUM
Daniel CUTBIRTH
William WELLS
Watson HARDIN
Elisha HUNTER
Robert NELSON
Samuel GOODRUM
Anthony J. TURNER
Hampton TURNER
Daniel PAYNE
James HANNAH

Jacob ROGERS
William WALLACE
Bird M. TURNER
John KENNEDY
William TIMMONS
Thomas POWERS
Ezekiel AIKIN
Green PRYOR
John MILLS
James PERCELL
Stephen SHEPHERD
Thomas SMITH
Alexander MOORE
Lyttleton ABERNATHY
James LOCKRIDGE
Edward SAUNDERS
James T. BYERS
James L. TURNER

page 325   Inventory of estate of John CAMPBELL, returned to
           court the 22nd of November 1817 by Elan CAMPBELL,
           administrator.

page 326   Widow's provision for Margarett COFFEY, widow of
           Chesley COFFEY, deceased. Laid out 3 March 1818 by
           Tyree DOLLINS, William RODGERS, and William EASTHAM.

page 326   Widow's provision of Polly CHERRY, widow of Jeremiah
           CHERRY, deceased. Set out 8 May 1821, by E. W. DALE,
           John T. MOORE, W. K. HILL.

page 326   Inventory of property of James CARR, deceased, 15
           July 1820, by Uzial HAWKINS.

page 327   Inventory of estate of John CHURCHWELL, deceased.
           "Wage due him from the U. S. for six months tour."
           By Elizabeth CHURCHWELL, administratrix, and Samuel
           B. MC KNIGHT, administrator. 15 May 1815.

page 327   Inventory of estate of Moses CHAFFIN, deceased. No
           date. Recorded 9 March 1824.

page 328   Sale of Chesley COFFEY, deceased, held 9 and 10
           November 1818. Buying:

Thomas ROPER
James TURNBOW
Joseph SOWELL
Edward HOUSTON
Jacob COFFEE
John TRANTHAM (?)
John COFFEE
Josiah HARREL
Griffith NICLES
Samuel FARIS
Landon COFFEE
Vincent STORY
William KENDRICK
John CURRY
Andrew TURNBOW

Elisha OGLESBY
Reuben BRAY
Isaac TOMASON
John BROWN
Thomas BILLINGSLEY
Nathan COFFEE
Amos JOHNSTON
Franklin HUSTON
James CURRY
John HAYS
William HOGAN
Silas ALEXANDER
Joel COFFEE
Arthur B. STEPHENS

page 329   Petition for dower for Polly CHERRY, widow of
           Jeremiah CHERRY, deceased, April session, 1824 (?).
           Signed Polly CHERRY, David CRAIGHEAD, her attorney.

| page 330 | Above petition granted and jury to return to next court, third Monday in April, 1821. |

| page 330 | 8 May 1821. Jurors, William K. HILL, Edward W. DALE, John HODGE, Andrew C. HAYS, Peter CHEATHAM, John L. ALDERSON, William VOORHIES, John T. MOORE, Thomas WHITE, Peter I. WOORHIES, John C. MC LEAN, and Alexander HENDERSON laid off to Polly CHERRY her "dowrey" of land...where Jeremiah CHERRY formerly lived. |

| page 330 | Inventory of estate of Thomas COX, deceased, by A. BULLOCK. Recorded 10 March 1824. |

| page 331 | Sale of property of John CAMPBELL, deceased, by Robert CAMPBELL and Philip JINKINS, executors. Purchasers: |

Thomas YOUNG
Esom (?) S. POLK
John POLK
Robert CAMPBELL, Sr.
James GOODRUM
Armstead ALDERSON
Alexander MOORE
Silas M. CALDWELL
John P. CAMPBELL
Moses F. ROBERTS
James T. SANDFORD
Joseph BOWERS (?)
Joseph POWERS
Richard CRAGG
Leonard THOMPSON
Elijah CRAGG
Ezekial M. CAMPBELL
John H. ESTES
William MC FARLIN
Joseph CHUMNEY
Colin CAMPBELL
Abdon ALEXANDER
Barton JENKINS

Joseph LEDBETTER
Bennet BLACKMAN
Jesse RODGERS
Langford FITZJARREL
John SHINALL
Allen RAINY
Samuel BEGGS
Charles LAVENDER
Joseph H. MILLER
Abram (?) WEDGE
Josiah ALDERSON
John MOORE
Robert RANKIN
Benjamin POLK
Simon TURNER
Bryan BAUGUS
Robert ALDERSON
Major WILLIS
John BOLLING (?)
Joseph CHUMLY
Luke BYNUM
Benjamin F. ALEXANDER
William MC KEE

| page 333 | Sale of property of William WHITESIDES, deceased, 10 April 1822, by Mary WHITESIDES, administratrix. |

| page 334 | Sale of estate of Jeremiah CHERRY, deceased, taken 10 May 1821, by James T. SANDFORD, administrator. Purchasers: |

Peter R. BOOKER
Merideth HELM
Polly CHERRY
Jeremiah CHERRY
P. CHEATHAM
S. RANKIN
J. S. ALDERSON
L. HITCHCOCK
William CHERRY
William A. FLEMING
William SMITH
James COLE
Mrs. CHERRY
Levi KETCHUM

Jacob ROGERS
H. IRELAND
K. (?) CHERRY
Edward W. DALE
V. RIDLEY
Isom J. ROGERS
R. MACK
John WHITE
Notes on Patsy MAN
J. GILBRETH
John HENDERSON
P. NELSON
Rosy CHERRY
Jacob DAIMEWOOD

Aaron BURNS   Ann BURNS
W. K. HILL   William COOPER
H. B. PORTER   William CLARK
Alex HENDERSON

Family Bible sold to P. CHERRY.

page 336   Inventory of estate of Edward CALLAHAN, deceased, 29 January 1821, by Thomas G. BLACK, executor.

page 336   April 20, 1819. "I do hereby relinquish my right of claim to the administration of Thomas COX, deceased, unto my father Allen BULLOCK. Betsy COX."

page 337   Sale of David COPELAND, deceased. No date. Purchasers:

More LUMKINS   John KERR
George WEBSTER   Archer MC KANEL
James COPELAND   A. M. COPELAND
Joshua ORR   Shade DUGGER
Robert LOGAN   George DAVIDSON
Daniel DAVIS   John JONES
M. NELSON   James GOODY (?)
Thomas ADAMS   John GILL
John HATCHETT   James KERR
John AVERETT   William W. CRAIG
John COWHAN   Joseph ROYAL
William BURROW   John MILLIGAN
Jesse MORTON   John OSBURN
Thomas BROWN   David MC ALISTER
Jeremiah BOBO   John WEBB
David COPELAND   Thomas GILL
Isaac BILLS   Frank GHOLSTON
David MILLS   John BOYD
Robert GILL   Robert LOGAN
James CRAIG   James VISAGE

By David and James COPELAND, administrators.

page 338   Inventory of property of John MC GIMSEY. Notes on Phelix GRUNDY, William FLYE, John MITCHELL. " I swear that the above is a true statement of the personal property that Colonel John MC GIMSEY, deceased, possess of in this state as far as it comes within my knowledge except a few head of cattle that by brother William MC GIMSEY and myself agreed should be given to Mathew HARBISON for his kindness to our father during his last illness. Signed: J. W. P. MC GIMSEY, administrator. 3 November 1821."

page 339   Inventory of estate of Mary CLARK, 30 January 1819, by D. DOBBIN and Wm. GILCHRIST, executors.

page 339   Sale of estate of Mary CLARK by D. DOBBIN and Wm. GILCHRIST, executors.

page 340   Inventory of property of Chesley COFFEE, deceased, 19 October 1818. Note on forgy and Wm. MAXWELL; note on Nathan COFFEE; note on Thomas ROPER; by Nathan COFFEE, Margaritt COFFEE, Landon COFFEE.

page 341   Apportionment for Margarett COFFEE, widow of Chesley
            COFFEE, deceased, by Tyree DOLLINS; William RODGERS;
            Wm. EASTHAM, this 3rd November 1818.

page 341   1 February 1822 - laid off for Widdow WHITESIDES...
            by Samuel MC CLENAHAN, Johnathan WHITESIDE, and Sam'l.
            WHITESIDE.

page 341   Inventory of property of Micajah DARK, deceased,
            16 October 1820, by Rebecca X DARK.

page 341   Sale of property of John DICKSON, deceased, 16 Nov-
            ember 1819. Purchasers:

James MITCHELL	John AUSTIN
Jas. JOHNSON	Robert MARTIN
Davis LISSLES	John MARTIN
Thomas DIXON	Jonathan BELEW
John BARLEY (?)	R. C. DICKSON
Wm. AKIN	Wm. WILLIAMS
Thos. NEELY	John HILL
Sterling TUCKER	William GOODJOIN
John GORDON	Elizabeth DICKSON
Stephen COOPER	Alex PICKARD
Wm. CURTIS	James ISOM
James BURKET	Philip PENN
A. T. CRISP	Robert NEELY
Solomon HOGUE	Alex BARNES
Samuel COWAN	Samuel COOPER
David HUGHES	Joshua HODGES
Jas. DICKSON	Jas. MC GOWIN
Jas. JONES	Ewd. COSTLOE
A. T. ISOM	Wm. CURTS
George KING	William PICKARD
Dudley ISOM	John CARTER
Wm. BRIANT	Sally HODGES
Wm. BURKET	Jas. STOCKARD

            by Robert C. DIXON, administrator.

page 344   Inventory of property of John DIXON, deceased..."10
            acres of standing corn in Lauderdale County, Alabama
            state"; notes on Joshua HODGES; John DAGBY; William
            CRISP; William BURNS; Nathaniel ROGERS. No date.
            By Robert C. DIXON, administrator.

page 345   Inventory of estate of George DIXON, deceased. (Bonds
            dated from November 1819 to April 1, 1823); by Thomas
            DIXON and Adam DIXON, executors.

page 346   Sale of property of Hor. DEPRIEST, Columbia, 16 Sep-
            tember 1820. Purchasers:

            SIMPSON & ROBERTS & HARRIS
            Loranso HITCHCOK & John JOHNSON
            Saml. MORGAN & John FARNEY
            Peter R. BOOKER
            James C. CRAIG & Edward B. LITTLEFIELD
            Robert L. COBBS & R. D. HARRIS
            Allen BROWN & B. PRINCE
            Thomas NORTON, J. GUEST, & Alex HENDERSON
            P. J. VOORHIES & Thomas NORTON

Jno. C. MC KAIN & Joseph _____
M. CARUTHERS & James WALKER
Robert MACK & Hugh B. PORTER
Samuel & P. CHEATHAM
A. BROWN & Alex HENDERSON
M. HELM & James PURSELL
Robin D. HARRIS & John Coffee
Jas. COE & Edward W. DALE

page 347   Widow's provision for Eliza G. DEPRIEST, widow of
            Horatio DEPRIEST, 15 September 1821, by John BROWN
            and James WALKER.

page 347   Inventory of Gilbreath DAVIDSON, deceased. Note on
            John E. DAVIDSON, due 1 January 1823. Note on Amis
            QUIN, due 28 December 1819.

page 348   25 December 1819. Inventory of estate of George
            DIXON, deceased, by John FARNEY; Henry TURNEY, and
            John SMISER.

page 349   Sale of Joseph DYAL, 15 February 1819. Purchasers:

            Joseph SEWELL   John TOMBS
            James COLE   John JONES
            Elizabeth DYAL (bought most of household furniture)

            by James DYAL, administrator.

page 349   Petition of Elizabeth DIAL, showing that in "1819
            Joseph DIAL of this county, husband of petitioner,
            departed this life possessed of 75 acres of land
            situate and lying in the county aforesaid on the
            waters of Fountain Creek bounded on the north by the
            land of Brackey DAVIDSON, on the south by the land
            of William _____, on the east by the land of
            Andrew KERR, and on the west by the land of WEEMES
            and THORNTON."....requests dower be laid off.
            Signed: Elizabeth X DIAL.

page 350   Division of negroes, lands, etc., in hands of Davis
            GURLEY, administrator, to estate of Thomas EDWARDS,
            deceased, "giving two thirds to him the only child
            of said deceased and one-third to said administrator."
            Divided as follows:

            Lot No. 1 drawn by said child
            Lot No. 3 drawn by Anne, the child...

            18 January 1820, by John MATTHEWS, Samuel GRIFFITH.

page 351   Additional inventory of estate of John ASKEW,
            deceased; rent of the lease sold to Thomas STREPLIN
            for the year 1818...18 October 1819, by Zephania
            NUNN, administrator.

page 351   List of negroes belonging to estate of L. B. ESTES,
            deceased, 28 December 1816, by L. (?) A. ESTES, D.
            MARTIN.

page 352   Inventory of property of Andrew FORGEY, deceased,
            21 October 1820.

page 351   No date. "Petition of Saly FREELAND respectfully shows that James FREELAND, her late husband, has not long since departed this life." Request her dower, Sally FREELAND by her attorney J. W. EGNEW.

page 353   Court orders Sally FREELAND's dower laid off as per application "of Sarah FREELAND for her dower of the estate of James FREELAND, that the heir of James FREELAND are all of lawfull age...." William HOLT, Alexander GILLASPIE, and Phillip ANTHONY appointed to divide the real estate of James FREELAND, deceased. No date.

page 353   Accounts of estate of Moses G. FRIERSON, 1814 - 1819. Persons named:

Sam'l FRIERSON	CRAIG & WASHINGTON
Samuel CRAIG	Robert FOSTER
Doctor D. N. SANSOM	David FRIERSON
Doctor Sam'l MAYS	John MC KEAN
Mr. ALDERSON	Nimrod PORTER
Wm. HENDERSON	Wm. MC FALL
CAMPBELL	A. BROWN
James R. PLUMMER	Wm. BRADSHAW
James C. O'RILEY	Patrick MAGUIRE
Benoni DICKEY	Elias FRIERSON
James WALKER	Samuel MC DOWELL
United States Tax, 1812	Edward H. CHAFFIN
Samuel H. WILLIAMSON	

28 April 1820, by George JOHNSTON, Sam'l MC DOWELL, administrators.

page 355   Inventory of personal property of James FREELAND, deceased, by Sally FREELAND, executrix; notes in hands of Joseph GIBSON; note of Demsey HUBBARD; E. PUCKETT by James FREELAND and Sally FREELAND. No date.

page 356   Sale of property of Andrew FITZPATRICK, deceased, sold on 15 June 1822. Buying: Selah FITZPATRICK, Littleton VAUGHAN, Stephen EDWARDS, Morgan FITZ-PATRICK; Selah FITZPATRICK bought most of the items.

page 357   Thomas STEPHENSON, James DOBBIN, and Samuel WITHER-SPOON appraised estate of Moses G. FRIERSON, deceased, and apportioned 1/8 part of the personal estate of William ARMSTRONG. 18 January 1819.

page 357   Inventory of estate of Robert FARIS by Moses ROBINSON.

page 358   No heading. Property settlement of estate of Moses G. FRIERSON, deceased. Accounts for 1819. By cash due, James M. FRIERSON; cash paid Rev. James W. STEPHENSON for ministerial services; _____ cash paid Wm. N. FRIERSON; cash paid the following: William D. FRIERSON, Ed. L. FRIERSON, COHEA, John HODGE, John BLACKBURN, Elias J. ARMSTRONG, Samuel BOWDERY, Mr. RICHARDSON, Elisha UZZELL for Wilson's wool hat, MC NEIL and MOORE, Mary T. FRIERSON, Thomas T. FLEMING for Davis schooling, Edward H. CHAFFIN, Caleb LANGLEY and Com., Joseph PORTER,

LEWNY and GRAVES, Elizabeth STEPHENSON, Thomas J.
FRIERSON, Patrick MAGUIRE, James R. PLUMMER, HITCHCOCK,
shoes for mother, John FINDLEY, Sam ROGERS for
teaching school, Samuel H. SMITH, John E. STEPHENSON,
Mr. CLICE, Hugh SHAW, Thomas YEATMAN; cash paid James
M. FRIERSON, his part of the money coming from the
estate of Moses G. FRIERSON. Henry E. TURNEY.

page 360   Inventory of estate of John A. FARIS, deceased: note
             on William HEMPHILL and Jacob GRAY; note on Moses
             ECHOLS; note on E. MILLER dated 25 October 1816;
             receipt on John KENDRICK for note on John G. PERRY;
             by John T. FRIERSON, administrator.

page 360   Inventory of estate of George FRIERSON, deceased,
             made 24 July 1820.

page 361   Inventory of estate of Andrew FITZPATRICK, deceased,
             22 April 1822, by Lelah (Selah) FITZPATRICK, admin-
             istrator. (Note: her name was Celia FITZPATRICK.)

page 361   Accounts of estate of Samuel FRIERSON. Paid out,
             years 1816 - 1817. Persons named:

             John WILLIAMS   Edward _____
             Thomas STEPHENSON   George DICKEY
             Doctor N. SANSOM   John BRADLEY
             Dr. O'RILEY   John C. MC CEAN
             John MC EAN   HICKES
             John T. MOORE   MC NEAL
             Allen BROWN   Caleb LANGLEY
             William G. ARMSTRONG   Edward B. LITTLEFIELD
             PORTER   James WALKER
             Mrs. PASETON   William BRADSHAW
             GOODMAN   Sam'l WEATHERSPOON
             James LEWIS   Robert DAVIDSON
             WHITE   Perry COHEA
             KELLY   John D. FLEMING
             FULTON & CROCKET   B. DICKEY
             David LEECH   Edward REESE (?)
             Margaret SAMPLE   Robert SMITH
             John GILL   Mrs. MC FALL
             MC GUIRE   John JONES
             Samuel CRAIG   JOHNSON
             UZELL   Elias FRIERSON
             Mother's expenses to Carolina and back again
             Alexander DOLLIN (for teaching music)
             Mary FRIERSON (for making Vincent's coat)

             Received; persons named:

             James T. SANDFORD   Paul FULTON
             James BIGHAM   John W. STEPHENSON
             Aron LANCASTER   James BIFLE

page 364   Year's provision for Charlett FARES, widow of Robert
             FARIS, deceased, 10 November 1821, by Will CATHEY,
             Geore OLIPHANT, Benjamin ROBERSON.

page 365   List of articles sold at sale of property of James
             FREELAND, deceased, by the administrators, James D.
             FREELAND and Sally FREELAND, widow of the deceased.
             No date.

page 365   Widow's provision for Elenor FORGEY, late widow of
            Andrew FORGEY, deceased, 11 November 1820, by V.
            RIDLEY, John MACK, Wm. PERRY, and Wm. A. MAXWELL.

page 366   "With James Madison FRIERSON Cr", accounts paid out
            1818. Persons named other than in above records:
            John HODGE, J. B. HARRISON, Edward DALE, S. (?) B.
            HARDIN, Kessiah FRIERSON, Richard JONES, William
            DEVERS, William NICHOLS, John LAYMASTER, Sam MC DOWELL,
            Mr. SHEROD, Mr. LONG, Thomas KELSOE, William LITTLE-
            FIELD, Mrs. WALKER.

page 368   Dr. estate of Samuel FRIERSON, 1818. Named: William
            JAGGERS, William NICHOLS, Rev. Duncan BROWN, William
            FRIERSON, James Madison FRIERSON for balance due him.

page 368   Inventory of estate of Joshua FRIERSON, deceased,
            made 8 August 1817 by William FRIERSON, Samuel MAYES,
            John FRIERSON.

page 369   Division of estate of George FRIERSON, deceased,
            between widow and her six children: to widow Mada
            A. FRIERSON and her two children Madison Squire and
            Mary - $3,093.25; to Kiziah SMITH - $925; to John
            MANTON - $1,141; to Eliza GAMBELL - $1,004; to
            Rebecah - $1,055. By Nathaniel WILLIS, Samuel MAYES,
            John FRIERSON, James ARMSTRONG, 28 January 1822.

page 370   "I relinquish my right to the administration of the
            estate of Andrew FORGEY, deceased, and pray that
            your honours would appoint Hugh FORGEY and Simpson
            PERRY, given under my hand this 21st day of October
            1820. Ellen X. FORGEY."

page 371   Sale of property of Andrew FORGEY, deceased, on 22
            November 1820. Buyers:

            Elenor FORGEY   John EDDLEMAN
            Polly FORGEY   Stephen SMITH
            Abner MATTHEWS   Andrew CARADIN
            Isaac J. THOMAS   Wm. L. MC KEE
            John MATTHEWS   John GOODMAN
            John MACK   Nancy FORGEY
            Samuel SCOTT   Pleasant JONES
            Joseph KENKINDE   John FORGEY
            Franklin R.(?) HOUSTON   Alexander OSBORN
            James FORGY   William PERRY
            Hugh FORGEY   James GUNN
            John M. JONES   Alexander L. HARRIS
            Abner OSBURN   James STOCKARD
            George W. JOHNSTON   James BOYD
            John RENFROW   Andrew BOYD

page 373   Inventory of property of Allen HAWKINS, deceased,
            12 January 1821.

page 373   Inventory of estate of Grant HAWKINS, deceased,
            taken 11 September 1815. One discharge for six
            months under the command of Major General Andrew
            JACKSON in Captain JACKSON's company, by William
            HAWKINS, administrator.

page 374   James HAMBLET, et al, vs. William YANCY, administrator - ordered that William COOPER, Jesse ROSS, Anthony
J. TURNER, James T. SANDFORD, and Swan HARDIN make
division of negroes between the heirs of Littleberry
HAMLETT, deceased, and return 3rd Monday in October
1818.

Division follows: James O'NEAL, lot no. 1; Berryman
HAMBLET, lot no. 2; Martha HAMBLET, lot no. 3;
William HAMBLET, lot no. 4; Thibble (Also Thibblety)
T. HUGHES, lot no. 5; James G. HAMBLET, lot no. 6.

page 375   Sale of property of William HAWKINS, deceased.
Purchasers:

Mary HAWKINS	Joseph CHOTE
Joshua NEWMAN	Reason L. BISHOP
John BRADSHAW	John BULLOCK
John CATHEY	Thos. SHELBY
William F. SCOTT	Nancy HOLLIS
Edward WILLIAMS	Seth HAWKINS
James ROBINSON	Elenor GATTEN
Daniel FORGUSON	Stephen HAWKINS
William HAWKINS	Hugh COWDEN
Leah FUGERSON	John COOKE
Thomas MC FALLS	Gideon STRICKLIN

9 December 1814, Mary and William HAWKINS, administrators.

page 377   Inventory of estate of Littleberry HAMBLET, deceased,
taken 20 December 1817, William YANCY, administrator.

page 378   Inventory of estate of Alexander HENDERSON, deceased,
taken 3 January 1822.

page 379   Inventory of estate of John HUCKABY, deceased, 2
October 1820. Accounts on:

Thos. YOUNG	Ephraigm BROWN
William TATE	Robert CAMPBELL
James BYERS	Nathan SIMON
Willie JOHNSON	John BLANTON
Joseph POWER	David LUCKEY
Barlett JINKINS	Burrell JOHNSON
John JENKINS	William LENE (LOVE)

page 380   Sale of property of Alexander HENDERSON, deceased,
made by E. W. DALE, administrator, 15 February 1822.

page 382   Inventory of estate of Uzzell HAWKINS, deceased,
taken by John SKIPPER 13 January 1821. Notes on
Samuel STRICKLIN, Senior; Francis WILLIS; E. DENHAM;
James L. (or S.) ROBISON.

page 383   Inventory of property of Alexd HENDERSON, deceased,
taken February 1822 by E. W. DALE, administrator.
Accounts found on books of Alexander HENDERSON:
James GULLET; Buford TURNER; Miss BITTLEMAN; John
LONGLEY; Joshua GUEST; E. P. OGLIVIE; Mr. KELSOE;
Bohan MARTIN; Henry GIPSON; David CAPBELL, James JOE;
Lewis JOHNSON; David JARROTT; Andrew HENDERSON;
William WALLIS; Lott FURGISON; JONES; W. TAYLOR;

Alexd LAIRD; George CAMPBELL; Jeremiah CHERRY; Elisha
UZZELL; Miss Ann BURNS; James WALKER; David CRAIGHEAD;
Joel B. SMITH; Jesse LEFTWICH; John W. LEMASTER;
Perry COHEA; Pleasant NELSON; James DOBBINS; J. B.
PORTER; Henry INLAND.

page 384 Inventory of estate of Rebecca HAMILTON, deceased,
by John C. HAMILTON, administrator; her life estate
in a negro boy Ishmael in the hands of William GILL
for whom there is a suit now pending, October term,
1820.

page 385 Inventory of property of James HAYS, deceased, by
John and Davis KILCREASE. Notes on:

John GORDON	David FORTNER
William KILCREASE	John WITT
Thomas CALDWELL	Marquis HOLLAND
Norman MC CLOUD	

Buyers at sale:

Willie SCOTT	Richard J. LOCKE
John KILCREASE	William ALLEN
William CALDWELL	Andrew MILLS
Jacob DAMEWOOD	the widow
Richard T. COCK	John BUTLER
Abner RHODES	Davis KILCREASE
James RANKIN	John BAUGUS
William KILCREASE	Thomas YOUNG
George NEWTON	Rubin SMITH
Richard SCOTT	John WITT

page 387 Apportionment for widow and children of James HAYS,
4 May 1822, by William KILCREASE, Jesse OVERTON,
Nathaniel LUNMAN (?).

page 387 Inventory. No name, no date. Note on Abraham
LOONEY, due 27 May 1823; Note on Robert CARUTHERS,
due 21 December 1820; note on James BALDRIDGE; two
due bills on David MARTIN; note on DOUGHERTY and
LONGLEY.

page 388 Sale of property of Allen HAWKINS, sold on 9 February
1821. Buyers:

Widow	Joseph JOINES
James JOSEY	John GRIMES
John ALDERSON	_____ GREENFIELD
William GORDON	John SKIPPER
Griffeth CATHEY	Andrew LETSINGER
William ERWIN	James FRIERSON
James LETSINGER	John KENDRICK
Charles SOWELL	William HAWKINS
Thomas B. MALONE	Joel ALEXANDER
Stephen HAWKINS	Joshua NEWMAN

Plantation rented to Samuel A. BAKER; signed: Hetty
HAWKINS and Joseph JOINES, administrators.

page 389 Widow's provision for Sophia HUCKABY, late widow of
John HUCKABY; 23 November 1820, by Willis WILLEFORD;
John D. BLANTON; William BUYERS.

page 389   Memorandum of goods and effects of William HOLDRIDGE, deceased. Accounts on John LITTLEFIELD; information of E. B. LITTLEFIELD and H. E. TURNER. 28 January 1822. Signed: Patrick MAGUIRE.

page 390   Additional inventory of estate of Benjamin HERNDON, deceased, by Joseph HERNDON, administrator; hire of negroes for year 1819.

page 390   Inventory of property of Enos HOLLAND, deceased, taken 17 May 1817 by John JOHNSON, administrator.

page 390   Inventory of the sale of Archibald HIGHT, deceased, by Richard B. HIGHT; buyers: Richard B. HIGHT, Robert HIGHT, Christian SHIRES, Sion HIGHT, William HIGHT, E. WILLICE, Michael ROBERTSON.

page 390   Sale of estate of David HINES, deceased, sold 27 November 1819 (?). Buyers:

John SELLERS	Benton BADGETT
John BOOKER	David MARTIN
Mark PIPKIN	Swan HARDIN
Joseph SANDFORD	Abner PARTEE
Thomas SUTHERLAND	Daniel PAINE
John GURLEY	Hardin TONEY
Samuel RUSH	Hez BROOKS

page 391   Inventory of property of Jeremiah HAMRICK at his decease on 21 March 1808, by Travas X HAMBRICK and Yelavan HAMRICK, administrators.

page 392   Inventory of personal property of Jesse HAYES, deceased, 17 March 1808.

page 392   Account of sales of James _____, deceased. No date. Buyers:

Wm. KING	Lewis JAMES (JOINES)
Prettyman DYE	Jesse THERMON
Blaxtin HARDIN	Jno. LORANCE
Wm. SHIELDS	Peter YOUNG
Robert CALVERT	William ALLEN
Andrew HAYES	James DUNCAN

page 393   Sale of John HAWKINS, deceased, 8 February 1821, by Edward BLACKBURN, administrator. Buyers:

Mrs. HAWKINS	John GILL
James M. FRIERSON	George HOGUE
Robert G. KELSEY	Uzzell HAWKINS
Samuel G. BRIGGS	William KIRK
Hugh DOUGLAS	Henry TURNEY
John ALEXANDER	John LAWDER
William HAWKINS	John J. BRIGGS
John BULLACK, Senior	Thomas KELSEY
John WALKER	Griffin WALKER
Edward MC FADDEN	George NICHOLS

"balance due John HAWKINS of his father's estate."

page 396   Account of sale of Duncan HILL, sold 20 May 1819.
            Buyers:

            Richard HILL   James BOONE
            Simson MARSH   Jeremiah GANT
            James VINCENT   Thomas GRANT
            Patsey HILL   Damon COALLMAN
            Robert HILL   Damon COLLENS (?)
            John WEAVER

            By Rd HILL, administrator.

page 397   Sale of Benjamin HAY, deceased, 7 July 1819 (?).
            Buyers:

            Sary HAY   Silas TOMPKINS
            George SWILLIVAN (?)   Robert HUNNELS

            List of perishable property belonging to Benj. HAY
            sold 6 February 1819 at Doctor TURNER's mill. Buyers:
            John PILLOW and William PILLOW.

page 398   Inventory of property of Benjamin HAY, deceased,
            18 January 1819, by Silas TOMPKINS, administrator.

page 398   Widow's provision for Sally HAY, widow of Benjamin
            HAY, deceased, for herself and four children; by
            John ALEXANDER, Jesse S. (?) ROSS, Henry E. TURNEY.

page 398   Sale of Uzzell HAWKINS, deceased, sold on 6 February
            1821. Buyers:

            James HAWEKENSON (?)   Alexander P. DENHAM
            Uzzell HAWKINS   A. J. ISOM
            Widow   Andrew WILEY
            William HINES   Samuel DAVIS
            Andrew BLAIR   John SKIPPER
            Noah JOINE   Jeney HAWKINS
            Squire CATHEY   Thomas KENDRICK
            Edward MCFADDEN   Abrayham WHITESIDES
            Daniel CHITHER (?)   Griffeth CATHEY
            Robert MALONE   Ezra C. BRISTE (?)
            James HICKMAN   Avanant B. (R.?) ENGLAND
            Alexander ERWIN   John POOL
            Polly HAWKINS

            By John SKIPPER, administrator.

page 402   Account books of Isaac B. HARDIN, deceased; persons
            name in Book A:

            Joseph C. MC DOWELL   Michael SANDS
            Elijah ROBERT   Thomas BROWN
            John M. GOODLOE   James D. MC CAIN
            Squire HUNT   John HENERY
            John MONTGOMERY   Robert O. DABNEY
            Joel REESE   John PAULEY
            Mark E. PIPKIN   Alexander MC CALLOW
            Nathan T. (or L.) SMITH John FITZPATRICK
            Jacob MC GHEE   William NORTON
            Silas M. CALDWELL   Robert MACK
                    CATHEY   Elizabeth OGLIVIE

Samuel OVERTON
Benjamin H. LEWIS
L. B. BOYD
Daniel LEATHERMAN
James WHITSON
Squire MC DOWELL
Temperance CATCHER
Andrew NEELY
David FRIERSON
Salam RASDALE
Samuel BROOKS
Park BROWN
Ann BURNS
Edward DUNN
Joseph SANDFORD
David & Sam CAMPBELL
Lasting POWEL
Carey NEWSON
Jethro JOINES
John LOFTAND

Abner PILLOW
Elijah PUCKET
Thomas James FRIERSON
Thomas PHELPS
William DAVIS
Agner HERYTON
DAUGHTERTY & LONGLY
Alphra ONEAL
Thomas WORTHAM
Merideth WEBB
Nancy ONEEL
Drusilla ABERNATHEY
John T. WHITE
Lewis DILLAHUNTY
Jeremiah SKELTON
Jeremiah CHERRY, Senior
James H. WILLIAMS
David SHANNON
John SIMS
Edom LOVE
Daniel DAVIS

Book B:

John GORDON, Esquire
Hugh SHAW
Jesse REEVES
Samuel LAWRENCE
William HALCOLM
John SHELTON
Jonathan WEBSTER
William ROPER
John C. DAVIDSON
Alexander HENDERSON
Charles U. BROWN
James BRANCH
Tilman A. CRISP
David GILLASPIE
John BITTLEMAN
Joseph HACKNEY
Amus JOHNSTON
Samuel S. ROGERS
James BARNS
Benjamin DOWEL
Samuel E. FRIERSON
Jeremiah FERGUSON
Edward HUDSON
William KIRK
David W. MCREE
Charles R. DILLEN
Samuel STRANLES (?)
James H. REECE
George TATE
James BLACKBURN
Zacheriah DOCKERY
Joseph GILMORE
A. B. MAYFIELD
Andrew B. HUDSON
Duncan MC INTYRE
Miner C. M. WILKS
Rolan CHAFFIN
John ONEAL
Reace B. PORTER

John D. RAMSEY
John LUCAS
George DAVIDSON
Edward WILLIAMS
Thomas GILL
Curtis WOOD
John SHADDEN
Wm. BRADSHAW
Mathis S. STEPHENSON
John ELLIOTT
Alexander GILLASPIE
Richard S. COCKE
Redding COUNCE
Joseph HART
John AYDLEMAN
Joshua GLOVER
John S. ALDERSON
Brittan S. (or J.) BAUCUM
William BROWN, Junior
David
Joseph HORTON
Joseph HERNDON
John W. LEMASTER
William ROGERS
Ebenezer SMITH
George COCKBURN
George DICKEY
James D. FREELAND
Gardner GILL
George HANCOCK
James LAIN
Samuel MC DOWEL, Va.
James REECE
Samuel STRICKLIN
Ezekial MOBLEY
Alexander CASTER
Reubin O. CARTER
George M. DICKEY
Henry GIPSON

Thomas C. FARIAS	Paul FULTON
James ONEEL	Samuel STRICKLAND
John RICHARDSON, Senior	William L. WILLEFORD
Peter S.(J) VOORHIES	Alexander MACKEY
Joseph H. MCEAUING	William JOHNSTON
James C. ORILEY	John HUNTER, Senior
Samuel RANKINS	Ephriagm E. MC CAIN
James White	James M. PARKER
James G. HAMLET	Shelby POLK
Abner JOHNSTON	Joseph B. PORTER
Henry TURNEY	A. O. HARRIS
Burrell CANNON	William MC NEEL
David CRAIGHEAD	Charles M. PARTEE
Solomon SHELTON	Tennessee ROPER
James OVERSTREET	John DAGLEY
Wm. H. STEPHENSON	Peter HOLLAND
Isom JACKSON	William SMITH
William CRAIG	Joseph SAUNDERS
Robert TATE	Moses TURNER
Seth BARNES	Thomas H. HOPKINS
Moses WHITE	William WEBB
Samuel SMITH	Aron SMITH
Augustin BROWN	Lewis DAVIS
John CARUTHERS	James RANKINS
Joseph CRENSHAW	James GULLET
Andrew H. GOFORTH	Pleasant NELSON
Merideth HELMS	David (Dosil?) SANDSOM
John HODGE	James BLACKMAN
John RICHARDSON, Junior	Kenneth CHERRY
William ROGERS	George SMITH
Arthur BEASLEY	John COOPER
Reubin DOWEL	Jesse THURMAN
Edward ENGLISH	William W. WOODS
Levi FERRIL	Thomas WHITE
Sarah HERNDON	Perry COHEA
Hall GERMAN	Joseph ALDERSON
William L. LEWIS	Thomas P. WINN
Andrew CARTEY	William VOORHIES
James SHELTON	Joseph YOUNG
William MC MINN	George CAMPBELL
Joseph MALCOMB	William T. LEWIS
Thomas H. KELSO	Henry PAYTON
John DAVIS	Jeremiah RANKINS
William GILMORE	Nathaniel WILLIS
Richard HART, Junior	Joseph PORTER
Robert TORSEL (?)	John BRANCH
John WATTS	Joseph COC (COE ?)
John RIGHT	Jeremiah CHERRY, Junior
Robert S. NELSON (J.?)	Joel MC KEE
John PORTER	Swan HARDIN
Malakiah PAMENTA	James ROBERSON
Ward S. WALLACE	A. C. HAYS
Patsey HAMBLET	Mary ROBERTS
John SMITH	Miner L. WILKS
Joseph BROWN, Sr.	George M. EGNEW
John MC KISICK	William LOVING
Richard ALLEN	Wilson WHITE
Henery E. TURNER	John WHITE
Benjamin THOMPSON	Reubbin BRAY
Westley WEATHERSPOON	John HATCHETT
James S. WALKER	Horacy COOPER
Joseph SHAW	Calvin SMITH
Thomas WALKER	Vincent PILLOW

Simon JOHNSTON
James H. BYRES
James R. DUN
David WEATHERSPOON
John WILLIAMS
Loreson HITCHCOCK
William MAXWELL
David WEAR
Edward H. CHAFFIN VC
Joseph DAVIS
Edwd DALE
Ely BYNUM
John CROSSWAIT
Richard HUSON
William C. HILL
Late FERGUSON
Joshua GUEST
Horatio DEPRIEST
James EDMINSTON

John M. FALLS
Samuel HERSTON
Robert CHAMP
Bird M. TURNER
Joseph HAMILTON
William RENFRO
James HOLLAND
John SIMPSON
James C. CRAIG
Henry SMITH
Barnett SATTEY
Mathias MARFIELD
Henry A. WILLIAMS
William DAVIS
David RUSSEL
John LINDSAY
Edward B. LITTLEFIELD
John W. BEASLEY
Alex M. WILLIAMS

page 406   Book R

Mark R. ROBERTS
Elisah SMITH
William POPE
James MC CANICO
Peggy RANDALE
Thomas SHELBEY
James STOCKARD, Senior
Nancy SANDERSON
Stephen RICE
William GOFORTH
Moses CHAFFIN
William POE (JOE?)
Elijah P. CHAMBERS
John BRADEN
Ephrem E. DAVIDSON
Samuel ELSWORTH
Joseph LAMASTER
Jeremiah TOBE (JOBE)
William PARKES
Jacob FRANCISCO
George GLASSCOCK
Moses RANKINS
William W. MORGAN
Alpha KINGSLEY
Noah LINGARD

George MITCHELL
Alexander LAND
Tammey STEPHENSON
David COPELAND
Moses HANKS
Blakey PETER
Stephen AKINS
George UMPH
James N. FLANIKIN
Adam KLICE
David CRAIG
Tapley BYNUM
Benjamin DAVIS
William M. CRAIG
William HANKS
Morgan BROWN
Bradshaw PHILE
Joseph ERWIN
Robert CAMPBELL
Nancy COOPER
Labram MC CARDEY (?)
Thomas NEELEY
William ALLEN
James R. PLUMMER

List of Notes:

Peter R. BOOKER
Joseph DAVIS
James COPLAND
John PEOBY (?)
Reubin O. CARTER
William BIRNUM
Perry COHEA
Richard J. COCKE
Richard C. HARRIS
Henry GIPSON
Joseph HACKNEY
William JOHNSON
George HANCOCK

Joshua GUEST
Gideon JOHNSTON
Benjamin HERNDON
David A. MILLS
Solomon P. MAXWELL
Isaac NEELLEY
J. B. MAYFIELD
Thompson PASETON
Abner PILLOW
Ezekiah MABBEY (MOBLEY)
James M. LEWIS
John TERRY
Abijah REDDING

Thomas RAMSEY	Nathaniel WILLIS
James (Ames) RICHARDSON	Bartel ESTES
Jeremiah CHERRY, Junior	John BAUCOMBE
George CAMPBELL	Mark EDWARDS
J. DOUGHERTY	Samuel BROOKS
John E. DAVIDSON	George DICKEY
George M. DICKEY	John DAVIS
Luke BYNUM	William DUNN acct.
James EDMINSON	E. P. CHAMBERS
John DICKEY	Edward HUDSON
John GORDON	Peter HOLLAND
Flanicin J. ROGERS	John HATCETT
Samuel FRIERSON	Richard HUGHSTON
Richard GUIN	John GRAVES
David MC COTISTER	James G. HAMBLET
Ireny JOHNSTON	Davis GURLEY
Meredith HELM	Gardner GILL
Joseph LAID	James PURSELE
Thisk PREWETT	David LOVE
Malikiah POMENTOR	Duncan MC INTYRE
Henry MILLER	John MAGILL
Thomas B. MALONE	Andrew MC CARTY
Robert PEARSELE	James ONEEL
Jehosiphat LADD	Edmand MAY
John MONTGOMERY	A. RODDEN
John T. STRONG	Buford TURNER
Henry E. TURNER	William SKELTON
Wm. M. THOMPSON	Samuel W. STAMLER
Jasper R. SUTTON	(or STRAMLER)

Officers report:

Robert MACK	Allen C. GATES
William P. EDDS	William WHITE
Benjamin HARDIN	William A. JOHNSTON
Thomas MC DONALD	Davis GARO

Cotton receipts: to Samuel B. MC NIGHT and T. P. MC NIGHT. C. M. SMITH states that the great part of the above cotton receipts are settled. "Given under our hands thirty July 1819. Its my opinion that money of the above accounts and notes never can be collected." No signatures or names.

page 408   Inventory of personal property of Swan B. HARDIN.

page 409   Account of sale of estate of Littleberry HAMLET, deceased, taken 8 January 1818. Evidently shoemaker. Names mentioned:

Col. Charles PARTEE	Robert WILLIAMS
Andrew RUSH	Major James G. HAMBLETT
Green WILLIAMSON	William RODGERS
Kibble T. HUGHS	Capt. James MC CLEAN (?)
George CAMPBELL	Shelby POLK
Samuel MC DOWELL	Watson HOWARD
Callaway HARDIN	Col. Samuel CRAWFORD
Jasper SUTTON, Esquire	Gardner GILL
Samuel FRIERSON	William YANCY
John BOOKER	Samuel BARSH (?)
Joshua GUEST	Mark PIPKIN
Mrs. Robert GOAD	Merideth HELM
Wm. WILLIAMS	Greenberry ROGERS

William SELLERS   Isaac SELLERS
John MILLS   Joseph ALDERSON
John SHERRALL

By William YANCY, administrator.

page 412   Inventory of estate of Thomas H. JENKINS, deceased, taken 9 May 1817. By Philip JENKINS, administrator.

page 413   Sale of William A. JOHNSON, deceased, by Andrew MC CASLIN and Abner JOHNSON. No date.

page 414   Account of sale of John JOHNSON, deceased. Buyers:

Joseph JOHNSON	Ed MOORE
Micajah DAVIS	William PILLOW
Mark HARDIN	James PURSELL
Wm. WILLIAMS	John SPENSER
Jacob DAMEWOOD	William DUNN
John MONTGOMERY	Jno. SMITH
John LOWDER	Perry COHEA
M. C. DAVIS	James HUEY
A. SMITH	William JOHNSON
James C. O'RILEY	D. OGLOVIE
Charles PARTEE	Davis CAMPBELL
Powell HALE	Elijah JOHNSON
Samuel HAYS	Joseph C. MC DOWELL
Dalency WAID	Jno. GORDON
Elijah JOHNSTON	Jno. ERWIN
David GLENN	Elisha UZZELL
Thomas ERWIN	Wm. P. CRAWFORD
John BICKERSTAFF	Peter CHEATHAM
L. B. ESTES	Callaway HARDIN
Isabella JOHNSON	Cades JOHNSON

By Jas. HENDERSON, Joseph JOHNSON, and JOHN MONT-
GOMERY, executors of John JOHNSON, deceased.

page 417   Jonathan WEBSTER, guardian's account with Miss Roxny (?) JOSEA. Accounts dated 1815 - 1816.

page 417   Additional inventory of estate of James JOHNSON, deceased: note on Isham JOHNSON, Junior; 31 July 1819 (or 1817) by Wm. RUSSELL, administrator.

page 418   Amount of sales of Jones KENDRICK, deceased, by Olsamus KENDRICK, administrator. No date. Buyers:

Hosea JAMESON	Solomon TUTTLE
Jones KENDRICK	William CRAIG
Wm. EMERSON	Midly (?) HESTER
Jesse EVANS	John ELLIOTT
Robert JOHNSON	Wm. ALLEN
Margt. KENDRICK	George FOSTER
Abner PREWETT	Betsey ALLEN
Olsimus KENDRICK	John GHOLSON
Jas. ORR	Lemuel PREWETT
Milly KENDRICK	

page 419   Sale of James KERR, deceased, sold on 3 August 1820. Buyers:

Ezekiel HAWKINS   John SKIPPER

Griffeth CATHEY   John KENDRICK
Jas. HINES   Eli LOVE
Alex. P. DENHAM   Uzial HAWKINS
A. T. ISOM   Benjamin ROBERTSON
William GARNER   And. CANEDY
Easter WEST   Arthur ISAM
George HOGUE

page 420   Inventory of Robert NEELY, deceased, 19 June 1811.
             Notes on:

John GILMORE   Henry BRANCH
Robert BROWN   Joshua DIAL
John NEELY   LATA
Thomas AYDELOTT   William ROGERS
William WINN   Thomas HEDGEPATH

Money due the estate in North Carolina.

By William NEELY and Abram WHITESIDES, administrators.
Return of sale:

Thomas KERR   Widow NEELY
Thomas HINES   Abram WHITESIDES
Mexmalen (?) REDDING   Harrison COOPER
William NEELY   Elijah P. CHAIMBERS
John NEELY   Hugh NEELY
Alexander READIN

page 422   November session 1816. John Jonathan BEAYTY (PEAYTY)
             (?) and Thomas STOCKARD, Esquire, or any two of them
             (?) settle with administrators of Robert NEELY,
             deceased.

page 422   Inventory of John NICHOLS, deceased. Buyers:

Charles T. REECE   William C. LONG
Robt. CHAFIN   John HART
David CRAIG   William MAY
Frances MC BRIDE   Robt. NICHOLS
James BARLOW   William FERRY
George GREEN   Peggy NICHOLS
James DUNCAN   Elia PEYTON
Benjamin ALLEN   Doctor JENNINGS

By Robert CHAFFIN.

page 423   Sale. No name. No date. Buyers:

Hugh NEELY   William TURNER
John MC GEE   Robert BROWN
Elijah P. CHAMBERS   Abram WHITESIDE
William TURNER   Andrew BROWN
Thos. HEDGEPATH   Maxmilen REDDING
Thos. WHITESIDE   Wm. BROWN
Jethrow BROWN   Thomas IDLET
John ISOM   Edw. WOLDREDGE
Peter POWELL   James B. MC CLAIN
Squire SHOAT   Ennis JOHNSON
Jonathan BROWN   Charles BROWN
Thomas W. J. SILLERNNER Mrs. TURNER
              (?)   Peter HERON
Thomas BOWMAN   Samuel WHITESIDE

Widow NEELY	Joseph SHORT
William JONES	Peter SATTERFIELD
John FERIS	Samuel ADKINSON
John NEELY	Starling BELL
Joshua WILLIAMS	Payton SHERRON
Archibald YOUNG	Caleb FARIS
Ephraim MC CLAIM	Robert MC CULLOUGH

page 425   Widow's provision for Mrs. Elizabeth OAKLEY, widow of Wm. OAKLEY, deceased. Set out 15 March 1822 by William EDMONSTON, William SHERROD, James DOTY.

page 426   Inventory of estate of William OAKLEY, deceased. _____ 10th, 1822 by Wm. GRAY.

page 426   15 April 1821. Inventory of estate of Aron ALDREDGE, deceased, by William ALDRIDGE.

page 427   List of accounts standing on the books of David OGLIVIE, deceased, and unsettled January 1817:

Peter CHEATHAM from year 1812
L. B. ESTES from 1811 - 1817

Jellso JOINER	John MONEY
Thomas WHITE	Gid. PILLOW
Mrs. BURNS	James DOBBINS
Mrs. LEONARD	Samuel CRAIG
Caleb LONGLEY	Elisha UZZELL
O. DAVIDSON	James DOOLEY
Wm. DUNN	D. N. SANSOM
Jas. C. MC DOWELL	Mrs. BROWN
John W. LEWIS	John SHELTON
Laurence ROSS	George CAMPBELL
Henry GIBSON	Wm. GIBSON
David COPELAND	Jno. WHITE
Samuel DAVIS	

"A list of notes, money, and property delivered to us by John HODGES - received of A. LEWIS in Virginia where OGLIVIE died is certified by Thomas N. BURNELL (BURWELL) and W. C. BOWAGDER(?)..."

John TEES, BAILES and MONTGOMERY, David C. LEWIS. By Elizabeth OGLIVER and Wm. BRADSHAW, administrators. Also signed by E. P. OGLOVER and William BRADSHAW.

page 428   Sale of property of David OGLOVE, deceased, sold on 15 October 1816. Buyers:

Isaac ROADS	E. P. OGLIVER
John BUTTER	Jno. SPENCER
Wm. DUNN	Thos. WHITE
Joshua GUEST	Buford TURNER
Jno. WHITE	Daniel EVANS
George M. MARTIN	L. L. MC KISTER (?)
Merideth HELMS	Jas. ALDERSON

page 429   Inventory of estate of James OAKLEY, deceased. 10 January 1822, by Wm. EDMUNISON.

page 430   Sale of James OAKLEY, 15 February 1822. Buyers: Elizabeth OAKLEY, Robert OAKLEY, Abraham MAYS,

Laban FIELDS, Moses HOLMNES, Alexander OAKLEY, John
GRIFFITH, Samuel OLIPHANT, Benoni PEREYMAN, Robt.
HOLMNES, George IRWIN, Jeremiah FLY, David R. MITCHELL,
Wm. FLY, Robert OVERLY; by William EDMUNDSON and
Elizabeth OAKLEY. 10 March 1822.

page 431   Sale of estate of Wm. OAKLEY, deceased, 15 March 1822.
           Buyers: Elizabeth OAKLEY, James DOTY, Wm. GRAY,
           David FLY, Joseph CHUMLEY; by Wm. GRAY.

page 432   Settlement of estate of George NICHOLSON, deceased,
           by John J. ZOLICOFER, executor, 1821, February:
           persons named: Nathaniel YOUNG, CAMPBELL and POLK,
           James PETERS, KERBY, JOINES and L. WALKER, MC NEAL
           and MOORE, James L. WALKER, Garret L. VOORHIES, Perry
           COHEA, Joshin ALDERSON, Andrew C. HAYES, Dr. MARTIN,
           Lemuel POPE, John POPE; by Swan HARDIN and James
           BLACK, 22 October 1822.

page 433   Sale of property of Isaac ROBERTS, deceased, sold on
           17 and 19 December 1819. Buyers:

           John B. ROBERTS   Rachael ROBERTS
           Polly ROBERTS   Robert WALLIS
           Swan HARDIN   Joshia ALDERSON
           Jeremiah CHERRY   Alexander KING
           Henry APPLEWHITE   Perry COHEA
           Wm. MILLER   Peter J. VOORHEIS
           Moses F. ROBERTS   Jacob ROGERS
           William SMITH   Joseph B. PORTER
           Major WILLIS   Horatio DEPRIEST
           Merideth HELM   John LAMASTER
           Samuel HAWKINS   Samuel SMITH
           William WEBB

           By Swan HARDIN and James WALKER, 24 January 1820.

page 435   Inventory of estate of Richard RUSSELL, deceased.
           No date. Note on Morgan FITZPATRICK.

page 435   Petition to divide estate of Isaac ROBERTS, deceased.
           April term 1820..."Mark R. ROBERTS (petitioner) is
           one of the children and heir of Isaac ROBERTS,
           deceased and that said Isaac died about year 1816
           leaving Polly VOORHIES, formerly Polly ROBERTS now
           deceased, she leaving three children her lawful heirs
           not yet of the age of 21, for whom Peter J. VOORHIES
           has been appointed guardian, Nancy HAWKINS, formerly
           Nancy ROBERTS, Mark R. ROBERTS, your petitioner,
           John ROBERTS, Moses F. ROBERTS, Rachael Persia
           ROBERTS, Patsey ROBERTS and William ROBERTS, his
           children and lawful heirs, the six last of whom are
           not yet of the age of 21 and for whom James T. SAND-
           FORD, Joseph B. PORTER, E. W. DALE, Polly ROBERTS,
           and George M. MARTIN have been appointed guardians
           that the said Isaac ROBERTS died possessed of 5
           tracts of land of 5,000 acres each lying in the
           western part of this state on the waters of the
           Obine, containing about 25,000 acres not yet included
           in any county as yet laid off, that your petitioner
           is of lawful age to wit twenty one years of age....
           his share of said lands as heir of Isaac ROBERTS,
           deceased, the same being a tenth part thereof to

each there being nine children or heirs and the widow taking a child's part." (Abstractor's note: Rachel ROBERTS, Persia had been marked out, then the children listed as above - probably two daughters, one Rachel and one Persia - still can count only eight children.)

page 436   Petition of Warner ROGERS....sheweth...that some time in year 1816 Carey N. (or W.) ROGERS of Smith County departed this life leaving your petitioner his only child some days after the mother of your petitioner died leaving your petitioner her only heir....is entitled to....to the amount of $10,000, that Thomas JONES was...appointed guardian to your petitioner and had the same amount in his hands....

page 437   Inventory of chattle property of Richard RUSSELL, deceased, sold on 1 May 1821 by me Catharine X. RUSSEL, administratrix.

page 438   16 July 1821. Amount of money in my hands of Egbert MEADOWS, legatee of Joseph MEADOWS, deceased, by Willis WILLIFORD, guardian.

page 439   Inventory of estate of Joel RIEVES, deceased, taken 22 January 1819. Bonds on COLEMAN and CARUTHERS; John LOVE; Elijah RIEVES; Derile BRIDGES.

page 439   Philip ANTHONY, John BILLS, and Willis BOBO appointed to lay out year's provision for Catharine RUSSEL. 23 April 1821.

page 440   Report of above returned, 30 April 1821.

page 440   Sale of property of Reubin REAVES, deceased. Buyers: Elijah REAVES, Hannah REAVES (widow), Susannah REAVES, Nancy REAVES, Wm. ADAMS, Joel REAVES, Henson BROWN, John CHISM, Thomas NATIONS, Thomas NIGHT, John WEBB, Derrel BRIDGES, Wm. C. HILL, Josiah ALDERSON, Wilson CURRY, John COOPER.

page 441   Inventory of estate of James W. ROGERS, deceased, taken 13 October 1820, by Thomas JONES; note on Wm. MC CLENNEHAN; Larkin DOUGLAS; Thomas JONES.

page 442   Sale of property of James W. ROGERS, deceased, 4 November 1820, by Thomas JONES, administrator. Buyers: Peggy ROGERS, Nicholas MC MILLAN, Edward BLEDSOE, William A. MAXWELL, Mathias LEE, James JONES, Daniel BROWN, Shadrick BROWN, William BROWN, John TERRILL, Thomas JONES, Alexander WILLIAMS, Abner JOHNSON, George LOVELL, David MITCHELL.

page 444   Inventory of property of Jeremiah SHELTON, deceased, 25 August 1817, by Isham MANGRUM.

page 444   Sale of Thos. SMITH, deceased, by Wm. T. COLE, administrator. Buyers: Katharine SMITH, John BAKER, Daniel CAMERON, Wm. JOPLIN, Jacob LANGSTON, George BLAIR, Moses CURTIS, James LOCKRIDGE, James ROGERS, David KERR, Benjamin CURTIS.

page 445   Sale of Wm. SELLERS, deceased, by James SELLERS, administrator. No date. Buyers: Major WILLIS,

Thomas POWERS, Bradford BUTTS, James BYNUM, Robin
GOOD, Rubin GOOD, Daniel PAIN, Luke SELLERS, Tos.
BOWERS, W. GRIFFIN, Isiah SELLERS, Shelby PARK.

page 445   Sale of William STONE, deceased, sold 9 November 1818,
            by John KNOX, administrator. Buyers: Jacob UTZMAN,
            Thomas GILASPIE, Richard JONES, Alexander HENDERSON,
            John HENDERSON, Wm. HENDERSON, _____ GULLET, Joshua
            BOWDERY.

page 446   Inventory of estate of Wm. STONE, deceased, by John
            KNOX, administrator, 9 October 1818.

page 446   Inventory of estate of Thomas SMITH, deceased, 18
            March 1822, by William T. COLE.

page 447   Sale of Jane SHAW, deceased, sold 15 December 1819,
            by David CRAIG, executor. Buyers:

William DICKSON	Andrew MC MAHAN
Mark GRIMES	James GORDON
William GRIMES (of Wm.)	John DAGBY
John GIBSON	William RICKETTS
Alexander GRIMES	John GORDON, Junior
James HICKMAN	William WILLIAMS
Philip PENN	James GRIMES
Levi SHAW	Robert NICHOLS
James BARLOW	John GORDON, Senior
William BURCHET	Francis SPENCER
William GRIMES	Hugh SHAW
William SHAW, Senior	Joseph STOCKARD
Daniel JOBE	Micajah NOLEN
William BLASINGAME	John HOWARD
William AKIN	William SHAW
Solomon HOGE	Alexander S. MC CLURE
Mary PICKARD	William ROBERTS
Dennis HARTY	Redding KOONCE
Michael BAILEY	William GORDON, Junior
Jane W. BURKET	Robert NICHOLS

            (Abstractor's note: in at least three instances,
            William GRIMES (of William) was listed as shown.)

page 449   Inventory of Malcolm GILCRIST, deceased, 25 July
            1821, by Malcolm GILCHRIST and William GILCHRIST,
            executors.

page 450   Petition for division: Washington NORWOOD petitioner
            in right of his wife Maria NORWOOD and Coller Thomas
            GANT by P. R. BOOKER, his guardian..."that on the day
            day of November 1816 William GANT of Maury departed
            this life leaving his wife Lesey and nine children,
            to wit, Maria GANT who has since intermarried with
            your petitioner Washington NORWOOD, Coller GANT....,
            and Amandy, Emmely, Jane, William, Eliza, John, and
            Robina, who are infant children of said William
            GANT." (wife of Washington NORWOOD also spelled
            Marina.)

page 451   Division of estate of William GANT, deceased, 29
            December 1819. Lese GANT, widow; Amanda GANT, his
            daughter; Robina, his daughter; John GANT, his son;

116

Collier GRANT, his son; William GRANT, his son;
Emmily GRANT, his daughter; Eliza GANT, his daughter;
Jane GANT, his daughter; Washington NORWOOD in right
of his wife Marina, a daughter of said decedent, by
Samuel H. WILLIAMS, John BROWN, Jas. HERNDON.

page 451   Poley JOST, wife of John JOST, deceased, relinquishes
right of administration unto Wm. JOST, brother to the
deceased, 19 October 1822, Polly X GOSTT. Witness:
Katharine GOSTT.

page 453   Sale of estate of William GANT, deceased, 26 December
1816. Buyers:

Mrs. Lisa GANT	John JENKINS
Elisha UZZELL	Major WILLIS
Robert ALDERSON	Henry PETTY
William GANT	Joshua GUEST
Anguish MC DUFFEY	Joseph DAVIS
Josiah ALDERSON	Samuel D. MC MAHAN
Jasper SUTTON	Alexander MOORE
Jethrow BROWN	Alfred WALLACE
Andrew MC MACKEN	Luke PATTERSON
William HARDIN	John MILLER
George CAMPBELL	Daniel GOODRUM
James D. MC LEAN	George COCKBURN
Joseph WINGFIELD	Isaiah HOGAN
Thomas H. PHILIPS	Phillip MEECE
William WADE	John S. ALDERSON
Green HILL	Andrew MC MAHON
Derril N. SANSOM	Aron LANCASTER
John MEECE	John BROWN
Thomas MAHON	Cullier GANT
William W. WOODS	Edmund HARRIS
James KNIGHT	James HAVY (?)
Robert GOAD	Eram DOOLEY

page 455   Davis GURLY petitions for division of estate of
Thomas EDWARDS...in 1814 Davis GURLY and the widow
were appointed administrators and in 1817 a settlement made. Thomas EDWARDS died leaving one child
only.

page 456   Sale of Mary GREEN, May session 1817. Buyers:

Thos. P. GREEN	Derom COLLINS
James DUNCAN	John DUNCAN
Stephen COOK	Susannah WILLIAMS
William CAUDLE	James Y. GREEN
Joshua CAUDLE	Harvey SMILEY
Laurence MC MANIS	Susannah MC MANUS
David ANDREWS	Robert ARNOLD
Isaac BAKER	Thomas S. GREEN
Abraham TALLEY	Asia BAKER
Asabel BAKER	Samuel MC MANUS
Susan MC MAHAN	Elisha HUNTER

by Joshua CAUDLE, administrator.

page 458   Inventory of estate of John GRIFFITH, deceased. Notes
on: DAUGHERTY and LONGLY; Robert NEELY; John GHOLSON;
by Samuel GRIFFITH and Amos JOHNSON, administrators.
25 January 1819.

page 459   Petition for distributive share: Washington NORWOOD
and Collen by his guardian Peter R. BOOKER vs.
Patrick MAGUIRE, Darrel N. SANSOM, and Peter R.
BOOKER, administrators of William GANT, deceased.

page 459   Inventory of property of John GOSSET, deceased,
19 October 1822.

page 460   More on petition for division of estate of William
GANT, deceased.

page 460   John MATTHEWS, Joseph HERNDON, and Samuel GRIFFITH
ordered to lay off, allot, and divide estate of
Thomas EDWARDS, deceased, allotting two/thirds to
Anna EDWARDS, the only child of Thomas EDWARDS.
D. GURLEY, petitioner.

page 461   Sale of Andrew H. GOFORTH, 2 June 1821. Buyers:

Nancy GOFORTH	Hiram GOFORTH
James HAYS	David RANKIN
John W. BEASLY	William SCOTT
Bennett W. MORE	William KILCREASE
Thomas CALDWELL	Samuel HAYS
Britton J. BAUCOMB	Shelton RENFRO
John BAUGERS	James RANKIN
William WALTON	Moses F. ROBERTS
Robert RANKIN	William JOHNSON
Alfred MILIN	John MILLS
Ezekial AKIN	John CILCREASE
Richard COCK	Bert RANKIN
Moses RANFROW	Wilie SCOTT
David FORTNER	Joseph MALCOMB
Drewry MORRIS	Samuel JOB

by Hiram GOFORTH, administrator, sold 23 July 1821.

page 462   Inventory of estate of Margarett GIBSON, deceased.
Notes on Mr. MC DILL, Bird SMITH; John CARTER,
administrator.

page 462   Account of sales of negroes of heirs of Joshua
GLOVER, deceased, by J. W. JONES, guardian.

page 463   Inventory of estate of Andrew H. GOFORTH, deceased,
14 April 1821. Notes on: Hiram GOFORTH, Abraham
JOB, Joseph HERNDON, Isaac RENFROW, Pugh CANNON,
Brittan J. BAUCOMB, _____ and STEPHENS; John
RENFROW, John CHISM, Marcus HOLLAND, Laurence
HOLCOLM, Powell HAIL, Moses RENFROW, L____RENFROW;
by Hiram GOFORTH, administrator.

page 464   Inventory of estate of William GIBSON, deceased,
20 February 1817, by Margarett GIBSON, administratrix.

page 464   Inventory of estate of William WHITE, deceased, by
Jane WHITE and E. B. DOOLEY, administrator.

page 464   "Silas WILLIAMSON a citizen of the State of Georgia
aged 23 years came to my house on 3rd of September
1821 and died on the 8th of October following...."
Inventory. Not signed.

page 465   Amount of sale of William WHITE, deceased. Notes on
                Alexander CARADIN, John L. SMITH, Edward B. LITTLE-
                FIELD, John W. LAYMASTER.

page 466   Elizabeth G. WEBB relinquishes right of administration
                of estate of John WEBB, deceased, to George P. TYLER,
                28 January 1822. Witness: Geo. HICKS.

page 467   A. LAIRD, Johns JOHNSON and Benjamin DAVIS allotted
                year's provision to Catharine WHITE, widow of James
                WHITE, deceased. 3 February 1821.

page 467   B. F. WINN, Thos. SIMS, C. B. WAKER (?), John WINN,
                legatees of late General Richard WINN agree to make
                a division, 25 October 1819.

page 468   Inventory of property of James WHITE, deceased,
                22 January 1821. Notes on: Lorenzae HIGHCOCKE,
                Madicin CARUTHERS, James L. WALKER, David HAMILTON,
                John RIM, Jesse W. EGNEW, David G. CAMPBELL, James
                HUEY, Martin SUTHERBE, William DAVIS, William COVEY,
                Henry GIBSON, Henry TUCKNISS, James LEWIS, Bartlett
                ESTES, Arthur BEATY, Jesse LEFTWICH, David FARRILL,
                David W. MC KEE, Henry MANGRIM, Thomas WHITE, Joseph
                RHODES, Richard SCOTT, George COCKBURN, P. J. VOOR-
                HIES, John S. LONGLEY, David MARTIN, John WHITE,
                Joshua GUEST.

page 470   Memorandum of property which WYKE, Senior, (?)
                deceased, possessed on 11 September 1820.

page 470   Jane WILSON, being one of the sisters and next of
                kin to William H. WILSON, deceased, do....relinquish
                my right to administer on the estate of my said
                deceased brother William H. to my brother-in-law
                Stephen SMITH and my nephew John W. SMITH...28 March
                1822.

page 471   Inventory of property of Richard WINN, deceased.

page 471   Widow's allotment for Patsey WILLIAMSON and children,
                4 February 1820, by Samuel SAVAGE, Thos. JONES, John
                HODGE.

page 472   Inventory of estate of Mary WARD, deceased, listed
                19 February 1816, by Benjamin SMITH, D. BROWNE,
                James T. SANDFORD, executors.

page 473   Sale of Green WILLIAMSON, deceased, 14 February 1820;
                by W. H. WILLIAMSON, administrator.

page 475   Inventory of Meshac WILLIS, deceased, 24 October
                1818. "Pention for 23rd of April 1818 to 24 October
                1818 at $8 per month" by Elizabeth WILLIS, administra-
                trix. (NOTE - Revolutionary Soldier)

page 475   Inventory of property of Suse WADE by J. SCOTT.

page 476   "Your petitioner Prissilea WINN, widow of Richard
                WINN, deceased; Benjamin WINN; John WINN; Thomas
                COLEMAN; Edward B. LITTLEFIELD hold by deed from
                Thomas WINN; Samuel WINN, Thomas SIMS and his wife

Mary SIMS in right of his said wife, Elijah BLOCKER in proper person and his wife Priscilla BLOCKER in her wright...by Samuel WINN trustee by the will... that General Richard WINN died about the 18 December 1818." Request for division of land. Request William FRIERSON, William WILLIFORD, Jonathan WEBSTER, George MITCHELL and James W. WITHERSPOON, Esquire, be appointed commissioners to divide land. October term 1819.

page 477   Inventory of articles chosen by Dolly WILLIAMS wife of Permineas WILLIAMS for her own use, 5 February 1821. By Edmd. WILLIAMS and Green B. WILLIAMS, executors. Inventory of debts due Permineas WILLIAMS, deceased - named: James PAYNE, Robert M. COOPER, Phillip P. WINN, John COLEMAN and Jeremiah ALMOND, William N. WILSON, Samuel GRIFFITH, Alexander MC DOWELL, Thomas FISHER, William SIMS, William JOHNSON, and Gideon HENDLY, William COOPER, Jr., William NEWSUM, Henry N. WHITMAN, Nicholas LONG, Lott HACKNEY.

page 478   Sale of Milly WALTON, deceased, sold 18 May 1822. Buyers:

Duncan COLLINS	Jonathan MC MANIS
Daniel G. BILLS	Thomas B. HARDISON
Andrew CULBERSON	Richard HILL
John B. FOWLER	Simeon MARSH (?)
Elisa MOORE	Isaac WILLIAMS
Alexander MEASE	Nancy DRAKE
Thomas RICHARDSON	Sally WATSON
Patsey HILL	Hubert DRAKE

By Duncan COLLINS, administrator.

page 479   Sales of negroes of Hungerford VINCENT, deceased, 27 November 1819. Buyers: John JENKINS, James T. SANDFORD, John BARNES, Phil JENKINS; by James T. SANDFORD, administrator.

page 480   Inventory of estate of Green WILLIAMSON; accounts:

S. CLARK	P. R. BOOKER
James WALKER	Abram WHITESIDES
Geo. CAMPBELL	P. MC GUIRE
D. W. MC KREE	W. VOORHIES
J. C. MC KEAN	James DOOLEY
John DAVIS	E. H. CHAFIN
John S. LONGLEY	E. W. DALE
James S. WALKER	P. CHEATHAM
G. W. EGNEW	

by Patsey WILLIAMSON and W. H. WILLIAMSON, administrators.

page 482   Inventory of estate of William H. WILSON, deceased. Return of articles sold; buyers: Drury BRACK, John GOODWIN, Alexander PICKARD, Jane WILSON, Russell BRACK, Warren BRISCOE, Phillip PENN, F. WILLIS, Stephen SMITH, Rice BUCKNER.

page 483   Inventory of estate of Milly WATON, deceased, 11 April 1822, Duncan COLLINS, administrator.

page 483   Sale of Daniel YEATS, deceased, 9 September 1815.
Roswell SETON bought everything except one item
bought by Adam ANDREWS. Debts not collected: note
on Gideon WARNER; "one discharge for three months
and three days serving in the service of the U. S.
at New Orleans by Daniel YEATS, due estate $24.70";
Jane BURNS; Roswell SETEN, administrator, 1 November
1815.

page 484   Provision for widow and family of Jno. B. WILKS,
deceased, July term, 1822; by Jno. HATCHETT, I. J.
BILLS, Jno. MACK.

page 485   Sale of Daniel WILSON, deceased. Buyers:

Miner WILKS	Benjamin WILKS
Edward HUDSON	Williamson ROGERS
_____ STILES (?)	Andrew COLE
Jno. W. JONES	Job. H. THOMAS
Aquilla W. MACK	Jessa WILKS
Joseph PIERCE	Robert W. SHEFFIELD
James GUNN	Wm. COMBS (?)
John DUCKEY	Isaac SIMPSON
Henry PERKINS	

23 November 1821, by Benjamin WILKS, Miner WILKS,
and Jesse WILKS, executors.

page 486   Provision for Elizabeth WEBB, widow of the late John
J. WEBB, deceased; "she being in a state of pregnancy."
given under our hands at Williams Port this 25th day
of February 1822. T. COLEMAN, Jas. G. SMITH, Geo.
HICKS.

page 487   Inventory of sale of James WHITE, deceased, on 1
March 1821. Buyers:

William HOLLAND	Samuel HESTEN
Samuel RANKIN	William COOPER
Richard COCKE	John JOHNSON
John BAUGUS	Henry MILLER
Alex HAMILTON	Joseph KELSA
Watson HARDIN	John L. SMITH
George M. MARTIN	George COCKBURN
James S. WALKER	James SUTHERLIN
Briant BAUGES	James HUEY
Daniel BROWN	

By Wilson WHITE, Catharine WHITE, administrators.

page 469   This page number should be 489.
Sale of property of Jon B. WILKS, deceased, 10 May
1822. Buyers:

Minor WILKS	Isaac BILLS
Wm. MITCHELL	Michael BALDRIDGE
Richard A. L. WILKS	Vincent STORY
John HATCHETT	William DANIEL
Beal GOODWIN	John WHITAKER
Joseph SEWELL	Drucilla GANNAWAY
John ADAMS	Constantine MACK
Mark JACKSON	John BRANCH
Alexr. JOHNSON	O. MARSH

Eliza L. WILKS
Jno. ANDERSON
Joseph KINGKAID
Jno. M. JONES
Robert ARNOLD
E. RICE
William A. JOHNSON
Minor C. M. WILKS
Levin COVEY
E. RICE, Senior
Benjamin THOMAS
William W. COVEY
George RICE

John KERR
Harburt JACKSON
James GUNN
John MACK
William RUST
Robert BULLER
T. M. BRANCH
Andrew NEELY
George GRAY
David KINGKAID
Jesse WILKS
Benjamin WILKS

page 470   Inventory of property of John B. WILKS.
(492)
page 473   Sale of Permeneas WILLIAMS, deceased. Buyers:
(493)

Robert B. NEWSOM
James HAYNES
David BROWN
Wm. MACON
David DOBBINS
Widow WILLIAMS
John SCRIBNER
James WORTHAM
Dolly WILLIAMS
Wm. STOCKARD
Peter JOYCE
Philip P. WINN
Allen JONES

Philip PENN
Alexander M. WILLIAMS
John T. JOHNSON
Redding SCRIBNER
James STOCKARD
John T. JOHNSON
Royal FURGERSON
Joseph R. SUTTON
Anderson WILLIAMS
Thomas WORTHAM
John CHISHOLM
Edmond WILLIAMS

By Edmund WILLIAMS and Green B. WILLIAMS, executors.

page 474   Sale of estate of Dr. Abram WHITESIDES, deceased,
            13 September 1821. Buyers:

Ephraim E. DAVIDSON
Ruth W. WHITESIDES
Silas M. CALDWELL
John BROWN
Perry COHEA
James L. WALKER
James HOLLAND
Abner MATHEWS
John MATHEWS
David FRIERSON
John HODGE
Henry E. TURNER
William MARCH
Samuel RANKIN
John DAVIDSON
Edward W. DALE
Patrick MAGUIRE
Samuel SAVAGE
Vincent RIDLEY
Isaac J. THOMAS

William YANCY
Thomas D. CLARK
William A. MAXWELL
Thomas BROWN
G. PINHARN (?)
John S. ALDERSON
Edward B. LITTLEFIELD
John O. DAVIDSON
Robert MACK
Peter CHEATHAM
William MC VEEL (?)
Gideon MILLS
Pleasant NELSON
Peter R. BOOKER
Joseph GILMORE
Andrew NEELY
Joel R. SMITH
Charles SUVILLIEN (?)
William G. DIXON

page 481   Sale of estate of John J. WEBB, deceased, sold in
            Williams Port, February 1822. Property listed. No
            names. Inventory follows.

page 486   Notes thought to be on solvent men - insolvent men,
           etc. Persons named:

Thomas WALKER   John M. DAVIS
John WOOLDRIDGE   George HICKS
Moses JOHNSON   W. T. G. TYLER
William GRIFFIN   Rachael BARNES
John GILBREATH   Neal HOPKINS
Vachel BARNHILL   John ERWIN
Howell BENNET of Va.   James H. GILLES
B. R. CHARTER   Samuel WINN
John C. HAMILTON   William TYLER
Thomas COLEMAN   Edward WALKER
William TALLEY   John MATHEWS
Nathan WILLIAMS   Kizza BROOM (?)

page 488   "A list of officers receipts for notes supposed to
           be on insolvent men":

Jesse OAKLEY for David MAYS
D. H. TRUE for John BRISCOE
William TOLEY   Peter PERVINE
Albert BEARD   Mark RUSHING
James KILOUGH   John WEEDAN
Stephen SANDERS of Virginia, due 3 February 1810
William CONE supposed of Virginia, dated 10 January
     1818

Accounts on men thought to be solvent:

Edward WILLIAMS   William YANCEY
James ERWIN   James DOBBINS
William TYLER, Senior   Samuel H. BAKER
George H. GANTT   Isaac FARIS
John PREWETT   David H. TRUE
Dolly GORDON   Jonathan WEBSTER
Daniel KUTCH   Joseph SHOATE
William V. AKIN   John C. HAMILTON
John WILSON   William ALDERSON
Luke WHITE   Jane THOMPSON
John SEELERS   John E. WILLIAMS
Richard ANDERSON   Jeremiah MC CINZIE
Thomas T. GREENFIELD   John GALE
William B. DICKEY   Suz GABRIEL
John WINN   William TALLEY
John KENDRICKS estate   James BECK
Jesse S. ROSS, Esquire   William PRUITT
James G. SMITH   Thomas CHOATE
Elijah BLOCKER   Col. John MC KINZIE
Joseph AYERS, Junior   Robert OAKLEY
Thomas P. MARTIN   George GANT
Edward MC FADDEN   James P. AYERS
Capt. John MITCHELL   William CHURCHWELL
Charles HICKS   John ROBERSON
Jonathan TALLEY   Gerrard T. GREENFIELD
John FORGERSON   Boiling GOODWIN
Arthur AYERS   James JOSEY
Doctor Charles SMOOT   George P. TYLER
George CRIVER   Edward W. DALE
Horatio CLAGETT   Charles SOWELL
John GORDON   Redmond CHOATE
William WHITESIDES   Thomas WEBB

Ebenezar ROSS
John DAVEY
William CRAWFORD
Neal HOPKINS
Nathaniel YOUNG
Thomas SIMMS
Abraham MAIZE
Samuel ROBERSON
John D. ALDERSON
Benjamin P. AYERS
Richard DAVIES
James BOOTH
Prudy CHOATE
Elisha WILLIAMS
John JONES
James WILLIE (?)
Job HUNT
Joab BROOKS
William BLACKBURN
Mrs. Henrietta OLIPHANT
Peter GRAHAM
Nathan WILLIAMS
Thomas SHELBY
John LUMPKINS
Claiborn PILLOW
Capt. John L. NEELY
Martha WILLIAMS
Jesse GRIFFIN
Leonard JONES
John PRIGGS
Samuel STRICKLAND
John BOAZ, Junior
Powhatten GORDON
David PISTOLE
Spencer TINSLEY
George COOK
Lambert C. OLIPHANT
Samuel SATTERFIELD
Alexander OAKLEY
James COHORN
Reubin ELLIOTT
Mary HAWKINS
Hugh WHITESIDE
Thomas CHOATE
George MITCHELL
James CHEAT
Alston JONES
James MITCHELL
Rubin WHITE
George GREER
Henry MORRACE
Hyrum RICHARDS
Robert HERRINGTON
William CRAWFORD
Council HEDGEPATH
James KILLOUGH
Eli SHELBY
Robert HAMILTON
William REGION
Samuel STRICTLAND
James JONES
John T. PRIMM

Capt. William FLY
John STEWART
Elisha SMITH
Henry JONES
Moses A. WILEY
Edward ENGLISH
Walter T. G. TYLER
Allen BULLOCK
Stewart STATIONS
F. D. ALDERSON
Allen PILLOW
Andrew MITCHELL
James DRUMMOND
Thomas KENDRICK
William GRIFFIN
John GRIFFETH
Edmund WALKER
David R. MITCHELL
James MONTGOMERY
William STRAHORN
Vincent PILLOW
Mrs.Edwards WILLIAMS
Robert AYERS
Edom LOVE
Daniel STEWART
Robert HOLMES
John RICHARDS
Jeremiah FORGUSON
Mrs. Mary PARKER
Thomas NEGHTON (?)
Ira CASEY
James LETSINGER
William HOGUE
Thomas AYDLETT
John CRINER
Ambrose R. RICHARDSON
Able FURGURSON
Campbell STRICKLAND
Daniel HOLKAM
Joseph AYRES, Senior
Charles PISTOLE
John MC FALL
George HAYS
Jesse OAKLEY
John GRIMES
Brittian GARNER
David ALLCOCK
Robert RICHARDS
William DANIEL
John AYDELETT
Peter GRAHAM
Cyrus GILES
Isaiah DAVIS
John TOLLEY
Stephen PILLOW
William FALLING
James TRAVERS
Robert PERRY
David COOK
James BIGHAM
John S. BROOKS
David KING

Thomas C. WALKER	Miss Polly JONES
Joseph ALLEN	John LEAPER
Adam COX	Thomas SILLEMAN
Isaac B. LINDSAY	James ERWIN

Still same records: A list of accounts found in an
old book kept whilst Jno WEBB did business in Hickman
County in the year 1820 and supposed to be all or
nearly all settled so far as the people could be
found, many of them having moved away. I have thought
it necessary to be thus particular as said accounts
are nearly all standing open and the persons many of
whom I called on have receipts. Signed: George P.
TYLER.

John NICKS	James LASSETER
Nathaniel KELLEM	Joseph CARROLL
John DUNCAN	William S. DUNKIN
Jacob PEELER	Barnet WADOO
Ephraim NORRIS	James M. BARNHILL
Doctor Charles SMOOT	William HICKS
Henry COCKRAM	Robert TOLLY, Senior
Edmund LOONEY	Edmund JANES
James SINGLETON	James LEWIS
Daniel PARET	Sailly ELLIOTT
Henry PICKETT	James PIGG
Robert ANDERSON	William RAGSDALE
John CRINER	Albert M. BAIRD, deceased
John ALDERSON	Dempsey HERRINGTON
Farney LASSETER	Patsey DUNCAN
John G. MALEY	Zebulin HOPHILL
Hill TOLLEY	David DUNCAN
Joseph M. BEARD	Benjamin MARTIN
Daniel COCHRAN	_____ COLEMAN
Edy LOSSETTER	George GREER
Daniel GRIGGS	Noel TONY
Garrett CAVANDER	William BRIGHT
Hugh HILL	Andrew LOFFERTY
Fielden L. GORDON	

page 493   List of sale, 9 May 1813, buyers: John FORGEY, John
CLANTON, Andrew FORGEY, Demsey TAILOR, John MACK,
Constant MACK, Lemuel MACK, A. OSBORN, J. SCOTT, A.
TAYLOR, James MACK.

page 494   Inventory of negroes of estate of Green WILLIAMSON,
deceased, 1 January 1821, by P. R. WILLIAMSON,
administratrix, and Will H. WILLIAMSON, administrator,
22 July 1821.

page 494   Second Inventory of estate of William WEEMS, deceased.
First, from Thomas ADAMS on an article for land;
second, from John WEEMS, deceased, estate.

page 494   Inventory of estate of Louisa WADE, deceased, by
Swan HARDIN, administrator, 23 July 1821.

page 494   Inventory of estate of Hungerford VINCENT, 24 October
1818, James T. SANDFORD, administrator.

page 495   Inventory of property of William HILL, deceased,
15 April 1822. 100 acres of land. Andrew HILL,
administrator.

page 495   Inventory of property of Archibald HIGHT, deceased,
           by Richard HIGHT, administrator.

page 495   Inventory of property of Andrew MILLER.

page 496   Inventory of estate of Hugh MARS, deceased; notes on
           Samuel BAKER, Richard LEWIS, Edmund WALKER, William
           B. ALDERSON. 28 October 1818. By John X PREWETTE,
           James MAIRS, administrators.

page 497   Sale of Hugh MAIRS, deceased, held 21 November 1818.
           Buyers:

Tolver BRADY   Robert MONTGOMERY
William REGION   James MONTGOMERY
James BEDFORD   James MEARS
Ebenezer ROSS   Elijah EMMONS
John PREWETT   Abram WHITESIDES
Richard JONES   James BRADY
John H. GATLIN   Lambert OLIPHANT
William MC INTOSH   John HARNEY
Betsey MEARS   John H. GATLIN
Alexander EVAN   James THOMPSON
Samuel STRICKLIN   James L. (or S.) ROBERTSON
John MIDDLETON   Ezra BRISTE
James CURRY   (sword, cap and coat)

           By James MEARS and John PREWETT, administrators.
           Estate settled 13 April 1820 by A. CATHEY and J.
           THOMPSON.

page 499   Litigation between John DEAN plaintiff and John
           SWEET prinicple. 17 October 1821. James SWEET,
           security.

page 500   Inventory of estate of Hugh MEARS, deceased.

page 501   Jane MC BRIDE, wife of Isaiah MC BRIDE, deceased,
           requests that Francis and Samuel MC BRIDE act as
           administrators. 15 May 1815.

page 501   Inventory of estate of John MUIRHEAD, deceased,
           taken 2 August 1813. Notes on: Joseph MC CRAVEN,
           John LOVE, Abner BLAIR, Permenas DRISCOE, Rizen L.
           BISHOP, Samuel MONTGOMERY, John SELSAR, MC LAUGHLIN,
           Joseph O'NEAL, Jacob MC KEE, Frederick B. _____,
           Robert ALFRED, Bene BROWN, Giles STEWART, Major
           Joseph LAYMASTER, James HUDSTOCK (?).

page 501   Inventory of John MUIRHEAD, deceased, "taken notice
           of the second day of August 1813 and now in possess-
           ion of Samuel OLIPHANT"...."now in possession Thomas
           DARKER"; notes in hands of Joseph MC CRAVEN, John
           LOVE; note on Abner BLAIR; Permenas BRISCOE; Rezin
           L. BISHOP; Sanuel MONTGOMERY; WILLIAMS; MC LAUGHLIN;
           Jacob MC KEE; Frederick B. C. SIMPSON; COOKE and
           LAMASTER; Robert ALFRED; Bene BROWN; Giles STEWART;
           Major Joseph LAYMASTER; Jap HERDSTOCK (?), COHEA
           and LAMASTER.

page 503   Settlement with administrator and administratrix of
           George Decd, 20 January 1825. Joseph B. WALLACE,
           Bird S. HURT.

126

page 503   Account of hiring of negroes of estate of John BARNES,
            deceased, for one year from first of January 1824;
            Mrs. BARNES account for one year from first of
            January 1825.

page 504   Settlement made 12 January 1825 with Jacob administra-
            tor of Louisa WADE, deceased. Vouchers on: SAMSON
            and HAYS, William MC NEEL, William J. JOHNSON, Samuel
            BLAKELY, Sarah WADE, Jacob SCOTT, John FIELD,
            Nathaniel YOUNG; settled with Jacob SCOTT, administra-
            tor of Louisa WADE, deceased; John MILLER, James
            BLACK.

page 505   Inventory of sale of Mathew SWAN, deceased, sold by
            Robert NICHOLS and Thomas BRAWLY, administrators,
            25 November 1824. Buyers:

            Sally LEE   Josiah GREEN
            Margaret SWAN (widow)   Samuel NORMAN
            Doctor BRISCOE   George BRISCOE
            Phillip PENN   Thomas WORTHAM
            Henry GIBSON   Widow SHAW
            Charles HARRIS   Elijah PETON
            E. KIRKMAN   Hugh SHAW
            Ruthy SWAN   Allen TAYLOR
            J. W. BRISCOE   Thomas ADKINSON
            Briant MOSLEY   Anderson BROOKES
            David VAUGHN   William BROWN
            William GETT   Robert F. MATHEWS
            Note on James ONEAL and Hiram GOFORTH, dated
               20 August 1819
            Note made by Thomas ROBINSON, dated 6 March 1819
            Due bill made by Joseph TERRILL, dated 15 September
               1822.

page 506   Account of hiring of negroes of William D. WILSON,
            deceased, by Stephen SMITH and John W. SMITH.

page 507   Sale of Benjamin CALOHAN, deceased. Buyers:

            Mareen DUVALL   Saml. M. KING
            Samuel SMITH   Samuel GALLOWAY
            Alexander SLAVEN   John CALAHAN
            John L. HADLEY   Hiram DAVIDSON
            John FIELDS   Elijah R. HURT
            Andrew BYRNES   Agnis KING
            Robinson ROSS   Bird S. HURT
            Nathaniel M. POWELL   Meshack MORRIS
            David GILLASPIE   John RYLES
            Eli ASKEW   Hugh B. KING
            John KING   Amos DUNKIN
            Benjamin DUVALL   Andrew FIELDS
            Thomas CASKY   James RUMMAGE

page 508   Settlement with executors of Jacob MC KEE, deceased,
            22 July 1824. Thomas MC KEE, executor; To Isaac
            MC KEE, deceased; Vouchers for PORTER; CHILDRESS;
            B. B. SMITH; W. COVEY; BOOKER; Samuel MC KEE; ALDER-
            SON; S. P. MAXWELL; GILMORE; Isaac BILLS; James
            WRIGHT; paid for boarding minor children; James
            HATCHETT, James L. BALDRIDGE.

page 509   Due Nathaniel GRAVES, administrator of John P. POOL,
            deceased. Notes on:

            Mordacy PILLOW   A. PILLOW
            John HART   R. G. KELSEY
            S. JONES   H. GILE
            Ed ENGLISH and H. TURNEY, not due till 25 December
              1824
            William POOL and Jas. WALKER
            Hire of negroes in 1823
            D. BRADLEY   Stephen JONES

            By Nathaniel WILLIS, Hugh DOUGLAS, Thomas J. FRIERSON.

            Accounts current with said estate credit: John W.
            BRASLY (?), Willis RIDLEY, R. G. THORNTON, William
            MILLER, James DOBBINS, William POOL, John G. HOUSE,
            Uzell HAWKINS, D. N. SANSOM, P. O. MALONE, Jas. JONES,
            Jas. G. SMITH, Jno. WALKER (for coffin), James K.
            POLK, Umphrey WILKINSON, Benjamin B. SMITH, DICKINSON
            and COOPER, Samuel STRICTLAND, William STRICKLIN, Wm.
            JOSEY, Geo. P. TYLER, J. J. WEBB (administrator of),
            Abraham MONTAGUE, John STRAYHORN, John BULLOCK, ERWIN
            and WEBB. 23 July 1824.

page 511   Sale of negro boy by Robert C. DICKSON, Alexander
            PICKARD, and James MC GOWEN, Guardians for minor heirs
            of John DICKSON, deceased, as order 14 February last
            on credit until 1 January 1825; Elizabeth DICKSON,
            late widow of John DICKSON, with James DICKSON,
            Return M. DICKSON, and William WILLIAMS her securitys.
            19 July 1824.

page 511   Inventory of property left by Wm. MC CORD at his
            decease on the 10th April 1824; Judgment on John
            EGNEW; note on John REDFORD. 19 July 1824, Richard
            A. L. WILKS, executor.

page 512   Settlement by James L. BALDRIDGE and Alex JOHNSON
            with Alex BALDRIDGE and Richard FAUCETT, guardians
            of minor heirs of James PURSELL; rent of plantation
            for 1824.

page 512   Division of estate of John P. POOL, deceased, between
            his widow Katharine KESTERSON and his son Lockland;
            guardian of said Lockland, 23 July 1824; Nathaniel
            willis and Hugh DOUGLAS, commissioners.

page 513   Will of James DOOLEY: grandson James Madison DOOLEY;
            son Esom; beloved wife Rachel: son Paris; son in law
            William WALLACE; grandson James Harvey WALLACE.
            Signed: James DOOLEY. Witnessed 5 May 1824 by John
            Thomas THOMAS and William E. ERWIN; proven January
            term 1825.

page 514   Will of Robert CRAFTON: son Bennet; daughter Nancy
            P. RICHERSON; heirs of Robert W. CRAFTON; daughter
            Ezann (?) RENFROW; (all above received $1.00);
            Samuel S. CRAFTON, ¼ section of land lying on Clear
            Creek; Paul CRAFTON, ¼ section of land lying on
            Clear Creek; daughter Mary B. CRAFTON, $300 plus;
            son Silas M. CRAFTON, $300 plus when he becomes of

age; son William W. CRAFTON, $300 plus when they becomes of age or married; wife Sarah CRAFTON...after paying three youngest children....also her portion that is left by her father...at her hands to be equally divided between all her children; wish this will to be recorded in Tennessee, Maury County, and all my property to be removed there....9 September 1823. Signed: Robert X CRAFTON; witnesses: William DIAL, David DIAL, David DIAL, Junior.

page 515   Settlement with Hugh DOUGLAS and William HAWKINS, administrators of Jehosaphat LADD, deceased; notes on John PRUETT; T. TRANTHAM; E. EMMONS; E. SHELBY; William PREWETT; J. DOTTY; Mary HUNTER; Benjamin BOWEN; T. KELSEY; 17 July 1824 by A. CATHEY, John O. COOK; vouchers on BROWN and MC GIMSEY; L. F. DOTY and J. DOTY; Archb HOMES; T. COLEMAN; E. CHAFFIN; E. WILLIAMS; L. SHELBY; P. FITZGERREL; E. MC FADDEN; C. LINSAY; J. C. HAMILTON; H. and N. PERKINS; T. B. MALONE; J. D. ALDERSON; N. PERKINS.

page 516   Inventory and sale of property of Joseph KINCAID, deceased, 10 July 1824, by Elizabeth KINKAID, administratrix, George W. EGNEW, administrator.

page 516   Inventory of property of Edward MC CAFFERTY, deceased, by Francis SPENCE, acting executor.

page 517   Year's provision for Penelope STRAYHORN, widow of David STRAYHORN, deceased, 6 May 1824, by A. CATHEY, Hugh DOUGLAS, John O. COOKE.

page 518   Sale of David STRAYHORN, deceased, sold 6 May 1824. Buyers:

Widow STRAYHORN	Daniel KUTCH
Katharine STRAYHORN	Jonathan WEBSTER
John HUNT	Joseph MC MARY, administrator
Joseph G. PRATE (?)	A. T. ISOM
Ezekiel NELMS	Andrew GRAY
P. J. W. JENNINGS	J. G. WEBSTER
Joseph MC MAURY	David THOMPSON
James JOSEY	H. STRAYHERN
George HAYS	

page 518   Inventory of Robert CRAFTON, deceased.

page 518   April term, 1824, allowance to Lidia DAVIS as guardian of her children, three children, two to school. By John MACK, Thos. GILL.

page 519   John MACK and John MATHEWS, commissioners, to settle with executors of William PERRY, deceased. Simpson PERRY, one of the executors. 15 July 1824.

page 519   Caleb HEADLEY and Jos. B. WALLACE, commissioners, to settle with John BATE and John L. (?) WOOD, executors of James REED, deceased. 24 June 1824.

page 520   Sale of William SILLEMAN, deceased; Buyers:

L. J. DICKSON	James CUNNINGAM
Joel MACKEY	Doctor HALL

Thomas N. SILLEMAN   J. M. DANNEL
Richard JENNINGS   James WORTHAM
Phillip PENN   John AKINS
John M. DANNEL

Sold in February or March 1824.

Signed: Thos. N. SILLEMAN.

MAURY COUNTY WILLS AND INVENTORIES - BOOK D

page 1   Josiah ALDERSON, deceased, to wife $.75. This entry
          marked out. No date.

page 4   Will of Thos. WHITESIDE of Maury County, recorded
          1 February 1826...beloved wife Margaritte to receive
          dwelling house and farm...my two sons James and Hugh
          ...son Robinson (later spelled Robertson)...a negro
          slave to go to his wife as slave Ann "we received
          her from her father by his will"...my three daughters
          Elinor, Jennett, Polly..."when sons James and Hugh
          come of age"...wife Margaret and son Robertson to be
          executors...signed Thomas WHITESIDES, 11 October 1825
          (or 1824)...witnessed by Charles TOM, A. WHITESIDES,
          Jas. CATHEY.

page 5   Memorandum of nuncupitive will of Abner J. DODSON,
          deceased, made 27 October 1825, recorded February
          1826, made in presence of Peter BIGGS and John WOLVER-
          TON..."wished his wife to sell certain coalt"...wife
          Elizabeth DODSON, his children. (children not named)

page 5   Peter (X) BRIGGS and John WOLVERTON appeared before
          Pleasant NELSON, J.P., 12 November 1825 and said
          Abner DODSON made his will in their presence.

page 5   Will of Isaac N. PORTER of Maury County, recorded
          2 February 1826...all real estate to my brother Thos.
          J. PORTER...my nephew Elijah PORTER and Alexander
          Newton PORTER, minor children of my brother John T.
          PORTER, to receive a negro Fan...my brother-in-law
          Robert CARETHERS...directs his executors to give
          title to land on Snow Creek sold to Edmond WILLIAMS
          as he has not yet given title to WILLIAMS...brother
          Thomas J. PORTER and brother-in-law Robert CARITHERS
          to be executors...signed 22 June 1825.

page 6   Will of James MORIS of Maury County, recorded Feb-
          ruary 1826...my beloved wife Kesiah - should she
          marry again she forfeits her claim; my son Henry G.
          MORRIS; each of my daughters: Lucinda MORRIS, Jane
          A. MORRIS, Rebecca C. MORRIS; my three daughters;
          desires that a colt be given to Lucy MC CORMACK; my
          four children; Calvin CURLEE, executor...signed
          James (X) MORRIS on 27 July 1825...witnesses: James
          SCOTT and Meshach MORRIS.

page 8   Will of William H. MOORE of Maury County, recorded
          23 February 1826...wife Priscilla MOORE...all my
          children...left land in Bertie County, N. C., to his

130

wife...mentions slaves...wife to be exeuctor...signed
11 November 1824. Witnesses: Jesse YATES, James
WHITESIDES.

page 9   Will of William LOVING, Senior, recorded 3 February
          1826...wife Elisabeth...four youngest children:
          David LOVING, Tennessee LOVING, Henry LOVING, and
          Malinda LOVING...my wife is pregnant..."when youngest
          comes of age", wife Elisabeth LOVING, Michael ROBERT-
          SON, Joseph HACKNEY, executors; signed 8 July 1824,
          William (X) LOVING...witnesses: William (X) ROPER,
          George CRAWFORD.

page 9   Will of Benjamin BOWEN of Maury County, recorded
          3 February 1826...mentions his mills and distilleries
          ...my children...sister Mary PALMER, sister Patsey
          KEITH, sister Nancy SHELTON, sister Cydia BOWEN...
          beloved wife Mary P. BOWEN...1/6 part to Euratte L.
          BOWEN, Mary A. BOWEN, and Jane G. BOWEN...wife to be
          executor...signed 19 September 1825, Benjamin BOWEN.
          Witnesses: Edward B. LITTLEFIELD, D. FITZGERALD,
          William B. BUTLER.

page 9   8 February 1826, William VINCENT in account with his
          guardian John JINKINS, for January 1824. Signed
          24 October 1825, James T. SANDFORD, James BLACK.

page 10   8 February 1825, settlement with John PICKARD, Senior
          in right of his wife Nancy PICKARD, formerly Nancy
          GRIMES, administrator of Luke GRIMES and heirs...
          former settlement made in 1817 with minor heirs of
          Luke GRIMES, deceased; Wilson GRIMES, guardian of
          Robert GRIMES, one of minor heirs...share of Henry
          GRIMES still remaining. Signed 5 July 1825, David
          CRAIG, William STOCKARD.

page 11   February 1826...Inventory of James BOYD, deceased...
          negro boy, negro woman, Tatta and her five children
          entailed to Elisabeth T. BOYD, wife of James BOYD,
          deceased, by the will of her father...notes on H. N.
          WHITMAN, James SMITH, Robert SHEFFIELD, John ALEX-
          ANDER, Samuel D. MACK, James BRANCH, James M. SIMMONS;
          account of Ebenezer RICE, WALKER and DAVIS, BROWN,
          MC GIMPSEY and SANDERS, Dr. HAYS, Willis RIDLEY;
          note of Andrew BOYD...signed William S. HENDERSON,
          John R. BOYD.

page 12   Inventory of William FARRIS, deceased, recorded
          22 November 1825...in his estate was negro boy Jack
          and negro woman and child...buyers: Jane or James
          FARRISS, Daniel MC LULLIN, James FARRIS, Samuel TURK,
          Senior, James CURRY, Senior, Samuel WHITESIDES, Thos.
          WALKER, Mikeal HAGGINGS, Jas. PATTON, Perry O. MALONE,
          James BOWMAN, Nathaniel WILLIS, Jacob BIFFLE, James
          B. FARRIS, Joseph LOFTIN, James ROBERTSON, William
          GARNER, James FORGEY, F. D. ALDERSON, C. W. KNIGHT,
          Jacob R. GARNER, John HAWK, Terrell GOODMAN, Joseph
          TOM, Samuel C. ALAPHANT, Hugh SHAW, Young KIRK, John
          MACON, John P. BLACKBURN, James JOSSEY, James HYNES,
          Joseph G. PRATT, James R. GARNER, G. B. CRAWFORD,
          William GRICCEF, Bett KITTPATRICK, Samuel H. JONES,
          Alexander CALK, John A. CHAMBERS, John L. DILLARD,

N. WALKER, Thos. WILLIAMS, Charles BURKET, William
CATHEY, William J. BURKET, Samuel REID, John BURNS,
H. BRADFORD, Bates BURNS, Jefferson FARIS; notes on
William GARNER, John CRAIG, Andrew BLAIR, Jacob
RODGER, Francis SPENCER, Jasper R. SUTTON, Thomas C.
FARRIS, (due 1819), Robert D. KELSEY (due 1818),
Thomas JONES, Abraham WHITESIDES, James J. (or S.)
ROBERTSON (due 1818); accounts of Moses ECHOLES,
William GARNER, James AYNES, Jonathan WHITESIDE,
James R. GARNER. Signed Jane FARISS and James FARIS,
administrators.

page 16 -   Amount of sale of Minor C. WILKS, deceased, sold
    19   13 August 1825, recorded 9 February 1825 (possibly
           meant to be 1826)...buyers: Lemuel PHILLIPS, William
           HENDERSON, Azra MITCHELL, John W. ANDERSON, John B.
           GOODING, Edward GANAWAY, Edmond THOMPSON, Andrew
           CALDWELL, Benjamin WILKS, Richard A. S. WILKS (bought
           NICHOLSON's encyclopedia), John W. JONES (bought
           Constitution of U. S. A.), Richard J. COCKS, William
           MORR, Robert M. DENHAM, James TOMLINSON, Dudley
           MC KINDRY, Edmond THOMAS, William M. ORR, John MYRICK,
           Lilth J. WILKINS, Joshua MORIS, Stephen W. SMITH,
           William R. HICKS, David KINKAID, John HATCHETT,
           Hezekiah OLIVER, William MITCHELL, Charles V. BROWN,
           Philip HOLDEGER, William WISEMAN, Thomas WISEMAN,
           Ebenezer W. ORR, Samuel PHILIPS, Benjamin WISEMAN,
           William COVEY, Richard FOSTER, Little John WILKINS,
           James ROSS, Robert CASKEY, Mark WHUTSES (?), Daniel
           DOUGLAS, Williby L. MANNING, John OSBURN...a great
           deal of seating plush and skirting sold at this sale
           ...returned October 1825. Signed: Richard A. WILKS,
           administrator.

page 19   Account of sale of Samuel FRIERSON, deceased, 10 Nov-
           ember 1825...buyers: Diana E. FRIERSON, Samuel H.
           ARMSTRONG, Samuel D. FRIERSON, William J. ARMSTRONG,
           David FRIERSON, D. E. FRIERSON, E. M. FORD, J. W.
           FRIERSON (bought Confession of Faith), T. J. FRIER-
           SON (bought Brooks Gazeteer), Samuel P. PEAK, William
           BLAKELY, John WALKER, H. TURNEY, J. W. BEAUFORD,
           Edward B. LITTLEFIELD, George DICKEY, John FRIERSON,
           James DOGGINS. Items of interest in sale were many
           books, a "Chatechism", a copy of the Constitution of
           the U. S. John FRIERSON, Samuel D. FRIERSON, admin-
           istrators.

page 23   11 February 1826...List of taxable property of Doct
           John KINDRICK of Williamsport...had house, one and
           one half acres, gold watch, globe, Pike's Arithmetick,
           Cicero's orations, two volumes of Virgil, First
           Principles of Polite Bearing, Walker's dictionary,
           Greek grammar, Morses geography...many books in this
           list...had $25 in pocket book in Nashville Bank...

page 24   Settlement with James P. SMITH, administrator of
           John KENDRICK, deceased...note on John CHAMBERS.
           Signed 17 January 1826, Alexander JOHNSTON, William
           EDMDES, commissioners.

page 24   James C. (?) SMITH, administrator of estate settle-
           ment of John KENDRICK, deceased. Receipt of Edward
           WALKER; notes on F. D. ALDERSON, Bowling GORDON,

David KING, Colonel COLEMAN, Jno. D. ALDERSON, G. T. GREENFIELD...receipt of John J. WEBB.

page 25   13 February 1826...Inventory of late Sally JOHNSTON, wife of William JOHNSTON, deceased...mentions her distributive share of the estate of Louisa WADE, deceased...Jacob SCOTT, administrator of Louisa WADE.

page 26   13 February 1826...Jonathan D. BILLS and James L. BALDRIDGE have made settlement with executors of James STEELE, deceased. Signed 5 January 1826.

page 27   13 February 1826...Commissioners met at Anderson WILLIAMS house and examined vouchers against estate of Mark CYRUMN (or CYNUM?), deceased...mentions hire of negro Stephen; accounts: Murdock MC LOY, John BOOKER, James KENNEDY, David H. TRUE, Robert CELLERS, James SELLERS, Charles D. CRAWFORD, Ribble (?) T. HUSS (?), Robert L. COBBS...mentions pork delivered to the widow...accounts: Hardy CELLERS, Micaja BROOKS, Luke BYRMON, Joseph G. HOLT or HATT, William WEBB, William CRAWFORD, Elisabeth CELLARS, A. Y. PARTEE, Joseph Y. HALL, Nobly W. BRISCOE, R. YEATMAN. Signed 5 October 1825, Nicholas J. LONG, Robert WORTHAM.

page 29   Amount of sale of land and negroes of Harman MILLER, deceased, recorded 13 February 1826, by Harman MILLER, Junior, administrator...buyers: James SANDERS, Walter S. JENKIN, Nancy MILLER, Joseph MILLER, James MILLER, Reuben SMITH, R. MILLER, Robert CRAWFORD.

page 29   Amount of sale of personal property of Harman MILLER, deceased, recorded 13 February 1826...mentions negroes he owned. Buyers: John DARNELL, Nancy MILLER, James BYERS, Pleasant AKIN, John BROGRES, James SANDERS, Allen AKIN, Anderson MILLER, Solomon BUNCH, Moses AKIN, Martin TONEY, Joseph JONES (?), William DARNELL, John MOORE, Jonathan MILLS, Elisha LANGFORD, Thomas WATSON, Andrew MILLS, Joseph NUMBEY (?), John TWOMS, Robert B. MONTGOMERY.

page 32   17 February 1826...Yearly allowance for maintenance of Elisabeth BOYD, widow of James BOYD, deceased... mentions that the white family numbered four and the black family number six. Signed 1 November 1825, Jno. MACK, George M. EGNEW, Solomon P. MACKWELL.

page 33   16 February 1826...Inventory of personal property of Samuel E. FRIERSON, deceased...had 17 negroes... owned a cotton gin. Signed: John FRIERSON, Samuel D. FRIERSON, administrators, October 1825.

page 34   18 February 1826...Settlement with Richard A. L. WILKS, executor of will of William MC ORD, deceased ...note on John HATCHER; judgement of A. M. HOUSTON; note of William BLACK, accounts of John BALDRIDGE, John WEBBER (?)...paid $1.25 to MITCHELL for coffin ...signed Alexander JOHNSTON, John HATCHETT, J.P.'s.

page 35   Recorded 12 February 1825...Ezekial M. CAMPBELL of Maury County sold to James ADKISON a negro named Sam, age 22, and Tom, age 20...his interest in said

negroes came from "my wife as one of heirs of William
AKIN, deceased." Signed 19 March 1825, Ezekial M.
CAMPBELL. Witnesses: H. GROVES, George PATTON.

page 35   Recorded 18 February 1825...Inventory of estate of
John GOSSETT, deceased, by William GOSSETT, administrator.

page 36   Recorded 18 February 1826...Account of James J.
JENKINS, guardian for Thomas W. VINCENT...items
included 18 - 3/4¢ expenses for whiskey at husking
...hire of negro Sabry and board for negro Mary.
Signed by James BLACK and James T. SANDFORD to settle
guardianship. (Guardian called John JENKINS in this
item also.)

page 37   Recorded 21 February 1826...Settlement with William
GOSSETT, administrator of John GOSSETT, deceased...
signed 11 January 1826 by B. S. HIRT and J. B.
WALLIENE. William GOSSETT paid for 53 days as
administrator of this estate in 1825 the amount of
$40.

page 37   List of sale of property of James BOYD, deceased...
Buyers: Abner MATTHEWS (bought constitution of
U.S.A.), Elizabeth MATHEWS, William J. HENDERSON,
Elizabeth P. BOYD, Andrew BOYD, Simpson PERRY,
Edward R. HOUSTON, Richard HENDERSON, John MIRICK,
Yancy BLEADSOE, A. C. ESLEMAN, George M. EGNEW,
Alexander S. HENDERSON, Benjamin WISEMAN, William
ALLEN, John MOORE, John R. BOYD, Nancy HENDERSON,
Lemuel PHILIPS, Leven COVEY, Robert SHEFFIELD,
Michael BALDRIDGE, Robert F. MATTHEWS, Ebenezer
RICE. Among items sold were shoemakers tools...
William S. HENDERSON, John R. BOYD, administrators.
Sale on 8 November 1825.

page 40   Recorded 22 February 1826...Settlement with William
RUTLEDGE, administrator of John EDLEMAN, deceased...
James PEYTON a buyer...notes on Alexander C. CROFFORD,
Thos. N. HARPER, Henry GIBSON, Thos. ADKISON, Thos.
WORTHAM, Robert WORTHAM, Charles B. HARRIS, Philip
PENN, Philip P. WINN, William STOCKARD, Thos. WORTHAM,
Nancy EDDLEMAN, Josiah GREEN, Robert F. MATTHEWS, O.
ALEXANDER, T. ROPER, E. PEYTON, James U. (?) JENKINS,
William PORTER...signed, David CRAIG, William STOCK-
ARD, J.P.'s, 20 January 1826.

page 41   Recorded 22 February 1826...Inventory of estate of
John S. LONGLEY, deceased, James W. (?) JOHNSTON,
administrator.

page 42   Recorded 21 March 1826...Will of John G. WEBSTER...
gold watch to brother Robert P. WEBSTER...wife Emily
L., "should she be delivered of a living child" -
the child would receive 2/3 of estate and wife 1/3,
if not, all to wife - if child is born within nine
months from present date...to brother-in-law, Col.
James DOBBINS "my interest in all land we have in
co-partnership with Maj. John BROWN"...signed John
P. WEBSTER...Witnesses: William C. GRAVES, John
KESTERSON, Thomas BROWN, Moses F. ROBERTS. A codicil

recorded desires that Patrick MC GUIRE, Nathaniel WILLIS, Col. James DOBBINS, and "my father" to be executors.

page 43   October term 1824...recorded 21 March 1826...Settlement made with John MILLER, treasurer of bridge commission.

page 44   Inventory of property sold by David REED and James PATTERSON, executors of Mary REED, deceased... property included a negro woman and three children... no date.

page 44   Recorded 21 March 1826...John GORDAN and John HATCHITT, Esquires,settled 22 ,July 1825 with Jesse BRIDGES, administrator, and Ester BRIDGES, administratrix, of Bains BRIDGES, deceased.

page 45   Recorded 22 March 1826...Return of hire of five negroes of William H. WILSON, deceased...signed Stephen SMITH, James W. SMITH, administrators.

page 45   Recorded 22 March 1826...Will of Nancy HARRIWAY of Maury County...to children of Elisabeth BROWN, my niece, the wife of Charles W. (?) BROWN, that is Peter A. BROWN, Martha Ann BROWN, Francis Elisabeth BROWN, Mildred Angeline BROWN, and James Price BROWN ...left negro to these children...signed Nancy (X) HARRIWAY...executors: Philip CHAPMAN, Benjamin CHAPMAN...signed 5 May 1822...witnesses: Allen HILL and Mariah (X) BOAZ.

page 46   Recorded 23 March 1826...A return of sail of property of William FARRIS, deceased...buyers included Harry HODGES, Robert WHITESIDE...signed by Jane FARRIS and James FARRIS, administrators.

page 46   Recorded 23 March 1826...Inventory of sale of property of William BESKIDE, deceased...Miles BURNS, administrator.

page 48   Inventory of property of John T. WARD, deceased... recorded 23 March 1826...John KNOX, administrator.

page 48   Recorded 23 March 1826...Inventory of sale of estate of Samuel FOX, deceased...among many items were two tomahawks, doctor books...held note on Joseph T. ELLIOTT...signed Matthew MOORE, executor.

page 51   Inventory of accounts of Solomon HERRING, deceased... recorded 23 March 1826 John MCFALLS, John W. MILLER, Jesse KENNEDY, Daniel BROWN, Junior, Elijah LANKFORD, Joseph DARNAL, John SHARP, Jesse LANGFORD, Robert GAING (?), Burrel AKIN, Thomas SMITH, Jesse B. RAINY, William TURNER, Shedrick CHANDLER, Joseph CHUMLEY, William YANCY, Sion BOON, Thornton MANDLER, Allaganna MAGUIRE, Nancy HOPSON, Robert SMITH, William KILCREASE, Joseph ROADS, George CASEY, John SUDDARDT, Thomas GRANT, Lemuel WATERS, William C. CLEMMONS, Richard VAUGHN, Abner ROADS...mentions hire of several negroes...

page 52   Supplement to inventory of James ISOM, deceased,
           recorded 23 March 1826...William CATHEY, Polly ISOM,
           administrators.

page 52   Recorded 24 March 1826...Inventory of personal estate
           of Thomas WATSON, deceased...Sion BOON, administrator.

page 53   Recorded 24 March 1826...Commissioners met at house
           of Mrs. Susanah WILLIAMS, it also being the residence
           of her deceased husband Greenbury WILLIAMS. The
           widow was to receive as her dower 1/3 part - four
           tracts of land, the mansion house...mentions a spring
           known as Elm Spring...the boundaries of the property
           mentioned and land calls were the sulphur spring at
           Pruit's Lick, the road from Columbia to Mt. Pleasant
           ...negroes included in estate...signed by William
           STOCARD, Nathl WILLIS, E. D. GONS (?), John SHIELD,
           Hugh SHAW, Alexander STAPLES, Samuel H. SMITH, John
           P. ELIOTT, David GLASS, Thos. M. GLASS, L. D. BREWS-
           TER, Nicholas LONG.

page 55   Recorded 24 March 1826...Inventory of estate of Isaac
           N. PORTER, deceased...notes on Edmond L. WILLIAMS...
           receipt of Jesse BRIDGES, R. H. BRANK, William
           TROUSDALE, Housa JAMISON, John W. COHANN, E. FLY,
           Henry CAPS, Johnathan GEORGE, Andrew SMITH, George
           M. MARTIN, Jesse BRIDGES, Samuel STOCKARD, William
           DENNY, John T. FARRIS, Thomas MC REE, John NIXON,
           Jacob SCOTT, William COVY, Elijah WOOD, Hugh DOUGLAS,
           Robert L. COBBS, Robert SELLARS, Solomon P. MAXWELL,
           Samuel CARUTHERS, John B. ALDERSON, John WILSON,
           William JOHNSTON, John T. RICHARDS, Simon JOHNSTON,
           David J. EVANS, James STOCKARD, Peter R. BOOKER,
           David CRAIGHEAD, Thos. B. CRAIGHEAD, John T. HUDSON,
           Lewis RENFRO, James K. POLK, John C.HAMILTON, Joseph
           B. PORTER, Isom CHERRY...property included "machine
           for impressing county seal", negro boy...Executors:
           Thomas Jefferson PORTER, Robert CARITHERS.

page 57   Recorded 25 March 1826...Settlement of commissioners
           with William WALLACE, guardian of George and John
           LUMPKINS, heirs of Robert LUMPKINS...mentions hire
           of negroes...signed 25 July 1825 Joel REESE, Joseph
           ERWIN.

page 58   List of vouchers for above included those on Richard
           HUSENFORD, Marshall DUNCAN, James C. KERR, Benjamin
           B. SMITH, James LONGLEY, SANSOM and HAYS, James R.
           PLUMMER.

page 58   Recorded 25 March 1826...Dr. the estate of Thos.
           LEWELLIN, deceased, in account with William R. MILLER,
           administrator...receipts, vouchers, or notes on C.
           GRANGER, James KENNEDY, John KENNEDY, William YANCY,
           ALDERSON and TUCKINS, James C. RILEY, Robert KENNEDY,
           James WALKER, Ruben SMITH...signed James BLACK, J.P.,
           and P. NELSON, J.P.

page 60   Dr William HAMLETT in account current with William
           COOPER...vouchers included one of account paid to
           Richard D. PASSAMORE for tuition on Nob Creek...
           mentions shoes and board for Philis - later mentions

hire of Philis, so Philis was presumably a negro
slave of estate...mentions accounts with Doctors
BROWN and MC GIMPSEY, Josiah ALDERSON, Moses HANKS,
William R. MILLER...signed 20 July 1825...Settlement
with William COOPER, guardian of William HAMLETT,
one of minor heirs of Littleberry HAMLETT, deceased
...signed Swan HARDIN, P. NELSON, J.P.'s.

page 61   Recorded 25 March 1826...Will of Ebenezer SMITH of
             Maury County...my wife Jane SMITH to receive the
             plantation and houses north of the spring branch
             except the Halter Shop, and some negroes...my eldest
             son William SMITH to receive one house and lot and
             halter shop in Mt. Pleasant...my son Robert SMITH to
             receive 1/5 part of tract of land...daughter Eliza-
             beth SMITH...son Zilman SMITH, 1/5 part of tract of
             land...son Ely SMITH, 1/5 part of tract of land...
             son Levy SMITH, 1/5 part of tract of land...son John
             SMITH, 1/5 part of tract of land...daughter Jane
             Porter SMITH...mentions my five sons - Robert, Ely,
             Levy, Zilman, John C...later wife is found as Jean...
             friend John GILCHRIST and Jean SMITH, administrators
             ...signed 9 December 1824, Ebenezer SMITH...witnesses:
             Robert DOAK, John GILCHRIST, George M. EGNEW.

page 64   Settlement with administrator of John GOSSETT, dec-
             eased...signed 13 July 1825 by Joseph B. WALLACE,
             Bird S. HURT, commissioners.

page 64   Recorded 28 March 1826...Settlement with Robert C.
             DICKSON, administrator of estate of John DICKSON,
             deceased...signed David CRAIG, William STOCORD.

page 65   Recorded 28 March 1826...Inventory of sale of John
             DAVIDSON, deceased...Buyers: Wesly G. NEELY, P. F.
             DOOLEY, Evander KENNEDY, E. B. DOOLEY, William
             MC KANLAS, Isaac GOFF, Ephragm G. DAVIDSON, John
             BROWN, Mathias WARFIELD, Ridley R. WESTBROOK, Joseph
             HANNA, James WILKINS, James MITCHELL, A. DICKSON.

page 67   Recorded 27 March 1826...Settlement with administra-
             tor of James BURNS, deceased...a voucher included
             "for his services in the United States Army" for $48.
             Signed James S. BALDRIDGE, Jno. W. RECORD, J.P.'s.

page 68   Recorded 27 March 1826...Inventory of estate of Anne
             MC INTYRE, deceased, by Nicholas P. SMITH, adminis-
             trator..."the said Duncan MC INTYRE resides at pre-
             sent in the state of Alabama."

page 69   Recorded 28 March 1826...Inventory of sail of pro-
             perty of Robert HULGAN, deceased...Buyers included
             John COOPER, William DIXON, Samuel KENNEDY, John
             FOSSETT, Meridath BLALOCK, Jesse KENNEDY; signed
             Samuel KENNEDY, administrator.

page 69   Recorded 28 March 1826...Additional return of sale
             of property of Ann MC INTIRE, deceased, by Duncan
             MC INTIRE, administrator...mentions one negro man
             sold in 1818 to James H. WILLIAMS. Signed: Duncan
             MC INTIRE.

page 69   Recorded 29 March 1826

page 70   Report of commissioners of examination of tax book
             of 1824 - 1825...pertaining to entries in the
             surveyor's office of the eighth District...signed by
             A. CATHEY, H. GROVES, Alexander JOHNSTON, Nicholas
             J. LONG.

page 70   Recorded 29 March 1826...List of property of Ann
             MC INTIRE, deceased, by Duncan MC INTIRE, administra-
             tor...mentions (possibly purchasers) Archd MC DONALD,
             Nancy WRIGHT, Catharine WRIGHT, Marshall SPAIN,
             Samuel GRIFFITH, John COFFEE, John POWELL, Duncan
             STEWARD, Edward DRAKE, Elisha SMITH, Sato NIGHT,
             William MACKEY, Charles CAMPBELL, John HUNTER, Henry
             PICKARD, John MC INTYRE, William HOLT, Cato NIGHT,
             James YOUNG, Malcolm MC INTYRE, Samuel SMITH, Kadis
             NIGHT, Duncan MC DUGGALD. Signed Duncan MC INTYRE,
             administrator.

page 72   Inventory of sale of estate of John SELLERS, deceased,
             recorded 27 March 1826...Buyers: Johnathan WHITESIDES,
             James CATHEY, Moses SMITH, Samuel WHITESIDES, Jr.,
             William HART, Daniel MC COLLUM, Thos. LANGFORD,
             Joseph HART, Hugh JONES, Robinson WHITESIDES, Samuel
             FARRIS, John MC GILL, Joseph MC MURRY, Uzzel HAWKINS,
             George ISOM, Polly SELLERS, James BRAIDY, Jane
             SELLERS (one Bible), Alexander ERVIN, William SCOTT,
             Thomas CRANTOM (?), J. HART for Betsy SELLERS, John
             SHELBY, Hugh JONES, Dudley ISOM, Green LEE, James
             PATTON, William SCOTT, J. RUDLE, James L. BELL, Andrew
             BLAIR, Joseph MC MURRY, Robert WILEY, Robinson YEATHAM.

page 74   Recorded 31 March 1826...Inventory of estate of Robert
             BURKETT, deceased.

page 75   Recorded 6 June 1826...Will of Squire SHERMAN of
             Person County, North Carolina, made 19 September 1815
             ...wife Dicy SHERMAN, daughter Nancy SHERMAN, son John
             Washington SHERMAN, son Abner SHERMAN, daughter Mary
             P. Martia SHERMAN (or possibly this entry could be
             read Mary and Martia SHERMAN), son Parsons SHERMAN...
             "she being at this time pregnant" (presumably this
             refers to his wife, although the wording of the will
             does not make it clear)...there was mention of
             negroes belonging to him...mention of land in Orange
             County, North Carolina...executors: friends Nicholas
             JONES, Samuel DICKENS, and William DICKENS. Signed
             Squire SHERMAN. Witnesses: Richard REED, Jno.
             BOWELS, Jr., William DUKE, Jno. DUKE. Certified by
             clerk of Person County, North Carolina.

page 77   Recorded 4 June 1826...Will of Jno. BALDRIDGE...
             beloved wife Isabella...all my children...daughter
             Isabella, daughter Margarette, daughter Elizabeth
             KENNEDY, son William L., son John, son James L.,
             executor...wanted his books left to the use of his
             family...owned negroes...signed 11 September 1823,
             with witnesses Ebenezer RICE, Junior, and John
             BALDRIDGE, Junior.

page 78   Recorded 4 June 1826...Will of Solomon HERRING..."my
              mother have a decent maintenance and she live with
              my family"...wife Nancy...son Robert, minor, and only
              child...owned negroes...Executor, John MILLER...
              signed 30 November 1824, Solomon (X) HERRING...
              Witnesses: James HUEY, James C. WISTLE (?).

page 79   recorded 4 June 1826...Will of John DAVIDSON of
              Maury County...Ruth C. DAVIDSON, daughter of my son
              Ephraigm E. DAVIDSON...Richard WHITESIDE, son of my
              daughter Ruth WHITESIDE...wife Francis...John G.
              DAVIDSON, son of my son Thomas DAVIDSON, deceased...
              B. C. DAVIDSON, son of my son Thomas DAVIDSON,
              deceased...son John O. DAVIDSON and son-in-law Paris
              F. DOOLEY to be executors...heirs of Thomas DAVIDSON
              in right of their father, Andrew NEELY and Jane his
              wife, Ephraigm E. DAVIDSON, John O. DAVIDSON, Parris
              F. DOOLEY and Cinthia his wife, to share and share
              alike...signed 15 June 1824, John DAVIDSON.
              Witnesses: Joseph B. PORTER, John MATTHEWS.

page 80   Recorded 4 June 1825...Will of James MATHEWS of
              Maury, dated 17 September 1819. Wife Mary...son
              Abner...mentions my surveying instruments...son
              Abner to be executor...signed James MATHEWS...
              Witnesses: Joel REESE, Moses D. HARPER, Isaac I.(J?)
              THOMAS.

page 81   Recorded 6 June 1826...Will of Polly J. VOORHIES
              made 4 July 1819...husband Peter J. VOORHIES to
              receive any real estate "which I might have descend
              to me from my father or mother, sisters or brothers."

page 81   Recorded 6 June 1826...Will of Simon TURNER of Maury
              County...wife Sarah...two youngest children - Martha
              W. TURNER and David B. TURNER - daughter Elisa SANDERS
              to receive land on Hatchee River, Tenth Surveyor's
              District, Western District, which he purchased from
              Col. William POLK of North Carolina...had land in
              Maury County adjoining William ALEXANDER...owned 15
              negroes...daughter Lucy PERKINS to also receive land
              in Western District purchased from POLK...daughter
              Nancy TURNER...two sons John T. TURNER and Simon T.
              TURNER..."when four youngest children reach age of
              21"...friends James P. PETERS and Fanning JONES,
              executors...signed Simon TURNER, 13 April 1824...
              Witnesses: Joseph HILL, Jones DAVID, James K. POLK.

page 85   Recorded 6 June 1826...Will of Mary TURLEDGE...
              balance of estate to be divided between Eastham B.
              DOOLEY and Parris F. DOOLEY, who were also executors
              ...all wearing apparel to be given to Mrs. Rachel
              DOOLEY and what "will not suit her to Mrs. Patsey
              DOOLEY, wife of Eastham B. DOOLEY and Mrs. Cinthia
              DOOLEY, wife of Parris F. DOOLEY." Signed 24 July
              1824, Mary RUTLEDGE. Witnesses: David MARTIN, Joel
              REESE, Nimrod PORTER.

page 85   Recorded 7 June 1826...Will of Joshua GRINDER of
              Maury County...wife Franky GRINDER...signed Joshua
              (X) GRINDER...Witnesses: Josiah BLACKBURN, Hensley
              WILLIAM, Sharp WILLIAM.

page 86   Recorded 7 June 1826...Will of Michael FOGLEMAN of
           Maury County...beloved wife...between my children.
           (Note: neither wife nor children were called by
           name in this will.) Signed Michael FOGLEMAN.
           Witnesses: Samuel FOGLEMAN, Nathaniel M. POWELL.

page 86   Recorded 7 June 1826...Will of John HODGE of Maury
           County...my wife and children...owned negroes...had
           land in Sumner County, and Giles County, Tennessee
           ...owned two lots in Pulaski, Tennessee...owned lot
           and a half in Gallatin, Tennessee...owned two lots
           in Columbia on which wool factory was located...wife
           Ann C. HODGE...left money for the raising of "her
           and our children"...children: James, Lewis, Joseph,
           John, Mary Euphemia, William Isaac, Robert Thomas,
           and Benjamin Lewis...till coming of age of my oldest
           son...family Bible left to his wife "in remembrance
           of me"...friends George M. MARTIN and Mathew D.
           COOPER, executors...signed 7 October 1825, John
           HODGE...Witnesses: famlin MC DOWELL, William MC
           NIEL, Thomas T. BROWN.

page 89   Return of commissioners...division of 1000 acre tract
           of land in Maury and Bedford Counties...divided into
           two equal parts in 1822...the heirs of MCLAIN to
           receive one part...and Benjamin LEVEL and Samuel
           BROWN to have other part...mentions Wilson SPRING in
           Bedford County...signed 31 October 1822, Jas. N.
           SMITH, Jos. MOORHEAD, Samuel SMITH.

page 90   Commissioners settlement with A. JOHNSTON, adminis-
           trator of Allen H. YOUNG, deceased...signed 20 Oct-
           ober 1824, James WALKER, Jos. B. WALLACE.

page 90   Juries return to lay off Sarah C. VOORHIES dower...
           she was late widdow of Benjamin HERNDON, deceased,
           and now Sarah VOORHIES...she was to receive one
           third part of land on Duck River, located seven
           miles above Columbia...mentions a linn spring on
           the property. Signed 17 March 1823 by James N. SMITH,
           Samuel SMITH, Smith JAMES, John L. RICHERSON, Alex.
           MOORE, John BUTLER.

page 91   Division of negroes, January 1825...to Jacob WILLIAMS
           and wife Jenny...to Terrill G. HUNTER...to Sarah
           HUNTER...to Hezekiah HUNTER...signed Willis TONS (?),
           George MITCHELL, Joshua WILLIAMS...Mary HUNTER,
           guardian of said minor children...Jacob BROOKS and
           Nancy his wife guardian of Comfort R. HUNTER.

page 93   Recorded 11 June 1826...Year's provision for Mrs.
           Elisabeth KINCAID...signed 15 January 1825 by Robert
           DOAK, John GILLESPIE, Abraham LOONEY.

page 93   Recorded 11 June 1826...Inventory of estate of
           Joseph KINCAID, deceased. George M. EGNEW and
           Elisabeth KINCAID, administrators.

page 94   Recorded 11 June 1826...Amount of property sold by
           John ALLISON, administrator, of James MORRIS, dec-
           eased, on 11 November 1824.

140

page 94	Recorded 11 June 1826...Inventory of estate of Sarah WADE, deceased...one negro man, age 50, was claimed by legatees of Dabney WADE, deceased, and so title to negro is doubtful...mentions Sarah WADE's share of the estate of Louisa WADE, deceased, whose estate was under Jacob SCOTT, administrator. John WOODRUFF, administrator of Sarah WADE, deceased.
page 94	Recorded 11 June 1826...Sale of estate of William BRADSHAW, deceased. George HARRISON, administrator.
page 94	Recorded 11 June 1826...Allottment to Winne WREN for year's support, signed 25 November 1824, by George A. PEELER, William SEGRIST, Nick CESOBBY (?).
page 95	Recorded 11 June 1826...Inventory of estate of Wright KERBY and sale...seven negroes in inventory...signed Allen RAINEY, administrator.
page 97 - 100	Recorded 11 June 1826...Inventory and account of sale of estate of William BRADSHAW, deceased...signed H. GOWER, administrator, and Elisabeth BRADSHAW, administratrix.
page 101	Recorded 13 June 1824...Settlement with Robert WORTHAM, Esquire, guardian of minor heirs of Green B. WILLIAMS, deceased...Susan WILLIAMS, widow, to receive her share of the crop. Signed 24 April 1826 by Nicholas J. LONG, David CRAIG, J.P.'s.
page 102	Recorded June 15, 1826...List of property belonging to estate of Staple CRAFTON, deceased, worth $275., total. Signed: Elisabeth CRAFTIN.
page 102	Recorded 15 June 1826...Allottment to Mary KIRBY, widow of Wright KIRBY, deceased, together with her six children...year's provision...signed 18 November 1824, Reuben SMITH, James BLACK, John KENNEDY, commissioners.
page 102	Recorded 15 June 1826...Inventory of estate of Isaac BILLS, deceased...inventory included negroes and a small library of books...Placebo M. BILLS and Lillus BILLS, administrators.
page 104	Recorded 15 June 1826...Inventory of estate of Sarah CAMPBELL, deceased, of Maury County...lists of notes and accounts and property...negroes included in estate as well as "note on bank of Marietta supposed to be counterfeit"...signed, John BROWN.
page 105	Recorded 15 June 1825...Peter J. VOORHIES and Sarah C. VOORHIES, his wife, sold to William FARROW the dower of Sarah, as relict of Benjamin HERNDON, deceased, which was land in Maury County on Duck River, "where Benjamin HERNDON resided during his lifetime"...signed 25 August 1825, Peter J. (or I.) VOORHIES and Sarah C. VOORHIES...witnesses: Will C. CHERRY and John S. LONGLEY.
page 106	Alexander PICKARD and James MC GOWIN, guardians for minor heirs of John DICKSON, deceased, rendered

account of estate at April term 1825...many receipts
and notes...notes on Elisabeth DICKSON, Robert C.
DIXON, James DICKSON...receipt of James K. POLK...
signed 18 July 1825, Richard STOCKARD, David CRAIG,
J.P.'s.

page 107   Recorded 11 June 1826...List of goods and chatles of
William LOVING, deceased...signed Michael ROBERTSON,
administrator.

page 108   Recorded 15 June _____...Settlement with Samuel MC LEAN,
guardian of minor heirs of William MC LEAN, deceased
...mentions taxes on lands in the Western District...
signed 24 April 1826, Richard B. PASSMORE, Robert
SELLERS, J.P.'s.

page 108   Recorded 15 June 1826...Inventory of goods and
chattles of John LINDSEY, deceased...many items
included...38 negroes listed as part of estate...
29 silver spoons...eleven beds and eight bedsteads...
notes...Sally LINDSAY and Guston (later found as
Agustus) KERNEY, administrators...signed 10 January
1826 by John HATCHETT.

page 110   Recorded 15 June 1826...Settlement with administrator
of Hopson ARNOLD, deceased...vouchers listed...signed
17 April 1826, James L. BALDRIDGE, P. D. BILLS, J.P.'s.

page 111   Recorded 11 June 1826...List of Sale of property of
John M. ALEXANDER, deceased...among the buyers were
James O. ALEXANDER, Siles ALEXANDER, Ozni ALEXANDER
...estate included many deer skins and stag skins.

page 112   List of judgements, notes, accounts for the above
estate. William R. ALEXANDER and James P. (?)
ALEXANDER found in this list.

page 113   Recorded 16 June 1826...Inventory of sale of personal property of John LINDSEY, deceased...among
items were smith tools and surveying chains...signed
17 April 1826, Sarah LINDSAY, Gustun KEARNEY,
executors.

page 113   Recorded 15 June 1825...List of property belonging
to estate of Samuel WASSON, deceased...Signed J.
WASSON and William MCONNELL.

page 114   Recorded 16 June 1826...Division of estate of John
GOSSETT, deceased...each distributee to receive
$220.50 2/3...signed 2 March 1826, Samuel DUNLAP,
John FIELDS, commissioners.

page 114   Recorded 16 June 1826...Settlement with Abraham
LOONEY, guardian of minor heirs of Jacob MC KEE,
deceased...accounts for the necessaries furnished
to Matilda MC KEE, Sally MC KEE, Malinda MC KEE,
Lucinda MC KEE, and Jacob H. MC KEE...signed Alex.
JOHNSTON, Robert CARUTHERS, commissioners.

page 115   Recorded 11 June 1825...Widow's provision for Jane
FARRIS, signed 10 November 1825, Will. CATHEY,
Samuel LUSK, Samuel W. ATKIN, Samuel WHITESIDE.

page 116	Amount of sale of estate of John T. WARD, deceased... total amount was $25...including a "kitt of shoe-maker tools"...John KNOX, administrator.
page 116	Recorded 16 June 1826...Provision for Elisabeth BRAD-SHAW, widdow of William BRADSHAW, deceased, for 1825 ...signed 13 December 1824, Peter R. BOOKER, John BOOKER, George M. MARTIN.
page 117	Recorded 16 June 1826...Will of Samuel WASSON of Maury County...negro slave Harry "to be emancipated" ...also gave other property to Harry...wife Cather-ine...son Abel...heirs of my son Abner...Executors: John WASSON, William MCONNELL, signed 11 March 1826, Samuel WASSON...Witnessed by Josiah WASSON, Samuel S. WASSON.
page 118	Recorded 16 June 1826...Settlement with Thomas GILLUM, executor of estate of John FORSYTHE, deceased... signed John GORDON, Robert E. HENDERSON, J.P.'s., 6 October 1825.
page 118	Recorded 16 June 1826...Inventory of estate of William WREN, deceased...items sold to Winefred WREN, Thomas WREN, Peter WREN, George WREN, Wingfield (also Winfield) WREN...signed Kinchen SPARKMAN, administrator.
page 119	Recorded 16 June 1828...Inventory of estate of Peter GLASSCOCK...only one item in estate, a negro named Jacob, age 20...James GLASSCOCK, administrator.
page 119	Recorded 16 June 1826...Inventory of property of Mathew SWAN.
page 119	Recorded 16 June 1826...Year's provision for Nancy HERRIN, relict of Solomon HERRIN, deceased...pro-vision for her and her families support...signed 18 January 1825 by Ruben SMITH, Robert CAMPBELL, Harman MILLER, James HUEY.
page 120	16 June 1826, recorded...Amount of estate of John GARRISON, deceased, on 29 May 1823...Total $114.60.
page 120	Recorded 17 June 1826...Amount of sale of estate of Robert BURKET, deceased.
page 122	Recorded 17 June 1826...William HAMBLETT, orphan of Littleburry HAMLETT, deceased, in account with his guardian.
page 122	Account of Sale of property of Sarah CAMPBELL, dec-eased...many accounts...mentions note on John CAMP-BELL...no date.
page 125	Recorded 17 June 1826...Inventory of estate of John HOLCOMBE, deceased, on 17 April 1826. Notes on Lawrence HOLCOMBE, and Lewis HOLCOMBE.
page 126	Recorded 16 June 1826...Guardians of William and Benjamin HARDIN, infant heirs of Isaac B. HARDIN, deceased, have been unable to obtain any money

belonging to said heirs...signed P. R. BOOKER, M. D. COOPER, who had been appointed guardians by the court.

page 126   Recorded 17 June 1826...Inventory of estate of Samuel MORGAN, deceased, late of Rutherford County, Tennessee ...note on John B. DUCKER of Mississippi...Allen BROWN, administrator.

page 127   Recorded 16 June 1826...Widow's provision for the Widdow EDDLEMAN...signed 11 November 1824 by James HAMMER, Moses D. HARPER.

page 127   Recorded 17 June 1826...Dr Francis WADE in account with Joseph WINGFIELD, guardian...mentions hire of negroes...signed James BLACK, John MILLER, J.P.

page 128   Recorded 17 June 1826...Sale of property of James DOOLEY, deceased...buyers included Ratchel DOOLEY, widdow of deceased; E. B. DOOLEY, Paris F. DOOLEY, Littleton DOOLEY, John B. BROWN, G. BROWN...Nimrod PORTER, Joseph ERWIN, administrators.

page 129   Recorded 17 June 1826...Inventory of estate of James ISOM, deceased...nine negroes...family Bibble...notes on Elisabeth ISOM, Dudly ISOM...account of Henry ISOM ...estate included $600 in U. S. money and $1.25 in Tennessee money...signed William CATHEY, Polly ISOM, administrators.

page 131   Recorded 17 June 1826...List of sale of estate of William LOVING, held 20 October 1824...Buyers included John LOVING, William LOVING, Tennessee ROPER, Malcom GILCHRIST...Signed Michael ROBERSON, Joseph HACKNEY, executors.

page 133   Inventory of John GRIFFITH...June 1826...Buyers: Samuel GRIFFITH, James GRIFFITH, John GRIFFITH, Susan GRIFFITH.

page 135   Recorded 11 November 1824...Account of inventory and sale of Charles WILSON, deceased...family Bible... "a legacy coming from the estate of Mrs. WILSON's father Thomas CATES, deceased"...one of the buyers was Elisabeth WILSON...Redrick DISHONGH, administrator.

page 137   Inventory of goods and affects of late Signor CAWLEY, deceased, as of 28 April 1823...mentions estate in Louisa (possibly Louisiana), in Mississippi, Tennessee, and Maury County...seven negroes...Samuel MORGAN, Patsey CAWLEY, administrators.

page 138   Inventory of estate of Obediah MASH, deceased... 18 October 1824...signed same date by Butler NOLES, Nimrod PORTER, administrators.

page 139   Inventory of property of Staples CRAFTIN, deceased... 26 July 1825, signed Elisabeth (X) CRAFTIN, administrator.

page 139   Inventory of estate and sale of Francis H. KENNEDY, deceased...buyers included E. STONE, James KENNEDY,

Mary KENNEDY (widow), Thomas KENNEDY, G. KENNEDY, M. KENNEDY; Thomas J. KENNEDY, George M. MARTIN, administrators.

page 144   Account of sale of William MCORD, deceased...R. A. L. WILKS, executor.

page 142   Inventory of property William REN, deceased. Kinchen
(note)   SPARKMAN, administrator.

page 142   Samuel MAYS, Alexander DOGGINS, Samuel WITHERSPOON, freeholders in Maury County, appraised personal estate of Moses J. FRIERSON, deceased, and found it to be $7,098.25...estate included negroes...have divided and given 1/7 part of Edward Livingston FRIERSON, one of heirs. Signed 25 January 1820?.

page 143   Widdow's provision for widdow of Mathew SWAN, deceased. (Note: not named)...signed Admiah TURNER, Mathew LEE, Robert WORTHAM, 16 November 1824.

page 143   Met at home of Mrs. Mary Jane FRIERSON, one of the guardians of the minor heirs of Moses J. FRIERSON, deceased...allotted to James A. FRIERSON in right of his wife Margarett A. FRIERSON...signed 11 February 1824, Nathaniel WILLIS, Alex. M. WILLIAMS, Henry TURNER.

page 144   Account of personal property of Isaac BILLS, deceased ...many books listed. Buyers included Lilles BILLS, P. M. BILLS, Ollivia BILLS...sale held on 12 and 13 November 1824...negroes in estate...Lilles BILLS, P. M. BILLS, administrators.

page 151   Inventory of estate of Solomon HERRING...18 January 1825...John MILLER, executor.

page 152   Settlement with Hugh DOUGLASS and William HAWKINS, administrators of the estate of Jehosaphat LADD, deceased...A. CATHEY, John O. COOKE, J.P.'s.

page 152   Inventory of goods and chatles of Chals WEEMS, deceased...sold on 20 August 1824...a buyer at this sale was Mary WEEMS.

page 153   Settlement with estate of Green B. WILLIAMS, deceased with administrator Alexander M. WILLIAMS...signed Robert WORTHAM, N. J. LONG, J.P...no date.

page 155   Inventory of estate of Robert FRIERSON, deceased... sold March 22 and divided among the heirs...Doctor Samuel MAYS, executor...signed 26 April 1824, James WALKER, J. S. ALDERSON, J.P.

page 156   Notes in hands of John T. FARRIS, administrator of James A. FARRIS, deceased...signed 26 April 1824, Hugh DOUGLASS, J. S. ALDERSON.

page 156   James T. SANDFORD and James BLACK appointed to divide the estate of John CAMPBELL, deceased...they found that there were eleven distributive shares, to wit: Joseph H. MILLER, Robert CAMPBELL, Alexander

CAMPBELL, Ezekial M. CAMPBELL, John P. CAMPBELL,
William C. CAMPBELL, Matilda T. CAMPBELL, Junius T.
CAMPBELL, Carolina H. CAMPBELL, Samuel P. CAMPBELL,
and Matilda G., widow of John CAMPBELL, deceased,
now Matilda G. JINKINS, wife of Philip G. JENKINS...
signed 19 December 1822.

page 157 Settlement of guardianship of Robert CAMPBELL,
guardian of Matilda I.(?) CAMPBELL and Caroline H.
CAMPBELL, heirs of John CAMPBELL, deceased. Signed
18 April 1825, James BLACK, Allen RAINEY, J.P.'s.

page 158 Commissioners settlement with administrator of
William WHITESIDES, deceased...signed A. CATHEY,
James GRAY, J.P.'s, 26 March 1824.

page 158 Settlement with Eli AMACK, guardian of minor heirs
of Aron ALDRIDGE, deceased...mentions estate of John
ALDRIDGE, deceased, one of the minor heirs of Aron
ALDRIDGE...Nancy ALDRIDGE one of Aron's minor heirs
...James ALDRIDGE, one of Aron's minor heirs...
Betsey ALDRIDGE, one of the minor heirs. Signed
14 April 1825 by Caleb HEADLEY, Jos. B. WALLACE,
justices of the peace.

page 159 Years provision for Elisabeth BURKET and family,
widow and children of William BURKET, deceased,
23 April 1825, by David CRAIG, James GRAY, J.P.

page 159 Account of Sale of Estate of Edward MC CAFFIRTY,
deceased, signed 25 October 1824 by Francis SPENCER.

page 160 Return of committee appointed to lay off to Lillis
BILLS and family, widow and relict of Isaac BILLS,
signed Temple TURNLEY, John GILLESPIE, John M. JONES.
No date.

page 160 Inventory of articles sold at sale of Charles BROWN,
deceased, on 18 August 1824 by Robert L. BROWN,
administrator. Among those buying were: .Mrs. BROWN,
Robert L. BROWN, Dr. J. (?) N. BROWN, William BROWN,
James BROWN.

page 164 10 April 1824, Settlement with Reubin SMITH, administrator of Silas WILLIAMSON, deceased. Signed 19
April 1824, James BLACK, Allen RAINEY, J.P.'s. $2.37
paid to R. A. RANKIN for coffin, among items listed.

page 165 Inventory of property of James DOOLEY, deceased,
signed 16 October 1824, by Nimrod PORTER and Joseph
ERWIN.

page 165 Account current with Estate of William FRIERSON,
deceased. Receipts listed...mention of E. J. FRIER-
SON in North Carolina...mention of collecting money
on J. PARSILL's estate. (PURCELL?) signed 19 July
1824 by James WALKER, Hugh DOUGLASS, J.P.'s.

page 168 Settlement of Guardian, of Tristam PATTON, guardian
of Malinda PICKINS, minor heir of David PICKENS,
deceased. Among the many items was a receipt for
money paid to John BROWN for tuition. Signed 16
April 1825 James BLACK, Allen RAINEY.

page 169   Settlement with administrators of Aron HUNTER, de-
            ceased...met at the home of Mrs. Mary HUNTER...signed
            9 November 1816 by L. (?) COLEMAN, Thos. HUDSPETH...
            Mary HUNTER "her ninth part" mentioned.

page 170   Settlement with Richard HIGHT, administrator of estate
            of Archibald HIGHT, deceased. Signed 19 July 1825, by
            Jos. B. WALLACE, Caleb HEADLEY, J.P.'s.

page 171   Commissioners settlement...Alex. JOHNSTON, Jno.
            HATCHETT, Robert MC DANIEL to settle with William
            and James BOGARD, administrators of Jacob BOGARD,
            deceased. 19 October 1824...negroes included in
            estate...mentions "Polk attorney fees", signed Alex
            JOHNSON, Robert MC DANIEL.

page 173   Year's provision for Polly BYNUM, widow of Mark
            BYNUM, deceased, for first year after BYNUM's death.
            Signed 4 February 1824, by Philip P. WINN, John P.
            ELLIOTT, John SHULL.

page 173   Distribution of personal estate of Abraham WHITESIDES,
            deceased...it was to be distributed "between Richard
            WHITESIDE, only son and heir, and Edward H. CHAFFIN,
            who has intermarried with the widow." Slaves included
            in estate. No date. Signed David CRAIGHEAD, John T.
            MOORE, H. GROVES.

page 174   January term 1824, settlement with William GRAY,
            administrator of estate of William OAKLEY, deceased
            ...widdow's allowance...mentions Jesse OAKLEY account.
            Signed 1 April 1824 by George MITCHELL, William
            EDMONSON, J.P.'s.

page 175   Settlement with Eli AMACK, guardian of Oron ALDRIDGE,
            deceased, minor heirs, who are John ALDRIDGE, Nancy
            ALDRIDGE, James ALDRIDGE, Betsey ALDRIDGE. Signed
            15 April 1825 by Caleb HEADLEY, Jos. B. WALLACE,J.P.'s

page 175   Settlement with Ezekial M. CAMPBELL, guardian of
            Junius and Samuel P. CAMPBELL, minor heirs of John
            CAMPBELL, deceased. Signed 18 April 1825, Richd. B.
            PASSMORE, Allen RAINEY, J.P.'s.

page 176   James L. BALDRIDGE and Jonathan D. BILLS, commission
            to settle with administrators of James PURSEL, de-
            ceased. Richard FAUSETT, one of the administrators.
            Signed 16 April 1824, James L. BALDRIDGE, Jonathan L.
            BILLS. (Abstractor's note: James PURSELL was an
            early builder of Columbia and died about 1821 accord-
            ing to "Youth and Old Age" by Nathan Vaught.)

page 176   Settlement with administrator of Daniel DAVIS, de-
            ceased...William BOAZ, administrator. January term
            1824. Signed by John MACK, Alex. JOHNSON.

page 178   Settlement with Samuel MC LEAN, guardian of minor
            heirs of William MC LEAN. Signed 18 April 1825 by
            R. B. PASSMORE, Robert SELLARS, J.P.'s.

page 178   Settlement with James N. BROWN, guardian for Joseph
            WALKER, a minor heir of Thos. WALKER, deceased.
            18 October 1824, A. CATHEY, James GRAY, J.P.'s.

page 179   Order for administrators of Jehosophat LAD to have a publick sale of six negroes. Signed 22 April 1825 by Hugh DOUGLASS, William HAWKINS, administrator.

page 179   Settlement with Jesse GOODMAN, administrator of Joseph SANDERS, deceased. 16 April 1824, John Mathews, George JOHNSTON, J.P.'s.

page 180   Settlement with William COOPER, guardian of William HAMBLETT, minor heir of Littleberry HAMBLETT, deceased...negroes in part of estate...signed Jno. S. ALDERSON, R. B. PASSMORE, J.P.'s.

page 181   Examination of Rebecca CAMPBELL, separately from her husband, and "she is willing to sign her right of said land and deeds without any constraint from her husband." 18 April 1825, signed Rebecca CAMPBELL. Witnesses: R. B. PASSMORE, Allen RAINEY, J.P.'s.

page 182   Settlement with John FERRIL, administrator of Levy FERRIL, deceased. Joel REESE and John MATHEWS, J.P.'s. No date.

page 183   Settlement with executors of William HENDERSON, deceased. Receipts of widow, John HENDERSON, Richard HENDERSON, William S. HENDERSON, Ezekial HENDERSON...mentions Elisabeth HENDERSON's claim... $2.00 was paid for coffin..."by mutual consent of executors and legatees, the books of the deceased are to remain in the possession of the widdow." Signed 18 February 1825 by John MACK, John MATHEWS, J.P.'s.

page 184   Recorded 3 August 1826, widow's provision for Susan B. WILLIAMS, widdow of Green B. WILLIAMS, deceased. Signed 9 June 1825 by James JONES, John SHULL, John P. ELLIOTT, commissioners.

page 185   Widow's provision for Mary ISOM, widow of James ISOM, deceased. Signed 31 January 1825 by A. CATHEY,Samuel LUSK, Robert LUSK, Joseph GRAY, J.P.'s.

page 185   Col. Simpson SHAW, guardian of Nancy SHERMAN... allowance made to minor heirs of Squire SHERMAN, signed 5 February 1824, by James WALKER, J. S. ALDERSON, J.P.'s.

page 186   August 3, 1826, paid William VOORHIES to imprisonment of Jno. RAGLAND on peace warrant. Signed Joseph B. PORTER, clerk.

page 186   Col. Simpson SHAW, guardian of John, Washington, Polly, Martha, and Person M. SHERMAN, minor heirs of Squire SHERMAN...receipts included "for teaching five children"..."for whipping Sam (costs incurred by judgement of Esquire SELLARS) $5.81-1/4." Signed 5 February 1824, James WALKER, John S. ALDERSON.

page 187   Peter R. BOOKER, James WALKER, Edward W. DALE, John S. ALDERSON, Patrick MC GUIRE appointed by court in 1824 to allot to Darrel N. SANSOM, 3/7 and 2/7 of one, 1/7 of two lots of land in Columbia, lots 64 and 61. Signed April 23, 1824.

page 188   Petition of Betsy SELLARS, William HART and Ratchel
          HART his wife (formerly Ratchel SELLERS), Jane SELLERS,
          Polly SELLERS, Elisabeth SELLERS (infant under 21),
          John SELLERS (infant under 21); and the petition of
          Ebenezer H. SELLERS, Serena S. SELLERS, minors by
          guardian James CATHEY...James SELLERS, Senior,
          husband of Betsy SELLERS, and father of other peti-
          tioners died in Maury County in 1824 without a will
          ...there were 21 negroes in his estate...this peti-
          tion for division of estate. (Note: At one place
          Serena SELLERS appears to be Sarah SELLERS.)

page 189   Division of negroes belong to estate of John SELLERS,
          deceased, by A. CATHEY, Samuel LUSK, William CATHEY,
          Samuel WHITESIDES, commissioners.

page 190   Lay off to duke WILLIAMS and Mary M. WILLIAMS, his
          wife, formerly Mary M. LONG, oldest daughter of John
          Joseph LONG, deceased...She is entitled to 1/6 part.
          Signed 18 April 1825 by Nathl. WILLIS, Jas. N. BROWN,
          Thos. J. FRIERSON.

page 191   George LUMPKINS versus William WALLACE, guardian of
          minor heirs of Robert LUMPKINS, deceased...petition
          for distribution...George LUMPKINS mentions "his
          father Robert", John M. LUMPKINS the other distri-
          butee...signed 27 July 1825 by Benjamin B. SMITH,
          Elisha UZZELL, E. W. DALE.

page 192   Commissioners settlement of estate of Jehosephat LADD,
          deceased...estate divided between James M. LADD, T.
          M. LADD, N. R. LADD, A. K. LADD. Hugh DOUGLASS and
          William HANKINS,administrators. Signed 23 January
          1826 by James WALKER and John COOKE.

page 194   5 October 1825...Settlement of estate of John S.
          ALDERSON...Taswell S. ALDERSON and Sarah B. ALDERSON,
          administrators...many accounts and notes listed...
          signed 24 July 1826 John HATCHETT and Robert HENDER-
          SON.

page 197   3 September 1827...John NICHOLSON's estate settlement
          ...mentions account of William R. NICHOLSON, hire of
          negroes, Mrs. Jane NICHOLSON, Malicia NICHOLSON,
          (no relationship given), and $12.10 for coffin.

page 198   Settlement with James SWANSON, executor of John
          NICHOLSON, deceased.

page 199   3 October 1826...Commissioners settlement with SHAW,
          guardian of minor heirs of Squire SHERMAN...paid
          $40.33 for Nancy SHERMAN's wedding dress...mentions
          board and clothes for Mary Martha and Person SHURMAN.
          Signed 16 July 1826, P. NELSON, James WALKER, J.P.'s.

page 200   3 October 1826...Commissioners report of settlement
          with William H. MACON, guardian of minor heirs of
          John J. LONG, deceased...negroes in estate...mentions
          receiving $72.64 from North Carolina legacy. Signed
          15 July 1826, Hugh DOUGLASS, John MATTHEWS, commis-
          sioners.

page 202   Commissioners settlement with P. M. BILLS, adminis-
            trator of Isaac BILLS, deceased, and former guardian
            of minor heirs of Alex. BRECKENRIDGE, 3 October 1826
            recorded. Signed 25 December 1826, A. JOHNSON,
            Robert CARUTHERS.

page 203   4 October 1826...Inventory and list of accounts of
            John S. ALEXANDER, deceased.

page 204 - Inventory of perishable property belonging to John S.
     206   ALDERSON, by Sarah ALDERSON and Taswell ALDERSON.

page 207   5 October 1826...Settlement with John LATTA, guardian
            of minor heirs of James LATTA, deceased. Signed
            15 October 1826, James BLACK, Allen RAINEY.

page 208   5 October 1826...Will of Daniel EVANS...wife Elisa-
            beth EVANS...my children, two oldest sons James R.
            EVANS and David J. EVANS to be executors...step
            daughter Nancy BEASLEY should not be included among
            legatees having already received her share. Signed
            21 July 1826, Daniel (X) EVANS. Witnesses: John
            BUTLER, J. W. P. MC GIMPSEY.

page 208   7 October 1826...Will of Sion RECORD..."my children,
            to wit, daughter Polly, Nealy WEAVER, Comfort GLASS-
            COCK, Mahala PICKENS, two sons: John RECORD, James
            RECORD." ...wife Penny...two youngest children come
            of age - William and Candres (?) RECORD...executors:
            Penny RECORD, John and James RECORD. Witnesses: S.
            T. THOMPSON, Sherwood WHITE.

page 210   11 October 1826...Commissioners report of estate of
            William BYNUM, deceased. Mentions hire of negroes
            ...schooling of Chestley BYNUM, receipt of James
            BYNUM, receipt of Norwood BYNUM, boarding for young-
            est child. Robert SELLERS, guardian.

page 211   11 October 1826...Will of James SCOTT of Maury County
            ...wife Dicy...my two children Siynetha Jane SCOTT
            and William SCOTT. Witnesses: John MATHEWS, Lemuel
            D. MACK.

page 212   Inventory of estate of Mark L. JACKSON, deceased,
            11 October 1826...negroes included in estate...
            signed 26 July 1826 by J. B. PORTER.

page 213   11 October 1826...Inventory of property of Powel HAIL,
            deceased. John C. HUCABY, administrator.

page 213   11 October 1826...Inventory of goods and chattles of
            Samuel MC DANIEL...administrator, Orren D. ALSTEN...
            negro slaves in estate - one of slaves claimed by
            Amos MC DANIEL and in dispute.

page 214   11 October 1826...Will of Mark L. JACKSON...daughters
            Sally, Betsy, Polly, Susannah (or Leanah), and Nancy.
            Son John...wife Susannah (or Leanah)...mother
            Jarnimiah LAMBERT...eight beloved children: Mark,
            David, Anna, Gilliam, Daniel, Andrew, Manerva, and
            Martha...wife and Mark JACKSON to be executors...
            signed 4 July 1823, Mark S. JACKSON...witnesses:
            Zephaniah NUNN and Caleb HEADLEY.

page 231   Settlement with George HARRISON, administrator of
William BRADSHAW, deceased...sworn in open court
16 April 1827.

page 232   Settlement with William STOCKARD, administrator of
John EDDLEMAN, deceased, recorded 8 May 1827...
William RUTLEDGE was the first administrator...signed
April 1827 by David CRAIG, Samuel GRIFFITH, J.P.'s.

page 233   Year's allowance for Hannah C. BERRYHILL, widow of
Andrew J. BERRYHILL...signed 23 April 1827 by John
BROWN, M. F. ROBERTS, H. B. PORTER.

page 233   Account of sale of estate of Solomon HERRING,
deceased, recorded 8 May 1827...Nancy HARRING was
one of the buyers; other buyers not copied.

WILL BOOK D - MAURY COUNTY

page 237   Joseph KINCAID - Settlement of estate of Joseph
KINCAID, decdased, recorded 9 May 1827...he had made
purchases of Samuel MC DOWELL, Samuel KINCAID, James
KINCAID, Polly KINCAID, and Elizabeth KINCAID...
borrowed $3 of James WARDEN...bought of T. A. CRISP,
O. J. NAGA, Yeatman EDES, H. CHAFFIN, David KINCKAID,
Signed Elizabeth KINKAID, 23. April 1827.

page 239   Nancy HERRING - Report of the jury who laid off dower
of Nancy HERRING, widdow of Solomon HERRING, deceased,
on 9 May 1827...land was on Rutherford Creek, mentions
a spring and a bluff...report signed by James N.SMITH
surveyor; commission included: G. L. VOORHIES, John
KENNEDY, William H. CALDWELL, Samuel HAWKINS, Bryant
BAUGUS, Alexr. YOUNGER, Jno. D. BLANTON, Jesse OVER-
TON, Robert CAMPBELL, James F. BYERS, John KILCREASE,
Hugh B. PORTER.

page 240   Isaac BILLS - Settlement with P. M. BILLS, Administrator of Isaac BILLS, deceased, former guardian of
minor heirs of Alexr. BRECKENRIDGE, deceased, 9 May
1827. Recorded Book D, page 202.

page 240   Burwell AKIN - Burwell AKIN mortgage to James T.
SANDFORD, 9 May 1827, for tract of land where "I now
live", also negroes, and furniture. Witnesses were
John MC HOME (?) and John J. ELLIOG(?).

page 241   Thomas J. BERRYHILL - Inventory of personal property
of Thomas J. BERRYHILL, recorded 9 May 1827. Notes
on Allison BERRYHILL, Samuel BERRYHILL, Ellison
BERRYHILL; signed Allison BERRYHILL, administrator,
and Hannah BERRYHILL, administratrix.

page 241   John CATHEY - Amount of perishable property of John
CATHEY on 15 May 1827. Buyers: G. KENNEDY, John
SKIPPER, Nathaniel ERWIN, William CHAMBERS, Andrew
MC MAHON, William ERWIN, Uzzel HAWKINS, Thos. B.
MALONE, John P. ERWIN, John ALEXANDER, John HINES,
James CATHEY, Alexr. CATHEY, Abnr. (?) CATHEY, John
WILIE, William CATHEY. Signed: Alexr G. CATHEY.

No page
number   James KIMBLE - Account of sale of James KIMBLE, de-
             ceased, 5 May 1827. Buyers were: Mary M. KIMBLE,
             B. H. WORTHAM, Isaac CURRY, S. R. KITTRELL, James W.
             WORTHAM, Duke WORTHAM, Johnson ROD (?), Robert PAYTON,
             David MANNING, Micklejohn KITTRELL, Wm. H. HUNTER,
             R. H. WORTHAM, James W. BRISCOE, Robert WORTHAM (?),
             Cried T. (?) WORTHAM, James PEYTON. Signed Wm. H.
             HUNTER, administrator.

page 246   James KIMBLE - Hire of negroes of James KIMBLE,
             deceased, 15 May 1827, to Gideon MILLS, Geo. W. JOHN-
             SON, Thos. WORTHAM, M. M. KIMBLE, John C. COLLINS,
             William WORTHAM, Senior, Samuel MC BRIDE, John SMITH,
             John H. MC CANLASS, Joseph HACKNEY, Samuel HANNAH,
             Anderson ROE, John FRY, Samuel CARUTHERS. Notes on
             David MARTIN, John H. FREEMAN, David MANNING. William
             H. HUNTER, administrator.

page 247   Abram PICKENS - Abram PICKENS, deceased, minor heirs
             - settlement with their guardian James N. SMITH,
             15 May 1827. Payment of Miss HANNAH's part; ballence
             due the two boys; settlement (February 1827) with
             John O. PICKENS, after he was of age. Settlement
             with Thomas PICKENS after he was of age...land pur-
             chased by Robert HANDERSON. Signed: James N. SMITH.

page 248   KIMBLE - Year's allowance for Mary M. KIMBLE - made
             15 May 1827; widow of James KIMBLE, deceased; allow-
             ance made 13 February 1827; commissioners: Robert
             WORTHAM, Thos. F. COLBOURNE, John MATHEW.

page 248   William FRIERSON - Samuel MAYS, guardian's agreement
             with Edwd. FRIERSON, minor heir of William FRIERSON,
             deceased...credits: COOPERS and HILL account, James
             S. WALKER, William BRIGGS, L. PRATO, SANSOM's note,
             LITTLEFIELD's note, DAVIS' note. Signed: Samuel
             MAYS, guardian, 24 April 1827.

page 249   John MC CORMACK - Will of John MC CORMACK, recorded
             15 May 1827 - son Charles, my little daughters, two
             youngest daughters, Nancy and Peggy; wife Elizabeth
             ...my eight children: William, Elisabeth, Daskhill,
             Sall MC CORMACK, Mary BURPO, Kesiah MORRIS, Lucinda
             MC CORMACK, Jane MORRIS, and Chas. MC CORMACK; wife
             Elisabeth, executrix; signed 22 February 1827 by
             John X. MC CORMACK; witnesses: B. S. HURT, James
             HURT.

page 251   Powel HAIL - Inventory of Powel HAIL, recorded 15
             May 1827; John C. HUCKABY, administrator.

page 251   MATHEWS - John MATHEWS, guardian of Margaritt A.
             MATHEWS makes settlement with court, recorded 15 May
             1827...mentions furniture now in possession of said
             child.

page 251   ARNOLD - Widow ARNOLD's year's allowance recorded
             15 May 1827 by James BALDRIDGE and James WRIGHT;
             she was widow of John ARNOLD, 18 November 1826.

page 252   GOINS - William STRATTON, guardian of Andrew GOINS'
             minor heirs makes settlement, recorded 15 May 1827.

Mentions cash paid to Lucy GOIN for minor; cash paid to John HOWES for tuition of Isaac and Levy GOINS, minor heirs.

page 252　LEWELLIN - Inventory of Charles LEWELLIN, deceased, recorded 15 May 1827...gives names and ages of six negroes. Administrator was P. I. VOORHIES, and administratrix was Sarah D. LEWELLIN.

page 253　TOMLINSON - Inventory of the property of Isaac B. TOMLINSON, recorded 16 May 1827...mentions six negroes, and 136 acres. Mary B. TOMLINSON, administrator.

page 253　FARRIS - Guardian report for year of Robert FARRIS by his guardian Samuel B. FARRIS, 15 May 1827.

page 253　WILKES - Heirs of Minor C. M. WILKES: Richard A. L. WILKES, guardian for minor heirs who were Sally D. WILKES, Unity H. WILKS, William B. WILKS, W. L. J. WILKS.

page 254　A schedule of property of Sally D., Unity H., Wm. B., and W. L. J. WILKS, minor heirs of Minor C. WILKS; signed R. A. L. WILKS, guardian.

page 254　GLOVER - Robert MC NUTT, guardian of Andrew GLOVER, report recorded 16 May 1827. John W. JONES was former guardian.

page 254　THORP - James THORP, guardian of other THORP heirs, report recorded 15 May 1827. Heirs to wit: Charles, Amos, Othi, Plesant, and Joel THORP.

page 255　FERRILL - Widdow FERRIL's dower recorded 19 June 1827, widow of Levy FERRILL, deceased. Report by Thos. JONES, James JONES, E. KENNEDY, Wm. M. RANDOLPH, James T. CROFFORD, Jno. THOMAS, Butler NOWLS, Obediah MASH, Elijah PEYTON, Paris F. DOOLEY, Joseph ERWIN, Esom B. DOOLEY.

page 256　James ISOM - Administrator's settlement of James ISOM, deceased; recorded 19 June 1827; Captain William CATHEY, administrator. Desperate notes: Samuel and William NORMAN, James BLACKBURN, Henry ISOM. Accounts: George NEXON, administrator of Jno. NIXON, Robinson YEATMAN and Company; Doctor SMITH; James PATTON; Thomas WEBB; Lambert C. OSSIPHANT; Dudley ISOM; William HARDIN; James MAYFIELD; Gideon STRICKLIN; Robert CROWBY; Joel DYER; Abraham WHITESIDES; James BOWMAN; Andrew MACON; Samuel WHITESIDES; Edward B. LITTLEFIELD; Doct. James N. BROWN; James CATHEY; John BULLOCK; William HART, administrator of John SELLERS; Robert L. COBBS; Nimrod PORTER.

page 257-8 John PICKARD - Account of sale of John PICKARD, deceased, recorded 19 June 1827; no names of buyers given; notes: Henry PICKARD, Junior, C. W. KNIGHT, A. MC MAHEN. Book accounts: John MC LEAN; Simon BACOMB, Samuel STUART, A. A. PICKENS, Jno. EDMONSON; Samuel STOCKARD, Senior; Henry HICKARD.

page 259　Henry MANGRUM - Account of Sales and Inventory of

Henry MANGRUM, deceased; recorded 19 June 1827; widow
bought bed and furniture; mentions "a negro man in
hands of ALLIN's heirs Mrs. MANGRAM's first husband:
Buyers: Mary MANGRUM, William F. BROWN, Thomas CALD-
WELL, Tincy ALLEN, William JOHNSON, James HUEY, John
SMITH, Theodorick RODSDALE, William P. CRANFORD,
Joseph MALCOM, Lusance MALCOM, William JOHNSON,
William HALCOM, William CALDWELL, Henry MANGRAM, Aron
THOMPSON, Wilie FARROW, Mose SWAIN; Francis SMITH,
William HARRISON; Shelton RANFRO; John SMITH; William
GUTHERY; David RANKIN; William WITT; James MANGRAM;
Hamblin ALLEN; Lawrence HALSOM; Henry WILSON; Vimon
JOHNSON; John R. TALLIFERRO; Robert TATE; William
DONNEY; Jno. CHATHAM. Signed G. G. FARRAR.

page 261-2 G. B. WILLIAMS - Report of guardian of minor heirs
of G. B. WILLIAMS, deceased; Susan B. WILLIAMS
received a balance; Credit Emily E. WILLIAMS for
boarding and schooling for 1825 and 1826; Nancy C.
WILLIAMS, boarding and schooling; James B. WILLIAMS,
boarding and schooling; Samuel N., boarding and
schooling; Martha S. WILLIAMS, boarding and clothing;
Penelope E. WILLIAMS, clothing and Dr. BRISCOE's
bill, also boarding and Dr. SANSOM's bill. Notes:
Alexr. PICKARD, John HUNTER, Philip P. WINN, Jno. B.
BONDS, Thomas HOUSER, Benj. WILSON, Guardian FRIER-
SON, Charles B. HARRIS; hire of negroes; John DAWSON
and KITTRELL rented land; signed: Robert WORTHAM
and Susan B. WILLIAMS, guardians, 18 April 1827.

page 263 BROWN - Thomas WALKER, guardian of Elizabeth H. BROWN,
report; recorded 19 June 1827; covered 1823 - 1827
period.

page 264 Mark BYNUM - Report of guardian of minor heirs of
Mark BYNUM, deceased; recorded 19 June 1827; widow
Dolly, hire of negroes; widow Dolly, her children
Jno. W., Elisabeth, Sally Ann, and Nimrod M. BYNUM.
Note of Joab RICHESON.

page 265 George PATTON - Inventory of property of George
PATTON, deceased...widow and minor heirs mentioned,
but not named; twelve negroes named and ages given;
signed Polly PATTON, recorded 19 June 1827.

page 266-7 Samuel SCOTT - Report of Isaac J. THOMAS, guardian
of minor heirs of Saml. SCOTT, deceased, recorded
19 June 1827; heirs: Sally N., James N., Jno. W.,
and Elisabeth SCOTT; Lewis NEEDHAM was administrator
of SCOTT's estate; interest received for September
1819 from William BROWN of North Carolina and in
hands of John ANDREWS; interest for July 1818 from
James H. HOUSTON by Samuel POLK; on 2 April 1824
paid to Sally N. SCOTT, now Sally N. OVERSTREET,
and Thomas OVERSTREET.

page 268 SCOTT - received from Minasse LOGUE, present guardian
of James N. SCOTT, son of Samuel SCOTT, deceased,
23 April 1827. Abner MATHEWS, jurat.

page 268 Jno. WILSON - Settlement of amount current of the
estate of Jno. WILSON by Samuel D. FRIERSON,
guardian of said minors. 23 April 1827.

page 269   RICHERSON - Account of money given James M. RICHERSON,
            guardian of _____ RICHERSON's minor heirs, recorded
            19 June 1827. James M. RICHERSON was guardian of
            William RICHARDSON, John RICHARDSON, and Thomas
            RICHARDSON.

page 269   William H. WILSON - Report of guardian of minor heirs
  - 270   of William H. WILSON, recorded 19 June 1827 - Jane
            WILSON was guardian and appointed October 1822.
            Accounts mentioned schooling for 1822 - 1826; WILSON's
            heirs were Jno. W. WILSON and James WILSON. Negroes
            named and ages given. Signed April 1827, Jenny
            WILSON and John W. SMITH.

page 270   Thos. WALKER - Settlement with Thos. WALKER's
            executors, recorded 19 June 1827. James N. BROWN
            was executor; J.P.'s were James GRAY and James CATHEY.

page 271   Samuel FRIERSON - Samuel E. FRIERSON, deceased, minor
            heirs were Sarah E. FRIERSON and guardian; recorded
            6 June 1827; settled with Jesse S. ROSS for lands,
            1822, 1825, 1826.

page 271   Daniel EVANS - Inventory of Daniel EVANS, recorded,
            24 June 1827; administrators were H. S. CRUTCHER and
            Francis SLAUGHTER; negroes named and ages. Accounts
            and notes (pages 272, 273, 274), Francis SMITH and
            Samuel SMITH; William MILLER and John MILLER; Thomas
            HARRIS and James RANKIN; Elisabeth EVANS, J. R. EVINS;
            Lemuel WALTERS, J. B. TURNER, Will JOHNSON, Tilmon
            MILLS, Jno. MILLS, Bryant BAUGUS, E. KENNEDY, James
            KENNEDY, William JOHNSON, William STRATTON, Jno. W.
            BEASLEY, D. J. EVANS, Jno. SMITH, P. J. AKIN, Alexr.
            MOORE, J. A. HALL, Herndon MC KEE, Daniel MC KEE,
            W. L. PARKER, J. C. WORMLEY, Henry SMITH, J. TRANUM,
            W. P. HOLCUM, W. F. GUTHRIE, William STANTON, Francis
            WILLIS, J. HART, Shedrick LOFTIN, Geo. W. LONG, Will
            REGDON, W. M. WITT, Thomas CALOWILL, Henry L. CRUTCHER,
            Hugh B. PORTER, Samuel MC DOWELL, S. JOHNS, Wm. M.
            DORCH, Elizabeth EVANS, Peter R. BOOKER, William
            SLAUGHTER, Dr. S. A. GILLISPIE, Martin TONEY. Elisa-
            beth EVANS was executrix and she refuses to give an
            account to the administrator. Notes on R. M. SMITH,
            Wm. K. HILL, D. FERRIL, Mrs. Lucy GANT, Jno. HARRIS,
            WALKER of Columbia, David FORTNER, Jesse E. EVANS.
            Inventory included set of small silver spoons.
            (page 275) Inventory taken 23 April 1827 by H. L.
            CRUTCHER and Francis SLAUGHTER.

page 275   Jacob MC KEE - Settlement with Abram LOONEY, guardian
            of minor heirs of Jacob MC KEE for 1824. Recorded
            25 June 1826. LOONEY appointed 1824 as guardian for
            Matilda, Sally, Malinda, Lucinda, and Hamilton H.
            MC KEE, minor heirs of Jacob MC KEE, deceased...had
            land with "some cabbins"...received items from P. M.
            BILLS, representative of Isaac BILLS, deceased, from
            guardian of said minor heirs...notes and accounts on
            Geo. M. EGNEW (tuition), Joseph GILMORE, E. SMITH,
            HOUSTON. (Page 277) "There are three other heirs
            of Jacob MC KEE who were married before I was guard-
            ian..." Isaac BILLS was former guardian. Account
            for schooling, bonnets, clothing, for Matilda MC KEE.

(Page 278) Account for Sally MC KEE - amount paid
LANGTRY for books for schooling; paid Mrs. BITTLEMAN
for making bonnet; paid Samuel MC KEE for shoes.
Malinda's accounts mentioned; Lucinda's accounts,
page 279.

page 280   A. J. BERRYHILL - List of Property of A. J. BERRYHILL,
            deceased, sold 9 February 1827; recorded 21 June
1   1827. Buyers: R. M. MONTGOMERY, Robert PAYNE,
            Allison BERRYHILL, Joseph G. HALL, Samuel BERRYHILL,
            A. H. FREEMAN, Jeramiah CRAFTON, Jesse CORCH, Josiah
            ANTER (?), B. B. MONTGOMERY, David DORCH, James
            COSTON; signed 23 April 1827 by A. J. BERRYHILL and
            Hannah BERRYHILL, administrators.

page 281   CAMPBELL - Robert CAMPBELL Guardian Report, recorded
            26 June 1827...Robert CAMPBELL, guardian for William
            C. CAMPBELL, minor heir of John CAMPBELL, deceased.

page 282   Robt. FARRIS - Robt. FARRIS, deceased, Inventory
            recorded 25 June 1827. Included "Schedule of pro-
            perty belonging to said orphans estate"; signed
            Samuel B. FARRIS, 16 April 1827. Estate included
            $75 in notes on good men and no other property has
            come into "my hands".

page 282   Daniel EVANS - Widow's provision for Daniel EVANS'
            widow, recorded 25 June 1827...provision for Elisa-
            beth EVANS, widow and relict. Made by John C. WORM-
            ELEY and Jno. MILLER and James BLACK in April 1827.

page 283   William H. WILSON - Inventory of William H. WILSON
            recorded 26 June 1827...Jane WILSON was guardian for
            the children...slaves named and ages given...signed
            Jane WILSON, 16 April 1827.

page 283   BROWN - Elizabeth H. BROWN's Guardian Thomas WALKER's
            report, recorded 26 June 1827...WALKER was guardian
            for Elizabeth H. BROWN...mentions "Yankey clock"
            sold to James WALKER. Signed 23 April 1827.

page 284   Dabney WADE - Rubin SMITH, Guardian for Sarah WADE,
            recorded 26 June 1827. In July 1822 SMITH was
            solicited by Mrs. Nancy WADE, relict of Dabney WADE,
            deceased, to take guardianship for her daughter
            Sarah WADE. Jacob SCOTT was administrator of estate
            of Levisey WADE, deceased, from whom the Little
            Legacy was to be paid me as guardian in October.
            Between July and October court the child died and
            SCOTT refused to pay saying he did not know to whom
            the legacy should go. SMITH asks court to appoint
            commission to make settlement.

page 285   James OGLISLEY - John M. JONES, guardian of James
            OGLISBY's minor heirs, recorded 25 June 1827. Heirs
            were Polly, Richard, Elisha, and Celia OGLISBY.
            Settlement made at October term 1820.

page 287   Francis ANDERSON - Francis T. ANDERSON's Dower -
            "refer to minutes April court 1827" "spread out at
            length", signed P. W. PORTER.

page 287   Thomas COLEMAN - Inventory of sale of personal estate
            of Thomas COLEMAN, sold 1st and 2nd of February 1827.
            Recorded 3 July 1827. Buyers were Jeremiah ALDERSON,
            Wm. ALDERSON, Jno. D. ALDERSON, Samuel S. PORTER, P.
            O. MALONE, Wm. P. POOL, James JOSEY, Thos. P. JOHNSON,
            Clarisa COLEMAN, Thos. S. SPENCER, John EDWARDS,
            Robert CRAWSBY, Saml. OLIPHANT, Thomas J. FRIERSON,
            Richard JONES (page 288) SQUIRE HARLOW, Geo. HAYS,
            W. W. COLEMAN, John GRIFFITH, Jackson DEATON, Edward
            D. WILLIAMS, James FORGEY, James CARTER, W. FURGUSON,
            And. WAGGONER, Eph. MC CALIB, Samuel H. SMITH, Bowlin
            GORDON, A. BRINKLEY. (page 289) Bonds, notes and
            accounts: William HENRY, David KING, Thomas HOOKS,
            Geo. HICKS, Archd. MC OMMILL, N. NOBLES, Noah WALKER,
            Jno. GRIFFITH, Jno. PHILLIPS, Allen PILLOW, Jno.
            WHEAT, James ONEAL, Josiah DAVIS, Daniel FURGUSON,
            Abram ROLTON, David PISTOLE, Charles PISTOLE, Wilie
            A. WHEAT, Robert BIRKS, William BIRK, A. BRINKLEY,
            A. FERGUSON, Samuel James CARTER (?), Thomas FRANKLIN,
            E. EMOS, A.JONES, Geo. MC OSSISTER, Charles GRAY,
            George GUIGLEY, Wiliam PILLOW. Signed Robert CRAWSBY,
            W. W. COLEMAN, executors of will of Thomas COLEMAN.

page 290   Jno. B. WILKES - Recorded 6 July 1827 - Commissioners
            settlement with Benjamin WILKES, administrator of
            estate of Jno. B. WILKES, deceased. Commissioners:
            Alexander JOHNSON and Ebenezer RICE. Minor C. M.
            WILKES, former administrator. Cash received from
            Joshua ORR, Robert BENTON, Jno. ELLIOTT's note; Jno.
            W. ANDERSON's note; Robert BUTLER's note; Isaac
            REDDING, cash; notes on William R. HICKS, William A.
            JOHNSON, William COVEY, John W. ANDERSON. (page 291)
            Elizabeth L. WILKES, widow of the deceased.

page 292   Joseph KINCAID - Account of Sale of personal property
            of Joseph KINCAID, deceased. Recorded 6 July 1827;
            signed Geo. M. EGNEW and Elisabeth KINKAID.

page 292-3 William RICHARDSON - Recorded 6 July 1827. Amount of
            notes in hands belonging to the estate of William
            RICHARDSON, deceased; notes on Simon CANNON, Thomas
            CASH, Amos QUINN, Thomas HILL, Saunders MILLS, William
            V. WHITE, Jno. CANNON, Amos RICHARDSON, and William
            L. WILLEFORD. Signed, James M. RICHARDSON, adminis-
            trator.

page 292   Thomas LINSTER - Inventory of account of Thomas W.
            LINSTER, deceased, recorded 6 July 1827 by Samuel
            CAMPBELL, administrator.

page 294   Francis H. KENNEDY - Recorded 21 August 1827 -
            Alexander JOHNSON, John W. RECORD, and Jonathan D.
            BILLS appointed to settle with Geo. M. MARTIN and
            Thos. J. KENNEDY, administrators, of Francis H.
            KENNEDY, deceased. Notes and accounts of Alexr.
            MC ALL, E. CRAIG, Aron SETTLE, F. J. KENNEDY, John
            MONEY, Bethia Lee RUE; William PILLOW, P. NELSON;
            (page 295) signed Alexander JOHNSON and John W.
            RECORD.

page 295   Benoni PERRYMAN - Inventory of Benoni PERRYMAN,
            recorded 30 August 1827, taken by J. C. PERRYMAN and

A. DARDEN. (page 296) Account of sale; buyers: Jerusha PERRYMAN, William FLY, William CAPPS, Henry CAPPS, Mark PIPPIN, Isaac PIPKIN, John W. COCHRON, Samuel WARREN, Isaac GAILEY, Robt. B. DUDLEY, Elisha FLY, James BAKER, James WARREN, Jacob MILLS, Edward MAINARD, George SELLER, Stephen POLARD (page 297) Joseph DUDLEY, Joseph WILLSON, Robert PAIN, William A. TOMPSON, John HALL, William SUITER, Amos WADDLE, Alfred DARDEN, Joseph DUDLEY, James THOMAS (page 298) Theolphlaus WILLIAMS. Signed Jerusha PERRYMAN and Alfred HARDIN, administrators.

page 298   WADE - Inventory or Schedule of property of Francis WADE...property received as guardian of Francis WADE ...negroes named; judgment against Jacob SCOTT; note on John WOODRUFF. Signed Joseph WINGFIELD, recorded 16 July 1827. (page 299) Francis WADE (non compes mentis), board and bills listed.

page 300   Littleberry HAMBLETT - William COOPER, guardian of
 - 302   William HAMLETT, minor of Littleberry HAMBLETT, deceased, report recorded 16 July 1827.

page 303   Harmon MILLER - Amount of Sale of Estate of Harmon MILLER, deceased. Vouchers listed. Signed: Harman MILLER, administrator of Harmon MILLER, deceased. No date.

page 304   James TURNBO - Will of James TURNBO - my beloved wife Philicia TURNBO...all my estate, lands, negroes, cattle, etc. to wife during her life or widdowhood... should she marry or die to be divided among my proper heirs. Friends Nathan COFFEY and Calvin COFFEY to be executors. Signed 29 July 1826; John GILBREATH and W. L. MACKEY, witnesses.

page 304   BROOKS - Commissioners settlement with John C. BROOKS, entry taker.

page 306   William R. ROBERTSON - Will of William R. ROBERTSON, written 5 July 1827 - my wife Alcey; children, Blount, Caroline, William, Henry, and Sharp ROBERTSON... oldest son Blunt...William B. PILLOW to be executor. Witnesses were Zebined CONKEY, John DICKEY, and Thomas LOWERY (or SOWERY). No recorded date.

page 307   Thrasher MC COLLUM - Settlement with Mary MC OLLUM, administratrix of estate of Thrasher MC OLLUM, deceased, made 14 July 1827; signed William FLY and William EDMONSON.

page 307   John EDDLEMAN - Thomas M.HARPER, guardian of minor heirs of John EDDLEMAN, deceased, reports notes on A. B. ALEXANDER, William STOCKARD, and Ozni ALEXANDER. Signed 16 July 1827, or recorded 16 July 1827.

page 308   HOBSON - Jeremiah HOBSON's Guardian J. BLACK reports. Signed James BLACK, guardian, recorded 16 July 1827.

page 309   David LOVE - Year's allowance for Polly LOVE, widow
 - 310   of David LOVE, deceased...to include "what may be earned by the mill to the first of December". Allowance made 9 July 1827 by Alexr. JOHNSON, Michael LANCASTER, and Stephen SMITH.

page 310   Allen MORRIS - Allen MORRIS' Inventory of notes in
            hands of former administrator John FIELDS: Henry
            MILLER, Stephen HARGRAVES, Zebidan CONKEY, Elijah
            MAYFIELD, Clement WALL, James BIZZELL, James KIRK,
            Senior, John ATKISON, Geo. WATKINS, Edmond MORRIS,
            Robason ROSS, Nathaniel M. POWELL, James ROGERS, Edw.
            W. DALE, John L. MADLEY. Signed B. S. HURT, adminis-
            trator, 16 July 1827.

page 311   William BYNUM - A. Y. PARTEE, guardian of four young-
            est children of William BYNUM, deceased, returns
            schedule of property of all description; recorded
            25 July 1827.

page 312   R. H. BRANK - R. H. BRANK's inventory - notes on
            James MC GIMSEY, Elijah and William MELTON, William
            WOODS, Grant A. JOHNSON, James GRAMMILL, Archibald
            BEDWELL, Benjamin MITCHELL, Andrew ATKISON, William
            SUFFOD, Silas ROCKBY, Solomon G. KIMBROUGH. Signed
            Ephrm. E. DAVIDSON, administrator. Recorded 25 July
            1827.

page 313   Simon BECUM - Inventory of Simon BACON (BECUM) -
            buyers were Mary BECUM, Stephen BECUM, William
            WILLIAMS, James RAY, John H. SMITH (page 314) G.
            DUKE. Signed Stephen BACON, administrator, recorded
            16 July 1827. (Abstractor's note: the surname was
            spelled several different ways in this one entry.)

page 314   Clerk's report to treasurer for 1825. There were
            20,089 acres of land for tax; 18 town lots for tax;
            seven ordinary licenses...signed Joseph B. PORTER,
            7 January 1826.

page 315   Jacob BOGARD - List of Jacob BOGARD's property sold
            on 21 February 1825. Buyers included James BOGARD,
            Abraham BOGARD, William BOGARD, Susannah BOGARD.
            Signed: James BOGARD and William BOGARD, administra-
            tors.

page 315   Isaac BILLS - Distribution of negro property of
  - 320   Isaac BILLS, deceased, to Lillias BILLS (deceased);
            to John H. BILLS; to Sally BILLS, married Robert F.
            MATTHEWS; to Placebo BILLS, to Octavia L. BILLS; to
            Isaac N. BILLS; to Martha Emily BILLS - the last
            three are minors...negroes divided into eight lots.
            Signed Alexander JOHNSON and John MACK commissioners,
            who were directed October 1826 to take division.

page 321   John LATTA, Senior - Inventory of Estate of John
            LATTA, Senior, deceased. (Abstractor's note: this
            was the complete entry.)

page 322   Daniel EVANS - Provisions for Elisabeth EVANS, widow
            of Daniel EVANS, set off by Thos. MAHON, John BROWN,
            Alexr. YOUNG, Jeremiah TRANUM, Thos. HARDIN, William
            JOHNS, John KILCREASE, Geo. W. TONEY, Henry S. WILSON,
            John WILSON, Jacob ROGERS, John BROWN, John BROWN (a
            second one), commissioners.

page 323   Daniel DAVIS - Will of Daniel DAVIS - beloved daugh-
            ter Mary ROSWELL; sons Joab DAVIS and Phillip DAVIS;

my two grandchildren, heirs of my daughter Elisabeth
SNELL; beloved wife Elisabeth; my three living children; son Phillip and friend James S. BALDRIDGE, executors, signed 27 July 1827 by Daniel DAVIS; witnesses, James L. BALDRIDGE and Phillip DAVIS.

page 324   Benjamin WILKES - Will of Benjamin WILKES - wife
           Polly...my youngest and unmarried children...(page
           325) my seven children, Richard A. L., Elisabeth L.
           PREWITT, Mary K. ORR, Sally D. WILKS, Unity K. WILKS,
           William B. WILKES, Washington L. J. WILKES...silver
           watch which formerly belonged to my deceased son
           Minor C. M. WILKES to go to William B. WILKES...
           Washington, my youngest son; son in law William M.
           ORR and son R. A. L. WILKES to be executors...signed
           6 October 1827, witnesses: E. RICE and Robert
           MC DANIEL.

page 327   David FOSTER - Will of David FOSTER - executors:
           William MC LUN and Joseph A. O'REILLY...school my
           children...my wife; witnesses: Ozni ALEXANDER and
           Richard KANDEE. Signed 11 August 1827.

page 328   John LATTA - Will of John LATTA - daughter Jane...
           daughter Rebecca (?), wife of Seth SPARKMAN...heirs
           of my daughter Elizabeth CHANDLER...my daughter Mary
           ROBISON...daughter Sarah MOORE...his brother John
           LATTA...signed 11 August 1827, Moses LATTA. (?)
           (This entry is questionable and hard to determine
           correct name.)

page 329   John SIMS - Will of John SIMS - beloved wife Sally...
           my children...all my children...all my children that
           is now unmarried...negroes named...son John D. SIMS;
           son Nicholas SIMS; daughter Mariah B. SIMS; daughter
           Sally G. SIMS; (page 330) daughter Lucy P. SIMS; son
           James SIMS...saddle to Hartwell C. L. D. SIMS (there
           appears to have been a paragraph of will left out)...
           children to get Good english schooling...John D. and
           Nicholas SIMS, executors; signed 5 August 1824 by
           John X SIMS; witnesses, Thomas SIMS, Joseph O. CROSS,
           John M. DANIELL.

page 331   FOSTER - Inventory of estate of David FOSTER, de-
           ceased...judgement against William MERRYMAN...two
           injunctions against Thos. L. ASHLTON; notes on
           William ELLISTON, John HOBSON, Joseph HALL and
           Charles WILLIAMS. No date.

page 332   Daniel DAVIS - Settlement with William BOAZ, adminis-
           trator of Daniel DAVIS, deceased, signed 18 August
           1827 by John MACK and Alexander JOHNSON.

page 333   G. C. NIGHTINGALE - Will of George Cortes NIGHTINGALE
           of Providence, Rhode Island, Providence Plantations
           merchant...wife Eliza,...wife Eliza and John S.
           DESTER, executors...signed 21 August 1812; witnesses,
           Saml. ANSET, Gardner DAGGETT, Amunah TINGLEY.

page 334   Jane FRIERSON - Jane C. FRIERSON's account, account
           of money spent. Signed Duncan BROWN, guardian,
           26 October 1827.

page 336 Thomas BRAWLEY - Inventory of property of Thomas BRAWLEY, deceased...silver watch...note on Hugh SHAW, James CUNNINGHAM...William WEAR is insolvent...note on William CHALKE...BRAWLEY in 1824 was appointed administrator of estate of Mathew SWAN and appointed guardian of Ruthey, Thomas, Catherine, Alexander, and James SWAN, minor heirs of Mathew SWAN. (Abstractor's note: there were no commas in the list of the minor heirs, these commas supplied by abstractor.) Receipt of N. W. BRISCOE, guardian of Jno. W. BRISCOE; notes of William BRAWLEY, David VAUGHN, E. W. LOVING, John and James ONEAL, H. GOFORTH, John M. GREENE. Signed, Henry SMITH, 24 October 1827.

page 337 Charles A. HOUSER - Schedule of property of Charles A. HOUSER, deceased;...silver watch...signed Henry TURNEY, 25 March 1827.

page 338 Lewis MC GRAW - Inventory of property of Lewis MC GRAW, deceased..."some valuable papers in hands of William MC GRAW"; note for 50 gallons of whiskey... "said Lewis MC GAW has left no wife and only one child." Signed Andrew EWING, 22 October 1827.

page 338 FULLERTON - Panel to examine Mrs. FULLERTON with respect "to the situation of her mind...our opinion is that she is partially deranged." Signed: Nathl. WILLIS, James RUTLEDGE, Robt. CAMPBELL, Stephen SMITH, James N. SMITH, Thos. BROOKS, P. H. JENKINS, George RUSE (?), Jno. D. LOVE, John ELLIOTT, E. E. DAVIDSON, W. NEWSUM, Junior, and R. P. WEBSTER.

page 339 Thomas WATSON - Account of Sales of Estate of Thomas WATSON, deceased...sold 11 February 1826...Buyers: Young CHUMBLEY, Joseph POWERS, James MOORE, Nathan WATSON, George CASEY, Andrew MILLS, Benjamin HOM, the Widdow (many items, including one Bible), Benjamin HORN, William WILLIAMS, Sion BOON, Solomon BUNCH (page 340) Demsey WATSON, Lemuel WATERS, Green AKIN. Signed: Sion BROWN, recorded 22 October 1827.

page 340 MANGRAM - Mary MANGRAM's relinquishment of right to administer on the estate of _____ MANGRAM, deceased ..."willing for George G. FARRAR to administer to my husband's estate"...signed 4 October 1826, Mary MANGRAM. Witnesses were William F. BROWN and Henry MANGRAM.

page 340 Isaac B. HARDIN - John HODGE and Robert MACK executors of Isaac B. HARDIN, in account 1825; receipts and notes on William ANDERSON, William MC NUTT, Thomas WHITE, Edward W. DALE, A. C. HAYS, James PURSELL, Alpha KINGLSEY, M. CARUTHERS, Edward ENGLISH, James WHITE, James R. PLUMMER, J. B. HOUSTON, S. B. and T. D. MC NIGHT, John S. ALDERSON, Samuel RANKIN, Adam KLICE, John WRIGHT, Samuel B. MC NIGHT, David W. MERU (?), Arther BEYTES (?), Perry COHEA, Samuel NORTHERN, Duncan MC NIGHT, Thomas J. FRIERSON, Kenneth CHERRY, James R. SHELTON, John C. MC KUNE, Wilson WHITE, William JOHNSTON, Samuel MC DOWELL, Joseph BOWEN and son; James C. CRAIG, William CRAIG, James WALKER, E. H. CHAFFIN, Geo. CAMPBELL, John W.

LEYMASTER, Pleasant NELSON, Agustin BROWN, David
LEATHERMAN, Joseph B. PORTER, N. PORTER, (page 342)
James C. O'RILEY, Nimrod PORTER, Madison CARUTHERS,
Thomas BROWN, John WHITE, David A. MILLS, Jeremiah
CHERRY, Samuel H. WILLIAMS, William K. HILL, James M.
LEWIS, Joseph _____ (?), George COATTES, WALTER and
HAYS, William H. EDWARDS, John DAGHY, Joseph CRENSHAW,
Isaac ACUFF, J. DAUGHTERTY, John E. DAVIDSON, William
DAVIS, William P. EDDS, William DUNN, (page 343),
David CRAIGHEAD, Rober PUIDEY, George M. MARTIN, N.
A. MC NAIRY, Alfred BALCH, Thos. HARDIMAN, L. HITCH-
COCK, J. P. CLARK, Matthew RHEA, Edmond DAYS, Sarah
P. HARDIN, Robert MACK, John HEDGES, Samuel GULLETT,
Richard C. HARRIS (page 344) John DERDAN, Lott FER-
GASON, John DAVIS, R. T. GUNN, G. GADE, Gideon HEMLY,
Abner JOHNSTON, Gardner GILL, Joseph HORTEN, HUCKS
and WINN, John HATCHETT, Alexander MC LOUGH, Alex.
LAIRD, James ONEAL, D. MC ALLISON, MAYALL and YOUNG,
W. B. LEWIS, Edmund MAYS, N. YOUNG, Isaac NEELY, John
TERRY, William SMITH, A. RARDIN, William H. STEPHENS,
Samuel M. STRAMGLES, E. WAL, Roderick BAUGHT; (page
345), the following probably cannot be collected:
Robert MACK, Nathaniel THOMPSON, Thomas RAYNOLDS, N.
PORTER, B. W. HARDIN, Mark HARDIN, John WHITE, N.
YOUNG, James KING, Benjamin HARDIN, William A. JOHNS-
TON, Josiah ALDERSON, Hugh B. PORTER, Luke BYNUM,
George CATTER, D. F. RANDOLPH, N. D. FORE (GORE?),
A. C. YATES, T. PHELPS (?), (page 346) James BLACK-
BURN, William ROGERS, E. E. MC LAIN, Lasting POWELL,
Reuben BRAGES, Thos. NEELY, George MITCHELL, Samuel
ELSWORTH, James PORTER, William CLARK, Samuel GIL-
BREATH, John P. SIMPSON (SIMMONS?), William MEDCALF.
Accounts: James STOCKARD, William W. CRAIG, George
GLASSCOCK, Nancy COOPER, Elisha SMITH, George MUM-
PHREYS, Nancy SANDERSON, William HANKS, Moses RANKINS,
Jeremiah JOB, Fany STEPHENS, E. P. CHAMBERS, James N.
FLANIGAN, Thomas NEELEY, James MC CARNIN (MC LARNIN?),
William GOFORTH, Benjamin BRADSHAW, David CRAIG,
Ephraim DAVIDSON, Cary NEWSUM, Elijah ROBERTS, Meson
OGLIVIE, Jethro JOINER (page 347) John M. GOODLOW,
John LOFTLAND, Squire HUNT, Benjamin H. LEWIS, Lard
B. BOYD, John MONTGOMERY, Mark PIPKIN, Jacob MC KEE,
John AMORY, Robert B. DABNEY, John POLNY, David and
Samuel CAMPBELL, James H. WILLIAMS, William BRADSHAW,
John BECARNS, Reubin A. CARTER, Charles R. DILLON,
Samuel M. STRANTES (?), Reece B. PORTER, Bird M.
TURNER, Josiah ALDERSON, William T. LEWIS, Minor S.
WILKES, D. N. SANDERS, Hannry A. WILLIAMS, James R.
STUTTON, Hall GUMAN, William CLARK. (page 348)
executors, John HODGE, Robert MACK, Swan HARDIN and
John C. WORMLEY appointed commissioners to settled
with executors and make return. Signed 27 January
1825.

page 349   James BROWN - Inventory and Account of Sale of James
- 350   BROWN, deceased; signed by Simpson BROWN, recorded
         16 October 1827. Buyers: Mrs. BROWN, John BROWN,
         David W. E. BROWN, McLintich BROWN, David BROWN,
         Archy BROWN, Archibald BROWN, Simpson BROWN, James H.
         BROWN, William RUSSELL, John HILL, John WEBB, John
         BILLS, John WILKINS, John BAITY, Harrison STEELE,
         John BALCH, James MC LINNEY, Jesse L. WILKINS, John
         MC KIBBON, Levy G. DILLAHAY, Saml. PAUL. Note on
         Andrew SMITH.

page 350   Elam ALEXANDER - Report of commission to value ____ acres of land on south side of Duck River belonging to Elam ALEXANDER of North Carolina, land opposite Samuel GALLOWAY's land, a little below KILPATRICK's big spring, valued at $5. (?) Signed 2 September 1824 by William STRATTON, Joseph LONG, Jacob D. BERRY, and James HARDIN.

page 351   Isaac BILLS - Settlement with Lillas BILLS, guardian
- 352   of minor heirs of Isaac BILLS, deceased: Olivia L. Isaac N. and Martha E. BILLS. Settlement made with commissioners Alexdr. JOHNSON and John MACK, who found in hands of the administrator of Isaac BILLS, deceased, $430. A settlement with all the heirs who had arrived at the age of 21 - Alvin W. BILLS, John H. BILLS, and Robert F. MATTHEWS. Sum is to be distributed between Placebo M., Ollivia L., Isaac N. and Martha E. BILLS and "myself", signed January 1827 Lillas BILLS, guardian.

page 352   BILLS - Plat of BILLS land - showing dower of Lillas
- 353   BILLS, wife and relict of Isaac BILLS, deceased... part of grant of 40 acres Number 310 and 30 acres Number 244. Signed 12 May 1827 by Alexander JOHNSON, Robert CARUTHERS, E. RICE, and Joel RUTE (?), commissioners.

page 353   BOYD - Widow BOYD's Dower of Land - commissioners to set off land for Elizabeth P. BOYD, widow of James BOYD, deceased...land calls for Andrew BOYD, William HENDERSON, Breckenridge LOONEY's south boundary line and Ezekiel HENDERSON line...tract of land on which James BOYD lived at time of his death. Signed on 13 June 1826 by John MATTHEWS, William E. MC KEE, John MACK, Isaac J. THOMAS, and Solomon Y. MAXWELL. (Page 354) Elisabeth P. BOYD relinquished right of administration of husband James BOYD, deceased, and recommends William S. HENDERSON and Jno. R. BOYD be appointed. Signed 17 October 1825 by Elisabeth P. BOYD.

page 354   BRADSHAW - Year's allowance for Kessiah BRADSHAW, signed 4 November 1826 by Charles SOWELL, Moses A. WILLEY and Sam. ROBINSON.

page 354   BALL - October 1826 Commissioners make year's allowance for Margarette BALL. Signed 1 November 1826 by James NEELEY, William GLASS, and Alexr. GLASS.

page 355   William B. ANDERSON - Account of Sale of William B.
- 357   ANDERSON; buyers: Fanny F. ANDERSON (most everything in household), John W. ANDERSON, John ALLEN, James BRANCH, Mathew G. COVEY, Stephen C. EUBANK, William ANDERSON, Jos. BROWN, Archibald W. WINN, John RICHARDS. Signed "administrators".

page 358   James BURNS - Provision for education and support - commissioners to let out four infant children of James BURNS, deceased, and make report. They reported they contracted with Mrs. Martha MC FALL for boarding, washing, and ledging of William and Henry BURNS, with James HILL for boarding of John and Milton BURNS. Wm. (or Mr.) OLLIVER hired as school master of said four boys. No date.

page 358   William BYNUM - Thomas HUDSPETH, James WALKER and
            Allen RAINEY to sell negroes belonging to estate of
            William BYNUM, deceased, on 13 March 1827 at court-
            house...negroes named and values given. Signed
            7 July 1826. (Page 359) Inventory of Property of
            William BYNUM, deceased, made 30 October 1824: eight
            negro men, seven negro women, five negro boys and two
            negro girls. Signed 29 October 1824, by H. GROVE and
            Elisabeth BRADSHAW.

page 359   William BURKETT - Inventory of William BURKETT, de-
            ceased, made on 15 April 1825. Signed 13 April 1825
            by Miles BURNS.

page 358   Francis F. ANDERSON - Widow's provision for Francis
(2d 358)   F. ANDERSON, widdow of William B. ANDERSON; signed
            Alex. JOHNSON, E. RICE, and N. W. WINN.

page 358   J. H. ARNOLD - Inventory of J. H. ARNOLD, deceased,
(3d 358)   signed William PERRY, administrator, 18 November 1826.

page 359   Charles BROWN - Inventory of Charles BROWN, deceased,
(2d 359)   made 14 April 1824, includes receipts from Thomas
            REED of York District, South Carolina. Signed:
            Robert L. BROWN and William BROWN.

page 360   Sterline BELL - Inventory of Sterling BELL; no date;
            Robert WHITESIDES and Mary BELL, executors.

page 360   Thomas G. BLACK - Inventory of Thomas G. BLACK, signed
            Mary BLACK; no date; had 156¼ acres.

page 361   Elias BRADSHAW - Inventory of Elias BRADSHAW, de-
            ceased, signed 4 November 1826 by John O. COOK, admin-
            istrator.

page 362   James AKIN, Junior - Dr the estate of James AKIN,
            Junior. Accounts: David N. SANSOM, William W. WOODS,
            Lemuel T. BROOKS, John DOWDY, Jacob RODGERS, John
            CHAMBERS, William BRADSHAW, Hezekiah BROOKS, Joab
            PATTERSON, James HIGGS, and John KENNEDY. Submitted
            28 January 1822. Mentions 1816 medical expenses due
            Darrel N. SANSOM.

page 362   CAMPBELL - Dr Ezekial M. CAMPBELL, guardian, 18 April
            1825, guardian settlement made. "Polk CAMPBELL"
            written in margin of page. (Page 363), in account
            with Samuel POLK, executor...money due from Jethro
            BROWN..."in month of May 1816 the negro boy Aron
            named in the will deceased", signed Samuel MC DOWELL,
            John S. ALDERSON. (Abstractor's note: not clear if
            entries on page 363 are with CAMPBELL account or not.)

page 363   Account of Samuel P. CAMPBELL; paid cash to William
            BLANTON for schooling; paid cash to John BROWN for
            schooling; paid R. B. PASSMORE's charge for making
            settlement. Signed E. M. CAMPBELL, Guardian, October
            182?.

page 364   CAMPBELL - Dr. Ezekiel CAMPBELL, guardian of_____.

page 364   DAVIDSON - Commission to settle with John DAVIDSON,
            deceased, estate; notes on Paris F. DOOLEY, Simon

165

JAGGERS, William PORTER, Adam KLYCE, John MATTHEWS, Vincent RIDLEY; amount of judgement versus E. E. DAVIDSON; money paid John O. DAVIDSON by E. E. DAVIDSON. Commissioners' investigation of the estate of John DAVIDSON, deceased, and passing the claims of John O. DAVIDSON and Paris F. DOOLEY, executors of John DAVIDSON, signed 13 July 1827 by John MATHEWS and Joseph ERWIN.

page 385   CAMPBELL - James CAMPBELL in account current; paid William BLANTON for schooling; paid John BROWN for schooling; signed E. M. CAMPBELL.

page 385   DAVIDSON - A/C current with John O. DAVIDSON and Paris F. DOOLEY, executors...accounts mentioned, William NOTTS, CHAFFIN, James K. POLK for costs of suit $15. Allowance for tombstone $100.00.

page 366   CAMPBELL - Robert CAMPBELL, guardian for Caroline W. CAMPBELL, on 5 February 1825, reports on 23 January 1827.

page 366   COURTHOUSE - October 1825 the court appointed commission to plan and contract with some person to enclose the courthouse in the town of Columbia. Report signed: Alexander JOHNSON, John C. WORMELEY, P. I. VOORHIES, commissioners.

page 367   Thomas COLEMAN - Will of Thomas COLEMAN - with respect to interment - direct that it be made in the family burial ground...without parade unnecessary expence or funeral sermon or oration...wife Clarissa, land on which I now live; youngest daughter Elvira COLEMAN...negroes named..son William White COLEMAN, land on road leading from Leiper's Lick Creek to Snow Creek...son Rufus...son Walter...daughters Nancy JOSEY, Clarissa ALDERSON, Julia EDWARDS, and Eliza P. CROSBY...other daughters Sophia E. MC EWING, Sarah T. COLEMAN and Carolina COLEMAN...others mentioned in will were John EDWARDS and Joseph H. MC EWING...oldest son Thomas B. COLEMAN died intestate ...son William W. and son in law John EDWARDS to be executors; signed 26 May 1824, Thomas COLEMAN; codicil dated 2 November 1826, appoints son-in-law R. CRAWSBY executor in place of John EDWARDS "he being in bad health".

page 370   DYEL - Sale of Joseph DYEL. Buyers: Elizabeth DYAL (household items), John JONES, Thomas GOODRUM, John TOMBS, Joseph GILL, Samuel CRAIG, James MC ORD, William MC_____(?). Signed: James DYAL, administrator.

page 371   Josiah CARTHELL - Will of Josiah CARTHELL - love and esteem for my wife Sarah CARTHELL...daughter Eliza CARTHELL...mentions Hannah, Kiron T. JONES, Nancy S. KILPATRICK, signed 10 February 1825. Witnesses, John CATHELL, Glover ALDREDGE.

page 372   DANILL - Widow's provision for Mary DANILL, widdow of Mary DANAL, deceased, for her and her family, signed 14 December 1826 by James L. BALDRIDGE, Alexander JOHNSON, Lewis L. COVEY, John D. LOVE.

page 372   Inventory of Estate of Jesse CAUDLE, deceased. No
 - 373   date. Notes on Henry DOBBS, Jessee BRAHEAN, Lawrence
           MC MEANS, John HART, James WHITE, Mayo BEEL, Elijah
           ROGERS, Baalam JEFF, Yearbey NIX, Elijah WILSON,
           William ROY, Nancy WRIGHT, Henry HOLT, S___ STRANGE-
           MAN, James HOUSTON, Claiborn PIGG, Shadrick WEAVER,
           Hugh HOUSTON. Signed Joshua CAUDLE, Francis BRIDGES,
           administrators.

page 373   William DANILL - Inventory of William DANILL, de-
           ceased, recorded 11 July 1828; notes and accounts on
           John HATCHETT, Archibald WINN, John ANDERSON and
           George DABBS. Signed, John J. ZOLLICEFFER, adminis-
           trator.

page 374   William DANIEL - Account of Sale of William DANIEL,
           deceased; buyers: Mary DANIEL (most of household
           items), Zachariah STYLES, Carolina DANIEL, Moore
           LUMPKIN, Isaac DANIEL, Richd. FOSTER, John WEBB
           (page 375) Alexander JOHNSON, John W. ANDERSON,
           Elisha ESTES, Archelaus W. WINN, John MYRICK, William
           COVEY, John D. LOVE, John WILKES, Minerva DANIEL,
           Levin COVEY, Andrew GOOD, Yancy BLEDSOE, William
           RENTFRO, John WILKINS, Granville PILLOW, Edward W.
           DALE, Robert DOAKE (two sets of mill stones), Ben-
           jamin WISEMAN, Woody TUCKER, Zachariah MURRELL,
           Samuel CRAFTIN, James BRANCH, Mason SANFORD, David
           TROUSDALE, John T. HUDSON (page 376), David RICE,
           Marvin G. DANIEL (silver watch), James T. CROFFORD.

page 376   J. CHERRY - Settlement with James T. SANDFORD, admin-
           istrator of estate of J. CHERRY, deceased, "too long
           to record here look at file of settlements". Signed
           21 October 1826.

page 376   RILLEY - Widow's provision for widdow of James RILLEY,
           deceased, order October 1827. Commissioners report
           on 17 November 1827, signed by James DIGHAM, James
           MC CONNELL, and James REEVES.

page 377   John B. WILKES - Richard A. L. WILKES, guardian of
           Ethelbert B. WILKES, minor heir of John B. WILKES,
           deceased, report signed 25 January 1828. Notes of
           estate: James WARDEN, Samuel M. WARDEN, John GILLES-
           PIE, A. M. COOPER, John KERR, A. M. COPELAND, John
           KERR, James KERR, John M. COOK, Thomas BROWN, Vincent
           RUST, William COOPER, John MYRICK, Wm. RENTFRO, Mark
           JACKSON, Habard JACKSON, Baalam METCALF, John ELLIOTT,
           Jordan HOBBS, Samuel MC DOWELL.

page 378   LAWRENCE - Dr Martha LAWRENCE in account with Willis
           H. BODDIE, guardian. Dr the children of Ricks
           LAWRENCE, Junior, in account with Willis BODDIE,
           guardian.

page 378   Jno. J. LONG - William H. MACON in account with
           estate of Jno. J. LONG, deceased. Cash received of
           Duke WILLIAMS, R. QUINN, Will BURKET, J. M. STAMPS.
           (Page 379) Accounts for year: Francis R. LONG, John
           Joseph LONG, George W. LONG, Nicholas LONG for 1826.
           Paid L. PHILLIPS; paid Geo. CHADDOCK for tuition of
           Jno. Joseph and George W. LONG; paid J. W. BRIGGS

for tuition of Nicholas LONG; paid E. M. LONG's expenses to Georgia; paid D. CRAIGHEAD for board of Jno. Joseph LONG; paid Duke WILLIAMS for board of Jno. Joseph LONG; paid Dr. SANSOM. Signed William H. MACON, guardian, 23 January 1828.

page 380   Wm. A. WILLSON - John W. SMITH return as guardian for John and H. WILLSON, infant heirs of William A. WILLSON...hired negroes to R. H. VAIL, Jane WILLSON and N. W. BRISCOE. Signed, John W. SMITH, January 1828.

page 380   Wm. RICHARDSON - Schedule of Property of minor heirs of Wm. RICHARDSON, deceased, John M. and Thomas RICHARDSON. Signed, James M. RICHARDSON, guardian. Also property of Thomas F. RICHARDSON. Signed 25 January 1828.

page 381   John SIMS - Inventory of Property of John SIMS, deceased...50 acres and nine negroes. Signed John D. SIMS and Nicholas SIMS, executors.

page 381   BILLS - Lillias BILLS, guardian of minor heirs of Isaac BILLS, makes report.

page 382   CAMPBELL - Robert CAMPBELL, guardian to Caroline H. CAMPBELL, makes report, signed 2 February 1828.

page 382   MANGRAM - Widow's provision for Jane MANGRAM, widdow of Edwin MANGRAM. Signed 1 December 1827 by Jno. HATCHETT, Peter WILLIAMS, and Edward PICKETT.

page 383   William FARRIS - Settlement with James FARRIS, administrator of William FARRIS, deceased. Signed 5 December 1827 by A. CATHEY and S. W. AKIN.

page 384   John NIXON - Administrator settlement of John NIXON, deceased...Dr. George NIXON, administrator of estate of John NIXON, deceased...vouchers of John MAGILL and Richard ANDERSON. Signed, 14 October 1826 by A. CATHEY and Jno. MACON.

page 384   KNOX - Settlement with Joshua NEWMAN, guardian of Polly TURNER and Peggy WILLIS, formerly Polly KNOX and Peggy KNOX. Signed G. MITCHELL, Wm. FLY.

page 384   OAKLEY - Amount of money in hands of Elisabeth OAKLEY, guardian of James OAKLEY's heirs: $114.50. Signed 13 January 1827, Elisabeth OAKLEY.

page 385   Wm. FARRIS - James FARRIS, administrator of William FARRIS, deceased...inventory...money. Signed 1 February 1828 by Samuel W. AKIN.

page 385   MEDDERS - Received of Willis WILLEFORD, my guardian, $552.85, my part of estate of Joseph MEDDERS, deceased. Signed 14 February 1827 by Egbert A. MEDDERS: witness, Hardy WILLIFORD.

page 386   SHAW - Settlement made between Simpson SHAW, guardian of minor heirs of _____, January 1826. (Abstractor's note: no deceased's name given.)

page 387   SHERMAN - Guardian of minor heirs of estate of Squire
_____, 1 January 1827...mentions boarding of Marsha
and Parson SHERMAN; signed Simpson SHAW, guardian...
Charles PARTEE former guardian.

page 388   THOMPSON - Receipt of guardian of Sarah THOMPSON's
guardian, William W. GOODSIN, signed 19 January 1829,
Jeph. D. MARCH.

page 388   CARRUTHERS - Report of commissioners to lay off year's
provision to Elizabeth CARUTHERS, widdow of Robert
CARRUTHERS, Senior, deceased, signed _____ 1828 by
Stephen SMITH, John SMIZER, Matthew RHEA.

page 389   WILKES - Report of R. A. L. WILKES, guardian of minor
heirs of _____. William B. WILKES, an heir of Minor
C. WILKES. Signed 25 January 1829, Richard A. L.
WILKES, guardian.

page 390   LONG - Dr to the minor heirs of John J. LONG...James
T. TURNER's rent; accounts of Stephen SMITH, Samuel
MAJORS; Barlow's rent; received of Duke WILLIAMS,
Edw. LONG, Edwd. FISHER; interest of E. M. LONG;
accounts for 1827 and 1829; George CHADDOCK for
tuition of J. J. LONG; G. W. BUFORD for board; E. M.
LONG for trip to North Carolina; R. L. COBBS, lawyer's
fee. Signed Will H. MACON.

page 391   FORTNER - A receipt of A. M. CAMPBELL, the present
guardian of Lewis FORTNER, appointed by court of
Logan County, Kentucky, to David CRAIG, former guardian in this county. David CRAIG was appointed guardian for the minor heirs of Lewis FORTNER, deceased,
that is Mourning FORKNER, Carolina FORKNER, Wilford
FORKNER, William P. FORKNER, and Rebecca FORKNER...
negroes named and ages given...signed 8 March 1821,
A. M. CAMPBELL. (Abstractor's note: name spelled
both ways in this entry.)

page 391   MOORHEAD - Inventory of estate of Joseph MOORHEAD,
deceased; signed by James N. SMITH, administrator.
No date.

page 393   HERRING - L. B. BOYD, guardian of Robert HERRING,
report; mentions hire of negroes; paid John BLOCKER
"agent for old Mrs. HERRING on her annual allowance
from estate"; paid A. O. HARRIS. Signed 26 January
1829, Laird B. BOYD, guardian of R. HERRING.

page 393   MARTIN - The Sale of Estate of Thos. W. MARTIN, de-
ceased, no date; buyers: Frederick FISHER, Widow
MARTIN, William HUGHS, John F. CARR, Robert WIGG,
Widder MARTN, John FOX, Wm. D. SMITH, George ROAN,
Hezekiah DAVID, Wm. ARNOLD (ALLREAD?), Boward HUGGINS,
James DARK, Benjamin M. JONES, Joseph C. BALCOM, John
RHEA, Josiah C. BALCOM, John TINDLEY (?), John K.
STEWART, Charles CARR. Signed, William CARR, admin-
istrator.

page 395   SELLERS - Account of Sale of Robert SELLERS, deceased.
Buyers: the Widow, John TROTTER, Kibble T. HUGHS,
C. ERWIN, Robert B. MONTGOMERY, James SELLERS, Isham

BOOKER, Radford BUTTS, Mark A. TONEY, Daniel PAINE, Polly SELLERS, Widow (the large Bibble), Dickey CHAPPEL, Luke SELLERS (page 396) William FIELDS, ("fishing on duck river"); Chesley HALES, Gray P. WEBB, Lorenzo DOWELL, James BYNUM, John BOOKER. Signed, Luke SELLERS, executor.

page 396 - 397

PATTON - Report of Mary PATTON, guardian of George PATTON's heirs, appointed January 1827...took or kept all twelve negroes and slaves - still with her; note of Robert MATTHEWS owed by estate; minor heirs; Petillo C. PATTON, Maria PATTON, Jane PATTON, Margaritte PATTON, Susan PATTON, George PATTON; signed 26 January 1829, Polly PATTON.

page 397 - 398

WILKES - Richard A. L. WILKES, guardian of Ethelbert WILKES, a minor heir of Jno. B. WILKES, makes report of cash and notes. Notes on Meredith HELM and Samuel MC DOWELL. Signed 25 January 1829.

page 396 (note)

BOAZ - Report of William BOAZ, Guardian of minor heirs of Daniel DAVIS..."schooling of the children for 1827".

page 397 (note)

BILLS - Report of Lillias BILLS, guardian of minor heirs of Isaac BILLS, deceased.

page 398

POWELL - Account of sale by James C. POWELL, administrator of Sarah POWELL, no date. Buyers: Rubin TILMON, William D. POWELL, James C. POWELL, Joseph SCOTT, Edward POWELL, Minor WILKES, Adam MASE, James GINNERS, Danl. B. BILLS, Wm. LONDON, Thomas BILLS, Larkin DEARIN (399), James MC CONNELL, Peter JONES, Adam MASH (?), James GRIMES, Jonathan MC MANNUS, Robert MC NUTT, Henry THOMPSON, H. W. K. MYRICK, Thomas DOGGETT, Gregory GANNAWAY, Adam MUSE, Durham COLLINS, James GENNINGS, Thomas JACKSON, Josiah DUNCAN, Richd. HILL, Jonathan BILLS, Alexander OSBOURNE, William LONDON, Thomas WILSON, Anderson PIGG, Isaac JACKSON, Danl. PARY, James DAVIS, Adam MEASE. Signed, James C. POWELL, administrator.

page 401

HERRING - Report of Laird B. BOYD, guardian of Robert HERRING, minor heir of Solomon HERRING, deceased...John MILLER, executor of last will... six negroes...notes of Harman MILLER, John MILLER, Anderson MILLER, and Thomas CALDWELL. Signed, 26 January 1829 by Laird B.BOYD.

page 402

RUSSELL - Report of money and notes due to the Widdow and minor heirs of Alexander RUSSELL, deceased... negroes named and ages given...a bond on A. D.MURPHY, North Carolina, to be discharged in western lands... cash for "moving residence and children from Haywood County to Maury"...tuition for Isabella...signed, David CRAIG, guardian, 26 January 1829.

page 403

MARTIN - 28 November 1828, commissioners appointed by court to lay off widow's provision for the widow of Thomas W. MARTIN. Commissioners: William LEGGETT, Brevard HUGGINS, John MILROY.

page 403   MC DANIEL - List of Sale of Property of Joel MC DANIEL,
           deceased, 10 November 1828, by Jane MC DANIEL, admin-
           istrator.

page 404   BURNS - Report of John W. LEMASTER, guardian of minor
           heirs of James BURNS, deceased...minor heirs were
           William, John, Milton, Harry, Martha, Pegg. "The two
           girls as yet in the state of Georgia." Signed John
           W. LEMASTER, guardian, January term 1829.

page 405   MITCHELL - Settlement with administrators of John
           MITCHELL, deceased, at court October 1828, required
           to make settlement with David CRAIG and James M.
           MITCHELL on estate. Accounts of LEE and HOGE, B. W.
           WILSON, N. W. BRISHOE, Thompson ARCHER, H. LANGTRY,
           (406) Drs. BROWN and MC GIMPSEY and SAUNDERS; HAMIL-
           TON and JORDAN; John W. SMITH; John R. RICHARDS; P.
           R. BOOKER; D. C. MITCHELL, Saml. C. MITCHELL. Signed
           24 January 1829, R. STOCKARD, Geo. NIXON, as commis-
           sioners.

page 407   MILLIKEN - Account of Sale of Estate of James MILLKEN,
           deceased, signed 19 September 1826 by Baxter MILLIKEN,
           administrator. Inventory of James MILLIKEN, deceased,
           taken by Widdow MILLIKEN and Baxter MILLIKEN; Baxter
           MILLIKEN, administrator.

page 408   MC DANIEL - Year's allowance for Jane MC DANIEL,
           widow of Joel MC DANIEL, made 10 November 1828 by
           P. NELSON, John T. MOORE, and William LITTLE.

page 408   MC DANIEL - Sale of Estate of Aron MC DANIEL, de-
           ceased. October. Buyers: Starca ROBINSON, James
           GULLETT, William LITTLE, Henry HILL, and Elizabeth
           MC DANIEL. William LITTLE, administrator. (Page
           409) Inventory of Aron MC DANIEL, deceased. Notes
           on James D. FREELAND, Joel MC DANIEL and Henry HILL.
           Accounts: Pleasant NELSON, John CHAPLAIN of Ruther-
           ford County, James GULLETT. Signed, Wm. LITTLE.

page 409   SWAN - Report of Duncan BAKER, guardian of minor
           heirs of Mathew SWAN, deceased...received money from
           Henry SMITH, administrator of estate of Thomas BRAW-
           LEY...five of the heirs of Mathew SWAN, deceased,
           were Ruth, Thomas, Alexander, Katherine, and James
           SWAN. (Page 410) Paid to William SPENCER and Ruth
           SPENCER. Signed, Duncan BAKER, guardian, 19 November
           1828.

page 410   WARR - James WARR as guardian of Elizabeth Ann WARR,
           minor heir of _____(not given). "I as guardian of
           Elizabeth Ann WALKER my own child hereby certify that
           I have not as yet received any part of the legacy due
           my ward and child which is yet due to me in the state
           of North Carolina..." signed, 21 January 1829, James
           WARR. (Abstractor's note: surnames given this way.)

page 411   Will of Elizabeth BROWN of Maury County...being sick
     412   ...daughters Patsey, Susan, Elizabeth...sons James,
           Bennedict W., Wiley D....three daughters...my brother
           Thomas WALKER, executor...witnesses, Thomas WALKER
           and Benjamin DAMERON. Signed 7 November 1827, Eliza-
           beth X BROWN.

page 413   FRIERSON - Will of John Witherspoon FRIERSON...beloved
            wife, property given her by her father...son Theodore
            "my lot in the division of my father's estate and in
            the division of the legacy left to my father's family
            by my grand Father WITHERSPOON"...son to be educated
            in the English language...if son dies property sold
            and given to American Bible Society and foreign
            missionary society. Guardians: John W. STEPHENSON,
            John FRIERSON, Robert Luther FRIERSON, James W. S.
            FRIERSON. Signed, 9 November 1828 by John Wither-
            spoon FRIERSON. Witnesses: Josiah FRIERSON, Samuel
            H. STEPHENSON.

page 414   WILKS - Will of Jane WILKS...son John J....son Wm. S.
            ...daughter Jane Ann WILKS...son William S. WILKS
            and brother in law William WILKS, executors; signed
            2 November 1828, Jane X WILKS. Witnesses: C. WILKS,
            Benj. MOON, Larkin DEARIN.

page 415   BINGHAM - Inventory of Sale of James BINGHAM, de-
            ceased. Buyers: B. R. CHARTER, John AYDELOTTE,
            Benjamin JOHNSON, Martin DODSON, Jannet BINGHAM,
            widow; John TALLEY, J. SOUTHERN, N. K. FITZGERALD,
            Thos. FITZGERALD, William D. STRAIN, J. N. BINGHAM,
            Flemming HALLOWAY, John MC FADDEN, Willis JONES,
            Thos. CLENDENON, John FIELDS, J. G. ROBINSON, Carnit
            B. MC LEAN, Isaac SOUTHERN, James FITZGERALD. Signed
            J. N. BINGHAM. No date.

page 416   CAMPBELL - To Caroline H. CAMPBELL, cash as guardian.
            Signed 5 February 1829, Robert CAMPBELL, guardian.

page 417   WILKINS - Little John WILKINS, guardian of William
            John W. Thomas Asa Lefts Wall Lucy M. Stamps, minor
            heirs of Boids STAMPS, deceased of Pittsylvania
            County, Virginia, reports nothing as come to his
            hands as guardian. Signed 27 January 1829 Little
            John WILKINS, guardian. (Note: no commas in list
            of heirs as shown.)

page 416   ARNOLD - Settlement with William PERRY, administrator
            of John H. ARNOLD, deceased, before James S. BALD-
            RIDGE and James WRIGHT, J.P.'s. Appointed October
            term 1828.

page 418   CALDWELL - Vincent RIDLEY, guardian of Thos. G. CALD-
            WELL in account with said ward. Signed 24 January
            1829 by V. RIDLEY.

page 419   MARTIN - Inventory of Thomas W. MARTIN, deceased,
            note on Robert L. FULLERTON, note on Edward BAUCOMB,
            doubtful. Signed Wm. CARR, administrator.

page 420   WHITE - Settlement with Esom B. DOOLEY, administrator
            of William WHITE, deceased; receipt of Dr. BROWN, Dr.
            MC GIMSEY, Elijah KING...schooling of children...Mrs.
            WHITE. Signed 20 January 1829, A. LOONEY, John L.
            SMITH, J.P.'s.

page 421   HOBSON - Report of James BLACK, guardian of Jeremiah
            HOBSON, estate of Jeramiah HOBSON...hire of negroes
            ...paid Robert M. SMITH for boarding Jeremiah 1827...
            signed 1 January 1829, James BLACK.

page 422   FARRIS - Samuel W. AKIN's report - Guardian of William FARRIS' heirs...hire of negroes...widow's part of hire...one saddle for benefit of Jefferson James and William...Jefferson's schooling...John's schooling... David's board...Betsey's board...Robert's board... mentions slave Betsy; one-ninth is the widow's part ...signed 1 January 1830, S. W. AKIN, guardian.

page 423   EWING - Sale of Andrew F. EWING...no buyers given. No date. Executor was Margarette EWING.

page 424   MC MANUS - Sale of William G. MC MANUS...buyers:
- 425   Joshua LAWHORN, James WHITE, Ann MC MANNUS, Jonathan GROVE, Elijah RUSTUN, Jonathan MC MANNUS, John MC LASLIN, W. M. RAY, Robert MC COY, Shadrick WEAVER, William HANLEY, James APPLEBY, James WHITE, William CAUDLE, William TILMON, B. SELF, William HOUSTON, Joseph DUNCAN, Joshua COGGINS, R. ARNOLD, John MC LASKIN. Signed, John MC CASLIN, administrator.

page 426   BARNS - Settlement with Mary BARNS, administrator of Jonathan BARNS, deceased. Signed 16 January 1829, Caleb HEADLEE, John STEELE, Wm. G. PICKENS, commissioners.

page 427   STONE - Inventory of property of Esubius STONE, deceased...no date..three trace chains...signed by Geo. (Jno.?) B. BOND, Saml. B. LEE, administrators.

page 427   RICHARDSON - Report of James M. RICHARDSON, guardian of John and Thos. P. (or T.) RICHARDSON.

page 428   LEECH - Report of Ann LEACH, guardian of David LEECH's heirs...board and clothing for five children...signed Ann LEECH, guardian. Dates went through 1828.

page 428   LAWRENCE - Willis H. BODDIE, guardian of minor heirs of Ricks LAWRENCE, deceased, report...boarding and clothing for Sabra LAWRENCE.

page 429   BOYD - Elizabeth P. BOYD, guardian of the minor heirs of James BOYD, deceased...guardian for Andrew F. and Nancy J. and John P. BOYD...received from Richd. HENDERSON, executor of estate of John TATE, deceased ...bills went through 1828. Signed, Elizabeth P. BOYD. No date.

page 430   OGLISBY - Report of John M. JONES, guardian of minor heirs of James OGLISBY, deceased...minor heirs were Richard, Elisha, and Celia OGLISBY. No date.

page 431   HINES - Division of Estate of David HINES, deceased ...lot one was the widow's dower, land bounded by John PATILLO; lot two went to James M. HINES, and mentioned PATILLO's line; lot three went to Chas. C. HINES; lot four went to George MOORE, representative of Nancy HINES, minor, his wife...signed by James DOBBINS, Rubin SMITH, John KENNEDY, commissioners appointed by October 1828 court. No date.

page 433   CARROTHERS - Inventory of Robert CARROTHERS, Senior, deceased...notes and receipts: John B. ALDERSON, A.

B. HUDSON, Robert CARROTHERS, Junior, Joseph PORTER, Robert CHAMP, Petillo PATTON, John L. PETILLO, John PETTILOW, Elizabeth JACKSON, John YOUNG, Thomas LYELL, John BURGIN, administrator of Millington PETTILO, deceased; Elizabeth CARUTHERS...mentioned "The LYTTLES line in the state of North Carolina"; "The BURGIN's line in the state of North Caroline"; "a note of mine which came from North Carolina" - Samuel CARUTHERS claims the above as a gift from his father. Signed, Robert CARROTHERS, administrator. Page 434 gives negroes and ages.

page 435   CAROTHERS - Account of Sale of Robert CAROTHERS, Senior, held on 21 and 22 November 1828. Buyers: James BRANCH, Samuel CAROTHERS, Polly PATTON, Andrew NEELY, Merideth HELM, John D. LOVE, Z. STYLES, Young S. SANFORD, Benjamin THOMAS, Elizabeth CARUTHERS, Jonathan WATSON, Merideth STONE, Stephen SMITH, John M. JONES, Clement FOX, Samuel RANKIN, Eli STROUD, P. R. BOOKER, R. M. WILLIAMSON, M. HELM, John WHITAKER, Nathan VAUGHT, Wm. C. HILL, William LEONARD, Pettilow PATTON, Henry SMITH, James M. MITCHELL, William ALLEN, John ELLIOTT, Robert F. MATTHEWS, William D. PETTICE (?). Signed 22 January 1829 by Robert CAROTHERS, John D. LOVE, administrators.

page 440   GANT - Report of James P. PETERS, guardian of Eliza M. GANT...cash from D. N. SANSOM, administrator of William GANT, deceased; signed 26 January 1829 by James P. PETERS. (Page 443-445) Report of James P. PETERS, guardian of John J. GANT, signed 26 January 1829, James P. PETERS. (Page 446-448) Report of James P. PETERS, guardian of Robina A. GANT, signed 26 January 1829, James P. PETERS. Paid John POLK for schooling; mentions Mrs. NORWOOD's bond.

page 449   MATHEWS - Settlement with John MATHEWS - John MATHEWS, guardian for Margaret A. MATHEWS from 16 April 1828 to 16 April 1829. Signed 16 April 1829, John MATHEWS.

page 449   CARUTHERS - Supplement to the inventory of Robert CARUTHERS, Senior, deceased, sold on 13 February 1829. Buyers: Petillo PATTON, Polly PATTON, James MOORE, J. D. LOVE, Samuel CARUTHERS.

page 450   KINKAID - Report of Elizabeth KINKAID, guardian of minor heirs of Joseph KINKAID, deceased. Signed 2 May 1829, Joel REESE, J.P.

page 451   MC CALLUM - Settlement of estate of Thrasher MC CALLUM, deceased, with Mary MC CALLUM, administrator. Mentions boarding and schooling of eight children. Signed 3 April 1829 by William EDMISTON and William KERSEY.

page 451   DALTON - Report of John F. CARR, guardian of minor heirs of Isaac DALTON, deceased. No date. "Went to Stokes County, North Caroline, in connection with estate."

page 452   SCOTT - Will of Samuel SCOTT - wife Sarah...daughter Agnes MATHEWS, wife of John MATHEWS...son James to get plantation where he lived and died...son Adam... daughter Jane LUSK, wife of Thomas LUSK...my single daughters Jenny, Sarah, Elizabeth, Mary and Martha SCOTT...my daughter Elizabeth is now in a low state of health...son Andrew SCOTT and William S. HENDERSON, executors...signed 2 September 1828, Samuel SCOTT. Witnesses: Richard HENDERSON, John R. BOYD, W. L. HENDERSON. (page 453), Codicil witnesses: William L. HENDERSON, Jonathan GALLOWAY.

page 453   HART - Will of Joseph HART...being old and inform... 1/3 to eldest son John L. HART...many debts left under control of executors for benefit of his family ...son Jessey HART...my son James HEMPHILL...daughters Nancy HART, Jane M. HART, Sally W. HART...son James ...six children...son Jessey HART and Alexander CATHEY to be executors...five youngest children... signed 29 October 1828. Witnesses: James CATHEY and John MORRISON.

page 456   ISOM - Account of the business in the hands of D. CRAIG, Esquire, and Polly, his wife, belonging to the estate of James ISOM, decest...mentions widdow's part ...mentions minor heirs...mentions David CRAIG and his wife Mary. Signed 16 February 1829 by A. T. ISOM and William CATHEY.

page 457   ISOM - Account of moneys laid out for use of minor heirs of James ISOM, deceast. Mentions J. O. COOK paid for surveying...paid Robert MACK, Dr. SANSOM, KINDLE, Actioneer; paid for Emaline and Robert's tuition...paid tuition to the Female Academy...mentions Sally's bill.

page 457   RODENY - Inventory of estate of Benjamin RODENY, signed 28 April 1827 by Winifred X RODERY.

page 459   FRIERSON - Return of Samuel MAYES, guardian of Edmund FRIERSON, for 1828...paid E. M. FORD for boarding.

page 459   CARUTHERS - Assignment of dower to Elisabeth CARUTHERS by Joel REESE, Nathl. T. MOORE, Stephen SMITH, John SIMSON, Zachariah MARTIN, 13 February 1829.

page 459   PATTON - Assignment of dower to Polly PATTON, widow
- 460   of George PATTON...land calls mention Abraham LOONEY's line, Lytle's Creek, and Robert CARUTHERS, deceased, corner...signed 19 December 1828 by Abraham LOONEY, Nathl. T. MOORE, Joel REESE, Mathew RHEA.

page 460   DAVIS - Dower of Lydia DAVIS, widow of Danl. DAVIS.
- 461   Signed 20 February 1827 by Milly P. ABERNATHY, James HOWARD, James H. EMERSON, James STOCKARD, George DAVIDSON, Joel REESE, Caleb THOMAS, deputy sheriff.

page 461   KIMBLE - Dower of Mary M. KIMBLE, signed 3 December 1828 by John W. SMITH, Duke WILLIAMS, Philip P. WINN, Samuel H. SMITH, R. H. VAIL, Joel REESE, surveyor.

page 461   COLEMAN - Return made by Clarissa COLEMAN, a guardian of her two sons Rufus and Walter for accounts up to 1 January 1829.

page 462   ADKINS - Will of Elijah P. ADKINS, written 27 February
           1829...very low and infirm - dear mother Jane ADKINS
           ...brother James ADKINS...sister Rebecca CAMPBELL...
           executors to be Wesley WITHERSPOON and Ezekiel M.
           CAMPBELL; signed 27 February 1829; witnesses, David
           STRAIN, Jackson FITZGERALD.

page 462   WILKES - Inventory of property of Jane WILKES, de-
           ceased...buyers were William WILKES, Jane A. WILKES,
           William DAVIS, Thomas ROBLY...amount of sale by
           William WEAKS and William L. WILKES, executors,
           27 April 1829.

page 464   MC CORD - William PERRY, guardian of Edmund, William,
           and Robert MC CORD, minor heirs of William MC CORD,
           deceased, makes report to April term 1829.

page 464   MC LEMORE - B. S. HURT, executor of Edward MC LEMORE
           makes report, signed 22 September 1829 by John C.
           WORMLEY, John SMITH, J.P.'s.

page 465   MILLICAN - Settlement with Baxter MILLICAN, adminis-
           trator, of estate of James MILLICAN. Signed 19 April
           1829 by R. STOCKARD and William STOCKARD, J.P.'s.

page 465   COLEMAN - Clarissa COLEMAN's account with Walter
           COLEMAN...rent for January 1829 recorded.

page 466   BODDY - Division of negroes - Willie BODDY to his
           grandchildren Matilda Becks LAURANCE, Jane Toole
           LAWRENCE, Sabra Boddie LAWRENCE and Martha LAWRENCE
           ...Jane is now Mrs. Jane T. JORDAN. Division made
           3 September 1814. (Note: date in question, hard to
           read.) Signed David CRAIG, John DAVISON, Micklejohn
           KITRELL, 4 February 1827.

page 466   DANIEL - Current account between Mary DANIEL, guardian
  - 469   of William W., John J., Elizabeth Franklin, and
           Martha Angeline DANIEL, minor heirs of William DANIEL,
           deceased. Signed 1 January 1830 by Mary DANIEL.

page 470   BROWN - Settlement with William BROWN, administrator
           of Charles BROWN...heirs of Charles BROWN were
           Elizabeth BROWN, Nancy, Archabald, Mary, John L.D.
           and Elizabeth M. R. BROWN. Signed 10 April 1829,
           A. CATHEY and S. W. AKIN, J.P.'s. (Abstractor's
           note: the name could also be Nancy Archabald instead
           of two names.)

page 471   DANIEL - Settlement with Mary DANIEL, administrator,
           and John J. ZOLLICOFFER, administrator of William
           DANIEL. Account of sale on 14 December 1826...buyers
           or accounts and receipts: John M. ANDERSON, George
           DOBBS, Samuel A. GILLESPIE, Benjamin B. SMITH, John
           MATTHEWS, Elisha ESTES, Leven COVY, Ebenezer RICE,
           John KIMES, Stephen EUBANKS, Moore LUMPKINS, James
           BRANCH, A. RANKIN, O. ALEXANDER, John MYRICK, R.
           CARUTHERS, Richard FOSTER, A. WILLIAMSON, Thomas
           NORTON, J. ALDERSON, A. O. HARRIS, G. L. JONES,
           William A. MAXWELL, John KERR, E. T. MITCHELL,
           Charles W. WEBBER, Doct. HUNT, A. W. WINER, J. W.
           DANIEL, Minerva DANIEL, Isaac K. W. DANIEL; (page
           473) signed by Alexander JOHNSON and Abraham LOONEY,
           commissioners.

page 473   HART - Inventory of estate of Joseph HART, deceased
...negroes named...signed Jesse HART and Alexander
CATHEY, executors. No date.

page 474   SELLERS - Settlement with Luke SELLERS, executor of
Robert SELLERS, deceased, receipts listed (abstractor's
note: not copied), signed 1 May 1829, John PORTER,
Samuel CRAWFORD, J.P.'s.

page 475   BALL - Settlement with James BALL, deceased, estate
...$7 paid for coffin...administrators were not
named. Signed 18 April 1829 by Jno. MACK, Joseph
IRWIN, J.P.'s.

page 476   TOM - Articles in Inventory of Estate of William TOM,
  - 477   deceased, by Nancy TOM, executrix of last will.
Signed 16 April 1829 by Nancy X. TOM.

page 477   WILLIAMS - Sale of perishable property of Nathaniel
WILLIAMS, deceased, by administrators on 19 December
1828. Buyers: Mrs. Leaner WILLIAMS, H. WILLIAMS,
John DAWSON, C. W. KNIGHT, Thomas WILLIAMS, D. WILLIAMS,
Francis MOODY, Alexander GOODMAN, William ROWSEY,
Joseph HACKNEY, Samuel SHULL, J. M. CRENSHAW, John
WATKINS, Samuel B. LEE, Jesse RENFROE, William KINDLE,
William NEELY, Jesse GOODMAN, D. G. JOHNSON, Joseph
GRIFFIN, Henry TUCKNISS, George CHADDOCK, Malachi
HELM, Robert MATHEWS, Eli NEELY, John WORTHAM, Joseph
HAWKINS, William SPENCER, Joseph O. CROSS, Duncan
BAKER, W. H. MACON, Alfred BROOKS, George W. JOHNSON,
Leml. PHILLIPS, O. BEKLEY, Mathias LEE, John SHULL,
Robert WORTHAM, George R. KELSEY, Samuel H. SMITH, Y.
MC CASLIN, William CURTIS, Moses PEYTON, David DOBBINS.
Administrators: Duke WILLIAMS, Frederick ZOLLICOFFER,
Harden WILLIAMS.

page 483   SELLERS - James CATHEY, guardian of Ebenezer SELLERS
  - 484   and Serena SELLERS, minor heirs of John SELLERS, make
report, signed 20 April 1829.

page 484   HOWARD - List of hire of negroes and sale of property
of John HOWARD, deceased, 30 December 1828. William
WHITTED was administrator. Buyers: Eleanor HOWARD,
Thomas C. HOWARD, McCagy SPRINKLES, William PICKARD,
George E. SKIPWORTH.

page 484   PURSELL - Richard FAWCETT, guardian of Benjamin F.,
Mary Ann, and Sarah PURSELL, makes report. Signed
20 April 1829. Paid to Sarah WADDLE, widow of the
deceased as her part of rent in right of dower.

page 485   BRAWLEY - Settlement with Henry SMITH, administrator
of estate of Thomas BRAWLEY, deceased. Notes: James
CUNNINGHAM, William WERE, William CHALK, and Elijah
KIRKMAN. Signed George JOHNSTON and Robert WORTHAM,
J.P.'s.

page 486   BLAIR - Account of sale of personal estate of Andrew
BLAIR, deceased, 23 January 1829. Buyers: J. T.
MACON, William ALDERSON, William BIFFLE, Charles J.
SOWELL, James C. O'RILEY, James BINGHAM, G. WEBSTER,
W. P. POOL, R. L. FRIERSON, Joseph MC MURRY, James
CATHEY, George LUTHES, Isaac D. VANHOOK, George KINSER,

James STRAYHORN, Peter JOICE, James YOUNGER, Jonathan
WEBSTER, Samuel LUCKETT, Alexr. WALKER, Elijah TURNER,
G. M. BUFORD, G. W. FRIERSON, J. W. L. FRIERSON,
Edward LONG, E. M. LONG, Thomas DEATON, Jonathan
BULLOCK, Samuel H. WILLIAMS, John BROWN, George SKIP-
WITH, Samuel LUCKET, John EAVES, William CAMPBELL,
William HART, Travis BOWDEN, George LUTHER, Crawford
BROWN, James HEAREY, James MC CORD, James JONES, John
SMITH, James JOSEY, William FLY, Thomas L. PATTON,
Stephen EDWARDS, W. WRIGHT, John HINES, William LEIGH,
Andrew CRAWFORD, Nathaniel WILLIS, John WALKER, Noah
B. TINDALE, Allen DODD, Henry TURNEY, Levi KETCHAM,
Thomas J. FRIERSON, N. B. TINDALL, J. D. VANHOOK,
Robert FOSTER, Joseph WALKER, James CATHEY, William
WHEAT, Alxr. CATHEY, Thomas HUDSON...mentions hire
of negroes...notes: Robert WEBSTER, John H. FISHER,
Thomas GARRET, Jonathan WEBSTER, John HART, Joseph
G. PRATT, David THOMPSON, James DOBBINS, James L.
ROBERTSON, John L. STRAYHORN, John G. BARRY, Ebenezer
MILLER. Book accounts: "William R. DICKEY living
in the Western District", Robert HARLOW, L. STRAYHORN,
Elias BUTLER, Mr. WHEAT. Signed James CATHEY, Jona.
WEBSTER.

page 491   GRAHAM - Inventory of Margaret GRAHAM. Purchasers:
Noah WHITE, Allen PILLOW, George G. MC CANNAN, James
MC CARDE, Temple HICKS, Noah B. TINDEL, William C.
CHAMBERS, Johnathan WEBSTER, Peter GRAHAM, Gilbert
HICKS, William RIGHTE, Dudley GRAHAM, Charles GRAHAM,
Melvina GRAHAM, Thomas J. FRIERSON, John EDWARDS,
Thomas DEATON, John FARIS, James GRAHAM, John M. FARIS,
Grean GRAHAM, Charles Robert FOSTER, Josiah AMOS.
Signed Green GRAHAM, administrator of Margaret GRAHAM.
No date.

page 493   DUNLAP - Inventory of Sale of Estate of Samuel DUNLAP,
deceased, on 27 November 1828. Buyers: Joseph DAVID-
SON, Bracket DAVIDSON, Jesse MOORE, A. L. KURHCTNER,
James RODGERS, William CRUTCHER, Robert D. WALKER,
William L. WADE, William A. STEPHENSON, Alanson HARROS,
Dennis STEPHENS, James D. BETTS, Alexander MC MILLAN,
John L. CRAWFORD, Robarson ROSS, Bogan C. WALLIS, A.
L. CRUTCHER, William RAYBURN, Clement WALL, David
EAGLE, James R. FOSTER, James M. STEPHENSON, William
BIZZELE, John ALDERSON, Samuel GRAHAM, Samuel D.
BETTS, Edward ROSS, William WOODSIDE, George CASKEY,
John A. COWLE, Samuel DUNLAP, Eliza DUNLAP, Emily
DUNLAP, James OLIVER, John STEPHENS, William GOSSETT,
Dennis STEPHENS, John R. DAOAL, George CASKEY. Notes
on John O'BRIANT, Bracket DAVIDSON, Moses SWIM.
(page 495) Negroes bequeathed to widow. Signed
April 1829, B. S. HURT, executor.

page 495   STONE - List of Property belonging to estate of
Esabius STONE, deceased. Buyers: Owen HUMPHREY,
Silas HARLIN, James RUSSELL, Miss STONE, Eli STONE,
John T. MACON, James J. SELLARS, Johnston CRAIG,
S. B. LEE, S. HARDIN, J. O. CROSS, Duke WILLIAMS,
Samuel B. LEE, A. H. BUCKNER, Elija HARDIN, Ward
STOCKARD, Jno. B. BOND, M. STONE, F. G. STONE, Napin
WILSON, James S. SELLERS, H. O. MILLER. Signed
Samuel B. LEE and John B. BOND. No date.

page 498   MC CORD - Inventory of Estate of William MC CORD, deceased, to be equally divided between his wife Nancy, now Nancy PERRY, and his three children, Edmond, William, and Robert MC CORD, according to last will... negroes named and ages given...signed 18 April 1829, Morgan FITZPATRICK, John JONES, William HOLT.

page 500   FRIERSON - Copy of the bill of estate of J. W. FRIERSON, sold 18 December 1828. Buyers: R. L. FRIERSON, J. FRIERSON, W. Joseph FRIERSON, W. G. FRIERSON, G. FRIERSON, G. Van BUREN, William MACON, J. BINGHAM, G. W. STEPHENSON, S. H. ARMSTRONG, S. MAYES, B. DENNON, G. KELSEY. Signed, John W. STEPHENSON, R. L. FRIERSON, Executors.

page 502   FRIERSON - Accounts of J. W. FRIERSON: J. FRIERSON, J. W. STEPHENSON, Thomas KELSEY, John ALEXANDER, G. Van BUREN, Rogeal FERGUSON, estate of B. DICKEY.

Maury County Will Book E

page 1   BROWN - Settlement with administrators of Thomas BROWN, deceased, recorded 24 August 1829. Balsaam METCALF, administrator of Thomas BROWN. Signed James WRIGHT and E. RICE, J.P.'s.

page 1   HACKNEY - Joseph GRIFFIN's receipt from Joseph HACKNEY for sale of David, age 18. Witnesses: Benjamin W. WILSON and John P. SPINDLE.

page 2   CAMPBELL - Robert CAMPBELL, guardian, return 24 August 1829, guardian of Caroline H. CAMPBELL. (Abstractor's note: this had been marked out.)

page 2   CALDWELL - Guardian account of CALDWELL's heirs, recorded 24 August 1829...Vincent RIDLEY settles with his ward, Thomas G. CALDWELL, on 24 January 1828.

page 3   Inventory of Estate of Andrew F. EWING, deceased,
- 4   recorded 24 August 1829...negroes named.

page 4   EVANS - Estate settlement of Daniel EVANS, deceased, with E. EVANS, recorded 24 August 1829. Accounts: Peter I. VOORHIES, S. A. GILLESPIE, Robert M. SMITH, Jesse G. WILKS, C. G. VOORHIES, Peter RAGSDALE, Amy JOHNSON, R. YEATMAN, William VOORHIES, James L. WATKINS, Barbara JONSTON, Samuel RANKIN, Chaffin, D. FALTNER, John WILSON; money received: John GORDON, D. and S. GILLESPIE, Mrs. GAUNT, William K. HILL. Signed 26 July 1827 by John C. WORMLEY, James BLACK.

page 5   CAMPBELL - Ezekiel CAMPBELL's guardian account for Junius P. CAMPBELL, minor, recorded 24 August 1829. Mentions Samuel P. CAMPBELL, a minor. Signed E. M. CAMPBELL.

page 5   DYER - Inventory of David DYER's estate, recorded 24 August 1829...mentions notes in South Carolina for collection, signed, James N. BROWN.

page 6   EVANS - Inventory of Estate of Daniel EVANS, deceased, recorded 24 August 1829, taken 18 October 1826. Notes and accounts: John GORDON, John W. BEASLEY, Robert M. SMITH, John EVANS, Martin TONEY (this is desperate), David FERRILE, ESTES, John WILSON...negroes named and ages given. Signed, Elizabeth X THOMAS.

page 7   COLEMAN - Recorded 24 August 1829...Schedule of Inventory of Sale of Estate of Thos. COLEMAN, deceased. Notes: Enos PIPKIN, R. CROSBY, John and Jeremiah ALDERSON, John L. SMITH, R. CROSBY, John G. EARLEY, William E. MC CARROLL, W. W. COLEMAN, Thomas P. JOHNSON, W. E. MC CARROLL, Square and William HARLOW. Signed 28 April 1828 by R. CROSBY.

page 7   ENGLISH - Susanna ENGLISH's allowance, recorded 25 August 1829...commission called on by Captn. George NIXON and Pair Edward F. ENGLISH, administrators of Thomas ENGLISH, deceased, to lay off property for Susannah ENGLISH, late widow of said deceased and family. Signed, David CRAIG, Ring. BUCKNER, Saml. WAKIN, 28 March 1829.

page 8   EASTWOOD - Will of Lydie EASTWOOD, recorded 25 August 1829 - nuncupative will...John WRIGHT and Samuel GULLETT reduce to writing her will...she departed this life, Wednesday, 28 January 1828...mentions grandchild Massey CARRINGTON, mentions Massey's mother Sally CARRINGTON (later found as Mary), signed 2 February 1828 John WRIGHT, Samuel GULLETT. (page 9) Inventory of property of Lydia EASTWOOD, deceased taken 31 January 1828, recorded 25 August 1829.

page 10   EDLEMAN - List of sales of John EDLEMAN, deceased, recorded 25 August 1829...William BALDRIDGE, Senior, James R. JENNINGS, Robert F. MATTHEWS, Robert WORTHAM, Ozni ALEXANDER, A. C. CROFFORD, William ALISON, Robert PEYTON, William PORTER, Henry SMITH, widow, Henry GIBSON, Anna EDDLEMAN, William MOSLEY, Josiah GREEN, William STOCKARD, Phillip PEN, Henry SMITH, William STOCARD, Philip P. WIN, Charles B. HARRIS, James PEYTON, Robert NICHOLAS. William RUTLER, Senior, administrator.

page 11   EDLEMAN - Thomas M. HARPER, guardian of minor heirs of John EDLEMAN, deceased, reports note on A. B. and Ozni ALEXANDER, recorded 25 August 1829.

page 11   HAMBLETT - William COOPER, guardian of William HAMBLETT, minor heir of Littleberry HAMBLETT makes return, recorded 25 August 1829. Note of Meredith HELM for "hire of Wilson and Phileir"; note on P. NELSON and Joshua GUEST for "hire of Parthena"; note on K. T. HUGHES. (Abstractor's note: slaves also found as Nelson and Phillis.) (Page 12) Paid EGGNEW for attending suit against William YANCEY...store account of Patrick MAGUIRE. Signed 21 July 1828.

page 12   ENGLISH - Dower of Susanna ENGLISH, recorded 25 August 1829, late widow of Thomas ENGLISH...land on Rigbigby in Range 3, Section 4, 169 acres, land belonging and being "last place of residence of the said Thomas

ENGLISH, deceased." Signed 17 April 1828 by David CRAIG, Thomas STONE, William GOODGION, William RICKETS, John STONE, Saml. WAKIN, James BAILEY, William W. GUIN, R. STOCKARD, Joel REESE, James W. GOODGON, Nimrod PORTER, sheriff.

page 13
- 16

Inventory of Sale of property of Thomas ENGLISH, deceased. Buyers: George NIXON, David CRAIG, Truman HEALTON, Hosea SKIPPER, Merrit MAXEY, Wilson (William?) WILLIAMS, Littleberry TURNER, Young KIRK, Thomas DEATON, James YOUNGER, William BLAKELEY, J. M. S. MAYES, James M. GOODGION, Joseph GRIFFIN, Young KIRK, Jacob RIFFLE, Samuel LIRBY (page 15) William CRAIG, E. F. ENGLISH, James TURNER, William GRAY, A. T. ISOM, Thos. N. WILLIAMS, M. J. KITRELL, Samuel GRAY, John EVES, James S. CRAIG, James MC GOWEN, George CHADDOCK, William NIXON, Saml. LILES, Ed. F. ENGLISH, Truman HEALTON, John EAVES, W. WILHAMS, John BULLOCK, Wm. HUNTER, James STOCKARD, John STONE, Saml. JENNINGS. Signed, Edward F. ENGLISH, George NIXON, administrators.

page 16

DUNLAP - Will of Samuel DUNLAP, recorded 25 August 1829...wife Nancy..."my new house"...settlement be made with Col. Aaron BOYD as guardian of the children of Nancy DUNLAP, formerly Nancy RIGGS...my two youngest children...my two youngest daughters Nancy FLEMING and Lydia ANDERSON...son Thomas when he arrives at the age 16..."the four children - Samuel DUNLAP, Eliza Jane, Emily, and Thomas H. DUNLAP"...the four oldest above named children. Bird S. HURT and W. M. GOSSETT to be executors. Signed 1 October 1828. Witnesses, Wm. GLENN, A. P. CRUTCHER, Saml. D.SAMATON.

page 17

CHEEK - List of Sale of Jesse CHEEK, recorded 26 August 1829. Buyers were Jane CHEEK and Peggy NEELY.

page 18

DANIEL - Dower for Widow DANIEL, wife of William DANIEL, deceased. He had 450 acres on Fountain Creek, mentions John LINDSEY's west boundary line, the mansion house, the still house, taken 13 October 1827, by James BRANCH, John GILLESPIE, Jarrett PATTERSON, John M. JONES, Robert MC DANIEL, Richard TIDWELL, John WHITAKER, John D. LOVE, John M. ANDERSON, Solomon P. MAXWELL, Joel REESE.

page 18-
19-20

EWING - Andrew F. EWING's will, recorded 26 August 1829...wife Margaret...daughter Malissa..."legacy due to me from the estate of my uncle James EWING, deceased, of Bedford County"...my wife's sister Mary F. CUNNINGHAM to have a home with my wife and daughter for herself and slaves during her natural life or celibacy...the legacy falling to me of my father's estate, after the death of my mother...until Malissa comes of age or marries unless my wife marries...my nephew Andrew Simpson EWING...brother in law Samuel T. CUNNINGHAM's first child that he has that lives to be grown...niece Jane Emeline EWING...niece Margaret Eleanor HILL...wife Margaret and brother George EWING to be executors...signed 13 September 1828...witnesses, Samuel EWING, Hezekiah OLIVER, Middleton HILL, Arthur M. SMITH. George EWING renounced his right as executor in open court.

181

page 21   BRAWLEY - Thomas BRAWLEY's list of sale, recorded
           26 August 1829. Buyers were Jonathan DOUGLAS, Robert
           F. MATHEW, William BRAWLEY, David MANNON, James CLAY-
           TON, Henry GIBSON, Ann BRAWLEY. Henry SMITH, admin-
           istrator.

page 21   BURKET - Settlement with Miles BURNS, administrator
           of estate of William BURKET, deceased, recorded 26
           August 1829. Vouchers of William H. MACON, BROWN
           and MC GIMSEY, David STREETE, Samuel MAJORS, Stephen
           SMITH, John BURNS, John NIXON, James GRAY.

page 22   BARNES - Valuation of property of James W. BARNES
           (or BARNER), deceased, taken by Jasper R. SUTTON and
           Obadiah ALEXANDER May 1828, recorded 26 August 1829;
           Thomas W. VINCENT, administrator.

page 22   BRIDGES - Guardian return for BRIDGES heirs, recorded
           26 August 1829...in 1827 Ester BRIDGES was guardian
           to William J., Olliver and Melita BRIDGES, minor
           heirs of Bain BRIDGES, signed Esther BRIDGES, 27 Jan-
           uary 1828.

page 23   BOYD - Guardian return for Andrew T., Nancy L., and
           John P. BOYD, minor heirs of James BOYD, deceased...
           receipt of William S. HENDERSON and John B. BOYD,
           administrators of estate of James BOYD...paid Mrs.
           Jane M. PATTON for schooling of Andrew T. and paid
           Joseph HANNAH for schooling of Andrew T. and Nancy
           L. Signed, Elizabeth P. BOYD, guardian.

page 24   BROWN - Inventory of William BROWN, recorded 26 Aug-
           ust 1829. Accounts: Willie D. BROWN, Benedict D.
           BROWN, Elizabeth BROWN, Saml. H. WILLIAMS, John
           FERRILL, James DOBBINS, Martha BROWN, Gideon PILLOW,
           Thos. WALKER, James BROWN, James BRADSHAW, Simeon
           DAMERON, Will G. ARMSTRONG, Priscilla MOORE, Susannah
           W. BROWN, Jas. W. JOHNSON, Elizabeth POTTS, Henry
           HILL, Hugh DOUGLAS, E. M. FORD. Signed W. G. ARM-
           STRONG, administrator.

page 24   BRECKENRIDGE - Guardian return of heirs of Alexander
           BRECKENRIDGE...note on Elisha ESTES; signed Benjamin
           THOMAS, recorded 28 August 1829.

page 25   JONES - Churchwell ANDREWS, one of the administrators
           of James JONES, deceased, makes return to court that
           nothing has come into his hands, recorded 26 August
           1829.

page 25   BROWN - Lurany BROWN's year allowance and provision
           recorded 26 August 1829, widow of Thomas BROWN,
           deceased, by John KERR, James KERR, Richard TIDWELL
           on 26 April 1828.

page 25   BROWN - Inventory of Thomas BROWN, deceased, recorded
     26   26 August 1829. Sold on Saturday, 23 February 1828;
           receipts on Wiley P. RICHARDSON, James S. STEELE,
           Elijah KIRKMAN, Drury MORRIS, Wright W. MANNING, Wm.
           C. HILL, James ALLEN. Buyers: Lurany BROWN, R. A.
           L. WILKES, John KERR, William L. LEONARD, William
           HORGIE, Balam METCALF, Francis WHEATLEY, Andrew M.
           KERR, William MURPHY, John THOMBS. Signed Balaam
           METCALF, administrator.

page 27- BADGET - Benton BADGET's distribution of property,
28   recorded 27 August 1829. "We, James P. PETERS, James
          DOBBINS, A. G. PORTER (A. Y. PARTEE?), Dickie CHAPPELL,
          Thomas HUDSPETH, Francis HILL appointed to lay off
          dower of Levisa BADGET out of estate of Benton BADGET,
          deceased"; Lot 1 to Samuel BADGET, Lot 2 to Jesse B.
          BADGETT; Lot 3 to William BADGET; Lot 4 to Levina
          BADGET; Lot 5 to Tennessee BADGET; Lot 6 to Noah
          BADGET; Lot 7 to Mary BADGET.

page 29   BELL - Inventory of Sale of James BELL, deceased,
          taken 28 July 1826, recorded 27 August 1829. Buyers:
          John WRIGHT, William KENNAMORE, Anna BELL, John W.
          KILPATRICK, James THOMAS, Waren MENSE, Thomas ROS-
          BOROUGH, Lemira BELL, William MC CONNELL, Louis MC
          GRAW, Edward WRIGHT, Gideon JOHNSON, Warren MEESE,
          Newman MOORE. Signed John W. KILPATRICK and James
          THOMAS.

page 30   BROWN - Thomas WALKER, guardian of Elizabeth H. BROWN,
          minor heir of William F. BROWN, deceased, report re-
          corded 27 August 1829.

page 30   BROWN - Account of Sale of Daniel BROWN, deceased,
          recorded 27 August 1829, sold 16 October 1828. Buy-
          ers: Osange HAM, Franklin E. POLK, John M. POINTER,
          Jas. P. PETERS, George MORE, Briton BAILEY, Caleb
          MANDLEY, Abraham HAMMONDS, Ezekiel AKIN, Saml. ATKIN-
          SON, Armstead A. POLK, John BAUGH, Benjamin ROODENY,
          Robt. EVANS, W. W. WILLIS, Wm. W. ROUNTREE, G. A.
          CONA (?), Richd. WILLIS, Francis HERRON, Dickie
          CHAPPEL, Wm. H. WORMACK, M. W. CAMPBELL, James NOT-
          GRASS, John MILLER, Young CHUMBLEY, Elijah HUNTER,
          Wm. M. WITTO (?), Joseph H. MILLER, Spivy MC KIISIC,
          Pleasant AKIN, Thomas MAHAN, John C. CAMPBELL, John
          KITRELL, Wm. M. DORTCH, Wm. C. CAMPBELL, Jefferson
          SHANNON, Nathanial CHEAIRS; note on Reddick DESHONGH
          (DESHOUGH?), William A. BAILEY. Signed Wm. H. HILL,
          administrator.

page 33   BROWN - Account of sale of Wm. BROWN, deceased, re-
          corded 27 August 1829; Elia J. ARMSTRONG, W. D. BROWN,
          widow, Jas. H. OLIPHANT, S. R. KITTREL, Wm. G. ARM-
          STRONG, S. H. WILLIAMS, Jessey YATES. Signed, W. G.
          ARNSTRONG.

page 34   BYNUM - Inventory of money in hands of guardian for
          P. BYNUM, minor heirs to William BYNOM, deceased.
          Signed, Thomas HUDSPETH, guardian, 27 August 1829.
          (Note: or C. BYNYM, minor heir of William BYNOM,
          deceased.)

page 34   ALEXANDER - John M. ALEXANDER's administrator settle-
          ment, 26 August 1829; Silas ALEXANDER was administra-
          tor. Vouchers and accounts: doctors bill, James
          KAVERCONES, Silas ALEXANDER, John GORDON, George
          JOHNSTONES, James O. ALEXANDER, A. B. ALEXANDER...
          whiskey for use at sale...head and footstone cost
          $10...signed John MATTHEWS, William CARR, 16 July
          1828.

page 35   ANDERSON - William B. ANDERSON's administrator settle-
          ment, recorded 26 August 1829. Francis T. ANDERSON

and John M. ANDERSON were administrators for William B. ANDERSON. Note on John G. BRANCH, mentions judgement in Kentucky...accounts of Saml. DAVIS, Joseph B. PORTER, Robert CARUTHERS, Jas. G. BRANCH...deficiency notes in widow's allowance for year...accounts of Benjamin WILKES and Doctor HUNTER...paid Francis T. ANDERSON for her services as administrator...signed Alex. JOHNSON, E. RICE.

page 36   BLAKELEY - Will of Jannet BLAKELEY, recorded 28 August 1829...daughter Sarah FRIERSON, widow of David FRIERSON...son William BLAKELEY...signed ____ July 1828, Janet BLAKELEY; witnesses, Ths. F. FLEMING, Jas. FRIERSON.

page 37   BRECKENRIDGE - Benjamin THOMAS, guardian for heirs of Alexander BRECKENRIDGE, deceased, makes return, recorded 28 August 1829...notes on Temple TURNEY and Peter R. BOOKER...receipts of B. B. SMITH, and Joel REESE, surveyor. Signed Benjamin THOMAS, 28 April 1829.

page 38   BILLS - Will of Placebo Milton BILLS, recorded 28 August 1829...mother, "I owe to my beloved mother the gratitude of a son for the many kind offices received at her hands in affection and where as she is Dwile (?) be engaged in keeping a public house," mother to have all my property...when my brother Isaac N. BILLS arrives at the age of 21..."beloved mother Lillias BILLS and James HOUSTON my beloved uncle to be executors...signed 20 October 1827. Witnesses were A. WILLIAMS, W. GILLESPIE, John GILLESPIE. Codicil dated 19 April 1828, "my black cloth coat to brother A. M. BILLS"...witnesses to codicil were John GILLESPIE and Archibald WILLIAMS ...Schedule also recorded, mentions land on Elk River.

page 40   AKIN - Amount of Sale of Property of James AKIN, deceased, on 12 May 1828; buyers were Robert RODGERS, Pleasant AKIN, Nancy MILLS, Jacob RODGERS, James AKIN, Jesse ROGERS, Robert ROGERS, Bryant BAUGAUS, Jane AKIN, Elizabeth AKIN, William COGGINS, Ezekial AKIN. Commissioners: John KILCREASE, Thomas MAHON, Alexander MOORE, signed 29 July 1828.

page 41   ALDERSON - Sarah ALDERSON's Dower, recorded 28 August 1829. Sarah ALDERSON, widow and relict of John G. ALDERSON, deceased...lot in Columbia where she now lives. Signed: James R. PLUMMER, Joseph ERWIN, Abraham LOONEY, Samuel MC DOWELL, Matthew RHEA, 29 August 1828.

page 41   ALDERSON - Division of Estate of John L. (S.?) ALDERSON, recorded 28 August 1829. Heirs, James R. SHELTON and wife, lot 1, which was lot 120 and lot 121 in Columbia; lot 2 to Emeline B. ALDERSON, lot at northwest corner of lot number 1; lot number 3 to Matilda D. ALDERSON; lot 4 to John B. ALDERSON; lot 5 to Taswell S. ALDERSON; lot 6 to David D. DEENS and wife, lots on high street...land on waters of Lytle Creek (granted to Elisha ESTES and deeded to John S. ALDERSON...slaves mentioned. Signed 31 October 1828 by M. HELM and Joseph HART.

page 44   BRANK - Account of Sale of Robert H. BRANK, deceased,
           recorded 28 August 1829...articles included Christiane
           BLACKSTONE (books), the U. S. Constitution, sorrel
           horse, saddle and bridle, and bay horse. Ephraim E.
           DAVIDSON, administrator. (Abstractor's note: BRANK
           was killed in duel by a Columbia lawyer; they went to
           Kentucky to fight the duel.)

page 44   BILLS - Recorded 28 August 1829, Inventory of P. M.
           BILLS...notes of J. B. PORTER, Young STANFORD,
           Robert F. MATTHEWS, Francis WILLIS and Jesse BRIDGES.
           Signed: James HOUSTON, Lillias BILLS, executors.

page 45   BLACKBURN - Administrator's Settlement of estate of
           Ambrose BLAKCBURN, deceased, recorded 29 August 1829.
           Signed by Peter I. VOORHIES and Samuel CRAWFORD.
           John BLACKBURN was administrator.

page 45   BEANLAND - Guardian settlement of minor heirs of
           Edward W. BEANLAND, deceased...Joseph BROWN was guard-
           ian...recorded 29 August 1829...Polly G. BEANLAND was
           widow of deceased...she drew pension from Government,
           was given tract of 134 acres purchased from Robert
           MC CORD and transferred by Polly BEANLAND on 5 April
           1817...mentions widow and her children...signed 22
           March 1828 by Alexander JOHNSON, E. RICE.

page 46   BARNES - Inventory of personal property of Jonathan
           BARNES, deceased, taken 28 April 1828, recorded 29
           August 1829...articles included some delft plates and
           some books...signed Mary X BARNES, administratrix.
           Account of sale of Jonathan BARNES, recorded 29 Aug-
           ust 1829, buyers included Mary BARNES and Josiah
           BARHAM. Signed 21 July 1828, by J. B. PORTER.

page 47   BARNES - Settlement with administrators of John
           BARNES, deceased, recorded 29 August 1829. Jasper
           SUTTON was acting administrator of estate of John
           BARNES, deceased. Included in estate was 1822
           receipt of Thomas M. FOWLER; notes on George ROSS,
           Andrew MC LACHLIN, Peter GRAVES or GRIMES, Thomas H.
           JENKINS, Robert G. KELSEY, Alexander WILEY. In 1823
           paid note to Selson LOVE. Accounts and notes of D.
           N. SANSOM, Wm. LITTLEFIELD, Noah WHITE, Perry O.
           MALONE, E. W. DALE; paid Francis L. CEVY tuition for
           children; John WALKER paid for making coffin; paid
           D. MALONE for attending to sick negro; C. M. SMITH's
           attorney fees; judgement in favor of E. H. CHAFFIN;
           paid J. G. HALE for boarding child; note on A. MC
           MACKIN, R. G. KELSEY, Peter GRIMES; mentions J.
           WALKER's account on Jane W. BARNES. Signed 23 July
           1828 by James WALKER and Garrett VOORHIES.

page 48   BROWN - Account of Sale of James H. BROWN, deceased,
           recorded 29 August 1829. Buyers: Morgan GARRETT,
           John BROWN, Thomas GARRET, Thomas MC LANE, John BATES,
           Simpson BROWN, Isaac H. HILL, David BROWN, Md. (Mcd)
           BROWN, C. B. HOLLIGER, George HENSLEY, L. J. WILKINS,
           William MOORE, John WEBB, Doctr MYRICK, Demsey HUBBARD.
           Signed MC LINTICK BROWN, administrator, April term
           1828.

page 49   BIGHAM - Inventory of property of James BIGHAM, deceased, recorded 29 August 1829...80 acres of land, one negro, carpenter tools...signed Jannet BIGHAM and J. N. BIGHAM.

page 50   WADE - Francis WADE (non compos mentis) - Paid to Joseph WINGFIELD, guardian, 1 July 1827 - guardian report.

page 50   BOYD - Will of Andrew BOYD, recorded 29 August 1829 ..."being old and infirm in body"...son John R. BOYD my plantation that I now live on...my two daughters Winifred and Sally when they get married or choose to leave him...a number of books...my son-in-law Thomas P. MC KNIGHT of Lauderdale County, Alabama, and daughter Sally 168 acres in name of Andrew BOYD and John HACHET in Gibson County, Tennessee, on waters of Obion River...signed 22 January 1828, Andrw. BOYD; witnesses were W. S. HENDERSON, John MATTHEWS, Zebina CONKEY. Cidicil, signed 26 January 1828, mentions son-in-law Lewis GLASS, 150 acres in Madison County on north fork of Forked Deer River. Witnesses were W. S. HENDERSON and Zebina CONKEY.

page 52   BRIDGE COMMISSIONERS - Recorded 27 August 1829 - Settlement with Bridge Commissioners...note of D. CRAIGHEAD; bank stock as per New Orleans...amounts from Robt. MACK, Saml. WITHERSPOON...paid T. G. BRADFORD, signed 28 January 1822 T. COLEMAN, I. N. BILLS, Allen RAINEY, J.P.'s.

page 52   BURKETT - Administrator's settlement of Robert BURKETT, deceased, with Robert CAMPBELL, administrator, recorded 31 August 1829. Amount of sale,buyers: HARRIS and POLK, E. H. CHAFFIN, James RAMAGE; vouchers, Bennet ROSS, B. B. SMITH, Jas. F. BYERS, Hillary LANTREE, Wm. F. BROWN, James RUMAGE, Thomas CALDWELL, John DARNALL. Signed 1 July 1827 by Robt. HENDERSON, John MILLER, J.P.'s.

page 53   BURKET - Mary BURKET's year's allowance, recorded 31 August 1829. Commissioners appointed to lay off provision for Mary BURKETT, the widow of Robert BURKETT, deceased. Signed 25 January 1826, Wm. H. BLANTON, Daniel B. MILLER, Solomon BUNCH.

page 53   ARNOLD - Inventory of John H. ARNOLD, deceased, re-
- 55   corded 31 August 1829, taken 18 November 1826. Buyers: Elizabeth ARNOLD (household furnishings), William COVEY, R. F. DENHAM, Abner RODES, Edward R. PUCKETT, Middleton HILL, John HILL, John RUMAGE, William HILL, James GARRETT, Lindsey ARNOLD, William PERRY, John M. KING, Willie L. FARROR, Littleton VAUGHAN, William MEDCALFE, James HILL, David WOOD, Edmund HARRIS, John W. LEMASTER, James WRIGHT, Stephen SMITH. William PERRY, administrator. (page 56) Inventory of property of John H. ARNOLD, deceased, recorded 31 August 1829, taken 18 November 1826 by William PERRY, administrator.

page 56   BELL - Inventory of Wm. BELL, deceased, recorded 31
- 57   August 1829, taken 18 February 1828. Buyers: James

186

BELL, Hugh SHAW, Jonathan WHITESIDE, Claiborn PILLOW, James BELL, John BELL, Samuel MC CLANAHAN, James BOWMAN, Joseph TOM, Abraham WHITESIDE, Hugh A. MC MACKIN, John HOAK, Thomas OLIPHANT, James NEELY, George CHAMBERS, William WHITESIDE, Francis SPENCER, John PEYTON, Alexander ERWIN, Green LEE, Theodore ERWIN, James PATTON, Robert LUSK, John A. JOHNSTON. Signed, James BELL, John BELL, executors.

page 57   BROWN - Additional inventory of James H. BROWN, de-
               ceased, recorded 31 August 1829, returned to court
               April term 1828...an order drawn by C. M. BILLS on
               Maj. Joseph B. PORTER on ____ October 1827, signed
               McLintoch BROWN...BROWN was administrator of James
               H. BROWN, deceased, 28 April 1828.

page 58   BOYD - Settlement with administrator of James BOYD,
 - 59   deceased, recorded 31 August 1829...administrators
               were William S. HENDERSON and John R. BOYD...signed
               John MACK, John MATTHEWS, J.P.

page 59   BELL - Will of William BELL of Maury County, recorded
 - 60   31 August 1829...beloved son James...son John...son
               Thomas...negroes mentioned...daughter Flanrance...
               daughter Elizabeth...rest of children: Thomas,
               Stevenson, Starling, Polly, Sally, Darius...Sally
               and Polly being deceased their part to be divided
               "amongst there children to wit Harding CUNNINGHAM,
               Elizabeth LOCK and William LOCK"...my daughter
               Darius (Danuss?) part to be divided among her child-
               ren...son James and son John BELL to be executors...
               signed 19 May 1821 by William X BELL. Witnesses,
               James LOVE, Francis SPENCER.

page 60   BELL - Inventory of William BELL, deceased, recorded
               31 August 1829 and taken 29 January 1828.

page 61   BLAIR - Will of Andrew BLAIR, recorded 31 August
               1829...my niece Honor B. CATHEY, wife of James...
               daughter Harriett WALKER if she should die before
               she is married then Thomas WALKER, my wife's father
               shall have negroes which came to me by my wife...
               notes I hold on James CARSON of Sumner County..."my
               daughter Harriett to continue to live at Jonathan
               WEBSTER's until she is of age or during Mrs. WEBSTER's
               life and that Mrs. WEBSTER be paid out of my estate
               for keeping her." James CATHEY and Jonathan WEBSTER
               to be co-executors, signed 3 October 1828 by Andrew
               BLAIR. Witnesses, James MC CORD, John L. STAUGHE.

page 62   LEVEL and BROWN - Division of land, recorded 1 Sept-
     63   ember 1829...land of LEVEL and BROWN, plat drawn in
               book. Land of Benjamin LEVEL of Gerrard County,
               Kentucky, and Samuel BROWN of Gipson, Tennessee,
               tract of 1,000 acres that was divided between the
               heirs of William MC LEAN and said LEVEL and BROWN...
               James N. SMITH of Maury County made survey...land on
               south bank of Duck River, at a ford near the Spring
               at Royal's port on the north side. (Abstractor's
               note: land appears to be in a large bend in Duck
               River from plat.) Signed 2 August 1828, J. M. CAR-
               THEL, Andrew STEELE, Jos. MOREHEAD, Caleb HEADLEE,
               John STEELE, commissioners.

page 63   BRAWLEY - Additional inventory of Thomas BRAWLEY, deceased, recorded 1 September 1829...entry to correct a mistake made.

page 63   WILLIAMS - Amended inventory of Permenas WILLIAMS,
- 64   deceased, recorded 1 September 1829...taken by Edmund WILLIAMS, executor...slaves were left to Dolly WILLIAMS, wife of Parmenus WILLIAMS, during her life ...slaves named and who has them presently...some were bequeathed to Nancy WORTHAM, some to Polly COLEMAN...slaves have been turned over...some negroes to Alexander WILLIAMS...some negroes were set at liberty by will and were to be sent to Indiana or Ohio or any other free state they might choose to go to; the woman declines to go but says she will go by or before next spring as her children are all young ...money has been collected from William HUNT of North Carolina...have collected from Jesse LEFTWICH ...paid David CRAIGHEAD...paid for education of James M. WORTHAM...Dolly WILLIAMS, wife of Parmenus WILLIAMS...signed 27 April 1829 by Edmund WILLIAMS, executor, surviving executor of estate; signed 29 April 1829 by P. H. PORTER.

page 65   LATTA - Report of John LATTA as guardian of Moses and John LATTA, minor heirs of James LATTA, deceased, recorded 1 September 1829. (Abstractor's note: this entry was marked out.)

page 65   LATTA - LATTA's Executor's settlement recorded 1 September 1829. Alexander MOORE, executor of John LATTA, deceased, settlement. Signed by Robert HENDERSON and John MILLER, J.P.'s.

page 66   FRIERSON - Additional inventory of John Witherspoon FRIERSON, recorded 1 September 1829...a note on William BARNS estate...signed Jno. W. STEPHENSON and Robt. Luther FRIERSON.

page 66   MILLS - Will of Gideon MILLS, recorded 1 September 1829...Francis S. PERRY certifies this to be will of Gideon MILLS, deceased, of Maury County, given "to me by himself the evening before his decease on friday the 29th day of May 1829:...committed to writing by PERRY on 6 June 1829...wife Rebecca MILLS should have all his estate as long as she remained a widow...his children...she was to raise his children and school them...but if she were to marry she would no longer possess or enjoy any part of his estate.

page 66   BUCHANAN - Will of Margaret BUCHANAN, recorded 1
- 67   September 1829...son Daniel BUCHANAN...son James BUCHANAN...daughter Margaret MC ARTHUR...grandson James BUCHANAN, son of John, all my land in Maury County on Enon Creek, 62 acres...negro boy Elija... two granddaughters Martha BUCHANAN and Mary Ann BUCHANAN, daughters of John BUCHANAN...my trusty friend John BROWN for the troubles and expense he has been at and yet may be at...my negro girl Clary ...daughter-in-law Catherine BUCHANAN and John BROWN to be executors...signed 25 October 1828 by Margaret X BUCHANAN. Witnesses: Hugh BROWN, Solomon BUNCH, Joseph F. BROWN.

page 67
- 68

MOORE - Will of Nathaniel MOORE, recorded 1 September 1829...wife Polly..."it is now probable that there will be issue from my marriage," four negroes to belong to said child as soon as it is born, then after wife's death negroes "shall go to my other children"...sons James and Nathaniel MOORE...daughter Betsy DOAK...son-in-law Robert DOAK...to "my negro woman Betsy, her liberty, also one cow and calf"... my negro man Henry remain and be the property of my children; my four daughters Betsy DOAK, Sally MC KENTTRA (?), Jane CAGE, Frances DILLARD. Robert DOAK and Leven COVEY, executors...signed 7 May 1829 by Nathl. MOORE. Witnesses were Mason SANFORD and Young S. SANFORD.

page 69
- 70

WILKES - Will of Minor WILKES, recorded 1 September 1829...wife Mary...my children: John WILKES, Burrell WILKES, Thomas W. WILKES, David L. WILKES, Sally WILKES, Elizabeth G. WILKES, William WILKES, Josier WILKES...son Richard...Jane S. WILKES, daughter...son Josier when he becomes of age "to be sent to school till he is learnt to reade and write and lernt the arithmetic through the Rule of Three"... 2/3 of my plantation to be rented...my other sons John, Benjamin, Thomas and David W., daughter Sally SPRING...signed 10 December 1828, Minor WILKES; witnesses, Constantine DAVIS, Minor WILKES.

page 71

WILKES - Inventory of Daniel WILKES, deceased, and his widow Elizabeth WILKES, deceased, recorded 1 September 1829...negroes named and ages given... inventory taken 30 July 1827 by Richard A. L. WILKES and Phineas THOMAS, administrators.

page 71
- 72

CAMPBELL - Settlement with Guardian of CAMPBELL's minors...E. M. CAMPBELL, guardian of James T. CAMPBELL, minor...account of Samuel P. CAMPBELL, minor.

page 72

BUCHANAN - Inventory of Margaret BUCHANAN, recorded 2 September 1829...negroes, large family Bible... taken by John BROWN, 28 July 1829.

page 72

BROOKS - Inventory of Isaac BROOKS, deceased, recorded 2 September 1829...50 acres on Carter's Creek, Maury County.

page 73

MILLS - Inventory of Gideon MILLS, recorded 2 September 1829...taken 20 July 1829...note on David FOSTER estate...note on James WARR. Signed, Francis S. PERRY.

page 73

WILLIAMSON - Settlement with WILLIAMSON's administrators, recorded 2 September 1829. Voucher of R. M. WILLIAMSON found.

page 74

WILLIAMSON - Inventory of Estate of William H. WILLIAMSON, deceased...negroes and their worth... list of accounts: P. R. BOOKER, E. M. FORD, M. J. KITTRELL, D. LEECH, H. BRADSHAW, J. M. THOMSON, P. F. DOOLEY, A. DICKSON, E. STONE, J. RECORD, H. LANGTRY, W. R. MILLER, WALKER and HARRIS, COOPER and HILL, M. R. RHEA, S. WILLIAMS, G. DICKEY, T. B. CRAIGHEAD,

A. LOONEY, W. KEYES, R. MACK, R. L. COBBS, J. DAWSON, J. W. EGNEW, J. HODGE, D. MARTIN, W. S. BARNEY, J. DOOLEY, G. WHITE, E. B. DOOLEY, _____ GINGER, J. KIMBLE...judgements against John SMITH and William SMITH, doubtful...note of W. S. BURNEY, good; note on James BROWN, good; note on D. MARTIN, doubtful; commissioners, Joseph ERWIN, Thomas WALKER.

page 75 - 76
BROWN - Inventory of Elizabeth BROWN, deceased, recorded 2 September 1829; amount of sale, no buyers names given.

page 76
WHITE - Settlement with Esom B. DOOLEY, administrator of William WHITE, deceased. Vouchers allowed: BROWN and MC GIMPSEY, Doctor BROWN, Elijah KING...allowance made to Mrs. WHITE for clothing and schooling of said children...signed Abraham LOONEY and John L. SMITH, J.P.'s.

page 78
MANGRAM - Settlement with Henry MANGRAM'S administrators...recorded 2 September 1829, George G. FARRAR. Signed 29 July 1829 by John GORDON, John SMITH.

page 79
BALL - Settlement with administrator of Tandy BALL, deceased...Johnston LONG, administrator...credits of James BISHOP, Doct. HAMILTON, B. W. WILSON, Green DUKE, Terry DOTSON, Saml. STOCKARD, Doct. BROWN, NIGHT and BREWSTER, Micajah SPRINKLES, So. HOGE, George LONG. Signed 24 July 1829 by David CRAIG, Wm. STOCKARD, R. STOCKARD, J.P.'s.

page 79
PATTERSON - Inventory of Jarred PATTERSON, recorded 2 September 1829, taken 27 July 1827...note on Samuel STUART due 1819; note on W. A. S. C. MANSODES; due to Robert PATTERSON from estate; due to W. P. SMITH from estate; note on Joshua RIGHT, Joseph IRVIN, John GILCHRIST; account of Joel REASE.

page 81
SMITH - Inventory of Samuel SMITH, deceased, recorded 2 September 1829...19 negroes...account of William MC LEAN...receipt of Cader JOHNSTON, Wm. HARDERSON, William WILLIAMS, William CARKER, Francis C. SMITH; note on William SLAUGHTER, Lodevick HARRISON, account of John WILSON, note of Henry SMITH, Spencer GRIFFIN. Signed 2 July 1829 by James M. BAKER, John WILKINS, administrators.

page 82
WADE - Frances WADE's guardian's account, recorded 3 September 1829, Frances WADE (non compos mentis) ...L. J. WINGFIELD, guardian...hire of negroes.

page 82
HILL - Inventory of James W. HILL, deceased, recorded 3 September 1829...taken 23 July 1829 by George W. WEAVER, administrator.

page 84
EVANS - Estate of Daniel EVANS, inventory, by commissioners, recorded 3 September 1829, taken 27 December 1828. (page 84) Estate has been divided and given to heirs to wit: to John SMITH, Henry SMITH, Henry L. CRUTCHER and wife, Francis SLAUGHTER and wife, James R. EVANS, David R. EVANS, Jesse EVANS, Pamela EVANS, Martha EVANS, Lucinda EVANS, Charity

EVANS, Mrs. E. EVANS. Signed: James N. SMITH, P. VOORHIES, John C. WORMLEY, John BROWN, John GORDON.

page 85 CATHEY - Settlement with John CATHEY's, deceased, executors...recorded 3 September 1829...Griffith and Alexander CATHEY, executors, signed 16 May 1829 by A. CATHEY and Richard ANDERSON, J.P.'s.

page 85 PERRYMAN - Perryman's guardian report, recorded 3 September 1829...guardian of Jane PERRYMAN and Madison PERRYMAN...Johnson RICHARDS, Guardian.

page 86 HARRIS - Inventory of Henry HARRIS, deceased, recorded 3 September 1829...sold 18 November 1827...Buyers: J. PENN, C. G. NIMMO, B. R. HARRIS, William WILLIAMS, Hardin WILLIAMS, James STOCKARD, James M. BRISCOE, B. W. WILSON, A. C. HARRIS. Benjamin R. HARRIS and Newt HARRIS, administrators.

page 86 MOREHEAD - Jane MOREHEAD's year's allowance, recorded 3 September 1829...dated 15 July 1829 by Matthew MOORE, Caleb HEADLEY.

page 86 - 87 MOREHEAD - Account of Sale of Joseph MOREHEAD, deceased, recorded 3 September 1829. Note of Matthew MOORE, Samuel MC CURDY's note, Mark JACKSON, Joseph M. CARTHEL, George HAKET, Nathaniel SMITH, Wm. D. SMITH, John RHYHE, Wm. HUGHES, Joseph ELKINS, Francis GILL, L. HARRISON, George ROANE, Charles HIGGINS, John K. STEWART, Williamson SMITH, Jonathan SMITH, Chas. S. SMITH, Caleb HEADLEE, Armistead MOREHEAD, James N. SMITH, Philip I. MOREHEAD, James M. MOREHEAD, John W. MOREHEAD. Signed, James N. SMITH, administrator.

page 87 WHITESIDES - William WHITESIDES, deceased - no date - Michael HIGGINS guardian's report in account with minor heirs of William WHITESIDES, deceased...boarding and schooling for two children, signed, Michael HIGGINS.

page 88 WHITSON - Will of Anne WHITSON - recorded 3 September 1829...son John WHITSON, son Thomas WHITSON, son James, son George, deceased, son William, daughter, Mary HARDIN, son Samuel, plantation where I now live ...land bordering Edmund L. WILLIAMS...negroes named ...daughter Sally WITHERSPOON..daughter Rebecca WILLIAMS to get land where she now lives...son James and son Samuel and Edmund L. WILLIAMS, executors... signed 29 April 1829. Witnesses, Elijah HANKS, Matthew HARBISON, J. WILLIAMS, Asa DODSON.

page 90 JENNINGS - Year's allowance for Judith JENNINGS, recorded 3 September 1829. Widow of Samuel JENNINGS. Signed 16 May 1829 by Johnston CRAIG, W. WILLIAMS.

page 90 SCOTT - Inventory of Samuel SCOTT, deceased, recorded 3 September 1829...negroes named...two Bibles, number of books...signed William S. HENDERSON, Andrew SCOTT, executors.

page 91 SCOTT - List of Sale of Samuel SCOTT, deceased, 21 May 1829. Buyers: Andrew SCOTT, John B. THOMAS,

William K. HILL, Robert HASKIN, Andrew NEELY, Grant
A. JOHNSTON, Joseph MATTHEWS, Albert L. CRAWFORD,
Robert T. MATTHEWS, James GALLOWAY, Richard FOSTER,
Wm. MACK, John R. BOYD.

page 92   SCOTT - List of sall of Samuel SCOTT, deceased,
continued: buyers: William K. HILL got SCOTT's
Bible, William P. HUDSON, Franklin R. HOUSTON,
Vincent RIDLEY, Lemuel D. MACK, Larkin PILKENTON,
John S. COOPER, John RENFRO, Abraham T. SHEPPARD,
John GALBREATH, Alexr. C. CRAWFORD, Andrew WALKER,
Andrew ZOLLOCOFFER, Thomas R. LUSK, notes of Robert
F. MATTHEWS, Zabina CONKEY, William WALKER, James
GALLOWAY, Alexander L. HAYNES. Signed, William S.
HENDERSON, Andrew SCOTT.

page 93   DAVIS - Jane DAVIS, Guardian Settlement, recorded
4 September 1829. James STOCKARD and Joseph ERWIN,
appointed commissioners at July 1828 term to settle
with Samuel DAVIS, guardian of Jane DAVIS (lunatic)
...vouchers on Alexander BROWN, Sampson DAVIS,
William KNOTT, Elijah DAVIS, Butler NOLES, Samuel
DAVIS, Isaac DAVIS.

page 94   COLEMAN - Inventory of estate of Thomas COLEMAN,
deceased, recorded 4 September 1829. W. W. COLEMAN,
executor. Notes on David KING, Thomas COOKE, Archi-
bald MC CONNELL, Nathaniel NOBLES, Noah WALKER, John
GRIFFITH, John PHELPS, James O'NEAL, Isaiah DAVIS,
David H. TRUE, John EDWARDS, John S. DANIEL, John
and William FERFERSON, Wiley S. WHEATE, Robert BAKER,
Samuel CRAWFORD, James CARTER, George MC COBSTER,
Charles GREY, John D. ALDERSON, J. G. EASLEY, William
MC CAROL, William W. COLEMAN, Thomas JOHNSON, John
EDWARDS, Robert CROSBY. Signed 18 June 1829 by Edw.
B. LITTLEFIELD, William EDMONSON, Edmund L. WILLIAMS,
commissioners to settle with executors.

page 96   BROWN - Account of Sale of James N. BROWN, recorded
4 September 1829. Buyers: Willis ERWIN, Wardemer
SHELBY, Widdow, John P. ERWIN, Thos. KINDRICK, Jas.
BECK, John KENDRICK, Arthur T. ISOM, John T. SMITH,
William BROWN, Griffith CATHEY, Josiah FARIS, William
PREWIT, El. BOSS (?), Eliza ERWIN (?), William PRUIT,
Richard ANDERSON, James BAXTER, James M. BROWN.
Signed James N. BROWN, administrator.

page 97   SAM - Report of Sale of SAM, recorded 4 September
1829...negro named in decree has been sold...Agree
ROGERS was highest bidder...30 August 1828, signed
by Hugh BROWN, William ALLEN, Laird B. BOYD, Robert
CAMPBELL.

page 97   GRIMES - GRIMES heirs guardian report, recorded 4
September 1829. John HATCHETT was appointed guardian
of minor heirs of James GRIMES, deceased, to wit:
Louisa, Nancy, Jack, James, William, and David GRIMES
in November 1827 (1824?)...he received of Frederick
B. SAWYER of Camden County, North Carolina, the "gds"
of the mother of said minors...accounts dating from
1821 mentioned.

page 98   EDDLEMAN - Eddleman's heirs guardian report, recorded
4 September 1829. Thomas M. HARPER in account with
minor heirs of John EDDLEMAN, deceased, as guardian
...note on Ozni and A. B. ALEXANDER.

page 98   SMITH - Account of sale of Samuel SMITH, recorded 24
- 103   September 1829, sold 22 May 1829...negroes mentioned
in estate...buyers: Martha SMITH, John SMITH, Samuel
SMITH, James SMITH, William SMITH, Francis SMITH,
John WILLIAMS, William WILLIAMS, James M. BAKER,
Jesse RAINEY, Silas WOLLARD, George W. WEAVER, Isaah
WEATHERLY, Humphrey HARDEN, M. J. MC KEE, Brown LONG,
William NEAL, Z. CAUSEY, Henry L. CRUTCHER, Amos
DUNCAN, John GARDNER, Harrison MC KEE, Scott M.J.
MC KEE, George MOORE, Smith WILLIS, L.B. HARRIS,
James MOORE, James A. ESTES, Joseph GILL, C. JONES,
P. B. HAMBLIN, Samuel KITTRELL, Joseph ROBERTSON,
John C. WORMLEY, C. T. BALDWIN, William HARDESON, K.
W. TRIGG, A. FUZZELL, William WILLIAMS, James M.
BAKER, H. MC KEE, William JOHNSON, Cohee F. SMITH,
P. RAGSDALE, John KITTRALL, John GORDON, W. BUNCOMB,
Jos. SMITH, T. R. COLEMAN, Geo. INGRAM, Samuel ALD-
RIDGE, John REILY, Marcus HOLLAND, Jesse RENFRO,
Thomas BLACKNALL, William MILTON, Arnold ARKER,
Ephraim BROWN, Armstead AIKEN; notes on James SMITH,
William SLAUGHTER, L. HARRISON, William PARKER,
Samuel KITTRELL, William WILLIAMS, John C. WILSON,
Isaah WEATHERLY, William HARDISON. Receipt on Cader
JOHNSON, doubtful to be collected...note on Spencer
GRIFFITH said to be dead and insolvent, due about
15 years...order on R. J. COOK.

page 105   FITZGERALD - Will of Christopher FITZGERALD, recorded
5 September 1829...wife Elizabeth, daughters Nancy
and Polly...negroes named...son Nathaniel, son Thomas
...land on north side of Duck River purchased of John
SPENCER...four sons, James, John, Nathaniel, and
Thomas. Signed, 13 January 1826, Christopher X.
FITZGERALD; witnesses, John NEELY, Samuel LATTA.
Codicil appointed Willis JONES, executor and witnessed by Nancy X DOTSON and Polly X FITZGERALD.

page 106   FRIERSON - John W. FRIERSON, Guardian settlement -
recorded 6 September 1829; April 1825 commissioners
appointed to settle with John FRIERSON, guardian of
John W. FRIERSON, appointed 1820...notes of Samuel E.
FRIERSON, John FRIERSON, and P. NELSON. Signed 19
April 1825 by Hugh DOUGLAS, David CRAIG, Swan HARDIN,
J.P.'s.

page 106   FARIS - Allotment of Dower for Jane FARIS, widow of
William FARIS - recorded 6 September 1829...land
bounded by Samuel FARIS, heirs to have privilege of
the spring...made 12 July 1826 by Will CATHEY, Samuel
W. AKIN, James CATHEY, James CURRY, Alexander CATHEY.

page 106   FERRELL - Amount of sale of Estate of Levi FERRELL,
deceased, held in 1821. Recorded 6 September 1829
by John FERRELL, administrator.

page 106   FRIERSON - Division of negroes of Samuel E. FRIERSON,
deceased, recorded 6 September 1829...Edward M. FORD,
Hugh DOUGLAS, and Samuel H. WILLIAMS to divide the

negroes...1/5 to Dianna E. FRIERSON...William FRIER-
SON, son and heir of deceased...Sarah FRIERSON,
daughter and heir of deceased...Isabella, daughter
and heir of deceased...signed E. M. FORD, Hugh DOUG-
LAS, Samuel H. WILLIAMS.

page 107   FOSTER - Inventory of David FOSTER, deceased, recorded 6 September 1829...taken 19 October 1829 by executor William E. MC KEE...judgement against William
MERRYMAN and Thomas L. ASH...note of William ELLISON,
Joseph HALL, George HOPSON, Charles WILLIAMS...
account of Thomas FOSTER...note on Samuel FLEMING
dated 1814 and desperate...note on Hugh GRAY dated
1813...memorandum of notes left in North Carolina...
negroes named and ages given...signed William E. MC
KEE.

page 109   GALLOWAY - Report of guardian of Samuel GALLOWAY's,
deceased, heirs...recorded 6 September 1829. Guardian was William M. GALLOWAY, signed 27 October 1828.

page 109   HOOD - Inventory of John HOOD, deceased, recorded
6 September 1829...155 acres of land, signed Agnes
HOOD.

page 110   HENDERSON - Allowance for widow of Ezkl. HENDERSON,
made 19 February 1828. (His name later found as
Ezekiel HENDERSON)...made by John MACK, Isaac T.
THOMAS, E. RICE.

page 110   GRIMES - Inventory of Goods and Chattels of Luke
GRIMES, deceased, recorded 6 September 1829...taken
15 September 1828...mentions notes in North Carolina
...signed by William GRIMES and Nancy GRIMES who
made inventory.

page 111   GOWEN - William STRATTON, guardian of heirs of Andrew
GOWEN makes report...recorded 6 September 1829...
mentions Isaac's part and Levi's part...schooling.
Signed April 1828 by William STRATTON.

page 111   FRIERSON - Guardian report of Jane C. FRIERSON, recorded 6 September 1829...Duncan BROWN appointed
guardian October 1827...mentions 535 acres...signed
1 November 1828.

page 111   FRY - Inventory of John F. FRY, deceased, recorded
- 112   6 September 1829...returned January 1827 by James H.
CLARK, administrator...mentions violin, flute, clari-
net, music books. (Abstractor's note: FRY was a
music teacher in Mt. Pleasant and was murdered by
George BRISCOE.)

page 112   HOWARD - Inventory of Estate of John HOWARD. (Abstractor's note: there was an ink blot on this entry and
could not be read.)

page 112   HENDERSON - List of Sale of William HENDERSON, de-
- 113   ceased...recorded 6 September 1829, sold 14 November
1822. Buyers: James BOYD, John BALDRIDGE, Ezekiel
HENDERSON, Thomas RAMEY, Nathan WILLIS, William S.
HENDERSON, George PATTON, James R. PLUMMER, Eliza
PATTON, Elias PEYTON, John MINOCK, John FORGEY, John

DALE, Lemuel D. MACK, John GILBREATH, John JONES,
Green MURPHEY, Larkin PILKENTON, George W. JOHNSON,
Simpson PERRY, John D. CURRY, E. W. DALE, Thomas
RAMSAY, Thomas W. STONE, John WEBB, John BILLS, James
BOMAN, Benj. WILKES, William MC KEE, Michael BALD-
RIDGE, James L. BALDRIDGE, John HENDERSON, Edward R.
HOUSTON.

page 114
- 115

HOWARD - List of Sale of John HOWARD, deceased, recorded 6 September 1829; sale held 3 January 1828 by
William WHITTEN, administrator...negro man hired out.

page 115
- 117

FRIERSON - Will of David FRIERSON, recorded 7 Sept-
ember 1829 - son James Armstrong FRIERSON...negroes
named...grandson David, son of James A....daughter
Elizabeth now wife of Samuel H. ARMSTRONG...grand-
daughter Elizabeth, daughter of my daughter Martha
Elizabeth...wife Sarah...my five children: Thomas
Gadsden, Benjamin Rush, Margaret Ann, Robert Wilson,
Sarah Louise, division to be equal...Samuel Henry
ARMSTRONG and James Armstrong FRIERSON to be execu-
tors...signed 25 February 1828. Witnesses: Jas.
ARMSTRONG, James BLAKLEY, John D. FLEMING.

page 117

JENNINGS - Inventory of Samuel JENNINGS, deceased,
recorded 7 September 1829; buyers: Doctor JENNINGS,
David GLASS, John POLLOCK, James W. JENNINGS, Ca___
JENNINGS, Sena JENNINGS, James JENNINGS, William
WILLIAMS, John DIXON, John READ, Jake JENNINGS, Moses
HOGE, John COOPER, Jade JENNINGS, Lena JENNINGS,
Archie JENNINGS, Juda JENNINGS, Isaac JENNINGS, John
GRIMES, Robert AKIN, William JOHNSTON, Widdow JENNINGS
...Inventory made 20 July 1829 by J. W. JENNINGS,
executor.

page 118

HUNTER - SANFORD - William K. HUNTER to James T.
SANFORD, recorded 7 September 1829...received of
James T. SANFORD, paid for occupant entry of John
WILLIAMSON on east fork of bigbigby...land was
deeded by WILLIAMS to SANFORD and by SANFORD to
HUNTER, 7 July 1829.

page 118

FOSTER - Recorded _?_ March 1815 the bill of personal
estate of Robert FOSTER, deceased, sold February
session 1815. Buyers: Jno. W. STEPHENSON, Mrs.
EVANS, Elias J. ARMSTRONG, David LEECH, Thomas
FLEMING, Thomas J. FRIERSON, Samuel FRIERSON, James
JOSSEY, Samuel WITHERSPOON, James GOSLEY, John P.
WHITE, James M. FRIERSON, Edward B. LITTLEFIELD,
Samuel MAYES, John BULLOCK, Thomas C. FARRIS, Moses
FRIERSON.

page 119

FRIERSON - Account of Sale of David FRIERSON, de-
ceased, recorded 7 September 1829...sold 8 July 1828
by executors; buyers: Widow, Samuel H. ARMSTRONG,
William J. FRIERSON, John Witherspoon FRIERSON,
James A. FRIERSON, J. W. STEPHENSON, D. D., William
G. ARMSTRONG, D. BROWN, D. D., E. J. ARMSTRONG, Jno.
Wm. FRIERSON, Thomas F. FLEMING, Henry TURNEY, Mum-
ford SMITH, Robert WILSON, Gardiner FRIERSON, John
WOODCUFF, William BLAKELEY, G. W. BUFORD, John
FERRILL, Saml. BLAKELY, T. H. ARMSTRONG, Jas. J.
FLEMING.

195

page 122   GOSSETT - John GOSSETT Guardian Report - recorded
8 September 1829. Accounts between Vandyke GOSSETT
and his wards Harvey M. GOSSETT and Clementine M.
GOSSETT, minor heirs of John GOSSETT, deceased,
signed 21 July 1828. Accounts "from their deceased
father's estate"..."William GOSSETT the administrator"
..."To there mother Mary GOSSETT."

page 126   FARRIS - Guardian report of William FARRIS, deceased
...recorded 9 September 1829...minor heirs of William
FARRIS, deceased...have received of Jacob FARRIS...
widdow Jane FARRIS, wife of said deceased...negroes
named and ages given. (Note: this entry quite
faded.)

page 127   HAWKINS - Additional inventory of John HAWKINS, deceased...recorded 9 September 1829...Edward BLAKCBURN
administrator.

page 127   GARRISON - Year's allowance for Delilah GARRISON,
recorded 9 September 1829...widow of John GARRISON.

page 128   HENDERSON - Additional inventory of Ezekiel HENDERSON
recorded 9 September 1829...a tract of land to the
sons and daughters of William HENDERSON, deceased,
by John TATE...signed Samuel HENDERSON and Richard
HENDERSON, administrators.

page 128   FULTON - Inventory of Archibald FULTON, deceased -
recorded 9 September 1829 - taken by William VOORHIES,
administrator...a negro Mary loaned by father of said
FULTON, deceased, during his life to Daniel BRIDGES
of Smith County, Tennessee...a negro hired to David
CRAIGHEAD of Nashville by father of said FULTON, deceased...negro hired to George CAMPBELL of Maury
County...notes on David WILEY, Junior, Jesse J.
BRIDGES.

page 130   FULTON - List of property belonging to estate of
Archibald FULTON...taken 13 May 1826. Sold to Benj.
B. SMITH, Elijah KIMBRO, Saml. GULLET, George CAMP-
BELL, Thomas CALDWELL, R. GOURD, Taxwell S. ALDERSON,
C. ERWIN, M. KITTRELL, Edmd. DILLAHUNTY, Patk.MAGUIRE,
William YOWELL, John KARNS, Daniel MC KEY, M. HELM,
Saml. RANKIN, Daniel MORRIS, Josiah ALDERSON, Polly
FULTON.

page 131   HENDERSON - Inventory of Ezekiel HENDERSON, recorded
9 September 1829...signed 21 January 1828 by Richard
and Samuel HENDERSON, administrators.

page 132   FRIERSON - Guardian report of Samuel FRIERSON's heirs
recorded 9 September 1829 - Sarah E. FRIERSON, infant
heir of Samuel E. FRIERSON, deceased...settlement
with Jesse ROSS for rest of land on 1 December 1827
...accounts with M. D. COOPER, G. W. BUFORD, Thos. R.
ENGLISH, S. D. FRIERSON, Lawren MARTIN...negroes
named...mentions "her father's estate".

page 132   HOWARD - Widow's allowance for John HOWARD's widow -
recorded 9 September 1829 - Elenor HOWARD, widow...
signed 3 December 1827 by Johnston CRAIG, David
DOBBINS, Wm. HUNTER.

page 133   HEROLD - Widow's allowance for Nancy HEROLD, Widow of Peter HEROLD - recorded 9 September 1829 - Nancy, widow of Peter HEROLD, and her "fore" children at October 1826 term. Signed Samuel GRIFFITH, Lazarus ANDERS.

page 133   FORKNER - Guardian return for heir of Lewis FORKNER recorded 9 September 1829 - guardian appointed 1820 for heirs: Manssey FORKNER, Carolina FORKNER, Milford F. FORKNER, William P. FORKNER, Rebecca FORKNER ...negroes named...Jonathan BAILEY was administrator of estate...signed David CRAIG, guardian.

page 134   CALLAHAN - Dower of CALLAHAN's widow - recorded 9 September 1829 - allowance made 1826 for Elizabeth CALLAHAN, now Elizabeth HAWTHORNE...signed 13 May 1826 by James L. BALDRIDGE, H. BILLS, __?__ ANTHONY.

page 134   HENDERSON - Account of Sale of Ezekiel HENDERSON - recorded 9 September 1829; buyers: widow, Richard HENDERSON, W. S. HENDERSON, Nancy HENDERSON, Michael BALDRIDGE, Doct. HUNT, D. G. JOHNSON, A. H. BUCKNER, William HENDERSON, James T. CROFFORD, John R. BOYD, James J. THOMAS, A. S. HENDERSON, James GALLOWAY, William KINDLE, Robert F. MATTHEWS, J. P. MAXWELL, G. B. SANDERS, Joseph WADKINS, Hugh PATTON, Lemuel PHILLIPS, Saml. H. SMITH, Wm. COVEY, BUCKNER and MITCHELL, E. R. HOUSTON, John B. HANNA, Dr. CONKEY, James WEAVER, Aquilla W. MACK, I. B. SANDERS, Abner MATTHEWS, Wm. LENARD, John H. HANNA, Henry SMITH, Simpson PERRY, John D. RAMSEY, James R. PLUMMER, Taswell S. ALDERSON...signed 14 February 1828 by Richard and Samuel HENDERSON, administrators.

page 137   HERRING - Guardian account for HERRING's heir - recorded 10 September 1829 - John MILLER, guardian for Robert HERRING, minor heir of Solomon HERRING - paid tuition to Reuben SMITH...hire of negroes.

page 138   FRIERSON - Settlement with administrators of Saml. E. FRIERSON - recorded 10 September 1829 - John and Samuel D. FRIERSON, administrators.

page 138   HOBSON - In 1826 Hugh BROWN, Reuben SMITH and John KENNEDY were appointed commissioners to divide and allot the estate of Jeremiah HOBSON, deceased, in hands of James T. SANFORD, administrator...have allotted to Robert M. SMITH...(Note: this one was blurred and hard to read)...James BLACK, guardian of Jeremiah HOBSON, his infant ward.

page 139   FRIERSON - Division of estate of George FRIERSON, deceased - recorded 10 September 1829 - commissioners were Edward B. LITTLEFIELD, Nathaniel WILLIS, James ARMSTRONG, Hugh DOUGLAS, and Joel REESE to let off to widow of George FRIERSON her dower...mentions mansion house...plat of land included.

page 141   FRIERSON - Division of land of Moses G. FRIERSON, recorded 10 September 1829. At July term 1824 Samuel H. WILLIAMS, Thomas WALKER, _____ M. WILLIAMS were made commissioners. Division was as follows, lot 1 to Isaac J. FRIERSON; lot 2 to James A. FRIERSON;

lot 3 to John D. FRIERSON; lot 4 to Elias FRIERSON; lot 5 to Mary J. FRIERSON; lot 6 to _____ E. FRIERSON. Signed 26 July 1826 by Joel REESE.

page 142   HERRING - Additional inventory of Solomon HERRING, deceased, recorded 10 September 1829: whiskey accounts: Lemuel WALLAM, John SWADLOR, Joseph ROADS, Robert SMITH, Robert YANCEY, John W. MILLER, Elijah LANFORD (LANGFORD), Shadrick CHANDLER, David UNDERWOOD, William YANCEY.

page 142   HARRIS - Inventory of Henry HARRIS, deceased, recorded 10 September 1829 - open accounts: John CRENSHAW, Rev. Wiley LEDBETTER, R. C. MARTIN, Philip PENN, William HARPER, J. H. CLARK, William HUMPHREY, N. K. RODGERS, Mansil CRISP, Johnathan MORGAN, Patrick HATTON, Wyatt HARRIS, John WEATHERLY, Mary ROBERTSON, Esquire WELSH, Doctor ECHOLS, Joel ECHOLS, Silas ALEXANDER, John GARRIGUS, Elijah WEAVER, _aiborne HARRIS, John MC KISSICK, Julius WOODWARD, Mrs. Polly BERRY, William EDWARDS, Susan ABERNATHY, A. G. YOUNGBLOOD, Mrs. ALEXANDER, William CRISP, Mrs. Esl___ CRISP, Tilman A. CRISP, William WORTHAM, Craig CROFFORD, Jesse WILLIAMS, William SIMS, Isaac CURRY, Peter H. ROBERTS, William MASON, Mrs. MC MANNIS, Elisha SMITH, W. P. SMITH, Thos. S. SPENCER, Joseph K. SMITH, Robt. MATTHEWS, A. B. ALEXANDER, Nathan COFFEE, Henry WILLIAMS, M. FARRIS, Moses SMITH, John JONES, I. G. HALL, B. M. KILPATRICK, Allen TAGLEY, C. G. NIMM, Zachariah WORTHAM, Edward GRIMES, Merret MANEY, Joshua RHODES, Dempsey TAYLOR, Henry TUCKNESS, James J. TUCKNESS, Carlisle W. KNIGHT, Benjamin DAVIS, _____ HARREL, Lot HACKNEY, Reddin TAYLOR, Thomas SIMS, Joseph _____, Edward WILLIAMS, Jacob COFFEE. Notes: George _____, William HUMPHREY, William K. HUNTER, Mathias GARRIGAS, Robert WORTHAM, Philip PENN, Elijah HARLAN, Thomas WILLIAMS, John AUSTIN, Joel WALKER, Sanders HASTIN, Stephen CARROLL... negroes named; signed Benj. R. HARRIS and West HARRIS.

page 144   GRIFFITH - Settlement with administrator of John GRIFFITH, deceased - recorded 10 September 1829 - Samuel GRIFFITH, administrator. Signed 25 October 1828 by David CRAIG and Wm. STOCKARD, J.P.'s.

page 144   HOBSON - Settlement with administrator of Jeremiah HOBSON - recorded 10 September 1829 - from 1822 settlements dating from 1822...vouchers for D. CHAPPELL, Robert RANKIN, William _____, Pleasant TODD, _____ MC KISSACK, J. ALDERSON, James PORTERS (PETERS?), Daniel BROWN, Reddick DISHONGH, James O'REILLY, SANDSOM and HUGHES, Joel FAGGESON, John KENNEDY, John N. LAVENDER, Edward H. CHAFFIN; signed John MILLER, and Allen RAINEY, J.P.'s.

page 145   HOLGON - Inventory of Robert HOLGON, deceased - recorded 10 September 1829 - made 18 March 1825 by Samuel KENNEDY, administrator.

page 146   HERRING - Account of sale of Solomon HERRING, deceased - recorded 10 September 1829 - made 10 February 1825 - buyers: Nancy HERRING, Benjamin RODENY, Thornton CHANDLER, William H. CALDWELL, Young CHUMBLEY,

Solomon BUNCH, John MILLER, Ezekiel AKIN, William
WILLIAMS, Elisha LANGFORD (LANKFORD), James HENRY,
Thomas MALCOMB, John BAUGUS, Meredith HELM, Robert
HENDERSON, Samuel POLK, Aron G. AKIN, Hugh B. PORTER,
Thomas GRANT, Alexander MOORE, Jonathan MILLS, James
MOORE, Joseph H. MILLER, Joseph GILL, Sion BOON,
Joseph POWERS, George J. WOODWARD, David UNDERWOOD,
Thomas YOUNG, James HUEY, John TURNER, Greenberry
GRANT, Earthalburk KERBY, Michael R. MOORE, John
TOLLIVER, Richard SCOTT, Robert HERRING, Aron THOMP-
SON, Harmon MILLER, Bryant BAUGUS, Ezekiel AKIN,
Robert A. RANKIN, John KENNADY. John MILLER, executor.

page 149   HALES - Settlement with Richard HALES, deceased,
            administrators...recorded 11 September 1829...paid
            Allen BROWN, DALE, TALLIFARO, B. HARMER, Thomas
            WHITBY, and widow...signed 24 July 1828 by John C.
            WORMLEY, John SMITH.

page 149   FOX - Settlement of estate of Lance FOX - recorded
            11 September 1829 - administrators were Caleb HEADLEY
            and MATHEW MOORE...note on John T. ELLIOTT...paid
            Jas. C. O'RILEY and William FOX...signed 27 October
            1828 by Jno. VINCENT, James BLACK, J.P.'s.

page 150   FRIERSON - Inventory of David FRIERSON, deceased -
            recorded 10 September 1829 - taken 2 May 1828...
            negroes listed by name...SCOTT's Family Bible...
            family Bible...signed Saml. H. ARMSTRONG, Jas. A.
            FRIERSON, administrators.

page 151   HERRING - Division of negroes of Solomon HERRING,
            deceased - recorded 11 September 1829 - commissioners
            appointed 16 December 1826 - negroes named...Robert
            HERRIN, minor heir...signed Reddick DISHONGH, Briant
            BAUGUS, John KILCREASE.

page 152   HODGE - Provision for Sally HODGE for year - recorded
            11 September 1829 - commissioners appointed 18 August
            1826, signed, James C. RECORD, Peter WILLIAMS, James
            KENNEDY.

page 152   HODGE - List of property of John HODGE, deceased -
            recorded 11 September 1829 - buyers were T. H.
            WILLIAMS, J. KENNEDY, L. HODGE...large Bible sold to
            L. (or S.) HODGE...J. WHITE, William AKIN, H. R.
            OSBURN...sold ___ September 1828, signed by R. R.
            BILES (BOLES), Sally HODGE, T. H. WILLIAMS.

page 153   HARDIN - Guardian return for heirs of Isaac B.
            HARDIN - recorded 11 September 1829 - 1 January 1827
            Peter R. BOOKER and A. D. COOPER, guardians of minor
            heirs of I. B. HARDIN, deceased, hired out negroes
            belonging to deceased...signed P. R. BOOKER, A. D.
            COOPER, 22 January 1827.

page 154   HOOD - Division of land of John HOOD, deceased -
            recorded 12 April 1829. To Eleanor ROSS, 35 acres,
            to Eliza HOOD, 45 acres, to Agnes RAMSEY, 27 acres,
            to Jane SIMMONS, 12 acres, to Mahala HOOD, 22 acres,
            and to John HOOD, 16 acres. Commissioners appointed
            April 1827...widow gave up her right of dower. Divi-
            sion went to Edward ROSS in right of his wife Eleanor,

formerly Eleanor HOOD; lot 3 went to John RAMSEY in right of his wife Agnes RAMSEY...to John SIMMONS in right of his wife Jane...land mentions CAMPBELL's line...Solomon BOND and Richard ALLEN were chain carriers during survey; James N. SMITH, surveyor; others on commission were James BLACK, John MILLER, William ALLEN, Robert HENDERSON.

page 156   PATTON - Additional Inventory of George PATTON, deceased - recorded 12 September 1829 - sold to Samuel CARUTHERS a silver watch; buyers: Zacheus STILES, Robert CARUTHERS...receipts of William B. ANDERSON, Elijah REAVES...receipt of John PETTILLO, said PETILLO had received too much of the estate of William ADKIN from the said PATTON, deceased, as administrator of said ADKIN's estate, PETTILLO being the heir of that estate...signed Robert CARUTHERS, administrator, 2 August 1828.

page 156   RODENY - Will of Benjamin RODENY - recorded 12 September 1829 - wife Winnefred...my children...cows and horses listed by name...estate to be divided among following children: Calvin B. RODENY, son; Sarah S. RODENY; Washington B. RODENY; daughter Nancy RODENY; daughter Elizabeth RODENY; James RODENY; Elizabeth RODENY; Elizabeth RODENY (Note: listed twice this was), son James RODENY; daughter Lucy RODENY; Benjamin RODENY...my daughter Norry OLIVER...signed 21 March 1829; witnesses were Reuben SMITH, James C. O'REILLY, T. H. MC KICHES.

page 158   POLK - Will of Samuel POLK - recorded 11 September 1829 - wife Jane, lot situated in town of Columbia ...land on Carter's Creek on Mount View tract... negroes named...son James K. POLK, in addition to what I have already given him, part of my woods lot enclosed around his stable...son Franklin E. land in Hardeman County granted to E. S. L. POLK, my woods lot lying west of James WALKER and John W. P. MC GIMSEY...son Marshall T. the HARDIN tract in Maury ...building north of my brick building on public square in Columbia...daughter Naomi HARRIS..land in Mc Nairy and Fayette counties, Tennessee...son John S. POLK...son William...son Samuel...daughter Maria J. WALKER...daughter Eliza CALDWELL...daughter Ophelia C. POLK...daughter Jane M. WALKER...daughter Lydia E. CALDWELL...daughters Naomi C. HARRIS and Ophelia C. POLK...son in law James WALKER...son James K. POLK, executor...signed 13 December 1826... witnesses: Silas M. CALDWELL, F. E. POLK, A. C. HAYS, Levi KETCHUM, John B. HAYS.

page 164   PERRYMAN - Settlement with administrator of Benoni PERRYMAN - recorded 14 September 1829 - signed 20 September 1828 William EDMONDS, William FLY, J.P.'s.

page 165   POWELL - Inventory of Sarah POWELL, deceased - recorded 14 September 1829; taken 21 October 1828, by James C. POWELL, administrator.

page 165   RIGGS - Inventory of Saml. RIGGS, deceased - recorded 12 September 1829. Buyers: Bennett BLACKBURN,

William WITT, John JAMISON, Robert CAMPBELL, Thomas
ROUNTREE, Jane RIGGS, Stephen ARNOLD, Moses BYSHOP,
Thomas MC CRACKIN, Robert A. RANKIN, Armstead AKIN,
Andrew HARDERSON, Andrew ROUNTREE, Ransom CATES, John
SATTERFIELD, Allen AKINS, John SOUTHALL, Joseph
CHUMBLY, Harmon MILLER, William TRIMBLE, Radford
BUTTS, Young CHUMBLEY, James BRINT, Balaam J. HICKS,
Allen RAINEY, Richard CRAGG, John P. CAMPBELL.
Returned by John JAMESON.

page 168   ROBERTSON - List of property of William R. ROBERTSON,
deceased - recorded 14 September 1829 - taken 12 Oct-
ober 1827 - buyers: Robert F. MATTHEWS, A. B. ALEX-
ANDER, John DICKEY, Joseph GILMORE, Edward WORTHAM,
Isaac G. SANDSBERRY, Elias PEYTON, James R. DICKEY,
Joseph HACKNEY, Silas ALEXANDER, Michael ROBERTSON,
Richard KINDLE, George W. JOHNSON, William B. PILLOW,
Thomas LOWERY, Jack FAGG, Alsey ROBERTSON. Signed
28 July 1828 by William B. PILLOW, executor, later
administrator.

page 168   PATTON - Account of sale of George PATTON, deceased -
recorded 15 September 1829, sold 17 August 1826.
Buyers: Robert CARUTHERS, John D. LOVE, Benjamin
WILKES, Saml. CARUTHERS, Abraham LOONEY, Mathew RHEA,
George M. MARTIN, Richard FOSTER, William MANING,
Elisha ESTES, Young S. SANDFORD, Thomas B. _____,
David TROUSDALE, John B. GOODIN, John T. HUDSON,
Zacheus STILES, Littleton VAUGHN, Widow PATTON,
Meredith HELM, Saml. MC KEE, Pattilo PATTON, James
HOWARD, Zacheriah MARTIN, William WILEY, Andrew
NEELY, Mason SANFORD, Joseph ALDERSON, John M. JONES,
Gilford PESSENS, John HATCHETT. Signed, Robert
CARRUTHERS, administrator.

page 172   PERRY - Recorded 15 September 1829 - as presented on
2 June 1828 at court house in Trenton, Gibson County,
Tennessee, last will and testament, made 6 May 1828:
"my niece Sarah E. MURPHY and brother" Silas a negro;
my negro "Rachel to be kept by mother until her death
and then sold"; all my brothers and sisters...sister
Lucy...my bedstead to Harriett...brother Francis...
brother Simpson...brother Isaiah..."dimity to
Charlotte"...my other brothers and sisters...signed
Sarah X PERRY; witnesses, H. S. DICKERSON, John H.
CRISP. Recorded in Gibson County.

page 173   PICKARD - Will of John PICKARD - recorded 15 September 1829 - son Isaac to get plantation..wife Nancy,
son John (a tract adjoining Sollomon HOGE's tract)...
my three daughters, Ruth, Catharine, and Sally...
negroes named...my three sons, Alexander, Young S.,
and Aron PICKARD...my daughters Margaret PICKARD,
Rebecca DODSON, Jane ROBBERSON, Delila KING, Ruth,
Mary, Catherine, Sally, and Mahaly...my youngest
daughter Rhoda...son Alexander PICKARD and son in law
William PICKARD to be executors...signed 27 October
1826 (or 1828), John X PICKARD; witnesses, David
CRAIG, William STOCKARD.

page 173   POLK - Codicil to Samuel POLK's will - recorded 15
September 1829.

page 176   RILEY - Account of sale of James RILEY, deceased -
recorded 15 September 1829 - sale held 17 November
1827. Buyers: Robert CRAWLEY, William EDMONDSON,
Joseph G. MC CRACKING, James EASON, Lemuel SHERROD,
J. G. ROBINSON, Mary GLASCOCK, Arthur SHERROD, James
HOSSE, John D. OLIPHANT, James B. WOLLARD, James
REAVES, Abraham MC CARLEY, Peggy RILEY, Jesse TEMPLE,
Charles MITCHELL, David H. TRUE, William ERVIN,
William BLACKBURN, Jacob G. ROBINSON, Goodwin MAYS,
James E. GLASCOCK, George W. MC CARLEY.

page 178   POWELL - List of Property of Ambrose POWELL - recorded 15 September 1827; taken 9 November 1821, signed
William HUDSPETH, 2I January 1828.

page 180   NIXON - Inventory of John NIXON, desist, recorded
16 September 1829, signed by George NIXON, administrator.

page 181   POWELL - Year's allowance for Margaret POWELL, recorded 16 September 1829 - widow of Ambrose POWELL, deceased, signed 9 December 1827 by Joshua SMITH,
Mechack WILLIS, Thomas HUDSPETH.

page 181   PETERS - Inventory of James PETERS, deceased -
recorded 16 September 1829 - taken 8 February 1827,
38 negroes named...deceased sold some negroes to
James P. PETERS...some negroes in his bequest to
Lucy PERKINS, Nancy TURNER, Simon TURNER and Nancy
SANDERS, his four grandchildren...signed James P.
PETERS, executor.

page 182   PATTON - Year's allowance for George PATTON's widow
...recorded 16 September 1829 - Polly PATTON, widow
and her family; signed Abraham LOONEY, Benjamin
THOMAS, Matthew RHEA.

page 182   RILEY - Inventory of James RILEY - recorded 16 September 1829; William EDMONDSON, administrator.

page 183   PATTON - Inventory of George PATTON - recorded 16
September 1829 - notes on William TROUSDALE, A. C.
EDALMAN, Joseph PORTER, Thomas H. FLETCHER, DICKESON
and COOPER, David CANE, George PATTON, Lake BYNUM,
P. NELSON...negroes names and ages...signed Robert
CARUTHERS, administrator, 24 July 1822.

page 185   OAKLEY - Guardian return for James OAKLEY's heirs -
recorded 16 September 1829 - Elisabeth OAKLEY,
guardian...signed 21 April 1828.

page 185   ROBERTSON - Inventory of Wm. R. ROBERTSON - recorded
16 September 1829 - taken 21 July 1827 - "support of
the family alowed by the will" - signed W. B. PILLOW.

page 185   PURSELL - Guardian return for PURSELL's heirs -
recorded 16 September 1829 - Richard FAUSETT, guard-
ian of his wards Benjamin F., Mary Ann and Sarah
PURSELL, signed 23 July 1827. A. LONG sued the
PURSELL estate...paid widow of the deceased...paid
R. L. MACK and N. P. SMITH...renting the plantation.

page 186 PERRYMAN - Account of notes of B. PERRYMAN, deceased
...recorded 16 September 1829...notes on Jonathan
BULLOCK, Robert HISATE, Asker P. FLY, Jeremiah FLY,
and James CAMEGON.

page 186 PAYTON - Inventory of Thomas PAYTON, deceased - re-
corded 16 September 1829; notes belonging to estate:
Robert WHITTEN (?), James NEELY, Jacob GARNOT,
William BIFFLE, Andrew WILEY, Jonathan WEBSTER,
Georg HERIN, Dudley ISOM, Peter KIRK, Michael HIGGAN,
John TROUSDALE, Eli BUNCH, Thomas BEARD, Gorge BROWN,
John WHITESIDE, Francis COOK, Cpt. Wm. CATHEY,
Joseph PAYTON, John BELL...a right to land for the
purposes of building a mill...signed 26 July 1828 by
Joseph PAYTON, administrator.

page 187 PERREMAN - Year's allowance for widow of B. PARREMAN
...recorded 16 September 1829..widow Jurusha PERREMAN,
widow of Benoni PERREMAN, "for herself and child" -
signed 29 September 1826, William FLY, William
EDMONDSON, J.P.'s.

page 187 OGLESBY - Guardian return for OGLESBY's heirs -
recorded 16 September 1829 - John M. JONES, guardian
of Richard OGLESBY, Elisha OGLESBY and Celia OGLESBY,
minor heirs of Jane OGLESBY, deceased...signed 25
May 1828, Joseph B. PORTER, clerk, John M. JONES.

page 188 OAKLEY - Guardian return for William OAKLEY's heirs -
recorded 17 September 1829 - amount of money received
by guardian of minor heirs of William OAKLEY, deceased...paid Ana OAKLEY another of said heirs; paid
Nancy OAKLEY; paid James OAKLEY, another of said
heirs; signed William GRAY, 18 October 1827.

page 188 RICHARDSON - Settlement with William RICHARDSON's
administrator...recorded 17 September 1829, Keziah
and James M. RICHARDSON, administrators...hire of
negroes mentioned...vouchers on Henry B. CANNON, H.
FERGUSON, Wm. WILLFORD, BROWN and MC GIMPSEY, Thompson BAXTER, Edward H. CHAFFIN...year's provision for
widow...signed Alex. JOHNSON, Thos. GILL, and E. RICE,
commissioners.

page 189 RAMSEY - Inventory of William RAMSEY, deceased -
recorded 17 September 1829 - taken October 1820 -
negroes named - to his son William, cash and Bible;
to his son James, tract of land where he now lives;
daughter Rachael; daughter Ann JACKSON; "my grandsons,
John and William JACKSON"; daughter Jane; notes on
Robert RAMSEY, Daniel DOUGLAS, Alexander GILLESPIE,
John M. FALLS, Shadrick DUGGER, Robert FLANIGAN, John
JONES, Saml. CUNNIGAM, James RAMSEY, Thomas RAMSEY,
Ann JACKSON. Signed James HILL and Thomas RAMSEY,
executors.

page 190 PERRY - Inventory of Sarah PERRY, deceased - recorded
17 September 1829 - estate included negroes..signed
Simpson PERRY, administrator, 20 October 1828.

page 190 PATTON - Settlement with administrators of George
PATTON - recorded 17 September 1829 - Alexander
JOHNSON and John MACK settled with Robert CARUTHERS,

administrator...three judgements on Richard HILL, two
on M. S. ROBERTS, and Luke BYNUM; vouchers for widow
PATTON, Young COLEMAN, Josiah ALDERSON, Benjamin
WILKES, et al...proven accounts and notes: Jane
ADKINS, John MATTHEWS, Jesse LEFTWICH, John J. ZOLLI-
COFFER, William PHELAN, Joel D____ , Simpson BROWN,
Caleb THOMAS, Joseph HART, James YORK, UZZEL and
KIRKPATRICK, Samuel RANKIN. L, HITCHCOCK, M. D.
COOPER, COOPER and HOLTS, Robert MATTHEWS, YEATMAN,
Henry EGNEW, MC GIMPSEY...

page 192   PORTER - Will of Joseph B. PORTER - recorded 17 September 1829 - wife Betsy the plantation on which I now
live...all my children...all my sons who profess
sufficent capacity shall be educated...a lot in
Columbia on Main Street between MC KEAN's and the
Methodist Church...tract of land on bigbigby creek
granted to Owen GRIFFIN and Reese BUCKNER...negroes
named...until my youngest child is of lawful age...
son Elias H. PORTER...my five youngest children...
daughter Elizabeth CARUTHERS, her husband Robert
CARUTHERS..."part of the portion coming to me from
Elizabeth DUFFLE"...son John T. PORTER..."my share
in POLK, PORTER and Company has been equally divided
between myself, James BROWN and said John T. PORTER"
...John T. PORTER to have land on which he now lives
in Madison County..."son Thomas J. PORTER confirms
part he now holds as division of Isaac N. PORTER"...
said Isaac N. PORTER's will...land in Obion County...
son Parry Washington PORTER...son James Madison
PORTER...son Joseph Young PORTER to get land adjoining town of Troy, Obion County; youngest son Elias
Humphreys PORTER when he comes of age...executors to
be Matthew RHEA, Robert CARUTHERS, wife Betsy, sons
Thomas J. and Parry W. and youngest sons when come
of age to be executors...signed 17 October 1828,
witnesses, P. R. BOOKER, Edmund DILLAHUNTY, Thos. C.
PORTER.

page 196   PEARSELL - Partition of land of James PEARSELL's
heirs - recorded 17 September 1829 - lot 1 to
William D. PEARSELL; lot 2 to Edward PEARSALL; lot 3
to Hugh D. PEARSALL; lot 4 to James PEARSELL; lot 5
to Jeremiah PEARSELL; lot 6 to Joseph D. PEARSELL;
signed Joel REESE, Samuel GRIFFIN, John MATTHEWS,
David CRAIG, William STOCKARD. (Abstractor's note:
this is thought to be the family of PEARSALLS
related to Revolutionary Soldier Joseph DICKSON of
Dickson County; see Tennessee Society DAR roster.)

page 198   RICHARDSON - Inventory of William RICHARDSON, deceased - recorded 18 September 1829 - James RICHARD-
SON, administrator.

page 200   RICHARDSON - Inventory of negroes of William RICHARD-
SON, deceased - recorded 18 September 1829 - taken
2 January 1827; negroes named and ages given.

page 200   RICHARDSON - Year's allowance for Keziah RICHARDSON,
widow of William - recorded 18 September 1829; taken
for her and said family by Jos. BROWN, Jas. SHIELD,
James HOWARD, David DUGGER, signed 10 July 1826.

page 201   RICHARDSON - Division of property of William RICHARD-
SON - recorded 18 September 1829 - heirs: Keziah,
widow; James M. RICHARDSON, oldest son; Amos RICHARD-
SON and Polly his wife, daughter of deceased; William
W. RICHARDSON, second son; John M. RICHARDSON, third
son; Thomas T. RICHARDSON, youngest son; signed, John
AMIS, Peter AKERS, James HOWARD, commissioners.

page 202   PETERS - Will of James PETERS, deceased - recorded
18 September 1829 - signed 24 April 1826 - wife Lucy
PETERS "the buildings I present occupy"; son James P.
PETERS; negroes named; emancipate negro Priscilla at
death of wife; James to pay Lucy PERKINS $300, Nancy
SANDERS $200, and Simon TURNER, $200; my grandchild-
ren, Lucy PERKINS, Nancy TURNER, Nancy SANDERS, and
Simon TURNER; daughter Susannah MC KISSACK; grand-
daughter Lucy DICKSON; son to be executor; witnesses,
Jos. HERNDON, M. D. COOPER.

page 203   POLK - Inventory of Samuel POLK - recorded 19 Sept-
ember 1829 - notes on Hardy C. KIRBY, James HUEY,
THOMPSON, Henry STRATTON, James S. WADDLE, Silas M.
CALDWELL, Alexander MC CORKLE, James WALKER, E.
WILKES, Joseph P. HALL, Samuel WATERS, Jonathan
WATSON, L. B. MANGRAM, John RAY, M. ELLISTON, Joseph
G. KELSO, John BATCHELOR, David SURRATT, Allen NANTY,
J. M. GREEN, Robert RIBERS (RIVERS), Wm. POLK, A. O.
HARRIS, J. W. FORT, Thos. MC NEAL, M. C. MORMAN (now
deceased), receipt of D. FENTRESS, E. P. MC NEAL, Wm.
STODDARD; James LANE's note; P. POWELL's note; notes
on Chas. FITZHUGH, William RAMSAY, William DENOVANT,
J. B. STOKES, James KENADY, R. and L. B. CAMPBELL;
accounts: John JENKINS, Hezekiah WARD, Thos. G. POLK,
Matthew RANAW, Saml. C. DICKENS, Mrs. LEETCH, Mark
ROBERTS, P. R. BOOKER, James K. POLK, Lewis BAND,
Thos. MAHAN, George CAMPBELL, POLK and PORTER, Samuel
PHILLIPS, George MORE, L. J. POLK, Benjamin POLK,
Spivy MC KISSACK, _____ MC DANIEL, Richard CHAPPELL,
Daniel C. BROWN, Harmon MILLER, E. M. CAMPBELL,
Redick DISHONGH, Isaac BROOKS, Thos. GRANT, James T.
WALKER, M. T. POLK, E. F. POLK; judgement on James
DAVIS of Wayne County.

page 207   MANGRUM - Inventory of Edwin MANGRUM - recorded 19
September 1829 - account of sale, no buyers given.
Signed, William A. JOHNSON, administrator.

page 207   MANGRUM - Inventory of Isham MANGRUM - recorded 19
September 1829 - taken 19 October 1818 - mentions
carpenter's tools...signed Patsey MANGRUM, Edwin
MANGRUM, administrators.

page 208   MC FALL - Inventory of John MC FALLS - recorded 19
September 1829 - taken 19 January 1827 - negroes
named; large Bible...signed Martha MC FALLS, Thomas
RAMSEY, administrators.

page 208   MALONE - Inventory of Robert MALONE, deceased - recorded 19 September 1829 - made 21 January 1828 -
included note on Henry JONES. Signed Thos. B. MALONE.

page 208   MADDING - Inventory of William MADDING, deceased -
recorded 19 September 1829 - mentions Sarah MADING.

page 209   ALLEN - Will of James ALLEN - recorded 20 January
1830 - daughter Caty REYNOLDS; daughter Nancy (sur-
name blurred); son William, son Charles, son Zachary,
son James (blurred); 1/6 part to lawful heirs of
Caty REYNOLDS; 1/6 part to lawful heirs of William
ALLEN; 1/6 part to lawful heirs of James ALLEN; 1/6
part to lawful heirs of Zacheriah ALLEN; two sons
William and Zacheriah to be executors; signed 16
August 1822; witnesses, Alex. JOHNSON and William A.
JOHNSON.

page 210   MOORE - Inventory of Nathaniel MOORE, deceased -
recorded 21 January 1830 - sold 13 August 1829 -
amount from sale of Jamtes T. MOORE; amounts from
Saml CARUTHERS, Nathaniel T. MOORE, John MATHEWS,
Larkin PILKINTON, John FLOWERS, Samuel KINKAID, David
KINKAID, John C. FLEMMINGS, Charles SIMMS (SIMMONS),
Alfred FARRIS, William O. FLEMMINGS, Elisha ESTES,
Young S. SANFORD, John W. HUDSON, Isaac HUDSON, John
B. THOMAS, Job H. THOMAS, Edward W. DALE, Christopher
TODD, Robert DOAK, William W. COVEY, Leven L. COVEY,
executor...sold negro man Henry according to direction
of testator's will.

page 211   WILKES - Inventory of Daniel WILKES, deceased - recorded 21 January 1830 - taken 24 September 1829 -
notes and accounts: John W. CLANTON, John C.
FLEMMINGS, William D. NELSON, Phineas THOMAS,
Richard FOSTER, Nathaniel THOMPSON.

page 211   ADKINS - Elijah ADKINS' inventory - recorded 22 January 1830.

page 212   ALSTON - Accounts against estate of Thos. (?) ALSTON
recorded 28 January 1830 - account of monies paid
out by ___?___ ALSTON against estate of Samuel MC
DANIEL, deceased - paid John MURRIL, $10; paid
Fanning JONES, other faded, paid BROWN and MC GIMPSEY,
Robert MC GOWEN, Jefferson PORTER, ROBISON for medical services, James N. SMITH; note on John PATTERSON,
Peter I. VOORHIES. (Abstractor's note: this entry
needs to be re-checked with original book.)

page 214   WILKES - Inventory of Elizabeth WILKES, deceased -
recorded 27 January 1830 - amount of sale on 24 Sept-
ember 1829 - buyers: John B. THOMAS, John C.FLEMMINGS,
Robert F. MATTHEWS, Dandridge POINDEXTER, John WILKES,
George W. BLEADSOE, Richd. A. L. WILKES, Wm. KENNE-
MORE, Richard FOSTER, ___thias J. WOODWARD, Andrew
SCOTT, John B. GOODING, William W. GALLOWAY, Robert
PATTERSON, William C. FLEMMINGS, Vincent RIDLEY,
Haywood BLEDSOE, Jonathan GILLESPIE, Daniel WILKES,
A. W. MACK, William KEER, two stone jars were claimed
by Jesse WILKES, two irons claimed by Benjamin WILKES,
one stay claimed by Mrs. GUINN; signed R. A. L.
WILKES, Phineas THOMAS.

page 215   FULTON - Archibald FULTON estate divided - recorded
30 January 1830 - his widow has now married Daniel
LITIRELL of "bed county, Virginia"...negroes named
...James FULTON, eldest heir of Archibald FULTON,
deceased and Polly his wife. Jackson FULTON, second

son of Archibald FULTON, deceased, and Polly his wife;
signed John T. MOORE, David MARTIN, John KNOR.

page 216   SCOT - James SCOT's guardian return - recorded 30
            January 1830 - for Cinthia Jane SCOT and William SCOT,
            heirs of James SCOT, deceased...signed Andrew SCOT,
            guardian.

page 216   BROWN - Duncan BROWN's settlement - recorded 30 Jan-
            uary 1830 - Duncan BROWN, guardian of Jane E. FRIER-
            SON in settlement with the court October 1828...paid
            E. W. DALE for tuition...signed, Duncan BROWN.

page 216   WHITSON - Inventory of Ann WHITSON, deceased, record-
            ed 30 January 1830 - returned by Samuel WHITSON and
            Edmund WILLIAMS, estate included 14 negroes...note
            on Westley WITHERSPOON, signed Samuel WHITSON and
            Edmund WILLIAMS.

page 217   OAKLEY - Elizabeth OAKLEY, guardian of the heirs of
            James OAKLEY, deceased, makes return to court -
            recorded 1 February 1830.

page 217   NEVILS - Inventory of John NEVILS, deceased - record-
            ed 1 February 1830 - had one negro...bond on M.
            WATKINS...account of Benjamin TATUM...account of
            William TATUM.

page 217   GALOWAY - William GALOWAY, guardian of Elizabeth
            GALOWAY, makes return - recorded 1 February 1830.

page 217   SWAN - Robert NICHOL, guardian of Mathew SWAN's
            heirs, makes return - recorded 1 February 1830 -
            taken 20 April 1828.

page 217   HUNTER - James H. HUNTER's settlement - recorded
            1 February 1830. (Abstractor's note: this entry
            had been crossed out, but will be included.) William
            H. HUNTER, administrator of estate of James KINDLE,
            paid Elias J. ARMSTRONG, Elijah PAYTON, and BROWN
            and MC GIMSEY, note on Robert MACK, tax receipt for
            taxes in Shelby County...allowance made to widow.

page 219   ALLEN - Inventory of personal estate of James ALLEN,
            deceased, taken at the request of his surviving
            friends "present at his death". Negroes named.
            Recorded 2 February 1830, signed E. RICE, Alex.
            JOHNSON.

page 220   KIMBLE - William H. HUNTER, administrator of James
            KIMBLE, deceased, makes settlement - recorded 3 Feb-
            ruary 1830 - hire of negroes - Doctor Bill BROWN...
            signed Nicholas J. LONG, Robert WORTHAM. (Abstract-
            or's note: this is believed to be the correct entry
            for the one marked out above.)

page 221   JACOBS - Alexander RAIMEY's settlement as administra-
            tor of William JACOBS, deceased - recorded 3 February
            1830 - with will annexed...vouchers for James NOT-
            GRASS, P. NELSON, P. MC GUIRE, BROWN and NOTGRASS,
            Finis SHANNON, Samuel W. AKIN, Richard CRAGG, Bennet
            BLACKBURN, Joh MOORE, William C. MC KEE, Daniel
            GOODRAM, Milton CARTER, Lemuel POPE, James C. NEELEY,

Nathaniel CROWDER, Robert L. COBBS, CURREN and MASON,
B. W. HARDIN, Hugh B. PORTER, Adkin NICHOLSON, Samuel
AKINS, Silas M. CALDWELL; signed 25 October 1829 by
Joe REESE, James BLACK, J.P.'s.

page 222   WHITSON - Inventory of amount of sale of Aney WHITSON,
            deceased - recorded 4 February 1830, sold 11 August
            1829; buyers: Samuel WHITSON, Westley WITHERSPOON,
            Edmond T. WILLIAMS, Even POLK, Mathew HARRINSON, Aron
            CULBERSON, Wm. D. WILLIAMS, Andy CULBERSON, James
            FITZGERALD, David H. TRUE, David DODSON, Danl. E.
            HAYDEN, Robert GASKEL, William HAMLET, Williamson
            BROWN, Thomas W. HARBINSON, Arthur CHURCH, Martin
            DODSON, Charles IRVIN, Asia DODSON, James RANDELL,
            James RUTLEDGE, John CATHEY, William COOPER, Kiaah
            BROOKS, James ERVIN, Allen MC LENHANEY, Mary HUNTER,
                        PARTEE, Beverly DODSON, Isom AVONDALE, Oby
            JOHNSON, Joshua WILLIAMS, Francis HILL, Robert
            GASCALL, William FLY, James ADKINS, Hugh N. JOHNSON;
            signed Samuel WHITSON and Edmund L. WILLIAMS,
            executors.

page 224   JOHNSON - Additional inventory of Amos JOHNSON -
            recorded 4 February 1830 - list of unsold articles
            belonging to estate; signed Elizabeth JOHNSON, admin-
            istrator.

page 224   PATTON (?) - William VOORHIES, administrator of
            Archibald FULTON (PATTON?) - settlement - recorded
            5 February 1830 - negroes were sold; received cash
            from George CAMPBELL; accounts and receipts of P. W.
            PORTER, Thos. J. PORTER, William R. MILLER, John
            KIMES, David MARTIN, Thos. S. DALE, Mrs. Polly
            FULTON, Jas. GULLET, E. BRIDGES, Doctor John B. HAYS,
            James M. ELLISON, William PHILIPS, Oren LARIMORE,
            Thos. J. BRIDGES, Elijah RIVERS, George M. MARTIN,
            BROWN and MC GIMSEY, Richard LANCASTER, Thos. N.
            EASON, Benj. B. SMITH, Augustus BROWN, John B. GROVES,
            Evan YOUNG, J. J. HUDSON, Chesly ESTES, Wm. BROOKS,
            Mrs. LAIRD, HAYS and DEANS, Lemuel PHILLIPS,
            DILAHUNTY, A. O. HARRIS, Thos. NORTON, Cufa WOODSON,
            Wm. WIBLE, Wm. PEALOW, John W. LAMASTER, John BARN-
            HILL, Doctor J. C. O'RILEY, Pleasant NELSON, John
            KNOX (or KNOR), Gray P. WIBLE, James S. WALKER,
            William LYTLE, James LANGTRY, J. ALDERSON, John B.
            ALDERSON, Daniel C. MORRIS. Signed, John KNOX, John
            T. MOORE.

page 227   HILL - Recorded 4 February 1830 - List of sale of
            James W. HILL, deceased - buyers: George W. WEAVER,
            Thompson GULLET, John SMITH, Simpson GABEL, Elias
            CHEEK, Cosby SCOTT, Alexander MC KEE, Thos. FORSYTH,
            Robert THOMPSON, Joseph H. AGNEW, Elizabeth HILL,
            Francis GILL, Parmela HILL, Francis SMITH, William
            GILLIAM, James N. SMITH, Margaret FINLEY, Pamela
            HILL, Samuel GULLETT, James C. FREELAND, John D.
            BAIN, signed G. W. WEAVER, administrator.

page 229   WILKS - Inventory of Minor WILKS, deceased - recorded
            8 February 1830 - buyers: Burwell WILKES, Richard
            WILKES, David WILKES, Thomas WILKES, Richard BENTLEY,
            George CAVENDER, James HASTEN, Larkin DEARIN, James

A. DENTON, William DAVIS, Thomas KETCHEM, Rease
HARRISON, some illegible names, Morgan FITZPATRICK,
Daniel BILLS, John HUEY, Walker MOORE, John J. WILKES,
Willis HUEY, Thos. GRANT, Joseph HARRISON, Giles
CRAFTEN, Wm. MC MEANES, James PHILLIPS, Jaret YOUNG,
Jeremiah HOLT, Adam MEASE, Robert CALVERT, James
DEAREN, Adam MEESE, Jonathan KETCHAM, Andrew SMITH,
David CAUDLE, Clement WADE, William J. WILKES, Mary
WILKES, James COOLEY, William D. HARDEY.

page 231   MC VANE - Robert MC NEILL, guardian report - recorded
8 February 1830 - Robert MC NEIL amount he received
from John MC VANES, former guardian, signed Robert
MC NEILL.

page 232   JOHNSTON - Inventory of sale of Amos JOHNSTON, de-
ceased - recorded 8 February 1830 - sold 27 and 28
August 1829 - buyers not named; notes on Lewis T.
JOHNSTON, James BLANKES, Wm. THOMPSON, Owen HUMPHREYS,
John GILCHRIST, Benjamin WORTHAM, Randolph PATE,
Willis TURNER, Nashville Bridge Company, Huntsville
banks, Bank of Alexandria (not good) - signed Eliza-
beth JOHNSTON, administratrix.

page 234   PETERS - Settlement with James P. PETERS - recorded
10 February 1830 - James P. PETERS makes settlement
as administrator (later executor) of Simon TURNER,
deceased...notes on Brittian SAND, Wm. LANE, David
JEFFRIES, Walter S. JENKINS, John ROY, James P.
PETERS, Francis GORDEN; allowance to guardian; paid
Allen RAINEY, Levi KETCHUM, Lewis HOLMAN; signed
24 January 1829 by James BLACK, Garret VOORHIES,
commissioners.

page 235   MILLS - Inventory of Gideon MILLS, deceased - recorded 10 February 1830 - taken 24 October 1829 - notes
on Jesse WILKES and Robt. SUFFIELD...note by W. W.
PARHAM of Franklin County, Alabama, signed Francis
S. PERRY, Executor.

page 236   MC KEE - A. LOONEY, guardian account - Jacob MC KEE,
heir of Jacob MC KEE, deceased in account with A.
LOONEY, guardian - payments made to John B. GOODING
for boarding and clothing; H. Milton MC KEE, heir of
Jacob MC KEE, deceased; Lucinda MC KEE, heir of Jacob
MC KEE, deceased - payment to Mr. H. PATTON for
tuition; Sally MC KEE, heir of Jacob MC KEE, deceased;
Matilda MC KEE, heir of Jacob MC KEE, deceased; July
1828 term.

page 238   HARRIS - Settlement with Benjamin R. and West HARRIS,
administrators of Henry HARRIS, deceased - recorded
12 February 1830. Notes payable to J. S. WALKER and
Company; receipts and notes of Nimrod PORTER, R. C.
MARTIN, Wiley LEDBETTER, William MACON, Aron MC MANIS,
FOSTER and SMITH, CRAWFORD, Wm. HARPER, Edmond
WILLIAMS, Benj. DAVIS, _____ TAYLOR, Robt. MATHEWS,
Graves HARWELL, several illegibles, James DAVIS,
Henry L. ROBERTSON (can't be found), Esquire WELCH,
Joel ECHOLS (insolvent), Doct. ECHOLS (western
district), Elijah WEAVER (broke and run away), WOOD-
WARD, Mrs. Elizabeth CRISP (can't be found), O. H.

ROBERTS (broke), N. K. RODGERS (broke), Jno. JONES
(broke), Zack WORTHAM (broke); note for tax in
Western District; Stephen GARRETT (cannot be found),
James W. CLARK (Western District)..."we have proceed-
ed to settle with administrators of Henry HARRIS,
deceased", signed Nicholas J. LONG and David CRAIG
on 14 October 1829.

page 240   FRIERSON - Recorded 15 February 1830 - Settlement -
accounts due James T. MOORE in right of his wife
Dannah E. MOORE, formerly Dannah E. FRIERSON, widow
of Samuel E. FRIERSON, deceased; Agginth, Jannette,
Isabella, Jason L. and William Y. FRIERSON, minor
heirs of Samuel E. FRIERSON; amounts due from
Jannette Isabella, Susan, William A. and Samuel S.
FRIERSON...paid DAMERON for teaching the children;
signed 25 October 1829 by Samuel CRAWFORD, John
PORTER, D. H. TRUE.

page 240   EVANS - Settlement with administrators of estate of
Daniel EVANS, deceased - recorded 15 February 1830 -
made 26 October 1828 - administrators H. S. CRUTCHER
and Francis SLAUTER..."for property retained by Mrs.
EVANS"...signed John C. WORMELEY and Peter I. VOOR-
HIES.

page 241   THOMPSON - Inventory of Sale of Estate of James
THOMPSON, deceased - recorded 18 February 1830 - no
buyers given.

page 244   TOMLINSON - Will of Isaac TOMLINSON - recorded 18
February 1830 - wife Mary B., son Edward Washington
TOMLINSON; my sister (blank) THOMPSON one of best
horses; wife and friends Edward B. LITTLEFIELD and
Nathaniel WILLIS, executors; signed 16 October 1826 -
witnesses, John KESTERSON, Edward ENGLISH, Edward F.
ENGLISH.

page 244   _____ - Supplement to inventory of Samuel S._____
(name not given), deceased - recorded 19 February
1830 - signed ___November 1829 by David CRAIG, Wm.
HUNTER, Hugh SHAW.

page 245   SCOT - Settlement with Lewis NEEDHAM and Hannah SCOT,
administrators of estate of Samuel SCOT, deceased -
recorded 19 February 1830 - George JOHNSTON and Tyree
DOLLINS were appointed February 1827 to settle with
administrators...mentions one bond on Rachel BROWN
...receipts of Isaac J. THOMAS "for said SCOTT's
serivces in States Army the last war"...bonds of
James S. BAILS, William CAMPBELL, Robert CLARKE,
Benjamin GOLSON; accounts, Amos SANON, Isaac J.
THOMAS, Robert DAVIDSON, Heskiah JONES, William MC
CONNELL, Ambrose HARWELL, Hugh BEARD; signed 17 May
1817, George JOHNSTON, Tyree DOLLINS. (Abstractor's
note: the date 1827 first given could possibly be
1817 also, hard to decipher.)

page 246   STRAYHORN - Joseph MC MURRAY, administrator of David
STRAYHORN, deceased, makes settlement - recorded
19 February 1830 - allowance for widow; vouchers,
accounts, etc.: Edward B. LITTLEFIELD, Arthur T.

ISOM, John SKIPPER, Joseph MC MURRAY, David SHAMPSON, Robison YEATMAN, John WALKER, John NIXON, WEBSTER and STRAYHORN, Docts. BROWN and MC GIMPSEY, William LITTLE-FIELD, Joseph HART, Joseph G. PRATT, Nathan SKIPER, Doctor Jas. G. SMITH, Robert B. LINN, Robert CROSBY, Timothy GEORGE, Penlope STRAYHORN, James JOSSEY, James M. MITCHELL, Nathaniel SANBORNS (receipt for indenture on barrels in state of Illinois); signed John O. COOK, George NIXON, J.P.

page 247 SELLERS - Inventory of Robert SELLERS, deceased - recorded 21 February 1830 - no buyers given.

page 248 SCOT - Settlement with executors of James SCOT - recorded 21 February 1830 - Andrew SCOT and James W. MATHEWS, executors...paid $10 to LINDSEY for coffin... amount for widdow...signed 10 October 1828 by John MACK and John MATHEWS, J.P.'s.

page 248 THOMPSON - Mrs. Sarah THOMPSON's accounts with W. W. GOODING - recorded 21 February 1830 - accounts beginning in 1823 - much clothing purchased.

page 250 BRAWLEY - Division of estate of Thomas BRAWLEY, deceased between his heirs - recorded 22 February 1830, Henry SMITH and Robert NICHOLS, administrators...also guardians of minor heirs of Mathew SWAN...to Robert NICHOLS, guardian for the children and the next friend to the widdow...Thos. BRAWLEY was former guardian of the children of Mathew SWAN...signed 14 April 1828, Nicholas J. LONG, David CRAIG, J.P.'s.

page 251 SHELBY - Inventory of personal estate of Thomas SHELBY, deceased, recorded 22 February 1820 - blacksmith tools - taken October 1822 term by Evan SHELBY and William SHELBY, executors.

page 251 THOMPSON - Petition of Jane THOMPSON for dower - recorded 22 February 1830 - made at October 1821 term, widow of James THOMPSON who "died about the year 1820" and he had 570 acres where widow now lives.

page 251 TOM - Will of William TOM - recorded 22 February 1830 - son William TOM; wife Nancy; daughter Elizabeth; son Joseph; daughter Nancy; son Charles; negroes named; wife Nancy and James N. BROWN, executors... signed 15 March 1826 William X TOM; witnesses, A. M. WILEY, Robert L. BROWN, William BROWN.

page 252 TATE - Recorded 23 February 1830 - Will of John TATE - to Ezekiel P. MC NEAL, eldest son of Thomas MC NEAL of Maury; "Thomas M. HARDEMAN, son of Thomas J. HARDE-MAN of Williamson County; to Marshal T. POLK, son of Samuel POLK and Rufus NEALEY, son of Charles NEALEY, deceased, all grandchildren of Ezekiel POLK, my tract of land granted to Elijah PATTON and conveyed to Sarah PATTON" 1000 acres in western district on waters of south fork and RUTHERFORD's fork of Obion River, to be equally divided...land granted to Edward HOUSTON and James BALDRIDGE, both of them sons-in-law of William HENDERSON, deceased, late of Maury, a certain tract granted to John TATE, 500 acres on east

side of Tennessee River in 8th surveyor's district on
the waters of big buffalo river, this to be divided
between Edward HOUSTON and James BALDRIDGE...I give
to Abner MATHEWS and James BOYD, both of Maury County,
sons in law of William HENDERSON, deceased, parcel of
land granted to John TATE, 640 acres on waters of big
buffalo river to be divided between them...land on
Knob Creek in Maury County, tract I once conveyed to
Thomas RAMSAY, to be sold and proceeds to (1) Prudence
T. MC NEAL, daughter of Thomas MC NEAL and granddaughter of Ezekiel POLK and (2) _____ L. POLK,
daughter of Samuel POLK, granddaughter of Ezekiel
POLK...balance to the lawful sons and daughters of
William HENDERSON, deceased, "at whose place of resi-
dence I now reside"...Richard HENDERSON and Samuel
POLK to be executors...signed 18 October 1822 by
John TATE; witnesses, James K. POLK, M. BALDRIDGE,
Alexander S. HENDERSON.

page 253   NICHOLSON - Calvin H. NICHOLSON's account, dating
            from April 1824...receipts of WALKER and HARRIS,
            Benjamin F. ALEXANDER, Samuel W. AKIN, Garrett L.
            VOORHIES, Mrs. NICHOLSON, J. KENNEDY.

page 257   WALKER - James S. WALKER's account from April 1823 -
            "James S. WALKER, my guardian" signed 23 February
            1827 by Calvin H. NICHOLSON. The above mentioned
            settlements and receipts recorded March 1830 term.

page 258   NICHOLSON - A. O. P. NICHOLSON's accounts - paid Sam
            POLK for "tuition kept"; sale of negroes...store
            account with WALKER and HARRIS..."cash sent you in
            Philadelphia"...receipts of M. J. KITRELL, Robert
            CAMPBELL, Col. S. POLK... Settlement made 19 January
            1830 by James S. WALKER, guardian of A. O. P. NICHOL-
            SON.

page 262   SCOTT - Job H. THOMAS, guardian of Jno. W. SCOTT and
            Elizabeth SCOTT, minor heirs of Samuel SCOTT, de-
            ceased...Isaac J. THOMAS, former guardian, from
            North Carolina...signed 29 June 1830 Job H. THOMAS.

page 270   NEVILS - Inventory of John NEVILS, deceased - record-
            ed 27 November 1830 - vouchers, receipts of G. M.
            WATKINS, Benjamin TATUM; signed 2 October 1830 by
            Clement NEVILS, guardian of P. NEVILS.

page 270   GALAWAY - William W. GALAWAY, guardian of Elizabeth
            GALAWAY, minor heir of Samuel GALAWAY, deceased,
            guardian report - recorded 21 November 1830, signed
            25 September 1830.

page 270   PERRY - Settlement with Sarah PERRY, deceased -
            recorded 27 November 1830 - Simpson PERRY, executor
            ...signed John MACK and Jasper R. SUTTON, J.P.'s.

page 271   PICKARD - Allowance for Fanny PICKARD, widow of John
            J. PICKARD - recorded 27 November 1830 - signed D.
            DOBBIN, Johnston CRAIG, William STOCKARD.

page 271   CALAHAN - Edward CALAHAN, deceased, heirs settlement
            - recorded 29 November 1830. Settlement with Mary B.

_____RICH, guardian of minor heirs of Edward CALAHAN, deceased, signed 24 September 1830 by John VINCENT, James L. BALDRIDGE, J.P.'s.

page 271 FRIERSON - Settlement with administrators of John W. FRIERSON - recorded 29 November 1830 - Tindal's School, received from estate of D. FRIERSON and from estate of B. DICKEY...paid Thos. KELY for tuition... paid John W. STEPHENSON for tuition...accounts of John ALEXANDER, Gerard VAN BUREN, Mrs. SESSAM...paid postage on letter from New Orleans, signed 29 September 1830, Joseph ERWIN, John E. STEVENSON.

page 262 FOX - Inventory of William FOX, deceased - recorded 25 November 1830 - notes and receipts on Joseph MOORE, George CRIPPEN, Willis BRIDGES, Abner FENTRESS, John RHYNE, Abraham FARRAR, James HOLCOMB, Solomon BRINTS, Samuel DUE...signed Jackson LEGGETT and Charles _____.

page 263 PUCKET - Account of sale of Edward PUCKET - recorded 25 November 1830 - buyers: Widow PUCKET, John H. HILL, William A. JOHNSTON, J. HUGGINS, E. M. HAYNES, Richard PENTLEY, M. STONE, G. STONE, J. W. DILLAHAY: signed John W. PUCKET, administrator.

page 263 DOOLEY - Inventory of Parris F. DOOLEY, deceased - recorded 25 November 1830; articles included Jackson press, "himm" book, Bible...signed 1 July 1830, by E. B. DOOLEY, administrator.

page 264 WREN - Inventory of sale of George WREN, deceased - recorded 25 November 1830 - no buyers listed, made 10 September 1830, Thos. WRENN, administrator.

page 265 PUCKET - Inventory of Edward PUCKET, deceased - recorded 25 November 1830 - signed Edward K. PUCKET, John W. PUCKET, administrators.

page 265 MILLER - Inventory of John B. MILLER, deceased - recorded 26 November 1830 - taken 22 September 1830 - note on Thomas CHANDLER, account of Jonathan MILLS, William S. TURNER, signed 22 September 1830 by James HUEY.

page 266 JOHNSON - Inventory of Cader JOHNSON - recorded 20 November 1830, taken 24 June 1830.

page 266 DOOLEY - Account of sale of Paris F. DOOLEY - recorded 26 November 1830; no buyers given; notes and accounts of Westley G. NEELEY, John C. NEELEY, E. E. DAVIDSON, James DOWDY, Yerby and Absalom ATKINSON, Wm. WALLIS, Isaac FERREL, William KNOT, George W. ELISON (considered desperate), Cyrus BRIGESS (very desperate), Joel B. SANDERS, George W. TONY, Isaac MOORE, Wilie W. BROWN (desperate), Taswell S. ALDERSON, Elias PEYTON, Dudley P. JOHNSON, William B. BROWN, Joshua BOWDRY (desperate), James KENEDY, Nathaniel CROWDER (desperate), David H. TRUE (desperate), Samuel MC BRIDE, John B. ALDERSON, Daniel MURDOCK, Peter HOLLAND, Jonathan WATSON (desperate), William PORTER. Signed, E. B. DOOLEY, administrator.

page 270   CALAHAN - Guardian return - recorded 20 November 1830
- on 15 September 1830 received of Marion DUVALL,
former guardian of minor heirs of Benjamin CALAHAN,
deceased, signed John DUVALL.

page 270   PERRAMAN - Guardian return - recorded 30 November
1830 - on 20 September 1830 received on Johnston
RITCHARDS, guardian of minor heirs of Benony PERRAMAN;
signed Johnson RICHARDS.

page 270   GIBBONS - Will of Samuel G. GIBBONS - recorded 30
November 1830 - signed 6 September 1816 - wife Elizabeth E. GIBBONS...my sister Honor...nephew John
ANDERSON..."in case my wife should have issue of my
body"..."do not wish any of my negroes ever to be
sold wishing them always to be retained by my wife"
...executors Edward W. DALE, Robert W. ROBERTS;
witnesses, John PHILIPS, Thomas DALE.

page 271   RENFRO - Will of William RENFRO - recorded 30 November 1830 - wife Jinny...farm whereon I now live...
sons John, Jesse, Moses...daughters Lidda HARRIS,
Nancy KENEDY, and Judy SIMMONS...son William to get
tract whereon I now live and all the negroes except
one...grandson John Shelburne RENFRO...signed 9 August 1825 William X RENFRO; witnesses, Jno. HATCHETT,
John KERR.

page 272   SCOTT - Guardian return - recorded 1 December 1830 -
guardian return for Cinthia J. SCOTT and William
SCOT, heirs of James SCOTT, deceased, 20 October
1829, by Andrew SCOTT.

page 272   DOOLEY - Widow allowance for Eliza DOOLEY, widow of
Parris F. DOOLEY, deceased - recorded 1 December
1830 - signed 20 September 1830 by John THOMAS, Adam
DIXON.

page 272   WHITESIDES - Guardian settlement - recorded 1 December 1830 - Michael HIGGINS, guardian to Robert N.
and Samuel D. WHITESIDES, signed Michael HIGGINS,
guardian.

page 276   WILLIAMS - Settlement with Duke WILLIAMS, Frederick
ZOLLICOFFER, and Harden WILLIAMS, administrators of
Nathaniel WILLIAMS, deceased - recorded 1 December
1830 - settled on 11 September 1830; estate included
slaves...paid Thomas ARCHER for coffin, $13.37 1/3;
receipts of Henry C. WILLIAMS, LEE and HODGE, John
GRIMES, Thos. WILLIAMS, Chiles MC GEE, Dr. D. N.
SANSOM, John B. HAYS, NICHOLSON and ESTES, DOBBS and
DILLAHUNTY, Henry HODGE, J. B. LEFTWICH, S. P.
JORDAN, CRAWFORD and SPINDLE, N. W. BRISCOE, WALKER
and VAIL, John MICHE, Benj. R. HARRIS, Thos. M.
HARPER, J. P. SPIDLE, E. H. CHAFFIN, J. J. ZOLLI-
COFFER, H. N. WHITMAN, Z. CONKEY, Thos. J. PORTER,
F. ZOLLICOFFER and Company, John W. SMITH, W. H.
BOWDER; signed September 1830 by Nicholas J. LONG
and Jno. B. BOND, J.P.'s.

page 277   SIMS - Sale of John SIMS, deceased - recorded 2 December 1830 - sold ____ 1828 - negroes named and ages

given...buyers were Jane W. GRIMES, C. W. KNIGHT, Thos. HOWARD, Anderson BROOKS..."sundry articles sold to the widow"...Mumford SMITH, Mathias LEE, Thomas SIMS. Signed John D. SIMS.

page 278   SIMS - Settlement with John D. SIMS, executor of John SIMS, deceased, made 11 September 1830 - recorded 2 December 1830; paid Leml. PHILLIPS, James STOCKARD, C. W. PORTER, Elisha RICHARD, Jno. W. SMITH, WALKER and VAIL, Jno. Y. BALDRIDGE, Benj. R. HARRIS, N. W. BRISCOE, COBBS and DILLAHUNTY, Jno. B. BOND, Thos. Y. WINN, Wm. E. GILASPIE, KNIGHT and BREWSTER, West HARRIS, Anderson BROOKS, O. ALEXANDER, LEE and HODGE, HAMILTON and JORDAN, Thos. HOWARD; signed Nicholas J. LONG and John B. BOND, commissioners.

page 279   BINUM - A. Y. PARTEE guardian settlement - recorded 2 December 1830 - lists A. Y. PARTEE's accounts with heirs of Wm. BINUM, deceased.

page 279   ADKINS - E. M. CAMPBELL settlement - recorded 2 December 1830 - E. M. CAMPBELL and Wesley WITHERSPOON, executors of Elijah ADKINS estate...receipts of G. W. CAMPBELL, CHAFFIN and HICKS, J. W. P. MC GIMPSEY; signed 16 September 1830 by Edmund L. WILLIAMS.

page 280   PERKINS - Inventory of Nancy PERKINS - recorded 3 December 1830 - rendered by her guardian, David PISTOLE, who was appointed October term 1827...a legacy paid Nancy by last will and testament of one Antony MILLS of Virginia and in hands of Antony MILLS' executor, Steven KENT, in Virginia...signed 19 September 1830, David PISTOLE...guardian was paid for traveling to and from Virginia.

page 281   CAMPBELL - E. M. CAMPBELL, guardian accounts - recorded 3 December 1830, as guardian of James T. and Samuel P. CAMPBELL.

page 281   MURPHY - Inventory of Nathaniel MURPHY, deceased - recorded 3 December 1830 - items included "one Yankee clock"...signed Robert MACK, administrator, 20 September 1830.

page 282   POLK - Settlement with James K. POLK and James WALKER, executors, of Samuel POLK, deceased - recorded 30 January 1830...paid E. P. MC NEILL, Samuel MC DOWELL, M. HELM, D. N. SANSOM, J. B. HAYS, John NIXON, S. F. CALDWELL, John CHAPMAN, Samuel RANKIN, J. S. WALKER and Company, BRADSHAW and KIMES, Polly ASTON, J. T. FARRIS, _____ BAKER, John KIMES, James H. PIPER (for tuition), W. PHELAN, D. MARTIN, Thos. J. HARRISON, Cuffy WOODSON, S. M. CALDWELL, J. P. HALL, H. LANGTRY, J. THOMPSON, George M. MARTIN (for Harden), Will B. CALDWELL, G. B. COCKBURN, F. E. POLK, illegible, M. D. COOPER, Will BROWN, James DOBBINS, L. E. CALDWELL, R. HENDERSON, J. NOTGRASS, Jane POLK, FREEMAN and ELISON, B. R. HARRIS and Company, R. H. POLK, B. TURNER, J. N. WALKER, WILL (shoemaker), L. KETCHUM, _____ KEESEE, James PURDY, James BROWN, R. J. NELSON, O. C. HAYS, James H. POPE, CRAIGHEAD and COBBS, A. JOHNSTON, A. O. HARRIS, J. W. POLK,

W. H. POLK, S. W. POLK, W. C. FLOURNOY, BERRYHILL,
D. LAIRD, William ALEXANDER, M. J. ROBERTSON...
expenses to go to Western District - 25 days self and
horse from 25 September to 23 October 1828...paid
William WILLIAMSON's boy Tom for assisting at funeral
of S. POLK, deceased...self and horse three days in
examining and surveying lands in bedford county...
paid James LANSDOWN for engraving on tombstone of
S. POLK.

page 287   POLK - James WALKER's executor of Samuel POLK accounts
            - many were the same as for James K. POLK as listed
            above...D. CHAPELL, J. P. HALL, H. G. KERBY, R. A.
            CARTER, P. KELSIE, M. O. LEETCH...judgements, sales
            of land, James POLK's share $1,000, William H. POLK's
            share $1,500., Samuel W. POLK's share, $1,500.,
            signed James WALKER.

page 292   WILSON - Guardian settlement - recorded 28 December
            1830 - minor heirs of Charles WILSON, Richard CRAIG,
            guardian..."Widow WILSON (Mrs. CRAIG's) portion"...
            "boarding and clothing for three minors"...accounts
            dating from 1826.

page 293   CARUTHERS - Robert CARUTHERS, deceased, inventory -
            recorded 28 December 1830 - buyers were John B. HAYS,
            Isaac K. DANIEL, Stoke SANFORD, note on Thomas LITTLE,
            of North Carolina, signed John D. LOVE, 20 December
            1830.

page 293   GLOVER - Guardian return - recorded 28 December 1830
            - Robert MC NUT to Andrew GLOVER as guardian, signed
            20 December 1830, Robert MC NUT.

page 293   PATTON - Polly PATTON, guardian, report - recorded
            28 December 1830 - minor heirs of George PATTON,
            deceased, with Mary PATTON as guardian. There are
            six wards: Pettillo C. PATTON, Mary M. PATTON,
            Elizabeth Jane PATTON, Margaret A. PATTON, Susan
            PATTON, and George W. C. PATTON, signed, Polly PATTON.

page 294   GIBBONS - Inventory of Samuel G. GIBBONS - recorded
            21 January 1831 - accounts of Robert S. SHARP, Swain
            W. WOOLARD (doubtful), Robert TURNER, Thos. S. LOGAN
            (doubtful), Daniel MC INTOSH, _____ CHEATHAM, Henry
            HOOK, Francis N. MORGAN (bad note), J. M. HOGUE (bad
            note)...one negro Joshua, blacksmith...negroes named
            ...Bible...many books, signed Edward W. DALE, executor.

page 295   CROW - Benjamin CROW'S inventory - recorded 5 January
            1831 - notes and accounts of Ephraim SHOCKLEY, David
            LAIRD, William VOORHIES, John MC CORPIN, William
            MILLER, James Tidwell, Joshua GUEST, John O. BROWN,
            Thomas MADDIN.

page 297   VINCENT - Inventory of Thomas W. VINCENT, deceased -
            recorded 5 January 1831 - six negroes named...notes
            on Allen DODD, George W. JENNINGS, Richard SCOT
            (desperate), C. BONE (desperate), J. HICKMAN (desper-
            ate), JOHNSTON and SAMPLE (?), George CAMPBELL, Royal
            FERGUSON...signed William B. VINCENT, administrator.

page 297   KENNEDY - Inventory of James KENNEDY - recorded 5
             January 1831 - buyers: Francis KENNEDY, Lucy G.
             DILEHAY, Joseph DAVIS, William M. KENNEDY, James
             SAWYERS, John YOUNG, John BALDRIDGE, Robert MC DANIEL,
             John BILLS, Mary KENNEDY, Jeremiah HOLT, Wm. OSBURN;
             signed Thomas and Francis KENNEDY, administrators.

page 298   MILLER - Inventory of John B. H. MILLER - recorded
             5 January 1831 - signed James HUEY, administrator.

page 299   HENDERSON - Inventory of property of James HENDERSON,
             deceased - recorded 14 May 1831 - included one negro,
             side saddle, and one watch...

page 299   WALKER - Account of Sale of Griffith WALKER, deceased
             - recorded 14 May 1831 - buyers: Doct. B. CRAWFORD,
             Green GRAYHAM, Geo. YOUNG, Thos. WALKER, John BULLOCK,
             Powton GORDON, Edward H. CHAFFIN, Noah SMITH, Elisha
             PAYTON, Charles SOWELL, signed Sealy WALKER and
             William P. POOL.

page 300   WEBSTER - Inventory of John G. WEBSTER, deceased -
             recorded 14 May 1831 - executors, Patrick MAGUIRE,
             James DOBBINS, and Jonathan WEBSTER; 18 negroes named.

page 301   EASTHAM - Inventory of William EASTHAM, deceased -
             recorded 16 May 1831 - note on Tennessee ROPER, due
             bill on Arthur POWELL (desperate)...negroes...note
             on P. PARCHMAN, dated 1823 (desperate)...signed
             Tennessee ROPER, administrator.

page 302   WILLIAMS - Account of Sale of Permenas WILLIAMS,
             deceased - recorded 17 May 1831 - made 30 January
             1830 - buyers: Mumford SMITH, Creed (Crud) T.
             WORTHAM, James S. CRAIG, Benjamin C. WORTHAM, Isaac
             CURRY, Wm. COCKRILL, Thos. SIMMS, C. W. KNIGHT. Thos.
             WORTHAM, Anderson WILLIAMS, James W. BRISCOE, Nathan-
             iel WILLIS, Marshall D. SPAIN, Robt. C. MARAN, George
             CRADDOCK, Thos. HOWARD, N. W. BRISCOE, Wm. GOODLOE,
             Isaac CHERRY, Anderson WILLIAMS retned BURKET's place
             ...signed Duke WILLIAMS.

page 303   HENDERSON - Account of Sale of James HENDERSON -
             recorded 17 May 1831 - buyers: John H. PHILIPS,
             Robert M. GALLOWAY, James SH____, Samuel PERKINS,
             Widow HENDERSON, Michael FRY, Robert ? , William
             USSERY, Wiley RICHARDSON, John GRADEN, Eli USSERY,
             John BRADEN, Wilson HENDERSON, Joseph FRY, Joseph
             PAULIN, Milton STACY, Samuel ? , Eli G. BRADSHAW,
             Wm. SHIELDS, Peter USERY, Wilie P. RICHESON, Robert
             A. CARUTHERS, Edmond ZANE, Felix BRADEN, Edmund LANE,
             John G. BRADEN, Newton SHIELDS, Malone STACY, Cather-
             ine PUCKET; Wilson HENDERSON and William USERY, admin-
             istrators.

page 305   WILKES - Inventory of John WILKES, deceased - record-
             ed 18 May 1831 - note on Edmond WILLES (WILKES)...
             note to be "paid at the death of the widow"...note on
             Joseph FRY, James DEARIN, John AMIS, Philip SMITH,
             William STONE; signed 12 June 1830, William WILKS,
             John WILKS, administrators.

page 306   GULLETT - List of sale of Samuel GULLETT, deceased - recorded 18 May 1831 - no buyers given; signed Samuel S. HOLDING. (Abstractor's note: his name was first given as James GULLETT in the entry.)

page 306   WILKS - List of sales of John WILKS, deceased - recorded 18 May 1831 - buyers: Richard BENTLY, Josiah ALDERSON, John BILLS, Joseph A. ROYALL, Samuel PATRICK, William MC WILLIAMS; administrators: William WILKS, John WILKS.

page 307   MILLIKEN - List of sale of Baxter MILLIKEN, deceased - 18 May 1831, recorded - buyers: Widow, John W. PICKARD, Mark GRIMES, Davis S. CRAIG, William MITCHELL, William B. CADES, Jas. STOCKARD, Caleb LINDSEY, Saml. DIXON, William STOCKARD, Joseph GLAWSON, Taylor PICKARD, David H. CRAIG, Samuel D. EDMONDS, Miss MILLICAN, Wm. CROMWELL, Jas. S. CRAIG, Wm. DUNCAN, Wm. PICKARD, John LINDSEY, Josiah HOLLAND, George LANG. Signed, Caleb LINDSEY, administrator.

page 308   MAYES - Account of sale of David MAYES - recorded 18 May 1831 - buyers: William GRAY, David FLY, Thomas OAKLEY, George A. PEELER, Sparkman SKELLEY, Benjamin GUNN, William ERWIN, Briton GARDNER, Elias P. MAYES, John KERSEY, Micagah PAINE, James OLIVER, Jorden ADKINSON, Jonathan ASHWORTH, Moses HANKS, Ransom HOWELL, William EDMONDSON, George MADOX, William KERSEY, William F. TWILLA, Robin OAKLEY, Roland OAKLEY, Moses C_____, _____ as OAKLEY, William OAKLEY, Willey MAYS, Goodwin MAYS, William GARNER, Stephen OAKLEY, Isom ANNAND, Robert OAKLEY, Jesse TEMPLES, Washington OAKLEY, Allen MC CASCALL ...signed 26 March 1830, William GRAY, administrator.

page 310   CRAIG - List of Sales of William CRAIG, deceased - recorded 20 May 1831 - buyers: Edmond WILLIAMS, Richard LEWIS, G. A. CONN, Abram BEARD, William BROWN, Turner NICHOLS, Aaron VESTALL, Moses LATTA, Robert CRAIG, A. J. ALEXANDER, John T. VESTAL, J. C. CRAIG, Richard CRAIG, Abraham BEARD, Abram ROGERS, John MOORE, C. B. HADLEY, James NOTGRASS, Sophia CRAIG, Ephraim WANTLIN...signed Robert CAMPBELL, Junior, administrator.

page 311   GULLETT - Inventory of James GULLET, deceased - recorded 21 May 1831 - notes on BROOKS, TURNER, WEATHERSPOON, JOHNSON...signed Samuel S. HOLDING, administrator.

page 311   HART - Inventory and account of sale of Moses HART, deceased - recorded 20 May 1831 - John Y. CARRONE, John APPLEBY, Robert FULLETON, William APPLEBY, Polly HART (bought quite a bit), Charles HARDISON, Mathew MOORE, A. BOSTICK, C. VARNER, John RAY, Elisha HURT, John RHEA, George FISHER, Robert BELL, Caleb HEADLEE, John VINCENT, James YARBOROUGH, James BRITAIN, James HUGHS, Joel HURT, William MC CLURE, John HILL, Robert WRIGHT, Samuel D. APPLEBY, John MACHLEHANNON, Jacob FISHER, Henry KOONCE, John F. CARR, George ROANE, George EWING...note on Joshua DAVIDSON...provision for widow, signed Caleb HEADLEE, administrator. (Abstractor's note: the surname appears both as HART and HURT.)

page 316   PATTERSON - List of sales of Jared PATTERSON, de-
            ceased - recorded 23 May 1831 - made 5 November 1829
            - buyers: Elias PEYTON, Michael John KITRELL, George
            W. MAXWELL, DALE and DUNCAN, ___ansbury, E. W. DALE,
            J. MARR, Dudley G. JOHNSON, C. TODD, J. S. CRAWFORD,
            Jno. W. JONES, Wm. COVEY, Robert MC DANIEL, Alexander
            J. HAINES, James MATHEWS, James BRANCH, Levin COVEY,
            Josiah PERRY, Samuel H. FARINGSORTH, John B. THOMAS,
            Merideth HELM, Robert RANSOM, William B. SMITH,
            Samuel NEELY, Ann PATTERSON, Jno. BARNS, Jane PATTER-
            SON, James WARR...signed Robert PATTERSON, administra-
            tor.

page 317   MOORE - List of sale of Nathaniel MOORE, deceased -
            recorded 23 May 1831 - sold 4 December 1829 - buyers:
            John B. THOMAS, James T. MOORE, William COVEY, Levin
            L. COVEY, Joseph BROWN, Wido ALDERSON...distributed
            to Widow MOORE items according to the will...signed
            Levin L. COVEY, executor.

page 318   PILLOW - Inventory of Gideon PILLOW, deceased -
            recorded 23 May 1831 - 15 negroes named...bond on
            Green WOODS, Joseph TALBOT; notes on Asa HOLLAND,
            Price M. GARNER, S. and C. BAYNE, John PORTER,
            William BELL, J. STILES, W. C. BLAKE, A. PILLOW...
            receipt of John PILLOW...note on William BALL, David
            LYNCH, James ROSS, Ezor EVANS, Z. PAY; title to a
            lot in Florence, Alabama...accounts against Peter
            JOHNSTON, Yerbey ADKERSON, W. MC CANDLASS, John
            BEAVER, Charles W__MAN, N. BOND; note on John SLOAN;
            A. B. BRADFORD's note...signed Granville A. PILLOW,
            Gideon J. PILLOW, administrators.

page 321   MAYS - Inventory of Abraham MAYS, deceased - recorded
            26 May 1831.

page 321   STOCKARD - Inventory of James STOCKARD - recorded
            26 May 1831 - sold 27 and 29 March 1829 - buyers
            were Susan STOCKARD, Joseph DAVIS, Doct. CONKEY,
            Joseph GILMORE, Nathan COFFEY, George JOHNSTON, John
            B. THOMAS, Robert MATTHEWS, illegibles, Andrew CALD-
            WELL, Alexr. OSBURN, Thomas CALDWELL, Grant A. JOHN-
            SON, John R. BOYD, John M__TONS, John MACK, S.PICKARD,
            J. H. CAMERON, A. LOONEY...rent on what is known as
            the BOAZE (BOASE) place or plantation...signed
            Abraham LOONEY, administrator.

page 324   WEBSTER - John G. WEBSTER, deceased, account of sale
            - recorded 26 May 1831 - sold ___ July 1826, no
            buyers given, signed Patrick MAGUIRE, Jonathan
            WEBSTER, James DOBBINS.

page 326   GALOWAY - Account of Sale of Samuel GALOWAY, deceased
            - recorded 30 May 1831 - sold 12 November 1829 -
            buyers: David CHADWELL, John GALLOWAY, E. H. MC
            GLANE, S. USERY, B. M. JONES, illegibles, ___
            ALDRIDGE, William HUGHS, N. W. WARD, John T. CARR,
            N. WOLLARD, James PATTERSON, Wm. BASS, Wm. APPLEBY,
            John M. WILLIAMS, George ALLEN, D. CHADWELL, Bill
            JONES, Thos. BLACKWELL, Andw. SLAUGHTER, E. C.
            MC CLAIN, Charles HARDISON, Moses HURT, Wm. ALDRIDGE,
            Saml. SMITH, Jeffrey BECK, Nancy ALDRIDGE, ___HANCOCK,

James LONG, David SHIRES, G. J. ALLEN, H. DARK, John
RAY, James LANE, Joseph BERRY, R. B. MC GOWAN, Tidance
LANE, DALE and DUNCAN, John JOHNSON, Spencer BROWN,
Jefrey BECK, Eli AMICK, Wm. ALDRDIGE, John GORDON,
Spencer C. BROWN, W. T. WILSON, Joseph ROBINSON,
Silas HOLLAND, John G. NAPIER, James RUSSELL, Jonathan
SMITH, James ROBISON, C. SHIRE, Peter HELTON, William
WALKER, Silas WOLLARD...signed Edward W. DALE, admin-
istrator.

page 329   KITRELL - List of sale of John A. KITRELL - recorded
1 June 1831 - Robert HENDERSON, administrator...
buyers, William HENDERSON, Arona CLARK, Amos DUNCAN,
Samuel KITRELL, Samuel SMITH...A list of notes on
men in Alabama "I don't know wheather they are good
or not: Matthew D. THOMASON, James THOMASON, Josiah
GOODING, H. S. THOMASON"...note on James HODGE of
Columbia...signed Robert HENDERSON.

page 330   WILKS - List of sale of Minor WILKS, deceased -
recorded 1 June 1831 - made 11 December 1829; buyers
were James PICKENS, James WALKER, James A. DLATON,
James MC CONNEL, Adam MEACE, William WILKES, Alexander
MEECE, Gregory GANOWAY, William GOOMM, D. BILLS, Bird
HALL, Hampton WADE, Thos. WILKS, Burrel WILKES, Siras
H. BARTLETT, John HUCKABY, John HUEY, David WILKS,
Joseph EDMONDSON, Cole COLLIER, Willis HUEY, Richard
WILKS, William H. PICKENS, James PHILIPS...signed
James CAMPBELL.

page 331   GILBREATH - Inventory of John GILBREATH, deceased -
recorded 1 June 1831 - John GILBREATH, Junior, admin-
istrator of John GILBREATH, Senior...claims on John
FISHER, Edward FISHER, Bowling FISHER, Daniel FISHER,
George FISHER, arising from trade of land...signed
John GALBREATH.

page 332   YOUNGBLOOD - Inventory and list of sale of A. G.
YOUNGBLOOD, deceased - recorded 1 June 1831 - taken
11 November 1830...notes of D. G. BRADLEY, J. G.
CRAIG, William HUNTER, John SPINDLE, E. M. LONG,
Peter JOHNSON, John S. SLAUGHTER, Wm. A. MAXWELL;
book accounts: KNIGHT and BREWSTER, Amos COHORN,
J. T. SMITH, John BLACK, Wm. P. PILLOW, Wm. KENDALL,
B. R. HARRIS, Thompson ARCHER, Mrs. Mary BERRY, W.
H. BALDRIDGE, MILLER and HUNTER, J. B. LEFTWICH, J.
P. SMITH, C. TURNER, J. Y. BALDRIDGE, Henry TUCKNESS,
John CRENSHAW, H. HOGE, Joseph GRIFFIN, S. P. JORDAN,
John ELLIOTT, Jas. SAMPTER (desperate), Amos JOHNSON
(desperate), J. P. BALLARD (desperate), P. PENN
(desperate), D. B. CRAWFORD (desperate), W. M. WILSON
(desperate), J. H. ALEXANDER (desperate), B. W.
WILSON (desperate), G. KELSEY (desperate), J. KIM-
BRELL (desperate), Z. L. GOUR, Jas. BISHOP, Jesse
ELFTWICH, M. L. BURNS, E. DOKE, Mrs. KIRK, John
JONES...hiring of slaves...some bank notes "counter-
feit"...signed A. H. BUCKNER, E. YOUNGBLOOD, administrator, administratrix.

page 334   HART - List of Sale of Joseph HART, deceased -
recorded 2 June 1831 - taken 11 December 1829 -
buyers: Isaac D. VANHOOK, John MAGIL, Hugh BRADFORD,

Jesse HART, Henry NIZER, A. C. REESE, Samuel AKIN,
Henry KINSLY, George BRADBURY, A. CATHEY, J. M.
RUSSELL, Henry RUSSELL, Josiah GLOTHY, John MC
MURRAY, James H. RUSSELL, Alexander CATHEY, A. T.
ISOM, James YOUNGER, Robert FOSTER, James T. TURNER,
James ROBERSON, James JOSEY, William WESTER, John
WALKER, Jonathan WEBSTER, Robert FRIERSON, Henry
KINZER, William HART, John MC GILL, Nancy HART,
William CATHEY, George KENNEDY, Jesse GRAY, John
HART, F. COOK, William LOCKE, George CHAMBERS,
William MALONE, Jane HART, Abner PASTOLE, Peter A.
KIRK, William DUE, James R. GARNER...slaves named
and to whom sold...signed Jesse HART, A. CATHEY,
administrators.

page 337   PICKARD - List of sales of John J. PICKARD, deceased
            - recorded 4 June 1831 - buyers were Francis PICKARD,
            Samuel STEWART, William STOCKARD, William WILLIAMS,
            Isaac PICKARD, Alexr. A. PICKARD, Robert HOWARD,
            Alten PICKARD, James MC GOWAN, John W. BAILEY, Joseph
            STOCKARD, William WHITTED, Allen PICKARD, Henry
            WILLIAMS, Robert GRIMES, John GRIMES...signed William
            PICKARD, administrator.

page 338   POLK - Inventory of Franklin E. POLK - recorded 6
            June 1831 - James WALKER, administrator...page 339,
            inventory of notes and accounts on books of Franklin
            E. POLK: D. C. BROWN, G. W. WEAVER, _____ FITZ-
            GERALD, E. HUNTER, Wm. HAMLETT, T. S. ROGERS, William
            C. CAMPBELL, Jno. D. ALDERSON, George C. HADDOCK,
            John B. _____, John MOORE, James M. WHITE, John H.
            WOOLRIDGE, Luke BYNUM, James A. WRIGHT, Wm. SIMMONS,
            Walter S. JENKINS, John S. CRAIG, Rebecca SLADE...
            paid "for blacksmith done in 1828" and remaining on
            books personal property conveyed "in trust to James
            K. POLK and myself"...consists of eight negroes,
            named, and for four negroes ages from 5 to 7 years...
            signed 14 March 1831, James WALKER, executor.

page 340   POLK - Will of Franklin E. POLK - recorded 7 June
            1831 - my father the late Samuel POLK...my nother
            Jane POLK...brother James K. POLK...brother in law
            James WALKER...all my brothers and sisters...James
            K. POLK to get "old watch chain"; "my land on which
            I live"...land in western district (Hardeman County)
            gotten from William LEECH...signed 18 January 1831,
            witnesses, George MOORE, _____ MOORE, Henry HADLEY.

page 340   FOSTER - Non-cupative Will of Booker FOSTER - record-
            ed 8 June 1831 - On 31 January 1831 "This day BOOKER
            FOSTER was wounded by the fall of a limb so that he
            died he called his brother in law and said that he
            wanted his wife to have all his property and that he
            did not want his brothers to have any part." Signed
            8 February 1831 by Carney FOSTER and Wilson HENDERSON.

page 341   WILLIS - Inventory of William W. WILLIS, deceased -
            recorded 8 June 1831 - taken 31 December 1830...
            negroes named and ages given...number of medical
            books...signed J. S. WILLIS.

page 341   VINCENT - List of sale of Thos. W. VINCENT - recorded
            8 June 1831 - held on 15 January 1831 - no buyers
            given.

221

page 342   WILLIS - List of notes and accounts of William W. WILLIS, deceased - recorded 8 June 1831. Notes: Jesse WHITLEY, Wm. H. EDWARDS, Jas. MOORE, Abell WALTON, Jesse WATSON, Wm. C. CAMPBELL, Armstead AKIN, estate of Right KERBY, Wm. Z. JONES, Thos. ROBERTS, James T. MORRIS, Hellen G. BOND, Solomon BUNCH, Geo. S. ARNOLD, Nathaniel CHEAIRS, D. DAWS, Josiah JACKSON, John YATES, Andrew NEELY, Reuben MAYS, Hugh BROWN, _____ KNOTGRASS, Senior, Bennett BLACKBURN, Robt. LOCKRIDGE, Edmond HOLT, Turner NICHOLS, _____ CHUMB-LEY, John ARON, Junior, Jno. C. SPILER, Britain BILY (or BARLY), Robert SHEEDON, Danl. C. BROWN, C. MORAN, Francis GORDON, James R. FOSTER, Wm. T. DOTSON, Jno. KILCREASE, Samuel DUNLAP, Zerrill MINOR, Thos. J. GOFF, R. H. SIMMONS, Joel B. SANDERS, Aligany MAGUIRE, Geo. S. ARNOLD, Milton CARTER, Doct. CRISP, Francis GORDON; signed John S. WILLIS, administrator of Doct. Wm. W. WILLIS, deceased.

page 343   SANFORD - Inventory of estate of James T. SANFORD, deceased - recorded 9 June 1831 - taken 3 January 1831; 1300 acres in Maury County...notes on Robert SANFORD...many negroes named...signed, James BLACK, administrator.

page 345   MC LEAN - Inventory of John MC LEAN, deceased - recorded 9 June 1831 - sold 4 January 1831 - Rowan C. BRALY, administrator...buyers were Mrs. MC LEAN, widow, John RICHIE, Thos. CHEEK, Rowan C. BRALY, Robt. PHILIPS, Davis WILIS, E. MC NIGHT, Wm. COLLINS, Isaac H. HILL, Henry COLLINS, Jos. NANCE, Levi COCHRON, Berry TALLY, Hugh B. BIGHAM, W. H. PHILIPS, Freeman HOLLINGSWORTH, Wm. NIX, John LONDON, Thos. PARKS, Harris CLARK, Alexr. OSBORN, Thos. ROSS. Wm. KENNEDY, Jas. KENNEDY, Bens RICHIE, Wm. TILMAN, John BOYL, Starling CARROLL, Jas. ELLIOTT.

page 348   MURPHY - List of sale of N. MURPHY, deceased - record-ed 9 June 1831 - buyers were M. P. MURPHY, T. REAVES, W. S. EMBRY, John HUCHASON, Wm. BROWN, Wm. BRIDGES, Jno. DILLAHAN, Stephen SMITH, J. H. NANCE, J. GARRETT, Jiles T. HARRIS, Robert CATESBY, John REAVES, Sally REAVES, Jas. HOLLAND, M. STONE, Jno. DILLAHAY, L. VAUGHAN, Jno. GORDON, Daniel ROANE, O. STEWARD; signed R. MACK, administrator.

page 349   GRAY - Non-cupative will of William GRAY, deceased - recorded 10 June 1831 - taken 22 February 1831 - deposition of Elizabeth FARRIS and Polly FARRIS who say: "they were present and called upon by William GRAY, deceased, during his last sickness, and the said William GRAY, deceased, at that time in his sound memory who verbally made his last will as follows": ...Elizabeth M. BARR, twin daughter of Hugh and Sarah BARR to get bed and furniture...will ordered to be admitted for probate.

page 350   PETTILLO - Inventory of John L. PETTILLO, deceased, recorded 16 June 1831 - negroes named and ages given; mentions one negro who was mortgaged to John D. LOVE; note on Luke BYNUM, Lindsay ARNOLD, John W. TASWELL, D. DEANS, William FIELDS, John ARNOLD, KNOX and CROW, J. PITTILLO, J. KENNEDY, J. C. PATTON; signed J. PETTILLO.

page 351   CHADDOCK - Inventory and account of sale of George
            CHADDOCK, deceased - recorded 18 June 1831 - taken
            1 October 1830 - buyers: Susan B. CHADDOCK, James
            G. FRIERSON, Jason B. CHADDOCK, E. A. NEELY, Thos.
            P. WORTHAM, Jas. J. CRAIG, Wm. C. BLAKE, John T.
            MACON, James W. BRISCOE, S. H. ARMSTRONG, Anderson
            BROOKS, Wiley BYNUM, Duke WILLIAMS, Harden WILLIAMS,
            Westley BYNUM, Edmond WILLIAMS, F. E. POLK, Henry
            WILLIAMS, Mumford SMITH, C. W. KNIGHT, Wm. WORTHAM,
            Elias PEYTON, Joseph O. CROSS, James BEAKLEY, Tolivar
            GOODMAN, Thos. C. GREENE, Wm. WISEMAN, William COOPER,
            Henry SMITH, William STOCKARD, William KINDLE, N. W.
            BRISCOE, Robert WORTHAM, G. W. SHERMAN, William
            SPENCER, some illegibles...notes, Alexander MC MILLAN,
            John BLACK, Andrew GOODE, Elijah H_____, Solomon
            WEBB; signed William H. HUNTER, 20 June 1830.

page 354   FARRIS - Guardian return on minor heirs of William
            FARRIS, deceased - recorded 21 June 1831 - mentions
            hire of negroes, widow's part, schooling James R.
            FARRIS, William FARRIS, John FARRIS, David FARRIS,
            Fanny's schooling, Elizabeth's schooling...settlement
            with Jefferson FARRIS...paid vouchers for James R.,
            William, John, Mary, Elizabeth, David, and Robert L.
            ...to make them equal with Mary FARRIS' part...signed
            1 January 1831...notes on S. PORTER, H. A. MEMAKIN,
            Jane FARRIS, rent of land..."The land is Joint
            between Jefferson FARRIS and the minor heirs"...
            negroes were joint between widow and minor heirs.

page 355   HILL - Will of James HILL, deceased - recorded 22
            June 1831 - wife Jane...daughter Olivia...son Alex-
            ander...daughter Matilda...son Middleton...son Thomas
            ...son William...daughter Jane CASKEY...son James B.
            ...land on Silver Creek...son William H. HILL, Execu-
            tor...signed 25 December 1830; witnesses were James
            BOWDEN, James M. BOWDEN.

page 356   WARDLOW - Will of William W. WARDLOW, deceased -
            recorded 22 June 1831 - nephew William W. EUSTACE a
            watch as a memorial of my affection...to Mrs. Sarah
            WATSON my wardrobe...my sister Mary Ann WARDLOW of
            Virginia...William H. NEWSOM of Maury County to be
            executor and to dispose of my drugs and medicine...
            signed William W. WARDLOW; witnesses, George G.
            SKIPWITH, D. N. SANSOM.

page 357   MIDDLETON - Will of John MIDDLETON, deceased -
            recorded 23 June 1831 - wife Rebecca...son Drury...
            "having heretofore given to each of my children"...
            son Alfred to be executor...signed 17 April 1831;
            witnesses, A. CATHEY, Wm. CHALK.

page 358   ALEXANDER - List of sale of Obediah ALEXANDER -
            recorded 23 June 1831 - taken 5 January 1831 - buyers
            were Jane ALEXANDER, W. D. BROWN, Alexander FARRIS,
            John ALEXANDER, Stephen JONES, Alexander F. WILIE,
            Thomas YOUNG, Anna ALEXANDER, Peter JOICE, Eli
            ALEXANDER, James COBB, Andrew ALEXANDER, Richard
            MILLER, William COOPER, Andrew HILL, Andrew BROWN,
            Jethro HOWELL, Tol GOODMAN, E. B. LITTLEFIELD,
            Richard YOUNG, Jesse GRAY, William GOB, Noah WHITE,

J. MC GAW, R. L. FURGASON, N. YOUNG, several illegibles...Nathaniel YOUNG, administrator.

page 359 GILLEY - Will of James GILLEY, deceased - recorded
   June 1831 - wife Jane...money in hand of Samuel
FARRIS and George M. WHELER..."for the schooling and
raising up of my poor little children"...son Alexander
..."my five beloved little daughters", Isabella M.
GILLEY, Eleanor A. GILLEY, Jane M. GILLEY, Martha
Matilda GILLEY, Mary Ann GILLEY..."also Sarah ROBERT-
SON, daughter of my wife"...signed James M. GILLEY,
25 May 1830; witnesses were William GARRETT, Josiah
WATSON, Hugh CAMPBELL.

page 361 WILLIS - List of sale of William W. WILLIS, deceased
- recorded 25 June 1831 - taken and sold 3 January
1831 - buyers: A. A. CAMPBELL, Jno. T. MACON, Jno.
S. WILLIS, A. GOOD, John WOOLRIDGE, R. GOAD, Thomas
HAYNES, William BROWN, Gilbert ELLIS, William HABLETT,
Chesley HALEY, G. BAKER, B. BLACKMAN, Jno. H. POINTER,
John POLK, Turner NICHOLS, B. F. ALEXANDER, James
BRIGGS, N. P. STONE, M. FITZGERALD, C. CAPERTON,
   KENNEDY, S. M. _____, James G. KELSO, Thomas
B. PORTER, George MOORE, John F. CRAIG, R. B. _____,
K___ CHERRY, G. L. VOORHIES, several illegibles,
Nancy B. WILKES.

page 363 HARDISON - List of sale of William HARDISON, deceased
- recorded 28 June 1831 - buyers were Humphrey
HARDISON, Jeremiah SWIM, Cosby SCOTT, John DERRYBERRY,
Charles HARDISON, Polly HARDISON, Joshua HARDISON,
   BONE, Park STREET, John SMITH, P. CROFT;
Ezra HARDISON, Eli HARDISON, Asa HARDISON, Ira HARDI-
SON, James HARDISON, Edward HARDISON, David EAGLE,
Joseph LONG, Robert CROFTON, John GORDEN, B. DAVIDSON,
John A. POWEL, James M. BAKER, Robert RANKIN, Jordon
THOMPSON, H. ALMON, William P. KETCHAM, Alexander
WILSON, John WILLIAMS, Joseph HARDISON, Jeremiah
SWAIM, Jackson POWEL...notes on William WILLIAMS,
David CAGLE, John POWELL, Lorenzo HITCHCOCK, Josiah
WEATHERBY, some illegibles, James JOHNSON, Solomon
K. JENKINS, _____ JACKSON, James ATKISON, Burrel
JOHNSON, John P. BOND, John A. POWELL, David CHADWELL,
C. SHIRES, John SMITH, Simon JOHNSTON, Samuel C. LOVE,
Samuel BLAKELY, David EAGLE, A. O. HARRIS, William
SMITH, Joseph B. WALLIS, Alexander SLAVOR, David
JACKSON, Isah WEATHERLY, Daniel C. BROWN, William
CHUN, Robert WALKER, Thomas LONG, John W. HANCOCK,
Thos. MURDOCK, Joshua HARDISON, Bird S. HURT.

page 366 FOX - Widow's allowance for Mary FOX - recorded
   June 1831 - widow of William FOX, deceased...
allowance made by Joel HARDISON and William LIGGET
and illegible.

page 367 BRIGGS - Inventory of estate of James BRIGGS, de-
ceased - recorded 29 June 1831 - made 18 April 1831
- negroes named...note on John ROWLAND, Walter S.
JENKINS, John BRIGGS, James C. O'RILEY, John CHEATHAM,
Henry D. DILLARD, Henry BRIGGS in North Carolina,
Detancy CHYSER in North Carolina, some illegibles,
Milton CARTER...signed Isaac BRIGGS, administrator
of James BRIGGS, deceased.

page 369   GLOVER - Inventory of Spicy GLOVER, deceased -
            recorded 31 June 1831 - by Joshua DAVIDSON...negroes
            named and ages given.

page 369   ATKINSON - Inventory of William ATKINSON, deceased -
            recorded 30 June 1831 - negroes named...signed
            14 March 1831 by John ATKINSON.

page 369   FOX - Inventory of sale of William FOX, deceased -
            recorded 30 June 1831; buyers were William LIGGETT,
            Mary FOX, John FOX, Charles HARDISON, Mathew MOORE,
            Joel HARDISON, Charles HUGGINS, George RONE, Nathan-
            iel WOLLARD, William E. SMITH, Mrs. FOX, Abraham
            FARRAR, B. M. JONES, Pervina FOX, George COX, George
            HASKEL, Nathaniel SMITH, A. BOSTICK, David TUTTLE,
            Miles MC AFEE, Pervinis FOX, Thomason GULLETT, George
            COCKE, Fendle MARTIN, John TOMBS, Isaac HUGGINS,
            William BARHAM, Chs. HARDISON, Josiah C. BANCOMB,
            Wyatt _____ HILL, Pleasant G. HARDEN.

page 371   STONE - Will of Richard STONE - recorded 5 July 1831
            - to Robert BLACKWELL and Charity his wife one
            dollar having given him a full proportion before...
            to Scarlot MADIN and Polly his wife one dollar having
            given him a full proportion before...Sally L. STONE,
            heir and representative of my deceased son Richard
            STONE...wife Sally...son William...daughter Nancy...
            signed 16 April 1831; witnesses were Michael ROBERTS,
            Archibald SCOTT, William ORR.

page 372   FARRIS - Account of sale of Josiah FARRIS, deceased -
            recorded 6 July 1831 - John MC GILL, administrator...
            buyers were John SMITH, John FARRIS, John MC GILL,
            Isaac L. FARRIS, Ned MC FADDEN, James H. COOPER,
            "The widdow", John N. BROWN, Caleb FARRIS, Andrew
            CRAWFORD, Elijah EDMONDS, John HEARST, Doctor SMITH,
            Campbell STRICKLIN, Simpson PATTON, Isham ECHOLS,
            Benjamin MC GAW, Robert HILL.

page 373   SMITH - List of sale of Joshua SMITH, deceased -
            recorded 6 July 1831 - buyers were Richard F. SMITH,
            John BOOKER, George HUDSPETH, Joel HUDSPETH, William
            HUDSPETH, George CAMPBELL, Robert CARTS, Robert
            COURTS, Thomas HUDSPETH, Elizabeth SOWELL, William
            SOWELL, John HOLCOMB...signed Richard F. SMITH,
            administrator.

page 374   DEAL - Settlement - Joseph DEAL - recorded 2 July
            1831, signed 12 May 1820...faded entry.

page 374   CHRISTIAN - Settlement of Isham CHRISTIAN, deceased -
            recorded 2 July 1831 - commissioners appointed
            December term 1813 and were John MATHEWS and Abner
            PILLOW...the legatees were Nathaniel CHRISTIAN,
            Patsy CHRISTIAN, Nancy CHRISTIAN, Jane CHRISTIAN,
            Betsy CHRISTIAN, Isham CHRISTIAN, Charles CHRISTIAN,
            Zelpha Charles CHRISTIAN, Rhody CHRISTIAN, sons and
            daughters of Isham CHRISTIAN and Nancy his wife...
            signed 10 November 1814 by John MATHEWS, Abner
            PILLOW. (Abstractor's note: Charles CHRISTIAN
            repeated twice through error of abstractor.)

page 375   MC CLEAN - List of sale of John MC CLEAN, deceased -
            recorded 29 August 1831 - inventory and amount of
            sale on 4 April 1831 - buyers were James C. RECORD,
            Simon MARSH, Rowan C. BRALY, sale of three negroes
            to William BINGHAM, Elias RAMBO, Alex. BALDRIDGE...
            amount due from North Carolina...amount due LEACY
            from ERWIN's estate in right of the widow from the
            estate of H. BRALY...ERWIN's administrator settle-
            ment made by R. C. BRALY...R. C. BRALY, administrator.

page 375   PETTILLO - Settlement of John L. PETTILLO, estate -
            recorded 30 August 1831 - signed 13 June 1831 by
            James BLACK, Edmund L. WILLIAMS, commissioners.

page 376   HART - Settlement with Joseph HART, deceased - re-
            corded 31 August 1831 - inventory given - hire of
            six negroes, "Phil the property of Campbell HART, a
            minor"...a negro the property of John HART, a negro
            the property of Nancy HART...signed 18 June 1831 -
            John O. CROW, Joseph MC MURRAY, administrators.

page 378   ERWIN - Will of Jonas ERWIN, deceased - recorded
            1 September 1831 - property to be divided between
            "my several heirs and legal representatives"...
            "Plantation on which I now live" to wife Mary ERWIN
            ...to Jane ERWIN wife of Ephraim ERWIN "provided it
            does not extend beyond the time when the youngest of
            the children of the afforesaid Ephraim and Jane shall
            arrive at full age"...in case Jane survive Ephraim,
            husband of Jane...then to (if she remarries) children
            of Ephraim and Jane: Mary J. KELLAM formerly Mary J.
            ERWIN, Susan A. ERWIN, Elizabeth J. ERWIN, William H.
            ERWIN, John F. ERWIN, Jonas N. ERWIN...signed 19 Feb-
            ruary 1830 by Jonas ERWIN...witnesses, H. GROVE, R.
            C. K. MARTIN, James T. CROFFORD.

page 380   LOVE - Supplemental inventory of David LOVE, deceased
            - recorded 9 September 1831 - negroes hired to John
            D. LOVE, SMITH, E. YOUNG, J. B. SANDERS; receipts of
            Thos. MEDCALF, illegibles, Mayson SANDFORD, James
            WRIGHT, Widow MOSLEY, Wright MANNING, W. MAXWELL,
            John ELLIOTT, J. WHITAKER.

page 382   POLK - Will of Marshall T. POLK of Charlotte, North
            Caroline - recorded 14 September 1831 - property
            purchased of Wm. J. ALEXANDER of the estate of the
            late Joseph WILSON to be conveyed to Mrs. Mary WILSON
            ...negroes now in Tennessee with my mother...my wife
            and children...wife Laura...executors to be Washing-
            ton MORRIS and James WALKER of Tennessee; signed 12
            April 1831 by M. T. POLK. Witnessed by D. R. DUNLAP,
            P. C. CALDWELL. Certified by clerk of Mecklenburg
            County, North Carolina by David R. DUNLAP and PINKNEY
            C. CALDWELL, signed Isaac ALEXANDER, clerk of
            Mecklenburg County.

page 383   MURPHY - List of sale of N. MURPHY, deceased - record-
            ed 16 September 1831 - buyers were M. P. MURPHY, W.
            S. EMBRY, T. REAVES, John HUCHERSON, William BROWN,
            William BUYERS, John DILLAHA, Stephen SMITH, John H.
            NANCE, John GARRET, E. REVES.

page 384   ANDREWS - Non-cupative will of John ANDREWS, deceased - recorded 6 October 1831 - the evidence of Levi G. DILLEHAY who swore that John ANDREWS told him "the day before he died" the whole of his property to continue in the hands of his wife, Elizabeth ANDREWS, to support herself and family...the whole of his children then to be divided...evidence of Isaac PATRICKSON also given, sworn 13 June 1831 before Peter WILLIAMS and James L. BALDRIDGE, J.P.'s.

page 384   RICE - Will of Ebenezer RICE, deceased - recorded 6 October 1831 - (faded) said wife...my lawful heirs ...wife Henrietta, son Ebenezer, Junior, daughter Sally MAYSON, son Abel RICE, daughter Patsy MOORE, son Joel, Sally RICE, daughter of my deceased son Rowland...Sally RICE to have one share when she arrives at the age of 18 or is married...to Ebenezer RICE son of the said Rowland RICE was intended to have a share but as "he was bound to me" until he was 21 and "has left me upwards of two years before his time was out" gets only one dollar...son Ebenezer ...signed 1 May (?) 1831, Ebenezer RICE, Senior; witnesses were Thomas MOORE and Richard A. L. WILKES.

page 385   HANKS - Will of Moses HANKS, of Maury County - recorded 6 October 1831 - "my beloved Agatha HANKS"...the whole of my children...son Elijah, executor... witnesses were William FIELDS, Westley WITHERSPOON, William SUIT. (?)

page 386   MC AFEE - List of Sale of Mills MC AFEE, deceased - recorded ___ September 1831 - taken 28 July 1831 (faded entry - buyers were several illegibles, James PATTERSON, David TUTTLE, Jedediah SAND___, Gideon FOX, _____ SCOTT, the Widow, The Widow Betsy MC AFEE, William W. BARHAM, George GLASSCOCK, Joel CURTIS, Cosby SCOTT, William SMITH, John L. CHEEK, Humphrey HARDISON, Robert HENDERS, Samil JACKSON, Charles HARDISON, Anderson HUGGINS, Permanas FOX, Larkin BARDAWAY, Pervines FOX, Robert FRY, John RHEA, Widow ROAN, Polly FOX, John FOX, J. LANDRETH, J. C. BAUCOM, Caleb HEADLEY, Joel HARDISON, George ROAD, George FISHER, John H. WRIGHT, Williamson SMITH, James E. GALLOWAY, Robert THOMPSON, Andrew RYNE, James R. FULLERTON, Mary FOX, Christopher RYNE... hire of negroes...notes and receipts...judgement against the estate of Samuel GULLETT, deceased...a list of notes found among the estate of Mills MC AFEE thought to be desperate...note given to Nancy REED, A. C. MARTIN, Joseph ROGERS, Obediah LANGTON, Jesse RHODES, William GRIFFITH.

page 390   SLACKS - List of sale of Abraham SLACKS, deceased - recorded 10 October 1831 - buyers were Dr. William ALLEN, John LAHR, J. R. DOWD, Joshua HOGG, Thomas SLACKS, Milly FORD, Charles ROBESON, P. CRAFT, Doc ALLEN, Doctor ALLEN, Austin N. WADE...signed Milly (his X mark) FORD.

page 382   RUTLEDGE - Inventory and list of sale of Thos. RUTLEDGE, deceased - recorded 12 October 1831 - no buyers named...note on _____ BILLS and John SMITH, I. N.

BILLS, Sterline CARROLL, John W. HANCOCK, Wiley G. HAYS, C. M. DERRYBERRY, Josiah HARDISON, Samuel KITRELL, B. S. HART, John RIGHT, John FANNING.

page 399   FARRIS - Inventory of Josiah FARRIS, deceased - recorded 14 October 1831 - John MC GILL, administrator...a mortgage on Coleman CHAFFIN.

page 399   PETTILLO - Inventory of John L. PETTILLO - recorded 14 October 1831 - taken 13 June 1831 by John PETTILLO.

page 399   GRAY - Inventory and List of Sale of William GRAY, deceased - recorded 14 October 1831 - buyers were Caleb HARRIS, Jesse GRAY, Robert FOSTER, Robert COCHRAN, by Jesse GRAY, administrator.

page 400   PUCKETT - Additional inventory of Edward PUCKETT, deceased - recorded 14 October 1831 - note on Littleton VAUGHN, A. T. MITCHELL and _____ MC DOWELL... signed E. PUCKETT, John W. PUCKETT, administrators.

page 400   EDWARDS - List of notes and accounts of Stephen EDWARDS, deceased - recorded 14 October 1831 - as of November 1830, T. T. GOODMAN, William FLY, Henry A. MILLER, Joshua MIDDLETON, William SHERMAN, Stephen SMITH, William DUE, John ALDERSON, Wm. GOODMAN, Jackson MIDDLETON, William ALLEN, Uriah HAMBRICK, John SMITH, Isaiah DAVIS, John A. BULLOCK, John C. WILLIAMS, Charles PISTOLE, Senior, Charles PISTOLE, Junior, John H. HOWELL, Isaac SIMPSON, Elijah BLOCKER, John GEORGE, John EDWARDS, James GLASSCOCK, Leonard JONES, Benjamin MYRICK, Levi BUSHBY...298 acres, 19 negroes...accounts of Celia EDWARDS, Robert L. TUSON (TRUSON), Robert HILL, James MORROW, Andrew CRAWFORD, Nathaniel WILLIS, James YOUNGER, William N. EDWARDS, Andrew BROWN, A. T. BLACKBURN, William ALDERSON, Moses A. WILEY, Peter JOICE, Daniel MC KENNON, Samuel TICER, Edward MC FADDEN, Robert L. FRIERSON, George WEBSTER, George NICHOLS, Isom ECHOLS, Thomas P. JOHNSON, John HARRIS, Ebbert TOMPSON (THOMPSON), Edward B. LITTLEFIELD, William P. POOL, William WHEAT, William M. EDWARDS, James RUSSELL, John D. ALDERSON, Charles PISTOLE, William ALDERSON, Thomas SOWELL, Ruben COCHRAN, George W. JINNINGS, Abner PISTOLE...signed Celia X EDWARDS, administratrix, William ALDERSON, administrator.

page 406   WILLIS - List of Sale of William W. WILLIS, deceased - recorded 18 October 1831 - buyers were A. A. CAMPBELL, John T. MACON, John S. MILLER, O. GOAD, Thomas HAYNES, Robert ELLIS, William BROWN, B. BLACKMAN, B. LEWIS, Turner NICHOLS, B. F. ALEXANDER, James BRIGGS, N. P. STONE, C. CAPERTON, several illegibles, James G. KELSOE, Thomas B. PORTER, George MOORE, John F. CRAIG, A. YOUNG, Nancy B. WILLOW, John C. WORMLEY... signed John S. WILLIS.

page 407   LAWRENCE - Guardian report of heirs of John LORANCE - recorded 26 October 1831 - negroes hired...bond with Willis H. BODDIE...account of Martha LAWRENCE...the children of Sabra LAWRENCE.

page 408   KELLY - Guardian return of Permelia P. KELLY, minor,
            recorded 24 October 1831 - Thomas JONES, guardian...
            accounts dated from 1826...hire of negroes...accounts
            of Robert L. COBBS, Thomas HAMILTON, N. W. BRISCOE,
            HARDIN and NIX, (they were paid for making coffin)...
            paid Ruth GUIN...signed 14 March 1831.

page 408   OGLESBY - Guardian return for heirs of James OGLESBY,
            deceased - recorded 25 October 1831 - minor heirs
            were Elisha OGLESBY and Celia OGLESBY...guardian was
            John H. JONES.

page 409   SHAW - William SHAW, Guardian return - recorded
            26 October 1831 - report of William SHAW's estate in
            my hands, signed Richard STOCKARD, guardian.

page 409   BROOKS - Administrator's settlement of Isaac BROOKS,
            deceased - recorded 26 October 1831 - Elisha HUNTER,
            administrator...vouchers of R. A. CARTER, Joseph Y.
            KELSO, James KENNEDY, E. H. CHAFFIN, M. MORRIS, James
            HALL, _____ M. CALDWELL, James T. SANDFORD, Saml. A.
            GILLESPIE, Luke BYNUM, E. HUNTER, U. R. MORGAN,
            Burial charge was $3.25, R. PASMORE, John KILCREASE,
            John MILLER, John KENNEDY, Samuel CRAIG, Samuel B.
            HILL, J. O. CURRIN, William PHELAN, John KNOX, William
            HUNTER, several illegibles...signed 9 June 1831 by
            James HUEY and John MILLER.

page 411   JENNINGS - Administrator's settlement of Samuel
            JENNINGS, deceased - recorded 26 October 1831 - hire
            of negroes...signed 7 June 1831 by David CRAIG,
            Richard STOCKARD, J.P.'s.

page 412   EDWARDS - Year's allowance for Celia EDWARDS - re-
            corded 27 October 1831 - widow of Stephen EDWARDS...
            signed 29 March 1831 by Nathl. WILLIS, John FRIERSON,
            Chas. SOWELL and William P. POOL.

page 412   MC LEAN - Year's allowance for Mrs. MC LEAN - record-
            ed 27 October 1831 - for widow of John MC LEAN,
            deceased - signed 3 January 1831 by James L. BALD-
            RIDGE, John S. RECORD, James ELLIOTT.

page 413   BRECKENRIDGE - Guardian return for Felix (?) BRECK-
            ENRIDGE's heirs...recorded 27 October 1831, signed
            Benjamin THOMAS, guardian. (Abstractor's note: the
            name could be Alex BRECKENRIDGE - faded entry.)

page 413   FRIERSON - Guardian return for Jane C. FRIERSON,
            minor - recorded 27 October 1831, by Duncan BROWN,
            guardian, signed 31 March 1831.

page 414   WILKS - Guardian report of Minor C. M. WILKS, de-
            ceased - recorded 27 October 1831 - Richard A. L.
            WILKS, guardian of William B., Washington L. J.,
            Unity K., WILKS, heirs of Minor C. M. WILKS.

page 415   ROBERTSON - Settlement with William R. ROBERTSON,
            deceased - recorded 28 October 1831 - William B.
            PILLOW, executor...vouchers of Silas ALEXANDER,
            James GILBREATH, James S. WALKER, Michael ROBERSON,
            A. B. ALEXANDER, N. W. BRISCOE, several illegibles,

Doct. HAYS, _____ HENSON, Thomas LOWRY...signed John
MACK, John H. THOMAS, J.P.'s, 14 March 1831.

page 415   WILKES - Guardian report of William B. WILKES, minor
            - recorded 28 October 1831 - minor heir of Benjamin
            WILKES, signed William M. ORR, guardian.

page 416   WILKS - Settlement of estate of Elizabeth WILKS,
            deceased - recorded 28 October 1831 - settlement made
            by Ebenezer RICE and John HATCHETT with Richard A. L.
            WILKES and Phineas THOMAS, administrators of Elizabeth
            WILKS, deceased...receipts of John B. THOMAS, John C.
            FLEMMING, Robert F. MATHEWS, Eundridge POINDEXTER,
            George W. BLEDSOE, William KENNEMORE, Richard FOSTER,
            _____ WOODWARD, Andrew SCOTT, John B. GOODING,
            William W. GALLOWAY, Robert PATTERSON, Vincent RIDLEY,
            _____ BLEDSOE, Johnathan GILLESPIE, Daniel WILKS, A.
            W. KOON, William KERR, John WILKS, Edward PUCKETT's
            account, John MEADOW's account for coffin, several
            illegibles, Frederick COFFER, William E. MC RIE.

page 417   WILSON - Guardian report, Charles WILSON, deceased -
            recorded 31 October 1831.

page 418   FOSTER - Settlement of estate of David FOSTER, de-
            ceased - recorded 1 November 1831 - vouchers of P.
            HILL, David FOSTER, Doct. CONKEY, A. C. CRAWFORD,
            Silas ALEXANDER, Joseph HACKNEY, Francis PERRY,
            illegibles, Isaac THOMAS, Nathan COFFEY, Thomas F.
            COBBURN, Claibourn HARRIS, BUCKNER and MITCHELL, A.
            B. ALEXANDER, William E. MC KUE, Joseph COWAN.

page 419   SELLERS - Guardian report of Serena SELLERS, minor
            heir of John SELLERS, deceased - recorded 2 November
            1831 - James CATHEY, guardian...hire of two negroes.

page 419   PERRYMAN - Benoni PERRYMAN, deceased, guardian report
            - recorded 4 November 1831.

page 419   HOBSON - Jeremiah HOBSON, minor, report - recorded
            4 November 1831, by John KENNEDY.

page 420   CARUTHERS - Settlement with estate of Robert
            CARUTHERS, Senior, deceased - recorded 4 November
            1831 - note on Joseph PORTER, Robert CHAME (CHAMP),
            J. SHELFORD, receipts of Samuel CARUTHERS, James R.
            PLUMMER, William ALLEN, Darrel N. SANSON, P. N.
            PORTER, H. LANGTRY, John PETTILLO, William B.
            SHAFFORD, Abner MATHEWS, William A. JOHNSON, R. J.
            FORTUNE, P. C. PATTON, John D. LOVE, traveling
            expenses to North Carolina...settlement with admin-
            istrators of R. CARUTHERS, Junior, deceased...
            Elizabeth B. CARUTHERS, administrator of Robert
            CARUTHERS, Junior, deceased, as was Parry W. PORTER
            ...William ALLEN was auctioneer...March term 1831,
            signed Alexander JOHNSON, and Abraham LOONEY.

page 422   ENGLISH - Edward W. ENGLISH, deceased, settlement -
            recorded 5 November 1831 - mentions George NIXON,
            Esquire, acting administrator of the estate of
            Thomas ENGLISH, deceased...signed 17 September 1831
            by David CRAIG, Samuel AKIN, J.P.'s.

page 422   EWING - Settlement with Andrew F. EWING, deceased -
recorded 8 November 1831 - by James WRIGHT and James
L. BALDRIDGE, J.P.'s, 7 May 1831.

page 423   WHITESIDE - Guardian report of William WHITESIDE's
heir - recorded 8 November 1831 - made 20 September
1831 by Richard HIGGINS, guardian for minor heirs
Robert K. WHITESIDE and Samuel WHITESIDE.

page 423   CAMPBELL - Samuel P. CAMPBELL's heirs - report -
recorded 8 November 1831 - return of the estate of
Samuel P. CAMPBELL by E. M. CAMPBELL.

page 423   CAMPBELL - James T. CAMPBELL's heirs - report -
recorded 8 November 1831, by E. M. CAMPBELL.

page 424   MARS - Mary Ann MARS minor - report - recorded 9 November 1831 - account with Mary Ann MARS, part of
Hugh MARS estate...accounts dating from 13 April
1820...paid John C. KELLY for tuition in 1828 and
Samuel WINN and Wm. WILIE for tuition in 1830...
signed John "P" PRUIT.

page 424   SCOTT - James SCOTT, deceased - report - recorded
9 November 1831 - guardian return for Cynthia J.
SCOTT and William SCOTT, heirs of James SCOTT,
signed by Andrew SCOTT.

page 425   GALLOWAY - Samuel GALLOWAY, deceased - report -
9 November 1831 - estate of Samuel GALLOWAY to
Thomas GALLOWAY for the minor heirs of said estate.

page 425   MOORE - Nathaniel MOORE, deceased - Settlement -
recorded 9 November 1831 - Levin L. COVEY, executor,
property sold 4 December 1829...specified legacy
paid to Mary MOORE, widow...paid Dudley MC KINDRICKS,
Joel B. SANDERS, Thomas BROWN, John MATHEWS, James
NEELY, Anthony MINTER, several illegibles...signed
Alexander JOHNSON, E. RICE.

page 426   ALDRIDGE - Elizabeth ALDRIDGE minor - report -
recorded 10 November 1831 - 8 April 1827 then due
Elizabeth ALDRIDGE from estate of Aron ALDRIDGE,
deceased.

page 426   OAKLEY - James OAKLEY's heirs - report - recorded
10 November 1831 - Elizabeth OAKLEY, guardian for
heirs of James OAKLEY, makes report.

page 426   MARTIN - Thomas W. MARTIN, deceased - Settlement -
recorded 10 November 1831 - settlement made with
William CARR, administrator...hire of negroes...
signed 20 June 1831 Mathew MOORE, Caleb HEADLEY,
commissioners.

page 427   HOWARD - Permenus HOWARD, deceased - Settlement -
recorded 11 November 1831 - account of James HOWARD,
executor...signed 22 April 1831 by Alexander JOHNSON,
John MACK.

page 428   BURNS - James BURNS' heirs - Guardian Settlement -
recorded 11 November 1831 - John M. LEMASTER, guardian of minor heirs of James BURNS, makes return...

got corn from Jeremiah DAVIS, cotton from Jane MAN-
GRAM...Jane MANGRAM rented the land...William BURNS,
one of the minor heirs paid for his expenses for
going to Dyer County...Milton BURNS' expenses paid.

page 429 POWELL - Sarah POWELL, deceased - Settlement - recorded 14 November 1831...settlement made 26 February
1831 with James C. POWELL, administrator...signed
James OSBURN and John W. RECORD, J.P.'s.

page 429 TATE - John TATE, deceased - Settlement - recorded
14 November 1831 - settlement made 14 September
1831 with Richard HENDERSON, executor...notes of
George and Robert PERRY, William ALEXANDER, James
WALKER; account on John HARRIS, and Richard B.
PASMORE's account...signed E. RICE, Jno. MACK,
commissioners.

page 430 SANDFORD - Wineford SANDFORD - recorded 15 November
1831 - widow and relict of James T. SANDFORD - allowance made 6 September 1831 by John C. WORMLEY, John
MILLER, John BROWN.

page 430 PICKARD - John J. PICKARD, deceased - Settlement -
recorded 15 November 1831 - William PICKARD, administrator...paid John J. PICKARD, Alexander A. PICK-
ARD, Tilman A. CRISP, widow's dower laid off -
William PICKARD's accounts against the estate...
signed Jno. B. BOND, James FORGEY, J.P.'s.

page 431 WILKS - Josiah WILKS minor - Guardian report -
recorded 15 November 1831 - Richard WILKS, guardian
of Josiah WILKS...mentions "bon" on Thomas WILKS...
signed 13 June 1831.

page 431 EDDLEMAN - John EDDLEMAN's heirs - Return - recorded
15 November 1831 - "Thomas M. HARPER in account with
the minor heirs of John EDDLEMAN, deceased"...notes
and accounts of Osni ALEXANDER, William GARRETT (for
schooling), McKay CAMPBELL, Thomas M. HARPER.

page 431 NEELY - Thos. NEELY's heirs - Guardian return -
recorded 15 November 1831 - John CHEEK, guardian...
paid Thomas NEELY 26 May 1831 for expenses in going
to North Carolina.

page 432 FRIERSON - David FRIERSON, deceased - Settlement -
recorded 15 November 1831 - settlement made with
executors on 14 March 1831 by Jno. E. STEPHENSON
and Saml. T. WILLIAMS.

page 432 MC CORD - William MC CORD's heirs - Guardian return -
recorded 16 November 1831 - William PERRY, guardian
of Edmond William and Robert MC CORD, minor heirs of
William MC CORD, deceased...hire of negroes.
(Abstractor's note: no commas as shown in list of
heirs.)

page 433 LEECH - David LEECH's heirs - Guardian return -
recorded 16 November 1831...for boarding Washington
and clothing five children...expenses on mill dam...
profits from said mill...signed 14 March 1831 by
David LEECH, Junior, guardian.

page 433   RICHARDSON - Thomas RICHARDSON minor - Guardian report - recorded 16 November 1831 - Thomas RICHARDSON, minor of William RICHARDSON...guardian was James W. RICHARDSON.

page 433   WILLIAMSON - Maria G. WILLIAMSON - minor - guardian report - recorded 16 November 1831 - paid Doct. Jno. B. HAYS, M. D. COOPER, D. MARTIN, H. LANGTRY, J. S. WALKER, boarding for year 1827...hire of negroes for 1827...signed P. C. WILLIAMSON, guardian of Maria G. WILLIAMSON.

page 434   HOWARD - Mary Ann HOWARD minor - Guardian return - recorded 17 November 1831 - note on Mira HOWARD and William WHITE...signed David DOBBINS.

page 535   HARDESON - Year's provision for William HARDESON's widow - recorded 17 November 1831...by John C. WORMLEY, Wyle BROWN, and H. ALMOND on 6 January 1831.

page 435   KIMBLE - James KIMBLE, deceased - Guardian return - recorded 17 November 1831; William HUNTER, guardian for orphans of James KIMBLE, deceased...hire of negroes to E. B. LITTLEFIELD, A. T. ISOM, F. T. MOODY, P. PERDUE, J. M. DANIEL, Joseph GRIFIN, A. BURKETT, Joseph WATKINS, J. M. CRENSHAW, H. TURNEY, J. W. JENNINGS, John B. LEFTWICH, M. J. KITRELL, William HUNTER, J. NEELY...paid William H. KIMBLE his portion of the auction...paid William H. KIMBLE for schooling, paid William H. BLAKE; land in Shelby County...paid Mrs. OVERSTREET for making clothes... Ann E. KIMBLE's accounts were for medical account of negroes paid to N. W. BRISCOE, paid John M. FRANCIS for schooling, paid Miss BLAKE for schooling... Accounts for Mary B. KIMBLE...paid Neils S. BROWN for schooling of Mary B. KIMBLE...

page 437   HOBSON - Jeremia HOBSON, minor - Guardian report - recorded 17 November 1831 - settlement of the guardianship of Jeremia HOBSON made 1 January 1831...

page 437   ISOM - James ISOM's heirs - Guardian report - recorded 18 November 1831 - exhibit of David CRAIG and his wife as guardian for minor heirs of James ISOM, deceased; hire of negroes...paid Doct. John P. SPINDLE, Doct. Eli E_____, A. T. ISOM, Sarah G. ISOM, William E. GILLESPIE, T. J. PORTER, Thomas D. ISOM, Elizabeth E. ISOM, Robert G. ISOM, "bad debts collected William K. HILL"...signed David CRAIG, guardian, 1 March 1831.

page 438   POWELL - Charles POWELL's heirs - Guardian report - recorded 18 November 1831 - James C. POWELL as guardian to minor heirs of Charles and Polly POWELL, deceased...wards were Mathew POWELL and Lucinda POWELL.

page 438   CAMPBELL - Caroline H. CAMPBELL, minor - Guardian report - recorded 18 November 1831 - signed 5 February 1831 by Robert CAMPBELL, guardian.

page 439   FALLEN - Jackson FALLEN minor - Guardian report - recorded 18 November 1831 - hiring of negroes...

signed William VOORHIES, guardian. (Abstractor's note: this name also appears as FULTON, believe FULTON is correct, although it appears more like FALLEN.)

page 439   FULTON - James FULTON minor - Guardian report - recorded 18 November 1831 - William VOORHIES, guardian...hire of negroes.

page 439   SCOTT - Samuel SCOTT, deceased - Settlement - recorded 18 November 1831 - 3 February 1831 settlement made with William S. HENDERSON and Andrew SCOTT, executors of Samuel SCOTT, deceased.

page 440   BRIGGS - Samuel BRIGGS, deceased - Settlement - recorded 19 November 1831 - settlement made with John JAMESON, administrator. (Abstractor's note: faded, could not read.)

page 440   HENDERSON - Ezekiel HENDERSON's heirs - Guardian Report - recorded 22 November 1831 - Richard HENDERSON, guardian for William Jnr.(?), minor heir of Ezekiel HENDERSON...tax paid on land in Maury and Gibson counties.

page 441   WILKS - Minor WILKS, deceased - settlement with executors - recorded 22 November 1831 - James CAMPBELL, executor...signed Robert MC NUTT and E. W. ORR, 12 _____ 1831.

page 441   BIGHAM - James BIGHAM, Deceased - Settlement - recorded 22 November 1831 - made 2 March 1831 by William EDMONDSON and John MC FADDEN, J.P.'s.

page 441   PLUMMER - Nancy PLUMMER, minor - Guardian Report - recorded 24 November 1831; Nancy PLUMMER minor heir of George PLUMMER, deceased...signed 14 March 1830 by George NIXON.

page 442   FOSTER - David FOSTER, deceased - List of Sale - recorded 24 November 1831 - made 30 November 1827; buyers were Benjamin ALLEN, Joseph HACKNEY, Silas ALEXANDER, Craig CRAWFORD, Andrew TURNBOW, Randol PATE, Edward WORTHAM, Mathew GARGAS, Jno. Y. ROPER, Franklin HOUSTON, _____ BENTON, Benjamin KILPATRICK, J. K. BOYD, signed William E. MC KEE, executor.

page 442   WILKS - Daniel WILKS, deceased - Settlement - recorded 24 November 1831 - R. A. L. WILKS and Phineas THOMAS, executors...cash from John W. CLANTON, John C. FLEMMINS, William WILSON.

page 443   BOID - BOID's heir - Guardian Report - recorded 24 November 1831 - William S. HENDERSON, GUARDIAN of Andrew T., Nancy S., and John P. BOID makes return ...note of John R. BOID...paid Johnathan GALLOWAY for schooling...taxes on land in Dyer County...signed William S. HENDERSON.

page 443   HERRING - Solomon HERRING's heirs - Guardian Report - recorded 24 November 1831 - balance of the capital of the estate of Robert HERRING "in my hands", signed Lard B. BOYD, guardian.

page 443   RUSSELL - A. H. RUSSELL, deceased - Guardian Report -
            recorded 25 November 1831 - David CRAIG, guardian of
            Alexander H. RUSSELL, deceased, and administrator of
            Elenor RUSSEL, late widow of said deceased, made
            return 12 March 1831 - money paid for sundries for
            widow and heirs of RUSSELL...note on A. T. MURPHY of
            North Carolina for land in western district.

page 444   JOHNSTON - Amos JOHNSTON, deceased - Settlement -
            recorded 25 November 1831 - Elizabeth JOHNSTON,
            executrix...notes on John BLANKS, John GILCHRIST,
            signed 7 September 1831, Joel REESE, J.P., David
            CRAIG, J.P., Nathan COFFEE, J.P.

page 445   SWAN - Mathew SWAN's heirs - Guardian report - record-
            ed 25 November 1831 - on 14 March 1831 Duncan BAKER,
            guardian of minor heirs of Mathew SWAN, deceased,
            paid Thomas SWAN one of the heirs his optional part.

page 445   WILLIAMS - Nathaniel WILLIAMS, deceased - Guardian
            return - recorded 15 November 1831 - return of
            Thomas WILLIAMS, guardian of Martha A. and Sophia
            WILLIAMS, minor heirs of Nathaniel WILLIAMS, deceased
            ...received of H. and D. WILLIAMS and F. ZOLLICOFFER
            administrators of deceased; hire of negroes to J. O.
            CROSS, Ed A. SALE, C. FARNEY, William WORTHAM,
            Thomas WILLIAMS, A. W. LONG, Doctor THEVENOT...
            Thomas WILLIAMS, guardian.

page 445   MATHEWS - Margaret A. MATHEWS, minor - Guardian
            report - recorded 28 November 1831 - settlement with
            guardian of Margaret A. MATHEWS, minor heir of
            William K. MATHEWS, deceased...rent for plantation
            for 1830...signed 23 March 1831, Thomas W. MATHEWS,
            guardian.

page 445   JONES - James JONES, deceased - Settlement - record-
            ed 28 November 1831 - David GLASS and Edward L. JONES,
            administrators of estate...sale of negroes mentioned.

page 446   BRECKENRIDGE - Alexander BRECKENRIDGE, deceased -
            Guardian report - recorded 1 December 1831 - receipt
            of N. PORTER and illegibles...note of P. R. BOOKER,
            Elisha ESTES...signed Benjamin THOMAS, guardian of
            minor heirs.

page 446   HOBSON - Jeremiah HOBSON, minor heir of Jeremiah
            HOBSON, deceased - guardian report - recorded 1 Dec-
            ember 1831, by John KENNEDY, guardian.

page 446   GRAHAM - Margaret GRAHAM, deceased - Settlement -
            recorded 1 November 1831 - paid H. E. TURNER,
            CROFFORD, illegible, FRIERSON, Johnathan WEBSTER,
            T. J. FRIERSON, signed Nicholas J. LONG, Joseph
            MC MURRAY, J.P.'s.

page 447   OAKLEY - William OAKLEY's heirs - Guardian return -
            recorded 2 November 1831 - illegible receipts...
            receipts of James OAKLEY, Milley OAKLEY, Jesse
            OAKLEY, Robert OAKLEY...

page 447   WILKS - Guardian returns for Unity K. WILKS, Washing-
    - 449   ton L. WILKS, and E. B. WILKS, minors, recorded 5 Dec-
            ember 1831.

page 449   DAVIS - David DAVIS, deceased - Guardian return for
            David DAVIS, deceased, heirs, recorded 3 November
            1831, signed William BOAZ on 12 March 1831.

page 450   STONE - E. STONE, deceased - Settlement - recorded
            5 November 1831 - John B. BOND and Samuel B. LEE,
            administrators...signed James FORGEY and David CRAIG,
            J.P.'s.

page 450   PAIN - Mildren N. PAIN, minor - Guardian Report -
            recorded 5 November 1831 - John ALEXANDER, guardian.

page 452   ROGERS - Aisly ROGERS, minor - Guardian report -
            recorded 8 November 1831 - signed Thomas JONES.

page 452   WILSON - William H. WILSON, deceased, heirs - Guard-
            ian report - recorded 8 November 1831 - mentions
            negroes belonging to late William H. WILSON, signed
            John W. SMITH, guardian.

page 453   BELL - William BELL, deceased - Settlement - recorded
            9 November 1831 - signed A. CATHEY, S. W. AKIN, J.P.'s.

page 453   KERBY - KERBY's heirs - guardian return - recorded
            9 November 1831 - made 15 March 1831 - Ethelbert
            KERBY, guardian for Mary M. KERBY...hire of negroes
            for 1827...mentions Enoch KERBY. (Abstractor's
            note: faded entry, may not be all.)

page 454   CRAWSON - Robert CRAWSON, deceased - Inventory -
            recorded 2 March 1832 - taken 21 December 1831...
            negroes named and ages given...F. ADAIR and William
            WILLIAMS owe small amount to the estate...signed
            J. B. RAINEY, Adam BYHARD, administrators.

page 455   GILLESPIE - Inventory of Jonathan GILLESPIE, deceased
            - recorded 2 March 1832 - taken December 1831 by
            Robert CRAIG, administrator...notes of Peter STUBBLE-
            FIELD (doubtful), W. JAMES for 27 notes on persons
            in York District, South Carolina (doubtful), George
            CORLAN (very doubtful), William B. PILLOW, Edward
            HALL (doubtful), Henry SMITH (doubtful), Joseph WAT-
            KINS' order on Samuel MC CAFFERTY; book accounts,
            Robert WADE, Thos. JAINS, Robert CRAIG, James STOCK-
            ARD, Josiah WASSON, James DAVIS, William MC CONNELL,
            Jesse PILKINTON, MAGRAW, William PORTER, William
            CONNAWAY, Edward WORTHAM, Thomas WORTHAM, Thomas
            RAMSEY, Robert MATHEWS, Taylor HARRIS, Harris HALL,
            Alexander D. ALEXANDER, John FARRIS, David PERANCE,
            McKee BRYSON, Joel REESE, Richard KINDLE, Silas
            ALEXANDER...negroes named and ages given; signed,
            Robert CRAIG, administrator.

page 456   GILLEY - James M. GILLEY, deceased - Inventory -
            recorded 4 March 1832 - bond on Samuel FARRIS,
            signed Jane GILLEY.

page 457   MC AFEE - Mills MC AFEE, deceased - List of Sale -
            recorded 4 March 1832 - sold 28 November 1831 -
            buyers Lahus MC AFEE, William W. BARHAM, Robert
            DRYDEN, Pleasant J. HARDIN, Edward HARRIS, Joel
            WRIGHT, Joel HARDISON, David TATTLE, Joseph HARDISON,
            John H. WRIGHT, John FOX...year's provision for widow.

page 457   ALEXANDER - Jane ALEXANDER, deceased - List of Sale -
            recorded 4 March 1832; buyers Eli ALEXANDER, Andrew
            ALEXANDER, John ALEXANDER, Ann ALEXANDER, Richard
            MILLER, Nathaniel YOUNG, William COOPER, D. ANDERSON,
            Andrew MILLER, Jesse GRAY, R. L. FRIERSON, T. THOMP-
            SON, John WYLIE, George W. SHURMAN; signed Alexander
            FARRIS, administrator.

page 458   HANKS - Moses HANKS, deceased - Supplemental Inventory
            - recorded 4 March 1831 - sold to Sarah HANKS two sows
            ...sold to David DODSON...signed 31 December 1831,
            Elijah HANKS.

page 458   GULLET - Samuel GULLET, deceased - List of Sale -
            recorded 4 March 1832 - buyers were William BARHAM,
            Rebecca GULLETT (bought most including Bible), Francis
            SMITH, William WILLIAMS, John GULLETT, Jackson LIGGETT,
            John GORDON, William FOX, G. GULLETT, Eli CHEEK, Mills
            MC AFEE, George ROAN, Nathaniel STEWART, Simon JOHNS-
            TON, Gideon FOX, Robert THOMPSON, Pervines FOX, Edmond
            FULLER, George GULLETT, William ALRED, William LYTLE,
            Thompson GULLETT, Pleasant G. HARDIN, Jessie YEATS,
            William FARRAR, James PENNY, Jesse YATES, Mark JACKS,
            J. B. M. JONES, Mark JACKSON, John CHEEK, Joseph
            ELKINS, A. V. STREET, John MC NEACE, A. BOSTICK,
            James WALKER, _____ FISHER, M. MOORE, John FOX,
            Joseph CLIMER, William D. SMITH, Simon ROANE.

page 460   GULLET - Samuel GULLET, deceased, inventory - record-
            ed 5 March 1832 - notes on John FLEMMING, David
            FOWLER, John FISHER, Hugh WALLACE, John KNOX, Amos
            MC DANIEL, P. WRIGHT, James CANNON, Joseph WILKINS,
            Thomas NICHOL, James HUNTER, E. HARRIS, S. HEMPHILL,
            John HARVILL, ROACH and WILSON, Wiles FARRAR, James
            SCOTT, Jerry CHEEK, John PORTER, J. C. ORILEY, Francis
            PARKER, Robert THOMPSON, David D. DEANS, John KIMES,
            Mary FRIERSON, Walter JENKINS, E. DILLAHUNTY.
            (Abstractor's note: with the exception of three,
            all were marked doubtful.)

page 461   RICE - Ebenezer RICE, Junior, deceased - List of Sale
            and Inventory - recorded 5 March 1832 - taken 18 Oct-
            ober 1831 - no buyers given...E. RICE was executor
            ...widow's allowance mentioned.

page 463   CARUTHERS - Robert CARUTHERS, deceased - Division of
            negroes - recorded 6 March 1832; Lot 1 drawn by Mary
            M. CARUTHERS, lot 2 by widow Elizabeth B. CARUTHERS,
            lot 3 by Susan J. CARUTHERS, lot 4 by Eliza T. CARU-
            THERS, lot 5 by Robert N. CARUTHERS, lot 6 by James
            M. CARUTHERS, lot 7 by Sarah H. CARUTHERS; signed
            6 January 1832 by John SMISER, M. HELM, James T.
            CROFFORD.

page 464   MILLS - Gideon MILLS - Administrator's Settlement -
            recorded 7 March 1832 - FOSTER's notes, account of
            William RAINEY, William HENDERSON; not of J. MEADOWS,
            Z.CONKEY, J. WARR, A. W. MACK, W. L. NEELEY, illegi-
            bles, J. W. BURRISS, D. G. JOHNSON...list of money
            paid against estate...paid W. BURRIS for coffin for
            child...paid for trip to Nashville "on pension
            business"...signed Francis S. PERRY.

page 466　　BRADSHAW - Elias BRADSHAW, deceased - Administrator's
Settlement - recorded 7 March 1832 - vouchers of
Robert CROSBY, Charles SOWELL, Moses A. WILEY, Hiram
HILL, William HAWKINS, Wm. ERWIN, L. F. DOTY, James
CARTER, And. LETSINGER, Hartwell DICKINSON, Thos.
WALKER, Jos. MC MURRAY, A. T. ISOM, P. GORDON, George
QUIGLEY, L. C. OLIPHANT, CRAWFORD and PORTER, the
widow, William CRAGG, "paid $6.50 for whiskey and
coffin"...signed John O. COOK, administrator...
signed 9 December 1831 by A. CATHEY, Joseph MC MURRAY,
J.P.'s.

page 467　　MILICAN - Baxter MILICAN, deceased - Administrator's
Settlement - recorded 7 March 1832 - Caleb LINDSEY,
administrator...note on Thomas PICKARD...signed
14 December 1831 by R. STOCKARD, David CRAIG, J.P.'s.

page 468　　MITCHELL - John MITCHELL, deceased - Administrator's
settlement - recorded 8 March 1832 - James MITCHELL,
administrator - vouchers on H. ALLEN, J. GROVES, J.
MC KIBBINS, W. J. RICHARDSON, B. WILKES, J. J. HUNTS,
SOWELL, W. A. GILLAM, J. MC CLANEY, M. WEBB, G.
HENSLEY, editor of the Whig and Banner, A. M. COPE-
LAND, A. O. HARRIS, widow's allowance...signed 18
December 1831 by Jno. HATCHETT and Will A. JOHNSTON.

page 468　　CROW - Benjamin CROW, lunatic - account - recorded
8 March 1832 - account with William VOORHIES, jailor,
for boarding in the common jail from 11 July 1829 to
20 December 1831...paid S. A. GILLESPIE, Joshua
GUEST for whiskey and tobacco furnished.

page 469　　MOOREHEAD - Joseph MOOREHEAD, deceased - administra-
tor's settlement - recorded 8 March 1832 - James K.
SMITH, administrator..."land which children have
taken in part of their legacy"...execution of James
MOOREHEAD of Richmond County, North Carolina, in
1818...vouchers: H. LANGTRY, William WILLIAMS,
BROWN and SANDERS, E. H. CHAFFIN, Thos. B. CRAIGHEAD,
note on Caleb HEADLEE, GROVE and JENKINS, note to
Isaiah REED, John K. STEWART, James PATTERSON,
Francis WRIGHT, James FULLERTON, William PHELAN,
Jonathan SMITH, Newman MOORE, Hugh B. PORTER, Chas.
HARDISON, L. LANDRICH (or LANDRITH), HANCOCK, Nimrod
PORTER, George M. MARTIN, Philip J. MOOREHEAD (a
receipt for legacy), Armstead MOOREHEAD's receipt
for the minor heirs of Joseph MOOREHEAD...Armstead
MOOREHEAD's receipt for legacy...widow's allowance...
signed, James HUEY, F. S. SLAUTER, J.P.'s.

page 470　　MC AFEE - Elissa MC AFEE's year allowance - recorded
10 March 1832 - wife of Mills MC AFEE, deceased...
allowance made by Mathew MOORE, Charles HARDISON,
Joel HARDISON, 17 September 1831.

page 471　　PATTERSON - Jarred PATTERSON, deceased - administrator's settlement - recorded 10 March 1832 - Robert
PATTERSON, administrator...note on Joseph SWIM
(doubtful), note on W. A. and S. P. MAXWELL, William
P. SMITH, Joshua WRIGHT, Joel REESE, John BURNS...
obligations to be paid at the death of the widow...
money from John GILBREATH...

page 472   GALLOWAY - Samuel GALLOWAY, deceased - Amount of Sale,
            Settlement - recorded 10 May 1832 - E. W. DALE, admin-
            istrator...cash from J. R. PLUMMER, C. N. SHIRES,
            William HARDISON, and Bogan WALLIS...paid James
            HARDISON, William STRATON, DALE and DUNCAN, HAYS and
            ESTES, B. B. SMITH, C. C. CATHEY, illegibles, Bird
            S. HURT, Catherine MC RORY, Sol K. JENKINS, Joseph
            B. WALLACE, G. W. FOGLEMAN, Jacob SHIRES, Louisiana
            MC REA, illegibles, signed 19 March 1832 by James
            WALKER, Abraham LOONEY, J.P.'s.

page 473   EASTHAM - William EASTHAM, deceased - Settlement -
            recorded 10 May 1832 - Tennessee ROPER, administrator
            ...note on P. PARKMAN insolvent...on Gaston POWELL,
            insolvent; signed 9 March 1832, W. B. PILLOW, George
            JOHNSON, J.P.'s.

page 474   GULLETT - Samuel GULLETT, deceased - Settlement -
            recorded 10 May 1832 - signed 15 December 1831,
            George GULLETT, administrator...vouchers of Hugh B.
            PORTER, William MC CLURE, Jno. KNOX, Rebecca GULLETT,
            Andrew RYONE, Gideon FOX, Willis JONES, Hugh BRADSHAW,
            J. B. REAVIS, Caleb THOMAS, Obediah LANDRETH, NICHOL-
            SON and ESTES, G. DUDLEY, Jno. FOX, G. W. CAMPBELL,
            Jesse YEATS, P. N. PORTER, R. H. MACK, Caleb THOMAS,
            Anthony MINTER, Joseph ELKINS, Jane WHITE, William
            LYTLE, James J. WALKER, Thomas KEESS, William P.
            MARTIN, Edmond DILLAHUNTY; notes of G. W. REAVES,
            Thompson GULLETT, Thomas NICHOLS, Jno. WARNER, Amos
            MC DANIEL, illegibles, Isaac MEADOWS, Elizabeth MC
            DANIEL, Jno. MARVELL, William HUNTER, P. WRIGHT, Jno.
            RION, Noah HERALUS, Esquire HERNDON, Jno. KIMES, John
            T. CARR, D. ANDERSON, Samuel HEMHILL, Jno. FLEMING,
            Joseph ELKINS, Milton BRIGHT, Newton PORTER...signed
            G. CAMPBELL, Frs. SLAUTER.

page 476   LOUELLIN - Josiah LOUELLIN, deceased, inventory -
            recorded 10 May 1832 - entire estate consisted of
            two old horses and an old saddle, signed Zibina
            CONKEY, administrator.

page 476   LOVE - David LOVE, deceased - Settlement - recorded
            11 May 1832 - John D. LOVE, administrator, corn due
            from Wilson PARKS; receipt of James K. POLK; account
            of Ebenezer RICE, Evan YOUNG, William A. JOHNSON,
            Robert MACK; vouchers: J. C. POWELL, J. W. P. MC
            GIMPSEY, William R. MILLER, James N. BOWMAN...note
            given L. PREWIT...allowance to widow Polly LOVE...
            accounts: John GILLESPIE, Iverson KELMS, Thomas T.
            HARRISON, Michael LANCASTER, Aron C. WILSON, Samuel
            CUNNINGHAM, Mary DANIEL, John MC KENNEDY, Martin
            WISEMAN, Rufus G. HENDERSON, Hezekiah OLIVER, allow-
            ance to widow Mary LOVE...amount D. LOVE, deceased,
            owed to the heirs of William HODGE, deceased.

page 479   DUNLAP - Samuel DUNLAP, deceased - Settlement -
            recorded 11 May 1832 - B. S. HURT, executor...vouch-
            ers: Felix KILPATRICK, Aaron BOID, William GOSSETT,
            Hugh COFFEY, John DEAN, William WOODSIDE, William
            HARDISON, George TILMAN, David JACKSON, John H.
            HANNAH, John STEPHENSON, WILLIAMS and ALDERSON, John
            RYLEE, Doct. G. OBRYAN, Doct. George W. FOGLEMAN,
            Thomas STANFIELD, James BEATY, B. CROW, Samuel

JACKSON...a receipt from William R. PADGETT "for part
of a legacy coming from his great grandfather John
CRANFORD of the state of Georgia and collected by
the deceased as guardian"...100 acres willed to
widow...paid James N. SMITH for survey for widow
Nancy DUNLAP...paid "Miss Emily DUNLAP note for
property bought at the sale"...James R. FOSTER's
note, doubtful...Thomas FERRILL's account...signed
21 October 1831 by S. K. JANKINS, J. A. POWELL, J.P.'s.

page 484   STACKS - Abraham STACKS, deceased - Settlement -
recorded 11 May 1832 - Milly FORD, administrator...
Nancy DUNLAP's note...receipt of B. S. HURT...
account of William ALLEN for medical attention...
account of Joshua HOGG...execution in favor of
Shaderick COSEY...signed J. A. POWELL, March 1832.
(Abstractor's note: name is given as SLACKS some-
times in same account of entries.)

page 484   MAYES - Abraham MAYES, deceased - Settlement -
recorded 15 May 1832 - Elias P. MAYES, administrator
...signed 8 March 1832 by Geo. A. PEELER, David FLY,
J.P.'s.

page 485   ISOM - James ISOM, deceased - Negroes divided -
recorded 12 May 1832 - to David CRAIG, Esquire, and
his wife Mary CRAIG, formerly Mary ISOM; to Jno. J.
CRAIG and his wife Sarah CRAIG, formerly Sarah ISOM
...signed 26 December 1831 by Jas. CATHEY, Jno.
DAWSON, Jos. GRIFFIN, commissioners.

page 485   WEBSTER - John G. WEBSTER, deceased - Settlement -
recorded 13 May 1832 - James DOBBINS, Patk. MAGUIRE
and Jona WEBSTER, executors...in account with estate
of G. W. WEBSTER, deceased...cash received of Jack-
son MIDDLETON, Jacob BIFFLE and AKIN, R. P. WEBSTER,
John L. SMITH...vouchers of Gardener FRIERSON,
Nathaniel LOVING, Jno. JOHNS, Vincent PILLOW, David
MARTIN, Jno. MC GILL, James S. WALKER, HARRIS and
POLK, COOPER and HILL, BRADFORD and STACK, William
R. MILLER, Robert LUSK, W. KILPATRICK, P. R. BOOKER,
E. B. LITTLEFIELD, NICHOL and SHAPPARD, Paul G.
CRAFTON, Iaac LANSBURY, John BROWN, James NEELEY,
Charles PISTOLE, Darrell N. SANSOM, William WALLIS,
Joseph G. POWELL, R. P. WEBSTER's note, Nathaniel
YOUNG, John JELKS, Vincent PILLOW, David MARTIN, Jno.
MC GILL, James W. WALKER, Lorenzo HITCHCOCK, Robert
LUSK, William J. BURKETT, HAYS and DEAN printing,
"Hartford BROWN for funeral ESTES"...Thomas J.
FRIERSON, David LUCK's executor...Doct. J. W. S.
FRIERSON, Joseph HERNDON, William C. GRAVES, Edward
H. CHAFFIN...paid A. O. HARRIS on account of tomb
...Jesse EGNEW, Mary PILLOW, James DOBBINS, Charles
PATTON, William STRAYHORN, Robert P. WEBSTER, COBBS
and DILLAHUNTY, Jno. B. HAYS, David THOMPSON, Thomas
STONE, Edward BLACKBURN...

page 488   DUNCAN - List of notes deliver Lemuel H. DUNCAN on
behalf of his wife as guardian for Emily Green
WEBSTER, daughter of John G. WEBSTER, deceased:
Jonn. WEBSTER, Edward ENGLISH, Vincent PILLOW, Mary
MACON, Robert P. WEBSTER, Henry TURNEY, Nathaniel

WILLIS, Noah B. TINDALL, Lucy GANT, Henry E. TURNER,
Andrw. BLAIR, Caleb LONGLEY, Eusebius STONE, Green
GRAHAM, Samuel MC REE, Meredith HELM, Benjamin THOMAS,
Edward B. LITTLEFIELD, Anthony MINTER, Jno. B. GOOD-
ING, Henry HOUSER, William COLLINS, Jerry CHERRY,
John M. FITZGERALD, Henry A. MILLER...negroes belong-
ing to Lemuel DUNCAN's wife delivered.

page 490   PORTER - Isaac N. PORTER, deceased - Settlement -
recorded 14 May 1832 - Robert CARUTHERS, Junior, one
of executors...paid Robert L. COBBS, Levi KETCHAM,
Jesse W. EGNEW, S. A. GILLESPIE, R. L. PHILIPS,
LEMASTER and FLIPPIN, M. HELM, Samuel NORTHERN, WALKER
and HARRIS, John T. PORTER, Samuel STOCKARD, P. NELSON,
Solomon P. MAXWELL, John WITT, D. HUMPHREYS, Isaac
SAMPSON, negro bought by Perry W. PORTER...signed
Thomas J. PORTER, executor of Isaac N. PORTER.

page 492   WARDEN - Will of James WARDEN, deceased - recorded
17 May 1832 - wife Polly for support of herself and
family to educate them the same as "my older have
been raised and educated"...son Samuel, son Richard,
each of my children...when they become of age...
Samuel to be executor...signed 1 December 1831, James
WARDEN; witnesses were John CAMPBELL, Richd. A. L.
WILKES.

page 493   JOSSEY - James JOSSEY, deceased - Widow's allowance -
recorded 17 May 1832 - year's provision for Nancy
JOSSEY, widow of James JOSSEY, signed by J. B.
HAMILTON, D. H. TRUE.

page 493   MC AFEE - Mills MC AFEE, deceased - Widow's allowance
- recorded 17 May 1832 - Elissa MC AFEE, widow...
signed 17 September 1831 by Mathew MOORE, Charles
HARDISON, Joel HARDISON.

page 493   MC AFEE - Mills MC AFEE, deceased - Widow's Dower -
recorded 17 May 1832 - laid off dower on eastern
part of the tract on which said MC AFEE lived on
meanders of Cedar Creek...signed 7 February 1832 by
Peter WILLIAMS, Robert HENDERSON, James L. BALDRIDGE,
Jno. VINCENT, Mathew MOORE, Joel REESE.

page 494   SOWELL - Will of Joseph SOWELL, deceased - recorded
17 May 1832 - wife Elizabeth...signed 17 January
1830, Joseph SEWELL; witnesses were Jno. HATCHETT,
John ALLEN.

page 494   MARTIN - Will of David MARTIN of Columbia - recorded
17 May 1832 - wife Sally A. MARTIN to be executor
and receive everything...signed 12 March 1827.

page 495   JOSEY - Inventory of property of James JOSEY, deceased - recorded 17 May 1832 - made 20 December
1831 - notes of Samuel MC DOWELL, Spencer TINSLEY,
William STRAYHORN, R. CROSBY, John L. STRAYHORN,
Zachariah HICKMAN, Elijah ROANE, Allen PILLOW, John
OWENS, J. JONES, Cornelius ____ NEY, Thomas GARRETT,
illegible, William FRYERSON...list of notes due the
estate: Thomas MC FALL, S. Y. BLACKBURN, Josiah
DAVIS (bad), M. P. PINKARD, _____ SLAYDEN, K. T.

TYLER (?), Samuel TICER, C. COLEMAN, John HAMILTON, Jerry ATKERSON, Thos. P. JOHNSON.

page 496   GILLESPIE - Jonathan GILLESPIE, deceased - Account of Sale - recorded 18 May 1832 - sold 16 January 1832. Buyers were Thos. J. CALDWELL, Robert CRAIG, James W. NEELEY, Wright EDWARDS, Darrel SANSOM, William HAIL, Simpson PERRY, several illegibles, Grant A. JOHNSON, Josiah HARRIS, Abner JOHNSON, Alfred GODWIN, Peter JOHNSON, Elizabeth SCOTT, Johnson GILLESPIE, Willis PEEDLE, Samuel HANCOCK, Samuel HOWELL, Robert MATHEWS, Charles S. WADE, Silas ALEXANDER, Allen TAILOR, John BENDERMAN, Robert WAID, Thomas WORTHAM, William GALLOWAY, Joseph WADKINS, Grant JOHNSON, Andrew SCOTT, Edward COLE, James GALLOWAY, Jonathan GILLASPIE, Pilmon COOL, A (?) WALKER, Samuel DAMRON...signed Robert CRAIG, administrator.

page 497   MOORE - John T. MOORE, deceased - Inventory and Account of Sale - recorded 17 May 1832, taken 27 October 183?...buyers were Thos. J. PORTER, Joel B. SANDERS, A. O. P. NICHOLSON, Lemuel PHILIPS, William W. KILPATRICK, Hugh TOMLINSON, Andrew MATHEWS, Joshua KILPATRICK, Mrs. Nancy MOORE (got most of items), James HITCHCOCK, John B. ALDERSON, Simon JOHNSON, William ROBERTS, John KIRK, John GAMBLE, James HITCH-COCK, John GORDEN, John L. SMITH, William B. BROWN, John WHITAKER, Hugh BRADSHAW, Meredith HELM, Joseph CHUMLEY, James JONES, Edward W. DALE, John WILSON, Joel B. SANDERS, Samuel SMITH, Asmond WILLIFORD, William W. CARTER, Jeremiah WHEATLEY...notes on Ruben A. CARTER, Sarah WHITE, Swan HARDIN, Thompson GULLETT, Henry PAYTON, William K. HILL, Samuel E. SLAYDEN, John A. POWELL, George P. KELSEY, James WHALING, P. H. MANLIFF, John HANKINS, Robert PIERCE, David STRONG, James SHIELDS, Mark PIPKIN, Needham JOHNSON, Novis WILLIAMS, Vincent DAVIS, William HENLEY, J. W. LIGGINS, W. W. WOOD, F. GHOLSON, Jesse BRIDGES, John MC FALLS, Joel HANKINS, A. B. HARDIN, Joseph GILL, Steward of M. E. Church, George PINKHORN, John DILL...doubtful notes: James GULLETT, William H. WILLIAMSON, Lorenzo HITCHCOCK, Josiah ALDERSON, Andrew EDMONDSON, Joel REESE...good notes on Charles C. MAYSON, B. BROWN, John BILLS, illegibles, Samuel RANKIN, John SMITH, L. and J. HITCHCOCK, James C. ORILEY, Joshua T. FLY, W. K. HILL; doubtful notes: Jas. CHUMLEY, L. RICHARDS ...good notes on William S. MOORE, Thomas GREGORY, J. M. SMITH...accounts most desperate and doubtful: J. T. DEWAGAN, Cuffy WOODSON (good), John KNOX, Capt. YANCY, Thomas DURANT, Samuel RANKIN, Benjamin B. SMITH, John K. BALCH, Allen BROWN, S. B. REAVES... signed Evan YOUNG.

page 503   POLK - CALDWELL's refunding bond - Samuel POLK, deceased - recorded 19 May 1832 - for amounts paid him, Silas M. CALDWELL, husband of Lydia E. CALDWELL, one of legatees, signed July 1830 by Silas M. CALD-WELL, A. C. HAYS, A. O. HARRIS.

page 504   POLK - Franklin E. POLK - refunding bond - recorded 19 May 1832 - acknowledges receipts from Samuel POLK, estate, witnesses were E. B. DUNCAN, S. P. WALKER...

signed 8 July 1830 F. E. POLK, Marshall T. POLK, James K. POLK, James WALKER. Page 505 refunding bond for Jane POLK; page 505 refunding bond for A. O. HARRIS in right of his wife Naomi L. HARRIS...page 506 refunding bond for John B. HAYES in right of his wife Ophelia C. HAYES, one of legatees; same for Marshall T. POLK, page 507; John L. POLK, page 507.

page 508   MC GIMPSEY - William MC GIMPSEY, deceased - Inventory recorded 21 May 1832 - Levin L. COVEY, administrator ...negroes named and ages given...a number of books and silver items.

page 508   PICKARD - John J. PICKARD - Supplemental Inventory - recorded 21 May 1832.

page 509   POLK - John L. POLK, deceased - Inventory and Notes - recorded 21 May 1832; notes of Jeremiah CHERRY, Moses MOORE, John B. HAYS, Mrs. Rebecca DARK, Joseph G. KELSO, Milton KELSON, John HOGAN, Kinros DARK, Jethro J. WADDLE, William J. JOURNEY, George MOORE, Ruben MORRIS, Jno. H. WOLDRIDGE, R. A. RANKIN, John MOORE, signed A. O. HARRIS.

page 510   ANDREWS - John ANDREWS, deceased - Inventory - recorded 21 May 1832 - by Elizabeth X ANDREWS.

page 510   SANFORD - James T. SANFORD, deceased - Account of Sale - recorded 22 May 1832 - sold 2 March 1831... buyers were H. LANGTRY, GEVE and JENKINS, William R. MILLER, signed James BLACK, administrator.

page 511   JOSSEY - James JOSSEY, deceased - Account of Sale - recorded 22 May 1832 - buyers were Nancy JOSSEY, Gilbert HICKS, J. B. HAMILTON, R. W. SOWELL, William ALDERSON, Senior, J. COLEMAN, William B. ALDERSON, S. S. PORTER, R. CROSBY, T. P. JOHNSON, John FERGASSON, J. M. KEY, William WALKER, D. A. MC COY, H. A. WILEY, P. GRAHAM, Esquire MC FADDEN, J. M. CAMPBELL, Seth BRADLEY, S. W. SLAYDEN, Capt. WEBSTER, G. WEBSTER, J. C. ALDERSON, John MC FADDIN, W. W. JOSSEY, John LATTA, J. COMPTON, David FLY, William M. EDWARDS, the widow, T. COLEMAN, William JOSSEY, J. G. ROBINSON, H. LEEPER, William COLEMAN, BLACKBURN and COLEMAN, J. DOBBINS, Mrs. JOSSEY...signed W. W. COLEMAN, administrator.

page 514   CROWSON - Robert CROWSON, deceased - recorded 22 May 1832 - sold 20 January 1832...buyers: Evander KENNEDY, Shadrick LOFTON, Jeremiah TRANNUM, William HARISON, Adam RYKARD, William COOPER, Pleasant AKIN, Jesse EVANS, Jesse OVERTON, James KENNEDY, Peter I. VOORHIES, Lorenzo DOWEL, David FORTNER, Jesse G. RAINEY, Hugh BROWN, George WILSON, Richard COOK, R. EVANS, Joseph CHUMBLY, John ADAIR, John GANT, Alexander WILSON, John GARET, Tilmon MILLS, Thos. CALDWELL, Newton GORDON, _____ JOHNSON (Bible), _____ WILLEFORD, James R. EVANS, Daniel BOOKER, John GORDON, Albert HUCKEBY, Thomas HARDISON, William H. ADAIR, Cornelius TRANNUM...signed J. G. RAINEY, Adam RYKARD, administrators.

page 516   HENDERSON - William S. HENDERSON - Guardian Report -
recorded 22 May 1832 - William S. HENDERSON, guardian
for Richard HENDERSON...part of a legacy of the
estate of John TATE, deceased...hire of negroes...
land in Gibson County.

page 517   WILKES - William B. WILKES, minor - Guardian Report -
recorded 23 May 1832 - William M. ORR, guardian...
heir of Benjamin WILKES, deceased.

page 517   WADE - Frances WADE, minor - Guardian Report - recorded 23 May 1832 - Joseph WINGFIELD, guardian...hire of
negroes.

page 517   FRIERSON - Theodore FRIERSON, minor - Guardian Report
- 23 May 1832 - hire of negroes...signed James N.
FRIERSON, guardian.

page 518   BOYD - BOYD's heirs - Guardian Report - recorded
24 May 1832 - William S. HENDERSON, guardian of
Andrew T., Nancy S., and John P. BOYD...paid Jonathan
AMIS for board 1831...paid Doct. CONKEY's visit...
paid James DAVIDSON for tuition of ward.

page 518   FARRIS - William FARRIS, deceased - Guardian Report -
recorded 25 May 1832 - amount to minor heirs of
William FARRIS, deceased, that is James, William,
David, John, Mary, Elizabeth and Robert FRANCIS...
hire of negroes...note on R. KELSEY, H. C. and P.
SOWELL, John AKIN...Jane FARRIS, widow...signed
12 March 1832 by Samuel W. AKIN, guardian.
(Abstractor's note: commas in list of children in
doubt.)

page 519   MARRS - Mary Ann MARRS, minor - Guardian Report -
recorded 25 May 1832 - William W. COLEMAN, guardian.

page 520   FRIERSON - Theodore FRIERSON, minor - Guardian Report
- recorded 25 May 1832 - James W. S. FRIERSON, guardian.

page 520   WILKES - William B. WILKES, minor, Guardian Report -
recorded 25 May 1832 - Richard A. L. WILKES, guardian
...William B. WILKES, an heir of Minor C. M. WILKES
and also of Nancy K. PREWIT...William B. WILKES
received from the division of Unity K. PREWIT estate.

page 520   WILKES - Washington L. J. WILKES, minor heir of
Benjamin WILKES, deceased - Guardian Report - record-
ed 26 May 1832...R. A. L. WILKES, guardian...Washing-
ton L. WILKES was an heir at law of Minor C. M.
WILKES and Unity K. PREWITT, signed 16 March 1832,
R. A. L. WILKES.

page 521   BEANLAND - BEANLAND's heir - Guardian Report -
recorded 20 May 1832 - Peter WILLIAMS was guardian
of E. Gibson BEANLAND and Priscilla BEANLAND...
Priscilla received from estate of her father..."to
Thomas C. KENNEDY the husband of said Priscilla"...
signed Peter WILLIAMS.

page 522   CAMPBELL - Carolina H. CAMPBELL - Guardian Report -
recorded 26 May 1832 - Robert CAMPBELL, guardian...
paid G. A. CANNS.

page 522   RODGERS - Ala RODGERS, minor - Guardian Report -
recorded 26 May 1832 - N. W. BRISCOE, guardian for
Aley RODGERS...Thomas JONES was former guardian...
paid John M. FRANCIS for schooling...paid Thomas
TURNER, Neil BROWN, Joseph CUNNINGHAM (paid by him
for schooling)...paid James CUNNINGHAM for her
boarding...signed 14 March 1832 by N. W. BRISCOE.

page 522   BAIRD - John BAIRD, deceased - Guardian Report -
recorded 26 May 1832 - Edward W. DALE, guardian...
receipts of David GRAHAM, MC EWIN and HOUSTON, Capt.
KINGLEY (KINGSLEY), C. BADDLE, SHAPPARD and YEATMAN,
SHIRLEY for rent of Academy Lot...receipt of Old
Sylvia rent of house on Academy lot...owned number
of houses for which rent received...signed 2 January
1832.

page 523   POWELL - Charles POWELL, deceased - Guardian Report -
recorded 26 May 1832 - James C. POWELL, guardian for
Mathew N. POWELL, minor heir of Charles and Sally
POWELL, deceased - Lucinda POWELL, minor heir of
Charles and Sally POWELL, deceased...signed James C.
POWELL.

ARMSTRONG, E.J. Cont. 195, 207; Elizabeth,195; James 012,050,059,102,197; Jas. 195; John,017; Joseph, 076; S.H.,179,223; Saml. H.,199; Samuel H.,050, 195; Samuel Henry,195; T.H.,195; Thomas J.,059; W.G.,182; Will G.,182; William G.,059,101,195; William J.,132; William P.,050; William 017,059, 100; Wm.G.,183
ARNOLD(ALLREAD), Wm.,169
ARNOLD, (Widow),153; Avery, 063; David,030,084; Elizabeth,186; Geo.S., 222; Hopson,030,063,082, 142; J.H.,165; James L., 063,064; John H.,172, 186; John Sr.,063; John 057,064,065,153,222; Lindsay,222; Lindsey, 065,186; R.,173; Robert, 117,122; Stephen,201; Thomas,032,063; William, 030; William Jr.,063; William Sr.,063
ARNSTRONG, W.G., 183
ARON, John Jr., 222
ASBURN, John,035; William 046
ASH, Thomas L.,194
ASHLTON, Thos.L.,161
ASHTON, Philip, 076
ASHWORTH, Jonathan, 218
ASKEW, Eli,127; John,039, 041,044,099
ASTON, Polly,215
ATKERSON, Jerry,242
ATKIN, Samuel W.,142
ATKINSON, A.,065; Absalom, 213; Armstead,093; John Sr.,093; John,011,089, 093,225; Nancy,092,093; Saml.,183; Samuel,092, 093; William,225; Yerby, 213; Samuel,041
ATKISON, Andrew,160; James, 224; John Sr.,017; John, 160
AUSBURN, John,030
AUSTIN, John,098,198
AVERETT, John,097
AVERY,(Dr.),051; Nathaniel, 075
AVEY,(Dr.),050
AVONDALE, Isom,208
AVORAL,Jacob,045
AYARES(?), James 030
AYDELETT, John, 124
AYDELOT,(?),013
AYDELOTT, Daniel,016; Jediah,018; Thomas,001, 016,112
AYDELOTTE, Arthur,014,018; Jodiah,014; John,172; Zador,027
AYDLEMAN, John,107
AYDLETT, Thomas,124
AYERS,Arthur,123; Benjamin P.,124; Gadwell,077; James P.,123; Joseph Jr., 123; Joseph,091; Robert, 124
AYNES, James,132
AYRES, Benjamin,084;James, 082; Joseph Sr.,085,124; Joseph,025

BACOMB, Simon,154
BACON, Simon,160
BACONS, Stephen,160
BADDES, Joshua,053

BADDLE, C.,245
BADGER, William,003
BADGET, Benton,183; Lavina, 183; Levisa,183; Mary, 183; Noah,183; Samuel, 183; Tennessee,183; William,183
BADGETT, Benton,088,105; Isaac,063; Jesse B.,183; Levenah,090
BADGETT(BAGETT?),Benton, 015
BAGSDALE(RAGSDALE?), Edward,086
BAGUS(BAGUES?), Briant,088
BAILES & MONTGOMERY,(?), 113
BAILES, James S.,031
BAILEY, Briton,183; Charles J.,062; James,181; John W.,221; Jonathan, 035,079,197; Joseph, 091; Michael,050,116; William A.,183
BAILS, James S.,210
BAIN, John D., 208
BAIRD, Albert M.,125; John, 245; Joseph M.,085
BAITY, James,082; John, 163
BAKER, ---,215; Aasbel, 117; Andrew,030,049; Asia,117; Duncan,171, 177,235; G.,224; Isaac, 117; James M.,190,193, 224; James,091,159; John, 115; Nicholas,092; Rickman,092; Robert,192; Samuel A.,044,084,104; Samuel H.,123; Samuel, 082,126; Thomas,010
BALCH, Alfred, 080,163; Amos P.,043; John K., 242; John,163; Theron E., 046
BALCOM, Joseph C.,169; Josiah C.,169
BALDRIDGE, Alex,087,128; Alex.,226; Alexander, 064,086; Benjamin,082; Isabella,138; James L., 127; J.Y.,220; James L., 066,087,092,128,133,138, 142,147,161,166,195,197, 213,227,229,231,241; James S.,137,161,172; James,066,104,153,211, 212; Jno.,138; Jno.Y., 215; John Jr.,138; John 066,082,138,194,217; M., 212; Manuel,075; Margaret,075; Margarette,138; Michael,121,134,195,197; Narcissa,075; W.H.,220; William L.,138; William Sr.,180
BALDWIN, C.T., 193
BALL, James,177; John,066; Margarette,164; Tanda, 151; Tandy,190; William, 219
BALLARD, J.P.,220
BALOH, Amos,044
BANCOMB, Josiah C.,225
BAND, Lewis,205
BANER, John,015
BARDAL(?), James,032
BARDAWAY, Larkin,227
BAREFOOT, Nancy,092
BARHAM, Josiah,185; William W.,227,236; William, 225,237
BARKE,(?),050
BARKER, Andrew,082;E.A.,51

BARLEY(?), John,098
BARLOW, James,059,065,112, 116
BARNER, James W.,182
BARNES, Alex.,098; James W., 182; Jane (Mrs.),089; Jane W.,089,185; Jane, 089; John,078,089,120, 127,185; Jonathan,185; Mary,185; Rachael,123; Seth,108
BARNET, Mabourne(?),020
BARNETT, Ruthy,020
BARNEY, W.S.,190
BARNHILL, (?),084; James M.,125; John,208; Vachel, 123
BARNS, James,107; Jno.,219; Jonathan,173; Mary,173; Wilkinson,091; Wilkison, 046; William,188
BARR, Elizabeth M.,222; Hugh,222; Sarah,222
BARROW, Joel,054
BARRY, John G.,027,178
BARSH(?), Samuel,110
BARTLET, Thomas,020
BARTLETT, Siras H.,220
BASKERVILLE, Richd.,013
BASKET, Malcolm Clark,078
BASS, Lawrence,018,033; Peter,002; Wm.,219
BATCH, Amos,037
BATCHELOR, John,205
BATE, John,129
BATES, John,185
BATSON, Richard,092
BATTEMAN, Simeon,017
BATY, (Major?),053; Thomas, 052
BAUCOM, J.C.,227
BAUCOMB, Brittan J.,118; Britton J.,118; Edward 172
BALCOMBE, John,110
BAUCUM, Brittain J.,049; Brittan S.(J.),107; William J. 049
BAUGAUS, Bryant,184
BAUGERS, John 118
BAUGES, Briant,121
BAUGH, John 183
BAUGHT, Roderick,163
BAUGUS, Briant 199; Bryan, 096; Bryant,152,156,199; John,104,121,199; Pleasant,092
BAUGUSS, Bryant,094
BAUTEL, Thomas,043
BAWSE, Pewell,092
BAWYER, Adam,018
BAXTER, James,192; Thompson,203
BAYNE, C.,219; S.,219
BAYRES, John M.,091
BEAKLEY, James,223
BEALL, Frederick,077
BEANLAND, E. Gibson,244; Ed.,038; Edw.,038; Edward W.,185; Edward,013,015; Polly G.,185; Polly,013, 038,185; Priscilla,244
BEARD, Abraham,218; Abram, 218; Albert,123; Hugh, 210; James,064; Joseph M.,125; Martin,055,094; Samuel,008,013; Thomas, 203; William,012,017
BEASLEY, (Mr.),054;Arthur, 108; Jno.W.,156; John W., 049,109,118,180; Nancy, 150
BEATY, Arthur,027,119;James 6,15,61,239; John,26,61

BOOKER, Peter R. Cont. 148,
156,184,199
BOOLER, John,015
BOON, Sion,135,136,162,199
BOONE, James,106
BOOTH, James,124
BOROUGH, William,086
BOSS(?), El.,192
BOSS, Mosy,092
BOSTICK, A.,218,225,237
BOWAGDER(?), W.C.,113
BOWDEN, Benjamin,131; James
M.,223; James,029,032;
Travis,178
BOWDER, W.H.,214
BOWDERY, Joshua,116;
Samuel,100
BOWDRY, Joshua,213
BOWELS, Jno. Jr.,138
BOWEN, Benjamin,129; Cydia,
131; Eurette L.,131;
Jane G.,131; Joseph,162;
Mary A.,131; Mary P.,131
BOWERS(?), Joseph,096
BOWERS, Tos.,116
BOWMAN, James H.,033;
James N.,239; James,066,
067,131,154,187; Thomas,
026,112
BOYAR, John,049
BOYCE, H.,034
BOYD, (Widow),164; Aaron
(Col),181; Andrew F.,
173; Andrew T.,182,244;
Andrew,021,048,091,102,
131,134,164,186; Andrw.,
186; Anny,073; Betsey
P.,075; Elisabeth T.,
131; Elizabeth,133; J.K.,
234; Jane,131; James,021,
066,102,131,133,134,164,
173,182,187,194,212; Jno.
R.,164; John B.,182;
John P.,173,182,244; John
R.,131,134,175,186,187,
192,197,219; John,046,
057,073,097; L.B.,107,
169; Laird B.,169,170,
192; Lard B.,017,163,234;
Nancy J.,173; Nancy L.,
182; Nancy S.,244; R.,
053; Sally,186; William,
045; Winifred,186
BOYET, James,022
BOYETT, Jesse,030
BOYL, John,222
BRACK, Drury,120; Russell,
120
BRACKENRIDGE, David,052;
Hannah,052
BRADBURY, Edmond,076;
George,076,221; Jacob,
076
BRADEN, Felix,217; John G.,
217; John,109,217
BRADEY, James,027
BRADFORD & STACK, (?),240
BRADFORD, A.B.,219; H.,132;
Hugh,028,220; T.G.,186
BRADLEY, D.,128; D.G.,220;
John,101; Seth,243;
William R.,011,094
BRADLY, Mary,074
BRADSHAW & KIMES, (?),215
BRADSHAW, Benjamin,163;
Eli G.,217; Elias,165,
238; Elisabeth,141,143,
165; H.,189; Hugh,239,
242; James,021,182; Jane,
021; John,103; Kessiah,
164; Sally,020; Samuel,
036; Sarah,051; Solomon,
061; Will,035; William
Jr.002,013,017,020,043,

BRADSHAW, William Cont.
046,053,054,101,113,141,
152,163,165; Wm.,100,107,
113
BRADY, James,009,027,126;
John,064; Thomas,083;
Toliver,009; Tolver,126;
William R.,012
BRAGES, Reuben,163
BRAHEAN, Jessee,167
BRAIDY, James,138
BRALY, H.,226; R.C.,226;
Rowan C.,222,226
BRANCH, Henry,005,013,037,
043,112; James,046,107,
131,164,167,174,176,181,
219; Jas.G.,184; John
G.,184; John,054,108,
121; Matthew,004,037;
Nancy,005; Nicholas,015,
036; T.M.,122
BRANFORD, William,086
BRANK, R.H.,136,160; Ro-
bert H.,185
BRASIN, Samuel,058
BRASLY(?), John W.,128
BRASSE, Jeremiah,092
BRATTON, William (Dr.),074
BRAWLEY, Ann 182; Thomas
162,171,177,182,188,211;
William,162,182
BRAWLY, Thomas,127
BRAY, Reubbin,108; Reuben,
095
BRAZEALE, Henry,075
BRECKENBRIDGE, George,015
BRECKENRIDGE, Alex.,150,
229; Alexander,057,182,
184,235; Alexr.,152;
Felix,229; Georg,035;
George,057
BRECKERSTAFF, George,056
BRECKHAM(?), David,027
BRECKINRIDGE, Alexander,
009; Ann,009; Edda Linn,
009; Elizabeth,009;
George,009; Jinny,009;
John,009; Polly,009;
Preston,009; Rachale,009;
Roddy H.,009; Washing-
ton,009
BRECKInRIDGE, Robert
James,009
BRESEL, Ezra,083
BRESINE, Sam,043
BREWSTER, L.D.,136
BRIANT, Wm.,098
BRIDGE, Barnes,090
BRIDGES, Bain,182; Bains,
135; Baynes,078; Daniel
G.,004,005; Daniel S.,
004,018; Daniel,024,029,
041,196; Derile,115;
Derrel,115; Drury,004,
005,024; E.,208; Ester,
135,182; Esther,182;
Francis,167; Jesse J.,
196; Jesse,056,068,078,
135,136,185,242; Melita,
182; Molley,004,024;
Poley,005; Terry,008;
Thos.J.,208; Willia,
070; William J.,182;
Willis,213; Wm.,222
BRIGESS, Cyrus,213
BRIGGS, (Maj.),054; Henry,
224; Isaac,224; J.W.,
167; James,224,228; John
J.,048,059,105; John
050,224; Peter,055,130;
Samuel G.,105; Samuel,
234; William,064,153
BRIGHT, Dennis,018; Milton,
239; William,125

BRINKLEY, A.,158; Timothy,
034
BRINS(?), Perminas,007
BRINT, James,201
BRINTS, Solomon,213
BRISCOE, (Dr.),155; Doctor,
127; George,127,194;
J.W.,127; James M.,191;
James W.,061,153,217,
223; Jno.W.,162; John,
062,123; N.W.,162,168,
214,215,217,223,229,233,
245; Nobly W.,133; Per-
menas,126; Warren,120
BRISCOD, George,053
BRISHOE, N.W.,171
BRISTE(?), Ezra C.,106
BRISTE, Ezra,126
BRITAIN, James,218
BROCK, Drewey,062; George
A.,008
BROGRES, John,133
BROKS, Hezakiah,015
BROOKES, Anderson,127
BROOKS, (?),218; Alfred,177;
Anderson,215,223; Bailey,
042; Baily,013; Dudley,
004,009,017; George,013;
H.(Widow),015; Hesekiah,
076; Hez,105; Hezakiah,
004,034,037,088,165;
Isaac,010,093,189,205,
229; Jacob,140; James,
004; Joab,124; John S.,
124; Keziah,076; Kiaah,
208; L.,051; Lemuel T.,
165; Maclaja,025; Meed-
jiah,076; Micaja,133;
Micajah,094; Nancy,140;
Richard,063; Samuel T.,
029; Samuel,029,055,076,
094,107,110; Stephen,004,
094; Thomas,001,010,013,
015,016,066,159; Thos.,
162; Widow H.,088; Wm.,
208
BROOM(?), Kizza,123
BROOM, Jonathan,030,090;
Mary,030
BROWN & GIMPSEY,(?),203
BROWN & LITTLEJOHN, (Firm),
036
BROWN & MCGIMPSEY,(?),206
BROWN & MCGIMSEY,(?),129,
182,190,207,208; (Firm),
048; (Firm?),061
BROWN & NOTGRASS,(?),207
BROWN & SANDERS,(?),238
BROWN,(?),131; (Dr.),137,
190,211; (Dr.),171,172;
(Mr.),081; (Mrs.),113;
146,163; A.,099,100;
Adam,008; Agustin,163;
Alexander,192; Allen,
098,101,144,199,242;
Andrew,112,223,228; Ann,
008; Archabald,176; Arch-
ibald,163; Archy,163;
Augustin,018,188; Augus-
tine,055; Augustus,059,
208; B.,242; Bene,126;
Benedict D.,182; Benedict,
067; Bennedict W.,171;
Bill (Dr.),207; Charles
U.,107; Charles V.,042,
132; Charles W.(?),135;
Charles,025,028,033,112,
146,165,176; Crawford,
178; D.,071,090,195;
D.C.,221; Daniel C.,068,
205,224; Daniel Jr.,093,
135; Daniel,011,014,018,
041,072,093,094,115,121,
183,198; Danl.C.,222;

COOK Cont. J.O.,175; John
M.,167; John O.,129,165,
211,238; John,039; R.J.,
193; Richard,243; Step-
hen,032,063,117
COOKE & LAMASTER,(?),126
COOKE, Henry,009; John O.,
052,129,145; John,043,
103,149; Thomas,192
COOKSEY, Phebe,092
COOL, Pilmon,242
COOLEY, James,209
COOPER & HILL,(?),189,240
COOPER & HOLTS,(?),204
COOPER,(?),050; A.D.,199;
A.M.,167; Harrison,005,
013,037,038,112; Horacy,
108; James H.,225; Jno.,
082; Joel,081; John S.,
192; John,015,017,034,
058,084,108,115,137,195;
M.D.,050,144,196,204,
205,215,233; Mary B.,087;
Mathew D.,140; Matthew
D.,059; Nancy,163,109;
Robert M.,027,120; Sally,
081; Samuel,098; Sarah,
087; Stephen,098; Willa-
im,137; William Jr.,120;
William,018,034,035,054,
094,097,103,121,136,148,
159,167,180,208,223,237,
243; Wm.,223
COOPERS & HILL,(?),153
COPELAND, A.M.,097,167,
238; A.W.,039; Anthony
M.,077; Anthony,002,033;
D.,057; David Sr.,077;
David,033,039,077,097,
109,113; Henry,033;
James,033,077,081,097;
Polly,077; Sally,077
COPLAND, A.M.,055; James,
109
CORBEAR, Thomas,039
CORCH, Jesse,157
CORLAN, George,236
COSEY, Shaderick,240
COSTELA, Edward,088
COSTELOW, Edmund,043
COSTET(?), Edward,016
COSTLOE, Edw.,098
COSTON, James,157
COTT, Casby,208
COTTLE, William,028
COTTON, Edward,051
COUNCE, Redding,107
COURT, Charles,010,011
COURTS, Robert,225
COUSAT, John,016
COVEY, Leven L.,206; Leven,
134,189; Levin L.,219,
231,243; Levin,044,122,
167,219; Lewis L.,166;
Mathew G.,164; W.,127;
William W.,122,206;
William,014,028,029,
031,048,091,119,132,158,
167,186; Wm.,197,219
COVY, Leven,176; William,
136
COWAN, Joseph,230; Robert,
008; Samuel,098
COWDEN, Hugh,103; Robert,
059
COWDER(?), William,030
COWEN, John 055; W.C.,053
COWHAN, John,097
COWLE, John A.,178
COX, Adam,125; Betsy,097;
Elizabeth,043; Faulker,
003; George,225; Thomas,
043,096,097
COIE, Joseph,072

CRADDOCK, George,217
CRAFFERD, James T.,062
CRAFFORD, James T.,058
CRAFT, P.,227
CRAFTEN, Giles,209
CRAFTIN, Elisabeth,141,
144; Samuel,167; Staples,
144
CRAFTON, Bennet,128; Jeremiah,157; Mary B.,128;
Paul G.,240; Paul,128;
Robert W.,128; Robert,
128,129; Samuel S.,128;
Sarah,129; Silas M.,
128; Staple,141; Robert,
129; William W.,129
CRAGG, Elijah,096; Richard,
096,201,207; William,238
CRAIG & WASHINGTON,(?),100;
(Firm),002
CRAIG, Betsy,029; D.,034,
175; David H.,218; David
Jr.,088; David,006,025,
026,027,050,051,058,
078,079,088,109,112,116,
131,134,137,141,142,151,
152,163,169,170,171,175,
176,180,181,190,193,197,
198,201,204,210,211,229,
230,233,235,236,238,240;
Davis S.,218; E.,158;
J.C.,218; J.G.,220;
James C.,098,109,162;
James S.,181,217; James.
002,097; Jas.J.,218;
Jas.S.,218; Jno.J.,240;
John F.,224,228; John P.,
015; John S.,221; John,
029,132; Johnson,001,015,
151; Johnston,042,178,
191,196,212; Mary,175,
240; Polly,077,175;
Richard,216; Robert,218,
236,242; Samuel,006,
018,029,055,100,101,113,
166,229; Sarah,240;
Sophia,218; Thomas,036;
William M.,109; William
W.,097,163; William,035,
040,056,093,108,111,162,
181,218
CRAIGE, John P.,018
CRAIGHEAD & COBBS,(?),215
CRAIGHEAD, D.,049,050,051,
168,186; Daniel,053;
David,095,104,108,136,
147,163,188,196; T.B.,
189; Thomas B.,080;
Thos.B.,136,238
CRANFORD, John,240; William P.,155
CRANTOM(?), Thomas,138
CRAWFORD & PORTER,(?),238
CRAWFORD & SPINDLE,(?),214
CRAWFORD, (Capt.),031; --
209; A.C.,230; Albert L.,
192; Alexander,037; Ale-
xr.C.,192; Andrew,178,
225,228; B.(Dr.),217;
Charles D.,133; Craig,
234; D.B.,220; G.B.,131;
George,131; Hardy W.,
062; J.S.,219; John L.,
178; John,043,058,079;
Robert,133; Sam (Capt.),
039; Samuel (Col.),110;
Samuel,014,026,041,055,
094,177,185,192,210;
Thomas,043,058,079;
William P.,062; William,
012,035,043,124,133;
Wm.P.,111
CRAWLEY, Robert,202
CRAWSBY, R.,166;Robert,158

CRAWSON, Isaac,027; Robert,
236
CRENSHAW, J.M.,177,233;
John,198,220; Joseph,
056,108,163; Thomas,017
CRESSWELL, Henry,027
CREW, Pleasant,055
CREWS, Pleasant,010,094
CRICNER, David,027
CRINER, John,124,125
CRIPPEN, George,213
CRISP, (Dr.),222; A.T.,
098; Elizabeth(Mrs.),
209; John H.,201; Mansil,
198; T.A.,152; Tilman A.,
059,107,198,232; William,
098
CRIVER, George,123
CROCKET, William,091
CROCKETTS, Andrew,037;
Robert,037
CROFFORD,(?),235; A.C.,180;
Alexander C.,134; Craig,
198; James T.,154,167,
197,226,237; Parson,001;
William,085
CROFT, P.,224
CROFTON, Robert,224
CROMWELL, Wm.,218
CROSBY, Eliza P.,166; R.,
180,241,243; Robert,192,
211,238
CROSS, J.O.,178,235; Joseph
O.,161,177,223; Oliver,
062
CROSSTHWAIT, John,066
CROSSWAIT, John,109
CROW, B.,239; Benjamin,
216,238; Isaac,002;
John O.,226
CROWBY, Robert,154
CROWDER, Nathaniel,208,213
CROWSON, Robert,243
CRUTCHER, A.L.,178; A.P.,
181; H.L.,156; H.S.,156,
210; Henry L.,156,190,
193; William,178
CUFFLE, Joshua,030
CULBERSON, Andrew,120;
Andy,208
CULBERSON, Aron,208
CUNNIGAM, Saml.,203
CUNNINGHAM, Aaron,076,094;
Harding,187; James,129,
162,177,245; Joseph,245;
Mary F.,181; Mary,020;
Samuel T.,181; Samuel,
056,239; W.W.,093;
William,040
CURLEE, Calvin,130
CURREN & MASON,(?),203
CURREY, William,055
CURRIN, J.O.,229; Robert
P.,006
CURRY, Isaac,153,198,217;
James,092,095,126,131,
193; John D.,195; John
S.,066; John,095; Willi-
am,042; William,115
CURTIS, Benjamin,115; Joel,
227; Moses,115; William,
177; Wm.,098
CURTS, Wm.,098
CUTBIRTH, Daniel,026,095
CUTTHAM, P.,017
CYRUMN (CYNUM?), Mark,133

DABBS, George,167
DABLES, Joel,041
DABNEY, Cornelius,010,056;
Robert B.,163; Robert
O.,106
DAGBY, John,098,116
DAGGETT, Gardner,161

DAGHY, John,163
DAGLEY, John,108
DAIMEWOOD, Jacob,096
DAIMWOOD, Jacob,009
DALE & DUNCAN,(?),219,220,
    239
DALE,(?),199; E.W.,057,
    058,065,080,084,086,095,
    103,114,120,149,185,195,
    207,219,239; Edwd.W.,
    081,160; Edward W.,047,
    048,049,051,052,056,057,
    066,070,073,096,099,122,
    123,148,162,167,206,214,
    216,220,242,245; Edward,
    102; Edwd.,109; John,
    195; Joshua,013,077,092;
    Thomas,214; Thos.S.,
    208; W.W.,049
DALTON, Isaac,174; James
    A.,220
DAMELEY, John,092
DAMERON, (Mr.),210; Benja-
    min,171; Simeon,182
DAMERWOOD, Jacob,094
DAMEWOOD, Jacob,056,104,
    111
DAMRON, Samuel,242
DAMSON, R.,053
DANDFORD, James T.,039
DANIEL, (Capt.),091;
    Widow,181; Carolina,167;
    Isaac K.,216; Isaac K.W.,
    176; Isaac,167; J.M.,233;
    J.W.,176; John J.,176;
    John M.,051,061,066,079;
    John S.,192; John,018;
    Martha Angeline,176;
    Marvin G.,167; Mary,167,
    176,239; Minerva,167;
    William W.,176; William,
    002,027,028,029,073,085,
    121,124,167,176,181
DANIELL, John M.,161
DANIEL, Minerva,176
DANILL, Mary,166; William
    167
DANILY, John,054
DANNEL, J.M.,130; John M.,
    130
DAOAL, John R.,178
DARDEN, A.,150; Alfred,
    159
DARK, H.,220; James,169;
    Kinros,243; Micajah,098;
    Rebecca (Mrs.),243;
    Rebecca,058,098
DARKER, Thomas,126
DARNAL, Joseph,135
DARNALL, John,186
DARNELL, John,133; Joseph,
    029; William,133
DAUGHERTY & LONGLY,(?),117
DAUGHTERTY & LONGLY,(?)107
DAUGHTERTY, J.,033
DAVEY, John,124
DAVID, Hezekiah,169; Jones,
    139; Samuel,066
DAVIDOSN, Ephrem E.,109
DAVIDSON, B.,224; B.C.,
    139; Bracket,178; Brac-
    key,099; E.,006,049;
    E.E.,040,048,162,166,
    213; Emeline,045; Eph-
    ragm G.,137; Ephraigm E.,
    139; Ephraim E.,073,
    079,122,185; Ephraim,
    163; Ephrm.E.,160;
    Francis,139; G.F.,006;
    George Jr.,046; George,
    001,005,006(2),045,046,
    061,062,097,107,175;
    Gilbreath F.,006,046,
    061; Gilbreath,046,099;

DAVIDSON Cont. Hiram,127;
    Isabella,045; James L.,
    006(2),046,061; James,
    244; Jane,046,061; John
    C.,107; John D.,009,042;
    John E.,045,046,099,110,
    163; John G.,139; John
    O.(?),048; John O.,122,
    139,166; John,122,137,
    139,165,166; Joshua,
    218,225; Louisa S.,006;
    Louisa,045; O.,113;
    Polly,046; Robert,046,
    101,210; Rosanna,045,
    046,061; Rosannah,062;
    Ruth C.,139; Sarah,045;
    Thomas,036,139
DAVIES, Richard,124
DAVIS,(?),153; Maj.016(2),
    038; Archelus,083; Bar-
    ten,033; Barton,008;
    Been,018; Benj.,209;
    Benjamin,109,119,198;
    Canstantine,189; Consta-
    tine,042; Daniel,042(3),
    052,054,097,107,147,160,
    161,170; Danl.,175;
    David,236; Elijah,192;
    Elisabeth,161; Henry,
    038; Hezekiah,053,063,
    064; Isaac,192; Isaiah,
    082,084,124,192,228;
    James,040,082,083,170,
    205,209,236; Jane,045,
    081,192; Jeremiah,232;
    Joab,160; John M.,123;
    John,003,009,028,034,
    038,108,110,120,163;
    Joseph,109,117,217,219;
    Joshiah,158; Joshua,054;
    Josiah,053,241; Lewis,
    108; Lidia,129; Lydia,
    042(2),175; M.C.,083,
    111; Magness,010; Magnus,
    016; Magnuss,026; Micaj-
    ah,111; Phillip,160,161;
    Saml.,184; Sampson,192;
    Samuel,049,087,091,106,
    113,192; Thomas,054;
    Vincent,242; William A.,
    017,054,062; William,
    010,016,026,034,038,056,
    107,109,119,163,176,209
DAVISON, George,036,081;
    Jane,045; John E.,006;
    John,002,176; Joseph,
    178; Robert,013
DAVY, John,085
DAWKIN, James,032
DAWS, D.,222
DAWSON, H.C.,090; Henry,
    090; J.,190; Jno.,240;
    John,087,155,177; Tho-
    mas,015
DAYS, Edmond,163
DE PRIEST, Horatio,006
DEADRIDGE, Samuel,025
DEAL, Joseph,225; Joshua,
    030,043
DEAN, Alexander,023; Alice,
    022; Benjamin,023;
    Eliza,022; Elizabeth,
    023; Hannah,022; John,
    022,023,126,239; Luke
    H.,009; Matilda,022;
    William,012,022,025,034
DEANS, D.,222; David D.,
    237; Luke H.,017
DEAREN, James,209
DEARIN, James,217; Larkin,
    170,172,208
DEATON, Jackson,158; Tho-
    mas,178,181
DEENS, David D.,184

DEER, Daniel,055
DEERIN, J.C.,054
DEGETT, William,064
DEIDRICK, Thomas,002
DEMOSS, Lewis,036; William
    036
DENHAM, Alex.P.,112; Alex-
    ander P.,039,106; E.,
    103; R.F.,186; Robert M.,
    132
DENNEY, William,049
DENNON, B.,179
DENNY, Margaret,058;
    William,136
DENNON, B.,179
DENNY, Margaret,058;
    William,136
DENOVANT, William,205
DENTON, Abram,079; Benja-
    min,079; Charles,079;
    Elenor,079; Elleanor,042;
    James A.,209; Joseph,
    042,079
DEPREIST, Horatio,114
DEPRIEST, Eliza G.,099;
    H.(Dr.),018; Hor.,043,
    098; Horatio (Doct.),
    029; Horatio,011,099,109
DERDAN, John,163
DERRYBERRY, C.M.,228; John,
    224
DESHONGH(DESHOUGH), Red-
    dick,183
DESTER, John S.,161
DEVER, Jane,006; Mary,006;
    William,006,058
DEVERS, William,102
DEWAGAN, J.T.,242
DEWANEY, James,017
DEWEARS, John,013
DEWOODY, George,067
DIAL, David Jr.,129; David,
    129; Elizabeth,099;
    Joshua,112; William,129
DICKENS, Saml.C.,205;
    William,138
DICKENSON, (Mr.),067;
    Archillus A.,072; Mary,
    072; Washington Ribon,
    072; William G.,048
DICKERSON, H.S.,201
DICKESON & COOPER,(?),202
DICKEY, B.,050,101,179,
    213; Banoni,053; Benona,
    025,043; Benone,016;
    Benoni,074,075,095,100;
    Benonin,059; G.,050,189;
    George M.,054,107,110;
    George,045,059,101,107,
    110,132; James R.,201;
    John Frierson,074; John,
    016,017,110,201; Ludlow,
    074; Nancy,016; W.R.,050;
    William B.,123; William
    R.,059,178
DICKIE, John,072
DICKINSON & COOPER,(?),128
DICKINSON, Hartwell,238;
    Nancy,072
DICKSON, A.,137,189; Amos,
    010; Elisabeth,142; Eliz-
    abeth,042,058,098,128;
    James,056,058,128,142;
    Jas.,239; John,042,098,
    128,137,141; Joseph,204;
    L.J.,129; Lucy,205; M.,
    128; R.C.,098; Robert C.,
    058,128,137; Thomas D.,
    049; William,116; John,
    058
DICKY, George,012
DIGHAM, James,167
DILAHUNTY, ---,208
DILEHAY, Lucy G.,217

DILL, John,242
DILLAHA, John,226
DILLAHAN, Jno.,222
DILLAHAY, J.W.,213; John,
222
DILLAHUNTY, E.,237; Edmd.,
196; Edmund,204; Lewis,
107
DILLANHAY, Levy G.,163
DILLARD, Frances,189;
Henry D.,224; John L.,
131
DILLEHAY, Levi G.,227
DILLEN, Charles R.,107
DILLIAN, Joseph,035
DILLIAMS, Nemrod,035
DILLON, Charles R.,163
DISHONGH, Reddick,198,199;
Redick,205; Redrick,144
DISON, William,049
DIXON, Adam,078,081,098,
214; Anna,078; George,
078,098,099; Gideon F.,
091; John,098,195; Mary,
078; Rachel,078; Robert
C.,098,142; Saml.,218;
Thomas,078,098; William
G.,122; William,137
DOAK, Betsy,189; Robert,
137,140,189,206
DOAKE, Robert,167
DOALDSON, Francis,027
DOBBIN, Catharine,975;
Catherine,078; D.,097,
212; David,078,085; James
052,100; Jennet Malvina,
078
DOBBINS, A.,050; Alexander,
059; David,041,082,122,
177,196,233; Isaac J.,
070; J.,243; James (Col)
134,135; James,002,008,
047,050,059,084,085,104,
113,123,128,173,178,182,
183,215,217,219,240;
Silas,033
DOBBS & DILLAHUNTY,(?),214
DOBBS, George,176; Henry,
167; Nathaniel,028
DOBING, James,028
DOBINS, Elexander,012;
James,025
DOBSON, George B.,004;
John,004; Phebe,004
DOCKERY, Zacheriah,107
DODD, Allen,089,178,216;
Mark,063
DODSON, Abner J.,130;
Abner,130; Asa,191; Asia,
208; Beverly,208; David,
208,237; Elizabeth,130;
George,019; John,019;
Martin,172,208; Pheby,
019; Rebecca,201; Willie,
068
DOGGETT, Thomas,170
DOGGINS, Alexander,145;
James,132
DOKE, E.,220
DOLLIN, Alexander,101
DOLLINGS, Jesse,048
DOLLINS, Alvira,079; Jere-
miah,079; Jesse,048;
John,079; Tyre,042;
Tyree,079,095,098,210;
Tyra,042; Widdow,042
DOLLISON, Barnabas,041
DONALDSON, Francis,020
DONLEY, William,038,048
DONNELS, Stockley,056
DONNEY, William,155
DOOLEY, Cinthia,139; Cyn-
thia,081; E.,072; E.B.,
072,118,137,144,190,213;

DOOLEY Cont. Eastham B.,
139; Eliza,214; Eram,
117; Esom B.,154,172,
190; Esom,128; J.,190;
James Madison,128; James,
113,120,128,144,146;
Jane,081; Levisa,081;
Littleton,144; P.F.,
137; Paris F.,139,144,
154,165,166,213; Paris,
128; Parris F.,139,213,
214; Patsey (Mrs.),139;
Rachel (Mrs.),139;
Rachel,128; Ratchel,144;
William,015,055,081;
P.F.,189
DOOLY, William,013
DORCH, David,157; Wm.M.,
156
DORTCH, Wm.M.,183
DOSS(?),Ayres,001,027;
Ayres,006
DOTSON, Nancy,193; Terry,
190; Wm.T.,222
DOTTSON, Lazarus,001
DOTTY, J.,129
DOTY, J.,129; James,113,
114; L.F.,128,238
DOUGHERTY, White,034
DOUGHERTY & LONGLEY,(?)
104
DOUGHERTY, J.,110
DOUGLAS, Daniel,132,203;
Hugh,051,071,083,089,
105,128,129,136,182,
193,194,197; John,005;
Jonathan,182; Larkin,
115
DOUGLASS, John,077; Daniel,
077; Hugh,013,016,145,
146,148,149; Margaret,
005
DOWD, J.R.,227
DOWDY, James,213; John,165
DOWEL, Benjamin,107; Lor-
enzo,243; Reubin,108;
William,091
DOWELL, Joel,032; Lorenzo,
170
DOWN, Conner,064
DOWNELLY, John,018
DRAKE, Annah,077; Demari-
us(?),077; Diana,077;
Edward,138; Eley,077,
078; Hubert,077,120;
Nancy,077,120; Z.,002
DRISCOE, Permenas,126
DRUMMOND, James,124
DRYDEN, Robert,236
DUCKER, John B.,144
DUCKEY, John,121
DUCKWORTH, John,010,016,
033,041,053,088; Mary,
077
DUDLEY, G.,239; Joseph,
159; Robt.B.,159; Willi-
am,005
DUE, Arthur W.,044; Samuel,
213; Thomas,042,054,056;
William,065,221,228
DUFF, Thomas,008,026
DUFFLE, Elizabeth,204
DUGGAR, Shadrach,062;
Shadrick,035
DUGGER, David,035,042,204;
Shade,097; Shadrick,203;
Shedrick,015
DUIN, Charles R.,056
DUKE, Green,190; Jno.,
138; William,138
DUN, James R.,109
DUNCAN,(?),050; Amos,193;
220; David,125; E.B.,
242; James,004,008,032,

DUNCAN, James Cont. 055,
083,105,112,117; John,
117,125; Joseph,065,173;
Josiah,170; Lemuel H.,
240; Lemuel,241; Marshall
136; Patsey,125; William
016,065; Wm.,218
DUNHAM, Alexander P.,027
DUNKIN, Amos,127; William
S.,125
DUNLAP, D.R.,226; David R.,
226; Eliza Jane,181;
Eliza,058,079,178; Emily,
178,181,240; Nancy,181,
240; Samuel,060,142,178,
181,222,239; Thomas H.,
058,079,181; Thomas,181
DUNN, Edward,107; William,
018,110,111,163; Wm.,113
DUNNAM, Robert,027
DUPREST, (?),050
DURANT, Thomas,242
DUTY, Littleton,027
DUVALL, Benjamin,127; John,
214; Mareen,127; Marion,
214
DYAL, Elizabeth,099,166;
James,099,166; Joseph,
042,099
DYE, Perteyman,056; Pretty-
man,105; Stephen,055
DYEL, Joseph,166
DYER, David,179; George,
093; Joel,154

EAGLE, David,178,224
EANCE, Nancy,092
EARLEY, John G.,180
EARTHMAN, (?),013
EASLEY, J.G.,192
EASON, James,202; Thos.N.,
208
EAST, Joseph,014,028
EASTHAM, William,095,217,
239; Wm.,098
EASTHOR, William,054
EASTWOOD, Lydia,180;
Lydie,180
EAVES, John,178,181
ECHOLES, Moses,132
ECHOLS, (Dr.),209; Doctor,
198; Isham,225; Isom,
228; Joel,198,209; Moses,
101
EDALMAN, A.C.,202
EDD, William O.,053
EDDLEMAN, (Widow),144;
Anna,180; John,102,152,
159,193,232; Nancy,134
EDDLEMON, David,042
EDDS, William P.,110,163
EDES, Yeatman,152
EDIMONSON, Thomas,055
EDLEMAN, John,134,180
EDLEMON, John,042
EDMDES, William,132
EDMINSON, James,110
EDMINSTON, James,109
EDMISTON, William,174
EDMON, John,062
EDMONDS, Elijah,225;
Samuel D.,218; William,
200
EDMONDSON, Andrew,242;
James,073; John,151;
Joseph,220; William,052,
159,202,203,218,234
EDMONSON, Jno.,154; William
147,192
EDMONSTON, William,113
EDMUNDSON, James E.,015;
William,114
EDMUNISON, Wm.,113
EDWARDS, Anna,118; Anne,99;

GILLEY, Alexander,224;
Eleanor A.,224; Isabella
M.,224; James M.,236;
James,224; Jane M.,224;
Jane,224,236; Martha
Matilda,224; Mary Ann
224
GILLIAM, J.M.,048; Joel,
064; Thomas,088; William
G.,017; William,040,055,
208; Wm.,088
GILLISPIE, S.A. (Dr.),156
GILLUM, Thomas,068,143
GILMOER, Joseph,073
GILMORE, (?),127; John,
013,043,112; Joseph,055,
107,122,156,201,219;
William,108
GINGER, --,190
GINNERS, James,170
GIPSON, Henry,053,055,057,
103,107,109; Margaret,
021; William,021
GIFTON(?), Willie,014
GIVEN, John,001
GIVINS, E.,035
GLASCOCK, James E.,202;
Mary,202
GLASGO, Nathan,030
GLASS, Alexr.,164; David,
063,136,195,235; Lewis,
186; Robert,151; Thos.
M.,136; William,042,164
GLASSCOCK, Comfort,150;
George,109,163,227;
James,058,143,228; Peter
058,143
GLAWSON, Joseph,218
GLENN, David,111; Wm.,181
GLOTHY, Josiah,221
GLOVER, Andrew,154,216;
Eleaner C.,060; Elenor
C.,047; J.,047; Jesse,
039; Joshua,083,107,118;
P.,047; Spicy,225
GOAD, O.,228; R.,224;
Robert (Mrs.),110; Ro-
bert,004,117; Rubin,094;
Thomas,010
GOALSBY, Jane,092
GOAN, Andrew,014
GOB, William,223
GODWIN, Alfred,242; Samuel
044
GOFF, Isaac,137; John,008,
046; Thos.J.,222
GOFORTH, Andrew H.,037,
049,108,118; Andrew,
003,037; H.,162; Hiram,
003,037,053,062,118,127;
Nancy,118; William,003,
086,163
GOIN, Lucy,154
GOINS, Andrew,153; Isaac,
154; Levy,154
GONS(?), E.D.,136
GOOD, A.,224; Andrew,167;
Peter,029; Reuben,014,
093; Robert,014,017,026,
094; Robin,116; Rubin,
116; Caleb,093
GOODAN, K.,066
GOODE, Andrew,223
GOODGION, James M.,181;
William,181
GOODGON, James W.,181
GOODIGHT, John,029
GOODIN, John B.,201
GOODING, Jno.B.,241; John
B.,230,132,206,209;
Josiah,220; W.W.,211
GOODJOIN, William,098
GOODLOE, (?),056; John M.,
002,003,015,033; Wm.,217

GOODLOW, John M.,017,025,
106,163; Maria Eliza,
025; Mary Hurt (?),025
GOODMAN,(?),101; Alexander
066,067; Alisha,059,065;
Fleming,063,065; Jesse,
050,065,067,148,177;
John,062,065,102; T.T.,
228; Terrell,131; Tol,
223; Tolivar,223; Toli-
ver,065; Wm.,228
GOODNIGHT, Henry,026
GOODNITE, Henry,014
GOODNOE, John,015
GOODRAM, Daniel,207
GOODRUM, Daniel,095,117;
James,096; Samuel,095;
Thomas,093,166
GOODSIN, William W.,169
GOODWIN, Beal,121; Boiling,
123; James,053; Jeremiah
062; John,120; Patsey,
091; William G.,052;
Willis,055
GOODY(?), James,097
GOOMM, William,220
GORDAN, John,135
GORDEN, Francis,209; John,
224,242
GORDON, (Capt.),039; Bow-
lin,158; Bowling,083,
132; Dolly (Mrs.),085;
Dolly,123; Fielden L.,
125; Fieldin,047; Fran-
cis,063,222; James,015,
018,116; Jesse M.,088;
Jno.,086,111; John
(Capt.),010; John Jr.,
116; John Sr.,116; John,
015,033,047,048,049,055,
062,067,068,083,084,094,
098,104,107,110,123,143,
179,180,183,190,191,193,
220,222,237,243; Newton,
243; P.,238; Powhatten,
124; Powton,217; Richard
049; Robin,083; William,
079,104
GORSON, John,012
GOSLEY, James,195
GOSSET, John,118
GOSSETT, Clementine M.,
196; Elijah,060; Harvey
M.,196; John,060,134,
137,142,196; Mary,196;
Polly,060; Tilman,091;
U.?,060; Vandyke,196;
W.M.,181; William,134,
178,196,239
GOSTT, Katharine,117;
Polly,117
GOUR, Z.L.,220
GOURD, R.,196
GOWEN, Andrew,194; Isaac,
194; Levi,194
GOWER, H.,141
GRADEN, John,217
GRAFFORD, A.S.,062
GRAHAM, Charles,178; David
245; Dudley,178; Grean,
178; Green,178,241;
James,178; Margaret,178,
235; Melvina,178; P.,
243; Peter,084,124,178;
Samuel,178
GRAHM, Daniel,025; Samuel,
021
GRAMMILL, James,160
GRANGER, C.,136
GRANT, Collier,117; Emmily
117; Greenberry,199;
Thomas,078,083,093,094,
106,135,199; Thos.,205,
209; William,010,117

GRAVES(GRIMES), Peter,185
GRAVES, Balias,032; Jacob,
032; John,054,110; Nath-
aniel,128; Nathn.,085;
William C.,134,240
GRAY, Andrew,129; Charles,
005,009,158; George,067,
122; Hugh,194; Jacob,101;
James D.,092; James,044,
146,147,156,182; Jesse,
221,223,228,237; John,
053; Joseph,148; Margaret
077; Samuel,181; Wm.,114;
William,036,147,181,203,
218,222,228; Wm.,113
GRAYHAM, Green,217
GREEN(GREER), William,037
GREEN, Andrew,045; George,
112; J.M.,205; James Y.,
022,030,054,065,117;
John W.,050,051; Josiah,
127,134,180; Mary,032,
117; Thomas S.,117;
Thomas,017; Thos.P.,117;
William,004,029,063
GREENE, John M.,162; Thos.
C.,223
GREENFIELD & SMITH,(Firm)
084
GREENFIELD, (?),104;
(Capt.),024,030; G.(Dr.),
017; G.T.,085,133;
Garrett (Dr.),005; Ger-
rard T.,123; T.T.,092;
Thomas T.,007,085,123;
Thomas,017,026
GREER, George,085,124,125;
Vance,091
GREGORY, Thomas,242
GREY, Charles,192
GRICCEF, William,131
GRIFFETH, John,124; Samuel
050
GRIFFIN, Jesse,084,124;
John,015,055; Jos.,240;
Joseph,177,179,181,220;
L--,015; Milley,028;
Owen,204; Samuel,204;
Spencer,001,017,190;
W.,116; Wiley,005;
William,094,123,124;
Willie,026; Wyley,037
GRIFFITH, (?),191; James,
144; Jno.,158; John,084,
114,117,144,158,192,198;
Samuel,010,016,026,058,
075,080,099,117,118,120,
138,144,152,197,198;
Spencer,193; Susan,144;
William,227
GRIFFON, Spencer,020
GRIFIN, Joseph,233
GRIGGS, Billy,076; Daniel,
125; Peggy,076; William,
021
GRIGORY, E.D.,045
GRIMES, Alexander,116;
Catherine,012; Cathy,006;
David,192; Henry,131;
Jack,192; James,026,116,
170,192; Jane W.,215;
John Sr.,027; John,006,
012,014,026,027,084,104,
124,195,214,221; Lloyd,
026; Louisa,192; Loyd,
012,026; Layed,006;
Luke,005,006,026,027,
131,194; Mark,116,218;
Nancy,006,131,192,194;
Peter,089,185; Robert,
131,221; William,006,
012,015,025,026,027,116,
192,194; Wilson,131;
Wortham,198

GRIMHAW(?), Milly,007
GRINDER, Franky,139;
  Joshua,139
GRISHAM, George,079;
  Sally,071,079
GROOMS, William,060
GROVE & JENKINS, (?),238
GROVE, H.,047,226; Jonathan
  173
GROVES & SMITH, (Firm),050
GROVES, H.,134,138,147; J.,
  238; John B.,208
GRUNDY, Felix,151; Phelix,
  097
GRYMES, Luke,012
GUEST, J.,098; Joshua,054,
  103,109,110,113,117,119,
  180,216,238
GUIGLEY, George,158
GUIN, Richard,110; Ruth,
  229; William W.,181
GUINN, (Mrs.),206
GUIST, Joshua,073
GULLET, --,116; George,
  073,086; James,002,009,
  103,108,218; Jas.,208;
  Saml.,196; Samuel,027,
  086,237; Thompson,208
GULLETT, G.,237; George,
  237,239; James,171,218,
  242; John,237; Rebecca,
  237,239; Samuel,163,180,
  208,218,227,239; Thoma-
  son,225; Thompson,237,
  239,242
GULLIT, James,017
GUM, Martin,054
GUMAN, Hall,163
GUMM, Norton,002
GUNN, Benjamin,218; Eliza-
  beth R.,072; James,066,
  102,121,122; R.T.,163
GURLEY, D.,118; David,034;
  Davis,010,011,034,038,
  099,110; Dee,034; Jere-
  miah,014,026,034,038,
  055,076; John,045,105;
  Polly,034,038
GURLY, Davis,117
GURT, Joshua,054
GUTHERY, William,155
GUTHRIE, W.F.,156
GWIN, Edmond,042

HAAZE, George,042
HABLETT, William,224
HACHET, John,186
HACKET, (?),091
HACKEY, Joseph,144,179
HACKNEY, Joseph,107,109,
  131,153,177,201,230,234;
  Lot,061,198; Lott,120;
  William,240
HADDEN, W.B.,092
HADDOCK, George C.,221
HADLEY, C.B.,218; Henry,
  221,John L.,127
HADNOT(?), Brice,026
HAGEPETH, Thomas,030
HAGGARD, Edmund,030,082
HAGGER, Edward,082
HAGGINS, Mikeal,131
HAIL, John,076; Nancy,
  076; Powel,150; Powell,
  118; Stephen M.,076;
  William,242
HAINES, Alexander J.,219
HAINESS, John,033
HALL, Powel,153
HAKET, George,191
HALCOLM, William,107
HALCOM, William,155
HALCOMB, B.,054; Daniel,
  083; John,054; Laurence,

HALCOMB Cont. Laurence,
  004,037; William,049,
  086; Wm.,003
HALCUM, Lawrence,049
HALE, Benjamin,030; J.G.,
  185; James,027,086; Powel
  049,063; Powell,111
HALEBET, John,040
HALES, Chesley,170; Rich-
  ard,199
HALEY, Chesley,224
HALIBERT, John,046
HALKIM, Daniel,033
HALL, (Dr.),061,129; Bird,
  220; E.J.,036; Edward,
  236; Harris,236; Henry,
  033,084; J.A.,156; J.P.,
  215,216; James,229; John
  065,159; Joseph G.,157;
  Joseph P.,205; Joseph
  Y.,133; Joseph,030,161,
  194; Powel,053
HALLOWAY, Flemming,172
HALSOM, Lawrence,155
HALL, I.G.,198
HAM, Osange,183
HAMBLET, Berryman,103;
  James G.,103,110; James,
  103; Littleberry,039,
  094,103; Martha,103;
  Patsey,108; William,103
HAMBLETT, James G.(Maj.),
  110; Littleberry,103,
  148,159,180; Littleburry
  143; William,143,148,180
HAMBLIN, P.B.,193
HAMBRICK, John,062; Travas
  105; Travis,055; Uriah
  228
HAMBUE, John,021
HAMES, Moses,030
HAMILTON & JORDAN, (?),
  171,215
HAMILTON, (Dr.),061,190;
  A.,091; Alex,121; Andrew
  028; David,119; J.,065;
  J.B.,241,243; J.C.,129;
  John B.,051; John C.,
  034,055,083,085,104,123,
  136; John,242; Joseph,
  043,109; Rebecca,104;
  Robert,085,124; Robert-
  son,092; Thomas,229
HAMLET, James G.,108;
  Littleberry,110; William
  208
HAMLETT, Littleberry,137;
  William (Dr.),136;
  William,137,159; Wm.,221
HAMMER, James,144
HAMMON, Abraham,068
HAMMONDS, Abraham,183
HAMPTON, Joseph,008
HAMRICK, Jeremiah,105;
  Traves,002; Travis,042;
  Yelavan,105
HANCOCK, (?),063,219,238;
  Elizabeth,063; George,
  107,109; J.W.,063; John
  W.,224,228; John,063;
  Lucinda,063; Richard C.,
  063; Samuel,242; Stephen
  M.,063
HANDERSON, Robert,153
HANEY, Calvin L.,055
HANKES, Thomas,090
HANKINS, David,014; Joel,
  242; John,242, William,
  149
HANKS, Agatha,227; Elijah,
  033,191,227,237; George,
  013; Moses,033,109,137,
  218,227,237; Mrs.,001;
  Polly,016; Richards,002;

HANKS Cont. Sarah,237;
  William,109,163
HANLEY, William,173
HANNA, John B.,197; John
  H.,197; Joseph,137
HANNAH, James,006,016,095;
  John H.,239; Joseph,182;
  Samuel,153
HANNUM, L.,022; Washington
  L.,052
HARBINSON, Matthew,035;
  Thomas W.,208
HARBISON, Mathew,097;
  Matthew,191
HARDAMAN, Thomas J.,010
HARDEMAN, Blackston,040;
  N.P.,083; Nicholas P.,
  083; Thomas J.,211;
  Thomas Jr.,040; Thomas
  M.,211
HARDEN, (?),215; Humphrey,
  193; Pleasant G.,225;
  Swan,046,049,050,073;
  Thomas H.,001,003
HARDERSON, Andrew,201
HARDESON, William,193,233
HARDEY, William D.,209
HARDIMAN, Tankersley N.P.,
  032; Thos.,163
HARDIN & NIX, (?),229
HARDIN, (Land),200; A.B.,
  242; Alfred,159; B.W.,
  163,208; Benjamin Frank-
  lin,075; Benjamin,110,
  143,163; Blaxtin,105;
  Callaway,041,094,110,111;
  Calloway,019; Cynthia,
  077; Elija,178; Henry,
  077; I.B.,199; Isaac B.,
  075,106,143,162,199;
  James,053,164; Martin,
  094; Mark,004,077,111,
  163; Martin,055,077;
  Mary,191; Pleasant G.,
  237; Pleasant J.,236;
  Richard,077; S.(?) B.,
  102; S.,178; Sally P.,
  075; Sarah P.,163; Sarah,
  077; Sion,054; Sucky,077;
  Swan B.,110; Swan,047,
  057,065,077,089,103,105,
  108,114,125,137,163,193,
  242; Thos.,160; Waston,
  009; Watson,095,121;
  William F.,075; William,
  077,094,117,143,154
HARDISON, Asa,077,224;
  Charles,218,219,224,225,
  227,238,241; Chas.,238;
  Chs.,225; Edward,224;
  Eli,224; Ezra,224; Hum-
  phrey,224,227; Ira,224;
  James,224,239; Jeremiah,
  070; Joel,224,225,227,
  236,241; Joseph,224,236;
  Joshua,224; Josiah,228;
  Mary,086; Polly,224;
  Thomas B.,120; Thomas,
  086,243; William,193,
  224,239
HARGRAVES, Stephen,160
HARISON, William,243
HARK, William,058
HARLAN, Elijah,198
HARLAND(?), Elijah,058
HARLIN, Elisabeth,007;
  Silas,178
HARLOW, Robert,178; Square
  (?),180; Squire,158;
  William,180
HARMER, B.,199
HARMICK, Anna,002; Jere-
  miah,002; Traves,002;
  Yelvanton,002

HARMON, Stephen,034; Willi-
am,052
HARNEY, James,092; John,
126; L.,053; Thomas,002
HARPER, Moses D.,051,139,
144; Moses,052; Thomas
M.,159,180,193,232; Thos.
M.,214; Thos.N.,134;
William,091; Wm.,209
HARPER, William,198
HARREL, (?),198; Josiah,
095; Richard,092
HARRELL, James,035
HARRING, Nancy,152; Robert
085
HARRINSON, Mathew,208
HARRIS & POLK, (?),186,240
HARRIS, Naomi C.,200;
?airborne,198; A.C.,191;
A.D.,066,108,169,176,
205,208,215,224,238,240,
242,243; Alexander L.,
102; B.R. (& Co.),215;
B.R.,191,220; Benj.R.,
214,215; Benjamin R.,
051,209; Benjamin,191;
Cabel,026; Caleb,228;
Calibourn,230; Charles
B.,134,155,180; Charles,
127; E.,237; Edmund,117,
186; Edward,081,236; Eli,
074; Elizabeth,005,
Henry West,074; Henry,
051,191,198,209,210;
Jiles T.,222; Jno.,156;
John,005,228,232; Josiah,
242; L.B.,193; Lidda,
214; Milly,074; Maomi L.,
243; Naomi,200; Newt,
191; Olive,051,074; R.,
198; R.D.,098; Richard
C.,053,086,109,163;
Robin D.,099; Simpson,
005,037,043,054; Stephen,
026; Taylor,236; Thomas,
156; West,048,051,074,
198,209,215; West.,013;
Wyatt,051,066,074,198
HARRISON, Daniel W.,027;
Edmund,003; George,089,
141,152; J.B.,102; Jo-
seph,209; L.,191,193;
Lodevick,190; Rease,209;
Sarah,004; Thomas T.,
239; Thos.J.,215; Willi-
am,004,155
HARRIWAY, Nancy,135
HARROD, John,055
HARROLD, Peter,151
HARROS, Alanson,178
HART, B.S.,228; Campbell,
226; J.,138,156; James,
175; Jane M.,175; Jane,
221; Jesse,177,221;
Jessey,175; John L.,175;
John,039,112,128,167,
178,221; Joseph,008,055,
107,138,175,177,184,204,
211,220,226; Moses,218;
Nancy,175,221; Polly,
218; Ratchel,149; Rich-
ard Jr.,108; Sally W.,
175; William,068,138,
149,154,178,221
HARTY, Dennis,116
HARVELL, Ambrose,042
HARVEY, Thomas G.,027,082;
Thomas,030
HARVILL, John,237
HARWELL, Ambrose,210;
Graves,209
HASKEL, George,225
HASKIN, Robert,192
HASTEN, James,208

HASTIN, Robert,192
HATCHER, John,054,133
HATCHETS, John,053
HATCHETT, James,127; Jno.,
121,147,168,214,238,241;
John,058,061,073,097,
108,110,121,132,133,142,
149,163,167,192,201,230
HATCHITT, John,135
HATT, Joseph G.,133
HATTON, Patrick,198
HAUTH, Andrew,046
HAVENDRE, Charles,053
HAVY(?), James,117
HAWEKENSON(?), James,106
HAWK, John,131
HAWKINS, (Mrs.),105; Allen
102,104; Esther,057;
Ezekiel,111; Grant,011,
014,102; Henry,029;
Hetty,104; Jeney,106;
John,016,105,196; Joseph
177; Mary,029,103,124;
Nancy,114; Polly,106;
Samuel,114,152; Seth,
103; Silas,026; Stephen,
103,104; Uzell,128;
Uzial,095,112; Uzzel,
138,152; Uzzell,103,105,
106; Uzzial,016; Willi-
am (Rev.),029; William,
011,014,029,059,082,102,
103,104,105,129,145,148,
238; Wm.,083; Allen,057
HAWTHORNE, Elizabeth,197
HAY, Benjamin,106; Sally,
106; Sary,106
HAYDEN, Danl.E.,208
HAYES, A.C.,080; Andrew
C.,114; Andrew,105;
Benjamin,053; Jesse,105;
John B.,243; Ophelia C.,
243; William,036
HAYNES, Alexander L.,192;
E.M.,213; James,076,
122; Robert,076; Sally,
076; Thomas,224,228
HAYNNIE, John,018
HAYS & DEAN, (?),240
HAYS & Dean, (?),208
HAYS & ESTES, (?),239
HAYS, (Dr.),131; A.C.,
108,162,200,242; Andrew
C.,096; David,094; Doct.
230; Eleanor,001; Elenor,
001,036; Geo.,158;
George,002,124,129; J.B.,
215; James,049,062,104,
118; Jesse,001,036;
Jno.B.(Dr.),233; Jno.B.,
068,200,214,216,243;
John,095; Jonathan,002;
Margaret,002; O.C.,215;
Samuel,049,111,118;
Wiley G.,228; William,
001,002
HAYWOOD, Doctor,054
HEADIN, Ann Maria,058;
Thomas H.,058
HEADLEE, Caleb,052,173,
187,191,218,238; Daniel,
060; David,060; Joseph,
060
HEADLEY, Caleb,129,146,
147,150,191,199,227,231
HEADLIE, Caleb,060
HEALTON, Truman,181
HEAREY, James,178
HEARMAN, Charles L.,056
HEARST, John,225
HEDGEPATH, Council,092,
124; Thomas,010,011,
013,037,112; Thos.,112
HEDGES, John,163

HELEY, Thomas,094
HELM, Joseph,177; M.,051,
066,099,174,184,196,215,
237,241; Meredith,110,
170,180,199,201,241,242;
Meridet,096; Merideth
L.F.,055; Merideth,110,
114,174,219; Meridith,
095
HELMS, Fielding,018; Mere-
dith,018,073; Merideth,
108,113; Sherwood,044
HELTON, Peter,220
HEMHILL, Samuel,239
HEMLY, Gideon,163
HEMPHILL, James,175; S.,
237; William,101
HENDERS, Robert,227
HENDERSON, (Widow),217;
A.S.,197; Alex,098;Alex.,
097,099; Alexander S.,
134,212; Alexander,050,
059,072,096,103,107,116;
Alexd.,103; Andrew,103;
Benjamin,086; Elisabeth,
148; Elizabeth,021;
Emeline,045,046,061;
Ezekial,066,148; Ezekiel,
075,164,194,196,197,234;
Ezkl.,194; James,021,217;
Jas.,111; Jesse Uria,021;
John,021,045,046,061,067,
096,116,148,195; Lowery,
058; Mary,021; Molley,
021; Nancy,075,134,197;
Pleasant,070; R.,215;
Richard,003,073,075,134,
148,175,196,197,212,232,
234,244; Richd.,173;
Robert E.,143; Robert,
018,027,035,086,149,188,
199,200,220,241; Robt.,
186; Rufus G.,239; Samuel
196,197; T.,033; W.L.,
175; W.S.,186,197; Wade
L.,053; William J.,134;
William Jr.,234; William
L.,175; William S.,048,
066,075,131,148,164,194,
196,197,211,212,220,237;
Wilson,021,061,062,217;
221; Wm.,100,116,190
HENDLY, Gideon,120
HENDRIX, Abner,013,019
HENDY, John,018
HENERY, John,106
HENLEY, Caleb,053,094;
William,026,242
HENRY, James,199; William,
014,158
HENSLEY(?), Ged,045
HENSLEY, G..238; George,
185; Giseon,053; William,
067
HENSLY, Gideon,055
HENSON, (?),230; William,
091
HENTY, William,010
HERALUS, Noah,239
HERAN, Solomon,094
HERDSTOCK, Jap,126
HERIN, Georg,203
HERNDON, (Esq.),050; Ben-
jamin Jr.,088; Benjamin,
062,086,105,109,140,141;
Esquire,239; James,049;
Jas.,117; Jos.,205;
Joseph,009,049,053,062,
064,070,105,107,118,240;
Sarah,062,108
HEROLD, Nancy,197; Peter,
197
HERON, Peter,112
HERRIN, Nancy,143; Robert

HOWARD, James Cont. 021,
046,072,175,201,204,205,
231; John,116,177,194,
195,196; Mary Ann,233;
Mira,233; Parmenas,151;
Parmenes,046; Permenus,
021; Permenus,231; Polley
003; Polly,021; Robert,
221; Shadrack,003; Thomas
C.,177; Thos.,215,217;
Watson,110
HOWEL & SAMPLE, (Firm?),
058
HOWELL, Jethro,223; John
H.,228; John,018; Joseph
B.,008; Ransom,218;
Samuel,242
HOWES, John,154; Josel,055
HUBBARD, Dempsey,185; Dem-
sey,082,100
HUCABY, John C.,150
HUCHASON, John,222
HUCHERSON, John,226
HUCKABY, John C.,153; John
080,103,104,220; Samuel,
080; Sophia,104
HUCKEBY, Albert,243
HUCKS & WINN, (?),163
HUDDLESTON, Joseph,027
HUDSO, A.B.,174
HUDSON, Andrew B.,107;
Edward,074,107,110,121;
Isaac,206; J.J.,208;
John T.,136,167,201;
John W.,206; Thomas,178;
William(?),028; William
P.,192
HUDSPETH, George,225; Joel
225; Moses,008; Thomas,
005,043,046,054,165,183,
202,225; Thos.,147;
William,202,225
HUDSTOCK(?), James,126
HUDSTOCK, David,007
HUEY, ?,088; James,009,
094,111,119,121,139,143,
155,199,205,213,217,229,
238; John,209,220; Willis
209,220
HUFF, Lenard,092
HUFFLESTUTLER, Solomon,039
HUFFSTATLER, Solomon,041
HUGGINS, Anderson,227;
Boward,169; Brevard,170;
Charles,225; Isaac,225;
J.,213
HUGHES, David,002,098;
James,014; K.T.,180;
Keblet,063; Thibble T.,
103; Thibblety T.,103;
Wm.,191
HUGHEY, John,001
HUGHS, James,218; Kibble
T.,110,169; William,
169,219
HUGHSTON, Richard,110
HULGAN, Robert,137
HULSEY, Charles,091
HUMPHREY, George W.,055;
Owen,178; William,198
HUMPHREYS, D.,241; Owen,
209
HUMPHRIES, G.W.,091
HUNNELS, Robert,106
HUNT, (Doct.),197; Daniel,
092; Doct.,176; Eliza-
beth,011,012,071; George,
018; J.,055; James,012,
018; Job,084,124; John,
129; Lucy A.,009; Lucy,
011; Minican,088; Spence,
091; Squire,106,163;
William,058,071,188
HUNTER, Dr.,184; (Mrs.)087;

HUNTER Cont. Aaron,001,
082; Aron,010,014,020,
030,147; Comfort R.,140;
E.,221,229; Elijah,183;
Elisah,030; Elisha,016,
022,030,040,041,095,117,
229; Eliza H.,087; Eliz-
abeth,022; Hezekiah,140;
Isaac,091; Jacob,087;
James H.,207; James,237;
John Sr.,108; John,011,
015,138,155; Mary,010,
014,020,083,129,140,147,
208; Patience,087; Sam-
uel,053; Sarah,140;
Terrill G.,140; William
H.,153,207; William K.,
195,198; William,006,
010,054,087,220,223,229,
233,239; Wm.,181,196,
210; Wm.H.,153
HUNTS, J.J.,238
HUNTSVILLE, (Banks),209
HURT(?), Lucy A.,009
HURT, B.S.,151,153,160,
176,178,239,240; Bird
S.,080,126,127,137,181,
224,239; Elijah R.,127;
Elisha,006,218; Eliza-
beth,006; Joel,218; Mary
092; Moses,219; James,
153
HUSENFORD, Richard,136
HUSON(HUDSON), Edward R.,
066; Richard,109
HUSS, Ribble(?) T.,133
HUSTER, William,091
HUSTON, Franklin,095
HUTCHESON, McDaniel,009
HUTIONG(?), Christopher,
014
HYNES, James,131

ICHOLSON, George,094
IDELOTT, Thomas,043
IDLET, Thomas,112
INGRAM, Geo.,193
HNLAND, Henry,104
IRELAND, H.,096
IRINA, Elijah,015
IRISH(?), Tilman,026
IRVIN, Charles,208; Jones,
078; Joseph,190
IRVINE, Charles E.,067
IRWIN, Joseph,005,177;
William,057
ISAM, Arthur,112; Eliza,
069; James,067
ISBY, Tapley,094
ISHAM, Arthur T.,041;
Arthur,006,028; Charles,
006,025,041; Dudley,006;
Elizabeth,007,040; Fanny
040; George,006,007,025,
028,040,041; Henry,006;
Janney,007; Jenny,040;
Jinny,007; John,007,040,
041; Jonathan,006,007,
040; Polly,007,040;
Sally,007,040; Ursula,
007,040; William,006,
007,028
ISOM, A.J.,106; A.T.,064,
098,112,129,175,181,221,
233,238; Arthur T.,192;
Arthur,210; Charles,028;
Dudley,092,098,138,154,
203; Dudly,144; Elisa-
beth,144; Elizabeth E.,
233; Emaline,175; George,
028,138; Henry,013,144,
154; James,024,028,036,
098,136,144,148,154,175,
233,240; John,024,112;

ISOM Cont. Mary,148,240;
Polly,136,144; Robert
G.,233; Robert,175; Sally
175; Sarah G.,233; Sarah
240; Thomas D.,233;
William,013,028
IVEY, ?,001
IXON, John,168

JACKS, Mark,237
JACKSON, (?),224; A.(Gen)
029; Allen,055; Andrew
(Maj.Gen.),102; Andrew,
020,150; Ann,203; Anna,
150; Betsy,150; Branch,
078; Daniel,150; David,
150,224; Elizabeth,174;
Gen.,014; Gilliam,150;
Habard,167; Harburt,122;
Henaritta,078; Isaac,170;
Isom,108; John,008(2);
053,150,203; Josiah,222;
Leanah,150; Maj.Gen.,012;
Manerva,150; Mark L.,150;
Mark S.,150; Mark,121,
150,167,191,237; Martha,
150; Nancy,150; Nelson,
027; Polly Ann,078; Polly
150; Sally,150; Samil,
227; Samuel,239; Susannah
150; Thomas,170; William,
203
JACKSON, David,239
JACOBS, Jesse,077; Joseph,
077; Rachel,077; Sally,
044,077; William,044,
077,094,095,207
JAGGERS, Simon,166; William
102
JAINKINS, Philip,096
JAINS, Thos.,236
JAMES(JOINES), Lewis,105
JAMES, Henry M.,091; John,
025; Smith,140; W.,236;
W.L.,054
JAMESON, (?),033; Hosea,
111; John,201,234
JAMISON, Allen,005; Eliza-
beth,005; George,005;
Housa,136; James,005;
John,005,201; Rhoda,005;
Robert,005; Samuel(?),005
JAMMESON, Hosea,028
JAMSION, Hosia(?),005
JANES, Edmund,125
JANKINS, S.K.,240
JARROTT, David,103
JARUS, William,043
JEFF, Baalam,167
JEFFRIES, David,209
JELETOTTE(?), Thomas,013
JELKS, John,240
JENKENS, Walter S.,014
JENKIN, Walter S.,133
JENKINS, Ann,031; Anney,
031; Barton,096; James
J.,134; James U.(?),134;
John,047,049,050,103,117,
120;134,205; Matilda G.,
134; P.H.,162; Phil,120;
Philip G.,146; Philip,
111; Sol K.,239; Solomon
K.,224; Thomas H.,009,
089,111,185; Walter S.,
209,221,224; Walter,042,
237; William,094
JENNINGS, (?),050; (Dr.),
195; 035; (Widow),195;
Archie,195; Ca--,195;
Doctor,112; George W.,
216; George,089; Isaac,
195; J.W.,195,233; Jade,
195; Jake,195; James R.,
180; James W.,195;

LONGLEY Cont., John,050, 059,103; R.,072; Rachael, 070
LOONEY, A.,172,190,209,219; Abraham,055,057,104,140, 142,175,176,184,190,201, 202,219,230,239; Abram, 156; Breckenridge,164; Edmund,125
LORANCE, Jno.,105; John, 228
LORENCE, John,083
LOSSETTER, Edy,125
LOUELLIN, Josiah,239
LOVE, Adam,030,083; Betsy, 004; D.,239; David,065, 110,159,226,239; Easter, 004; Edam,030; Edom,004, 082,085,107,124; Eli,004, 083,112; J.D.,174; James, 005,008,025,026,029,036, 037,055,187; Jane,004; Jno.D.,162; Joel,004, 030,053,082; John D., 166,167,174,181,201,216, 222,226,230,239; John, 002,004,007(2),009,030, 082,083,115,126; Mary Lee(?),004; Mary,002, 239; Nathan,004; Nathaniel,083; Polly,159,239; Robert,002,004,030,082; Samuel C.,224; Selson, 185; Wilson,004,030,082
LOVELL, George,115; William,028
LOVING, David,131; E.W., 162; Elizabeth,131; Gabriel,055; Henry,131; John,144; Malinda,131; Nathaniel,240; Tennessee, 131; William Sr.,131; William,108,142,144
LOVNY, William,131
LOWD(?), Joseph,027
LOWD, Thomas,005
LOWDER, John,111
LOWERY(SOWERY), Thomas,159
LOWERY, Thomas,201
LOWRANCE, Elenor,076; John, 076; Sam,092
LOWRY, Thomas,230
LUCAS, John,107
LUCK, Catharine (Mrs.)043; Cinthia,043; David,037, 043,045,240; Henry,037
LUCKETT, Samuel,178
LUCKEY, David,103
LUMKINS, More,097
LUMPKIN, Moore,167
LUMPKINS, George,136,149; John M.,149; John,124, 136; Moore,176; Robert, 018,035,036,043,136,149
LUNMAN(?), Nathaniel,104
LURK, James,013
LUSK, Elander,076; Henry, 004,043; James,004,043, 076,084; Jane,174; Margaret,076; Robert,056, 076,084,148,187,240; Samuel,028,056,076,084, 142,148,149; Thomas R., 192; Thomas,174
LUTHER, George,178
LUTHES, George,177
LYELL, Robert,027; Thomas, 174
LYLE, David,030; George P.,044; Robert,026
LYNCH, David,219; James, 042
LYNN, Joseph,008
LYON, John,002; Peter,009;

LYON Cont., Richard,031; William,012
LYONS, Elizabeth,071; James 071; John,071; Peter, 012,071; William,071
LYTLE, William,208,237,239

MABA, Thomas,054
MABBEY(MOBLEY), Ezekiah,109
MACHLEHANNON, John,218
MACK(?), Samuel D.,067
MACK, A.W.,206,237; Aquilla W.,121; C.,061; Constant 125; Constantine,021,121; James H.,021; James,021, 125; Jno.,121,133,177, 232; John,021,025,046, 052,074,083,102,122,125, 129,147,148,151,160,161, 164,187,194,203,211,212, 219,230,231; Lemuel D., 150,192,195; Lemuel,125; R.,096,190,222; R.H., 239; R.L.,202; Robert, 006,021,031,054,067,075, 099,106,110,122,162,163, 175,207,215,239; Robt., 004,186; Samuel D.,131; Sarah,021; William,021; Wm.,192
MACKEY, Alexander,050,108; H.M.,090; Joel,129; Jonathan,090; W.L.,159; William,138
MACKWELL, Solomon P.,133
MACON, Andrew,154; J.T., 177; Jno.,168; Jno.T., 224; John T.,178,223, 228; John,049,053,085, 131; Mary,240; W.H.,177; Will H.,169; William H., 081,149,167,168,182; William,051,179,209; Wm., 122
MADDEN, Robert,030
MADDIN, Thomas,216; William,046
MADDING, William,205
MADEN, Robert,082
MADIN, Polly,225; Scarlot, 225
MADING, Sarah,205
MADLEY, John L.,160
MADOX, George,218
MAGE, Chiles,037
MAGIL, John,220
MAGILL, John,110,168
MAGRAM, Henry,190
MAGRIM, Henry,119
MAGRUM, Isham,115
MAGUIR, P.,048
MAGUIRE, Aligany,222; Allaganna,135; Patk., 196,240; Patrick,025; 048,049,100,101,105, 118,122,217,219
MAHAN, Thomas,183; Thos., 205
MAHON, Thomas,094,117,184; Thos.,004,160
MAICK, Eli,220
MAINARD, Edward,159
MAIRS, James,126
MAIZE & CRAWFORD (?),094
MAIZE, Abraham,124
MAJORS, Samuel,169,182
MAKIN, James W.(Capt.), 029; Thomas,004; W.,039
MAKINS, Andrew,054
MALCOM, Joseph,155; Lusance,155
MALCOMB, James,049; Joseph 108,118; Thomas,199
MALEY, John G.,125

MALOEN, Perry O.,085
MALONE, Caty,071; D.,185; Hallery,009; Henry,012, 071; Jane,009; P.O.,128, 158; Perry O.,131,185; Robert,106,205; T.B., 129; Thomas B.,083,104, 110; Thomas,007; Thos., 205; Thos.B.,152; William 221
MAN, Patsy,096
MANDLER, Thornton,135
MANDLEY, Caleb,183
MANEY, Merret,198
MANGEE, Mrs.,018
MANGRAM, Edwin,168; Henry, 155,162; James,155; Jane, 168,232; L.B.,205; Mary, 162
MANGRUM, Edwin,205; Henry, 154,155; Isham,205; Mary,155; Patsey,205
MANING, William,201
MANLIFF, P.H.,242
MANNING, David,153; Williby L.,132; Wright W., 132; Wright,226
MANNON, David,182
MANSODES, W.A.S.C.,190
MANTON, John,102
MARAN, Robt.C.,217
MARCH, William B.,049; William,122
MARCUS, P.,034; Phillip, 037
MARFIELD, Mathias,109
MARLOW, James,053
MARR, J.,219
MARRS, Mary Ann,244
MARS, Hugh,126,231; Mary Ann,231
MARSH(?), Simeon,120
MARSH, O.,121; Simon,226; Simson,106
MARTEN, J.R.,036; James C., 018; William,045
MARTIN, (Dr.),114; (Widow) 169; A.C.,227; Alexander, 007,060,070; Benjamin H.,085; Benjamin,125; Bohan,103; D.,099,190, 215,233; David,018,025, 048,050,053,104,105,119, 139,153,207,208,240,241; Fendle,225; Geo.M.,158; George M.,057,080,084, 113,114,121,136,140,143, 145,163,201,208,215,238; George,008,025,027,048, 054; John,098; L.,057; Lawren,196; R.C.,198, 209; R.C.K.,226; Robert, 098; Sally A.,241; Samuel,094; Thomas J.,085; Thomas P.,123; Thomas W., 170,172,231; Thomas,030; Thos.W.,169; William B., 047; William P.,239; Zachariah,175; Zacheriah, 201
MARVELL, Jno.,239
MASH(?), Adam,170
MASH, Obediah,144,154
MASON, John,066; William, 198
MASSEY, John,086
MASSINGALE, Kinshen,002
MASSON, John,021
MATHEW, John,153; Robert F.,182
MATHEWS, Abner,122,139, 155,212,230; Agnes,174; Andrew,242; Elizabeth, 134; James W.,211;

MATHEWS Cont., James,139,
219; John,122,123,129,
148,150,153,174,206,211,
225,231; Mararitt A.,153;
Margaret A.,174,235;
Mary,139; Robert F.,127,
230; Robert,177,236,242;
Robt.,209; Thomas W.,
235; William K.,235
MATHIS, John,011
MATTHEWS, Abner,102,134,
197; Asenath,075; Hannah,
073; James D.,063; John,
013,046,047,051,061,062,
066,074,080,081,099,102,
118,139,149,164,166,176,
183,186,187,204; Joseph,
063,192; Lewis,039;
Margaret Ann,052,073;
Robert F.,062,134,160,
164,174,180,185,192,197,
201,206; Robert T.,192;
Robert,073,074,170,204,
219; Robt.,198; William
K.,052; William R.,062
MATTOS, John,005
MAXEY, Merrit,181; William
010
MAXWELL, George W.,219;
J.P.,197; James J.,064;
S.P.,127,238; Solomon
P.,044,048,051,073,109,
136,181,241; Solomon Y.,
164; W.,226; W.A.,238;
William A.,006,040,044,
053,115,122,176; William
109; Wm.,097; Wm.A.,102,
220
MAY, Daniel,044; Edmand,
110; Edmund,030; Moses,
042; William,112
MAYALJ, & YOUNG, ?,163
MAYBERRY, Abram,028,036,
041; David,028; Frede-
rick,025,028; Henry,
036; Michael,036
MAYES, Abraham,240; David,
218; Dr.,050; Elias P.,
218,240; J.M.S.,181;
James,055; S.,179; Sam-
uel (Dr.),042; Samuel,
084,102,175,195
MAYFIELD, A.B.,018,044,
048,054,066,073,107;
Elija,160; J.B.,109;
James,154; Samuel,028,
036; Susannah,021; W.C.,
053; William,028,067
MAYS, Abraham,113,219;
Abram,092; David,092,123,
218; Mary,004; Reuben,
222; Sally,036; Sam'l.
(Dr.),100; Samuel (Dr.),
145; Samuel (Dr.),004;
Samuel,024,080,145,153;
Willey,218
MAYSE, John,030
MAYSON, Charles C.,242;
Sally,227
MC--(?), William,166
MCAFEE, Betsy,227; Elissa,
238,241; Lahus,236;
Miles,225; Mills,227,
236,238,241
MCAFERTY, Sally,009
MCAFFEE, Moses,092
MCALISTER, David,097; J.R.
085; James,013
MCALL, Alexr.,158
MCALLISON, D.,163
MCARTHUR, Margaret,188
MCBEE, ?,035
MCBRIDE, Frances,112;

MCBRIDE Cont., Francis,
011,020,126; Isaish,011,
126; Jane,016,126; Jo-
siah,055; Samuel,011,126,
153,213; William,003,
032,033
MCCABE, Hugh,084
MCCAFERTY, J.,042; James,
042
MCCAFFERTY, Edward,129;
Samuel,236; Sarah,008
MCCAFFIRTY, Edward,146
MCCAIN, Amos,003; Eli,021;
Elizabeth,027; Ephriagm
E.,108; James D.,106;
James,053; Robert,021,
027,046; Robt.,003
MCCALIB, Eph.,158
MCCALL, James A.,060;
Thomas,027,029,086
MCCALLOW, Alexander,106
MCCALLUM, Isaac,080; Mary,
174; Thrasher,174
MCCAMMEL, John,074
MCCANDLASS, W.,219
MCCANICO, James,109
MCCANLASS, John H.,153
MCCANNAN, George G.,178
MCCARDE, James,178
MCCARDEY(?), Labram,109
MCCARLEY, Abraham,202;
George W.,202
MCCARNIN, James,163
MCCARNISH(?), Betsey,077
MCCAROL, John,192
MCCARROLL, William E.,180
MCCARTER, Andrew,054;
Robert,007,054; William
053
MCCARTY, Andrew,051,066,
110; James,016; Kathe-
rine,016; Nancy,016;
Nathaniel,016; Polly,
016; Sarah,005
MCCASCALL, Allen,218
MCCASLIN, Andrew,111;
John,173; Y.,177
MCCASTER, Robert,007,027
MCCAULEY, James,016,034
MCCAVEN, Joseph,007
MCCAWLEY, Catherine,016,
026; James,016,026;
Nancy,026; Nathaniel,
026; Polley,026
MCCEAN, John C.,101
MCCINZIE, Jeremiah,123
MCCLAIM, Ephraim,113
MCCLAIN, E.C.,219; James
B.,112
MCCLANAHAN, Samuel,187
MCCLANE, Murdock,063
MCCLANEY, J.,238
MCCLEAN(?), James (Capt.)
110
MCCLEAN, Doctor,013; James
015; John,226; Samuel,
015
MCCLELLAND, John,010;
Rosanna,010; Rosy,010
MCCLENAHAN, Samuel,098
MCCLENNEHAN, Wm.,115
MCCLEUR, James,046
MCCLISH, John,041
MCCLOUD, Norman,104
MCCLURE, Alexander S.,116;
William,218,239
MCCLUSKEY, Samuel,002
MCCOBSTER, George,192
MCCOLLISTER, Turkey,007
MCCOLLUM, Daniel,025,033,
138; Isaac,005,030,082;
Mary,013,041; Thrasher,
013,159; Thresher,041
MCCOLOUGH, Alen,054;

MCCOLOUGH Cont., Alexander
054
MCCONNEL, Amanaud(?),076;
James,220
MCCONNELL, Archibald,192;
James,167,170; Walter,
042; William,079,142,
183,210,236
MCCORD, Edmond William,232;
Edmond,179; Edmund,176;
James,178,187; Nancy,179;
Robert,176,179,185,232;
William,176,179,232;
Wm.,128
MCCORKLE, Alexander,205
MCCORMACK, Charles,153;
Chas.,153; Daskhill,153;
Elisabeth,153; Elizabeth,
153; John X.,153; John,
153; Lucinda,153; Lucy,
130; Nancy,153; Peggy,
153; Sall,153; William,
153
MCCORNAL, Fanney,091
MCCORPIN, John,216
MCCOTISTER, David,110
MCCOY, D.A.,243; Robert,
173
MCCRACKIN, Thomas,201
MCCRACKING, Joseph G.,202
MCCRAVEN, Joseph,126
MCCRERY, John,046
MCCULLA, Henry,012
MCCULLOCK, Robert,034,043
MCCULLOUGH, Robert,113
MCCURDY, Samuel,191
MCCURLEY, John,001
MCCUTCHEN, Rhoda,079
MCCUTCHINS, James,053
MCDANIEL, (?),205; Amos,
150,237,239; Aron,171;
Elizabeth,171,239; Jane,
171; Joel,171; Robert,
093,147,161,181,217,219;
Samuel,068,150,206;
William,140; samuel,059
MCDAVID, Samuel,044
MCDILL, (Mr.),118
MCDINEL, Thomas,053
MCDONALD, Alexander,001,
038; Archd.,138; Catha-
rine,018,041; Catherine,
041; Daniel,018; Donald,
041; James,001; John,
001,038,062; Joseph,001,
038; Richard,001; Robert,
001,045; Samuel M.,018;
Thomas,110
MCDOWD, Joseph C.,034
MCDOWEL, H.,057; Samuel,
107
MCDOWELL, (?),228; Alexan-
der,120; Famlin,140;
Jas.C.,113; Joseph C.,
018,106,111; Joshew,017;
Sam,102; Saml.,084;
Samuel,048,075,084,100,
110,152,156,162,165,167,
170,184,215,241; Squire,
107
MCDUFFEY, Anguish,117
MCDUGGALD, Duncan,138
MCDUGLE, Hugh,073
MCEAN, John,101
MCEAUING, Joseph H.,108
MCEWIN & HOUSTON, (?),245
MCEWING, Joseph H.,044,
166; Sophia E.,166
MCFADDEN, E.,129; Edward
Jr.,071; Edward,071,083,
105,106,123,228; Esquire,
243; John,172,234; Ned,
225
MCFADDIN, John,243

MCFADE, Edward,055
MCFALL, (Mrs.),101; George
E.,047; George,053; John
025,055,124; Martha(Mrs.)
164; Thomas,241; Wm.,100
MCFALLS, George Sr.,092;
John Jr.,044; John,022,
032,040,044,092,135,205,
242; Martha,205; Thomas,
043,103
MCFARLIN, William,096
MCFAWLS, John,025
MCGAW, Benjamin,225; J.,
224
MCGEE, C.,007; Chiles,008,
016,075,214; John,112;
Joseph (Rev.),007;
Joseph,007,008; Polly
Jr.,008; Thomas,008;
William,002,016
MCGERVIN, Nancy,077
MCGHEE, Jacob,106
MCGILBERT, Alexander,002
MCGILL, Jno.,240; John,
076,138,221,225,228
MCGIMPSEY & SANDERS, (?),
131
MCGIMPSEY, (?),204; (Dr.),
137,211; (Dr.),171;
J.W.P.,150,215,239; Tho-
mas,089; William,243
MCGIMSEY, (?),052; (Dr.),
081,172; J.W.P.,097;
James,160; John W.P.,049;
John,033,097; William,
097
MCGINNIS, John,091
MCGLANE, E.H.,219
MCGOWAN, James,221; R.B.,
220
MCGOWEN, James,058,128,
181; Robert,206; Samuel,
091
MCGOWIN, James,141; Jas,
098; Nancy,077
MCGRATT, Thos.,003
MCGRAW, (?),236; Lewis,
162; Louis,183; William,
162
MCGREARY, Pleasant,016
MCGRIMSEY, John W.P.,200
MCGUIRE, (?),101; P.,050,
120,207; Patrick,009,
029,033,043,051,055,059,
135,148,180
MCHOME, John,152
MCINTERE, Duncan,017; John
015
MCINTIRE, Alexander,073;
Ann,043; Anney,076;
Archibald,076; Christian,
076; John,041,076; Polly
073
MCINTOSH, Daniel,216;
William,005,064,092,126
MCINTYRE, Alexander,057;
Ann,138; Anne,137; Dun-
can,048,054,107,110,137,
138; Malcolm,138
MCKAIN, Jno.C.,099
MCKANEL, Archer,097
MCKANLAS, William,137
MCKAY, Alexander,050
MCKEA, David W.,054
MCKEACHEN, Ephraim,071
MCKEAN, Elizabeth,004;
J.C.,048,120; John,100;
Robert,004
MCKEE, ---,018; Alexander,
055,073,208; Anne,040;
Betsey Malinda,073;
Betsy,040; Daniel,156;
David W.,094,119; Eliza-
beth,040; H.,193; H.

MCKEE Cont., Milton,209;
Hamilton,156; Harrison,
193; Herndon,156; Isaac,
127; Jacob B.,142; Jacob
Hamilton,073; Jacob,
007,040,044,057,073,126,
127,142,156,163,209;
Jane,040,073; Joel,108;
Lucinda,142,156,157,209;
M.J.,193; Malinda,040,
073,142,156,157; Matilda
040,142,156,209; Minerva
040; Nancy Lucinda,040,
073; Polly,040; Sally,
040,073,142,156,157,209;
Saml.,201; Samuel,073,
127,157; Scott M.J.,193;
Thomas,040,066,073,127;
William C.,207; William
E.,164,194,234; William,
096,195; Wm.L.,102
MCKENNEDY, John,239
MCKENNON, Daniel,071,228
MCKENON, ---,018
MCKENSEY, J.,084
MCKENTTRA(?), Sally,189
MCKENZIE, J.H.,074
MCKEY, Daniel,196
MCKIBBONS, J.,238
MCKIBBON, John,163
MCKICHES, T.H.,200
MCKIISIC(MCKISSOCK),Spivy,
183
MCKINDRICKS, Dudley,231
MCKINDRY, Dudley,132
MCKINDSY, A.,054
MCKINZIE, John (Col.),123
MCKISICK, John,108
MCKISSACK (?),198; Spivy,
205; Susannah,205
MCKISSICK, John,198
MCKISTER(?), L.L.,113
MCKITE, Samuel B.,019
MCKNIGHT, Arabella W.,075;
John,001; S.B.,016;
Sam'l.B.,011; Samuel B.,
006,019,095; Thomas P.,
186
MCKNITE, Samuel B.,013
MCKREE, D.W.,120
MCKUE, William E.,230
MCKUNE, John C.,162
MCLACHLIN, Andrew,185
MCLAFFERTY, James,079
MCLAIN, (?),140; E.E.,163;
Jesse,030
MCLANE, Robert,002; Thomas
185
MCLARNIN, James,163
MCLASKIN, John,173
MCLASLILN, John,173
MCLAUGHLEN, Thomas,027
MCLAUGHLIN, (?),126; Tho-
mas,001
MCLAYER, Isaac,092
MCLEAL(?), James,088
MCLEAN, (Mrs.),222,229;
Alvey,079; Andrew M.,
151; Andrew,082; Betsey,
079; Carnit B.,172;
Cavel B.,079; Cynthia,
079; Ephr.,088; Ephraem,
015; Ephraim Jr.,079;
Ephraim,010,079; Ephraim
010,079; Ephriam,002;
Harvey William,082;
James B.,014,079; James
D.,026,034,117; Jesse,
008; John C.,096; John,
048,079,154,222,229;
Margaret,033; Margarett,
033; Nancy,008,082;
Patsey,079; Polly,079;
Sam P.,011; Samuel,014,

MCCLEAN, Samuel Cont.,026,
033,035,041,058,082,088,
142,147,151; William,
011,029,033,058,082,142,
147,151,187,190; peggy,
029
MCLEDEN(MCLERLEN?), Hugh,
086
MCLEMORE, Edward J.,151;
Edward,176; Thomas,018
MCLEOD, William,052
MCLINNEY, James,163
MCLISH, John,036
MCLOUGH, Alexander,163
MCLOY, Murdock,133
MCLULLIN, Daniel,131
MCLULLIN, Daniel,131
MCLUN, William,161
MCMACKEN, Andrew,117
MCMACKIN, Andrew,089; Hugh
A.,187
MCMAHAN, Andrew,116; John
B.,004; Richard,055;
Samuel D.,094,117; Susan,
117; William,094
MCMAHEN, A.,154; Capt.,012;
James,018,019; Richard,
019; Robert,019; Samuel,
018
MCMAHON, Andrew,117,152;
James,019,041; Polly,019;
R.,019,041; Richard,004;
Thomas,004
MCMAKIN, A.,185; Andrew,028
MCMAN, William,054
MCMANIS, Aron,209; Jonathan
120; Laurence,030,117
MCMANNAS, Jonathan,016
MCMANNIS, (Mrs.),198
MCMANNUS, Jonathan,170,173
MCMANUS, John,009; Samuel,
117; Susannah,117; Willi-
am G.,173
MCMARY, Joseph,129
MCMAURY, Joseph,129
MCMEANES, Wm.,209
MCMEANS, Lawrence,167
MCMEEN, John,021
MCMILLAN, Alexander,178,
223; Catherine,078;
Nicholas,115; Sarah,075,
078
MCMINAS, Lawrence,052
MCMINN, William,108
MCMORRIS, Jonathan,030
MCMUNN, W.,074; William,
039,094
MCMURRAY, Jos.,238; Joseph,
210,211,226,235,238
MCMURRY, John,221; Joseph,
138,177
MCNAIRY, N.A.,163
MCNANNUS, Ann,173
MCNEACE, John,237
MCNEAL & MOON, (Firm),034
MCNEAL & MOORE, (?),114
MCNEAL & MORE,(Firm?),051
MCNEAL, (?),101; (Dr.),067;
E.P.,205; Ezekiel P.,212;
Prudence T.,212; Thomas,
020,025,094,211,212;
William,067
MCNEEAL, Thos.,205
MCNEEL, William,108,127
MCNEIL & MOORE, (?),100
MCNEIL, Robert,209; Thomas,
026,031; William,048
MCNEILE, William,084
MCNEILL, E.P.,215; Robert,
209
MCNICK & MOORE, (Firm),034
MCNIGHT, Duncan,162; E.,
222; S.B.,162; Samuel B.,
110,162; T.D.,162;T.P.,110

NOTTS, William,166
NOW(?), Aguiler,001
NOWLIN, Jabus,002,003
NOWLS, Butler,154
NULTS(?), John,012
NUMBEY(?), Joseph,133
NUNN, Zephanaiah,044;
   Zephania,099; Zephaniah,
   039,041,150
NUNNALE, Edward,027
NUNNALEE, Edward,027
NUTT, William,027

O'BRIANT, John,178
O'NEAL & WITHERSPOON
   (Firm),034
O'NEAL, James,092,103,192;
   Joseph,007,126; Margaret
   006; Marmaduke,028;
   Thomas H.,028
O'REILLY, J.C.,078; James
   C.,(Dr),078; James C.,
   062,064,200; James,198;
   Joseph A.,161
O'RIELEY, J.C.,(Dr.),067
O'RIELY, James C.,070
O'RILEY, (Dr.),101; J.C.,
   054,208; James C.,100,
   111,163,177,224; Jas.C.,
   199
OAKLEY, --as,218; Alexan-
   der,085,114,124; Ana,
   203; Elisabeth,168,202;
   Elizabeth (Mrs.),043;
   Elizabeth,113,114,207,
   231; James,043,113,168,
   202,203,207,231,235;
   Jesse,085,091,123,124,
   147,235; Jessee,027;
   Milley,235; Nancy,203;
   Robert,036,113,123,218,
   235; Robin,218; Roland,
   218; Stephen,218; Tho-
   mas,218; Washington,218;
   William,113,147,203,218,
   235; Wm.,113,114
OBRYAN, G.,(Dr.),239
ODIL, Mary,077
OGLESBY, Celia,203,229;
   Daniel,028; Elisha,095,
   203,229; James,005,028,
   049,229; Jane,203;
   Richard,203
OGLEVIE, David,018,035;
   Elizabeth,035
OGLISBY, Celia,157,173;
   Elisha,157,173; James,
   157,173; Polly,157;
   Richard,157,173
OGLISLEY, James,157
OGLIVER, E.P.,113; Eliza-
   beth,113
OGLIVIE, David,113; Eliza-
   beth,106,Mason,163
OGLOVE, David,113
OGLOVER, E.P.,113
OGLOVIE, D.,111
OLA, Thomas,050
OLDHAM & O'NEAL,(Firm)002
OLDHAM, Abram,094
OLIPHANT, Geore(?),101;
   Henrietta (Mrs.),124;
   Jas.H.,183; John D.,202;
   L.C.,050,064,238; Lam-
   bert C.,124; Lambert,
   126; Lembert C.,059;
   Robert,005,005,007; S.,
   047; Saml.,158; Samuel,
   006,007,008,009,017,114,
   126; Thomas,187
OLIVER, Hezekiah,132,181,
   239; James,178,218;
   Norry,200
OLLIPHANT, James,033;

OLLIPHANT, Cont.,Samuel,
   033
OLLIVER, William J.,182;
   Wm.164
ONEAL, Alphra,107; James,
   010,055,127,158,162,163;
   John,107,162; Marmaduke,
   038,043; Thomas H.,038
ONEEL, James,108,110;
   Nancy,107
ORILEY, J.C.,237; James C.
   049,108,242
ORR, E.W.,234; Ebenezer
   W.,132; James,083; Jas.,
   111; Joshua,035,054,097,
   158; Mary K.,161; Willi-
   am M.,132,161,230,244;
   William,225
ORTERE(?), David,002
ORTON, Richard,002
OSBORN, A.,125; Abner,102;
   Alexander,102; Alexr.,
   222; Thomas,055
OSBOURNE, Alexander,170;
   Noble,010
OSBURN, Alexr.,219; H.R.,
   199; James,232; John,
   097,132; Thomas,066;
   Wm.,217
OSBURNE, Thomas,042
OSSIPHANT(?), Lambert C.,
   154
OTEY, James H.,051
OVELL, Thomas,017
OVERLY, Robert,114
OVERSTREET, (Mrs.),233;
   James,108; Sally N.,155;
   Thomas,155
OVERTON, Jesse,094,104,
   152,243; John,004; Sam-
   uel,107
OWEN, James,030,082;
   William,068
OWENS, John,241; Reuben,
   041

PACE, John,028; William,
   083
PACERLY, James,015
PACKEY, William,051
PADGETT, William R.,240
PAGET, Drury,042
PAIN, Daniel,116; Micager,
   016,093; Micajah,088;
   Mildren N.,236; Robert,
   159; Wiley B.,091
PAINE, Daniel,105,170;
   Micajah,218
PAISLEY, James,004,024
PALMER, John,002; Mary,
   131
PAMENTA, Malakiah,108
PARCHMAN, P.,217
PARET, Daniel,125
PARHAM, W.W.,209
PARK, Shelby,116
PARKER, (Mrs.),080;
   Artimus,025; Francis,
   005,237; James M.,108;
   Mary (Mrs.),124; Molley,
   025; Peter,035; Thomas,
   025; W.L.,156; William,
   193
PARKES, William,109
PARKINS, N.,045
PARKMAN, P.,239
PARKS, Robert,086; Thos.,
   222; Wilson,239
PARREMAN, B.,203
PARRIS, Miager(?),088
PARRISH, Caleb,092; E.,
   092; Harberd,092
PARSILL, J.,146
PARTEE, A.,030,088; A.Y.,

PARTEE, A.Y. Cont.,063,090,
   133,160,183,215; Abner,
   016,032,105; Charles
   (Col.),100; Charles M.,
   015,088,108; Charles,
   011,030,050,061,063,088,
   090,111; Hiram,016,088,
   090; Lockar,030; Locker,
   030; Martha,030; ---,208
PARY, Danl.,170
PASETON, (Mrs.),101; Thomp-
   son,109
PASMORE, R.,229; Richard
   B.,232
PASSAMORE, Richard D.,136
PASSMORE, R.B.,147,148,165;
   Richard B.,048,050,058,
   081,082,142; Richd.B.,
   147
PASTOLE, Abner,221
PATAN, Robert,003
PATE, Chales(Charles),004;
   Randol,234; Randolph,209
PATERN, Isaac,018; Samuel,
   017,018
PATERSON, Joab,019; Nancy,
   019
PATILLO, John,085,173
PATRICK, Samuel,218
PATRICKSON, Isaac,227
PATTEN, Robert,031
PATTERN, Isaac,017
PATTERSON, (Mr.),062; Ann,
   219; Jacob,019; James,
   060,069,135,219,227,238;
   Jane,219; Jared,219,238;
   Jarred,190; Jarrett,181;
   Joab,165; Joel,088; John,
   085,206; Luke,010,117;
   Polly,069; Robert,190,
   206,219,230,238; William
   042
PATTEN, William H.,058
PATTON, (Widow),201,204;
   Charles,240; Elijah,041,
   211; Eliza,194; Elizabeth
   Jane,216; George W.C.,
   216; George,041,066,085,
   134,151,155,170,175,194,
   200,201,202,203,216; H.,
   209; Hugh,197; J.C.,222;
   James,021,138,154,187;
   Jane M.(Mrs.),182; Jane,
   170; Jas.,131; John,084;
   Margaret A.,216; Margaritte,170; Maria,170;
   Mary M.,216; Mary,170,
   216; P.C.,230; Pattillo,
   201; Petillo C.,170;
   Petillo,174; Pettillo C.,
   216; Pettilow,174; Polly
   155,170,174,175,202,216;
   Sarah,211; Simpson,225;
   Susan,170,216; Tristam,
   146; William,022
PAUL,Saml.,163
PAULEY, John,106; Valentine
   050
PAULIN, Joseph,217
PAY, Z.,219
PAYNE, (Mr.),067; Daniel,
   018,033,063,095; James,
   120; Micajah,094; Robert
   063,094,157
PAYTON, Elijah,207; Elisha,
   217; Henry,003,007,008,
   032,108,242; John,007,
   065; Joseph,013,028,040,
   203; Josephh,006; Moses
   D.,056,062,066; Moses,
   004,032; Peggy,008;
   Robert,008,032,153;
   Thomas,203
PEAK, Samuel P.,132

POLK Cont., Shelby,044,
108,110; Thos.G.,205;
W.H.,216; William H.,
216; William (Col.),139;
William,030,200; Wm.,
205
POLLOCK, John,195
POLNY, John,163
POMENTOR, Malikiah,110
POOL, Catherine,085; John
P.,085,128; John,106;
Lockland,128; W.P.,177;
William P.,217,228,229;
William,026,128; Wm.P.,
158
POPE, J.,069; James H.,
215; John,114; Lemuel,
114,207; William,109
PORGEY, Andrew J.,013
PORTER, (?),101,127; A.G.,
183; Alexander Newton,
130; Betsy,204; C.W.,
215; Charles & Sons,053;
Elendor(?),021; Elias H.
204; Elias Humphreys,
204; Elijah,130; Francis
062; H.B.,097,152; Hugh
B.,021,053,099,152,256,
163,199,208,238,239;
Isaac N.,130,136,204,241;
J.B.,045,048,104,150,185;
James Madison,204; James
014,025,026,033,041,094,
163; Jefferson,206; John
T.,048,056,130,204,241;
John,053,108,177,210,
219,237; Joseph B.(Maj.),
187; Joseph B.,002,018,
028,052,054,057,108,114,
136,139,148,151,160,163,
184,203,204; Joseph
Young,204; Joseph,100,
108,174,202,230; N.,055,
057,163,235; Newton,239;
Nimrod,021,038,056,059,
089,100,139,144,146,154,
163,181,209,238; P.H.,
188; P.N.,230,239; P.W.,
157,208; Parry W.,204,
230; Parry Washington,
204; Perry W.,241; R.B.,
054; Reace B.,107;
Reece B.,163; Reese,042;
S.,223; S.S.,243; Samuel
S.,158; T.J.,233; Thomas
B.,224,228; Thomas J.,
130,204,214,241; Thomas
Jefferson,136; Thomas,
015; Thompson,061; Thos.
C.,204; Thos.J.,130,242;
William,134,166,180,213,
236
PORTERS, James,198
PORTOR, Nimrod,055
POTTS, Elizabeth,182
POWEL, Ambrose,011,013;
Charles,039,047,072;
Elisha,013; Flora,013,
029; Jackson,224; John
A.,224; John,037; Last-
ing,107; Nancy,047,072;
Sally,040,047,072; Sely
H.,074; Thomas,013,029;
William D.,039; William,
047,072; Zepparah,013
POWELL, Ambrose,005,101,
202; Anderson,030;
Arthur,217; Charles,039,
233,245; D.(Mrs.),039;
Edward,170; Elisha,029;
Gaston,239; Isom,092;
J.A.,240; J.C.,239;
James C.,170,200,232,
233,245; John A.,065,

POWELL, John A. Cont.,224,
242; John G.,053; John
P.,010; John,004,092,
138,224; Joseph G.,240;
Lasting,163; Lucinda,
233,245; Mathew N.,245;
Mathew,233; Nathaniel
M.,127,140,160; P.,205;
Peggy,006; Peter,112;
Polly,233; Sally,245;
Sarah,170,200,232; Tho-
mas,004; William D.,170
POWER, Joseph,103
POWERS, Joseph,096,162,
199; Thomas,095,116
POWEL, Sally,047
PRATE(?), Joseph G.,129
PRATO, L.,153
PRATT, Joseph G.,131,178,
211
PRENIE, F.,055
PREWETT, Abner,033,111;
John,083,123,126; Lem-
uel,015,022,111; Thisk,
110; William,083,084,
129
PREWETTE, John,126
PREWIT, Abner,008; L.,239;
Nancy K.,244; Nancy,008;
Unity K.,244; William,
192
PREWITT, Abner,007; Elisa-
beth L.,161; John,008,
033; Lemuel,016,054;
Michael,008; Nancy,007
PRIGGS, John,124
PRIMM, John T.,124
PRINCE, B.,098
PRIOR, Green,055; Peter,
056
PROWEL, Sampson,027
PROWELL, Thomas,035
PRUETT, John,129
PRUIT, Joel,036; John "P",
231; William,192
PRUITT, William,123
PRUNETT, William,064
PRUVETT(?), John,064
PRYERSON, Samuel,033
PRYOR, Green,095
PUCKET, (Widow),213; Asa,
044; Catherine,217;
Edward K.,213; Edward,
087,213; Elijah,107;
John W.,213; Joseph,093
PUCKETT, E.,100,228; Edw.,
018; Edward R.,186;
Edward,228,230; John W.,
228
PUIDEY, Rober,163
PULIN, Anna,022
PUMMER, Nancy,234
PURCELL, J.,050
PURDON, George J.,064
PURDY, James,215; William,
004
PUREY, Robert,008
PURNELL, William,043
PURNETT, (Mr.),067
PURSEL, James,147
PURSELE, James,110
PURSELL, Benjamin F.,177,
202; James,006,059,099,
111,128,147,162; Mary
Ann,177,202; Sarah,177,
202
PURSWELL, James,073

QUIGLEY, George,238
QUILLEN, William,036
QUIN, Amis,099
QUINN, Amos,158; R.,167
RADFORD, Hannah,032; Jesse
016,032; John,030

RAGGEN, Richard,082
RAGLAND, Jno.,148
RAGSDALE, P.,193; Peter,
053,179; William,036,125
RAIL, James,028
RAIMEY, Alexander,207
RAINEY, Allen(?),044;
Allen,077,141,146,147,
148,150,165,186,198,201,
209; Isaac,050; J.B.,
236; J.G.,243; Jesse G.,
243; Jesse,193; William,
237
RAINS, John,002
RAINY, Allen,010,096; Jesse
B.,135
RAMAGE, James,186
RAMBO, Elias,226
RAMEY, Thomas,194
RAMSAY, Thomas,195,212;
William,205
RAMSEY, (Mr.),048; Agnes,
199,200; James,203;
Jane,203; John D.,107,
197; John,200; Rachael,
203; Robert,203; Susanna
075; Thomas,066,110,203,
205,236; William H.,017,
018; William,054,203
RANAW, Matthew,205
RANDAL, Thomas,026,094
RANDALE, Peggy,109
RANDELL, James,208
RANDLE, Thomas,011,014
RANDOLPH, D.F.,163; John,
041; Wm.M.,154
RANFRO, Shelton,155
RANFROW, Moses,118
RANKIN, A.,176; Bert,118;
David,049,118,155; James
049,062,078,104,156;
James,064; Moses,049;
R.A.,146,243; Robert A.,
199; Robert S.,201;
Robert,049,096,118,198,
224; S.,096; Saml.,196;
Samuel,049,121,122,162,
174;179,204,215,242
RANKINS, James,108; Jere-
miah,108; John,054; Moses
109,163; Samuel,108
RANSOM, Robert,219
RARDIN, A.,163
RASDALE, Salam,107
RAY, J.L.,092; James,160;
John M.,092; John,064,
205,218,220; W.,092;
W.M.,173; William,013
RAYBURN, William,178
RAYE, A.W.,003; Jane,003
RAYNOLDS, Thomas,163
REA(?), Josiah(Bird),027
READ, James,054; John,195
READIN, Alexander,112
REAH, Matthew,048
REANY, Margaret,001
REASE(REESE?), Joel,190
REAVES, Elijah,115,200;
G.W.,239; Hannah,115;
James,071,202; Joel,078,
115; John,222; Nancy,115;
Reubin,115; S.B.,242;
Sally,222; Susannah,115;
T.,222,226
REAVIS, J.B.,239
REBB, John,056
RECORD, Candres,150; Cum-
ford,030; George W.,065;
J.,189; James C.,030,
063,065,082,199,226;
James P.,066; James,150;
Jno.W.,137; John Jr.,022;
John M.,041; John S.,229;
John W.,016,030,052,065,

RECORD Cont., John W., Cont.
073,151,158,232; John,
022,041,150; Mary,016,
022,030,041,065; Penny,
150; Polly,150; Shear-
wood P.,063; Sherwood P.
065; Sherwood,030; Shur-
wood,064; Sion P.,065;
Sion S.,041; Sion,016,
022,030,063,150,151;
William,030,150
REDDIN, Max Miller,038
REDDING, Abijah,081; Arm-
stead,035,093; Isaac,
158; Maxmilen,112; Mex-
malen(?),112
REDENGRIDE, Marker Mellon,
013
REECE, Charles T.,112;
Henry,056; James H.,107;
James, 013,107; John,
053; Jordon,018
REED, Asar,027; Daniel,
060,064,069; David,135;
Elizabeth,006; Henry,
027,041; Hugh,059,060,
068,069; Isaiah,238;
Jacob,008; James,059,
060,129; John,006,059,
060,069; Josiah,059,060;
Mary,069,135; Nancy,227;
Peggy,069; Polly Elenor,
069; Richard,138; Robert
018,053; Samuel,027,069;
Thomas,165; William Bell,
069; William,059
REEDE (RUDE), James,054
REEDE, Isaiah,068; James,
068; John,068; Mary,068;
William,068
REESE(?), A.W.,032; Ed-
ward,101; James,032
REESE, A.C.,221; Charles,
053; Elenor,076; James,
068; Joe,208; Joel,106,
136,139,148,174,175,181,
184,197,198,204,235,236,
238,241,242
REEVES, Elijah,053; James,
167; Jesse,107; Joel,
054,090; Reubin,053;
Srigley,027
REFORD, John,128
REFROE, Jesse,177
REGDON, Will,156
REGION, William,008,064,
084,124,126
REID, Daniel,086; Hugh,
027; Isiah,029,086; Ro-
bert,086; Samuel,132
REILY, John,193
REN, William,145
RENFRO, Jesse,193,214;
Jinny,214; John Shel-
burne,214; John,016,066,
192,214; Lewis,136;
Moses,214; Shelton,118;
William,035,109,214
RENFROE, John,065
RENFROW, Ezann(?),128;
Isaac,049,118; John,
049,050,059,102,118;
L---,118; Lewis,049;
Moses,118; Shelton,049
RENTFORD, Isaac,027
RENTFRO, William,167
REVES, E.,226
REYNOLD, Benjamin,054
REYNOLDS, Caty,206; Jane,
008; Thomas,053
RHEA, John,169,218,227;
M.R.,189; Mathew,175,
201; Matthew,163,169,
184,202,204

RHINE, John,057
RHODES, (Widow),027,036;
Abner,104; Cynthia,070;
Elisha,027,035,036;
Jesse,227; Joseph,002,
054,119; Joshua,198;
Kinchen,027; Rebecca,
036; Sarah,035; Tyree,
070
RHYHE, John,191
RHYNE, John,213
RIBERS, Robert,205
RICE, Abel,227; David,167;
E.,122,161,164,165,179,
184,185,194,203,207,231,
232,237; E.Sr.,122;
Ebenezar,014,031; Ebe-
nezer Jr.,138,227;
Ebenezer,022,061,131,
134,158,176,227,230,237,
239; Fereby,011; George,
122; Henrietta,227; Jesse
227; Josiah,019; Pherr-
by,015; Pherreby,011;
Pherriba,016; Roland,
015,016; Rowland,227;
Sally,227; Stephen,109
RICH, Mary B.,213
RICHARD, Elisha,215
RICHARDS, Ambrose B.,079;
Ambrose R.,085; Hyrum,
124; John R.,171; John
T.,136; John,124; John-
son,191,214; Jonah,018;
L.,242; Robert,124;
William,042
RICHARDSON, (Mr.),100;
Absalom,007; Allen,022,
042; Alpia,017; Ambrose
R.,124; Amos,022,158,
205; Frances,022; Hulda,
022; James M.,158,168,
173,203,205; James W.,
233; James,110,204;
Jane,022; Jinny,022;
John Jr.,108; John M.,
168,204; John Sr.,108;
John,022,036,042,091,
156,173; Keziah,203,204,
205; Levoy,022; Polly,
205; Robert M.,042;
Samuel,092; Thomas F.,
168; Thomas T.,205;
Thomas,022,036,120,156,
168,233; Thos.P.,173;
W.J.,238; Wiley P.,182;
Wiley,022,217; William
W.,205; William,042,
058,156,158,203,204,205,
233; Willis,018,022,042;
Wm.168
RICHARSON, Asa,038
RICHERSON, James M.,156;
John L.,140; John T.,
070; Josiah,070; Nancy
P.,128
RICHESON, Joab,155; Wilie
P.,217
RICHIE, Bens,222; John,
222
RICHMOND, William,027
RICKETS, William,181
RICKETTS, William,116
RICLEY, J.T.,033
RIDGWAY, Jonathan,027
RIDLEY, V.,040,096,102,
172; Vincent,122,166,
172,179,192,206,230;
Willia,059; Willis,128,
131
RIEVE, Presley,086
RIEVES, Elijah,115; Joel,
115; Presley,027
RIFFLE, Jacob,181

RIGGAN, William,083
RIGGS, Jane,201; Nancy,181;
Saml.,200
RIGHT, John,108,228; Jo-
seph,028; Joshua,190;
Rhoderick,027; Roderick,
028
RIGHTE, William,178
RILEY, James C.,136; James
S.,041; James,091,202;
Peggy,202
RILLEY, James,167
RIM, John,119
RING, Lewis,082
RION, Jno.,239
RITCHARDS, Johnston,214
RIVERS, Elijah,208; Robert,
205
RIVES, G.M.,058
ROACH & WILSON, (?),237
ROACH, Simeon,036
ROAD, George,227
ROADS, Abner,135; Isaac,
113; Joseph,135,198;
Richard,041
ROAN, (Widow),227; George,
064,084,169,237
ROANE, Daniel,222; Elijah,
241; George,191,218;
Simon,237
ROBB, Ann,025; John,025;
Joseph,025,035
ROBBERSON, Jane,201
ROBBINS, Samuel,084
ROBERSON, Benjamin,101;
James,108,221; John,123;
Michael,144,229; Samuel,
124
ROBERT, Elija,106
ROBERTS, E.,038,045; Eli-
jah,022,163; Isaac (Gen)
022,043; Isaac,002,003,
022,038,057,114; John B.,
114; John,114; Joseph,
092; M.F.,152; M.S.,204;
Mack,056; Mark R.,109,
114; Mark,022,205; Mary,
108; Michael,225; Moses
F.,096,114,118,134; Moses
Firk,022; Nancy,022,114;
O.H.,210; Patsey,114;
Persia,115; Peter H.,
198; Polly (Mrs.),057;
Polly,022,038,043,045,
114; Rachael Persia,114;
Rachael,114; Rachel,115;
Richard,008; Robert W.,
214; Thos.,222; William
J.,050; William T.,057;
William,085,114,116,242
ROBERTSON, ---(?),022;
Absalom,092; Alcey,159;
Alsey,201; B.,030; Ben-
jamin,112; Blount,159;
Caroline,159; Charles,
043; Eldridge B.,051;
Elijah,022,051; Henry L.
209; Henry,159; James J.
(S.?),126; James S.,036;
James,027,029,091,131;
John L.,178; John,092;
Joseph,193; M.J.,216;
Mary,198; Michael,105,
131,142,201; Moses,036;
R.,035; Reddick,037;
Redrick,094; Sarah,224;
Sharp,159; Sterling C.,
030,051; Tyre,055,094;
William R.,159,201,229;
William,054,094,095,159;
Wm.R.,202
ROBESON, Charles,227;
James,045
ROBINS, Moses F.,049

ROBINSON, Betsey,077; Charles,077; David,077; Elizabeth,077; J.G.,172,202,243; Jacob G.,202; James L.,053; James,040,059,103; Joseph,220; Mark,077; Martha,077; Moses,052,100; Nancy,077; Sam.,164; Starca,171; Thomas,127
ROBISON, --,206; Benjamin,069; James L.(S.?),103; James,220; John D.,053; Mary,161; Moses,020,069,071; Reddick,005
ROBLY, Thomas,176
ROCHARDS, John,164
ROCKBY, Silas,160
ROD(?), Johnson,153
RODDEN, A.,110
RODENY, Banjamin,198; Benjamin,175
RODERY, Winifred,175
RODES, Abner,186
RODGER, Jacob,132
RODGERS, Ala,245; Aley,245; Eilliam,016; Jacob,019,165,184; James,178; Jesse,096; N.K.,198,210; Robert,184; William,013,029,042,043,095,098,110
RODNEY, Benjamin,200; Calvin B.,200; Elizabeth,200; James,200; Lucy,200; Nancy,200; Sarah S.,200; Washington B.,200; Winnefred,200
RODSDALE, Theodorick,155
ROE, Anderson,153
ROGERS, Abram,218; Agree,192; Aisly,236; Alexander G.,007; Ali,080; Carey N.(W.?),115; Elijah,167(Flanicin J.,110; Green B.,010,014,094; Greenberry,110; Isom J.,096; Jacob,004,064,088,094,095,096,114,160; James W.,091,115; James,115,160; Jesse,184; Joseph,227; N.,056; Nathaniel,098; Peggy,091,115; Richard,063; Robert,080,184; Sam,101; Samuel J.,006,045,046,059,061,062; Samuel S.,107; Samuel,035; Sarah C.,045,046; Sarah,061; Sion,040; T.S.,221; Warner,115; William,094,107,108,112,163; Williamson,073,121
ROLSTON, (?),091
ROLTON, Abram,158
RONE, George,225
ROODENY, Benjamin,183
ROOLER, Eskard,063
ROOTS, James,036
ROPER, Jno.Y.,234; T.,134; Tennessee,108,144,217,239; Thomas,095,097; William,042,107,131
ROSEBOROUGH, Thomas,183
ROSS & RUSSEL,(Firm?),053
ROSS(?), Elezar,083
ROSS, (Mr.),053; (?),001; Bennet,186; Ebenezar,064,124; Ebenezer,084,126; Edward,178,199; Eleanor,199; George,089,185; Hugh,001,018,037; Isaac,045; James,045,132,219; Jesse S.(?),106; Jesse S.,085,123,156;

ROSS Cont., Jesse T.,048; Jesse,103,196; John,018; Laurence,113; Robarson,178; Robason,160; Robinson,127; Robison,060; Thomas,064; Thos.,222; William,017
ROSSE, Jesse,056
ROSWELL, Mary,160; Solomon,040
ROUNTREE, Andrew,201; Thomas,201; Wm.W.,183
ROW, George,060
ROWLAND, John,224
ROY, John,209; William,167
ROYAL, Catharine,072; John Sr.,063; John,058,072; Joseph,035,072,097; Richard,035,072; Sally,072; Susannah,072; William,072
ROYALL, Joseph A.,218
RUDD, William,031
RUDLE, J.,138
RUE, Bethia Lee,158
RULEDGE, James,088
RUMAGE, James,186; John,186
RUMMAGE, James,055,127
RUSE(?), George,162
RUSH, Andrew,110; Samuel,105
RUSHING, Mark,123
RUSSEL, Albert (Col.),009; Catharine,115; David,056,109; Elenor,235; John,002
RUSSELL, (Widow),170; A.H.,235; Albert,011; Alexander H.,235; Alexander,170; Co.,001; D.,077; David,033,050,089; Henry 221; J.M.,221; James H.,221; James,178,220,228; Richard,114,115; William 011,035,055,111,163
RUST, Vincent,167; William 035,122
RUSTUN, Elijah,173
RUTE(?), Joel,164
RUTLEDGE, James,016,034,054,162,208; Osphia,006; Samuel,056; Thos.,227; William,018,054,134,152
RUTLER, William Sr.,180
RYKARD, Adam,243
RYLEE, John,239
RYLES, John,127
RYNE, Andrew,227; Christopher,227
RYONE, Andrew,239

SADDEN, Martin,056
SADERS, Elisa,139
SAGE, John,031
SALE, Ed A.,235
SAMATON, Saml.D.,181
SAMPLE, John,046; Margaret,101
SAMPSON, Isaac,241
SAMPTER, Jas.,220
SAMSON & HAYS, (?),127
SANBORNS, Nathaniel,211
SAND, Brittian,209; Jedeiah,227
SANDEFORD, James T.,017
SANDERS, (Widow),065;D.N.,163; G.B.,197; I.B.,197; J.B.,226; James,018,031,133; Jane,009; Jenny,071; Jesse,055; Joel B.,213,222,231,242; Joseph,056,065,148; Nancy,202,205; Peter,009,071;

SANDERS Cont., Stephen,123; William,009,071
SANDERSON, Nancy,109,163
SANFORD, James T.,003,014,024,031,039,045,047,052,057,062,064,068,093,094,096,101,103,114,119,120,125,131,134,145,152,167,229,232; Joseph,031,033,039,045,105,107; Mayson,226; Wineford,232; Young S.,201
SANDS, Michael,106; William 042
SANDSBERRY, Isaac G.,201
SANDSOM & HUGHES, (?),198
SAMDSP,. David (Dosil?),108
SANFORD, James S.,016,033,040,054,056,195,197,222,243; Mason,167,189,201; Robert,222; Stoke,216; Young S.,174,189,206
SANON, Amos,210
SANSOM & HAYS, (?),136; (Firm?),057,067
SANSOM, (?),153; (Dr.),006,061,155,168,175; D.N. (Dr.),100;214; D.N.,025,048,051,113,128,174,185,215,223; Darrel N.,040,080,118,148,165,230; Darrel,242; Darrell N.,240; David N.,165; Derril N.,117; Dorrel N.,048; James,060; N.(Dr.),101
SARRAGE, Matthew,048
SASSELMAN, Abrom,055
SATERFIELD, Samuel,084
SATTERFIELD, John,201; Peter,113; Samuel,124; Terry,092
SATTEY, Barnett,109
SAULTERS, Joseph,009
SAUNDERS, (Dr.),171; Edward,090,095; John,044; Joseph,067,108; Polly,043
SAVAGE, (?),050; (Capt.),050; Samuel,049,053,058,119,122; William,083
SAWYER, Frederick B.,192
SAWYERS, Betsy,034; James,217
SCOT, Andrew,207,211; Cinthia Jane,207; Hannah,210; James,207,211; Richard,216; Samuel,210; William F.,016; William,207,214
SCOTT, (?),157,227; (Mrs.),066; Adam,174; Andrew,175,191,192,206,214,230,231,234,242; Archibald,225; Cinthia J.,214; Cosby,224,227; Cynthia J.231; Dicy,150; Elisabeth,155; Elizabeth,175,212,242; Esther,068,069; Hannah,011,013,031; J.,119,125; Jacob,067,127,133,136,141,157,159; James N.,155; James,032,059,062,092,130,150,174,214,231,237; Jane,068,069; Jenny,175; Jno.W.,155,212; Joseph,170; Martha,175; Mary,175; Nathaniel,011; Polley,003; Rachel,069; Rebecca,003; Richad,063; Richard,003,063,104,119,199; Robert,079; Sally N.,155;

SLADE, Rebecca,221
SLATER, Andrew,081; George
  081; Patsey,082; William
  091
SLAUGHTER, Andw.,219;
  Francis,064,156,190;
  George,061; John S.,220;
  Patsey,081,082; William
  156,190,193
SLAUTER, F.S.,238; Francis,
  210; Frs.,239
SLAVE(?), David,179
SLAVE, Ann,130; Aron,165;
  Betsy,173,189; Clary,
  188; Easter,077; Elija,
  188; Fan,130; Harry,143;
  Henry,189,206; Ishmael,
  104; Jack,131; Jacob,
  143; Joshua,216; Lucy,
  003; Mary,134,196; Nel-
  son,180; Parthena,180;
  Phil,226; Phileir,180;
  Philis,136,137; Phillis,
  180; Priscilla,205;
  Rachel,025,201; Sabry,
  134; Sam,133,148,192;
  Sharp,003; Silas,201;
  Stephen,133; Tatta,131;
  Tenny,003; Tom,133; Wil-
  son,180
SLAVEN, Alexander,127
SLAVOR, Alexander,224
SLAYDEN, (?),241; S.W.,
  243; Samuel E.,242
SLENS(?), William,088
SLOAN, John,219
SMART, Samuel,055
SMILEY, Harvey,117
SMISER, John,059,067,078,
  081,099,237; Smith(?),
  James G.(Dr),028
SMITH, (?),226; (Dr.),154,
  225; A.,111; A.A.,058;
  Aaron,056; Alexander B.,
  080; Alexander,018;
  Andrew,052,136,163,209;
  Aron,043,108; Arthur
  M.,181; B.B.,127,184,
  186,239; Benj.,B.,196,
  208; Benjamin (Capt),
  009; Benjamin B.,048,
  092,128,136,149,176,
  242; Benjamin,016,024,
  035,119; Bird,118; C.M.,
  110,185; Calvin,108;
  Charles,024; Chas.S.,
  191; Cohee F.,193;
  Drewey,094; E.,054,156;
  Elisha,124; Ebenezer,
  038,073,107,137; Eli,
  044; Elisah,109; Elisha,
  138,163,198; Elizabeth,
  137; Ely,137; Ezekial,
  028; Francis C.,190;
  Francis,155,156,193,
  208,237; George,036,
  108; Henry,109,156,162,
  171,174,177,180,182,190,
  197,211,223,236; Hiram,
  090; J.G.(Capt),024;
  J.M.,242; J.P.,220; J.T.
  220; James C.,132; James
  G.(Dr),052; James G.,
  044,045,123; James K.,
  238; James N.,069,086,
  140,152,153,162,169,187,
  191,200,206,208,240;
  James P.,132; James W.,
  080,135; James,019,024,
  042,077,086,131,193;
  Jane Porter,137; Jane,
  080,137; Jas.G.(Dr.),
  211; Jas.G.,121,128;
  Jas.N.,140; Jean,137;

SMITH Cont., Jno.,156;
  Jno.W.,215; Joel B.,104;
  Joel R.,048,122; John
  C.,137; John H.,160;
  John L.,054,057,089,119,
  121,172,180,190,240,242;
  John T.,192; John W.,
  085,119,127,156,168,171,
  175,214,236; John,064,
  075,088,108,111,137,153,
  155,176,178,190,193,199,
  208,224,225,227,228,242;
  Johnathan,060; Jonathan,
  063,191,220,238; Jos.,
  193; Joseph K.,198;
  Joshua,006,018,202,225;
  Katharine,115; Kiziah,
  102; Levy,137; Martha,
  076,193; Moses,075,138,
  198; Mumford,195,215,
  217,223; N.P.,202; Nat-
  han T.(L.?),106; Nathan,
  044; Nathaniel,055,060,
  191,225; Nicholas P.,
  137; Noah,217; Patsy,
  036; Phebe,079; Philip,
  217; R.M.,156; Reuben,
  042,086,090,133,141,197,
  200; Reubin,057,071,146;
  Richard F.,225; Richard,
  080; Robert M.,172,179,
  180,197; Robert,101,135,
  137,198; Ruben,136,143;
  Rubin,104,157,173; Saml.
  219; Saml.H.,197; Sam-
  uel G.,080; Samuel H.,
  061,101,136,158,175,177;
  Samuel Jr.,094; Samuel,
  019,044,056,062,072,076,
  077,086,108,114,127,138,
  140,156,190,193,220,242;
  Sarah,015; Stephen,080,
  085,091,102,119,120,127,
  132,135,159,162,169,174,
  175,182,186,222,226,228;
  Thomas O.(?),015; Thomas
  011,030,057,068,094,095,
  116,135; Thos..115;
  Tilman(?),137; W.P.,190,
  198; William B.,219;
  William D.,237; William
  E.,225; William P.,238;
  William,001,033,064,080,
  096,108,114,137,163,190,
  193,224,227; Williamson,
  063,191,227; Wm.D.,169,
  191; Zilman,137
SMIZER, John,169
SMOOT, Charles (Dr),123,
  125; John C.,003;
  Samuel,056
SMOTHERS, John,059
SNELL, Elisabeth,161;
  Stephen,053
SNOODY, Samuel,008
SONFORD, James T.(Col),009
SOPELAND, David,073
SOUTHALL, John,201
SOUTHERLAND, Thomas,018
SOUTHERN, Isaac,172; J.,
  172
SOWEL, Charles,084
SOWELL, (?),238; Charles
  J.,177; Charles,104,
  123,164,217,238; Chas.,
  229; Elizabeth,225,242;
  H.C.,244; Joseph,095,
  241; P.,244; R.W.,243;
  Thomas,228; William,225
SPACE, Thomas,072
SPADLING, James,044
SPAIN, Marshall D.,217;
  Marshall,138
SPARKMAN, Kinchen,143,145;

SPARKMAN Cont., Rebecca(?),
  161; Seth,161; William,
  036
SPARKS, (?),094
SPEAN, Patten,091
SPENCE, Francis,129
SPENCER, Francis,116,132,
  146,187; Hyrney,061;
  Jno.,113; John,002,003,
  031,091,193; Ruth,171;
  Thos.S.,158,198; William,
  171,177,223; Zebinon,010;
  Zilman,013
SPENSER, Francis,056; John,
  111
SPICER, Claborn,091
SPIDLE, J.P.,214
SPILER, Jno.C.,222
SPINDLE, John P.(Dr),233;
  John P.,179; John,220
SPRADLING, James,044
SPRING, Sally,189; Wilson,
  140
SPRINKLE, Moses,037
SPRINKLES, McCagey,177;
  Micajah,190
SPICLEY, (?),015
SPRIGLEY, Rachel,015; Sam-
  uel,014
SRYGLEY, Samuel,015
STARBOUGH, John,036
STACKS, Abraham,240
STACY, James,055; Malone,
  217; Milton,217
STAGGS, Martin,015; William
  015
STAGS, Abner,056; John,
  015
STALLINGS, Stewat,084
STAMFIELD, (?),069
STAMLER, Samuel W.,110
STAMPS. Asa,172; Boids,
  172; J.M.,167; John W.,
  172; Lefts Wall,172;
  Lucy M.,172; Thomas,172
STANDPACE, Orin,013
STANFELL, Jonathan,034
STANFIELD, Isaac,005,008,
  025,026; Jackson,005,
  028; Jacob,005; James,
  005; John,005,007,008;
  Jonathan J.,008,028;
  Jonathan,005; Rebecca,
  005; Sarah,005; Thomas,
  005,239; William,009,
  017,064,092
STANFILE, Jackson,008; John
  008; Jonathan,008
STANFILL, Isaac,008; Jacob
  033; Rebecca,009; Sarah
  008
STANFORD, Ann(?),013;
  Young,185
STANTON, William,156
STAPLES, Alexander,136
STARLING, Shadrack,053
STATIONS, Stewart,124
STATLER, Chares,018
STAUGHE, John L.,187
STEAL, C.,092
STEEL(?), Robert,035
STEEL, Elizabeth,068; H.,
  083; Hannah,068; James,
  068,069,083; John,059;
  Nathaniel H.,059,069;
  Rachel,068; Samuel,059;
  William,059,069
STEELE, Aaron,059,066,069,
  080; Andrew,060,187;
  Harrison,163; James S.,
  182; James,066,069,080,
  133; Janey,068; Jinney,
  068; John,060,068,173,
  187; Martha,068;

VOORHIES, William Cont.,
091,096,108,148,179,196,
208,216,234,238; William
057
VORRHIES, William,042

W--MAN, Charles,219
WADDE(?), John W.,093
WADDLE, A.,025; Amos,159;
James S.,205; Jethro J.,
243; John S.,094; Sarah,
177
WADE, Austin N.,227;
Charles S.,242; Clement,
209; Dabney,034,056,141,
157; Frances,067,190;
Francis (Dr),144; Fran-
cis,067,159,186,244;
Hampton,220; John S.,
029; Levisey,157; Louisa
067,125,127,133,141;
Nancy(Mrs),157; Nancy,
094; Noah,077; Robert,
236; Sarah,127,141,157;
Suse,119; W.J.,066;
William J.,034; William
L.,178; William,009,
062,117
WADKINS, Joseph,197,242
WADOO, Barnet,125
WADSWORTH, Nancy,015
WAFOR, Isaiah,046
WAGGONER, And.,158;
William,050,059
WAID, Dalency,111; Robert,
242
WAKEFIELD, Joseph,034
WAKER(?), C.B.,119
WAKIN, Saml.,180,181
WAL, E.,163
WALDROP, --kiah,005;
Michel,054
WALDRUP, Ezekial,033; Hez-
ekiah,008; Michael,045
WALES, Joseph,005
WALKER & DAVIS, (?),131
WALKER & HARRIS, (?),189,
212,241; (Firm?),052,057
WALKER & HAYS, (Firm?),052
WALKER & HODGE, (Firm?),
051
WALKER & VAIL, (?),214,215
WALKER, (?),050,156; (Mrs)
102; A.(?),242; Alexr.,
178; Andrew,068,076,192;
Edmund,124,126; Edward,
123,132; Elijah,036;
Elizabeth Ann,171; Eliz-
abeth,019,038,039;
George H.,091; Griffin,
105; Griffith,217; Harr-
iett,187; J.,185; J.N.,
215; J.S.(& Co.),215;
J.S.,209,233; Jacob,092;
James J.,239; James L.,
052,087,119,122; James
S.,050,056,108,120,121,
153,208,212,229,240;
James T.,057,205; James
W.,057,240; James,018,
034,048,052,080,085,086,
090,095,099,100,101,104,
114,120,136,140,145,146,
148,149,157,162,265,185,
200,205,215,216,220,221,
226,232,237,239,243;
Jane,068,200; Jas.,128;
Jno.,128; Joel,198; John
068,083,089,105,132,278,
185,211,221; Joseph,068,
147,178; Maria,069;
Maria J.,200; Maria,070;
Mary Ann,071; N.,132;
Nixen,068; Noah,158,192;

WALKER Cont., Randolf,083;
Robert D.,178; Robert,
224; S.P.,242; Sealy,
217; Shadrick,053;
Simpson,050,059; Stephen
013; Thomas C.,125;
Thomas,044,060,068,076,
085,108,123,155,157,171,
183,187,190,197; Thos.,
131,147,156,182,217,238;
Washington,019,028,038,
039; William,192,220,243
WALL, Clement,160,178
WALLACE, (?),056; Alfred,
053; Hugh,237; James
Harvey,128; Jos.B.,129,
140,146,147; Joseph B.,
052,126,137,239; Robert,
073; Thomas,084; Ward
S.,108; William,082,095,
128,136,249
WALLAM, Lemuel,198
WALLER, John L.,056
WALLIENE, J.B.,134
WALLIS, Bogan C.,178; Bo-
gan,239; Joseph B.,224;
Robert,044,114; William,
032,103,240; Wm.,213
WALLS, Joseph,037; Thomas,
068
WALSON, James,003
WALTER & HAYS, (?),163
WALTER, Jesse,056
WALTERS, Lemuel,156
WALTON, A.J.,018; Abell,
222; Jesse,062; Milly,
120; Mrs.,001; William,
049,118
WANTLIN, Ephraim,218
WARD, Eli,008; Elijah,086;
Hezekiah,205; John T.,
135,143; Mary,016,024,
119; N.W.,219
WARDEN, James,152,167,241;
Polly,241; Richard,241;
Samuel M.,167; Samuel,
241
WARDLOW, Mary Ann,223;
William W.,223
WARFIELD, Mathas,056;
Mathias,137
WARNER, Gideon,121; Jno.,
239
WARNERSON, John,015
WARR, Elizabeth Ann,171;
J.,237; James,171,189,
219
WARREN, James,159; John
W.,067; John,027,084;
Samuel,159
WARRINGTON, Daley,036;
James,036
WASHINGTON, James J.,027
WASSON, Able,143; Abner,
143; Catherine,143; J.,
142; John,042,143;
Josiah,143,236; Samuel
S.,143; Samuel,142,143
WAST, Polly,091
WATERS, Lemuel,135,162;
Samuel,205
WATKINS, G.M.,212; Geo.,
160; Gregory,028; James
L.,179; John,177; Jo-
seph,233,236; M.,207;
Samuel,026; Solomin,017
WATON, Milly,120
WATSON, Dempsey,162; J.,
079; Jesse,222; Jonat-
han,174,213; Josiah,224;
Nathan,162; Sally,120;
Sarah (Mrs.),223; Tho-
mas,133,136,162
WATTES(?), Benjamin,092

WATTS, Andrew,010; Ann,010;
James,010; Jane,010; John
010,017,026,108; Margaret
010; Mary,010; Rebeccah,
010; Rosanna,010; William
010
WEAKLEY, Robert,002
WEAKS, William,176
WEALTEY, Robert,021
WEAR, David,109; William,
162
WEATHERBY, Josiah,224
WEATHERINTON, Joseph,041
WEATHERLY, Isaah,193; Isah,
224; John,198
WEATHERS, James,055
WEATHERSPOON, (?),218;
David,033,035,109; Sam'l.
101; Samuel,037,045;
Westley,108; Westly,035
WEATHERTON, Abraham,041
WEAVER, Elijah,198,209;
G.W.,208,221; George W.,
190,193,208; James,197;
John,106; Joseph,030;
Nealy,150; Shadrick,167,
173
WEBB, (Mrs.),085; Elizabeth
G.,040,119; Elizabeth,
121; Gray P.,170; J.J.,
128; Jno.,125; John J.,
040,052,121,122,133;
John,054,058,059,066,
083,097,115,119,163,167,
285,195; M.,238; Merideth
042,107; Solomon,223;
Thomas,085,123,154;
William,009,010,012,056,
068,108,114,133
WEBBER, Charles W.,176;
George,056; John,133
WEBSTER & STRAYHORN,(?)211
WEBSTER, (Capt),243; (Mrs)
187; (?),020; Emily Green
240; Emily,134; G.,177,
243; George,008,014,044,
097,228; J.,016; J.G.,
129; John G.,134,217,219,
240; John P.,134; Johna-
than,178,235; Jona,240;
Jona.,178; Jonathan,016,
018,055,085,107,111,120,
123,129,178,187,203,217,
219,221; John,240; R.P.,
162,240; Robert P.,134,
240; Robert T.,240;
Robert,178
WEDGE, Abram(?),096
WEEDAN, John,123
WEEK(?), Benjamin,029
WEEMES, (?),099; William,
087
WEEMS, Chals,145; Charles,
087; John,125; Mary,145;
William,125
WEGSTER, G.W.,240
WEIR, Thomas,038
WELCH, (Esquire),209;
James,002; William,067
WELL, Meredith,083
WELLS, John,001; William,
095
WELSH, Esquire,198; James,
002,003
WERE, William,177
WEST, Easter,112
WESTBROOK, Ridley R.,137
WESTER(?), William,221
WHALING, James,242
WHARTON, David,018
WHATSON, (?),013
WHEAT, (Mr.),178; Jno.,
158; Wilie A.,158; Willi-
am,178,228

WHEATE, Wiley S.,192
WHEATLEY, Francis,182;
 Jeremiah,242
WHEELER, George M.,224
WHERTON, A.,013; David,
 010
WHIG & BANNER, (Paper)238
WHITAKER, J.,226; John,
 028,121,174,181,242
WHITBY, Thomas,199
WHITE, (?),101; (Mrs.),
 172,190; Alexander,052;
 Alfred,018; Andrew,094;
 Benjamin,042; Catharine,
 057,119,121; Edward,040;
 Eliza,057; G.,190; George
 042; Isaac,024; J.,199;
 J.T.,033; James M.,221;
 James W.,057; James,018,
 030,056,082,108,119,121,
 162,167,173; Jane,118,
 239; Jno.,113; John F.,
 045; John P.,195; John
 T.,107; John,002,018,
 055,057,096,108,119,163;
 Josiah,008; Lucy,002;
 Luke,085,089; Matthew
 L.,077; Moses,108; Noah,
 178,185,223; Phillemon,
 037; Robert,094; Rubin,
 124; Sarah,242; Sherwood,
 010,150; Thomas,018,057,
 072,078,096,108,113,119,
 162; Thos.,113; William
 V.,158; William,018,110,
 118,119,172,190,233;
 Wilson,057,108,121,162
WHITEMAN, H.N.,131
WHITESIDE & WILLIS, (Firm?)
 092
WHITESIDE, A.(Dr),009,018;
 A.,056; Abraham (Dr),
 049; Abraham,016,048,187;
 Abram,025,043,055,112;
 Elenor,076; Elinor,130;
 Hugh,008,085,124,130;
 James,130; Jennett,130;
 John,028,035,203; Johna-
 than,098; Jonathan,132,
 187; Margaret,130; Mar-
 garitte,130; Polly,130;
 Richard,139,147; Robert
 K.,231; Robert,056,076,
 135; Robertson,130;
 Robinson(Robertson),130;
 Ruth,139; Sam'l.,098;
 Samuel,035,089,112,142,
 231; Thomas,025,056;
 Thos.,112,130; William,
 187,231; Wm.,085
WHITESIDES, (Dr),046;
 (Mrs.),049; (Widow),098;
 A.,130; Abraham,051,132,
 147,154; Abram (Dr),122;
 Abram,112,120,126; Abray-
 ham,106; James,131; John-
 athan,138; Mary,096;
 R.(Mrs.),049; Richard,
 049; Robert N.,214; Ro-
 bert,165; Robinson,138;
 Ruth M.,049; Ruth W.,
 122; Samuel D.,214;
 Samuel Jr.,138; Samuel,
 050,059,131,149,154;
 Thomas,130; William,041,
 096,123,146,191
WHITLEY, Jesse,222
WHITMAN, H.N.,214; Henry
 N.,120
WHITNEY, Mary,077
WHITSON, (Widow),043;
 Aney,208; Ann,001,207;
 Anne,191; Elizabeth,031;
 George,191; Isaac,055;

WHITSON Cont., James,045,
 055,107,191; John,001,
 191; Joseph,001; Samuel,
 191,207,208; Thomas,001,
 027,191; William,001,
 025,191
WHITTED, William,177,221
WHITTEN, Robert,203; Willi-
 am,195
WHITTON, James,008
WHUTSES(?), Mark,132
WIBLE, Gray P.,208; John,
 003; Wm.,208
WIGG, Robert,169
WIGGS, Matthew,063
WIKES, Benjamin,061
WILCOXEN, Aron,042
WILEFORD, W.L.,061
WILEY, A.M.,211; Alexander
 078,089,185; Allen,089;
 Andrew,078,106,203; Dav-
 id,196; H.A.,243; John,
 009,021,023,078; Marga-
 ret,078; Moses A.,092,
 124,228,238; Moses R.,
 084; Moses,026,078;
 Polly,078; Robert,017,
 078,089,138; Sarah,078;
 Thomas,078; William,078,
 201
WILIE, Alexander F.,223;
 John,033,152; Wm.,231
WILIS, Davis,222
WILKASE, Jacob,053
WILKES, (Mr.), Jr.,54;
 A.L.,167; B.,238; Benja-
 min,189; Benj.,195;
 Benjamin,045,061,072,
 158,161,184,201,204,206,
 230,244; Betsy,072; Bur-
 rel,220; Burrell,189;
 Burwell,208; C.M.,154,
 158,244; Daniel,061,072,
 189,206; David L.,189;
 David W.,189; David,208;
 E.,080,205; Elizabeth
 G.,189; Elizabeth R.,072;
 Elizabeth,061,158,189,
 206; Ethelbert B.,167;
 Ethelbert,170; Heneriter
 072; Henrietta,061; Hen-
 ritta,072; Jane A.,176;
 Jane S.,189; Jane,176;
 Jesse,061,072,206,209;
 Jno.B.,158,170; John B.,
 046,167; John J.,209;
 John,056,072,093,167,
 189,206,217; Josier,189;
 Mary,189,209; Minor C.,
 169; Minor C.M.,161;
 Minor L.,055; Minor S.,
 163; Minor,061,072,170,
 189; Nancy B.,224; Polly
 072,161; R.A.L.,161,169,
 182,206,244; Richard A.
 L.,154,161,169,170,189,
 227,230,244; Richard,
 057,189,208; Richd.A.L.,
 206,241; Sally D.,154;
 Sally,189; Thomas W.,
 189; Thomas,189,208;
 Washington L.J.,161,244;
 William B.,161,169,230,
 244; William J.,209;
 William,176,189,220
WILKINS, Alexander,091;
 James,055,137; Jesse L.,
 163; John,063,163,167,
 172,190; Joseph,237;
 L.J.,185; Lilth J.,132;
 Little John,132,172
WILKINSON, Umphrey,128
WILKS, Benjamin,121,122,
 132; C.,172; Daniel,230,

WILKS, Daniel Cont., 234;
 David,220; E.B.,235;
 Eliza L.,122; Elizabeth,
 046,230; Jane Ann,172;
 Jane,172; Jessa,121;
 Jesse G.,179; Jesse,121,
 122; Jno.B.,121; John
 B.,122; John J.,172;
 John,217,218,230; Jon B.,
 121; Josiah,232; Miner
 C.M.,107; Niner L.,108;
 Miner,121; Minor C.,132,
 154; Minor C.M.,122,229;
 Minor,121,208,220,234;
 R.A.L.,145,154,234;
 Richard A.,132; Richard
 A.L.,121,128,133,229;
 Richard A.S.,132; Rich-
 ard,220,232; Sally D.,
 161; Thomas,232; Thos.,
 220; Unity K.,161,229,
 235; Unity,154; W.L.J.,
 154; Washington L.,235;
 Washington L.J.,229;
 William B.,154,229; Willi-
 am S.,172; William,172,
 217,218; Wm.S.,172
WILLAMS, E.,129
WILLEFORD, (?),243; W.L.,
 057; William L.,108,158;
 Willis,104,168
WILLES(WILKES), Edmond,217
WILLEY, Alexander,025;
 Jonith,092; Moses A.,164;
 William,079
WILLFORD, Wm.,203
WILLIAM & LEE, (Firm?),051
WILLIAM, Hensley,139; Sharp
 139
WILLIAMS & ALDERSON, (?),
 239
WILLIAMS, (?), M.,197; (?),
 126; (Widow),122; A.,184;
 Alex M.,109,145; Alexan-
 der M.,071,079,091,122,
 145; Alexander,050,059,
 061,115,188; Anderson,
 058,060,063,093,122,133,
 217; Archibald,184; Asa,
 089; Basel,060; Bennett,
 074,075,079; Betsey,070;
 Betsy,074; Boswell,064;
 Charles,092,161,194; D.,
 177,235; Daniel,051,074;
 Dolly,070,071,120,122,
 188; Duke,058,080,149,
 167,168,169,175,177,178,
 214,217,223; Edmd.,120;
 Edmond L.,136; Edmond T.,
 208; Edmond,061,122,129,
 209,218,223; Edmund L.,
 191,192,208,215,226;
 Edmund,058,070,071,079,
 122,188,207; Edward D.,
 158; Edward,044,084,103,
 107,123,198; Edwards
 (Mrs),124; Elisha,124;
 Emily E.,071,155; G.B.
 (Dr),050; G.B.,034,155;
 Green B.,061,079,120,122,
 141,145,148; Greenberry,
 056,058,070,071; Green-
 bury,136; H.,177,235;
 Hannry A.,163; Harden,
 177,214,223; Hardin,061,
 191; Henry A.,109; Henry
 C.,214; Henry,198,221,
 223; Isaac W.,082; Isaac,
 013,066,120; J.,067,191;
 Jacob,013,046,051,140;
 James B.,155; James H.,
 056,079,107,137; James,
 033; Jenny,140; Jesse,
 198; John C.,228; John E.,

WILLIAMS, John E., Cont.,
084,123; John M.,219;
John,001,002,004,008,
009,032,051,065,066,101,
109,193,224; Jonathan,
044; Joseph,026; Joshua,
030,048,113,140,208;
Leaner (Mrs),177; Leon-
ard(?),074; Margaret,074,
077; Martha S.,155;
Martha,029,124,235; Mary
M.,149; Milly H.,093;
Nancy C.,155; Nancy,070,
074; Nathan,123,124;
Nathaniel,177,214; Nath-
niel,235; Novis,242;
Oliver,042,093; Parmenus
056,188; Penelope E.,155;
Permenas,058,070,071,188,
217; Permeneas,122; Per-
mineas,120; Peter,168,
199,227,241,244; Polly,
070; Rebecca,191; Ro-
bert,033,110; S.,189;
S.H.,183; Saml.H.,182;
Saml.T.,232; Samuel H.,
(Col),018; Samuel H.,
004,013,027,028,037,046,
055,117,163,178,193,194,
197; Samuel N.,155;
Samuel,001,034; Sophia,
235; Susan B.,148,155;
Susan,141; Susanah (Mrs)
136; Susanna B.,061;
Susannah,117; T.H.,199;
Theolphlaus,159; Thomas,
029,039,070,071,177,198,
235; Thos.,132,214; Thos.
N.,181; Veneable,056;
W.,181,191; William H.,
085; William,006,018,026,
029,033,062,064,074,077,
116,128,160,162,190,191,
193,195,199,221,224,236,
237,238; Wilson(William?)
181; Wm.098,110,111; Wm.
D.,208; Zachariah,074
WILLIAMSON, (Mrs.),048;
-- H.,047; A.,176; Ann
H.K.,046,048,081; Eliza-
beth P.,046; Green,006,
033,046,055,110,119,120,
125; John,195; Maria G.,
048,081,233; Mariah G.?
048; Martha A.,046;
Martha,048,081; Marthey,
047; P.C.,233; P.R.,125;
Patsey H.,047; Patsey,
119,120; R.M.,081,174,
189; Russel M.,046;
Russell McCord,048;
Samuel H.,100; Silas,
118,146; Tom,216; W.H.,
119,120; Will H.,125;
William H.,047,048,189,
242; William,216
WILLIAMSOM, Mariah G.,046
WILLICE, E.,105
WILLICO, (?),056
WILLIE(?), James,124
WILLIE, James,084
WILLIFORD, Asmond,242;
Hardy,168; William,120;
Willis,115
WILLIS, (Col),080; (Maj),
009,096,115,117; Augus-
tine,048; Elizabeth,119;
F.,120; Francis,103,156,
185; J.S.,221; James,
094; Jno.S.,224; John S.,
222,228; John,027,089;
Major,114; Mechack,202;
Meshac,119; N.,066;
Nathaiel,039; Nathan,194;

WILLIS Cont., Nathaniel,
024,043,051,066,102,108,
110,128,131,135,145,178,
197,210,217,228,241;
Nathl.,136,149,162,229;
Oscar,048; Peggy,168;
Piety,027; Richd.,183;
Robert,018; Samuel,009,
027,029; Smith,193;
Thomas,045; W.W.,183;
William W.(Dr),222;
William W.,221,222,224,
228; William,089; Wright
035
WILLIAMS, James H.,163
WILLOFORD, Thomas,054
WILLOW, Nancy B.,228
WILLS, John B.,007;
Nathaniel,074; Thomas,
063; William,094
WILLSFORD, William L.,054
WILLSON, H.,168; Jane,168;
John,054,168; Joseph,
159; William A.,168;
William H.,056; William,
060; Wm.A.,168
WILSON, (Mrs),144; (Widow)
216; Aaron,060; Abe,
093; Abel,004,009,034;
Alexander,086,224,243;
Anney,086; Aron C.,239;
B.W.,171,190,191,220;
Benj.,155; Benjamin W.,
179; Charles,144,216,
230; Cornelius,086;
Daniel,121; Elijah,167;
Elisabeth,144; George,
243; Henry S.,160; Henry
Stephens,086; Henry,086,
155; James,156; Jane,
119,120,157; Jenny,156;
Jno.,155; Jno.W.,156;
John C.,193; John,039,
084,086,123,136,160,179,
180,190,242; Joseph,226;
Martin,039; Mary (Mrs.),
226; Nancy,086; Napin,
178; Robert,195; Thomas,
074,170; W.M.,220; W.T.,
220; William D.,127;
William H.,087,119,120,
135,156,157,236; William
N.,120; William,234
WIMS, Mary,039; William,
039
WIN, Fred,064; Philip P.,
180
WINCALE, Sarah,072
WINDFORD, William,012
WINER, A.W.,176
WINGFIELD, Joseph,010,
067,117,144,159,186,244;
L.J.,190
WINKFIELD, Joseph,012
WINN, Archelaus W.,167;
Archibald W.,093,164;
Archibald,167; B.F.,119;
Benjamin,074,119; Cris-
tine,074; Jenny,007;
John,050,074,084,119,
123; Margaret,074; Miner
064; N.W.,165; P.P.,062,
Philip P.,122,134,147,
155,175; Phillip P.,
120; Phillips P.,056;
Priscilla,074; Prissi-
lea,119; Richard (Gen)
018,119,120; Richard,
074,119; Samuel,054,
074,084,119,120,123,
231; Thomas P.,108;
Thomas,074,119; Thos.Y.,
215; William,043,074,112
WINNS, Charles,035,039;

WINNS Cont., Mary,039;
Nancy,035; William,035,
039
WINSTEAD, Johnston,035
WIRE, Phiip,061
WIRIGATE, William,091
WISE, John,026
WISEMAN, Benjamin,132,134,
167; Martin,239; Thomas,
132; William,132; Wm.,
223
WISTLE(?), James C.,139
WITHERSPOON, James W.,120;
Sally,191; Saml.,186;
Samuel,100,145,195; Wes-
ley,176,215; Westley,
207,208,227
WITT, John,104,241; W.M.,
156; William,155,201
WITTO(?), Wm.M.,183
WOFIELD, Mathias,086
WOLDREDGE, Edw.,112
WOLDRIDGE, Jno.H.,243
WOLLARD, James B.,202; N.,
219; Silas,077,193,220
WOLVERTON, James,090
WOMBLE, Redding,006
WOOD, Curtis, 084,107;
David,186; Elijah,136;
John L.(?),129; John L.,
018,055,059,068; John
S.,060,068; Samuel,064;
W.W.,242; William W.,055
WOODARD, Julius,095
WOODCUFF, John,195
WOODRIDGE, John,084
WOODRUFF, John,141,159
WOODS, Curtis,027; Green,
219; James,010; Jean,
010; Jonah,019; William
W.,073,108,117,165;
William,160; Wm.,006
WOODSIDE, William,178,239
WOODSON, Cufa,208; Cuffy,
215,242
WOODWARD, (?),230; ---,209;
--thias J.,206; George
J.,199; Julius,198
WOODY, Curtis,044
WOOLARD, Nathaniel,064,225;
Swain W.,216
WOOLDRIDGE, John,084,123
WOOLRIDGE, John H.,221;
John,224
WOOSLEY, Peter,069,070
WOOTON, Benjamin,002
WORMACK, Wm.H.,183
WORMBRY, John C.,018
WORMELEY, John C.,049,067,
166,210
WORMLEY, J.C.,156; John C.,
056,157,163,176,179,191,
193,199,228,232,233
WORTHAM, Alfred H.,062;
B.H.,153; Benjamin C.,
217; Benjamin,209; Creed
(Crud) T.,217; Cried T.
(?),153; Duke,153; Ed-
ward,201,234,236; James
M..188; James W.,153;
James,122,130; John,177;
Nancy,071,188; R.,065;
R.H.,153; Robert,042,
056,066,075,133,134,141,
145,153,155,177,180,198,
207,223; Thomas,008,061,
062,074,075,080,107,122,
127,236,242; Thos.,134,
153,217; Thos.P.,223;
William H.,075; William,
153,198,235; Wm.,223;
Zachariah,198; Zack,210
WREN, George,143,213;
James,001; Peter,143;

www.ingramcontent.com/pod-product-compliance
Lightning Source LLC
Chambersburg PA
CBHW021854020426
42334CB00013B/328